Redefining Comparative Constitutional Law

OXFORD COMPARATIVE CONSTITUTIONALISM

Series Editors

RICHARD ALBERT

William Stamps Farish Professor of Law,
The University of Texas at Austin School of Law

ROBERT SCHÜTZE

Professor of European and Global Law,
Durham University and College of Europe

Comparative constitutional law has a long and distinguished history in intellectual thought and in the construction of public law. As political actors and the people who create or modify their constitutional orders, they often wish to learn from the experience and learning of others. This cross-fertilization and mutual interaction has only accelerated with the onset of globalization, which has transformed the world into an interconnected web that facilitates dialogue and linkages across international and regional structures. Oxford Comparative Constitutionalism seeks to publish scholarship of the highest quality in constitutional law that deepens our knowledge of local, national, regional, and global phenomena through the lens of comparative public law.

Also Published in this Series

Foreign Relations Federalism
The EU in Comparative Perspective
Thomas Verellen

Responsive Judicial Review
Democracy and Dysfunction in the Modern Age
Rosalind Dixon

Outsourcing Rulemaking Powers
Constitutional Limits and National Safeguards
Cedric Jenart

Abusive Constitutional Borrowing
Legal Globalization and the Subversion of Liberal Democracy
Rosalind Dixon and David Landau

A Theory of African Constitutionalism
Berihun Adugna Gebeye

Eternity Clauses in Democratic Constitutionalism
Silvia Suteu

Deliberative Peace Referendums
Ron Levy, Ian O'Flynn, Hoi L. Kong

Scales of Memory Constitutional Justice and Historical Evil
Justin Collings

Redefining Comparative Constitutional Law

Essays for Mark Tushnet

Edited by

VICKI C. JACKSON
MADHAV KHOSLA

OXFORD
UNIVERSITY PRESS

OXFORD
UNIVERSITY PRESS

Great Clarendon Street, Oxford, OX2 6DP,
United Kingdom

Oxford University Press is a department of the University of Oxford.
It furthers the University's objective of excellence in research, scholarship,
and education by publishing worldwide. Oxford is a registered trade mark of
Oxford University Press in the UK and in certain other countries

Published in the United States of America by Oxford University Press
198 Madison Avenue, New York, NY 10016, United States of America

British Library Cataloguing in Publication Data

Data available

Library of Congress Control Number: 2024944351

ISBN 9780198891451

DOI: 10.1093/9780191996344.001.0001

The manufacturer's authorised representative in the EU for product safety is Oxford University Press España S.A. of El Parque Empresarial San Fernando de Henares, Avenida de Castilla, 2 – 28830 Madrid (www.oup.es/en or product.safety@oup.com). OUP España S.A. also acts as importer into Spain of products made by the manufacturer.

Acknowledgments

We are grateful to each of the contributors for their engagement with Mark Tushnet's work, and for their patience and steadfastness in the process of moving from a conference in his honor to this scholarly volume. We are grateful to our law schools, Harvard and Columbia, and to their deans and staff for supporting this intellectual project. Meng Ye at Columbia Law School provided superb research assistance. Our primary debt is, of course, to Mark—for his many contributions to the field and to each of our scholarly works, and for his encouragement of this volume.

Contents

Contributors

Richard Albert is William Stamps Farish Professor in Law, University of Texas at Austin School of Law

Aharon Barak is Professor, Reichman University Harry Radzyner Law School

Bojan Bugarič is Professor of Law, University of Sheffield

Peter Cane is Emeritus Distinguished Professor of Law, Australian National University

Cora Chan is Professor of Law, University of Hong Kong Faculty of Law

Sujit Choudhry is Head of Chambers for Hāki Chambers Global

Erin F. Delaney is Professor of Law, Northwestern Pritzker School of Law

Rosalind Dixon is Professor of Law, School of Global & Public Law, University of New South Wales

David C. Donald is Professor Emeritus, Chinese University of Hong Kong

Tom Ginsburg is Leo Spitz Professor of International Law, University of Chicago Law School

Jamal Greene is Dwight Professor of Law, Columbia Law School

Dieter Grimm is Professor Emertius of Law, Humboldt University

Ran Hirschl is David R. Cameron Distinguished Professor in Law and Politics, University of Toronto

Vicki C. Jackson is Laurence H. Tribe Professor of Constitutional Law, Harvard Law School

Madhav Khosla is Dr. B. R. Ambedkar Professor of Indian Constitutional Law, Columbia Law School

David Landau is Mason Ladd Professor and Associate Dean for International Programs, Florida State University College of Law

David S. Law is E. James Kelly, Jr., Class of 1965 Research Professor of Law, University of Virginia School of Law

Sanford Levinson is W. St. John Garwood and W. St. John Garwood, Jr. Centennial Chair in Law Professor, University of Texas at Austin School of Law

Pratap Bhanu Mehta is Laurence S. Rockefeller Visiting Professor for Distinguished Teaching, Princeton University

Frank I. Michelman is Robert Walmsley University Professor, Emeritus, Harvard Law School

Catherine O'Regan is Professor of Human Rights Law and Director, Bonavero Institute of Human Rights, University of Oxford

Yaniv Roznai is Vice Dean and Co-Director, Rubinstein Center for Constitutional Challenges, Reichman University Harry Radzyner Law School

Cheryl Saunders is Laureate Professor Emeritus, Melbourne Law School

Kim Lane Scheppele is Laurance S. Rockefeller Professor of Sociology and International Affairs in the Woodrow Wilson School and the University Center for Human Values, Princeton University

Mark Tushnet is William Nelson Cromwell Professor of Law, Emeritus, Harvard Law School

Mila Versteeg is Henry L. and Grace Doherty Charitable Foundation Professor of Law, University of Virginia School of Law

Maartje De Visser is Professor of Law, Singapore Management University Yong Pung How School of Law

Jeremy Waldron is University Professor, New York University School of Law

Po Jen Yap is Professor, University of Hong Kong Faculty of Law

Tushnet and the Future of Comparative Constitutional Law

Vicki C. Jackson and Madhav Khosla

This volume is inspired by the remarkable and ongoing work of Professor Mark Tushnet in the field of comparative constitutional law. A conference in his honor was held in June 2021, to celebrate and mark his retirement from Harvard Law School. Most of those who attended have contributed to this volume—contributors span the globe, with background and/or experience in Africa, Europe, Russia, South America, the UK, New Zealand, Australia, East Asia, India, and North America. Tushnet has made enormous contributions, both on normative questions and on positive understandings of constitutions and constitutionalism. On the positive side, Tushnet's many analyses of different constitutional questions impart a methodological rigor, a refusal to see issues as neatly determined or one-sided, and an attention to the interrelationships between law, politics, and sociology that has provided a model for so many. On the normative side, as Mark Graber explained in his contribution to the conference out of which this book arose, Tushnet "is a twenty-first century inclusive/pluralist populist."[1] This normative commitment has led to another large body of work, including Tushnet's concluding chapter in this volume, exploring different modalities through which popular movements and publics can define and redefine their polities.

We begin with some general observations about Mark Tushnet's work and how it relates to this volume. We then turn to the contributions, briefly considering their intervention in the field of comparative constitutional law. In closing, we speculate on the future of the discipline.

Tushnet as Inspiration

The editors initially identified a distinct set of themes in Tushnet's work that have been of foundational importance in the development of this field, and invited

[1] Quoted with Mark Graber's permission.

contributions on those themes. The contributions, in turn, sharpened and refined these themes into five broad categories: (1) methodological questions and approaches ("Curiosity, Epistemic Caution, and Methodologies"); (2) the nature and limits of constituent power and constitutional authority ("Constituting Constitutions: Law, Power, and Authority"); (3) courts, rights, and review; 4) constitutional design and nonjudicial structures to protect democracy; and (5) varieties of constitutionalism.

Tushnet's 1999 paper, "The Possibilities of Comparative Constitutional Law," famously developed three different ways in which thinking about constitutional law comparatively might be helpful in understanding US law.[2] First, he suggested that functional understandings of how different systems meet common problems could illuminate choices that are not experienced as such from within a single domestic system. Second, in contrast to the functional approach, he suggested that constitutions might be understood in some respects as rather particularized expressions of specific national identities. Third, he suggested that studies of actual constitution-making revealed a degree of "bricolage" in their construction, of a borrowing of what happened to be at hand, in ways that might undermine strong assumptions of coherence in constitutional texts and thus bear on interpretation.

Much comparative constitutional work, especially in what Ran Hirschl calls "constitutional studies,"[3] is functional in character, trying to understand how different constitutional schemes, or approaches to making constitutions, contribute to different distributions of power or other results; for example, do constitutions drafted by special constitutional conventions outperform (on a number of metrics) constitutions drafted by parliaments?[4] The "expressivist" character of constitutions is a lively subject in contemporary work, reflected in studies, for example, of the language of preambles, and in work by Tarunabh Khaitan on the "expressive accommodation of dissenters";[5] in this volume, Maartje de Visser's chapter on the role of language in constitution-making and interpretation is a reminder of how powerfully expressive that choice can be.[6] The point about bricolage is vividly

[2] Mark Tushnet, *The Possibilities of Comparative Constitutional Law*, 108 Yale L.J. 1225, 1225 (1999).

[3] In addition to Professor Hirschl's contribution to this volume, *see, e.g.*, Ran Hirschl, Comparative Matters: The Renaissance of Comparative Constitutional Law (2014).

[4] *Compare, e.g.*, Jon Elster, *Forces and Mechanisms in the Constitution-Making Process*, 45 Duke L.J. 364 (1995) and Bruce Ackerman, The Future of LIberal Revolution (1992) *with* Gabriel L. Negretto, *Democratic Constitution-Making Bodies: The Perils of a Partisan Convention*, 16 Int'l J. Const. L. 254 (2018).

[5] Tarunabh Khaitan, *Directive Principles and the Expressive Accommodation of Ideological Dissenters*, 16 Int'l J. Const. L. 389 (2018). *See also* Jeff King, *Constitutions as Mission Statements*, *in* Social and Political Foundations of Constitutions 73 (Denis J. Galligan & Mila Versteeg eds., 2013); Madhav Khosla, India's Founding Moment: The Constitution of a Most Surprising Democracy 44–55 (2020).

[6] *Compare* Ford v. Quebec (Attorney General), [1988] 2 SCR 712.

illustrated in a number of recent works, including Linda Colley's book *The Gun, the Ship, and the Pen*, as well as in the work of Günter Frankenberg.[7]

Tushnet's work on the core feature of constitutions—the fact that they *constitute* power and authority—has similarly had a major impact in comparative study. In his essay "Peasants with Pitchforks, and Toilers with Twitter," for example, Tushnet explored the idea of unconstitutional constitutional amendments, and used the theme to reflect on the meaning and exercise of "constituent power."[8] In doing so, Tushnet questioned assumptions about how much law could control outcomes in situations where the people want a significant constitutional change. He also noted that, as an analytic matter, a constitutional amendment process may in particular cases be more justifiably viewed as emanating from a decision of "the people" as a whole than a formal new constitution. When Mark Tushnet and his co-editor sketched an agenda for *Defining the Field of Comparative Constitutional Law* in 2002,[9] limits on constitutional amendments were not a major topic on the horizon for most comparative constitutional law scholars in the West.[10] Such limits had, however, been a subject of considerable scholarly and juridical attention elsewhere, including in India.[11] Indeed, as Madhav Khosla's recent work suggests, India has a number of important contributions to comparative constitutionalism warranting greater study.[12] In Aharon Barak's chapter, we find an account of limits on constituent power—and an argument for the importance of judicial review to determine if such power has been exceeded. Catherine O'Regan's contribution turns to a similar theme, but analyzes the matter in a very specific context: that of the recent Kenyan decision that considered whether there are substantive limitations on the power to amend the 2010 Kenyan Constitution. David Landau, by

[7] *See* Linda Colley, The Gun, the Ship and the Pen: Warfare and the Making of Modern Constitutions (2021); Günter Frankenberg, Comparative Constitutional Studies: Between Magic and Deceit (2018).

[8] Mark Tushnet, *Peasants with Pitchforks, and Toilers with Twitter: Constitutional Revolutions and the Constituent Power*, 13 Int'l J. Const. L. 639 (2015). *See also* Mark Tushnet, *Constitution-Making: An Introduction*, 91 Tex. L. Rev. 1983 (2013); Mark Tushnet, *Amendment Theory and Constituent Power*, *in* Comparative Constitutional Theory 317 (Gary Jacobsohn & Miguel Schor eds., 2018).

[9] Defining the Field of Comparative Constitutional Law (Vicki C. Jackson & Mark Tushnet eds., 2002).

[10] For an early collection some of whose essays bear on the question, *see* Responding to Imperfection: The Theory and Practice of Constitutional Amendment (Sanford Levinson ed., 1995).

[11] *See, e.g.*, P.K. Tripathi, Some Insights into Fundamental Rights 1–44 (1972); Fundamental Rights Case: The Critics Speak (Surendra Malik ed., 1975); H.M. Seervai, *The Fundamental Rights Case: At the Cross-Roads*, 74 Bombay L.R. 47 (1973); Indian Constitution: Trends and Issues (Rajeev Dhavan & Alice Jacob eds., 1978); Upendra Baxi, Courage, Craft, and Contention: The Indian Supreme Court in the Eighties 64–97 (1985). *See generally* Madhav Khosla, *Constitutional Amendment*, *in* Oxford Handbook of the Indian Constitution 232 (Sujit Choudhry, Madhav Khosla & Pratap Bhanu Mehta eds., 2016). For discussion of related issues concerning the "theoretical limits constitutional amendment," *see* Kazuyuki Takahashi, *Why Do We Study Constitutional Laws of Foreign Countries, and How?*, *in* Defining the Field of Comparative Constitutional Law, *supra* note 9, at 35, 43.

[12] *See* Khosla, India's Founding Moment, *supra* note 5.

contrast, reflects on the nature of constituent power by considering the range of actions sometimes taken by constitution-making bodies. On both conceptual and positive grounds, there are reasons, Landau suggests, for caution about imposing limitations on the functions that these bodies can perform.

The relationship between constitutionalism and sovereign authority also informs, though in very different ways, Frank Michelman's effort at exploring the role that constitutionalism plays in procedural visions of democracy; Michelman engages deeply with Tushnet's commitments to democracy in the context of exploring Rawlsian justifications for judicial review. In Erin Delaney's emphasis on "coercive constitutionalism," the nature and exercise of sovereignty, and the tensions that it involves, are unpacked in an entirely different context: what she describes as a "coercive continuum" of postcolonial transitions. Throughout, these chapters negotiate the tension between the constitutive conditions that make constitutionalism possible and the popular authority to determine those conditions.

Mark Tushnet's work on rights and judicial review has likewise been enormously generative, inspiring a raft of scholarship on various approaches to "weak form" review and on legislative roles in the constitutional protection of rights.[13] In *Weak Courts, Strong Rights*, Tushnet explored examples of courts whose remedial powers were not exercised with the finality associated with judgments of the US courts, but which nonetheless, he argued, contributed to stronger rights enforcement.[14] The possibility of judicial review that is not strong-form in character continues to provoke debate, as seen by Aileen Kavanagh's new book on *The Collaborative Constitution*.[15] In this volume, Jeremy Waldron takes up questions inspired by this work, in his exploration of why weaker forms of review have not typically been discussed in connection with questions of constitutional structure. Dieter Grimm approaches the overall theme from a quite different perspective as he defends the role of distinctively legal reasoning in legitimating judicial review of rights issues.

Several other chapters engage with questions of constitutional structure and constitutional design from a variety of perspectives. Peter Cane offers a comparative and historical analysis, arguing that "(three-branch) separation of powers theory" is no longer useful in understanding changes in the distribution of government power in the UK or the US "in the 200 years since Montesquieu"; instead,

[13] For a recent examination, *see, e.g.*, *Symposium: Weak-Form Review in Comparative Perspective*, 17 INT'L J. CONST. L. 807 (2019) (featuring contributions by Mark Tushnet, Swati Jhaveri, Po Jen Yap and Francis Chung, Kent Roach, Scott Stephenson, Rosalind Dixon, and Stephen Gardbaum).

[14] MARK TUSHNET, WEAK COURTS, STRONG RIGHTS: JUDICIAL REVIEW AND SOCIAL WELFARE RIGHTS IN COMPARATIVE CONSTITUTIONAL LAW (2008). *See also* Mark Tushnet, *The Rise of Weak-Form Judicial Review*, *in* COMPARATIVE CONSTITUTIONAL LAW 321 (Tom Ginsburg & Rosalind Dixon eds., 2011); Mark Tushnet, *The Relation Between Political Constitutionalism and Weak-Form Judicial Review*, 14 GERMAN L.J. 2249 (2013). For other roughly contemporaneous efforts at exploring weaker forms of judicial review, *see* STEPHEN GARDBAUM, THE NEW COMMONWEALTH MODEL OF CONSTITUTIONALISM: THEORY AND PRACTICE (2013).

[15] AILEEN KAVANAGH, THE COLLABORATIVE CONSTITUTION (2023).

he suggests, envisioning "a spectrum with high concentration of power and high diffusion of power at either end is more helpful than separation of powers," with the implication that courts' functions may vary considerably among different systems. In a different vein, Richard Albert explores design strategies by which the "globalization of constitutional law" has occurred. What techniques have been used to create a kind of supranational overlapping constitutional consensus, as it were? The chapters by Jackson and Choudhry consider institutions that are usually understudied but are of great significance. Jackson turns to legislatures and their role in the constitutional system, a turn that relates to Tushnet's interest in emphasizing the role of other institutions in the protection of rights. Choudhry looks at political parties, whose importance Tushnet has repeatedly emphasized both in *Why the Constitution Matters* and in *The New Fourth Branch*, and puts forth a taxonomy for how constitutional texts address, regulate, and empower political parties with their design framework.[16]

Tushnet's work on the varieties of constitutionalism reflects his great intellectual curiosity, as well as his skepticism about strong versions of judicial supremacy and strong entrenchment of legal norms against popular revision. His work, as seen for example in his coedited collection on "unstable constitutionalism" in South Asia, has long moved beyond the standard set of Western constitutional democracies and has been vital to the field's taking constitutionalism seriously in all its forms and challenges.[17] In their introduction to *Defining the Field of Comparative Constitutional Law*, Tushnet and his coauthor noted the difficulty in finding a term to juxtapose with "constitutional law," in the way that one can juxtapose and contrast civil law and common law. In order to counterpose constitutional law with some other concept, it would be important, they observed, to inquire into normative questions pertaining to the goals of constitutions.[18] Tushnet's paper on "Authoritarian Constitutionalism" can be viewed as an effort to overcome the narrowed normativity of many analyses of constitutionalism by arguing that one could envision a system that had some of the rule of law attributes associated with constitutionalism, with only moderate degrees of democratic participation and moderate to low levels of rights protection, as in the way he characterized Singapore.[19] The benefit of this category, he suggested, was, among other things, to expand the field of study for comparative constitutional scholars. In this volume, Cora Chan's chapter on "Pluralizing Constitutionalism" takes up Tushnet's invitation to think beyond liberal constitutionalism by focusing on Ernst Fraenkel's

[16] Mark Tushnet, Why the Constitution Matters (2011); Mark Tushnet, The New Fourth Branch: Institutions for Protecting Constitutional Democracy (2021).

[17] Unstable Constitutionalism: Law and Politics in South Asia (Mark Tushnet & Madhav Khosla eds., 2015).

[18] Vicki C. Jackson & Mark Tushnet, *Introduction*, in Defining the Field of Comparative Constitutional Law, *supra* note 9, at xv–xvi.

[19] Mark Tushnet, *Authoritarian Constitutionalism*, 100 Cornell L. Rev. 391 (2015).

idea of the dual state and its application in the context of Hong Kong.[20] Po Jen Yap connects Tushnet's work on dialogic judicial review and on authoritarian constitutionalism by considering how constitutional courts function in "First World autocracies" such as Singapore and Hong Kong, thereby allowing us to think about the nature of judicial review across regime types. Interestingly, as readers will see, the contributions for this volume have illuminated other areas in which Tushnet's work has played a leadership role, broadening normativity in a different direction. Cheryl Saunders' chapter, arguing for deeper engagements between international law and constitutional law, is an instantiation and elaboration of perspectives Mark has raised repeatedly in his scholarship.[21]

In studying the varieties of constitutionalism, Tushnet has, of course, been a key voice in the ongoing conversation on democratic backsliding and authoritarian populism.[22] In particular, he has suggested that we must be sensitive to different forms of populism, and we must not view all populist endeavors as equally authoritarian or regressive in character.[23] This suggestion, developed at length in his coauthored book with Bojan Bugarič, *Power to the People*, has been central to problematizing the idea of populism.[24] In his chapter in the volume, Bugarič draws on this work and connects it to Tushnet's prior writing on popular constitutionalism. It is important, Bugarič reminds us, to notice the deep democratic character of certain populist movements. The chapters by Khosla and Mehta similarly engage with the theme of populism. For Khosla, *Power to the People* offers an invitation to consider what kinds of political formations may follow from our present populist moment, and outlines a sketch for competitive populism as a particular regime type. Mehta, in turn, looks at how features of democratic mobilization can themselves pose a challenge to liberal democracy, focusing in particular on the challenges posed by dissent and nationalism.

From his collection on *Unstable Constitutionalism*, which held up for consideration Global South forms of constitutionalism and innovations in constitution-making and constitutional law, to his repeated efforts at joinder with other fields

[20] *See* Ernst Fraenkel, The Dual State: A Contribution to the Theory of Dictatorship (2017 [1941]).

[21] *See, e.g.*, Jackson & Tushnet, *supra* note 18, at xix (emphasizing as a theme the importance of globalization in understanding comparative constitutional law); *id.* at xi (noting that "constitutionalism has spread in tandem with the growth of international law commitments to human rights law and the development of transnational legal regimes for trade and commerce"); Mark Tushnet, *Federalism and International Human Rights in the New Constitutional Order*, 41 Wayne L. Rev. 841 (2001) (exploring federalism-based obstacles to integrating international human rights law in the US constitutional order); Mark Tushnet, *The Canon(s) of Constitutional Law: An Introduction*, 17 Const. Comment. 187, 193 (2000) (discussing arguments from "cosmopolitanism" that the canon of US constitutional law should include more consideration of international law).

[22] *See* Constitutional Democracy in Crisis? (Mark A. Graber, Sanford Levinson & Mark Tushnet eds., 2018).

[23] *See* Mark Tushnet, *Varieties of Populism*, 20 German L.J. 382 (2019).

[24] Mark Tushnet & Bojan Bugarič, Power to the People: Constitutionalism in the Age of Populism 36–53 (2022).

to improve more contextualized understandings of law, Tushnet has long sought to expand the range of our learning both across and beyond legal systems.[25] As Tushnet and his coauthor observed in their early collection: "If it is correct that both constitutional law and constitutional systems depend importantly on popular understandings and the political-social environment, then the work of constitutional law and comparative constitutional law cannot carry forward in intellectual isolation from the work of other disciplines of political science, sociology, cultural anthropology, the cognitive sciences, or economics."[26] They hoped that "comparative constitutional study will revive interest in the direction of broader understandings of relevant knowledge."[27] As the contributions of Cheryl Saunders, Tom Ginsburg and Mila Versteeg, Ran Hirschl, and David Law—both to this volume and in their other work—reveal, this suggestion has been quite strongly taken up.

Tushnet has long made clear that the "relevant knowledge" also extends to history—that is, he has argued that the study of constitutional law and constitutionalism "requires greater knowledge of and engagement with the broader context in which law and legal decisions occur," including history.[28] In this spirit, Catherine O'Regan's chapter draws on five decades of history and political development in Kenya to explain the significance of the Supreme Court's *BBI* decision and its interpretations of the 2010 constitution. Erin Delaney draws attention to the significance of histories of colonialism and degrees of coercion in different constitution-making contexts.

Tushnet's skepticism about broad normative claims for constitutional law has never been more prescient than in the past decade. The 1990s, when Mark Tushnet first started working in this field, were a time of great optimism about the "possibilities of comparative constitutional law."[29] In many countries, authoritarian, dominant-party regimes were collapsing—and new constitutions committed to democracy, the protection of human rights, independent courts, and separation of powers were being written and put into effect. The last decade and a half, however, has been one of declining faith in liberal democracy and in the aspects of constitutionalism that consist of constraints on popular majorities. As Madhav Kkosla discusses in his chapter, it is an era where politics now persists without institutions as postwar constitutional democrats had envisaged them, and where the (ab) use of the forms of legality are being used to—in another of Tushnet's insightful

[25] *See, e.g.*, Tushnet, *Possibilities of Comparative Constitutional Law*, *supra* note 2, at 1285–86 (explaining the concept of bricolage developed by French anthropologist Claude Lévi-Strauss); Mark Tushnet, *Interdisicplinary Legal Scholarship: The Case of History-in-Law*, 71 Chi.-Kent L. Rev. 909 (1996) (exploring different approaches to history, including how a historian might question even the best of "law-office history").

[26] Jackson & Tushnet, *Introduction*, *supra* note 18, at xviii.

[27] *Id.*

[28] Jackson & Tushnet, *Introduction*, *supra* note 18, at xvii; *see* Tushnet, *The Possibilities of Comparative Constitutional Law*, *supra* note 2, at 1270–78 (discussing how distinct national histories may be expressed in constitutions or constitutional law).

[29] Tushnet, *The Possibilities of Comparative Constitutional Law*, *supra* note 2.

phrases—"pus[h] the envelope" of what is lawful in directions that move away from the realm of liberal democracy.[30]

Mark Tushnet has applied his typical curiosity and sense of skepticism to claims being made about this time. There is a question mark at the end of the book he coedited on *Constitutional Democracy in Crisis?*[31] And in his work with Bojan Bugarič Mark has questioned whether "populism" should be treated as an undifferentiated political phenomena, from an empirical and normative point of view. David Donald's chapter, for example, deploys a skepticism analogous to Tushnet's about the role of common law adjudication in the construction of markets, reflecting on the relationship between legal reasoning and constitutional political economy. Other contributors acknowledge the skepticism—both in the past and today—while also, as in O'Regan's chapter, noting Tushnet's insistence on the possibility that a sense of law's autonomy may matter to the internal logic of legal decisionmakers.

The Contributions Toward Redefining the Field

The contributions in this volume have been organized in five parts that correspond to the themes identified above.

Part I addresses large questions of methodology and attitude in doing comparative constitutional work. Rosalind Dixon provides a helpful explication of five differing modalities of comparative constitutional law: studies of the migration of constitutional ideas; deliberative comparisons of foreign courts and their reasoning on similar issues; empirical or functional comparisons; dialogical or expressive approaches; and moral cosmopolitanism. The chapters following hers provide echoes of broader debates in the field about comparative constitutional law and comparative constitutional studies.[32] Hirschl argues that the field of comparative constitutional law has expanded and been transformed—transformed to embrace a wider field of comparative constitutional studies as reflected in methodologies used, and broadened to include new subject matters entirely (including, e.g., environmental constitutionalism). Ginsburg and Versteeg argue against the

[30] Mark Tushnet, *Constitutional Hardball*, 37 J. Marshall L. Rev. 523, 535 (2004); *cf. id* at 523 ("A shorthand sketch of constitutional hardball is this: it consists of political claims and practices—legislative and executive initiatives—that are without much question within the bounds of existing constitutional doctrine and practice but that are nonetheless in some tension with existing *pre*-constitutional understandings").

[31] Constitutional Democracy in Crisis?, *supra* note 22.

[32] *See generally* Hirschl, Comparative Matters, *supra* note 3; Vicki C. Jackson, *Comparative Constitutional Law, Legal Realism, and Empirical Legal Science*, 96 B.U. L. Rev. 1359 (2016); Stephen Gardbaum, *How Do and Should We Compare Constitutional Law?*, *in* Comparing Comparative Law 109 (Samantha Besson et al. eds., 2017); Theunis Roux, *Comparative Constitutional Studies: Two Fields or One?*, 13 Ann. Rev. L. & Soc. Sci. 123 (2017); Madhav Khosla, *Is a Science of Comparative Constitutionalism Possible?*, 135 Harv. L. Rev. 2110 (2022).

proposition that the indeterminacy of constitutional texts without interpretation, and the wide varieties of interpretation of similar words, stand as obstacles to meaningful empirical comparisons of constitutional texts. Sandy Levinson reminds us of, and emphasizes, the role of epistemic modesty in Tushnet's own approach to his research work, and explores how such modesty contributes to "true complexity of his particular form of engagement" with comparative constitutional law. David Law explores the idea of "canon" in comparative constitutional law, identifying the exclusionary risks of "canonical" approaches (e.g., compounding disadvantages for scholars from non-canonical countries), but offering new ways of thinking about the selection of materials that are taught, focusing on choosing particular works for their "representative" (rather than "canonical") character. Kim Scheppele offers a new conceptualization of the work in the entire field, based on the networking of ant colonies in their projects—so not an approach "resting on a coherent normative theory" but rather an approach "developed out of mutual constitution between texts, practices, histories, people, objects and animating ideas" in "particular historical and cultural backgrounds." Maartje De Visser explores how language itself poses challenges for the field of comparative law, in four different respects: "literal translation; . . . legal-conceptual translation; a multilingual discourse that is marked by fragmentation; and expectations in communication with a foreign or international readership."

Part II addresses how constitutions come to be constituted. Contributions from Frank Michelman and Pratap Bhanu Mehta explore the presuppositions of and challenges to liberal constitutionalism. Michelman considers what a background commitment to constitutional democracy demands. Does it, in particular, require an institutional adoption of an independent tribunal with powers of review? For Mehta, both the impossibility of full and complete consent of all members of the population to any basic law, and the identity-based challenges of nationalism, pose obstacles for implementing liberal constitutionalism today. Peter Cane explores the varying forms of constitutional architecture that different systems can follow in allocating powers and functions (including the functions of, for example, "implementing and interpreting" and "oversight") among different parts of the government, with ensuing implications for what each part does. Richard Albert and Aharon Barak explore limits on the constituent power to make or amend constitutions. Albert describes several different modalities by which courts around the world have undertaken to subject domestic constitutions to international legal values, and suggests consideration of an "international constitutional court." Barak argues that the initial terms on which a people's self-conception is defined—in Israel, in its Declaration of Independence—may operate as an external limit on the constituent power. Cheryl Saunders then calls attention to the increased role of international actors in the initial construction of constitutions, often functioning as peace agreements in civil conflicts. And David Landau analyzes the phenomenon of "ancillary powers" exercised by conventions called to write constitutions, and, while noting potential abuses, explores difficulties with attempts to limit their exercise of other governmental powers.

In Part III, the roles of rights and of courts are considered from different perspectives. Both Grimm and O'Regan (perhaps not coincidentally, both former members of their countries' constitutional courts) defend the role of legal reasoning in constitutional adjudication and urge the importance of taking legal reasoning seriously in evaluating judicial decisions. Scholarship that looks only at the outcomes of litigation or political processes misses something important, they argue, if such examinations fail to excavate the reasoning relied upon. Grimm interestingly suggests that perhaps the German Constitutional Court's procedures are more conducive to the justices deliberating together than in the United States. O'Regan discusses why the Supreme Court of Kenya rejected adopting an "unconstitutional constitutional amendment" doctrine in light of the tiered amending procedures already found in its constitution. Jeremy Waldron asks why "weak-form" judicial review is associated with constitutional challenges based on rights, rather than on structures, suggesting that the answer might have to do with whether for structural issues it is more important for the issue to be settled than for it to be settled correctly. In a spirit of skepticism about courts and about attacks on government regulation of markets not dissimilar to Tushnet's, David Donald explores "how the academy and governments alike . . . advocated the peeling away of unnatural legal and governmental layers of law and regulation;" "Liberating the natural forces of self-interest valorized common law as a lighter, plaintiff-driven substitute for *ex ante* regulation," he argues. Finally, Po Jen Yap explores "dialogic" review in the relatively rare context of "First World autocracies," arguing that weak forms of review (through statutory interpretation, or through highly calibrated uses of the power to declare laws unconstitutional only in areas not at the core of the dominant regime's interests) are necessary to sustain "a constructive and sustainable model of rights-protection" in these regimes.

In Part IV, three chapters explore the role of nonjudicial actors in sustaining constitutionalism. Yaniv Roznai offers a reconstruction of recent Israeli politics as an example of a mobilized people functioning as the ultimate check on abusive government, in the context of efforts by the ruling coalition to limit judicial review; Roznai's effort reminds us of the possibilities of popular mobilization to safeguard constitutional democracy. Sujit Choudhry calls attention to the very significant role of political parties in constitutional systems—a subject that has not always received due attention—and documents how different constitutions in the world address the role of political parties. Vicki Jackson takes up the need for a sense of civic obligation on the part of public representatives, as well as the public, and explores approaches to the cultivation of such attitudes.

The final section is devoted to varieties of constitutionalism, as one of Mark Tushnet's signal contributions is his call, in *Authoritarian Constitutionalism*, for constitutional scholars to broaden their understanding of what systems could be called "constitutional" and should be studied.[33] Bojan Bugarič elaborates on the different forms of popular constitutionalism, extending a theme explored in his recent book with Tushnet. Cora Chan's "pluralizing" of constitutionalism calls attention to "mixed constitutions," and in particular to the way in which some contemporary regimes, notably Hong Kong, are "dual states" under Fraenkel's influential theory. Madhav Khosla argues that for the foreseeable future a "competitive" set of populisms will be vying for constitutional power, after authoritarian populists have torn down prior liberal constitutional organs, with the possible result being that of entering a "phase of democracy without institutions." And Erin Delaney introduces yet another new category for consideration, which she calls "coercive constitutionalism" and which applies not only to the well-known cases of constitutions drafted under the constraint of occupying military powers but also to a much wider range of constitutions that emerge after colonial empires dissolve.

In Part V, the Epilogue, Jamal Greene offers personal reflections on Tushnet's contributions and how he has avoided the pitfalls of "constitutional tourism" while at the same time traveling, in the deep sense of the word, to other constitutional systems. Finally, Mark Tushnet himself joins the conversation. He offers a provocative reflection on constituent power, arguing that "the concept of constituent power is properly used only retrospectively," and also on language and the contexts in which working knowledge of other languages (do and do not) matter to the quality of the scholarship being produced.

Toward the Future

The chapters in this collection are a testament to the progress in the field of comparative constitutional law since the initial effort by Tushnet and his coeditor at *Defining the Field of Comparative Constitutional Law* more than two decades ago. At the time, the effort was to acknowledge the value of comparative study and to contribute toward a creation of "a community of scholars with the ability to learn about other systems, to analyze those systems and constitutional practices, and to communicate with one another about foreign and domestic experiences."[34] The question that informed this initial, preliminary effort at the creation of a field involved matters such as the relationship between comparative constitutional law and comparative law; the legitimacy of considering foreign constitutional law in domestic adjudication; the interactions among globalization, international law and other transnational forces, and domestic constitutional law, such as in the field of human rights; constitutionalism and popular understandings; the "dilemmas of equality"; and so forth. We have moved on from that initial phase in key ways,

[33] Tushnet, *Authoritarian Constitutionalism*, *supra* note 19.
[34] Jackson & Tushnet, *Introduction*, *supra* note 18, at xii.

perhaps above all in the sense that the case for comparative constitutional law today no longer needs so much of an argument in its support and that the field is now a more robust and diverse community across themes and jurisdictions.[35] There is, of course, much work that still remains to be done.

So, what is the future of comparative constitutional law as a field of study? Some longstanding debates are likely to endure—over the wisdom and viability of various forms of judicial review (strong and weak) as compared with various forms of political constitutionalism, or over different approaches to constitutional interpretation.[36] Others, such as the heated debate over inclusion of social welfare rights in the 1990s, have morphed, as increasing numbers of jurisdictions have taken various approaches to their inclusion and interpretation; as Mark Tushnet has said on many occasions, major constitutional questions over welfare rights now are less about whether to include them than how to implement them.

Innovations in constitutional design, many from Global South countries, have now been in place long enough to support empirical as well as conceptual study. How will future scholarship evaluate, for example, the "Fourth Branch" institutions about which Tushnet has written, such as those provided for in the 1996 South African constitution?[37] Or the various moves toward more participatory,

[35] In addition to the jurisdictions and forms of constitutionalism already noted, consider the expanding group of scholars now writing in English on constitutionalism in the Middle East and in Islamic states. *See, e.g.*, Yvonne Tew, *Stealth Theocracy*, 58 VA. J. INT'L L. 31 (2018); Intisar Rabb, *The Least Religious Branch? Judicial Review and the New Islamic Constitutionalism*, 17 UCLA J. INT'L L. & FOR. AFF. 75 (2013); Kristen Stilt, *"Islam is the Solution": Constitutional Visions of the Egyptian Muslim Brotherhood*, 46 TEX. INT'L L. J. 73 (2010); ZAID AL-ALI, ARAB CONSTITUTIONALISM: THE COMING REVOLUTION (2021); FEDERALISM AND DECENTRALIZATION IN THE CONTEMPORARY MIDDLE EAST AND NORTH AFRICA (Asli Ü. Bâli & Omar M. Dajani eds., 2023); THE RULE OF LAW IN THE ISLAMIC REPUBLIC OF IRAN: POWER, INSTITUTIONS, AND THE LIMITS OF REFORM (Hadi Enayat & Mirjam Künkler eds., forthcoming 2024). Although English is still a dominant language in transnational discourse about constitutions and constitutionalism, it is noteworthy that recently at least one leading English-language journal, the *International Journal of Constitutional Law*, has begun sometimes publishing in Spanish. *See* Gráinne de Búrca & J.H.H. Weiler, *Editorial: I•CON in Spanish—I•CON en Español*, 19 INT'L J. CONST. L. 786 (2021).

[36] One important debate, for example, relates to how rights are understood, interpreted, and enforced. *See generally* AHARON BARAK, PROPORTIONALITY: CONSTITUTIONAL RIGHTS AND THEIR LIMITATIONS (2012); PROPORTIONALITY AND THE RULE OF LAW: RIGHTS, JUSTIFICATION, REASONING (Grant Huscroft, Bradley W. Miller & Grégoire Webber eds., 2014); PROPORTIONALITY: NEW FRONTIERS, NEW CHALLENGES (Vicki C. Jackson & Mark Tushnet eds., 2017); NIELS PETERSEN, PROPORTIONALITY AND JUDICIAL ACTIVISM FUNDAMENTAL RIGHTS ADJUDICATION IN CANADA, GERMANY AND SOUTH AFRICA (2017); FRANCISCO J. URBINA, A CRITIQUE OF PROPORTIONALITY AND BALANCING (2017); PROPORTIONALITY IN ASIA (Po Jen Yap ed., 2020); JAMAL GREENE, HOW RIGHTS WENT WRONG: WHY OUR OBSESSION WITH RIGHTS IS TEARING AMERICA APART (2021).

[37] TUSHNET, THE NEW FOURTH BRANCH, *supra* note 16. *See also* Tarunabh Khaitan, *Guarantor Institutions*, 16 ASIAN J. COMP. L. s40 (2021). In addition to these well-known Chapter 9 organs in South Africa, future constitutional studies may well focus on provisions designed to preserve an independent and impartial civil service. *See, e.g.*, 1991 Const. of Colombia arts. 209–10; Case C-588 (Const. Ct, Colombia, 2009) (holding a constitutional amendment an impermissible "substitution" where it impaired requirements for merit-based civil service); Vicki C. Jackson, *Knowledge Institutions and Democratic Backsliding: A Research Agenda*, *in* THE RESEARCH HANDBOOK ON LAW AND DEMOCRACY (Glenn Patmore ed., forthcoming 2025). For reflections on fourth branch institutions in the context of welfare constitutionalism, *see* Raymond A. Atuguba & Katharine G. Young, *Developmental*

inclusive, and/or consultative modes of governance that have emerged across countries of the world in constitution-making and implementation?[38]

Larger questions shadow the field: If the field was, at one time, only or primarily about liberal democratic constitutionalism, do less democratic, more autocratic forms of constitutionalism now demand more systematic attention, as Professor Tushnet has argued? Have some countries—India, or the United States—grown too large or too polarized for constitutionalism of a neat, clear variety to work? What is the relationship of corruption to constitutionalism?[39] In many parts of the world administrative law is seen as closely connected to constitutional law, though this is much less the case in the United States. Is public administration an essential aspect of (liberal forms of) constitutionalism?[40] Will right-leaning governments around the world reshape constitutional law in more statist, or more libertarian, or more conservative directions? Is there value across regimes of having relatively independent structures within overall governance? How can constitutionalists, especially those trained in the close analysis of particular provisions or doctrines, respond to the challenges Kim Scheppele has posed in explaining how systemic, interactive constitutional elements combine together to create unconstitutional conditions?[41]

Perhaps the largest challenges for the future arise from (actual or perceived) differences among the countries of the world and their public law practices. When Jackson and Tushnet published the first edition of their *Comparative Constitutional Law Casebook* in 1999,[42] many perceived clear divisions in the world between countries that were democratic and constitutionalist and those that were authoritarian and nonconstitutionalist. Moreover, at that time differences between constitutions and constitutional law, and other sources of public law (international law, domestic statutes, domestic administrative regulation, domestic common law, and so on), loomed large, and served to narrow the scope of what was considered part of the field of comparative constitutional law.

Constitutionalism and the Fourth Branch: Ghana's Independent Constitutional Bodies and the Redress of Poverty and Inequality, 51 FED. L. REV. 399 (2023).

[38] Consider here the "citizens' assemblies" now used in Ireland as a preliminary vehicle for considering and adopting constitutional amendments, or the many countries that now impose or authorize gender parity (as in France) or gender quota (as in Rwanda and India) rules on the composition of legislative bodies, or even in the conventions to draft constitutions (as in Chile).

[39] *See* Matthew C. Stephenson, *Constitutionalism and Public Corruption*, *in* CONSTITUTIONALISM AND A RIGHT TO EFFECTIVE GOVERNMENT? 247 (Vicki C. Jackson & Yasmin Dawood eds., 2022).

[40] *See, e.g.*, José Ignacio Hernández G., *Administrative Procedure Acts in Latian America*, THE REGULATORY REVIEW (Nov. 3, 2022), https://www.theregreview.org/2022/11/03/hernandez-administrative-procedure-acts-in-latin-america/ (noting Jorge Fernández Ruiz's argument "that Latin American administrative law is the concretization of constitutional law").

[41] *See* Kim Lane Scheppele, *The Rule of Law and the Frankenstate: Why Governance Checklists Do Not Work*, 26 GOVERNANCE 559 (2013).

[42] VICKI C. JACKSON & MARK TUSHNET, COMPARATIVE CONSTITUTIONAL LAW (1999).

Today, both sets of bifurcations—between constitutional democracies and other polities, and between constitutional law and other sources of law—have weakened in their descriptive power; the categories have become much more permeable. Much scholarly work today is being done on "small c" constitutionalism; thus, for example, the mere enactment or reactivation of laws on sedition, criminal defamation, and the like, may be studied and understood as part of a matrix of constitutionalism, even if the events occur at the level of statutory enactment or enforcement decisions. In order to understand constitutionalism in Hungary, scholars today are unlikely to focus only on the formal constitution and its interpretation but also on the practices of the government. Even in the United States, courses are now being offered that study the constitutionalist aspects of public administration.[43]

Moreover, as this collection powerfully demonstrates, the division of countries into a binary—of liberal democratic versus authoritarian governments—no longer seems to capture the lived reality of modern constitutional experience. The United States, which was in the 1990s perceived as a reasonably free, reasonably liberal, functioning democracy, has fallen sharply in international rankings of civil rights and civil liberties, and has begun to suffer the kind of violence and attempted *coups d'état* that were thought to characterize more authoritarian regimes. Hungary and Poland have likewise swung from being well-rated liberal democracies to falling sharply in evaluations of protection of civil rights and civil liberties and in the quality of democracy, though the recent election in Poland suggests it might be moving in a different direction. Seemingly well-established constitutional courts, as in Israel and Hungary, came under fire and (sometimes successful) attack to turn what had been independent judicial bodies into dependent arms of the government in power. Elements of constitutionalism have been identified as existing in an authoritarian system such as that of Singapore, dubbed by Mark Tushnet as a form of authoritarian constitutionalism. There has been much movement of particular countries on evaluations of democracy, judicial independence, and respect for rights, and there has been an increased perception that democracy and respect for rights must be evaluated on a spectrum, not through bipolar categories.

These changes in recent decades—the degree to which prior certainties and categories are now up for grabs—have implications for the study and subject matter of comparative constitutional law. Generally, it has become much more difficult to decide on what to study, what to compare. This is true both with respect to particular countries, and with respect to particular laws (constitutional or nonconstitutional). It is the hope of the editors—and all of the contributors—that Professor Tushnet will long continue to shed light on these issues and guide the field for many more years to come.

[43] *See, e.g.*, Harvard Law School, Constitutional Dimensions of the Administrative State: Comparative Perspectives (reading Group, offered Spring and Fall 2023, Prof. Vicki C. Jackson).

1

How to Compare Constitutionally: An Essay in Honor of Mark Tushnet

Rosalind Dixon[*]

It is a real honor and pleasure to have the opportunity to join in celebrating Mark Tushnet's contribution to the field of comparative constitutional law.[1] Tushnet has been one of the pioneers of the field in the US, and a wonderful mentor and interlocutor to scholars in the field around the world. I certainly count myself as extremely fortunate to have had Tushnet play both these roles in my scholarly career.

Tushnet was a key influence in encouraging my own scholarly interest in 'weak' forms of judicial review.[2] I remember reading Tushnet's work on *Taking the Constitution Away from the Courts* and *Alternative Forms of Judicial Review*,[3] and being inspired to study comparative constitutional 'dialogue' as an SJD at Harvard Law School.[4] Tushnet also examined my SJD thesis and gave extremely generous feedback and encouragement in pursuing the idea of dialogue and weak-form review in a broader comparative context, and in 2011, coauthored with me a piece on

* The author thanks participants at online workshops of papers for helpful comments on previous versions of the chapter, the ARC and Manos Foundation for research support, and Hayden Clift for outstanding research assistance. A prior version of parts of this chapter previously appeared in Spanish in the *Latin American Law Review*. The author thanks the LALR for permission to reprint parts of that article in translated form. The chapter also overlaps in its substantive focus with Rosalind Dixon, *Comparative Constitutional Modalities: Towards a Rigorous but Realistic Comparative Constitutional Studies*, 2 Comp. Const. Stud. (2024); Rosalind Dixon, "Constitutional Comparison and Case Selection" in Dixon, Langford and Law, *Comparative Constitutional Method: a Reader* (Forthcoming, Elgar 2024).

1 Ran Hirschl, Comparative Matters: The Renaissance of Comparative Constitutional Law (2014).

2 The concept has a variety of meanings, but is generally used to refer to models of judicial review in which there is broad scope for legislative override: *see generally* Mark Tushnet, Weak Courts, Strong Rights: Judicial Review and Social Welfare Rights in Comparative Constitutional Law (2009); Rosalind Dixon, *Creating Dialogue about Socioeconomic Rights: Strong-Form versus Weak-Form Judicial Review Revisited*, 5 Int'l J. Const. L. 391 (2007); Rosalind Dixon, *The Forms, Functions and Varieties of Weak(ened) Review*, 17 Int'l J. Const. L. 904 (2019).

3 Mark Tushnet, Taking the Constitution Away from the Courts (2000); Mark Tushnet, *Alternative Forms of Judicial Review*, 101 Mich. L. Rev. 2781 (2002).

4 Tushnet's Weak Courts, Strong Rights, *supra* note 2, came later when I was already nearly finished. I was also influenced in this context by Stephen Gardbaum, The New Commonwealth Model of Constitutionalism: Theory and Practice (2013); Stephen Gardbaum, *The New Commonwealth Model of Constitutionalism*, 49 Am. J. Comp. L. 707 (2001).

Rosalind Dixon, *How to Compare Constitutionally: An Essay in Honor of Mark Tushnet* In: *Redefining Comparative Constitutional Law*. Edited by: Vicki C. Jackson and Madhav Khosla, Oxford University Press. © Rosalind Dixon 2025.
DOI: 10.1093/9780191996344.003.0001

weak review in Asia.[5] Since then, Tushnet has also been a tireless friend and interlocutor on almost all the major comparative projects I have undertaken.

Tushnet is not the traditional mentor for a female constitutional scholar from Australia: he would be unlikely to be found at any mentoring event, let alone one for junior or mid-career women (from Australia). But over many years and emails, he has provided a consistent stream of encouragement and criticism, which has played a vital role in my development as a scholar. My academic work would certainly have been poorer, and my career lonelier, but for his engagement.

In the remainder of this chapter, however, I want to focus on a specific topic on which Tushnet has written and where his words have had a powerful impact on my thinking: the topic of comparative methodology. Tushnet has contributed to debate on methodology at three key levels: first, by providing a useful taxonomy for thinking about different modes of comparison (taxonomy); second, by using and citing a variety of different methods of comparison (mixed methods); and third, by engaging in rigorous if under-theorized modes of comparison.

I therefore want to pay tribute to Tushnet's role in the field by celebrating this implicit methodological contribution. The remainder of the chapter is divided into four sections. Section 1 provides a taxonomy of different modes of comparison and relates those to the modes of comparison identified by Tushnet and others in previous work. Section 2 considers the different modes or forms of comparison implicit in Tushnet's work, as exemplifying his own methodological eclecticism. Section 3 notes the rigorous principles of case selection implicit in these various approaches, and section 4 offers a brief conclusion considering the link between these lessons and Tushnet's contribution to the field.

Five Modes of Constitutional Comparison

Practices of constitutional comparison can be organized or conceptualized in a variety of different ways.[6] Tushnet himself, in his essay in the *Yale Law Journal* on the "Possibilities of Comparative Constitutional Law," identified three broad modes of comparison as having some potential relevance to the construction of the US Constitution: "functionalism," "expressivism," and "bricolage."[7] In my own

[5] Mark Tushnet & Rosalind Dixon, *Weak-Form Review and Its Constitutional Relatives: An Asian Perspective*, *in* COMPARATIVE CONSTITUTIONAL LAW IN ASIA 102 (Rosalind Dixon & Tom Ginsburg eds., 2014) (exploring the normative and practical political preconditions for weakened forms of review).

[6] *See generally* Vicki C. Jackson, *Foreword—Comment: Constitutional Comparisons, Convergence, Resistance, Engagement*, 119 HARV. L. REV. 109 (2005); Mark Tushnet, *The Possibilities of Comparative Constitutional Law*, 108 YALE L.J. 1225 (1999); Sujit Choudhry, *Globalization in Search of Justification: Toward a Theory of Comparative Constitutional Interpretation*, 74 IND. L.J. 819 (1999); Nicholas Aroney, *Comparative Law in Australian Constitutional Jurisprudence*, 26 UNIV. QUEENSL. L.J. 317 (2007).

[7] Tushnet, *supra* note 6.

work, I have suggested that if we go beyond the US constitutional context and consider the full possible universe of comparison, it may be useful to think of there being five, rather than three, broad modes of comparison. But these modes inevitably overlap with those identified by Tushnet and may themselves be "thin" or "thick," and "positive" or "negative" (or "aversive"), in influence.[8]

The first mode of comparison is oriented toward the "migration" or "transfer" of constitutional ideas,[9] or what Vicki Jackson has called a form of constitutional "convergence."[10] The purpose of comparison of this kind is to identify constitutional *language*, *structures* or *doctrines* from other jurisdictions that might be "borrowed," or "transferred" to one's own jurisdiction, or that have already influenced domestic constitutional design. For constitutional drafters, the focus will generally be on constitutional language and structures, whereas for lawyers and judges it will be on *doctrines* that can usefully be borrowed. But in both cases, the aim is to identify useful practices for borrowing or adaptation.

At "time 2," borrowing of this kind can also invite "genetic" or "genealogical" forms of comparison.[11] Genetic modes of comparison involve looking to how another jurisdiction understood or interpreted a constitutional provision at the time it was borrowed, whereas forms of "genealogical" comparison involve a consideration of how all countries with common constitutional structures or norms have interpreted those norms over time. In both cases, however, the logic of comparison is borrowing-based and backward-looking in nature.[12]

A second form of comparison is "deliberative" in nature. It involves considering how foreign lawyers and courts have framed arguments around the construction of common or similar constitutional provisions.

A third mode of comparison is "empirical" or "functional" in nature.[13] It focuses on the actual practices, rather than forms, decisions, or arguments adopted

[8] Richard Primus, *A Brooding Omnipresence: Totalitarianism in Postwar Constitutional Thought*, 106 YALE L.J. 423 (1996); Kim Lane Scheppele, *Aspirational and Aversive Constitutionalism: The Case for Studying Cross-Constitutional Influence through Negative Models*, 1 INT'L J. CONST. L. 296 (2003). For examples, *see, e.g.*, the influence of the US Constitution on the South African Constitution equality clause, as discussed in Pretoria City Council v. Walker, 1998 (2) SALR 363 (CC): *see* Po-Jen Yap, *Four Models of Equality*, 27 LOY. L.A. INT'L & COMP. L. REV. 63, 77 (2005). *See also* Sujit Choudhry, *The Lochner Era and Comparative Constitutionalism*, 2 INT'L J. CONST. L. 1 (2004).

[9] *See, e.g.*, GÜNTER FRANKENBERG, ORDER FROM TRANSFER: COMPARATIVE CONSTITUTIONAL DESIGN AND LEGAL CULTURE (2013); Vlad Perju, *Constitutional Transplants, Borrowing, and Migrations*, *in* THE OXFORD HANDBOOK OF COMPARATIVE CONSTITUTIONAL LAW 1304 (Michel Rosenfeld & Andras Sajo eds., 2012); Günter Frankenberg, *Constitutional Transfer: The IKEA Theory Revisited*, 8 INT'L J. CONST. L. 563 (2010); THE MIGRATION OF CONSTITUTIONAL IDEAS (Sujit Choudhry ed., 2006); Lee Epstein & Jack Knight, *Constitutional Borrowing and Nonborrowing*, 1 INT'L J. CONST. L. 196 (2003).

[10] VICKI JACKSON, CONSTITUTIONAL ENGAGEMENT IN A TRANSNATIONAL ERA (2013).

[11] Louis Henkin, *A New Birth of Constitutionalism: Genetic Influences and Genetic Defects*, 14 CARDOZO L. REV. 533 (1993); Choudhry, *supra* note 6.

[12] Choudhry, *supra* note 6, at 838–39.

[13] *Compare* Tushnet, *supra* note 6; Rosalind Dixon, *A Democratic Theory of Constitutional Comparison*, 56 AM. J. COMP. L. 947 (2008).

in foreign constitutional systems, and in some cases, the origins and consequences of those practices.

A fourth mode is "reflective"[14] in nature, though it is also called "reflexive"[15] or "dialogic"[16] or understood as looking in the mirror.[17] Tushnet called this form of comparison "expressive."[18] It involves attempting to understand the self, or, in a constitutional context, our collective constitutional identity and values, through confronting countries with both similar and different values and traditions.[19] Hence, it can be both "aversive" or negative and positive or recognition-based in nature.[20]

And a fifth mode of comparison is "moral–cosmopolitan" in nature. It proceeds from the assumption that there are universal answers to certain common global problems and that by looking around the world, we can get a better sense of what those answers might be. And while comparison of this kind is often focused on human rights norms, it can also extend—as David Landau and I have shown—to structural constitutional contexts, and thus help shed light on notions such as the "minimum core" requirements of constitutional democracy.[21]

Each of the different modes of comparison may also be used in "thinner" or "thicker" ways.[22] Thinner forms of comparison will be those focused on constitutional text, or the formal features or a constitution or particular legal system, where thicker approaches will extend to considering the context for the adoption and implementation of legal norms, and their real-world effects.

There are also hybrid approaches, which combine elements of these different approaches. Tushnet, for instance, has highlighted the potential combination of reflective/expressive and more "bricolage"-oriented forms of comparison. The idea of bricolage, as Tushnet notes, draws on the work of Claude Levi Strauss, who coined the term to describe "the assembly of something new from whatever materials are at hand."[23] Comparison of this kind has clear empirical or functional dimensions, but also reflective benefits. As Tushnet notes, "thinking about constitution-making as a process of bricolage . . . casts doubt on a form of textualism that attributes to the

[14] Dixon, *supra* note 13, at 959–60.

[15] *See* Tushnet, *supra* note 6, at 1268.

[16] Choudhry, *supra* note 6, at 835–38.

[17] Frank I. Michelman, *Reflection: Symposium: Comparative Avenues in Constitutional Law—Borrowing*, 82 Tex. L. Rev. 1737 (2004).

[18] Tushnet, *supra* note 6, at 1304.

[19] Elsewhere I have suggested that this mode can be further subdivided into static and dynamic forms of reflective comparison: Dixon, *supra* note 13.

[20] Primus, *supra* note 8; Scheppele, *supra* note 8.

[21] Rosalind Dixon & David Landau, *Transnational Constitutionalism and a Limited Doctrine of Unconstitutional Constitutional Amendment*, 13 Int'l J. Const. L. 606 (2015); David Landau & Rosalind Dixon, *Constraining Constitutional Change*, 50 Wake Forest L. Rev. 859 (2015).

[22] Compare the idea of thick description: Clifford Geertz, The Interpretation of Cultures (1973); Immy Holloway, Basic Concepts for Qualitative Research (1997); Yvonna S. Lincoln and Egon G. Guba, Naturalistic Inquiry (1985); Gilbert Ryle, The Concept of Mind (1949).

[23] Tushnet, *supra* note 6, at 1229.

constitution's writers a purpose of creating a tightly integrated document governed by a form of conceptual determinism."[24]

Another important question, when we think about constitutional comparison, is who is engaging in comparison, for what purpose, and in what context and with what audience in mind. In the US, for instance, there remains vigorous debate about whether constitutional comparison is useful and legitimate, where in most other countries the question is not whether to compare, but rather when or how much, or with what kind of focus. This can also influence how judges and lawyers approach the task of comparison, and how scholars—including Tushnet himself – framed their interventions in defense (or critique) of comparative constitutional engagement.

Take early decisions of the US Supreme Court and Constitutional Court of South Africa (CCSA) on LBGTQI+ rights. In the US, in *Lawrence v Texas*, in overturning *Bowers v Hardwick* and holding unconstitutional Texas' ban on same-sex intercourse, the Court engaged in a broad-ranging form of moral cosmopolitan comparison, noting that the right claimed "has been accepted as an integral part of human freedom in many other countries." But it placed greater emphasis on a more limited form of moral–cosmopolitan comparison—to the UK and Europe—aimed at *rebutting* the claim in *Bowers* that same-sex intimacy was contrary to Western tradition and "Judeo-Christian moral and ethical standards."[25]

In South Africa, in contrast, different forms of comparative engagement run throughout the decisions of the court in this same context. In *National Coalition I*, in considering the constitutionality of apartheid-era legislation banning consensual (anal) intercourse between adult men, the CCSA engaged in *doctrinal* comparison by surveying the constitutional practices of a large number of other constitutional democracies. In doing so, it also engaged in a form of *moral–cosmopolitan* comparison: it linked these practices to the question of whether the relevant limitations on the petitioners' rights to privacy, dignity and equality were reasonable and justifiable in a "open and democratic society."[26] At the same time, in doing so, it took a skeptical view of the representativeness of *Bowers v Hardwick*, as a statement of the contemporary US position on this question: in addition to highlighting important textual differences between the US and South African Constitutions in this context, in writing for the CCSA Justice Ackermann engaged in *thick contextual* analysis of the US position—noting that Bowers had been subject to "sustained criticism" in the US—and further implied that it was inconsistent with the decision of the US Supreme Court in *Romer v Evans*, which "struck down

[24] Tushnet, *supra* note 6, at 1300.

[25] Lawrence v. Texas, 539 US 558, 572–74 (2013).

[26] National Coalition for Gay and Lesbian Equality v. Minister of Justice, 1998 ZACC 15, at paras. 33–57.

an amendment to the Colorado State Constitution which prohibited public measures designed to protect persons based on their sexual orientation."[27]

It is not surprising, therefore, that comparative constitutional scholarship coming out of the US and South Africa around the same time has had a somewhat different focus and audience in mind. In South Africa the task is to continue an appropriately rigorous comparative constitutional dialogue,[28] whereas in the US it is often to defend the very legitimacy and utility of such a dialogue. Witness Tushnet's own writing in this vein, in articles such as *The Possibilities of Comparative Constitutional Law.*[29]

Methodological Eclecticism

In the course of his long and varied comparative constitutional career, Tushnet himself has also engaged in forms of comparison that span these different modes. He has long been a leading practitioner of theoretically focused, reflective modes of comparison of this kind. While his focus has not been on values *per se* but on broader constitutional logics, structures, and commitments, he has used reflective comparison to shed light on the underpinnings of a variety of dimensions to US constitutionalism—including the state action doctrine. In *Weak Courts, Strong Rights*, he engaged in a detailed and nuanced discussion of the state action doctrine in Canada, suggesting that the lessons for the US in this context were several, including: that the state action doctrine in the US is closely linked to limits on the capacity of courts (such as the US Supreme Court) to decide cases involving background rules of property, contract, and tort law, and to limits on the commitment of US constitutional culture to social and economic rights.[30] The concerns that "animate a state action doctrine," Tushnet suggested, largely "disappear where the courts can easily regulate private activity with no greater difficulties than legislatures can" (i.e. courts have broad, general jurisdiction).[31] But they are also inextricably linked to the scope of commitments to social and economic rights, or state provision.[32]

Tushnet also goes further and suggests that a comparative approach to the state action doctrine can reveal theoretical tensions in the relationship between commitments to social provision and the "private" sphere. Social democracies, Tushnet suggests, "are always incomplete, in that social provision is not, and

27 *Id.* at para. 54.

28 *See, e.g.*, L.W.H. Ackermann, *Constitutionalism Comparativism in South Africa*, 123 S. Afr. Law J. 497 (2006).

29 Tushnet, *supra* note 6.

30 Tushnet, *supra* note 2, at 198.

31 *Id.* at 203.

32 *Id.* at 198, 218–19.

probably never can be, comprehensive. Social democracies are also characterized by a public commitment to civil and political liberties. One aspect of that commitment is a commitment to maintaining some private domain free from public regulation."[33] This "incomplete system of social provision induces constitutional courts to consider that the actual level and distribution of material goods is consistent with the nation's constitutional commitment to social provision. The need to preserve a private domain leads constitutional courts to develop a state action doctrine. But preserving a private domain undermines efforts to sustain a constitutionally acceptable level and distribution of material goods."[34]

In other work, Tushnet has also engaged in wide-ranging forms of (albeit relatively thin forms of) empirical comparison. For instance, in his work on weak-form review, Tushnet has offered important empirical insights about the potential instability in weakened models of review, suggesting that there is often a tendency for weak review to become nonexistent or closer to strong-form review. One danger arises because legislatures may be (too) quick to use formal powers of legislative override in response to court decisions under such a system, and thereby create broad popular acceptance of the routine use of such powers.[35] The result will be that weak-form review becomes largely indistinguishable from a system of parliamentary supremacy.[36] And the opposite danger arises because if legislatures hesitate to use their powers of override—in part because there are no court decisions that meet clear majority disapproval, or courts are seen as providing "objective" interpretations of the constitution—something like a de facto convention may arise whereby legislators believe that they are not entitled to rely on such a power simply to express ordinary forms of (reasonable) democratic disagreement.[37] This time the result will be a system of de facto strong-form review.[38]

In our coauthored work on the topic, Tushnet has also led the way in combining both descriptive, normative, and empirical insights. In exploring weak-form review in Asia, Tushnet and I noted the degree to which the existence of a (single) dominant party tends to produce at least de facto weak review: in Japan, we noted the development of sub-constitutional forms of review by the Japanese Supreme Court, as creating a form of de facto weak review;[39] and in India, we likewise noted the role of (quite frequent) formal constitutional amendment in weakening the finality of decisions of the Supreme Court of India.[40] Beyond these descriptive

[33] *Id.* at 218.
[34] *Id.*
[35] *Id.* at 44–47.
[36] *Id.*
[37] *Id.* at 47–62.
[38] *Compare* Dixon, *Forms and Functions*, *supra* note 2, at 917.
[39] Tushnet & Dixon, *supra* note 5, at 108. *Compare* Dan T. Coenen, *A Constitution of Collaboration: Protecting Fundamental Values with Second-Look Rules of Interbranch Dialogue*, 42 Wm. & Mary L. Rev. 1575 (2001).
[40] Tushnet & Dixon, *supra* note 5, at 108–13, though we also note limits on this power imposed by the doctrine of unconstitutional constitutional amendment: at 112–13. *See also* David E. Landau, Rosalind

insights, however, we noted that a key contributing factor seemed to be the "persistent" domination of the legislature by a "single political party" in ways that have influenced norms of judicial appointment (in Japan), and the functional ease of amendment (in India).[41]

Methodological Rigor

Tushnet has often expressed skepticism about overtheorizing questions of comparative method and case selection, but he has also exemplified a rigorous approach to comparative case selection—even if only implicitly and in an incompletely theorized way.

Some forms of comparison raise few challenges of "case selection." Either the focus of comparative study will be largely self-evident, or there will be broad discretion as to what countries to focus on.

For historically focused modes of comparison, for example, there will be little choice as to what countries to look to for comparative insights: the scope of comparison will logically be restricted to those countries that historically had a meaningful influence on the drafting of a written constitution, or that shared the same historical constitutional norms and structures. This also extends to both "genetic" and "genealogical" modes of comparison.

For moral–cosmopolitan forms of comparison, the potential universe of comparison will likewise be fixed—by the need to consider either all constitutional systems, or all democratic constitutional systems. Reflective modes of comparison, in contrast, are almost entirely open-ended in scope. They can focus on countries with a high degree of similarity *or* difference to one's own: the expectation is that comparison may yield either positive or negative or "aversive" forms of reaction, both of which may be informative in clarifying domestic constitutional values and commitments.[42] The only constraint on the scope of comparison of this kind will arise where the focus of comparison is dynamic rather than static in nature. Here, there will be a requirement of ingoing general and topical similarity between countries.[43]

The same is true for deliberative modes of comparison. The usefulness of comparative arguments may vary, depending on the degree of similarity between the

Dixon & Yaniv Roznai, *From an Unconstitutional Constitutional Amendment to an Unconstitutional Constitution? Lessons from Honduras*, 8 GLOB. CONSTITUTIONALISM 40 (2019); Dixon & Landau, *supra* note 21; Landau & Dixon, *supra* note 21; Yaniv Roznai, *Unconstitutional Constitutional Amendments: The Migration and Success of a Constitutional Idea*, 61 AM. J. COMP. L. 657 (2013).

41 Tushnet & Dixon, *supra* note 5, at 113.
42 Primus, *supra* note 8; Scheppele *supra* note 8.
43 Dixon, *supra* note 13, at 979.

original and new constitutional setting. But they almost always have some relevance or utility.

However, there are two categories of comparison that *do* squarely raise issues of case selection: borrowing-oriented (and especially doctrinal) and empirical modes of comparison. Constitutional doctrines or structures developed elsewhere should only be borrowed—as opposed to redesigned and repurposed[44]—where there is a relatively high degree of ingoing similarity between constitutional systems. Similarity of this kind can also be measured across four broad levels, that is, similarities in (i) constitutional language or text; (ii) constitutional history; (iii) constitutional system and structures; and (iv) socio-political context and understandings.

Empirical forms of comparison likewise often call for quite demanding approaches to case selection. The thinnest forms of empirical comparison simply focus on foreign practices as a *possible* outcome of particular constitutional choices. But thicker forms of empirical comparison—or what Tushnet labels "functional" models of comparison—seek to understand the actual causal origins or impact of specific legal and constitutional choices.

This will also involve a turn either to large-n constitutional studies or small-n approaches that involve rigorous approaches to case selection. Large-n approaches have the virtue of being comprehensive.[45] But they also tend to focus on constitutional text as compared to the other features of a constitutional order.[46] And they are often only able to identify statistical correlations, as opposed to true causal relationships.[47]

Many comparative constitutional scholars (including Tushnet) have therefore tended to favor small over large-n approaches. And this has necessitated a rigorous approach to case selection. The leading approach in this context is one identified by Ran Hirschl, drawing on the insights of comparative politics. It involves adopting one or all of five principles, namely (i) the "most similar cases" principle, (ii) the "most different cases" principle, (iii) the "prototypical cases" principle, (iv) the "most difficult cases" principle, and (v) the "outlier cases" principle.[48]

[44] Tushnet, *supra* note 6, at 1285–1306.

[45] Hirschl, *supra* note 1, at 225.

[46] *See e.g.* Madhav Khosla, *Is a Science of Comparative Constitutionalism Possible?*, 135 Harv. L. Rev. 2110 (2022); Mark Tushnet, *"Sometimes the Magic Works. Sometimes It Doesn't": A Comment on Chilton and Versteeg*, Univ. Chi. L. Rev. Online (Apr. 5, 2021), https://lawreviewblog.uchicago.edu/2021/04/05/cv-tushnet/.

[47] Rosalind Dixon and Richard Holden, *Comparative Constitutional Matching: From Most Similar Cases to Synthetic Control?*, Univ. Chi. L. Rev. Online, https://lawreviewblog.uchicago.edu/2021/04/05/cv-dixon-holden/.

[48] *See* Ran Hirschl, *The Questions of Case Selection in Comparative Constitutional Law*, 53 Am. J. Comp. L. 125, 134 (2005) (most similar cases: "researchers should compare cases that have similar characteristics, or cases that are matched on all variables or potential explanations that are not central to the study, but vary in the values on the key independent and dependent variables"); 139 (most different cases: "researchers should compare cases that are different on all variables that are not central to the study but match in terms that are"); 142 (prototypical cases: "a prototypical case serves as a representative exemplar of other cases exhibiting similar pertinent characteristics"); 147 (outlier cases: "selecting

These are also all principles that Tushnet himself has employed at various times, albeit often implicitly rather than explicitly. In writing about weak review, for example, he has implicitly relied on a form of the "most similar cases" principle. Unlike Stephen Gardbaum, Tushnet does not regard the link between weak-form review and British parliamentary traditions, or "Commonwealth models" of constitutionalism, as definitional.[49] In principle, he could thus consider weak-form review in a wide variety of settings—including in Poland, Mongolia, Belgium, Luxembourg, and Finland.[50] But instead, he has focused on the use of weak-form review in countries such as New Zealand, the United Kingdom, and Canada.[51] This could be explained on more than one ground.

One is that these are effectively the "most similar" cases to the US—that is, countries that are "reasonably well-functioning democracies in which civil liberties and civil rights are reasonably well protected" in the same way as they are in the US, and thus which provide a meaningful comparator for US constitutionalists interested in the effect of weak versus strong models of judicial review.[52] But another is more practical: other than perhaps Mongolia, many other weak-form systems have a history of legislative rights protection. But Tushnet does not read Polish, Mongolian, Flemish, Finnish or (much) French, and German, and assessing the impact of weak-form review requires quite thick forms of comparison, which require attention to foreign decisions, legislative debate, and scholarly writing. In this sense, Tushnet clearly engaged in a form of realistic, provisional approach to comparison: he chose to focus on the cases where his own skills and knowledge could be used to best effect, but then continued to test and refine these ideas in subsequent studies of other countries,[53] and to encourage others to do so.[54]

Similarly, in writing about the judicial enforcement of social rights, in *Weak Courts, Strong Rights*, Tushnet chose to focus on Ireland and South Africa as examples of 'declaratory' and "weak" versus "strong" rights enforcement,[55] when logically he could just as easily have chosen to focus on India, Nepal, and Bangladesh, or Colombia or Brazil.[56] Again, this could have been justified on more

a number of outlier cases that cannot be explained by existing theories helps substantiate the new cause, explanation or argument through the a-priori elimination of alternative explanations").

[49] *See* Tushnet, *supra* note 2, at 24.

[50] Gardbaum, *supra* note 4.

[51] Tushnet, *supra* note 2, at 21.

[52] *Id.* at 24. But compare also at 75 (noting that there may be reasons why strong-form review is better for the US).

[53] *See, e.g.*, Tushnet & Dixon, *supra* note 5.

[54] He has done this both through his scholarship and supervision of masters and doctoral students. For example, he was a supervisor to Po Jen Yap, who has been one of the leading voices on weak-form review in common law Asia: *see* Po Jen Yap, Constitutional Dialogue in Common Law Asia (2015).

[55] Tushnet, *supra* note 2, at 238–50.

[56] On these jurisdictions, *see* Madhav Khosla, *Making Social Rights Conditional: Lessons from India*, 8 Int'l J. Const. L. 739 (2010); Farrah Ahmed & Tarunabh Khaitan, *Constitutional Avoidance in Social Rights Adjudication*, 35 Oxford J. Legal Stud. 607 (2015); Malcolm Langford & Ananda Mohan

than one ground: either as an application of the most similar cases principle, with a US constitutional audience in mind,[57] *or* as a realistic judgment about country expertise and language skills. At the time, Tushnet was quite familiar with Ireland and South African constitutional experience but had more limited knowledge of South Asian and Latin American constitutionalism.[58] And he does not read Portuguese or Spanish. Yet in later work, he has extended this analysis to consider a wide variety of other jurisdictions, including analyzing social rights in the context of recent neo-Bolivarian constitutional models.[59]

Conclusion

One of the *many* reasons to celebrate Tushnet as a pioneer of comparative constitutional law is because of his methodological contribution to the field. He has decried the idea of complex comparative methodology, yet at the same time provided a useful taxonomy of comparative modes, and used a mixture of different comparative methods. He has also sought to match relevant methods with the scope and subject-matter of the project.

Tushnet's work thus reminds us that paying attention to constitutional methodology need not mean treating that methodology as highly theoretical or complex. Comparative method can be implicit and undertheorized, and yet still rigorous and well-designed. Should we ever doubt this, we only need to return to Tushnet's vast body of comparative work to remind us.

Bhattarai, *Constitutional Rights and Social Exclusion in Nepal*, 18 INT'L J. MINORITY & GROUP RTS. 387 (2011); Awal Hossain Mollah, *Judicial Activism and Human Rights in Bangladesh: A Critique*, 56 INT'L J.L. & MANAGEMENT 475 (2014); Daniel M. Brinks & Varun Gauri, *The Law's Majestic Equality? The Distributive Impact of Judicializing Social and Economic Rights*, 12 PERSP. POL. 375 (2014); David Landau, *The Reality of Social Rights Enforcement*, 53 HARV. INT'L L.J. 189 (2012).

[57] Hirschl, *supra* note 1, at 241–42.

[58] For earlier writings on Ireland and South Africa, *see* Mark Tushnet, *Social Welfare Rights and the Forms of Judicial Review*, 82 TEX. L. REV. 1895 (2003); .Mark Tushnet, *State Action, Social Welfare Rights, and the Judicial Role: Some Comparative Observations*, 3 CHI. J. INT'L L. 435 (2002); Mark Tushnet, *The Issue of State Action/Horizontal Effect in Comparative Constitutional Law*, 1 INT'L J. CONST. L. 79 (2003). Subsequently, Mark has also become increasingly expert on South Asia and Latin America: *see* UNSTABLE CONSTITUTIONALISM: LAW AND POLITICS IN SOUTH ASIA (Mark Tushnet & Madhav Khosla eds., 2015); Mark Tushnet, *The New "Bolivarian" Constitutions: A Textual Analysis, in* COMPARATIVE CONSTITUTIONAL LAW IN LATIN AMERICA 126 (Rosalind Dixon & Tom Ginsburg eds., 2017).

[59] Tushnet, *The New "Bolivarian" Constitutions*, *supra* note 58.

2

Comparative Constitutional Law: Reflections on a Field Transformed

*Ran Hirschl**

In the second half of his illustrious career, Mark Tushnet has made invaluable contributions to the study of constitutional law and constitutional institutions across time and place. His expressly comparative writings over the past 25 years range from leading textbooks and primers on comparative constitutional law to advanced analyses of key constitutional phenomena in all four corners of the world. The sheer scope of his comparative work is remarkable—even more so when one considers the fact that it was not until the 1990s that comparative constitutional law became one of Tushnet's main areas of interest. His understanding of Canadian constitutional law and his mastery of the Supreme Court of Canada's jurisprudential output in the Charter era, to pick just one example, is second to none outside of Canada and easily matches that of the very top Canadian constitutional scholars.

Tushnet's "The Possibilities of Comparative Constitutional Law"—published in the *Yale Law Journal* back in 1999[1]—may be considered an early epistemological field definer in comparative constitutional law. Even in a piece on a subject that was not central to Tushnet's other areas of interests up until the mid-1990s, and despite his statement in the piece that his "claim is, in the end, rather modest: U.S. courts can sometimes gain insights into the appropriate interpretation of the U.S. Constitution by a cautious and careful analysis of constitutional experience elsewhere,"[2] Tushnet managed to make a long-lasting contribution by identifying several main directions, aims, and modalities of what was back then a fairly modest scholarly enterprise.

While some scholars at the time acknowledged the constitutional transformation of Europe, or studied dilemmas of constitutional design in the postauthoritarian and postcommunist world, the full extent of the global spread of constitutionalism

* The author thanks the volume editors and the participants at the Conference in Honor of Mark Tushnet's Contributions to Comparative Constitutional Law (June 2021) for their helpful comments and suggestions on a preliminary draft of this chapter, as well as Julius Ott, Julianne Schmidt, and Zachary Rosen for their superb research and editorial assistance.

[1] Mark Tushnet, *The Possibilities of Comparative Constitutional Law*, 108 Yale L.J. 1225, 1225–1309 (1999).

[2] *Id.* at 1228.

Ran Hirschl, *Comparative Constitutional Law: Reflections on a Field Transformed* In: *Redefining Comparative Constitutional Law*. Edited by: Vicki C. Jackson and Madhav Khosla, Oxford University Press. © Ran Hirschl 2025.
DOI: 10.1093/9780191996344.003.0002

and judicial review was not yet obvious to many. Nor was the ever-increasing reliance on constitutional courts worldwide to address some of the most fundamental predicaments a polity can contemplate. Tushnet is to be credited for being one of the first to identify a global constitutional trend, the scope, nature, and implications of which only a handful of observers could grasp at the time.

A Field Transformed

Today, nearly a quarter of a century after the publication of Tushnet's seminal piece, the field of comparative constitutionalism is very different.[3] From its beginnings as a relatively obscure and esoteric subject studied by a devoted few, comparative constitutionalism has developed into a thriving area of contemporary legal scholarship, and has become a cornerstone of constitutional jurisprudence and constitution-making worldwide. Perhaps more importantly, comparative constitutional law has expanded its epistemological and methodological boundaries to form what I have termed elsewhere *comparative constitutional studies.*[4]

Everyday indicators of the comparative turn in constitutional law are plentiful. Virtually all reputable peak courts across the globe maintain websites on which thousands of rulings, including those released the same day, may be browsed with ease and downloaded within seconds. New online portals allow jurists, scholars, and policymakers to retrieve and compare the entire corpus of constitutional texts around the world, from the late 18th century to the present. Lively discussions about current developments in constitutional law, theory, and design abound in blogs devoted exclusively to comparative constitutionalism. These new platforms have proven particularly important in recent years in enabling real-time commentary on and analysis of increasingly common threats to liberal and democratic constitutionalism worldwide. And the comparative revolution has certainly not been limited to the digital world: scholarly books dealing with comparative constitutional law in all its epistemological, methodological, and normative varieties are no longer considered a rarity; new periodicals and symposia are dedicated to the comparative study of constitutions and constitutionalism; and top-ranked law schools in the United States and elsewhere have begun to introduce their students to a distinctly more cosmopolitan and comparatively informed view of constitutional law and legal institutions. Nor has this shift been limited to the academy: constitutional drafters from Latin America to the Middle East openly debate comparative constitutional experiences in making choices about what constitutional features to

[3] Tom Ginsburg, *The State of the Field*, *in* CONSTITUTIONALISM IN CONTEXT 23, 23–40 (David S. Law ed., 2022).

[4] RAN HIRSCHL, COMPARATIVE MATTERS: THE RENAISSANCE OF COMPARATIVE CONSTITUTIONAL LAW (2014); Ran Hirschl, *From Comparative Constitutional Law to Comparative Constitutional Studies*, 11 INT'L J. CONST. L. 1, 1–12 (2013).

adopt or to avoid. Meanwhile, prominent constitutional court judges commonly lecture about, write on, and refer to the constitutional laws of others. Inasmuch as the current "global market" of citation sources offers an indication of the field's novel jurisprudential trends, it is quite common to note that the Supreme Court of Canada, the German Federal Constitutional Court, and the European Court of Human Rights have emerged as three of the most frequently cited courts in the world, while other high courts (e.g. the South Africa Constitutional Court and the Supreme Court of India) are developing a greater international reputation.

Taken as a whole, it is hard to overstate the incredible intellectual renaissance of comparative constitutional law over the past two decades. This development reflects a confluence of factors, chief among which are the worldwide trend toward constitutionalization; the proliferation of courts equipped with wide, constitutionally entrenched review powers; the internationalization of the legal profession and of legal education; and the rise of communication and information technologies that facilitate the diffusion of constitutional concepts and foster crossnational jurisprudential and academic dialogue. The result of the transnational migration of constitutional ideas has been an explosion of interest among scholars, judges, practitioners, and policymakers in the comparative study of constitutions and of constitutionalism more generally.

The Turn to Constitutional Studies

A few years ago, I called upon constitutional scholars and political scientists alike to engage more closely with each other's insights and methodologies, and invited scholars of all pertinent persuasions to lower the traditional disciplinary boundaries between the study of constitutional law as an exclusively legal field and the study of the constitutional sphere as part of the broader political context within which it operates. I suggested, in a nutshell, that the minimal communication between different academic communities studying the same set of phenomena was artificial and driven by intellectual path dependence and sociology of knowledge factors, rather than by political and constitutional realities. Just as concepts such as "religion," "cities," or "climate change" may not be fully grasped using the methods and insights of a single discipline, nor can "constitutionalism."

With or without connection to my writings, the field has endorsed, by and large, the call for epistemological correction. An increasing number of doctrinal constitutional analyses, certain discussions in constitutional theory, and most prominently the constitutional studies literature, all now commonly incorporate comparative approaches.[5] In recent years, a new generation of scholars has deployed new

[5] Ran Hirschl, *Methodology and Research Design in Comparative Constitutionalism*, *in* CONSTITUTIONALISM IN CONTEXT 41–58 (David S. Law ed., 2022); Ran Hirschl, *Comparative*

research methods to study the constitutional sphere; engage in interdisciplinary conversations about constitutional law and its intersection with political science, sociology, history, and economics; and develop new concepts and insights that purport to analyze, taxonomize, and explain constitutional phenomena across time and place.[6] Taken as a whole, these studies illustrate that the call to blend the field of comparative constitutional law with the study of comparative politics to form a field called *constitutional studies* has largely been vindicated.

The tremendous interdisciplinary work in support of constitutional democracy, done by constitutional scholars studying "democratic backsliding," "constitutional capture," "constitutional retrogression," "autocratic legalism," "stealth authoritarianism," "illiberal constitutionalism," "abusive constitutionalism," and so on, are a case in point.[7] As is well known, the rise of populism, in particular of the ethno-nationalist variety, has put liberal constitutional democracy and its core principles under threat in an increasing number of polities worldwide. Backlash against global constitutionalism, liberal rights discourse, and what is framed as a large-scale usurpation of power by supposedly overprogressive constitutional courts and judges ensues. Comparative constitutionalists have taken the lead in examining (and, oftentimes, warning against and responding to) this trend. As this burgeoning body of literature suggests, some of the shrewdest governments, parties, and leaders in the world today invest tremendous energy in hollowing out and ultimately subverting the constitutional order to suit their a-democratic interests and illiberal agendas. Importantly, these a-democratic actors often continue to adhere to the formal symbols, institutions, and procedures of constitutionalism and the rule of law even as they undermine democracy and subvert liberalism more generally. Relatedly, leading comparative constitutionalists, including Tushnet, have turned their attention to imagining new institutional designs aimed at safeguarding democracy and democratic political institutions against autocratic and illiberal threats.[8] In so doing, these studies build on the rich literature on regime

Methodologies, *in* CAMBRIDGE COMPANION TO COMPARATIVE CONSTITUTIONAL LAW 11–39 (Roger Masterman & Robert Schütze eds., 2019).

[6] *See, e.g.*, ADAM CHILTON & MILA VERSTEEG, HOW CONSTITUTIONAL RIGHTS MATTER (2020). For a taste of the debate concerning the deployment of quantitative methods in comparative constitutional studies, see Madhav Khosla, *Is a Science of Comparative Constitutionalism Possible?*, 135 HARV. L. REV. 2110, 2110–49 (2022); Zachary Elkins & Tom Ginsburg, *On Disruption and Leximetrics*, 19 INT'L J. CONST. L. 1835, 1835–41 (2022).

[7] *See, e.g.*, David Landau, *Abusive Constitutionalism*, 47 U.C. DAVIS L. REV. 189 (2013); Kim Lane Scheppele, *Autocratic Legalism*, 85 U. CHI. L. REV. 545 (2018); CONSTITUTIONAL DEMOCRACY IN CRISIS? (Mark A. Graber, Sanford Levinson & Mark Tushnet eds., 2018); WOJCIECH SADURSKI, POLAND'S CONSTITUTIONAL BREAKDOWN (2019); ROSALIND DIXON & DAVID LANDAU, ABUSIVE CONSTITUTIONAL BORROWING: ABUSIVE CONSTITUTIONAL BORROWING: LEGAL GLOBALIZATION AND THE SUBVERSION OF LIBERAL DEMOCRACY (2021); WOJCIECH SADURSKI, A PANDEMIC OF POPULISTS (2022).

[8] *See, e.g.*, TOM GINSBURG & AZIZ HUQ, HOW TO SAVE A CONSTITUTIONAL DEMOCRACY (2019); Stephen Gardbaum, *The Counter-Playbook: Resisting the Populist Assault on Separation of Powers*, 59 COLUM. J. TRANSNAT'L L. 1 (2020); MARK TUSHNET, THE NEW FOURTH BRANCH (2021).

types, constitutional design, and the transition to and consolidation of democracy, which has been developed by political scientists. More than anything else, then, these comparative constitutional studies illustrate how any successful attempt to understand one of the most important political phenomena of our time must acknowledge the fluidity of the law/politics distinction and appreciate the significance of the political context (e.g. political ideologies, institutions, actors, and incentives) with which the constitutional sphere constantly interacts.

One of the markers of a great scholar is her ability to acknowledge and endorse an epistemological shift when it is timely, analytically warranted, and empirically supported. Tushnet lived up to this criterion by endorsing the move toward constitutional studies. More than any of the thousands of pages of Tushnet's prolific and influential comparative constitutional writings, the last paragraph of the Introduction to a short book he wrote in 2018—the second edition to his *Advanced Introduction to Comparative Constitutional Law*, described by one reviewer as "probably the best advanced introduction to comparative constitutional law you can find in under 150 pages"—reflects Tushnet's endorsement of a move from comparative constitutional law to comparative constitutional studies. Nearly two decades after "The Possibilities of Comparative Constitutional Law," Tushnet writes:

> [O]ne theme running through many discussions that follow should be made explicit at the outset: A great deal of interest in the field turns less on a constitution's language or the wording of judicial opinions than on the nation's party structure—whether the nation has an authoritarian party in charge, a dominant party, a multi-party system with relatively stable parties, a multi-party system with parties popping in and out of existence freely, or a stable two-party system. Some aspects of the party system are loosely coupled with constitutional structure: Multi-party systems are more common in systems with proportional representation, for example. As Ran Hirschl has suggested, perhaps we should understand the field of comparative constitutional law to be blended with the study of comparative politics into a field to be called 'constitutional studies' (Hirschl 2014).[9]

I could not agree more!

As remarkable as the turn to comparative constitutionalism has been, we would be remiss if we did not acknowledge an apparent disparity between the acknowledgment of the importance of political science insights by leading comparative constitutional scholars such as Mark Tushnet and others, and the failure to do the converse by political scientists. Although we are nearly 20 years into the current "golden age" of comparative constitutional inquiry, and a few years into the rise of comparative constitutional studies as an interdisciplinary bridge between

[9] Mark Tushnet, Advanced Introduction to Comparative Constitutional Law 9 (2nd ed., 2018).

legal academics and social scientists, not all disciplines have taken up the mantle with equal enthusiasm. Many of the doctrinal biases commonly reflected in the legal analysis of constitutional law and courts as inherently apolitical enterprises are mirrored in social science—in particular, in political scientists' lack of serious attention to constitutional doctrine, to the professional ethics of constitutional courts and judges, and to the role of reasoning in constitutional adjudication. Instead, judgments are often treated as merely post-hoc rationalization, and as little more than professional dialect that thinly covers what is "really" going on.[10]

To be sure, virtually all grandmasters of 20th-century constitutional design literature—Arend Lijphart, Donald Horowitz, Juan Linz, Giovani Sartori, or Guillermo O'Donnell, to mention a few prominent names—are political scientists. The same generally holds true with respect to the literature on the transition to and consolidation of democracy following waves of democratization in Latin America, Asia, and most notably southern, central, and eastern Europe; many prominent authors (e.g. Jon Elster, Stephen Holmes, Adam Przeworski, or Andrew Arato) are political scientists, even if they do hold joint appointments in law schools. Likewise, institutional economists and political scientists have developed theories of constitutional transformation that see the development of constitutions and judicial review as mechanisms to mitigate systemic collective-action concerns such as commitment, enforcement, and information problems. One such explanation that derives directly from Max Weber's work (advanced by Nobel Prize Laureate Douglass North, among others) sees the development of constitutions and independent judiciaries as an efficient institutional answer to the problem of "credible commitments."[11] The constitutional entrenchment of limitations on a given regime's ability to behave unpredictably (e.g. property rights, independent judicial monitoring of legislative and executive branches) is seen as an effective way of increasing that regime's credibility vis-à-vis potential lenders and investors. However, the "golden age" of this scholarship within political science is largely over. And at any rate, even during its intellectual height in the final third of the 20th century, little attention was paid by political scientists to a comparative analysis of courts, judges, and jurisprudence as independent or at least semi-autonomous political actors.

This stark gap has widened in recent years, with the ever-growing significance of courts and tribunals worldwide in dealing with core questions that define and divide entire nations. Just as comparative constitutional law scholars must appreciate the social and political context within which the constitutional realm is embedded and operates, there is an equally urgent need for scholars of comparative

[10] *See, e.g.*, Barry Friedman, *Taking Law Seriously*, 4 PERSPECTIVES ON POL. 261, 261–76 (2006).

[11] Barry Weingast, *Constitutions as Governance Structures: The Political Foundations of Secure Markets*, 149 J. INSTITUTIONAL & THEORETICAL ECON. 286, 286–311 (1993); Barry Weingast, *The Political Foundations of Democracy and the Rule of Law*, 91 AM. POL. SCI. REV. 245, 245–63 (1997).

politics to understand constitutional vocabulary and its comparative practice and implications. It is unfortunate that many (though, happily, not all) of the leading departments of political science overlook this plain truth. Most leading political science departments in North America, and to my knowledge elsewhere, devote limited attention to public law and courts as an independent area of research. Consequently, landmark US Supreme Court rulings concerning voting rights and the electoral process—think of *Bush v Gore* (2000); *Citizens United* (2010); *Shelby County v Holder* (2013); or *Rucho v Common Cause* (2019)—are often covered in passing in "American politics" classes, without detailed consideration of the lines of reasoning, ideational platforms, or views of the role of the court in the American political system featured in these decisions. A similar oversight is evident in Canada, where public law has been largely subsumed within "Canadian politics." Even in Europe, where national and supranational courts repeatedly address the question at the core of the European integration project—namely, the status of each individual member state's constitutional order, tradition and identity vis-à-vis the emerging pan-European constitutional and political order—landmark rulings of the German Federal Constitutional Court (e.g. the *Maastricht Case* of 1993, the *Lisbon Treaty Case* of 2009, and the *European Central Bank Case* of 2020), the European Court of Human Rights' momentous decisions in the cases of *Sejdić and Finci v Bosnia and Herzegovina* (2009), *Lautsi v Italy* (2011), and *S.A.S. v France* (2014), and the ECJ rulings in *European Commission v Poland* (2019) and *V.M.A. v Bulgaria* (2021) are commonly considered materials "for lawyers," not for political scientists.

Consequently, key elements of contemporary constitutional jurisprudence, interpretation, and reasoning, let alone the intricacies of major court rulings—such as the UK Supreme Court's landmark decisions in the *Miller I* (2017) and *Miller II* (2019) cases dealing, respectively, with the constitutional preconditions for the Brexit process to launch, and with the constitutionality of the Boris Johnson government's decision to prorogue parliament to avoid unfavorable votes on the Brexit process; the Spanish Constitutional Court's rulings on the status of Catalonia; the Colombian Constitutional Tribunal on the status of the historic peace agreement in that country; or the Supreme Court of Pakistan landmark rulings in the Nawaz Sharif cases (ousting elected Prime Minister Nawaz Sharif and later banning him from politics for life, following his conviction for capital and tax evasion), or the court's landmark ruling (2022) overriding PM Imran Khan's decision to dismiss parliament in order to avoid a crucial no-confidence vote (2022), thereby paving the way for a change of government—remain nearly unreachable to political science students, despite the considerable political weight each of these landmark cases carry.

With the exception of a handful of departments, a PhD student in political science who is interested in topical subjects involving constitutional law and constitutional courts would need to enroll in a comparative constitutional law course at a nearby law school in order to grasp the full significance of constitutional discourse on any and all of these issues. This stark deficiency is alarming considering the ever-increasing significance of constitutional law and courts, regional and transnational human rights regimes, and international tribunals to politics and policymaking worldwide.

As Aharon Barak, former President of the Supreme Court of Israel, noted, "The world is filled with law; anything and everything is justiciable."[12] The ever-increasing political significance of constitutional law, constitutional courts, and constitutional discourse is one of the hallmarks of 21st-century government, and a core element in understanding many key political issues. Not a week goes by without a national high court or international tribunal somewhere in the world releasing a landmark judgment concerning core moral predicaments, the scope of fundamental rights and liberties, key policymaking challenges, and contentious political questions that define and divide entire nations. Scholars have identified this trend as the "judicialization of politics";[13] "governing with judges";[14] and "juristocracy,"[15] conceptualizing judges as "legislators in robes"[16] and suggesting that our time may well be defined as the "Judicial Era."[17] In short, "courts in ever more countries are issuing ever more decisions about seemingly ever more important questions."[18] The rise of law, courts, and judges as a critical force in comparative and world politics suggests that politics and law are becoming ever more intertwined, affecting each other in intricate ways that are seldom acknowledged by doctrinal analyses. Consequently, traditional disciplinary boundaries between the study of law and politics are increasingly difficult to sustain.

Yet the inexplicable disciplinary divide between law schools and political science departments, and the overarching belief that "constitutional law is for lawyers," render a full understanding of constitutional rulings virtually unattainable for most political scientists. And so, quite ironically, while Mark Tushnet, alongside many other comparative constitutional law professors, has endorsed the core epistemological claims of comparative constitutional studies—namely that the complex symbioses of today's world admit neither constitutionalism-free political systems nor apolitical constitutional law—most leading political scientists, and the discipline of political science more generally, continue to overlook it.

[12] Aharon Barak, *Judicial Philosophy and Judicial Activism*, 17 Iyunei Mishpat 475, 475–502 (1993).

[13] The Global Expansion of Judicial Power (Neal C. Tate & Torbjörn Vallinder eds., 1995).

[14] Alec Stone Sweet, Governing with Judges: Constitutional Politics in Europe (2000).

[15] Ran Hirschl, Towards Juristocracy: The Origins and Consequences of the New Constitutionalism (2004).

[16] Kenneth Shepsle, *Old Questions and New Answers About Institutions: The Riker Objection Revisited*, *in* The Oxford Handbook of Political Economy 1031, 1031–49 (Barry R. Weingast & Donald Wittman eds., 2006).

[17] Comparative Judicial Review (Erin Delaney & Rosalind Dixon eds., 2018).

[18] *See* Ginsburg, *supra* note 3, at 25.

The Persisting "Global South" Challenge

Among Mark Tushnet's many contributions to the renaissance of comparative constitutional inquiry is his interest in constitutional law in the so-called Global South.[19] In his book *The New Fourth Branch*, to pick just one recent example, Tushnet addresses in detail the rise, status, and impact of fourth-branch institutions protecting democracy in South Africa, Brazil, India, and South Korea.[20] He is not alone in turning his gaze southward; a growing number of monographs, edited collections, and journal articles focus on important constitutional trends and phenomena in under-explored countries and regions.[21] However, these works remain the exception, as the share of studies of canonical constitutional settings remains disproportionally high. As admirable and analytically called for as the geographical diversification of comparative constitutional explorations is, the oversight of constitutional law, constitutional institutions, and constitutional politics in the Global South continues to hamper the field's ability to advance purportedly universal insights that in reality are based on the constitutional experience of a limited number of often-studied countries.

In an earlier work, I suggested that the field of comparative constitutional law tends to draw on "a small number of overanalyzed, 'usual suspect' constitutional settings and court rulings."[22] The constitutional sphere in the United States, the UK, Canada, and Germany are honorable members of that commonly explored (to put it mildly) "platinum club." With notable exceptions such as South Africa, India, and Colombia (commonly invoked supposed posterchildren of "Global Southness"), much of the so-called Global South is infrequently explored or represented. Consequently, "the constitutional experiences of entire regions . . . remain largely uncharted terrain, understudied and generally overlooked."[23] The question here is how truly "comparative" or generalizable is a body of knowledge that seldom draws on or refers to the constitutional experience, law, and institutions of the Global South? A similar sentiment has been echoed and further advanced by other authors.[24] To be sure, the global spread of constitutionalism; the corresponding

[19] Mark Tushnet, *Authoritarian Constitutionalism*, 100 Cornell L. Rev. 391, 391–462 (2015); Antoni Abat I. Ninet & Mark Tushnet, The Arab Spring: An Essay on Revolution and Constitutionalism (2015).

[20] *See* Tushnet, *supra* note 8.

[21] *See, e.g.*, Tom Ginsburg, Judicial Review in New Democracies: Constitutional Courts in Asian Cases (2003); Ran Hirschl, Constitutional Theocracy (2010); Berihun Gebeye, A Theory of African Constitutionalism (2021); The Oxford Handbook of Caribbean Constitutions (Richard Albert, Derek O'Brien & Se-shauna Wheatle eds., 2020); Comparative Constitutional Law in Africa (Rosalind Dixon, Tom Ginsburg & Adem K. Abebe eds., 2022). There are of course many other examples: some are genuinely focused on the Global South; others resort to what may be seen as Global South tokenism.

[22] *See* Hirschl, *supra* note 4, 192–223.

[23] *Id.*

[24] *See, e.g.*, The Global South and Comparative Constitutional Law (Philipp Dann, Michael Riegner & Maxim Bönnemann eds., 2020).

rise in scholarly interest in the study of constitutionalism across time and place; and the emergence of new, more open, and accessible discussion and dissemination venues in the field, have all had some mitigating effect. Likewise, the groundbreaking advisory work done by bodies such as International IDEA foster interest in and awareness to challenges of constitution-making and constitutional governance in Africa, Asia, Latin America, and the Pacific. The void has been further alleviated in recent years, with an increasing number of works focusing on democratic backsliding and constitutional retrogression. Even so, here too a few constitutional settings (e.g. Hungary and Poland) have become the routine, near-cliché reference points for any discussion in that area.

The "unofficial canon" phenomenon poses a set of normative, epistemological, and methodological challenges for a field that purports to advance universal, generalizable, scientifically sound insights. When it comes to materializing the potential of comparative constitutional inquiry, however, extensive focus on a dozen frequently explored constitutional settings is not only a matter of representation, fairness, or justice, but also a missed opportunity to engage with a living laboratory of constitutional innovation concerning some of the greatest challenges of our time. Unlike the largely stagnant national constitution-making enterprise throughout much of the Global North, many of the most daring and innovative constitutional experiments concerning issues such as climate change, urbanization, and democratic renewal have taken place in the Global South. The vast majority of these settings lie well beyond the contours of the oft-studied comparative constitutional "canon."

Consider climate change and environmental protection—arguably the most significant global challenge currently facing humanity. As early as 1994, the revised constitution of Argentina included an unalienable right to the environment. Article 41 warrants that "all inhabitants enjoy the right to a healthful, balanced environment fit for human development, so that productive activities satisfy current needs without compromising those of future generations, and have the duty to preserve the environment. Environmental damage shall generate as a priority the obligation to repair it under the terms that the law shall establish." Article 43 further frames environmental rights as collective rights and provides for the *acción de amparo* (an appeal for the protection of constitutional rights and guarantees) and the class action (lawsuits regarding collective rights that can be filed by those affected by environmental pollution or risks, by the National Ombudsman, and by civil associations representing diffuse interests).[25]

Ecuador (2008) was the first country to enshrine the rights of the environment in its constitution. Article 71 is dedicated to Pachamama (Andean "Mother Earth"), providing for nature's "right to integral respect for its existence, the maintenance

[25] Lucas G. Christel & Ricardo A. Gutiérrez, *Making Rights Come Alive: Environmental Rights and Modes of Participation*, 26 ARGENTINA J. ENV'T & DEV. 322, 322–47 (2017).

and regeneration of its life cycles, structure, functions and its evolutionary processes . . . All persons, communities, peoples and nations can call upon public authorities to enforce the rights of nature . . . The State shall give incentives to protect nature and to promote respect for ecosystems." Article 414 further states that: "The State shall adopt adequate and cross-cutting measures for the mitigation of climate change, by limiting greenhouse gas emissions, deforestation, and air pollution; it shall take measures for the conservation of the forests and vegetation; and it shall protect the population at risk."

As of 2023, the national constitutions of ten countries—all in the Global South—have followed Ecuador's precedent. Neighboring Venezuela (2009) and Bolivia (2009) adopted a constitutional provision on the right and duty of the state and present generations to future generations. Vietnam (2013), Tunisia (2014), and the Dominican Republic (2015) similarly outlined the state's policy to protect the environment and respond to climate change. Zambia (2016) included a broad commitment to implement mechanisms to address climate change. Thailand (2017) provided for a national reform of water resource management to respond to climate change. Cuba's (2019) climate clause is explicitly framed by political language vowing to respond to climate change as part of a commitment to "anti-imperialism" and a more "equitable international economic order." Both Côte d'Ivoire (2016) and Algeria (2020) include a commitment to climate protection in their constitutional preambles. To be sure, politics plays a key role in any constitutional transformation; not all, or even most, of these constitutional commitments were driven by genuine care for the environment. But the fact remains that these innovations provide constitutional drafters and constitutional scholars alike with a range of new design options to consider.

At the subnational level too, the environmental protection agenda has taken hold. The constitution of Mexico City (since 2017 an autonomous state within the Mexican confederation), to pick one example, states that "The City-State Government will develop a long-term plan for adaptation to climate change" (Art. 16 I (2)); that "the authorities shall guarantee the right to a healthy environment. They shall apply the necessary measures to reduce the causes, prevent, mitigate and reverse the consequences of climate change" (Art. 16A(4)); and that "Environmental damage or deterioration generates liability. Those who cause them are obliged to compensate and fully repair the damage, without prejudice to criminal or administrative sanctions established by law" (Art. 16A(7)).

Trends in constitutional jurisprudence parallel the adoption of climate clauses. Most cases taking a constitutional rights-based approach to climate litigation are found in the Global South. A textbook illustration is the 2018 Colombian case of *Future Generations v Ministry of the Environment and Others*.[26] Here, 25 youth

[26] Corte Suprema de Justicia [C.S.J.] [Supreme Court] abril 5, 2018, 4360-2018, no. 11001-22-03-000-2018-00319-00 (Colom.).

plaintiffs sued the Colombian government, alleging that its failure to take steps toward a target of zero-net deforestation in the Colombian Amazon by 2020 (as agreed under the Paris Agreement and the National Development Plan 2014–2018), threatened their fundamental rights. The Colombian Supreme Court of Justice, analyzing the Constitution from a "green" perspective, elevated the environment to the category of a fundamental right. The court recognized that the rights of life, health, freedom, and human dignity are substantially linked and determined by the environment and the ecosystem.[27]

Another clear indication of the Global South lead in climate change jurisprudence is the recent Supreme Court of Brazil ruling (June 2022) to recognize the Paris Agreement as a human rights treaty.[28] Such designation as human rights treaty—the first of its kind concerning the Paris Agreement worldwide—establishes a basis for requiring the federal government to reactivate its national climate fund and allocate resources from it to fight extensive deforestation in Brazil, acknowledged by the court as a major source of emission and as jeopardizing attempts to effectively fight climate change. In January 2023, to pick another recent example, Chile and Colombia filed a request for an advisory opinion from the Inter-American Court of Human Rights regarding the scope of state obligations for responding to climate emergency under the frame of international human rights law.[29] The request acknowledged the human rights effects of the climate emergency, especially highlighting the vulnerability of communities and ecosystems in Latin America. In this line, Colombia and Chile emphasized the need for regional standards to accelerate action to confront climate change.

In contrast, there has been limited constitutional innovation with respect to climate change and environmental protection in national constitutions of the Global North.[30] The US Supreme Court ruling of June 30, 2022 in *West Virginia*

[27] In Juliana v. United States, 947 F.3d 1159 (9th Cir. 2020), the Ninth Circuit dismissed a roughly similar claim by 21 young plaintiffs and the environmental organization Earth Guardians, who argued that the federal government's failure to adequately address climate change violated their constitutional rights to life, liberty, and property (similar to *Future Generations* above). The case was dismissed for lack of Article III standing because the plaintiffs' requested relief (requiring the federal government to implement a plan to phase out fossil fuel emissions) involved policy decisions delegated to the executive and legislative branches. This reversed Judge Aiken's 2016 decision for the US District Court for the District of Oregon, which held that "a right to a climate system capable of sustaining human life is fundamental to a free and ordered society."

[28] PSB et al. v. Brazil, S.T.F., ADPF 708, 01.07.2022 (Braz.). The national climate fund was established in 2009; however, in 2019 the Bolsonaro administration failed to allocate the available resources from it, thereby making the fund inactive: *See* Isabella Kaminski, *Brazilian court world's first to recognise Paris Agreement as human rights treaty*, https://www.climatechangenews.com/2022/07/07/brazilian-court-worlds-first-to-recognise-paris-agreement-as-human-rights-treaty/ (last visited Jul. 7, 2022).

[29] *See* Request for an advisory opinion on the scope of the state obligations for responding to the climate emergency, Global Climate Change Litigation Database, http://climatecasechart.com/non-us-case/request-for-an-advisory-opinion-on-the-scope-of-the-state-obligations-for-responding-to-the-climate-emergency/ (last accessed Nov. 25, 2023).

[30] While the Global North holds the majority of climate cases globally, only a handful have been based on constitutional claims. *See* Jacqueline Peel & Jolene Lin, *Transnational Climate Litigation: The Contribution of the Global South*, 113 Am. J. of Int'l L., 711, 711–12 (2019).

v Environmental Protection Agency speaks for itself.[31] France's failure to reach a constitutional referendum on a climate amendment in 2021 further illustrates the Global North's disparate experience in constitutionally addressing climate change. Iceland, poised for potential "crisis-change" amendments in the aftermath of the 2008 financial crisis, failed to reach a consensus among opposing political parties on new constitutional provisions. No climate clause was adopted.

An important breakthrough may emanate from the jurisprudential front. In its landmark ruling in the *Urgenda* case (2019), the Dutch Supreme Court upheld lower court rulings stating that the Dutch government has a duty to urgently and effectively slash the country's planet-warming emissions.[32] Specifically, the court ordered the government to set higher emission reduction targets in accordance with the UN Intergovernmental Panel on Climate Change (IPCC) and the goals of the 2015 Paris Agreement. *Urgenda* was also the first ruling to hold a government legally accountable for its international commitments and national targets regarding emission cuts. In 2024, the Constitutional Court of South Korea held in what was the first such case in Asia that most of the country's climate goals failed to meet constitutional rights commitments (e.g., the right to life and the right to a healthy environment) towards younger generations.[33] A couple of years earlier, in its landmark ruling in *Neubauer et al v Germany* (March 2021), the German Federal Constitutional Court (FCC) struck down parts of Germany's Federal Climate Protection Act as they set insufficient greenhouse gas emissions reduction targets beyond 2030, thereby failing to properly consider future generations' constitutional rights to life and physical integrity. The court found that Article 20(a) of the Basic Law obliges the legislature to protect the climate.[34] However, in the follow-up case, the FCC refused to hear the claim that subnational-unit climate change legislation was insufficient, noting that the constitutional complaints lacked "any prospect of success."[35] It determined that, while the federal government is obligated to implement emissions reduction targets, this obligation does not exist at the state level. A second follow-up case, *Steinmetz et al v Germany*, was

[31] West Virginia v. Env't Prot. Agency, 142 S. Ct. 2587 (2022).

[32] Urgenda Foundation v. Netherlands, Case Number 19/00135, Dec. 20, 2019 (Netherlands). The ruling emanated from a suit filed by a Dutch environmental group, the Urgenda Foundation, alongside 900 Dutch citizens that required the Dutch government to do more to prevent global climate change. The court ordered the government to set emission reduction targets to 25 percent below 1990 levels by 2020, finding the government's existing pledge to reduce emissions by 17 percent was insufficient to meet the country's fair contribution toward the UN goal of keeping global temperature increases within two degrees Celsius of pre-industrial conditions.

[33] The plaintiffs in all four consolidated petitions on the matter were children and young environment activists. One of the petitions listed "Woodpecker"—an embryo (now born)—as lead complainant. Consequently, the case has come to be known as "Woodpecker et al. v. South Korea" (decided on August 28, 2024).

[34] Bundesverfassungsgericht [BVerfG] [Federal Constitutional Court], March 24, 2021, Case no. BvR 2656/18/1, BvR 78/20/1, BvR 96/20/1, BvR 288/20 (Ger.).

[35] Bundesverfassungsgericht [BVerfG] [Federal Constitutional Court], January 18, 2022, Case no. 1 BvR 1565/21 (Ger.).

filed in 2022. Claimants argue the emission reduction measures taken by the federal government post-*Neubauer* are insufficient. Interestingly, even in the realm of commitment to future generations in matters related to climate change and environmental protection, one of the first pertinent apex court rulings is the Supreme Court of the Philippines' 1993 decision in *Minors Oposa v Factorani*.[36] Here the court accepted a petition against massive deforestation schemes, based on Section 16 of Article II of the Constitution (which provides that the "State shall protect and advance the right of the people to a balanced and healthful ecology in accord with the rhythm and harmony of nature"). In its ruling, the court acknowledged that in the context of deforestation's considerable environmental damage, "every generation has a responsibility to the next to preserve [nature's] rhythm and harmony."

Another vivid illustration of the "Northern stagnation versus Southern innovation" pattern in contemporary constitutional design is the North/South constitutional split concerning urbanization and cities. Urban agglomeration is one of the most significant phenomena of our time. The figures are striking: within the past century, the world's urban population has increased nearly 30-fold;[37] UN projections suggest that by 2100, the world's 100 largest cities will host a quarter of the planet's population. Megacities of 50 million or even 100 million inhabitants will emerge by the end of the century, mostly in the Global South. In many Global South megacities, density has already reached near-dystopian levels.[38] In short, what has been termed the "urban era" and "the century of the city" marks a major and unprecedented transformation of the organization of society, both spatially and geopolitically.

Although we live in the century of the city, comparative constitutional studies, let alone mainstream constitutional theory and its overarching Global North tilt, are still the captives of constitutional structures, doctrines, perceptions, and expectations that were developed alongside the modern nation-state and evolved in a historical process that saw the sovereign city become increasingly subjugated to those states. Most current constitutional orders and virtually all those adopted prior to the great urbanization of the last few decades, treat cities—including some of the world's most significant urban centers—as "creatures of the state," fully submerged within a Westphalian constitutional framework, and assigned limited administrative local governance authority.[39] The constitutional orders of the United

[36] Republic of the Philippines Supreme Court July 30, 1993, G.R. No. 101083 (224 S.C.R.A. 792).

[37] In 1900, approximately 150 million people—representing fewer than 10 percent of the world population at that time—lived in cities, while 90 percent lived in nonurban settings. As of 2023, approximately 4.8 billion people, or 58 percent of the world population, live in cities.

[38] In Dhaka and Manila, for example, citywide density is approximately 120,000 people per square mile. It is 5 times denser than New York City, 7 times denser than Hong Kong, 12 times denser than Paris, 16 times denser than Toronto, and nearly 30 times denser than Melbourne. If the entire world population (8 billion) lived in similar density conditions as Dhaka or Manila, it would fit within an area the size of Oklahoma.

[39] For a full account of these trends, *see* RAN HIRSCHL, CITY, STATE: CONSTITUTIONALISM AND THE MEGACITY (2020).

States and Canada are "exhibit A" and "exhibit B" in the constitutional oversight of cities and the subjugation of the urban to dated spatial constitutional imagination. (In contrast with the area of climate change and environmental protection, where conceptualizing US states as laboratories of democracy and innovative experimentalism has some purchase, when it comes to urbanization and city power, that conceptualization has proven futile; in fact, resistance for city constitutional emancipation and constant curbing of city power emanates from states/provinces.)[40]

When we turn our gaze to constitutional orders in the Global South, a different picture emerges. Major attempts to bolster the constitutional status of cities have taken place in Global South countries as diverse as Brazil (1988)—the first national constitutional to recognize Henri Lefebvre's *Right to the City* (*Le droit à la ville*); India (the 73rd and 74th amendments, 1992); and South Africa (1996)—arguably the most extensive constitutional design experiment to date in the context of nationwide constitutional empowerment of cities.[41] At the same time, we have seen the constitutional empowerment of large cities in both federal countries in the Global South (typically by designating them as autonomous states, as with Mexico City, Buenos Aires, and Addis Ababa) and formally unitary countries such as South Korea, Vietnam, China, and Taiwan.[42]

With respect to constitutional jurisprudence on city status too, apex courts in the Global South have taken the lead. In a series of decisions over the last two decades, the South African Constitutional Court reinforced the autonomy of South African cities with respect to municipal planning, including zoning and land use management.[43] It went on to decide that while intergovernmental cooperation is to be favored, a national competence may be limited by the exercise of a municipal competence.[44] Meanwhile, in a ruling that would be unthinkable in the constitutional context of the United States or Canada, the Supreme Court of Nigeria, for example, ruled in July 2024 that local government in that country is an independent

[40] The notion of US states as laboratories of democracy is commonly associated with Justice Brandeis's dissenting opinion in *New State Ice Co. v. Liebmann*, 285 U.S. 262 (1932). For a critical account, *see, e.g.*, Charles W. Tyler & Heather K. Gerken, *The Myth of Laboratories of Democracy* (GWU Legal Stud. Rsch. Paper No. 2021-46, 2021).

[41] Article 40(1) of the South Africa constitution (1997) holds that "government is constituted as national, provincial, and local spheres of government which are distinctive, interdependent and interrelated." Chapter 7 (sections 151–64) of the constitution further marks a fundamental shift away from the pre-1996 order. It builds upon and operationalizes Article 40(1) by giving municipalities the ability to legislate and administer regulations in a number of areas (e.g., municipal planning, health services, public transport, trade), and, most importantly, the ability to raise funds in these areas, subject to some oversight by provincial and national governments. The contrast with the constitutional nonstatus of cities in the United States or Canada is striking.

[42] The Constitution of South Korea, for example, establishes 17 subnational units, of which eight are designated "first-level" cities (including Busan, Daegu, Gwangju, Incheon, and Seoul), with Sejong as a special self-governing city.

[43] See City of Johannesburg Metropolitan Municipality v. Gauteng Development Tribunal 2010 (2) SA 554 (SCA); confirmed by the Constitutional Court in City of Johannesburg Metropolitan Municipality v. Gauteng Development Tribunal 2010 (6) SA 182 (CC). See also Telkom SA SOC Ltd. v. City of Cape Town 2021 (1) SA 1 (CC).

[44] Maccsand (Pty) Ltd. v. City of Cape Town 2012 (4) SA 181 (CC).

tier of the Nigerian federation and enjoys financial autonomy vis-à-vis state governments.[45] Accordingly, all federal monies allocated to Nigeria's 774 local governments, the Court ruled, must be transferred directly to them, without withholding or monitoring by state governors as has been the practice since the adoption of the Nigerian Constitution (1999). Not surprisingly, observers described the ruling as one of the most remarkable constitutional judgments in the history of the country.

In short, while not all the attempts in the Global South to constitutionally bolster city status have proven equally successful (some in fact have been outright failures; a notable example of this is India), the fact remains that constitutional innovation in this key area occurs largely outside of North America or Europe.[46]A similar pattern is evident when we look at the closely related issue of the urban/rural divide—one of the most significant social, economic, cultural, and political rifts of our time.[47] Here, too, constitution-drafters in the Global South have taken the lead in institutionalizing formal constitutional recognition of the urban/rural divide in national constitutions as a response to the rural experience of feeling "left behind." In several Global South constitutional orders, direct reference is made to the need to balance urban and rural interests. In other Global South settings, most notably in Latin America, the "rural" intersects with other constitutionally recognized categories, notably peasant and indigenous populations. In fact, the core economic objectives listed in the constitutions of at least two dozen countries in Africa and Asia include improvement in the quality of life in rural communities and redressing economic imbalances between rural and urban communities.

Southern innovation in addressing the urban/rural challenge goes even further. One obvious characteristic of what counts as "urban" or as "rural" is high and low human density. An interesting possibility in this context is to give people living in dense inner-city neighborhoods or remote rural areas added power in key policy decisions related directly to the density conditions in which they live. We can plausibly speculate that these measures, when applied to policy issues directly affected by very high or very low density, hold some potential in alleviating alienation in both poor, densely populated city neighborhoods and left-behind, sparsely populated rural areas. The idea of varying democratic voice based on density is also likely to increase pressure on elected officials to pay attention to the grievances of those whose quality of life and range of opportunities are affected.

This idea is not purely hypothetical. Initial experimentation with density-sensitive representation matrices is already endorsed by several national constitutions worldwide. As of 2023, 27 national constitutions—25 of which are of countries in the Global South—recognize density-based deviation from the

[45] Attorney General of the Federation v. Attorney General of Abia State & 35 Ors (Supreme Court of Nigeria) SC/CV/343/2024 (decision released July 11, 2024).

[46] A notable exception is Italy, where a motley reform in this area has taken place.

[47] Ran Hirschl, *Constitutional Design and the Urban/Rural Divide*, 16 LAW & ETHICS HUM. RTS. 1, 1–39 (2022).

baseline principle of equal number of voters per electoral district in order to enhance representation of high-density neighborhoods in cities or in remote, sparsely populated regions. A few recent examples include the constitution of Sierra Leone (2013), Nepal (2015, revised in 2020), Jamaica (2015), the Dominican Republic (2015), Botswana (2016), Malawi (2017), Uganda (2017), and the Gambia (2020). Likewise, the constitutions of several small island nations (e.g. Bahamas, Trinidad & Tobago, Saint Vincent and the Grenadines, St Lucia, Tuvalu) entrench enhanced representation for sparsely populated areas. In Nepal, to pick one example, a constitutionally protected (and non-challengeable for 20 years) corrective of 10 percent in seats allocation is granted to sparsely populated provinces where the proportional space share far exceeds the overall population share. Consequently, the province of Gandaki, with 15 percent of the country's total area but only 9 percent of the population, has 11 percent (18) of the seats in parliament (165). Likewise, the province of Karnali, with 18 percent of the territory and 6 percent of the population, has 7.2 percent (12) of the seats in parliament.[48]

The list of recent Global South constitutional innovations goes on and on. Some of these initiatives have been more successful than others. From experimenting with constitutionally entrenched gender equality quotas across government and the public sector (e.g. the constitution of Kenya of 2010),[49] to embarking on massive public participation campaigns of constitution-making at the national (e.g. Brazil 1987–1988; Uganda 1988–1995; South Africa 1993–1996; Fiji 1993–1997 and in 2012–2013; deliberative polling on constitutional amendments in Mongolia 2017; large-scale public input in constitution-making in Chile 2021–2022; the current constitutional renewal process in Jamaica) or at the local level (e.g., extensive solicitation of public input in the constitutional transformation of Mexico City from a federal district to an autonomous state within the Mexican confederation—the largest constitution-making crowdsourcing at the local/municipal level to date), Global South constitution-making, politically subservient as it sometimes is, is filled with fresh ideas and daring experimentation. While experimentation with

[48] Article 286(5) of Nepal's revised constitution (2020) states: "While determining election constituencies pursuant to this Article, the Election Constituency Delimitation Commission shall, subject to sub-clause (a) of clause (1) of Article 84, determine the constituencies in a Province in accordance with the federal law, *having regard to the population as the main basis and geography as the second basis for representation*, and there shall be at least one election constituency in each district within the Province." Article 286(6) states that: "While delimitating election constituencies pursuant to clause (5), attention shall be required to be given, inter alia, *to the population and geographical convenience, density of population, geographical specificity, administrative and transportation convenience, community and cultural aspects of the constituencies*." According to the Constituency Delimitation Commission (2017), these overarching guidelines are to be translated such that 90 percent weight is given to population and 10 percent to proportional space.

[49] Article 27(8) of the constitution of Kenya (2010) states, "The State shall take legislative and other measures to implement the principle that not more than two-thirds of the members of elective or appointive bodies shall be of the same gender." Article 81(b) stipulates that the electoral system shall comply with the principle that "not more than two-thirds of the members of elective public bodies shall be of the same gender."

public participation in constitution-making certainly occurs in the Global North too (e.g. the oft-discussed yet ultimately failed crowdsourcing of a new constitution in Iceland, public consultations concerning rights protections in Australia, or experiments with citizen convention and assemblies in Ireland), its level does not match the near-canonical status Global North constitutionalism commonly enjoys.

Mission: Partly Accomplished

Over the past two decades, comparative constitutional inquiry has witnessed tremendous intellectual renaissance. The scholarly pursuits of Mark Tushnet—one of America's foremost constitutional thinkers—reflect and embody this remarkable transformation. His many comparative constitutional writings—articles, monographs, and textbooks—over the past quarter-century have contributed considerably to the advancement and canonization of comparative constitutional inquiry in the American legal academy. And his willingness to engage with pertinent concepts and ideas from political science helped foster a culture of interdisciplinarity that characterizes contemporary comparative constitutional studies. This reflects the acceptance of comparative discourse by leading constitutional scholars, some of whom have contributed to this volume. The critical contribution of comparative constitutional scholars to our understanding of what has been termed democratic backsliding, constitutional retrogression, and illiberal constitutionalism is a case in point. Unfortunately, the recent contribution of political scientists to comparative constitutional studies has been rather modest. Given the critical significance of constitutional law, constitutional courts, and constitutional politics worldwide, this shortcoming is becoming ever harder to justify.

A second persisting obstacle is the Global South challenge. If comparative constitutional scholars are serious about the potential of comparative constitutional inquiry to offer effective remedies to some of the burning challenges of our time, closer attention to Global South constitutionalism is the call of the hour. The generalizability of insights based on a limited and often-studied corpus of constitutional settings is questionable. However, the need to account for the diverse constitutional experiences of the Global South is not merely or even primarily a matter of justice or representation. Rather, it is a matter of practical utility. Alongside other non-canonical constitutional orders (e.g. supranational, subnational), the Global South constitutional universe has become a bustling lab of innovation that in many respects is more promising than its Northern counterpart. To remain relevant in an ever more challenging world, constitutional design scholars will not only have to take core challenges such as climate change or urban agglomeration more seriously: They will have to set their gaze southward.

3

Are Constitutions So Indeterminate that We Cannot Compare Them?

Tom Ginsburg and Mila Versteeg

Introduction

One of the most famous examples in jurisprudence is H.L.A. Hart's description of the sign "no vehicles in the park."[1] To most, this basic rule will be clear.[2] Those operating a truck, car, or scooter will, upon noticing the sign, likely interpret it as prohibiting them from entering the park. But outside of what Hart called the "core" of the rule, there is also a "debatable fringe" or a "penumbra."[3] What about a dad pushing little kids in a stroller? Should he turn around? Is a stroller a vehicle, and if not, what makes it different from a truck, car, or scooter?

Now, consider an example from constitutional law. Most constitutions contain a simple rule that "no one shall be subjected to torture" or "cruel, inhuman and degrading treatment."[4] Most of the time, this rule is clear. Government officials will know that if they were to intentionally inflict severe physical or mental pain or suffering on those in their care, they would violate this rule and face legal consequences. This might then deter them from engaging in those acts or, alternatively, encourage them to cover their tracks. Regardless, in many real-world situations, the basic rule will be clear enough. But even for the prohibition of torture, there is a debatable fringe. Is rape a form of torture,[5] and if it is, is it also torture when it happens within the context of a marriage?[6] Is sleep deprivation caused by playing loud music a form of torture, or is it merely cruel treatment?[7] What if the evidence

[1] Fredrick Schauer, Thinking Like a Lawyer 19 (2018).

[2] *Id.*

[3] *Id.*, at 20 (describing the "debatable fringe").

[4] Adam S. Chilton & Mila Versteeg, *The Failure of Constitutional Torture Prohibitions*, 44 J. Legal Stud. 417, 424–25 (2015).

[5] *See* Nigel S. Rodley, *The Definition(s) of Torture in International Law*, 55 Current Legal Probs. 467, 479–80 (2002).

[6] *See* Melanie Randall & Vasanthi Venkatesh, *The Right to No: The Crime of Marital Rape, Women's Human Rights, and International Law*, 41 Brook. J. Int'l L. 153, 179–83 (2015) (arguing that marital rape is an act of torture under international human rights).

[7] *See* Case of Ireland v. The United Kingdom, 2 Eur. Ct. H.R. 25 paras. 96, 167 (1978) (finding that subjecting a detainee in "a room where there was a continuous loud and hissing noise" is a form of cruel treatment or punishment but falls short of torture).

Tom Ginsburg and Mila Versteeg, *Are Constitutions So Indeterminate that We Cannot Compare Them?* In: *Redefining Comparative Constitutional Law*. Edited by: Vicki C. Jackson and Madhav Khosla, Oxford University Press.
 DOI: 10.1093/9780191996344.003.0003

of torture is invisible?[8] Again, we can look outside the clear core to the penumbra of the torture prohibition to try to answer these and similar questions.

If we accept that *all* constitutional rules have a clear core and a debatable fringe, how much can we learn from studying constitutional text alone? In separate recent contributions, Professor Mark Tushnet and Professor Madhav Khosla take the position that constitutional text is so indeterminate that (i) we can only understand its meaning once it has been interpreted and (ii) that interpretation depends on context.[9] The implication is that a comparison of constitutional texts across legal systems can be a meaningless exercise. They sometimes make these points in response to our own prior work, which has coded and compared written rules in constitutions, including constitutional rights provisions. To be sure, this is not their only critique of our work, but it is the one on which we focus in this short chapter.

For Tushnet, comparing constitutional texts, and especially constitutional rights provisions, without further inquiry on how these provisions have been interpreted is based on a "super-formalist jurisprudence."[10] Khosla likewise reflects that it is not possible "to know what content a right has . . . without interpreting the right."[11] Khosla takes this argument one step further than Tushnet, and argues that identical rules can take very different meanings in different contexts to the point that we cannot compare them.[12] Khosla's critique uses the prohibition of torture as a running example.[13]

In this chapter, we respond to both these critiques. In the remainder of this chapter, we first take up the critique that we cannot understand constitutional texts without interpretation. The essence of this critique is that constitutional text is so indeterminate that studying and comparing it without inquiry into relevant (judicial) interpretations is a pointless exercise. Our position is *not* that texts do not require interpretation; characterizing our position as otherwise is a straw man. But there is a point of disagreement. To us, the relevant question is how much of the everyday application of constitutional rules falls within the clear core, and how

[8] Darius Rejali, Torture and Democracy 400 (2007) (discussing "clean tortures" which are difficult to identify as torture).

[9] *See* Madhav Khosla, *Is a Science of Comparative Constitutionalism Possible?* 135 Harv. L. Rev. 2110, 2130–40 (2022); Mark Tushnet, *"Sometimes the Magic Works, Sometimes It Doesn't": A Comment on Chilton and Versteeg*, 2021 U. Chi. L. Rev. Online 1 (2021).

[10] Tushnet, *supra* note 9, at 2–3. See also Mark Tushnet, *Introduction*, *in* The Routledge Handbook on Constitutional Law (Mark Tushnet, Thomas Fleiner & Cheryl Saunders eds., 2013) ("fully understanding any nation's domestic law will require attention to details that vary substantially from nation to nation").

[11] Khosla, *supra* note 9, at 2131.

[12] *Id.* ("Constitutions can contain similar—even identical—expressions but radically different rights. Indeed, on certain occasions, the specific intention will be to ensure that expressions that appear similar mean something very different").

[13] *Id.* at 2117.

much falls within the debatable fringe. This is an empirical question, and one that is not easy to answer in a general way. But in our view, instead of simply assuming that text is indeterminate, it is more useful to engage in empirical inquiries of when constitutional text is indeed indeterminate, and when it is not.

We next take up the argument that constitutional texts not only need interpretation but that *how* they are interpreted radically differs from country to country, to the point that comparison is impossible. A first observation we make is that, if one believes that constitutional rules depend on culture all the way down, it is not obvious that a nation-state is the right unit of observation at all; there are also cultural differences within states, especially states as large and diverse as India or the United States. If words and concepts are not stable across contexts, why should we accept that these national contexts are stable locales in which interpretation can take place? As we will argue, one cannot deploy the indeterminacy argument in limited and selective ways—choosing this route ultimately leads down a deconstructionist path with no end.[14]

But more importantly, the claim that interpretations are radically different across countries runs contrary to an entire literature that has documented substantial transnational judicial dialogue in constitutional interpretation. Constitutions, and especially constitutional rights, are part of a transnational legal order.[15] Thus, when high courts are asked to interpret the outer boundaries and debatable fringes of rights, they do not operate in a vacuum. They generally take meaning from international law, and can draw on prior decisions from peer courts around the world.[16] They use similar tools for interpretation, such as proportionality review, and are in direct dialogue with one another.[17] In doing so, they can expand or contract the clear core of a constitutional right, and create understandings that cross national boundaries. This insight, which has been documented by scholars from many regions of the world, should give pause to those who assert that constitutional rules reflect culture all the way down.

[14] Yasuo Hasebe & Cesare Pinelli, *Constitutions*, *in* The Routledge Handbook on Constitutional Law 9 (Mark Tushnet, Thomas Fleiner & Cheryl Saunders eds., 2013).

[15] *See* Terrence Halliday & Gregory Shaffer, *Transnational Legal Orders*, *in* Transnational Legal Orders 3 (Terrence Halliday & Gregory Shaffer eds., 2016).

[16] Wen-Chen Chang & Jiunn-Rong Yeh, *Internationalization of Constitutional Law*, *in* The Oxford Handbook of Comparative Constitutional Law 1165 (Michel Rosenfeld & András Sajó eds., 2012); Sujit Choudhry, *Globalization in Search of Justification: Toward a Theory of Comparative Constitutional Interpretation*, 74 Indiana L.J. 819, 822 (1999); Christopher McCrudden, *A Common Law of Human Rights? Transnational Judicial Conversations on Constitutional Rights*, 20 O.J.L.S. 499 (2000); Anne Marie Slaughter, *A Global Community of Courts*, 44 Harv. Int'l L.J. 191 (2003).

[17] Kai Möller, The Global Model of Constitutional Rights (2015); Vicki C. Jackson and Mark Tushnet, eds. Proportionality: New Frontiers, New Challenges (2017).

Claim 1: We Cannot Understand Constitutions Without Interpretation

Tushnet's and Khosla's core objections to our work, which compares constitutional texts across many constitutional systems, are that constitutional texts themselves do not reveal very much, as texts take meaning through interpretation. Applied to rights, this means that it is only when constitutional rights have been interpreted, presumably by courts, that we understand the contours and meaning of specific rights.

Of course, the notion that written law is indeterminate and only acquires meaning through interpretation is not new. It is one of the core premises of the legal realist tradition. The legal realists, such as Jerome Frank and Karl Lewellyn, have long held that legal texts do not dictate the outcome of actual cases, but that instead the personal attributes and political preferences of judges play an important role.[18] This same premise is also present in much of the work coming out of the Critical Legal Studies (CLS) movement. Tushnet himself, writing during the heyday of the CLS movement, argued in the pages of the *Harvard Law Review* that judges' political ideology, not constitutional text, explains judicial decision-making.[19]

We do not disagree that constitutional provisions need interpretation. Instead, for us, the core question is how much of constitutional law is clear on its face and how much is not. Or, to borrow H.L.A. Hart's distinction, what we need to know is how much of the everyday application of constitutional law falls within the clear core, and how much falls within the debatable fringe. This, in our view, is ultimately an empirical question involving an assessment of interpersonal agreement on meaning.

We do not have a definitive answer to this question, and measurement would be thorny (though perhaps not impossible). But we do have a hunch that constitutional scholars steeped in the American constitutional tradition might have a skewed view of how much of constitutional law is indeterminate. Law teaching tends to focus on the "hard cases," not the easy ones in which the law is clear, thus creating a selection effect in how we view constitutional law.[20] What is more,

[18] Schauer, *supra* note 1, at 127–34.

[19] Mark V. Tushnet, *Following the Rules Laid Down: A Critique of Interpretivism and Neutral Principles*, 96 Harv. L. Rev. 781, 784 (1981) ("Over time, however, it became clear—as a result, for example, of the first era of substantive due process and the legal realists' destructive rule skepticism—that judges no less than legislators were political actors, motivated primarily by their own interests and values").

[20] Schauer, *supra* note 1, at 23 ("The selection effect is the major factor in determining which disputes or law-controlled events wind up in litigation, but the effect is even greater as we proceed up the appellate ladder . . . Very much the same dynamic applies to the cases selected for law school casebooks. What makes those cases interesting and pedagogically valuable is, usually, that they are hard cases, ones in which the lawyers on both sides can make strong arguments and in which the students can analyze and evaluate the opposing positions . . . Appellate courts and law school classrooms have good reasons for operating in the gray areas of rules—on the fuzzy edges. But it is a big mistake to assume that rules are nothing but gray areas and fuzzy edges").

because it is so old and brief, the U.S. Constitution may be more indeterminate than most other national charters.[21]

Let us use the example of torture. We use this example because Khosla uses it as the running example in his critique of our work. The prohibition of torture is enumerated in several international human rights treaties, and in the vast majority of written constitutions. One typical formulation is the 2013 Constitution of Zimbabwe, which simply states that "[n]o person may be subjected to physical or psychological torture or to cruel, inhuman or degrading treatment or punishment."[22] Likewise, the Russian Constitution states that "[n]obody should be subjected to torture, violence, or other severe or humiliating treatment or punishment."[23]

It seems to us that torture is a particularly bad example for Khosla to argue that we cannot understand the constitution without interpretation. There is a remarkable agreement across legal systems that the prohibition of torture is absolute, even in times of emergency.[24] The language of torture prohibitions in different countries is rather similar. And the moral consensus that torture ought to be outlawed is near universal, with legal philosophers invariably condemning torture as a "moral and legal abomination,"[25] "the sort of evil that arouses human rights passions and drives human rights campaigns,"[26] or an act that is on the "never list" of "forbiddens" in international politics.[27]

Perhaps more important for our purposes, we suspect that, most of the time, torture is something of which you can say "you know it when you see it," to borrow Justice Potter Stewart's famous description of pornography.[28] Government officials and others in positions of power will likely be aware that many actions that they might contemplate are not permitted, and that this prohibition is absolute. We do not want to argue that this means that this rule will always be followed; enforcing

[21] Mila Versteeg & Emily Zackin, *American Constitutional Exceptionalism Revisited*, 81 U. Chi. L. Rev. 1641, 1654 (2014).

[22] Constitution of Zimbabwe, art. 53 (2013).

[23] Конституция Российской Федерации [Constitution of the Russian Federation], art. 21.2 (1993).

[24] Torture is absolutely prohibited, not just by international human rights law (Convention Against Torture and Other Cruel, Inhuman or Degrading Treatment or Punishment, art. 2, *adopted* Dec. 10, 1984, 108 Stat. 382, 1465 U.N.T.S. 85 [hereinafter Convention Against Torture]; Universal Declaration of Human Rights, art. 5, *adopted* Dec 10, 1948, G.A. Res. 217A, U.N. GAOR, 3d Sess., 1st plen. mtg., U.N. Doc. A/810), but also by international humanitarian law (*see, e.g.*, Geneva Convention (I) for the Amelioration of the Condition of the Wounded and Sick in Armed Forces in the Field. Geneva, art. 50, *adopted* Aug. 12, 1949, 6 U.S.T. 3114, 75 U.N.T.S. 31 [hereinafter Geneva Convention (I)]) and by international criminal law (Rome Statute of the International Criminal Court, art. 7.1.f, *adopted* July 17, 1998, 2187 U.N.T.S. 90 [hereinafter Rome Statute]).

[25] Jeremy Waldron, Torture, Terror and Trade-Offs: Philosophy for the White House 4 (2010) ("Torture was and remains a moral *as well as a* legal abomination").

[26] *Id.* at 253.

[27] Jean Bethke Elshtain, *Reflection on the Problem of "Dirty Hands"*, *in* Torture: A Collection 77, 77 (Sanford Levinson ed., 2004).

[28] Jacobellis v. Ohio, 378 U.S. 184, 197 (1964) (Stewart, J., concurring).

constitutional law is challenging and raises its own set of analytic issues.[29] There is no doubt that torture takes place in secret, making it especially difficult to detect. Our claim is more modest: much of the time, torturers will know that they are engaged in illegal conduct. Indeed, this is one reason why torturers take care to hide their activity.

We thus expect that, for torture, there is a substantial clear core of behavior that would meet the definition. What is more, there is reason to believe that there is substantial agreement on the basic rules across communities and countries. The human experience of pain does not differ radically across time and place, and many ordinary people will agree that certain acts ought to be designated as torture. If asked whether a particular practice meets the definition of involving "severe pain or suffering, whether physical or mental . . . intentionally inflicted on a person" for one of the designated purposes under the Convention against Torture, we suspect many people would likely agree with one another. That is, there will likely be very large zones of inter-subjective agreement among ordinary people across cultures when confronted with certain practices. Some evidence for the shared experience of torture is that torture victims from settings as disparate as the South Side of Chicago and Camp X Ray at Guantanamo Bay see commonalities in their own experiences, and indeed have created bonds around their shared trauma.[30]

This is not to say that there will never be room for interpretation. There will undoubtedly be situations that will fall outside of the clear core of the prohibition. For example, it is only relatively recently that rape has been recognized as a form of torture.[31] What precisely constitutes severe mental distress is open to varying interpretations. Some behavior that is colloquially understood as torture may not meet the legal definition because of the requirement that there be an intent to coerce on the part of the perpetrator.[32] In addition, the conceptual relationship between torture and the categories of cruel, inhuman and degrading treatment is subject to debate among human rights lawyers and judges.[33]

[29] Adam Chilton & Mila Versteeg, How Constitutional Rights Matter 7–8 (2020); Chilton & Versteeg, *supra* note 4, at 421–23.

[30] *See* Remaking the Exceptional: Tea, Torture and Reparations from Chicago to Guantanamo (Aliya Hussein, Audry Petty, Amber Ginsburg & Aaron Hughes eds., 2022). We should note that, in our view, interpretations by ordinary people are important. Constitutions notoriously lack outside enforcers. It is therefore important for ordinary people to be able to detect when government actions cross the bounds set by the constitution. When they can, they can punish officials who transgress their power. Chilton & Versteeg, *supra* note 29.

[31] Rodley, *supra* note 5.

[32] Convention Against Torture, *supra* note 24, art. 1.

[33] The Convention Against Torture prohibits cruel, inhuman and degrading punishment as well as torture, and the CAT Committee has made clear that it is not possible to draw the line between the two. U.N. Comm. Against Torture, *General Comment No. 2: Implementation of Article 2 by States Parties*, U.N. Doc. CAT/C/GC/2 (Jan. 24, 2008). *See also* U.N. Human Rights Comm., *General Comment No. 20: Article 7 (Prohibition of Torture, or Other Cruel, Inhuman or Degrading Treatment or Punishment)*, *in* 1 International Human Rights Instruments: Compilation of General Comments and General Recommendations adopted by Human Rights Treaty Bodies 204, U.N. Doc HRI/GEN/1/Rev.9 (Vol. I) (May 27, 2008), https://www.ohchr.org/Documents/HRBodies/TB/HRI-GEN-1-REV-9-VOL-I_en.doc.

Judges and other legal professionals might deliberately look for the debatable fringe, in order to define practices as being outside of the definition of torture, so as to insulate perpetrators.[34] For example, during the administration of George W. Bush, law professor John Yoo and now-judge Jay Bybee famously constructed a definition of torture that was far more limited than that found in the Convention against Torture.[35] Their memos defined torture as requiring specific intent on the part of the perpetrator and interpreted severe pain as "serious physical injury, such as organ failure, impairment of bodily function, or even death."[36] One might see this kind of cynical move as illustrating the CLS point that interpretation is plastic and reflects the political goals of those who engage in it. But the fact that the Yoo-Bybee interpretations were nearly universally rejected by experts suggests that it is not so easy to undermine the clear core of the torture prohibition. An interpretative community—in this case, a transnational one, to which we will return below—rejected a new interpretation of an old concept.[37]

Our point is a simple one. Even if a debatable fringe exists, we believe that much, if not most, of the time it is easy to detect whether the prohibition of torture has been violated. The Crit scholar focuses on the indeterminacy in legal language; the torture victim seeking redress, the activist, and the empiricist prefer to focus on the core areas of agreement.

To summarize, it seems to us that the indeterminacy critique hinges on the question of how much of everyday constitutional law is in the clear core and how much is in the debatable fringe. This is ultimately an empirical question, and one on which more research is needed. The answer to this question will likely be contingent, and may also depend on the constitutional rule itself. For example, it might be the case that it is easier to detect violations of the prohibition of torture without interpretation than violations of free speech. But importantly, in order to believe that constitutional texts tell us next to nothing about how constitutional law actually works, one has to believe that virtually all applications lie in the debatable fringe. Such a position seems unattainable without further empirical evidence.

[34] Nick Cheeseman, *Torture in Thailand at the Limits of Law*, 48 Law & Soc. Inquiry 236 (2023) (providing examples of cases where courts deny the facticity of torture or interpret legal duties to render torture excusable).

[35] Memorandum from Jay S. Bybee, Assistant Att'y Gen., Office of Legal Counsel, to Alberto R. Gonzalez, Counsel to the President (Aug. 1, 2002) [hereinafter Bybee Memorandum], http://www.justice.gov/olc/docs/memo-gonzales-aug2002.pdf.

[36] *Id.* at 1.

[37] *See, e.g.*, Bruce Ackerman, The Decline and Fall of the American Republic 6 (2010) ("the justly notorious "torture memos"); W. Bradley Wendel, *Legal Ethics and the Separation of Law and Morals*, 91 Cornell L. Rev. 67, 68 (2005) ("[t]he overwhelming response by experts in criminal, international, constitutional, and military law was that the legal analysis in the [torture memos] was so faulty that the lawyers' advice was incompetent"); Jenny S. Martinez, *Process and Substance in the "War on Terror,"* 108 Colum. L. Rev. 1013, 1072 (2008); Jordan J. Paust, *Executive Plans and Authorizations to Violate International Law Concerning Treatment and Interrogation of Detainees*, 43 Colum. J. Transnat'l L. 811, 811 (2005) ("Not since the Nazi era have so many lawyers been so clearly involved in international crimes concerning the treatment and interrogation of persons detained during war").

And because they are empirical questions, empirical methods are necessary, even if they are always imperfect.

Claim 2: Interpretation and Meaning Will Vary from Country to Country, So that We Cannot Compare

One might believe that constitutions not only need interpretation, but also that interpretations are radically different from one country to the next, to the point that the comparison of constitutional texts is an entirely useless exercise. Madhav Khosla explicitly develops this argument, though we suspect that Tushnet might be sympathetic to it.

We observe that this claim is also consistent with the CLS perspective. A core CLS premise is that doctrine reflects power structures that serve certain segments or classes in society.[38] As Frederick Schauer puts it, "one of the important claims of Critical Legal Studies was that legal doctrine could best be understood as a reflection of contingent political and ideological decisions."[39] If doctrine indeed reflects contingent political decisions, then one might expect that the meanings of constitutional texts, as interpreted by courts, vary from place to place. The implication is that, even if we had taken account of how constitutional provisions had been interpreted—rather than merely considering the language of constitutional rules—we would still be unable to compare constitutional law across countries.

The critique also bears some similarity with French structuralism, associated with Pierre LeGrand in comparative law.[40] Under LeGrand's oft-stated and long-debated view, laws or norms cannot be meaningfully compared across boundaries, because once a norm enters a new legal system, it interacts with aspects of culture and legal order to *become a completely different norm*.[41] Whether or not Tushnet

[38] Schauer, *supra* note 1, at 146.

[39] *Id.*

[40] *See, e.g.*, Pierre Legrand, *The Same and the Different*, *in* Comparative Legal Studies: Traditions and Transitions 240, 303 (Pierre Legrand & R. Munday eds., 2003) ("The point is to displace the precedence of (purported) sameness-in-the-law in order to show that behind the mask of universality lies a differentiation which has been repressed and which, although unsettling to the dominant and dogmatic discourse, can be recovered in its expressive and excessive dimensions. The point is to reject a topology and propose a topography. The point is to analyse the specific as the specific. The point is to foster hyper-awareness. The point is, rather than impose a framework upon something, to derive a framework from something. The point is to impel the comparatist toward an ethical encounter with the other-in-the law").

[41] Pierre Legrand, *The Return of the Repressed: Moving Comparative Legal Studies Beyond Pleasure* 75 Tul. L. Rev. 1033, 1046 (2001) ("the 'uniformity' thesis can only hold if its proponents are prepared to pretend that the problems which the law addresses and the solutions which the law provides to these problems are somehow unconnected to the cultural environment from which the problems and solutions arise"), *and* Pierre Legrand, *The Impossibility of Legal Transplants*, 4 Maastricht J. Eur. & Compar. L. 111, 114 (1997) ("[L]egal transplants are impossible"), *with* Alan Watson, Legal Transplants: An Approach to Comparative Law 21 (1974).

and Khosla go this far, they share with LaGrand a plea to understand context, and in Khosla's case a desire to undermine cross-cultural understanding of concepts.

We make two points here. First, the reification of culture as the unit of analysis is subject to the same critical moves deployed by the CLS practitioners. If words and concepts are not stable across contexts, why should we accept that these contexts are themselves stable locales in which interpretation can take place? As we will argue, one cannot deploy the indeterminacy argument in limited and selective ways—choosing this route ultimately leads down a deconstructionist path with no end.

Our second point is that in our era, interpretation is increasingly a transnational process, in which courts and practitioners communicate across borders. Context and culture, it turns out, are less important than they used to be, precisely because interpretation is often produced within a transnational legal order. Another way of stating this is that the "cultures of interpretation" are not contained within any particular nation-state. This has important methodological implications that push in the direction of broader comparative work.

Start with the reification of culture. "How do we know," Khosla asks, "that we are actually comparing torture across two cultures without an assessment of how the cultures understand the infliction of pain and the character of violence?"[42] Methodologically, this leads Khosla to favor single country studies, rather than cross-national approaches.[43] But why is there not indeterminacy all the way down? Why treat a single country as presenting a coherent unit of analysis while eschewing the possibility of transnational comparison? Indeed, the very diversity of Khosla's home jurisdiction presents particular challenges. How does one know that torture means the same thing to a speaker of Malayalam as to one of Bengali? Or for that matter, that an understanding of torture is the same in Kolata, Howra, and Siliguri, to take three cities in West Bengal? Taking indeterminacy seriously requires destabilizing any unit of analysis. Taken to the limit, this means that not only is comparison impossible, but conversation entirely.

To restate our point above, we suspect that the vast majority of acts of torture would be understood as such, regardless of which of the three cities in West Bengal one was asking the question. And whether those understandings are systematically different from those in Kerala is, in the end, an empirical question rather than a conceptual one. There is also the issue of whether a single national high court, such as the Supreme Court of India, can contribute to common cultural understandings through its jurisprudence. But answering these questions requires the methods of empirical social science.

This leads to our second point. Instead of such atomization of interpretive communities, we are observing precisely the opposite. A growing comparative

[42] Khosla, *supra* note 9, at 2135.
[43] *Id.* at 2146.

literature has documented remarkable similarities in rights interpretation across legal system.[44] That is, when asked to interpret the debatable fringe of rights, many interpretations will be similar across legal systems. There are several reasons for that. First, most rights found in domestic legal systems are also found in international human rights law. The international and domestic legal orders do not operate in a vacuum; they draw meaning from one another.[45] In fact, in a growing number of countries, international human rights treaties are directly incorporated into the domestic constitutional order.[46] Second, domestic courts are in dialogue with one another when interpreting their constitution. A body of literature has shown that constitutional courts in different legal systems are in ongoing conversation with one another.[47] Relatedly, the interpretative toolkits used by these courts are remarkably similar. Notably, many courts rely on proportionality analysis to adjudicate rights disputes.[48] Khosla himself has observed that proportionality "serves as the uniform standard of rights review in jurisdictions as diverse as Israel, Germany, Canada, and South Africa."[49]

As a result, many view rights as an example of what Terrence Halliday and Gregory Shaffer call a "transnational legal order," that is, "a collection of formalized legal norms and associated organizations and actors that authoritatively order the understanding and practice of law across national jurisdictions."[50] Halliday and Shaffer exhaustively document the existence of norms and institutions that inform each other and interact across local, national, regional, and global levels.[51] Local legal cultures are not stable units of analysis here—they are terrains on which norms, actors, and institutions operate, recursively affecting the local culture.

[44] Ran Hirschl, Comparative Matters: The Renaissance Of Comparative Constitutional Law 233 (2014) (observing that "constitutional jurisprudence in Germany, Spain, Israel, Canada, and South Africa looks increasingly similar"); David S. Law, *Generic Constitutional Law*, 89 Minn. L. Rev. 652, 659 (2005) ("Commonalities emerge across jurisdictions because constitutional law develops within a web of reciprocal influences, in response to shared theoretical and practical challenges. These commonalities are at points so thick and prominent that the result may fairly be described as *generic constitutional law*—a skeletal body of constitutional theory, practice, and doctrine that belongs uniquely to no particular jurisdiction").

[45] Neha Jain & Mila Versteeg, *Comparative Human Rights Law, Introduction to the Field*, *in* The Oxford Handbook of Comparative Human Rights Law (2024 forthcoming).

[46] *See, e.g.*, Manuel Eduardo Gongora-Mera, *The Block of Constitutionality as the Doctrinal Pivot of a Ius Commune*, *in* Transformative Constitutionalism in Latin America 235 (Armin von Bogdandy et al. eds., 2017). Note that many constitutions also explicitly state that human rights treaties are part of the constitution.

[47] *See, e.g.*, Sujit Choudhry, *Globalization in Search of Justification: Toward a Theory of Comparative Constitutional Interpretation*, 74 Indiana L.J. 819, 822 (1999); Christopher McCrudden, *A Common Law of Human Rights? Transnational Judicial Conversations on Constitutional Rights*, 20 O.J.L.S. 499 (2000); Anne Marie Slaughter, *A Global Community of Courts*, 44 Harv. Int'l L.J. 191 (2003).

[48] Kai Möller, The Global Model of Constitutional Rights 13 (2012) ("Different courts use different formulations of what is essentially the same [proportionality] test"); Alec Stone Sweet & Jud Mathews, *Proportionality Balancing and Global Constitutionalism*, 47 Colum. J. Transnat'l L. 72, 111–59 (2008).

[49] Madhav Khosla, *Proportionality: An Assault on Human Rights?: A Reply*, 8 Int'l J. Const. L. 298, 298 (2010).

[50] Halliday & Shaffer, *supra* note 15, at 11.

[51] *Id.*

Take again the example of torture, surely the object of a transnational legal order. There is a substantial consensus, reflected in international law, that the prohibition of torture is absolute, and that torture is not allowed under any circumstances, including times of emergency.[52] The norm is reflected in regional, national, and local law. Its interpretation is undertaken by diverse institutions, including the Committee on Torture, the Human Rights Committee, the European Court of Human Rights, the Inter-American Court of Human Rights, and numerous national courts such as the Supreme Courts of Israel and the United States. When studying the doctrine of these courts, one will not find radically different approaches on what kind of treatments constitute torture. What is more, torture is also a focal point of non-governmental organizations, such as Amnesty International, the Center for Constitutional Rights, and the World Organization against Torture. As Halliday and Shaffer argue, there may be significant complexity in the interpretation of the norm, but there is also no doubt that the norm has "settled" in the sense that there is no contestation over the core prohibition.

Again, the settlement of a norm does not require universal agreement on every case. Such a demanding standard would be impossible to meet. But when there are transnational understandings of a legal norm, this means that there is substantial agreement even across national systems of the clear core of the rule. In addition, because there is transnational dialogue over the debatable fringes, the clear core itself can expand. To appreciate this point, consider again the torture memos. It is because of settled transnational understandings that the Yoo/Bybee interpretation was easily rejected. Thus, we take Halliday and Shaffer's notion of settlement as meaning that there is substantial consensus on a core set of cases, even across legal systems, even if there is an outer zone of indeterminacy.

Conclusion

Both Khosla and Tushnet have written up various criticisms of our work. In this chapter we respond to one such criticism, which is that constitutional texts are characterized by such indeterminacy that looking at text tells us very little, and cross-national comparison is impossible.

In our view, the extent to which constitutional text is indeterminate is ultimately an empirical question. And blanket rejection of empiricism is not helpful in making progress in how constitutions operate, and the extent to which constitutional texts

[52] *See* Convention Against Torture, *supra* note 24, art. 2.2; Geneva Convention (I), *supra* note 24, art. 50, Aug. 12, 1949, 6 U.S.T. 3114, 75 U.N.T.S. 31; and Rome Statute, *supra* note 24, art. 7.1.f. The prohibition is also considered to be customary international law. See Restatement (Third) of the Foreign Relations Law of the United States § 702 (1987). Moral philosophers have invariably condemned torture, widely regarding it as a "moral and legal abomination" and "the sort of evil that arouses human rights passions and drives human rights campaigns." *See* Waldron, *supra* note 25.

themselves can create stable understandings among ordinary people. To the extent that our own prior work is imperfect (and it surely is) we need more and better empirical methods, not to substitute them with beliefs or critical claims of radical indeterminacy.

We end with two final observations on interpretation. The first concerns Tushnet's criticism that Chilton and Versteeg's approach would have been less formalist had they considered limitations clauses. We are a bit puzzled by this critique, as it appears to assume that the basic rules stated in the constitution are indeterminate, but somehow limitation clauses are not. We expect that, when it comes to the outer zones of agreement on rights, transnational understandings are far more important than the exact phrasing of the limitation clause. Whatever the exact language of the limitation clause, limitation clauses are operationalized through proportionality review, and this test itself is part of a transnational legal order.

The second concerns Khosla's criticism of Melton et al.'s study on the interpretability of constitutional texts.[53] In this study, the authors used a measure of intercoder reliability to determine how easy it is for educated readers to agree on the meaning of a text. In this case, it is the Crit rather than the empiricist who exhibits a thin nominalism. Khosla's primary objection, it seems to us, is about the use of the term "interpretability" in the title of the article: "interpretability is not merely the same thing as agreement, which is what is actually being measured. It is substantially different. Interpretability is a hermeneutic enterprise involving an application of mind rather than a fact about a text or the world that is, in some sense, existing in physical space. There is, plainly put, no metric of 'correctness' in the interpretation of a constitution."[54] We have no great stake in whether Elkins et al.'s measure, which captures the extent of agreement by two reasonably intelligent coders as to whether a text does or does not represent a particular concept, meets some platonic concept of "interpretation." Perhaps the coders did not grasp the true and deep meaning of the terms, as a critical seer might have it. But the coders were engaged in the everyday practice of reading texts, and coming to intersubjective agreement in the vast majority of cases. This is precisely the kind of empirical exercise which is needed in order to answer the question of whether intersubjective meaning exists; if we discard empirical work, all we have is a potentially infinite regress of critique.

These remarks, of course, do not in any way diminish how much we have learned from Mark Tushnet, one of the great comparative constitutional lawyers. His voracious scholarship and generosity of spirit are inspirations to all who follow him.

[53] Khosla, *supra* note 9, at 2133–34. Khosla critiques James Melton et al., *On the Interpretability of Law: Lessons from the Decoding of National Constitutions*, 43 Brit. J. Pol. Sci. 399, 400 (2012).

[54] *Id.* at 2133–34.

4

Mark Tushnet's Central Contribution—and Challenge—to the Enterprise of Comparative Constitutionalism

Sanford Levinson

There are many reasons I am delighted to participate in this truly worldwide and well-deserved celebration of the career of Mark Tushnet. I have known Mark for a half century. He has been in a number of ways a major influence on my own scholarly life. I was very pleased to be able to dedicate my 2006 book *Our Undemocratic Constitution* to Mark as an "old friend . . . and model . . . of scholarly engagement," both of which are happily true and continue to be true.[1] This chapter, like all of the other contributions to this volume, was initially prepared on the occasion of his formal retirement from Harvard Law School—but it is important, though, to celebrate as well the fact that he has retired only from the duties of teaching law. Fortunately, he continues to be one of our premier scholars and commentators about whatever he wishes to write about, including, of course, comparative constitutional law.

What I want to talk about, though, is the true complexity of his particular form of engagement. I begin with what I think is a telling anecdote. Sometime I think in the early 1990s, Mark mentioned that he was going to Poland to talk with Poles engaged in drafting a new constitution for the country. I asked him what advice he was going to give. What struck me was his reply. He said that he had no advice to give, because he just did not know enough about the country and its culture. Perhaps he could ask informed questions, but he was not going over there in order to deliver a model constitution that they could simply use as a template for their own unique polity. I remember at the time thinking that he was being too modest. I had, one or two years before, given a somewhat similar answer to a Brazilian journalist who wanted to interview me about the drafting of a new constitution for that society. But I surely had much to be modest about. At that time, I had never traveled to Brazil, nor did I really know much at all about its current political situation. More to the point, I really knew almost nothing about the then

[1] Sanford Levinson, Our Undemocratic Constitution: Where the Constitution Goes Wrong (And How We the People Can Correct It) (2006).

Sanford Levinson, *Mark Tushnet's Central Contribution—and Challenge—to the Enterprise of Comparative Constitutionalism* In: *Redefining Comparative Constitutional Law*. Edited by: Vicki C. Jackson and Madhav Khosla, Oxford University Press. © Sanford Levinson 2025. DOI: 10.1093/9780191996344.003.0004

nascent field of comparative constitutional law. But Mark had already become a remarkably cosmopolitan world traveler. And he was famous as well for "reading everything," something not always true of people who publish as copiously as he does. He would, in 1999, with Vicki Jackson, publish the first edition of their important casebook on comparative constitutional law.[2] If anybody was entitled to offer advice, surely it was Mark. Surely he might suggest one or another design as constituting a "best practice." After all, wasn't that one of the points of doing comparative analysis? Perhaps I was thinking, at the time, of Justice Brandeis' too often quoted reference to American states as "little laboratories of experimentation." The analogue, I suppose, is that I was willing to believe at the time that whole countries could be viewed as similar "laboratories." It followed, then, that the master comparativists, such as Mark, would bring the news to others as to which were the successful experiments, to be adopted presumably worldwide, and which were not. Looking back, I am appalled at my blithe assumptions and more impressed than ever by Mark's completely un-false modesty.

As we are all aware, American law professors at the time were scarcely hesitant to press their views on those living abroad. I will never forget an article in a suitably glossy magazine published by a distinguished law school, about one of its most distinguished members. He wrote of his travels to the former Soviet Republic of Georgia and of his efforts to impress upon the Georgians the importance of adopting the American form of judicial review. I have no doubt at all that he was sincerely committed both to helping to strengthen the nascent system of liberal constitutionalism struggling to establish itself in Georgia and to the belief that the American practice of a decidedly "strong" system of judicial review would be efficacious to achieving that goal. For better or worse, I cannot think of any American law professor less likely to be an evangelist for American judicial review than Mark Tushnet, even though I am confident that Mark would join in the hope that the newly emergent independent countries in Eastern Europe would establish themselves as flourishing liberal democracies. But, of course, that required a nuanced, and inevitably controversial, understanding of what one meant by "liberal democracy" in general and, in particular, what role courts should play in defining such a democracy. Thus 1999 saw not only his and Jackson's casebook, but also his book *Taking the Constitution Away from the Courts*.[3]

Many things have happened since that conversation now at least a quarter-century ago. One of them is that I myself have become more involved in the enterprise of "comparative constitutional design" than I was at the time. But I emphasize the importance of the noun. It speaks to the fact that I have become ever more

[2] Vicki C. Jackson & Mark Tushnet, Comparative Constitutional Law (3rd ed., 2014). *See also* Defining the Field of Comparative Constitutional Law (Vicki C. Jackson & Mark Tushnet eds., 2002); Mark Tushnet, Advanced Introduction to Comparative Constitutional Law (2nd ed., 2018).

[3] Mark Tushnet, Taking the Constitution Away from the Courts (1999).

deeply convinced of the relative importance of constitutional *structures*, as against the *rights* that continue to draw special—and I believe undue—attention both from students and their professors. What this means is that I spend relatively little time in my courses on judicial opinions involving such issues as abortion or freedom of speech, however interesting they undoubtedly are. Like James Madison, I have come to believe that rights provisions as a general matter are almost always mere "parchment barriers,"[4] quite permeable to what Oliver Wendell Holmes called the "felt necessities of the times."[5] This is, of course, especially true, if the times in question are thought to be especially challenging, even "emergencies." One need not read Carl Schmitt in this regard. James Madison will do, as in passage from the rarely read or discussed *Federalist* No. 41:

> The means of security can only be regulated by the means and the danger of attack . . . It is in vain to oppose Constitutional barriers to the impulse of self-preservation. It is worse than in vain; because it plants in the Constitution itself necessary usurpations of power, every precedent of which is a germ of unnecessary and multiplied repetitions.[6]

Far better, it appears, to place almost nothing in a constitution that might be read as placing "barriers" in the way of doing what is necessary for self-preservation, inasmuch as such barriers will inevitably be breached—and serve as precedents for future breaches—when it is thought "necessary" to do so. A modern lawyer, after all, might see this as an ancestor of what today call the "compelling interest" test that functions to legitimate state power that a naïve textualist might believe to be forbidden by the constitution. This is, perhaps, one form of the "critique of rights" that Tushnet was associated with during the heyday of Critical Legal Studies. What is ultimately important is deciding who might be trustworthy to make the determinations that a "felt necessity" justifies the abridgment of any given right.

But, perhaps, comparativists might have useful things to say about various rights controversies inasmuch as they basically become proxies for classical debates in liberal political theory about what rights individuals (or groups) should possess. If one looks at most casebooks in comparative constitutionalism, one finds a heavy emphasis on the variation around the world with regard to such obvious problems

[4] THE FEDERALIST NO. 48 (1788) ("What this security ought to be, is the great problem to be solved. Will it be sufficient . . . to trust to these parchment barriers against the encroaching spirit of power?"), https://avalon.law.yale.edu/18th_century/fed48.asp.

[5] OLIVER WENDELL HOLMES, THE COMMON LAW 1 (1881) ("The life of the law has not been logic: it has been experience. The felt necessities of the time, the prevalent moral and political theories, intuitions of public policy, avowed or unconscious, even the prejudices which judges share with their fellow-men, have had a good deal more to do than the syllogism in determining the rules by which men should be governed").

[6] THE FEDERALIST NO. 41 (1788), https://avalon.law.yale.edu/18th_century/fed41.asp. *See also* SANFORD LEVINSON, AN ARGUMENT OPEN TO ALL: READING "THE FEDERALIST" IN THE 21ST CENTURY 152–54 (2015).

as abortion, "hate speech" as a protected mode of "expression," linguistic autonomy, or affirmative action. All of these are obviously both interesting and controversial. American students certainly can benefit from learning that we are basically outliers with regard to our zeal to protect "hate speech" and that many other countries that we generally view as within the family of "liberal democracies" or liberal constitutional orders find it altogether proper to limit such speech.

That being said, I find myself less and less pedagogically interested in these controversies. In my book *Framed*,[7] I suggested a distinction between what I call "the constitution of conversation" and the "constitution of settlement." By the former, I meant to refer to the kinds of issues overwhelmingly raised and taught in courses on American constitutional law and, for that matter, reflected as well in casebooks on constitutional law, including the ones in which Tushnet and I participate.[8] That is, students are most often introduced to issues that are the subject of litigation before the United States Supreme Court, about which both lawyers and the justices themselves are often in sharp disagreement. Certainly my own attraction to what was called the "indeterminacy" critique of traditional notions of "rule of law" was very much promoted by the simple fact that the subject matter of "constitutional law" was almost exclusively drawn from the "constitution of conversation." So, not surprisingly, I was exhilarated to read Tushnet's classic 1983 essay in the *Harvard Law Review* on what it might possibly mean to "follow the rules laid down."[9] No single essay more completely demonstrates the fatuity of Antonin Scalia's attempt to define "the rule of law" as "the law of rules."[10]

But, as indicated, I have come to the conclusion that the legal academy's obsession with the constitution of conversation, whatever its undoubted importance, has blinded us in important ways to the existence of the constitution of settlement, by which I mean to refer to the basic structures set out in the texts of constitutions that rarely, if ever, raise the kinds of "interpretive" disputes about "meaning" that is true of the constitution of conversation. As I use the term, the "constitution of settlement" generates important questions about *wisdom* and not *meaning*, at least as that term is defined by constitutional scholars. I should emphasize, incidentally, that my notion of "settlement" has nothing in common with the notion of Henry Hart and Albert Sachs that legal disputes become "settled" by a "legal process" of "reasoned elaboration" in which the law "works itself pure" largely through canonical judicial opinions. My own view of what "settlement" means is much more what some might call mindlessly textualist, where "reasoned elaboration" takes

[7] Sanford Levinson, Framed: America's 51 Constitutions and the Crisis of Governance (2012).

[8] *See* Geoffrey R. Stone, et al. Constitutional Law (9th ed., 2023) (the list of authors includes Tushnet); Paul Brest et al. Processes of Constitutional Decisionmaking: Cases and Materials (8th ed., 2022) (the list of authors includes Levinson).

[9] Mark V. Tushnet, *Following the Rules Laid Down: A Critique of Interpretivism and Neutral Principles*, 96 Harv. L. Rev. 781 (1982–83).

[10] Antonin Scalia, *The Rule of Law as a Law of Rules*, 56 U. Chi. L. Rev. 1175 (1989).

second place to the simple questions "what part of two" or of "January 20 do you not understand?" To that extent, perhaps I am conceding that important parts of American constitutional law *can* be reduced to a Scalian "law of rules," though the paradox is that those aspects of the Constitution almost never appear in front of the courts precisely because challenging what is accepted as their clear meanings would so clearly be fruitless and, indeed, liable to dismissal as "frivolous."

For what it is worth, my own form of textualism does not depend on a particular theory of linguistic determinacy. Rather, I am making only the pragmatic argument that all of us in our ordinary lives recognize the difference between a truly controverted matter and one in which appeal to the text does indeed work to stop further conversation about meaning. Illustrations certainly include the assignment of seats in the Senate or the day on which we inaugurate new presidents. As it happens, I think that both are stupid and truly indefensible in terms of either normative legitimacy (as with the Senate) or simply sound policy, as with Inauguration Day. But I am confident that both now and in the foreseeable future, any arguments that they were "unconstitutional" would be deemed "frivolous" by any adjudicator to whom one presented such arguments. The "correct" response would be, "you may be right, but you'll have to amend the Constitution in order to overcome its clear present meaning." As I have written elsewhere, I doubt that Ronald Dworkin's "Hercules" could come up with a cogent argument that the assignment of equal voting power in the Senate is "unconstitutional" instead of (merely?) indefensible under any modern theory of "equal concern and respect."[11] But Dworkin in fact never wrote anything about structural design. "Hercules" was devoted exclusively to thinking about "rights" and what it meant to "take them seriously" as subjects of adjudication.

Mark has suggested, at least on occasion, that there is always the prospect of constructing clever "workarounds" that would minimize the apparent importance of the textual requirements. Still, the necessity for such "workarounds," assuming they are truly available, is caused by the apparent textual hurdles, and one must always ask about the actual practicality of any suggested workaround. What can be imagined around a seminar table is very different from what might actually gain purchase in the court of public opinion or, of course, among legislators who might view themselves as benefiting from maintaining the status quo. Were it not for the 20th Amendment, for example, Congress could simply reset the day for inaugurating new presidents, assuming, of course, that Congress at the same time could provide an adequate solution to the problems presented by the Electoral College as a mechanism for choosing presidents in the first place. We would not be treated to, say, Akhil Reed Amar's theoretically available "workaround" by which a

[11] *See* Sanford Levinson, *Reflections on What Constitutes "a Constitution": The Importance of "Constitutions of Settlement" and the Potential Irrelevance of Herculean Lawyering*, *in* PHILOSOPHICAL FOUNDATIONS OF CONSTITUTIONAL LAW 75 (David Dyzenhaus & Malcolm Thorburn eds., 2016).

defeated president would be such a good sport as to (a) force the vice president to resign; (b) appoint the winning candidate as the successor; (c) arrange with members of the defeated incumbent's own party, who might control the House or the Senate, to confirm the new nominee for the vice presidency immediately; and then (d) and, finally, resign the presidency so that the new vice president could immediately take over.[12] This strikes me as more akin to a Rube Goldberg cartoon than to serious constitutional analysis, especially as American politics have developed—perhaps the better word is degenerated—since the time that Amar offered his initial suggestion.

So in spite of the interest in and importance of what we usually think of as "constitutional rights," I have concentrated far more on the extent to which other institutions, including legislatures and executive branches, do or do not respond adequately to the challenges facing their particular polities. Surely the canonical modern example is response to climate change, as well as more mundane examples involving, say, the costs of healthcare or the various financial crises facing an aging American population that will need a variety of caretaking. Courts are undoubtedly of some importance, and they are not ignored, but it is vitally important to recognize their limitations. Even if one wishes to rail at the extent of judicial power in the United States, say, it must be recognized that the assertion by Tocqueville almost two centuries ago that in the United States all political issues are turned into legal issues that are then resolved by the judiciary was false at the time[13] and has become even less true today, even if it is true that the federal courts within the United States have an unusual degree of power. But, of course, it has been suggested by Gerald Rosenberg that, more often than not, they act as a "hollow hope" for those who look to the judiciary as the institution that can bring about needed major reforms.[14] Moreover, as Mark would no doubt be the first to insist, one is dreadfully mistaken if one assumes that the Supreme Court throughout its history has acted as a progressive force in American politics. The infatuation with the Warren Court, which Mark never fully shared, led all too many American scholars to ignore the actual history of the Court in this regard.

In any event, my course, usually taught with Spanish professor Victor Comella Ferreres, who visits the University of Texas Law School from Barcelona every spring for seven weeks, began years ago with a decidedly technocratic flavor. That is, we focused on what might indeed be the "best practices" for any country, anywhere, designing a new constitution. We looked at, say, presidentialism versus parliamentarianism (or, in the modern era, "semi-presidentialism") and other institutions that were, so to speak, on offer, to constitutional designers. I would not

[12] Akhil Reed Amar, *Electoral College Reform, Lincoln-Style*, 112 Nw. U. L. Rev. 63, 77–79 (2017).

[13] *See* Mark A. Graber, *Resolving Political Questions into Judicial Questions: Tocqueville's Thesis Revisited*, 21 Const. Comment. 485, 487 (2004).

[14] Gerald N. Rosenberg, The Hollow Hope: Can Courts Bring About Social Change? (3rd ed., 2023).

describe myself as a committed technocrat; I was certainly aware that there were significant debates about the merits of one design over another, but it remained true that a primary purpose of the course was to introduce students to the vigorous debates among empirically oriented social scientists and to encourage them to come to decisions on their own as to who persuaded them. I described the course as one that, ideally, could offer students passing it a document attesting to their status as a "certified constitutional designer" that they could display when getting off planes in countries around the world eager to hire them as consultants. That is, they would not necessarily display Tushnetian modesty about their capacity to offer advice!

Over the years, however, our course has become ever less technocratic, even if its formal title remains "comparative constitutional design." A major reason is an ever-diminishing confidence about the extent of truly useful knowledge about the consequences of our own constitutional system(s) even in America, let alone those that would accompany their adoption across the world. Perhaps it is relevant to note that I have become extremely impatient with those fond of quoting Brandeis on the empirical value of federalism.[15] As Malcolm Feeley and Ed Rubin noted some years ago, in their book on American federalism,[16] these purported "experiments" are almost never accompanied by any genuine rigor with regard to testing their consequences. The Brandeis quote is used to lend a false sense of what might be termed "scientism" to what are most often simply political or ideological preferences as to what government should do in responding to certain problems. Indicative of my own development, I organized a major conference at the University of Texas at Austin in 2008 (published in June 2009 in the *Texas Law Review*) around the question "what, if anything, do we know about constitutional design?"[17] Many luminaries contributed, including, of course, Mark. One might summarize the conclusion as "much less than would be desirable," especially if one purports to give advice to constitution drafters around the world.

So how does this relate to the initial anecdote about Mark's trip to Poland? The answer, I think, is something like this: If the major controversies involved only what particular rights to place in the constitution, then it seems altogether possible that someone from abroad might indeed have much to contribute with regard to understanding, or unpacking the meanings, of terms like "freedom of expression" or even a "right to education" or "medical care." (Should a right to state-provided education include law school, or one to medical care include heart transplants?)

[15] *See* John M. Golden & Sanford Levinson, *Splitting the Atom of False Scientism in Constitutional Law*, 66 Arizona L. Rev. 1 (2024) (arguing that there is no useful analogy between genuine scientific "experimentation" and the vagaries of American federalism).

[16] Malcolm M. Feeley & Edward Rubin, Federalism: Political Identity and Tragic Compromise (2008).

[17] *See* Sanford Levinson, *Symposium: What, If Anything, Do We Know About Constitutional Design? Foreword: "I Read the News Today, Oh Boy": The Increasing Centrality of Constitutional Design*, 87 Texas L. Rev. 1265 (2009).

Even if one believes that the specific answers one will ultimately choose will be a function of the culture—or resources—of a given polity, it is still of obvious value to realize that there are multiple positions instantiating important values. As an American liberal, I tend to be antagonistic both to French notions of laïcité and the attempts in such countries as Greece and Russia to prevent Jehovah's Witnesses from seeking converts away from the established churches in those two countries. These are, of course, not simply abstract classroom controversies inasmuch as all there of these countries are adherents of the European Convention on Human Rights; this means that cases can be taken to Strasbourg to be litigated. One can certainly provoke good discussions in classrooms either in the United States or abroad by presenting examples of what values are emphasized, or suppressed, in various constitutional orders. Consider, for example, the problem of "militant democracy," where Tushnet has set out American approaches to the problem in an edited collection comparing a number of countries with one another.[18]

What becomes far trickier, I have come to believe, are discussions not of abstract principles, but, rather, of designing institutions that will ostensibly work to achieve these principles. Start with what is often the most basic decision, which is whether to adopt a parliamentary or presidentialist (or now, "semi-presidentialist") system. And, whatever decision is made, by what process should one choose the officials, and how long will they be permitted to retain their seats until the next election? And so on through what I now regard as in its own way perhaps the most crucial of all: how easy or hard will it be to engage in formal constitutional amendment should choices made at Time X appear to be unwise and needing change? My own view is that the most truly regrettable of what I regard as an increasingly dysfunctional United States Constitution is the difficulty placed in the way of amendment by Article V. Unfortunately, Madison's call in *Federalist* No. 49 for "veneration" has proved to be more influential than his bracing call in *Federalist* No. 14 that we heed the "lessons of experience" and be willing to shed established ways of doing things when they are recognized to be no longer efficacious.

It is hard not to accept the proposition that arguments often draw on the teachings, if any, of political scientists as to the empirical consequences of adopting one institutional structure over another. And lawyers are often not comfortable with assessing such empirical arguments. They certainly receive no relevant training in most law schools, and Supreme Court opinions are far more likely to quote *The Federalist* or Tocqueville as sage observers of what might be viewed as "eternal truths" about the American experiment than as distinctly time- and culture-bound writers whose views, however interesting, might be very much in need of revision.

It turns out to be extremely difficult to have a confident views about the virtues of presidentialism as against parliamentarianism and, even more, about the

[18] *See* THE "MILITANT DEMOCRACY" PRINCIPLE IN MODERN DEMOCRACIES (Markus Thiel ed., 2009).

many sub-issues, which may or not be handled constitutionally, that quickly arise. Should one have a "unitary" executive or should instead department heads themselves be relatively independent of presidential control? Here, incidentally, to ride a hobby-horse of mine, it would be wonderful if American comparativists paid more attention to American *state* constitutions and the fact that very few of them adopt anything close to the "unitary executive." As Christopher Berry and Jacob Gerson have noted,[19] almost all states have adopted what they call an "unbundled" executive, that is, a system in which governors do *not*, as the result of winning office, also gain the right to appoint what one might think of as her "cabinet," that is, the heads of various and sundry executive branch departments. Many such officials are separately elected, owing no fealty at all to the ostensible "chief executive" of the state. My home state of Texas is perhaps at one end of the spectrum in the number of "executive" offices that are elected by the voters and, concomitantly, not appointed by, or accountable to, the governor, but it is scarcely truly atypical. The overwhelming number of state attorney generals (AGs), for example, are independent of their governors, and it is not unusual for the AG to come from the "opposite party" of the governor or, even if notionally from the same party, to be gunning for the governor's job and thus quite independent of gubernatorial desires. Even New Jersey, which is perhaps the closest analogue in design to the national government, prohibits its governors from firing the attorney general, even though they gained their position through gubernatorial appointment, unless there is good cause to do so, which, presumably, could be tested before a court. Devotees of "the rule of law" may legitimately wonder at the wisdom of placing the head of the Department of Justice, as is the case with the American national government, under the control of a president who might, quite obviously, be wary of excessive "independence" on the part of the Attorney General particularly with regard to the power to investigate and, ultimately, bring charges against malfeasance in office.

American states are also far more open than the national constitutional order to varieties of "direct democracy," as are, of course, a number of foreign countries ranging from Ireland and Switzerland to Australia and New Zealand. But looking at California, Ohio, or Maine deprives critics of the opportunity to suggest that "American exceptionalism" means that there is nothing really to learn from looking at the way that other countries structure their polities. It is hard to deny that California, Ohio, and Maine are all part of what must be defined as "American constitutionalism." This means that the national constitution might itself be recognized as a significant "outlier" not only in the general world, which is clearly the case in important respects, but also, and far more importantly, within the United States itself. One can scarcely argue that the United States Constitution

[19] *See* Christopher R. Berry and Jacob E. Gersen, *The Unbundled Executive*, 75 U. Chi. L. Rev. 1385 (2008). *See also* William P. Marshall, *Break Up the Presidency? Governors, State Attorneys General, and Lessons from the Divided Executive*, 115 Yale L.J. 2445 (2006).

is "unAmerican." But a familiarity, say, with John Dinan's important book *The American State Constitutional Tradition* makes it crystal clear that there are *multiple* conceptions of constitutional government within the United States, and it is entirely misleading to assume that one can understand "American constitutionalism" by studying only one of the literally dozens of constitutions that comprise it. One of my own ambitions is to get students vigorously to argue with one another as to whether the United States or, say, the Oregon or Wisconsin constitution is better with regard to the opportunities that are (or are not) provided for some degree of active "self-government" by an aroused electorate. If they wish to allude as well to Switzerland or Ireland, all the better, but it is not at all necessary to look outside the borders to find the materials for comparative analysis and debate.

Unfortunately, no American state has chosen to adopt a parliamentary system, in which one would have to decide whether, for example, a no-confidence vote should require, as in Germany, the presentation of a substitute for the present Chancellor. Or should such a vote, even without the presentation of an alternative, simply depose an incumbent and trigger either a complex negotiation process or the holding of new elections? Of course, several American states, including California and Wisconsin, do allow the calling of "recall elections," by which the electorate can depose a governor (or other public officials). That is how Arnold Schwarzenegger came to be Governor of California after Grey Davis was recalled. One could go on and on.

Is there, for example, in fact a "best practice" with regard to designing judiciaries? As one looks at various constitutions both at home and abroad, one discovers extremely interesting differences as to criteria for initial selection, length of term, even the toleration or disallowance of concurring or dissenting opinions by members of multi-member courts. Is faith in "the rule of law" reinforced or diminished by allowing the publication of vigorous dissents? Germany prohibited such dissents until 1971 and then chose to allow them, though they are rare. The European Court of Justice, unlike the European Court of Human Rights, continues to rely on singular opinions of "the court"; it has been suggested to me that this is explained as an attempt to reduce the pressure on individual justices, appointed, after all, by their own countries, to hew to a particular nationalist conception about how best to interpret the European treaties. Or perhaps one's answer might depend on the degree to which dissenting opinions include the kind of "trash talk" that was frequent in Antonin Scalia's dissents throughout his career, where, notably, he accused his colleagues of "not acting like judges" or otherwise being mere agents of "elite" agendas rather than faithful servants of the law?[20] And might his friend Ruth Ginsburg's most enduring legacy, far more than her relatively infrequent majority opinions in major cases, be the overwhelming realization that life tenure on apex

[20] *See* Sanford Levinson, *Trash Talk at the Supreme Court: Reflections on David Pozen's* Constitutional Bad Faith, 129 Harv. L. Rev. F. 166 (2016).

courts is a dreadful mistake, especially given the now-baked-in politicization of the appointment process? But is the preferable alternative a fixed term—say 10, 12, or even 18 years—or placing an age barrier that would have forced her to retire, as is common throughout the United States and the world, when reaching 70 or 75?

I think it is safe to say that courses on comparative constitutional law—or their casebooks—rarely spend many pages on such topics, in part because students may find them far less interesting than, say, materials on hate speech or abortion. But it may also be a function of the fact that it is far harder exactly to know what follows from introducing students to the variation that is present across the world with regard to institutional design, especially if, as is increasingly common in so-called large-n studies, understanding the argument may require some degree of comfort with regression analyses. I will confess that though I have a PhD in political science, I do not have the requisite knowledge of statistics to be able to assess a regression analysis. I must take their author's arguments on faith, which is scarcely satisfactory. There is also the fact that American law schools expect their students to "discuss" the issues raised by cases, and it is far easier to do this with regard to "rights" or other abstract values that are thought to be independent of empirical data. Do we really expect students to be able to say very much of interest with regard to their preferences for presidential as against parliamentary systems, especially as the analyses get ever more empirical or, for that matter, historical? Is it relevant that almost never will judicial opinions be the source of relevant material inasmuch as they simply presuppose the basic structural features rather than submit them to analysis?

Consider, for example, Juan Linz's well-known critiques of presidentialism,[21] adopted by Bruce Ackerman in his own work.[22] Linz argued that presidentialism is far more likely to decay into forms of authoritarian rule, either by dictatorial presidents or by coups overthrowing unusually strong presidents. Linz relies for much of his argument on evidence drawn from Latin America. Why exactly would we expect students untrained in political science to be able to adjudicate Jose Antonio Chiebub's critique of Linz, which depends, among other things, on one's confidence in various regression analyses, not to mention fairly detailed knowledge of the histories of particular countries?[23] Or consider in this context the recent important work by Rosalind Dixon and David Landau on the adoption by would-be autocrats of institutions present in "liberal democracies."[24] However, in quite different contexts, including the presence of autocrats who wish to bolster their own

[21] *See, e.g.*, Juan Linz, *The Perils of Presidentialism*, 1 J. Democracy 51 (1960).
[22] *See* Bruce Ackerman, *The New Separation of Powers*, 113 Harv. L. Rev. 633 (2000).
[23] Jose Antonio Cheibub, Presidentialism, Parliamentarism, and Democracy (2006).
[24] Rosalind Dixon & David Landau, Abusive Constitutional Borrowing (2021). *See also* Sanford Levinson, *Assessing "Abusive Constitutionalism" in a Complex Political Universe*, 7 Canadian Journal of Comparative and Contemporary Law 14 (2021) (reviewing Rosalind Dixon & David Landau, Abusive Constitutional Borrowing).

power, the important of such institutions can become the source of what they call "abusive constitutionalism." Kim Scheppele has led the way in emphasizing that one only rarely today sees old-fashioned military coups; instead, as in Hungary especially, well-trained lawyers are capable of defending their adoption of certain practices against the (justified) outrage of liberals such as Scheppele.[25] But how exactly does one recognize "abuse" when the practice being adopted is part and parcel of what is defined as a "liberal constitutional order"?

I am not alone, for example, in denouncing the efforts by Israeli Prime Minister Benjamin Netanyahu to eviscerate the current system of judicial independence in Israel by giving the parliamentary majority basically unlimited power to appoint its own favorites to the courts. But it is an embarrassing truth that Netanyahu could simply assert that he wishes to adopt the system of judicial appointment found at the national level in the United States or, for that matter, in Australia or New Zealand. In the United States, especially, judicial appointments are increasingly viewed as a "spoil" of election. A successful candidate for the presidency, if accompanied by a politically compatible Senate, can "pack" the federal judiciary almost without any vaunted "checks and balances." Concomitantly, a Senate controlled by the "opposition" party can simply refuse even to grant a hearing to a nominee of the president, as notably happened with President Barack Obama's nomination of Merrick Garland to succeed Antonin Scalia upon his death in 2016.

I recall being quite stunned several years ago, when visiting Australia, to read that the Australian Prime Minister had named a new Chief Justice and that that was the end of the matter. There were no parliamentary hearings or formal confirmation. But, I was told by people I trusted, that that was not a problem, because the Prime Minister was an honorable man who in fact picked someone from the opposition party on meritocratic principles. Or, of course, one could look at most of the state judges in the United States, who are either directly elected or, at least, subject or one or another form of ultimate electoral accountability. If we are willing to tolerate either of those systems as part of a "liberal constitutional order" in the United States or elsewhere, then what exactly makes it "abusive" if Netanyahu and his collaborators wish to make Israel look more like the national United States or New Zealand, the latter another small country with a unicameral legislature and no practice of American-style "judicial review"? The answer, surely, requires looking not only at legal formalities, but also the nature of Israel's (or New Zealand's) political culture and, importantly, the degree to which one actually trusts Netanyahu's own commitment to "liberal democracy."

Mark is famous for suggesting that "it depends," when asked about the desirability or consequences of adopting any given policy. I think he is basically

[25] *See* Kim Lane Scheppele, *The Rule of Law and the Frankenstate: Why Governance Checklists Do Not Work*, 26 Governance 559 (2013). *But see* Mark Tushnet & Bojan Bugarič, Power to the People: Constitutionalism in the Age of Populism (2022), ch. 5.

correct, but this conclusion can be dispiriting to anyone seeking advice, such as those drafting new constitutions, or to students who take a course on comparative constitutional design. Both might hope that they will learn what constitute "best practices" with regard to putting in place institutions that will guarantee the implementation of the "constitutional values" that might generate a desire for constitutional design in the first place. To be told that "it depends" and that highly provisional answers might depend on the ability to develop social-scientific skills that are rarely taught in the legal academy will not be deemed very helpful, especially if, as is almost certainly the case, the constitutional designers are working under the pressures of time and exigent political circumstances. To revert to Brandeis's aphorism again, even if one takes seriously the notion that a given state might be engaging in an experiment from which the rest of us can learn, an all-important question is how long it will take genuinely to learn all of the effects, both positive and negative, of the experiment in question. There is a reason, after all, that one often sees quoted the comment attributed to Zhou Enlai, responding to a question from Henry Kissinger about the consequences of the French Revolution and the Paris Commune. "It's too early to say," Zhou apparently replied. And would it really be any more comforting if the Chinese Prime Minister were, as some have suggested, being asked in 1973 only about the consequences of the French uprising in 1968?

In my own work, I am increasingly obsessed with trying to determine how consequential the United States Constitution has actually been within the United States itself. More particularly, can we say with confidence when we have been unequivocally aided by the constitution, when we have been just as unequivocally harmed by its presence, and when—I suspect most of the time—it really has been of little, if any, importance? Mark has often suggested that the constitution—and judicial opinions—generate a kind of "noise" that, empirically, has relatively little consequence. How would one test that proposition? I have often been extremely critical of the statement by Thomas Friedman, a pundit whom I often admire, and his co-author Michael Mandelbaum, that "for America's remarkable history, the Constitution deserves a large share of the credit."[26] It is not only that I am skeptical about how exactly one would demonstrate this, but I am also flabbergasted that they do not balance their praise of the Constitution, which, by stipulation, might even be deserved, with the recognition, as I would prefer to phrase it, that "for much that has gone wrong in America's remarkable history, the Constitution deserves a large share of the blame." I am personally confident that this latter formulation is at least as correct as their far more optimistic rendering, but, again, how exactly would one prove either assertion to a skeptic? And, more broadly, can a comparativist say with any confidence that *any* constitution not only deserves

[26] Thomas L. Friedman & Michael Mandelbaum, That Used to Be Us: How America Fell Behind in the World It Invented and How We Can Come Back 33 (2011).

great praise or blame within its particular country of origin, but also that its features merit either adoption or rejection perhaps halfway across the globe?

That, I think, is the great challenge facing anyone who professes to be interested in comparative constitutionalism, which I think should include all of us. Mark Tushnet's most valuable contribution might well be to encourage the kind of modesty that has characterized his career. Back in the day, he responded to some critics of Critical Legal Theory that "critique is all there is,"[27] that he could provide no "blueprint" by which a presumptively better society might be achieved. But "constitutional design" ultimately is all about specs and blueprints. I would like to think that we know at least a bit, that is, that there are *some* "lessons of experience" we might have cautious confidence in believing, but, at the end of the day, it is absolutely crucial always to recall Mark's consistent willingness to challenge all confident certainties. There are many worse lessons that we can teach our students than the necessity of challenging their own priors and being open to other perspectives even as it does become necessary to choose one or another of them. Mark remains a model of what scholarly engagement requires.

[27] *See, e.g.*, MARK V. TUSHNET, RED, WHITE, AND BLUE: A CRITICAL ANALYSIS OF CONSTITUTIONAL LAW 318 (1988).

5

Canon and Comparative Constitutional Law

*David S. Law**

Introduction: Four Varieties of Canon

Some have suggested that the time is ripe for the conscious articulation of a "canon" in comparative constitutional law (CCL).[1] Indeed, there is much reason to think that CCL already has a canon in some sense. The qualification "in some sense" is, however, doing a lot of work. There is canon, and then there is *canon*: this is a concept that can be innocuous or pernicious, and we fail to distinguish among the various species of canon at our own peril. In what ways and why does the idea of canon come up in CCL? What might we mean when we talk about "canon" in CCL, and what does the existence of this conversation tell us about the field? There are at least four possibilities, which are not mutually exclusive[2] and court very different levels of controversy.

1. Descriptive canon: We could talk in a purely descriptive way about whether something tantamount to a "canon" exists, and, if so, why it exists and what it contains, without valorizing either its existence or its content.
2. Normative canon: We could talk about canon in an explicitly normative way as an intellectually rewarding and worthwhile project of identifying and anointing the worthy that any mature field ought to pursue.

* Many thanks to Jack Balkin, Sandy Levinson, and Ron Krotoszynski, and especially to Mark Tushnet himself for lighting the way and encouraging me to "write this up" in the first place. Special thanks to the volume editors, Vicki Jackson and Madhav Khosla, for going above and beyond the call of duty to see this chapter into print.

[1] *See, e.g.*, Global Canons in an Age of Contestation: Debating Foundational Texts of Constitutional Democracy and Human Rights (Sujit Choudhry, Michaela Hailbronner & Mattias Kumm eds., 2024); Michaela Hailbronner, *Constructing the Global Constitutional Canon: Between Authority and* Criticism, 69 U. Toronto L.J. 248 (2019). Comparative constitutional studies (CCS) is, for most purposes and for the various reasons identified by Ran Hirschl, a preferable term but may not be suitable in this specific context because—to its credit—it denotes a broader enterprise, less focused on judicial decisions, that is correspondingly less susceptible to any impulse toward "canonization" of the type discussed here. *See* Ran Hirschl, *Comparative Constitutional Law: A Field Transformed*, in this volume.

[2] J.M. Balkin & Sanford Levinson, *The Canons of Constitutional Law*, 111 Harv. L. Rev. 963, 969–70 (1998) ("Because legal materials have multiple audiences and functions, there is no reason to think that law, or any field of law, has a single canon.").

David S. Law, *Canon and Comparative Constitutional Law* In: *Redefining Comparative Constitutional Law*. Edited by: Vicki C. Jackson and Madhav Khosla, Oxford University Press.
DOI: 10.1093/9780191996344.003.0005

3. Pedagogical canon: We could seek to develop a canon as something that is instrumentally useful for pedagogical purposes and worth cultivating for that reason. There are "thin" and "thick" ways of defining and justifying a classroom canon, the arguments for which will vary accordingly.
4. Discursive canon: We could seek to develop a canon that would operate as an intellectual lingua franca or common framework for discussion, which CCL may especially need because its lack of geographical or disciplinary boundaries threatens to fragment the field and undermines the prospects for shared discourse or a coherent and cumulative research agenda.

Descriptive Canon: The Inescapability of Conventionality

The emergence of something resembling a canon in content, if not in name, may be an inevitable byproduct of the growth and maturation of CCL as a field. As an empirical matter, as any field matures, some materials are bound to be used more frequently than others. It would be strange and surprising indeed if CCL scholars were to spend an exactly equal amount of time and energy on all possible objects of study—every jurisdiction, every court, every doctrine, every opinion the beneficiary of equal attention. And that is, of course, not what has happened.

What we have instead is a "de facto canon" or "unofficial canon."[3] It is a canon neither in the original sense of church diktat, nor in the updated sense of embodying standards of judgment or authority,[4] but only in the narrow, empirical sense that its contents are widely used and discussed to the point of being unavoidable, and that scholars generally agree on its contours as a descriptive matter, regardless of how they may feel about it on the merits. It consists of around "[t]wo dozen" or so judicial decisions,[5] focused mainly on rights protection and drawn from "a standard and relatively limited set of cases"—mainly "South Africa, Israel, Germany, Canada, the United Kingdom, New Zealand, the United States,"[6] "and the European Court of Human Rights alongside . . . an occasional tribute to India or Australia."[7] To note the emergence and contours of this de facto canon is not to celebrate its existence or endorse its content. On the contrary, scholars writing in

[3] Ran Hirschl, Comparative Matters: The Renaissance of Comparative Constitutional Law 192–223 (2014).

[4] Balkin & Levinson, *supra* note 2, at 968 n.24.

[5] Hirschl, *supra* note 3, at 163; *see also, e.g., id.* at 40–41; Rosalind Dixon & Tom Ginsburg, *Introduction: Comparative Constitutional Law, in* Comparative Constitutional Law 1, 13 (Tom Ginsburg & Rosalind Dixon eds., 2011) ("It is probably the case that 90% of comparative work in the English language covers the same ten countries, for which materials are easily accessible in English").

[6] Sujit Choudhry, *Bridging Comparative Politics and Comparative Constitutional Law: Constitutional Design in Divided Societies, in* Constitutional Design for Divided Societies: Integration or Accommodation? 3, 8 (Sujit Choudhry ed., 2008).

[7] Hirschl, *supra* note 3, at 163; *see also, e.g., id.* at 40–41.

this descriptive vein are often openly critical of its biases and blind spots.[8] And this is as it should be. There is a critical distinction between what *receives* our attention and what *deserves* our attention. Our preoccupations do not always align with our ideals.

Language, for example, plays an outsized role and is correlated or intertwined with a variety of other factors that tilt the playing field.[9] Countries with English-speaking judges and lawyers, in particular, make up the vast bulk of the "usual suspects." Thus, for example, the extant literature dwells at much greater length on the work of the Israeli Supreme Court and the South African Constitutional Court than on, say, the Korean Constitutional Court or the Taiwanese Constitutional Court, and that is not because the former make more sophisticated or extensive use of comparative law than the latter (false), or because the former have superior democratic bona fides (again, false). To be sure, the judicial style of the Israeli and South African courts produces more grist for the mill in the form of relatively verbose opinions. But the simple fact is that the sheer accessibility of their decisions to the English-speaking world matters greatly.

"Accessibility," in this case, has more than one dimension. It is a function of not only the availability of the decisions themselves in English—for the Korean and Taiwanese decisions satisfy that relatively modest condition—but also the social and professional networks that define the scholarly conversation and bring certain materials and not others to the attention of the legal community. These networks both embody and perpetuate the dominance of the usual suspects. Accordingly, it will take more than the online availability of English-language translations from other jurisdictions to disrupt the status quo.

These upstream advantages are compounded over time by a combination of mechanisms including path dependence and cascade effects. Linguistic accessibility can lead to the early inclusion of certain materials and not others in a casebook that turns out to be especially influential;[10] a generation of scholars is trained in a particular set of materials as a result; initial popularity begets further popularity; and a snowball effect kicks in. The sociology of CCL as a field encourages people to pile on. "People cluster around a certain set of materials and topics because they see that other people do, and they think"—perhaps correctly—"that doing so will make them part of the conversation."[11] In all of these ways, one lingua franca spawns another: the lingua franca of English serves as the point of departure for the lingua franca of CCL. To those who have, more shall be given.

The emergence and articulation of a de facto canon may also be a natural by-product of efforts to understand and describe an increasingly complex field.

[8] *See, e.g., id.*
[9] Maartje De Visser, *Constitutional Comparisons and Language*, in this volume.
[10] *See, e.g.*, Vicki C. Jackson & Mark Tushnet, Comparative Constitutional Law (3d ed. 2014).
[11] Thanks to Jack Balkin for this formulation.

A fast-growing and increasingly diverse field like CCL is defined by a proliferation of knowledge: more jurisdictions, more disciplines, more perspectives, more everything. The practical result is what Tom Ginsburg calls "the encyclopedic turn"[12]—the growing need for, and popularity of, tools and resources that rationalize, summarize, organize, and synthesize this sprawling mass. The popularity and proliferation of research handbooks is one manifestation of this demand. But the idea of canon—the promise of a pared-down, one-stop shop for the essentials—scratches the same itch.

Above all, the emergence of de facto canon may simply reflect the maturation of the field. With the benefit of experience, established patterns and practices come into focus. Systematization and repetition suggest themselves as rational strategies: they save time and effort and appeal to our confidence in the tried and true. It may be, however, that this kind of maturation is something we ought to resist rather than embrace.

For around a quarter-century now—a period roughly coinciding with the life of the Jackson and Tushnet casebook,[13] which has arguably been akin in its impact to the opening of the Northwest Passage—CCL has been a great field for those of us who in some sense do not want to grow up. The youth of the field—defined in part by the lack of any sense of canon—meant that getting into CCL at the turn of the 21st century came with the luxury of charting one's own path and marching to the beat of one's own drum, largely free of the weight of expectations and the anxiety of influence. An enormously attractive thing about the field—at least to me, at the time—was that one did not have to color within the lines, because there were no lines, or at least no lines that were not themselves up for grabs. There were emerging topics and objects of discussion, but they were not valorized or framed as "canonical." People often discussed certain cases and countries more than others, but not necessarily with any sense of obligation to do so, and the agenda remained plastic. Of the field, it could genuinely be said: everything was so new that everything remained possible. Whatever defined the field was whatever people chose to do. So why work to end this now?

For some, this experience of everything being up for grabs may be profoundly liberating. For others, however, it could activate yearning for the structure and stricture of canon. It is precisely at times of "ferment, growth, change, and innovation," observe Balkin and Levinson, "that anxieties about canons arise in any discipline. The discipline seeks either to reconstitute itself or to close ranks by considering what, if anything, can be said to be canonical about its practices, its methods, or its materials of study."[14] CCL is not a field on the brink of reconstituting itself. More

[12] Tom Ginsburg, *The State of the Field*, *in* CONSTITUTIONALISM IN CONTEXT 23, 37 (David S. Law ed., 2022).

[13] JACKSON & TUSHNET, *supra* note 10; *see* David Fontana, *The Rise and Fall of Comparative Constitutional Law in the Postwar Era*, 36 YALE J. INT'L L. 1, 46–53 (2011).

[14] Balkin & Levinson, *supra* note 2, at 969.

likely, therefore, is a closing of ranks. In this context, canon doubles as both a sign and a form of ossification. A field that lacks a canon, by contrast, is a field that does not purport to already know what is worth knowing; because it cannot rest on its laurels, it tends instead toward growth and experimentation. These are the hallmarks of neoteny—extended youth—and there is much to be said for remaining as young as we can, for as long as we can.

Normative Canon: Towering Judges, Great Cases?

Canon is in some sense the high-toned, academic version of the top ten list or the hall of fame. That is not an inherently bad thing. Top ten lists can be interesting, fun, and informative. They can be informative in the sense of identifying highlights that any newcomer or outsider with limited bandwidth ought to know. But canon also aspires to be more than just a highbrow beauty contest. Does CCL as a field not possess intellectual or technical standards of merit and excellence, if not also substantive values? What is the point of having standards or values if we do not strive to apply them? And what better way could there be to apply and refine our benchmarks than to identify and celebrate the materials that score the highest? At its best, canon-making pushes us to articulate and reflect upon what we are trying to do, what we value, and why.[15]

To many, this kind of curation may sound like an unobjectionable and indeed self-evidently worthwhile endeavor. To others—including even the most casual observers of academic politics over the last 30 years—it may set off alarm bells. Most concerns can be divided into two categories, implementation and consequences. Implementation alone poses formidable, if not insurmountable, challenges: it would require agreement not only on what standards and values to apply, but also on how to apply them in specific cases.[16] Then comes the question of what consequences we might reap from our efforts. Slow but meaningful progress? Wasted effort? Something worse?

On both counts, there are lessons to be had from experience. Basic prudence demands that we consider how the idea of canon has worked out in other corners of academia. The short answer is that it has proved a bloody quagmire. Efforts to construct "core courses" that introduce students to a Great Works or Western canon have come under intense criticism from a variety of directions, and rightfully so. The idea of the Great Works canon triggered years of pitched conflict in the form of the "canon wars" of the late 1980s and early 1990s, in which "traditionalists in favor of centering the curriculum on classic works of literature faced off against

[15] *See, e.g.*, *id.*; Hailbronner, *supra* note 1, at 261–62, 274.

[16] *See* Hailbronner, *supra* note 1, at 274 ("[T]he idea that we might achieve anything like a comprehensive agreement on the canon's contents is doubtless fanciful").

multiculturalists who wanted to include more works by women and members of minorities"—and by and large, the pro-canon traditionalists lost.[17]

There is little reason to think that the construction of a canon in CCL would escape these difficulties.[18] On the contrary, by reifying a problematic and truncated understanding of what people ought to study, the project of canonization might instead entrench and reinforce some of the worst tendencies of a field already characterized by a poorly justified preoccupation with certain jurisdictions and topics. Just as the idea of Western canon runs the risk of devolving into a reactionary and stereotypical ode to dead White men, a CCL version of canon runs the risk of fetishizing the predominantly White, Western, and/or English-speaking usual suspects. To be sure, progress has been made as of late,[19] but that is perhaps all the more reason to refrain from picking favorites now. Establishing a canon at a time when the field is expanding and diversifying is akin to locking in a permanent wardrobe at age 15: the choices may fit now, but there is every reason to question whether they will age well.

The timing is, if anything, even less ripe for the idea of an intellectual canon now than it was in the 1980s. The last 30 years in academia, if not also society more broadly, have by and large been a story of growing sensitivity and attention to issues of diversity, inclusion, and identity, and of striving to unearth and reckon with structural bias. Why should the field of CCL court such criticism and controversy, in apparent defiance of the lessons of recent history? What wisdom is there in turning our efforts to an innately retrograde project and throwing ourselves upon the third rail of academic politics in the process?

It is impossible to elevate one set of fetish objects to the status of canon without marginalizing everything that is left out. Canon is not just characterized but *defined* by the act of exclusion: what gives canon its content, and what gives its content authority, is precisely its exclusivity. This is why outsiders are often suspicious of the idea of canon, and rightfully so. Can the field be trusted to perform this exclusion well and wisely, when so much work remains to be done? Are good intentions enough to prevent us from enshrining our own blind spots and biases? How confident can we be that a canon constructed today, even with conscious attention paid to questions of diversity and inclusion, will actually be a diverse and inclusive canon? We remain very far from being able to claim that we have systematically

[17] Rachel Donadio, *Revisiting the Canon Wars*, N.Y. Times, Sept. 16, 2007, at 716, https://perma.cc/EM2P-PNE5; *see, e.g.*, Harold Bloom, The Closing of the American Mind: How Higher Education Has Failed Democracy and Impoverished the Souls of Today's Students 62–67, 336–82 (1987); Harold Bloom, The Western Canon: The Books and School of the Ages 15–41, 517–28 (1994); Irving Howe, *The Value of the Canon*, New Republic, Feb. 18, 1991, at 40, https://perma.cc/J5FS-JS4T.

[18] This paragraph is adapted from David S. Law, *Pedagogy and Conceptualization of the Field, in* Constitutionalism in Context, *supra* note 12, at 3, 12.

[19] *See, e.g.*, Ginsburg, *supra* note 12, at 27, 37–40; Ran Hirschl, *Methodology and Research Design*, in Constitutionalism in Context, *supra* note 12, at 41–58.

canvassed constitutionalism around the world in all its shapes and forms and are now in a position to bestow ribbons and sashes. On the contrary, any current effort at canon-making is likely as a methodological matter to rely heavily on word of mouth and the reach and quality of the canon-maker's networks.

The same abundance of new frontiers and underexplored or unexplored reaches that continues to make CCL such an inviting field full of possibility for veterans and newcomers alike also dooms the normative canon-making project to fail at its goals. Canon of the normative variety is supposed to consist of what we ought to know. The problem is, however, that we do not know what we ought to know. We do not know everything, and what we do not know invariably includes a lot of things that are worth knowing. The only canon we are capable of fashioning is one that consists of what we already know, and what we *already* know is not the same as what we *ought* to know.

What we know of the de facto canon that already exists—not to mention the past experience of the humanities—strongly suggests that we will end up with the CCL equivalent of a literary canon of Great Works by Dead White Men that invites (and deserves) attack from a variety of perspectives. The CCL equivalent will probably consist in large part of Great Cases written, presumably, by Towering Judges (and, by way of negative example, a few Great Mistakes authored by The Judges Whom Towering Judges Tower Over).[20] Construction of a canon today, with the intellectual and human capital available to us now, will have predictable, systematic, self-reinforcing, and lamentable results, such as the marginalization of the Global South (with the exception of a handful of largely English-speaking and/or common law "platinum club" members such as South Africa and India).

This is the opposite of a diverse and inclusive enterprise. Those on the outside have every reason to reject the articulation of a canon—and, with it, a codified self-understanding of the field—that marginalizes them. It is hard to imagine how creation of a canon could make it easier for students and lawyers and scholars in Taiwan, or South Korea, or Hong Kong, or Thailand, or Indonesia (or indeed most of the Global South, or the Muslim world) to relate to the work of the field. None of this bodes well for the growth and vitality of the field.

Again, there are lessons to be learned from the recent past. Where American conservatives went wrong in the canon wars was in failing to recognize that what people generally long for in literature is not so much "book camp," or a crash course in Western citizenship, as self-recognition.[21] The same could be said of CCL. When students and lawyers and scholars in much (most) of the world look to what currently passes for canon, they largely fail to see themselves reflected or represented. It is not clear why a consciously crafted canon—curated by the same

[20] *Cf.* Towering Judges: A Comparative Study of Constitutional Judges (Rehan Aberatyne ed., 2021). This turn of phrase is borrowed without permission from Mark Tushnet.

[21] Donadio, *supra* note 17 (quoting Mark Lilla).

cast of characters, from the same raw materials—would do much better. Indeed, it could do worse. The gatekeeping that goes into the construction of a canon is inescapably an exercise of judgment and power. What we study, and especially what we study habitually and automatically, is both indicative and constitutive of power dynamics.

Hence, canon is divisive. Its response to troubling conditions of hegemony, marginalization, and exclusion is to double down—to draw and celebrate an explicit line between the deserving insiders and the undeserving outsiders. The enterprise of canonization may reveal more about the tastes and aptitudes and power dynamics of those doing the canonizing than about what works are truly great and in what order of greatness. Efforts to graft broader representation onto existing canon, meanwhile, tend to reek of tokenism because that is all too often what they are.[22]

What is at stake, however, is not just diversity for the sake of diversity, or inclusion for the sake of inclusion, or the critical examination and rectification of structural bias. A field that defines itself around an imbalanced and backward-looking canon risks failing to serve the pressing practical needs of a genuinely global enterprise and may fail in particular to serve the needs of those most in need. The field has much to offer those interested in improving and tweaking the judicial implementation of liberal constitutional democracy at the margins. The pressing concerns of much of the rest of the world, however, are already marginalized. Highly consequential countries are often dismissed or excluded from study altogether because they are judged to lack "real" judicial review, or "real" democracy, or "real" constitutions, or "real" constitutionalism.[23]

What reason is there to think that an explicit project of canonization will do anything but formalize and even celebrate these blind spots and omissions?[24] What will the canon have to say to those in countries that do not already have judicial review? What will it have to say to the growing numbers living under the yoke of authoritarian rule?[25] What will the canon have to teach us about the systems that are least like our own—and therefore the ones about which we most urgently need to learn?

[22] Part of this paragraph is adapted from Law, *supra* note 18.

[23] *See, e.g.*, *id.* at 7 n.7 (discussing the reasons given by the editors for the deliberate exclusion of Russia and China from a recent CCL casebook); Wen-Chen Chang & David S. Law, *Constitutional Dissonance in China*, *in* Comparative Constitutional Theory 476, 476–91, 491–513 (Gary Jacobsohn & Miguel Schor eds., 2018); Hailbronner, *supra* note 1, at 263 (arguing that "sincere engagement with shared values and principles" is a sine qua non of inclusion in any CCL canon).

[24] *See* Hailbronner, *supra* note 1, at 249 (noting the tendency of canons to "exclude and marginalize" and "reflect existing societal and intra-disciplinary hierarchies").

[25] *See, e.g.*, Freedom House, Freedom in the World 2021: Democracy Under Siege 1–3 (2021), https://perma.cc/U9H8-RWU7 (noting the "15th consecutive year of decline in global freedom," and reporting that less than 20 percent of the world's population now lives in a free country, the lowest proportion since 1995).

In this field as in any other, reflection on what is best or most worthwhile can be a valuable exercise. The danger lies in insisting that this process of reflection yields right or best answers—in other words, a canon—as opposed to highly contingent answers that reflect the predilections and limitations of those doing the reflecting.

Pedagogical Canon: The Teacher's Pets

One might argue that, even if it is difficult to justify a Great Works/Great Cases canon for its own sake on normative grounds, there are nevertheless compelling practical reasons to develop a CCL canon of sorts for teaching purposes. Whether the idea of a classroom canon is in fact easier to defend, or instead invites all of the same objections and perhaps a few more to boot, depends on what kind of classroom canon we have in mind. We could imagine both a "thin," efficacy-driven version and a "thick," substance-driven version, with the former being much easier to swallow than the latter.

Consider first the efficacy-based or "thin" version. Even if it is a fool's errand to seek to pin down the "best" or "most important" materials in the field from a substantive perspective, that does not mean that instructors should pick teaching materials at random. Some materials may simply be better suited for teaching use or offer greater bang for their buck than others: in other words, they happen to be effective delivery mechanisms. In the context of CCL, it could be that a particular case does a good job of isolating and clearly explaining a particular issue, without unwelcome complications or diversions. Or, conversely, a case might be valuable for classroom use because it raises multiple issues at once and thus highlights the interaction of those issues, or allows more ground to be covered more quickly, or the like. The fact that a particular case proves through experience to be especially attention-grabbing or easy for students to intuit, or to elicit especially lively engagement and discussion, is another good reason for instructors to treat it as canonical, at least for teaching purposes.

On this "thin" understanding of classroom canon, the *existence* of a canon for pedagogical purposes is a good thing, but the *contents* of the canon are not necessarily valorized as masterpieces for the ages. Indeed, they may not even be inherently superior to other potential teaching materials. All that can be said about them is that they get the job done and are widely used. The inclusion of a particular item in the canon means merely that it is a time-tested and efficient vehicle for conveying content, eliciting discussion, and so on. Indeed, the very fact of its inclusion—its entry into the collective lore of law students past, present, and future—tends to enhance its utility as a teaching tool. For example, the "hairy hand" case[26] is canonical

[26] Hawkins v. McGee, 84 N.H. 114 (1929).

for teaching purposes not because it is an especially unique or groundbreaking case as a matter of contract law—for it is not—but rather because it covers key points and raises important questions in a memorable, familiar, and illuminating fashion that lends itself to retelling and discussion across generations as part of the shared culture and traditions of American legal education.

The emergence of a classroom canon in a thin sense is probably not only inevitable as an empirical matter, but also unobjectionable in principle. In practice, however, it may still have unintended or even undesirable consequences. For example, a desire for materials that thoroughly explain legal doctrines may lead instructors to favor the verbose judicial style of common law jurisdictions, which may in turn leave students with a misleading or unrepresentative picture of constitutionalism around the world. Still, there are ways to mitigate such concerns (such as the selection of quasi-official or otherwise authoritative commentary from civil law jurisdictions).

Vastly more problematic is the idea of a "thick" classroom canon with more ambitious goals and pretensions. One might say that the goal is to distill the field down to the "essentials" of what students must know. Or perhaps the goal is to produce lawyers or scholars who are in some objective sense "well-read" in the subject matter, which requires us to first determine what ought to be read—or, in other words, what is canonical. But these amount to different ways of framing the same general enterprise. Although the contents of "thin" and "thick" classroom canon may well overlap in practice, the selection criteria are different. The first is about pedagogical efficiency; the second is about substantive prioritization. "Thin" classroom canon is the accretion of pedagogical experience as to what materials elicit the desired student response. By contrast, "thick" classroom canon calls on instructors to identify materials that ought to be studied in their own right. The key consideration is not how students respond to the material, but what instructors think about the merits of the material.

A "thick" version of classroom canon faces at least two problems. First, it is indistinguishable from, and raises the same concerns as, the "Great Cases" variety of canon discussed above: it will marginalize and exclude in ways that perpetuate and entrench the blind spots and structural biases of the field. The fact that our goals happen to be pedagogical in nature—that classroom canon is for the sake of shaping young minds and thus implicates the reproduction and future of the field—does nothing to address these concerns, but instead aggravates them.

Second, "thick" canon does not solve much as a practical matter and may indeed compromise other teaching goals. Much of the appetite for thick canon is driven by the perennial problem of instructional capacity. In every field, there is always too much content to cover and too little time in which to cover it, and the problem is even worse than usual in an international, interdisciplinary, expanding field like CCL.[27] In theory, canon suggests itself as the solution: what better way to survey a

[27] Law, *supra* note 18, at 3–22.

vast field in a short amount of time than to lean on a condensed, prepackaged selection of the "best" or "most worthwhile" or "most important" materials that the field has to offer? In practice, however, it does not take much immersion in CCL to realize that the prospects for distilling the "best" or the "essentials" of such a sprawling field into a semester's worth of instructional time or a single casebook are poor and only getting worse.

The solution of classroom canon is thus no solution at all. On the one hand, if we stick to our principles and canonize everything that deserves canonization, we fail to solve the problem of capacity and instead pass the buck to individual instructors, which defeats the purpose. A canon that consists of x, y, and z does not solve the problem of what to teach if there is only time to teach x, y, *or* z.

On the other hand, there is no good way of cutting the canon down to classroom size. Determining what to cut is a constant headache for instructors. Relabeling that task one of "canon-culling" rather than "syllabus-culling" does not magically make it easier or unlock new solutions. At best, this move narrows down the field of candidates, but it also leaves us with hard choices and no obvious criteria for further triage. There is a world of difference, for example, between saying that both Machiavelli and Sun Tzu belong in the canon (relatively easy to argue), and saying that Machiavelli should be retained at the expense of Sun Tzu (much harder).

One might respond by doubling down and attempting to unearth some basis for further ranking everything *within* the canon, with the goal of prioritizing the *most* canonical materials. Even assuming that some "mini-canon" or "super-canon" can be discerned within the canon, however, its use is likely to cause further headaches. If one starts with an unrepresentative canon, then makes further cuts using a stepped-up version of the same criteria that produced an unrepresentative canon in the first place, it stands to reason that the resulting "mini-canon" will do even worse at capturing the range of constitutional experience and diversity that merits classroom coverage.

There are better ways of tackling the problem of capacity while also doing justice to the diversity of the field. In particular, one might instead conceptualize CCL pedagogy as an exercise in *sampling*. Social scientists continually face the challenge of learning about populations that are too vast to be studied in their entirety, and they respond to this challenge by seeking to draw samples that capture and represent the diversity of these populations. CCL pedagogy might adopt an approach analogous to stratified sampling. We could divide the universe of constitutionalism into its major dimensions of variation and categories of interest (liberal or not, democratic or not, judicial review or not, West or Global South, etc.) then draw a sample from each subpopulation, with the aim of representing the range and diversity of constitutional experience. The goal, in other words, is to cover not the "best" materials, but rather a representative sample of what we are trying to study.[28]

[28] *See id.* at 17–18 (contrasting an anticanonical "representation model" of CCL pedagogy with existing approaches). Representativeness is an attractive principle, but not all approaches to

The sampling paradigm has several advantages over the canon paradigm as a way of dealing with the problem of capacity. First, it refrains from valorizing its subjects and thus avoids all the objections that plague that enterprise. On the contrary, it recognizes that there are other cases we could have picked with equal validity. Second, unlike the canon paradigm, the sampling paradigm hails from a methodological rather than a theological tradition and thus draws our attention to the need to be transparent, reflective, and self-critical about methodology—about the way we choose what to include and what to leave out.[29]

Discursive Canon: The Lingua Franca

Canon might also emerge out of a conscious effort to establish common points of reference or a kind of lingua franca for our far-flung field. Every field has its lingo and shorthand, and this is a good thing. Among other things, a precise conceptual and intellectual vocabulary fosters the articulation and advancement of a common research agenda and prevents people from talking past each other. The need for a common baseline may be particularly pronounced in the case of CCL, which is defined by weak to nonexistent disciplinary and geographical boundaries. Indeed, the field consists at its core of exchange across disciplines and borders. Without a shared vocabulary or language, how is exchange to occur? Without shared points of reference or objects of inquiry, how can there be a common enterprise? In the face of so much material and so many choices, where are newcomers to begin? It is arguably the very diversity of the field that necessitates the equivalent of a canon in substance, if not in name. If so, why not help the process along by actively cultivating what already exists in substance, if not also in name? Why not guide the development of the lingua franca in a thoughtful and deliberate way, instead of letting the chips fall where they may?

This line of thinking has undeniable intuitive appeal but immediately runs into several problems. One is conceptual; another is distributional.

representativeness necessarily live up to the name. For example, Choudhry et al. claim to agree that a CCL canon should be constructed on the basis of "representativeness," but what should be represented or sampled in their view are "ways of thinking about certain key themes of constitutional democracy." GLOBAL CANONS IN AN AGE OF CONTESTATION, *supra* note 1, at 5. However, unless one takes the discredited triumphalist view that constitutional democracy dominates the world—*see* CONSTITUTIONAL DEMOCRACY IN CRISIS? (Mark A. Graber, Sanford Levinson & Mark Tushnet eds., 2018); *supra* notes 23–25 and accompanying text—restriction of the sample to the realm of constitutional democracy amounts at best to a representative sample of an unrepresentative subset. By contrast, the idea of representativeness proposed here and in earlier work, *see* Law, *supra* note 18, entails sampling along all major dimensions of constitutional variation, not just the dimensions that Western liberals find normatively agreeable or amenable to importation.

[29] Law, *supra* note 18, at 17–18.

(a) The conceptual problem. It may be a conceptual error to think of canon as performing the role of a common language or medium of communication. Needless to say, a canon cannot constitute a language in a literal sense. It can do so only in a metaphorical sense, and at least in the context of CCL, the metaphor may be misleading. CCL certainly has its fair share of concepts and terms of art—amparo, tutela, soft review, and so on—and the more numerous and widely known such terms and concepts are, the better the prospects for broad participation in productive scholarly dialogue. Generally, though, when we speak of canon in CCL, we probably do not have specific words or terms in mind. We are more often talking about things like particular judicial decisions (*Makwanyane*,[30] *Lüth*[31]), doctrines ("basic structure,"[32] "constitutional block"[33]), institutions ("fourth-branch institutions"[34]), and examples or specimens of various phenomena ("notwithstanding clause"[35]).

The result is less a language than a set of intellectual touchstones or interpretive artifacts. Potentially canonical materials in CCL are not, for the most part, discrete words or concepts that lend themselves to unambiguous and uncontroversial definition and thus to use as a means of communication. Instead, the field traffics heavily in materials that are (a) rooted in specific factual and legal contexts, and/or (b) in need of interpretation, unpacking, or translation of some sort, all of which renders them poor vehicles for transnational communication. They are widely known and widely invoked, but they are at best points of reference—arguably more akin to campfire stories, or parables, or nursery rhymes than to dictionary entries. They have to be unpacked, they can be unpacked in different ways, and the process of unpacking them and discussing how to unpack them is itself constitutive of the field.

(b) The distributional problem. This reconceptualization of canon as an object of discourse rather than a medium of communication leads us to the distributional problem with the enterprise. The field of CCL is, among other things, an interpretive community,[36] and there can be no interpretive community without something to interpret. To stipulate which interpretive artifacts are indispensable

[30] State v. Makwanyane, 1995 (3) SALR 391.

[31] BVerfGE, 1 BvR 400/51, Jan. 15, 1958.

[32] David S. Law & Hsiang-Yang Hsieh, *Judicial Review of Constitutional Amendments: Taiwan*, in Constitutionalism in Context, *supra* note 12, at 191–92.

[33] Justin O. Frosini, Constitutional Preambles at a Crossroads Between Politics and Law 67–70 (2012) (discussing France and Colombia).

[34] Mark Tushnet, *Fourth-Branch Institutions: South Africa, in* Constitutionalism in Context, *supra* note 12, at 426–46.

[35] §33(2), Canadian Charter of Rights and Freedoms, Part I of the Constitution Act, 1982, *being* Schedule B to the Canada Act, 1982, c. 11 (U.K.); *see* David S. Law & Mark Tushnet, *The Politics of Judicial Dialogue, in* Research Handbook on the Politics of Constitutional Law 286, 299–303 (Mark Tushnet & Dimitry Kochenov eds., 2023).

[36] *See, e.g.*, Stanley Fish, Is There a Text in This Class? The Authority of Interpretive Communities 14–18 (1980).

is to regulate membership and participation in the interpretive community. Canon in CCL thus performs the critical role of gatekeeper or barrier to entry into the discourse. To adopt a canon is to impose, as Bourdieu might put it, a capital requirement.[37]

As a practical matter, successful entry into any field (petroleum extraction, literary criticism, comparative constitutional law) demands at least some kind of capital (financial, educational, intellectual, social, etc.). Moreover, some will inevitably be endowed with more capital, or more valuable forms of capital, than others, and some forms of capital will be more useful in some settings than others. That is just the way of the world. To decree that knowledge of x, y, and z is foundational to discourse and participation in a particular field, however, is to specify that one must possess at least certain forms and levels of intellectual and educational capital in order to obtain the profits of membership and attain dominance in that field. Claims about canon, in other words, are claim about the rules of the game: what must one have in order to play, much less succeed?

To understand scholarly canon as a formalized capital requirement imposed on would-be participants is to highlight both the profound distributional consequences of canon and the need for contestation and resistance. Who has a say in the content of the canon and thus the rules of the game? Those with influence and resources—in other words, those who already have power and privilege.[38] What will they choose to canonize? The powerful will inevitably require others to know what they know, not necessarily out of a desire to oppress or exclude, but rather because all they know is what they already know. Asked to devise a literacy test, English-speakers cannot help but devise a test that is in English. Likewise, in the context of CCL, logic and experience alike suggest that the canon will oversample the most familiar corners of the world and under-sample the least familiar, simply because those responsible for fashioning the canon are only familiar with what is already familiar to them.

The result is a canon that not only underrepresents many jurisdictions and varieties of constitutional experience, but also disproportionately burdens would-be scholars who are not from certain White and/or English-speaking countries. Those who do not hail from canonical jurisdictions rife with canonical materials start at a disadvantage for that reason alone. It's good to be Canadian, bad to be Cambodian; good to be German, bad to be Ghanaian. Once again, the privileged become further privileged. This inequity is, moreover, entirely of our own making.

[37] Pierre Bourdieu, The Rules of Art: Genesis and Structure of the Literary Field 231 (Susan Emanuel trans., 1995) (defining the "structure of the field" as "the structure and distribution of those kinds of capital (or of power) whose possession governs the obtaining of specific profits . . . put into play in the field").

[38] *See id.* at 224–26 (observing inter alia that "the field of cultural production" is characterized by ongoing power struggles over who belongs in the field, and who has the right to participate in deciding who belongs in the field).

This is not akin to a situation in which some countries happen to have minerals or oil and others do not, and that is just the way things are. On the contrary, the idea of a canon in CCL that favors the privileged is the epitome of a socially constructed phenomenon. It is the product of explicit claims about value and worth by members of a privileged in-group.[39]

Is it any justification to say that this is done in the name of facilitating scholarly dialogue? Should we say to most of the world, "we know that this CCL pantheon we have ordained is under-representative in content and regressive in effect, and moreover, we cannot purport to defend this underrepresentation on the merits because we are largely ignorant of what we are underrepresenting, but please go along with it for the sake of fostering shared discourse?" Is this not akin to English-speakers solving the problem of linguistic diversity by insisting that others speak English? If the goal of fostering shared discourse or scholarly dialogue is not a satisfactory reason to exclude African or Asian or Latinx authors from a literary canon, why should it be a satisfactory answer to lawyers and scholars throughout most of Africa, Asia, and Latin America?

Conclusion: Toward Representation and Generality

It is tempting to assume that there must be some way of mitigating these harms, and of reforming and improving the project of canon instead of abandoning it altogether. But identifying and fostering a canonical set of touchstones and artifacts that is fit for a genuinely global and inclusive hermeneutic community and gives voice to all with something to say—not just those with the loudest voices—is much easier said than done. Inequalities embedded in the structure of the field—differences in resources, prestige, market size, and so on—do much to determine who has a say over the contents of the canon and what will be considered canonical. The creation of a canon may not cause these inequalities in the first place, but it does codify and perpetuate them.

Insofar as the distributional and exclusionary concerns associated with canon are rooted in both the structure of the field and the very concept of canon, we should not expect an easy or simple fix. A normatively palatable conception of canon in CCL is likely to require a paradigm shift. How might such a shift look? Consider in this vein the possibility of a canon defined by principles of *representation* and *generality*.

Representation, in this context, has both procedural and substantive dimensions. As a matter of process, definition of the canon cannot be left to a privileged coterie of Western scholars. Left to their own devices, insiders can be expected to favor

[39] *See id.* at 229; Hailbronner, *supra* note 1, at 256, 258.

other insiders and to lean on what they know best: to ask Canadian and German scholars what is canonical is to ensure that Canadian and German materials will be represented in the canon. Outsiders must have a seat at the table. At the level of substance, the idea is to adopt the sampling paradigm and canvass the diversity of constitutional experience around the world—not just the parts and aspects that are already familiar to insiders.[40]

Generality refers to the notion that, as much as possible, the contents of the canon can and should be framed and defined in universalistic or generic fashion. Relatively abstract and portable terms and concepts should be favored for canonization over specific cases, courts, and countries. All are then invited to flesh out these generic terms and concepts with context and examples from their own countries or regions, rather than being forced to make their own experience fit into the pigeonhole of a specific example from a high-profile foreign country.

For instance, we might canonize the concepts of "soft review" and "legislative override clauses" (generic) as opposed to the "notwithstanding clause"[41] (country-specific). Likewise, we might expect others to know the terms "amendment-review" or "super-hard review"[42] (generic), but not necessarily the "basic structure doctrine"[43] (country-specific). In other words, we canonize the concept but not the specific case of Canada or India as the starting point or baseline for understanding or defining the concept. This move opens the door to the use and acceptance of non-canonical jurisdictions,[44] as examples in addition to, or even instead of, the usual suspects. In this way, all examples and manifestations of the term or concept are validated and valued, regardless of where they are found: all are framed as elaborations of a generic concept rather than deviations from a specific foreign template.

Ideally, the result is akin to a generic language of CCL—one that is abstract enough to be applicable everywhere, yet also comprehensive enough to be adapted and applied to local conditions everywhere. Generality, in this sense, serves the goal of inclusiveness: just as there is no reason to prefer gender-specific pronouns over gender-neutral pronouns when referring to non-gender-specific phenomena, there is no reason to demand country-specific terminology over generic terminology when referring to non-country-specific phenomena. But generality of this sort also serves to level the playing field and equalize barriers to participation. In

[40] *Cf.* Law, *supra* note 18, at 17–18 (articulating a "representation model" of CCL pedagogy that aims to sample "the main dimensions of constitutional variation and the diversity of constitutional experience around the world").

[41] *See* Tushnet, *supra* note 34.

[42] *See* Law & Hsieh, *supra* note 32, at 192–93 (using these terms to identify judicial review of constitutional amendments, and to distinguish it from judicial review of legislation).

[43] Kesavananda Bharati v. State of Kerala, 4 SCC 225 (1973); *see* Law & Hsieh, *supra* note 32, at 195–96.

[44] *See, e.g.*, Law & Hsieh, *supra* note 32, at 193 (treating Hong Kong as an example of "soft review"); *id.* at 204–11 (using Taiwan as an example of amendment-review).

the context of CCL, canon of a conventional variety confers upon those who are already privileged the further advantage of speaking from and about their own experience, while forcing others to learn their language. When canon is instead deliberately pitched at a high level of generality, however, everyone learns to speak the constitutional equivalent of Esperanto—a synthetic mix that mimics no specific language yet offers something familiar to everyone. No one starts from scratch, but no one starts at the finish line either.

This unorthodox rendition of the concept of canon is no doubt open to its own share of objections—practical, conceptual, perhaps even normative. And there may well be other, better ways of reconciling the project of canon-making with the study of constitutionalism in all its real-world diversity. What cannot be right for this field, however, is a rehash of what has already proven wrong for other fields.

6

Foxes, Hedgehogs, and Ants

Kim Lane Scheppele

Most everyone in this volume has their revealing Tushnet Tale that captures something about the way Mark Tushnet works. I recall running into Mark quite by surprise in the Philadelphia airport as he was changing planes. (Pardon my referring to him on a first name basis, but we have been friends for too long for it to be easy to address him by only his last name!) Where are you going, I asked? The Faroe Islands, he replied. The Faroese were drafting a new constitution and they had called upon him to help.[1]

Mark must have seen my puzzled look, because he first had to explain to me where the Faroe Islands were (north of Scotland between Iceland and Norway) and then what their constitutional problems looked like (shoring up their status as an autonomous territory within the Kingdom of Denmark). And then, in typical Mark style, he said that he didn't think he had much to add to their discussion but he was curious to learn something about the place. So he was going—for a few days.

Mark has learned a lot about a lot of places, often on consulting trips like this, often by attending every conference on offer with a preference for those in remote locations, and always by reading. Mark travels and reads a prodigious amount. Plus, he writes more about a wider variety of places, topics, and historical periods than almost anyone else. This has made him a distinctive kind of comparative constitutionalist. In the conceptual ordering of the world explained by Isaiah Berlin,[2] Mark is a constitutional fox who knows many things and tends to think of his own analyses as contingent and tentative without an overarching theory to unite them all. By contrast, some in the field (famously Ronald Dworkin) are hedgehogs,[3] who tend to know one big thing anchored by a strong normative political theory.

In this short chapter, I will introduce another form of animal constitutionalism—ant constitutionalism—that sees the world of comparative constitutional law not as

[1] More than 20 years later the Faroese have still not adopted a new constitution, though the Constitutional Committee placed a draft before Parliament in 2017. It still awaits passage because passage requires more consensus than has been generated for this draft so far. *See* The Government of the Faroe Islands, *The Constitutional Status of the Faroe Islands*, https://www.government.fo/en/foreign-relations/constitutional-status. *See also Faroese Constitutional Referendum Unlikely to Be Held in the Short Term*, NATIONALIA (Dec. 13, 2018), https://www.nationalia.info/brief/11155/faroese-constitutional-referendum-unlikely-to-be-held-in-the-short-term.

[2] ISAIAH BERLIN, THE HEDGEHOG AND THE FOX: AN ESSAY ON TOLSTOY'S VIEW OF HISTORY (1953).

[3] RONALD DWORKIN, JUSTICE FOR HEDGEHOGS (2011).

Kim Lane Scheppele, *Foxes, Hedgehogs, and Ants* In: *Redefining Comparative Constitutional Law*. Edited by: Vicki C. Jackson and Madhav Khosla, Oxford University Press. © Kim Lane Scheppele 2025. DOI: 10.1093/9780191996344.003.0006

powered by contingent insights (fox constitutionalism) or as resting on a coherent normative theory (hedgehog constitutionalism), but instead as developed out of mutual constitution between texts, practices, histories, people, objects, and animating ideas understood against particular historical and cultural backgrounds. "Ant" not only identifies the animal species with the most complex divisions of labor and resulting mutual dependencies but has also become the acronym for the Actor–Network Theory of Bruno Latour,[4] who emphasizes relations among elements rather than the elements themselves in understanding how societies work. Ant constitutionalists see constitutions not as disaggregatable sets of rules but as interdependent systems of networked links.

But let's start with Isaiah Berlin:

> For there exists a great chasm between those, on one side, who relate everything to a single central vision, one system, less or more coherent or articulate, in terms of which they understand, think and feel—a single, universal, organising principle in terms of which alone all that they are and say has significance—and, on the other side, those who pursue many ends, often unrelated and even contradictory, connected, if at all, only in some de facto way, for some psychological or physiological cause, related to no moral or aesthetic principle. These last lead lives, perform acts and entertain ideas that are centrifugal rather than centripetal; their thought is scattered or diffused, moving on many levels, seizing upon the essence of a vast variety of experiences and objects for what they are in themselves, without, consciously or unconsciously, seeking to fit them into, or exclude them from, any one unchanging, all-embracing, sometimes self-contradictory and incomplete, at times fanatical, unitary inner vision. The first kind of intellectual and artistic personality belongs to the hedgehogs, the second to the foxes . . .[5]

According to Berlin, the foxes are delightfully unsystematic while the hedgehogs prioritize the universal over the particular and the systematic over the scattered insight. If one had to classify Mark as one or the other, Mark would be a constitutional fox by self-definition. He collects a vast array of things, and mixes and matches far-flung examples into typologies (strong and weak judicial review)[6] and nontypologies (populism and constitutionalism do not go together in predictable ways).[7] But he always presents his insights as contingent and deliberately unsystematic. No wonder he calls this method *bricolage,* borrowing from Claude

[4] For an introduction, *see* BRUNO LATOUR, REASSEMBLING THE SOCIAL (2005).

[5] Berlin, *supra* note 2, at 2.

[6] MARK TUSHNET, WEAK COURTS, STRONG RIGHTS: JUDICIAL REVIEW AND SOCIAL WELFARE RIGHTS IN COMPARATIVE CONSTITUTIONAL LAW (2009).

[7] MARK TUSHNET & BOJAN BUGARIČ, POWER TO THE PEOPLE: CONSTITUTIONALISM IN THE AGE OF POPULISM (2022).

Levi-Strauss the description of composing something new from whatever is to hand.[8]

As other chapters in our Tushnet-Fest have emphasized, Mark has always been skeptical of the grand normative theories that drive constitutional analysis, which makes him critical of the hedgehogs of our field. Because Mark has engaged in travel across time (delving deeply into US history) as well as across space (visiting more countries and cities and remote outposts than most people on earth), he knows that there is no one-size-fits-all approach that makes sense of all of the constitutions of the world, let alone any one constitution over a substantial period of time. He is enough of a sociolegal/empirical thinker to know that the contours of any actually existing constitutional system are bound to be contingent on many things. Moreover, he knows that arrangements that work tolerably well in one place clearly do not work at all in others and, however much comparative constitutional law may enlighten all those who study it, comparative constitutionalists would be ill-advised to plunk down a closely reasoned German constitutional judgment in the middle of American or even Canadian case law and presume that it can be made to fit. Constitutions are too various and changeable to be swept up in a single theory and the constitutional history of even one constitution standing alone provides reason to doubt that there is a single normative vision that can capture either what did happen or what should have. Comparing constitutions can be done for so many different reasons that the field itself cannot have a single coherent starting point from which to set out on quests for answers to all problems. Mark has demonstrated this over and over again in his immense body of work.

In Mark's latest book, written with Bojan Bugarič, *Power to the People*, the authors stay away from grand theories and stick to a "thin" conception of constitutionalism—which requires only that majority preferences dictate most policy decisions while reserving rights and structures for greater entrenchment, that judges are independent of politicians, and that politicians are dependent on parties for seeking popular support.[9] There is no greater democratic theory to explain the relationship of parties to democratic will-formation; no normative account of why certain issues should be entrenched while others need not be—or for that matter how to separate policy from structures or rights; no grander argument about why politicians should be organized in parties (rather than, say, social movements) or why judges should be held strongly accountable under laws passed by politicians but not at all accountable directly to politicians. Mark's and Bojan's positions are entirely sensible, of course, and they put this thin theory of constitutionalism to good use as they explore the relationship between this conception of constitutionalism and various versions of populism throughout the book. And for

[8] Mark Tushnet, *The Possibilities of Comparative Constitutional Law*, 108 YALE L.J. 1225, 1229 (1999).

[9] Tushnet & Bugarič, *supra* note 7, ch. 1.

them—and for Mark's fans in general—the point of theory in comparative constitutional law is to organize the comparisons, not to build castles in the air.

The hedgehogs among us will surely complain precisely because the judgments about minimal constitutionalism seem ad hoc even if intuitively plausible. Hedgehoggishness tends to demand that even the obvious be justified at great length even if no one seemed to question it before the hedgehogs went to work. Hedgehogs will also demand a coherent overall account of any concept to ensure its consistent use. In Mark's work generally, as in his new book with Bojan, giant jurisprudential questions are left off to the side to get a working definition that is useful for a specific argument. If I were a hedgehog, I would demand more (and some hedgehogs no doubt will), but the point of this analysis—as of so much of Mark's writing—is to get on with making a point about how constitutions are comparatively organized and how they work (well or badly) in practice. Hedgehoggishness bogs that sort of comparative analysis down, to no particular good effect, says the fox. Foxiness underplays the crucial importance of sound justification and theoretical coherence, says the hedgehog. Such is the state of the field.

If one looks closely enough, however, there is often a bit of foxiness in hedgehogs and a bit of hedgehoggishness in foxes. For all of Mark's foxiness, he harbors a hedgehog hiding behind the scenes. After all, Mark's "Crit" origins[10] do in fact provide him with deeply held normative commitments. Mark is a revolutionary of the Left at heart, living in a world in which most functional constitutions are relentlessly (neo)liberal at best, opposed to all progressive change at worst, and certainly not in general capable of realizing a revolutionary program of equality and justice. The drive for a better world, combined with a disdain for constitutional roadblocks that stand in the way, has animated much of Mark's work. He does work with a general theory, in which constitutions are perhaps more often roadblocks than they are key facilitators.

Realizing equality and justice as a political project is far more important to Mark than parsing the words of constitutions to find deep values, especially when constitutions themselves are likely to be a product of normalizing forces that do not share the values of the Left. After all, as Mark said in his *Yale Law Journal* article on the history of Critical Legal Studies (CLS):

> These themes (of CLS scholarship) converged in the programmatic statement that law is politics, all the way down . . . We saw law as a form of human activity in which political conflicts were worked out in ways that contributed to the stability of the social order ("legitimation") in part by constituting personality and social institutions in ways that came to seem natural.[11]

[10] Mark Tushnet, *Critical Legal Studies: A Political History*, 100 YALE L.J. 1515 (1991).
[11] *Id.* at 1536.

Given this view, it must have seemed natural to Mark that taking the values baked into a constitutional order as worthy of an independent normative defense was a mistake. Given the way that law is constituted, it would be surprising to find worthy values embedded in constitutions instead of in political debates that did not take the existing legal order for granted. Over and over again, Mark attacks hedgehog constitutionalists for leaving too little space for the people to take matters into their own hands, especially when that involves upending a constitutional order to make the world better.

But rather than refuting hedgehogism, these debates reveal that Mark has a hedgehoggish streak of his own. For Mark, constitutions (like concepts) are useful only insofar as they make possible certain results. Constitutions cannot satisfy the drive for justice as long as they merely naturalize the status quo. Besides, many constitutions do not strive for justice and equality as first-order goals in any event, given that they are generally obsessed with proceduralism rather than concrete outcomes. In this respect, Mark as hedgehog sides with Marx's Thesis Eleven: "The philosophers have only interpreted the world, in various ways; the point is to change it."[12] One can guess from Mark's work that he believes that the standards of what would be a worthwhile revolutionary change will not come from constitutions themselves but from political action that stands outside the constitutional framework and sometimes in opposition to it. The dream of realizing a comprehensively Left program is Mark's hiding hedgehog.

As a result, Mark's normative advice scattered across his many writings on constitutions might read something like this: If I wanted to change the world, I certainly would not start with constitutionalism. But if you insist on starting with constitutionalism, then at least don't allow the design of constitutions to destroy the possibility of progressive social change.

Power to the People adds to this law-is-politics-all-the-way-down theme in Mark's work. We have seen this theme before in Mark's work when he has argued for sidelining rigid constitutional constraints, courts, and strong-form judicial review, precisely in order to leave more space for politics. For someone with a history of advocating "taking the constitution away from the courts"[13] in order to allow political debate to settle constitutional questions, however, populism poses a serious challenge—especially when it emerges in the personae of Donald Trump, Viktor Orbán, Recep Tayyib Erdoğan, and more. Are those representatives of "the people" the ones who should decide fateful matters, especially when they destroy constitutional guardrails along the way? In this newest book, then, Mark and Bojan take up the challenge of electoral populism, evidenced when the people rise

[12] KARL MARX, *Theses on Feuerbach, in* 1 MARX/ENGELS SELECTED WORKS 15, XI (W. Lough trans., Progress Publishers 1969) (1888), https://www.marxists.org/archive/marx/works/1845/theses/theses.htm (last accessed Nov. 27, 2023).

[13] MARK TUSHNET, TAKING THE CONSTITUTION AWAY FROM THE COURTS (2000).

up in revolt against an existing order and sometimes show themselves eager to run off the rails of the constitutions that they have inherited by electing leaders whose respect for existing constitutional norms is not their calling. But is populism the greatest danger of our time, or can it have a silver lining? Can populism underwrite the progressive politics that Mark has always longed for, or is it always regressive? *Power to the People* explores these questions.

The overall argument of *Power to the People* is that not all forms of populism undermine constitutionalism. Some forms do but other forms do not. Constitutions are in danger and populists will sometimes overthrow them when they block what majorities (or particular "populist" leaders) want. They can become a target of attack if their speedbumps and roadblocks thwart popular will—or at least popular will as defined by populists. But some populist leaders will see the point of honoring a constitution that allows for policy to flow from democratic deliberation, itself constituted and structured by the institutions created by the constitution itself. If a constitution encourages popular preferences to flow into policy without too many roadblocks, then a constitution will not usually interfere with "power to the people" and populists will not attack it.

In keeping with Mark's earlier work, Mark and Bojan do not want to defend proceduralism against populism. As they argue, sometimes populism *should* overturn the existing constitutional order in order to strive for a better world. This explains the different treatment in the book of Right populisms (bad on policy and often toxic to constitutional forms) from Left populisms (which they argue are empirically less often destructive of constitutional forms but which might be more justified in rejecting constitutional constraint should they choose to do so).[14] Thus, Right populism emerges as generally bad, Left populism as potentially good. Mark and Bojan want to make the constitutional world safe for the demands of Left populism, even when those demands would be destructive of existing constitutional institutions. At the same time, they want to shore up constitutional defenses against Right populism when it tries to undermine constitutionalism in the name of real or fictive majorities.

This two-tailed argument—more permissive of constitutional deconstruction on the Left side of the political spectrum than on the Right side—has all of the characteristics of foxiness. The argument depends precisely on a deeply *political* conception of normative desirability rather than building a general normative *legal* view with which all could agree because it is independent of political leanings (the typical stance of hedgehogs). It starts with the conclusions (Left is good) and reasons backward to figure out what institutional arrangements make the good possible, justifying along the way the dismantling of institutional arrangements

[14] Tushnet & Bugarič, *supra* note 7.

(in the name of "good governance") that interfere with reaching legitimate political goals.

In particular, Mark and Bojan challenge one common view of constitutionalism—that it provides a set of necessary speed bumps or veto points to constrain power. Why are checks on power a good thing, they argue, if these constraints block the advancement of the public good? Why should power be limited if it can be deployed to change the world for the better? Taking the example of independent institutions (courts, for example) that are controlled by incumbents appointed by previous governments who no longer have the support of the people, Mark and Bojan question the legitimacy of a veto power exercised by a discredited political force. They therefore explore various opportunities for court-packing and other workarounds for use when checking institutions do not match the politics of the day. As Mark and Bojan put it:

> Facing a veto gate controlled by people who no longer have the people's confidence, an incoming party with such an agenda, whether the party is populist or otherwise, will think seriously about ways of evading the veto gate or, if the thing being blocked is truly important (as the party sees it) dismantling the veto gate either entirely or with respect to the program of concern. Institutional reform might be necessary to carry out the party's agenda, and sometimes the reforms will be justified by that fact alone—that is, where the agenda is quite a good one and is being thwarted by an institution controlled by those the people have repudiated, changing the institution might be justified even if we acknowledge that there's a cost associated with dismantling *any* veto gate.[15]

For them, evading veto points or engaging in institutional reform to eliminate barriers to good policy is not dangerous constitutional destruction; it can be considered legitimate political action if it is based on the results of an election, if it occurs within the procedural boundaries of constitutionalism (unless it doesn't), and if it represents "fine-tuning" an institution rather than smashing it. Ultimately, however, they argue that a progressive political program that the people have voted for should be enacted even if it means removing constitutional speed bumps. This is the hedgehog poking his nose out from behind the fox—that progressive ends justify the unconstitutional means (within limits)—because instrumentalism is also a well-known general theory.

So maybe foxes are not always foxes. The same may be true of hedgehogs.[16] But I want to convince Mark that there is a third constitutional approach that merits consideration and that he might want to consider adopting.

[15] *Id.* at 150.

[16] I am reminded that the Hedgehog in Chief, Ronald Dworkin, had his foxy moments—which are evident in his most hedgehoggy work of all, *Law's Empire*. In the index, under the entry "Distinctions, binary," one can find a reasonably complete catalogue of all of the places where his argument ran into

The third way in the pantheon of animal constitutionalisms is ant constitutionalism. Ants are distinguished by their complex division of labor. A colony depends on the contributions of all—but can pick up and move, restore itself after disruptions, and otherwise act as an organic entity, shape-shifting over time. (By the way, lest you think that ants are boring or all the same, recent research shows ants of a similar type within the colony develop leadership structures so that mass emigrations to new colonies seem to be organized by a few dissident leaders who corner the market on information.[17]) What matters for the metaphor, however, is that—to an ant constitutionalist—constitutional systems are organized like ant colonies, with complex interdependencies among the various elements which include not only the living things (the ants) but also their living spaces, ecosystems, systems of communication, ordinary practices, and more. Similarly, constitutionalism comprises legal texts, legal actors, norms, objects, and publics with varying connections to "the law." Thus, what matters is not one particular rule or one particular practice or even a particular set of actors, taken alone, but the way in which the complex systems of which they are a part fit together and develop interdependencies. The ant constitutionalist asks what it means to think of a constitutional order as a network containing all of these things, each of which both contributes to the whole and defines what it is.

This is not functionalism, explaining how everything contributes to harmony and in which everything is defined by its purpose. Disruptions in crucial interdependencies can cause constitutional systems to crash or to morph in non-responsive ways. Disruptions can, following Mark and Bojan, also improve constitutional governance and allow voters' preferences to be less often thwarted. Like ant colonies, constitutional governments are complex systems comprising a myriad of elements all holding each other up and together constituting a common reality—until they do not. To an ant constitutionalist, however, picking any one actor or rule or practice in isolation does not tell you much about what is going on. You have to see what the thing you are staring at is connected to, how changes in one part of the network ramify through the system, how other actors and entities respond to the changes, how the systems adapt (or don't). One ant does not a colony make, just as one text or one rule does not a constitutional system make.

Ant constitutionalism can refer metaphorically to the practices of ants, but it can also be a reference to Bruno Latour's Actor–Network Theory, also known as ANT. Latour (whose book on the French *Conseil d'État*[18] marked his entry into

inconvenient complexities. Whenever reality counseled contingency, Dworkin tended to distinguish away the problematic cases, in the spirit of a common law lawyer.

[17] Gabriele Valentini et al., *Division of Labour Promotes the Spread of Information in Colony Emigrations by the Ant Temnothorax Rugatulus*, 287 Proc. Royal Soc'y B 287 (2020).

[18] Bruno Latour, The Making of Law: An Ethnography of the Conseil d'État (Marina Brilman et al. trans., 2009) (2002).

the sociology of law) famously obliterated the first principle of sociology (or anthropology)—which is that the field is centrally about people. Nonsense, argued Latour first in his studies of scientific laboratories. People alone don't produce science. It is the interaction between the people and the objects they study, including also instruments used for measuring particular aspects of the world together with the way that "nature" interacts with these instruments and the way that scientific knowledge is summarized in a mathematical symbolic system and communicated across natural languages, tested against other bits of nature elsewhere with different people using different instruments . . . all of this taken together creates the practices of science. To say that science is what scientists produce may have an analogy in the idea that constitutions are what lawyers and judges produce, but all those of us living in reasonably functioning (even if not always perfectly functioning) constitutional systems know that is incomplete. A legal system is made up not only of the people who act within it (including democratic publics) but also it is composed of texts, histories, practices, objects, and places. Complex systems of thought produced through human effort and interactions with a messy world are not just about the thoughts or intentions of individual people. And to understand how they work, one must get a sense of the whole network together.

At the *Conseil d'État,* Latour became fascinated with "the file" as a carrier of law, with legal vocabulary (see his long meditation on the word *moyen*), with the way that some offices in the building were part of the judiciary and others were part of the executive (and what that meant for their work and whom they could work with), with how the architecture carried traces of the history of the institution and how a precedent-based court in a code system worked with other institutions with different operating logics. Not all of Latour's key nodes in the network constituting law in France were people. Instead Latour saw France's top administrative court as a network of people, objects, spaces, words, and pronouncements, located in a history and a broader political system.

Latour does not linger on people or their intentions. Nor do those who study ants. By contrast, Mark and Bojan in *Power to the People* believe that the only way to distinguish good constitutional change from bad constitutional change is through analyzing the intentions of those doing the changing. Are those smashing constitutional norms motivated by progressive aims or by self-dealing? Are they trying to do what they promised voters they would do or are they trying to stay in power forever? Despite the fact that Mark and Bojan nod to the proposition that "the analysis of specific populisms and their policies in relation to constitutionalism must be highly sensitive to context,"[19] context drops out of the analysis of most of their cases. And therein lies the problem with the way that Mark and Bojan have conceptualized the constitutional world to someone who is an ant constitutionalist.

[19] Tushnet & Bugarič, *supra* note 7, at 147.

Context matters to ant constitutionalists. To illustrate, let me take up a topic where my approach strongly differs from the one that Bojan and Mark use when they discuss my idea of the "Frankenstate" in Chapter 5 of *Power to the People.* In my original essay,[20] the Frankenstein metaphor was meant to call attention to the fact that Frankenstein's monster was composed of body parts from normal people, dug up and stitched together to create a novel and threatening form (though, as Mark and Bojan note, sometimes the monster could generate sympathy with his plight). Similarly, a Frankenstate emerges when constitutional rules, roles, institutions, and ideas that work perfectly well in one political system are mixed and matched with those from different political systems so that the rules or practices in the new context turn out to do mischief because what made the rules, institutions, and ideas operate without producing mass pathology in their country of origin was not also transposed with them. As Mary Shelley's story reminds us, body parts are not interchangeable across people without a great deal of medical work in transplant surgery, just as constitutional parts are not interchangeable across political systems without similar careful work to make sure that they do not have disturbing side effects. While the two examples I gave in that very brief essay showed how one constitutional clause could interact badly with another (because they were easily to explain), the general idea of the Frankenstate also covers the situation in which a new rule transplanted from a healthy democracy can sicken a weak democracy because it cannot be sustained by other elements of the constitutional system, understood as a Latourian network.

To take examples from (what else?) Orbán's Hungary: Orbán modified the jurisdiction of the Constitutional Court in 2012 to limit abstract review by getting rid of the *actio popularis* jurisdiction that had been a signature element of Hungarian constitutional law after 1989. In its place, the new rules of abstract review permitted only certain actors to bring cases to the Court, all actors who were appointed by the government (and therefore unlikely to rock the boat) except for the case in which one quarter of the parliament could to bring a new law to the Court. That is exactly the same rule as in Germany. But in Hungary, the opposition in the parliament controlled only one-third of the seats, divided equally between a far-right party and varying parties on the left who would never work together to bring a case to the Constitutional Court. The rule on the size of the parliamentary group that could bring abstract review cases to the Constitutional Court might have looked reasonable in Germany where the distribution of party seats in the parliament ensures that there is almost always a group of MPs able to bring a meritorious case to the Court precisely because the election law guarantees that parties in parliament are represented proportionally to the votes they receive. But the party system in Hungary was different; the Fidesz party presently has 67 percent of

[20] Kim Lane Scheppele, *The Rule of Law and the Frankenstate: Why Governance Checklists Do Not Work*, 26 GOVERNANCE 559 (2013).

the parliamentary seats having won less than half the vote ever since 2014. Indeed, there were no cases of abstract review brought before the Constitutional Court in the first eight years under the rule change. The transplanted rule shut down the flow of abstract review cases to the Court while looking completely reasonable because a "good democracy" had the same rule. Given the difference in electoral systems between Hungary and Germany, there was no way for the parliamentary opposition in Hungary to ever challenge the laws that had been pushed through the parliament with only the votes of the governing party.

But, as the example illustrates, the rule about how to bring a case to the Constitutional Court for abstract review does not operate alone: The parliament holds virtually no debates and offers virtually no opportunities for the opposition to propose amendments or other input into legislation. The rule change on access to the Constitutional Court meant that the opposition parties also lost their ability to challenge a law once it passed after they had already been stripped of the ability to have any meaningful input into these laws in the first place. Of course, since 2013, the Constitutional Court has been packed with Orbán supporters, so the opposition would not get a friendly reception if it took a case to that court in any event. But while the more restrictive rule of access to the Constitutional Court may make sense by itself because it just is the German rule that operates perfectly well there, this rule must be understood as part of a package in which all ways for the opposition to challenge the government have been blocked.

Mark and Bojan would say: What is so bad about this? What if the laws that Fidesz rushes through the parliament were terrific? Why slow down the process of putting the people's will into action by tying things up at the Constitutional Court? But—I would answer—how would you know what the people's will was if there were little political competition and certainly not a level playing field on which parties were competing? The broadcast and major print media said hardly anything at all about the opposition's arguments because most of the media are controlled by the governing party. The rules of parliamentary procedure were altered so that MPs were fined personally when they challenged rulings of the speaker, who always ruled opposition interventions out of order. And, from 2014 on, the election rules were changed to make it virtually impossible for the opposition to win elections.[21] You do not have to rely on Orbán's intentions or on the assessment of what kind of populist he says he is to find that the near-total shutdown of political competition means that the political system is no longer a democracy because the people—whose power Mark and Bojan want to preserve—cannot change their leaders if they want to. So we should not just consider the one rule about how to bring challenges to the Constitutional Court, but the web of rules and practices

[21] The Frankenstate quality of the election law reform was truly ingenious, but it operated so that only one particular party could win. For my analysis of the election rules, *see* Kim Lane Scheppele, *How Viktor Orbán Wins*, 33 J. DEMOCRACY 45 (2023).

that has made it impossible for the opposition parties to get their message out, to participate in debates over what the laws should be, and to have any chance of winning future elections. Even on Bojan's and Mark's thin version of constitutionalism, this set of practices disqualifies Hungary from being a democratic constitutional order—regardless of what kind of populist Orbán is.

To take another example from Mark's and Bojan's discussion of the Frankenstate, they resurrect and discuss a report that the Hungarian government commissioned to support its view that the Fourth Amendment to the Hungarian Constitution in 2013 (one year after their new constitution went into force) met European standards. (Conflict of interest warning: That report was commissioned by the Hungarian government to counter a report that a group of Hungarian constitutional lawyers—including me—had submitted to the Venice Commission explaining the context of the Fourth Amendment so the Venice Commission would understand how the amendment fit into the Hungarian legal system more generally.) The experts that the Hungarian government located were conservatives likely to be sympathetic to Orbán, as Mark and Bojan point out, but ideological fellow-traveling was not their problem, in my view. The Hungarian government's foreign experts only had before them the French translation of the Fourth Amendment and the constitution itself, without knowing anything else about the Hungarian legal system and without being able to speak the language to find out more. (Given the content of the expert analysis, there were also reasons to believe that they were working with a problematic translation that did not adequately convey the Hungarian original.) The experts assessed each provision of the Fourth Amendment as if each one were not connected to any of the others.

Among other things, as Bojan and Mark point out, the foreign experts said that it was perfectly reasonable for the Fourth Amendment to nullify the entire jurisprudence of the Hungarian Constitutional Court interpreting the old constitution because the new constitution required the Court to start over. What the experts did not know was that the not-yet-packed Constitutional Court had said that it would only refer to the previous case law of the Court when the old and new constitutions were identically worded, which was the case for most of the rights provisions. If the case law disappeared as a source of law specifying how constitutional rights were to be understood in Hungary, the practical application of rights would be up for grabs without the case law to concretize what abstract pronouncements meant. In fact, since the Fourth Amendment, the government has violated many of the prior decisions of the Court—for example, linking databases across agencies to generate complete Orwellian portraits of all Hungarians in violation of the personal identifier number opinion of the Court and even floating the idea of bringing back the death penalty which the Court had abolished. Because those specifications of rights were solidly grounded in the case law, the government had never bothered to pass statutes shoring up those court decisions, so the abolition of the deep body of case law meant that the Hungarian government was free to violate rights that Hungarians had come to expect would be honored. Again, I take Mark's and Bojan's point that perhaps Hungarian voters wanted to be liberated from rights to which they had become accustomed, but since the wholesale change in the meaning of rights had never been a subject of public discussion, voters would have had no idea that this would happen when they voted for Fidesz.

What does an ant's-eye view contribute to all of this? Against Mark's and Bojan's suggestions, ant constitutionalism absolutely ignores the intentions of the actors, takes no account of the Leftward or Rightward direction of the changes and understands the effects of constitutional reform only in the specific context where the changes occur, not against some hypothetical different world in which the changes might be justified in general. Of course, if voters elect a conservative government, they have every right to get a government that governs conservatively. I might even go so far as to say that if voters voted to shut down democratic government in their country, then their preferences should be honored as long as there were sufficient guarantees that the voters knew what they were doing and the election were free and fair. My objection to Orbán is not that he is conservative. My objection is instead that he has been building a web of laws and practices that make it impossible for the people to change their government. He has put in place a system that looks perfectly reasonable if you take one element at a time, rip it out of context, and imagine some situation in which it would not be a problem to do that one thing. Deconstructing his changes one by one is precisely what he wants outside observers to do because his defense always is to decontextualize—to show how the new system of privatized universities is just like that put in place in Finland;[22] how the use of emergency powers to control the pandemic is just like what many European countries have done;[23] and how the election law mirrors Germany's.[24] Decontextualization is the method Orbán uses to defend himself and it is alarming to see Mark and Bojan falling into the trap of doing precisely what Orbán urges. They do not intend to vindicate Orbán, of course, but they play his game precisely the way he wants them to. Orbán would love for this debate to be over conflicting political visions—in which his nationalism is pitted against the cosmopolitanism of his critics. Framing the debate in that way distracts from the interdependent and complex system Orbán has been constructing in order to stay in power for as long as he wants. And I would hope that, in a book called *Power to the People*, Bojan and Mark would agree that this is an illegitimate goal of democratic politics—whether from the Left or from the Right.

[22] Benjamin Novak, *Hungary Transfers 11 Universities to Foundations Led by Orbán Allies*, N.Y. Times (Apr. 29, 2021), https://www.nytimes.com/2021/04/27/world/europe/hungary-universities-orban.html.

[23] Gábor Halmai, Gábor Mészáros & Kim Lane Scheppele, *So It Goes—Part I*, Verfassungsblog (Nov. 19, 2020), https://verfassungsblog.de/so-it-goes-part-i/.

[24] Scheppele, *supra* note 21.

Ant constitutionalism is un-fox-like because it tends to delve deeply into specific legal systems to see how the pieces of the legal network constitute the whole. Ants do not move fox-like among different legal systems looking for similarities and differences at the level of the individual rule. Ant constitutionalism is un-hedgehog-like because the orienting principles come from inside the systems that are being analyzed rather than from outside sources as standards against which to compare the local practices. The internal normative order of a legal system is one of the elements in the network to be studied. As I wrote in my essay on "Constitutional Ethnography"[25] years ago, the point of what I am now calling ant constitutionalism is to see legal systems as wholes and to use comparative constitutional law not to compare one free speech clause with another or to examine executive decree power across many systems, but to understand the ways in which the various pieces of particular systems relate to each other in a specific cultural and historical space and then compare those intact and complexly woven systems with analyses of how other whole systems are organized. Fox constitutionalism and ant constitutionalism counsel different empirical practices. The fox constitutionalist may go to the Faroe Islands for a few days to check out the constitutional conversation there and use it to compare constitutional drafting processes, to add to the catalog of problems of regional autonomy and more—but the ant constitutionalist will learn languages, move to a country for years and immerse herself in the local culture and history with the goal of understanding not just what people talk about at moments of transition, but what is taken for granted, what triggers historical memories and how elements inside the legal system relate to elements outside. The fox will, in Isaiah Berlin's words, "pursue many ends, often unrelated and even contradictory, connected, if at all, only in some de facto way," while the ant will show that legal cultures are complex social systems with mutually interdependent parts that can only be understood as wholes.

[25] Kim Lane Scheppele, *Constitutional Ethnography*, 38 LAW & SOC'Y REV. 389 (2004).

7

Constitutional Comparisons and Language

Maartje De Visser

Introduction

In a 2017 essay, Mark Tushnet candidly shared that in his view, "the measure of a study's value is not its methodological rigor, but whether it is, as I put it, 'interesting' or productive of further thinking."[1] By way of explanation he pointed to his academic upbringing in the United States, with its "pragmatic scholarly tradition."[2] A "just do it" approach resonates with many of the scholars, judges, legislators, and drafters who engage with constitutional approaches and ideas from elsewhere in their own work—and for good reason. From an academic perspective, becoming preoccupied with the finer details of methodological quandaries could distract those already belonging to the "in-crowd" from producing substantive comparative knowledge that fosters our collective thinking on matters pertaining to the design and daily (mal)functioning of constitutional orders. We should further be wary of the danger of developing an overly sophisticated methodological matrix that may be perceived as impenetrable by newcomers, who might consequently be deterred from joining the comparative constitutional law community. However, even if not explicitly addressed, each substantive comparative study entails multiple methodological determinations, including deciding what to compare, the number and choice of jurisdictions to be examined, the selection and mode of collecting the (extra-)legal data to be analyzed, or the way materials will be presented and evaluated. A balance, thus, needs to be struck between recognizing that questions of method inevitably rear their head and engaging with such questions in such a manner and to the extent that it improves the value of the comparative study.

In this chapter, I aim to discuss one pervasive challenge that is usually mentioned only in passing, if at all: the interplay between comparative law and language. This may seem an eminently practical issue, but it also relates to context, local knowledge, conceptual nuances, and systemic idiosyncrasies—and as such, it is intended to be evocative of the principal leitmotivs that have informed Mark's approach to comparative constitutionalism.[3] At its most fundamental, "language

[1] Mark Tushnet, *The Boundaries of Comparative Law*, 13 Eur. Const. L. Rev. 13, 14 (2017).
[2] *Id.*
[3] His concern with taking context seriously is evident in, among others, Mark Tushnet, *Some Skepticism about Normative Constitutional Advice*, 49 Wm. & Mary L. Rev. 1473 (2008); Mark Tushnet, *Interpreting Constitutions Comparatively: Some Cautionary Notes, with Reference to Affirmative Action*, 36 Conn. L. Rev. 649 (2004).

Maartje De Visser, *Constitutional Comparisons and Language* In: *Redefining Comparative Constitutional Law*.
Edited by: Vicki C. Jackson and Madhav Khosla, Oxford University Press. © Maartje De Visser 2025.
DOI: 10.1093/9780191996344.003.0007

is law's way of existing in the world":[4] capturing thoughts and ideas in the mind in words, thinking about the best way to convey these to the imagined addressees, with the latter engaging in decoding and sometimes reconstructing legal meaning all involve linguistic processing. Language is an important consideration for all legal scholars, and even more so for comparatists who must engage with materials from elsewhere. Yet, although we know that law is intricately connected to language, their interrelationship, and the implications thereof for comparative constitutional scholarship, are underexplored.

In this chapter, I aim to discuss four ways in which language matters when engaging in constitutional comparisons: the problem of literal translation; the problem of legal-conceptual translation; a multilingual discourse that is marked by fragmentation; and expectations in communication with a foreign or international readership.[5] The approach taken is constructive, with efforts to identify possible coping techniques to alleviate the challenges identified.

The Problem of Literal Translation

I begin with the most obvious problem of literal translation, which arises when the materials regarding one or more of the legal systems selected for study are in a foreign language. Whether to translate foreign law has been a source of disagreement among general comparatists.[6] The majority argues that translation is a necessity to allow the benefits commonly associated with comparing to materialize.[7] Attention accordingly shifts to practical issues, which are also of interest for the field of comparative constitutional law. Should this be done at an individual level, with the comparatist attempting her own translation or should this be seen as a community-wide endeavor? While (highest) courts in particular have begun to publish some of their decisions in foreign languages, the linguistic accuracy of those versions may vary, as such translations are not always prepared by trained legal linguists. So, is the comparatist permitted, or even expected, to provide a different translation of the judgment if she believes that her translation offers a "better" rendition of the foreign legal text? I am inclined to think so: after all, the foreign versions of a judgment are typically explicitly stated not to be authoritative. The reader should, however, be alerted to this difference in translation as well as the writer's reasons

[4] Jeanne Gaakeer, *Iudex Translator: The Reign of Finitude*, *in* METHODS OF COMPARATIVE LAW 253 (Pier Giuseppe Monateri ed., 2012); also R. Arntz, *The Roman Heritage in German Legal Language*, *in* THE DEVELOPMENT OF LEGAL LANGUAGE 33 (H. Mattila ed., 2002) ("Law comes to life through language").

[5] My analysis is relevant not only to legal texts, but also legal practices that might not be reflected in discrete documents that could be translated.

[6] A succinct overview of the different positions is presented in MATHIAS SIEMS, COMPARATIVE LAW 17–18 (2014).

[7] *See e.g.* ENGAGING WITH FOREIGN LAW (Basil Markesinis & Jörg Fedtke eds., 2009).

for preferring another choice of word, to enable her to understand the writer's cognitive assumptions and epistemological frame.

In contrast, other comparatists have expressed reservations on the question of translation. Their apprehension is that important nuances are literally being lost in translation. For example, scholarly work by Armin von Bogdandy and Laurent Pech comparing national versions of what in English is known as the rule of law have convincingly shown that the French *État de droit*, the Greek *kratoz dikaiou*, the German *Rechtsstaatlichkeit*, or the Italian *stato di diritto* cannot be treated as identical concepts.[8] As such, using "rule of law" to refer to those varied national understandings would be misleading, suggesting a false sense of similarity across jurisdictions. This would be particularly problematic for readers who are unable to self-correct such misconceptions because they are unable to take cognizance of relevant materials from the jurisdictions covered in the comparative work.

A common coping strategy advocated by the "legal-culturists" is to leave the concept in its original language and provide an approximate rendition in the author's working language. While intuitively appealing, this way of proceeding is however not foolproof: words may not translate well or may require substantial explanation to flesh out the attributes that are encapsulated by the foreign word so that their meaning becomes intelligible to the non-native comparatist. To give one example: the Dutch discourse distinguishes between the country's *Grondwet*—the official name of its written foundational text, customarily referred to in English as the constitution—and the *constitutie*, which denotes all the principles and norms that are considered to have a constitutional quality. This notably includes unwritten principles, but is sometimes taken to also encompass rules of international and European law that are binding on Dutch state institutions by virtue of the provisions in the *Grondwet* that set out a modulated form of monism.[9] While the fundamental distinction[10] between *Grondwet* and *constitutie* is familiar to every first-year law student in the Netherlands, it is largely ignored in the (limited) English literature about this jurisdiction, arguably in part due to the absence of a suitable shorthand reference that would enlighten rather than confuse the reader. In a related vein, in the French and Spanish constitutional discourse, among others, the *bloc de constitutionnalité* and the *bloque de constitucionalidad*

[8] Armin von Bogdandy, *Ways to Frame the European Rule of Law: Rechtsgemeinschaft, Trust, Revolution and Kantian Peace*, 14 Eur. Const. L. Rev. 675 (2018); Laurent Pech, *A Union Founded on the Rule of Law: Meaning and Reality of the Rule of Law as a Constitutional Principle of EU Law*, 6 Eur. Const. Law. Rev. 359 (2010); *see also* Constance Grewe & Hélène Ruiz Fabri, Droit constitutionnels européens (1995).

[9] Dutch Constitution, Arts. 93 and 94.

[10] This distinction, *inter alia*, matters for the approach taken to constitutional review and more broadly helps to explain the relative lack of visibility and relevance that the *Grondwet* enjoys in the Netherlands as compared to nondomestic norms, among elites as well as the citizenry at large.

respectively occupy a central place.[11] While a literal translation as the "constitutionality block" might give a sense of the gist of these notions, it does not convey what is part of this block, let alone how this *bloc/bloque* conceptually "breaks up" the conventional distinction between the big-C and the small-c constitution. This reality also means that the advent of technology, and having recourse to automated translation, will not alleviate the challenge of literal translation entirely: much will depend on the legal skills and sensibilities of those who have done the programming and a premium should be placed in this regard on the use of properly trained lawyer-linguists.[12]

The Problem of Legal-conceptual Translation

The issue of translation also matters for comparative legal research beyond the lexical aspect, in a deeper and more conceptual manner. The words found in legal texts, from constitutions to statutes to contracts, are not only linguistic expressions in a language that can be transformed, if need be, with the help of a dictionary, into the corresponding terms in another language: they are also part of a special "legal language."[13] This legal language is a subset of ordinary "human language," with added layers of technicality and conceptual meaning. Its creation involves a process of translating extralegal realities into legal constructs, and those in charge of this process (constitutional drafters, legislatures, courts, executives, etc.) rely upon epistemological assumptions in doing so. These can encompass professional terms of art—for a constitutionalist, the word "review" may evoke something different than it does for a layperson—and extend to the prevailing national sociocultural matrices within which law is embedded. Vivian Curran has referred to this as "cognitive lock-in."[14] Compared to other legal texts, constitutions generally contain more value-laden language given their functions as a national covenant and official autobiography of a polity's constitutional identity. The corollary, as Husa reminds us, is that the comparatist must contend with a set of "triple hermeneutics": she must understand social reality, the legal system's normative dimension and interpret the foreign system through her own (reconstructed) observation of

[11] *See in greater detail* LOUIS FAVOREU & F RUBIO LLORENTE, EL BLOQUE DE LA CONSTITUCIONALIDAD: SIMPOSIUM FRANCO-ESPAÑOL DE DERECHO CONSTITUCIONAL (1991); MAARTJE DE VISSER, CONSTITUTIONAL REVIEW IN EUROPE: A COMPARATIVE ANALYSIS 243–49, 263–64 (2015).

[12] The European Union may offer an inspiring example, relying as it does on thousands of such lawyer-linguists to translate EU documents into all the Union's official languages. On these professionals, *see e.g.* Madis Vunder & Claude-Oliver Lacroix, *Training Lawyer Linguists at the Court of Justice of the European Union, in* INSTITUTIONAL TRANSLATOR TRAINING (Tomás Svoboda, Lucja Biel & Vilelmini Sosoni eds., 2022).

[13] *Cf.* HEIKKI MATTILA, COMPARATIVE LEGAL LINGUISTICS (2006).

[14] Vivian Grosswald Curran, *Cultural Immersion, Difference and Categories in U.S. Comparative Law*, 46 AM. J. COMP. L. 43 (1999).

that system.[15] The need for and importance of this form of legal-conceptual translation is not diminished by the ascendency of English as the lingua franca (which I address below). As an aside, conceptual translational challenges may be particularly pronounced in relation to countries or cultures marked by legal pluralism, with indigenous customary or religious systems that operate on a different logic or with different concepts than those associated with the typical "modern" constitutional order.

The challenge posed by the legal-conceptual mode of translation is familiar terrain for traditional comparatists: "the same label may well capture different realities (rules, concepts, etc.)—and a different label, similar realities, in different legal systems."[16] The French *Conseil d'État* may share its English name with the Danish *Statsrådet*—both are "Councils of State"—but its advisory role has closer parallels with those exercised by the Japanese Cabinet Legislation Bureau or Singapore's Attorney General Chambers, while the role performed by the Danish *Statsrådet* is more akin to that of the United Kingdom's Privy Council when it comes to the exercise of the royal prerogative. By way of another example, commentators have noted that while it is common for courts across jurisdictions to engage in "balancing" in the context of fundamental rights protection, the exact understanding of what this requires judges to do is far from uniform.[17]

The risks of proceeding based on system-specific labels are equally well known: a comparison that is prejudiced in its design and hence liable to produce misperceptions and dislocations.[18] How should we deal with this? David Nelken has suggested that it may require the development of a "socio-legal Esperanto which abstracts from the language used by members of different cultures."[19] This is perhaps appealing in principle, but it is difficult to fathom how a multilingual community with members trained in different national-legal epistemological traditions would be able to formulate such a neutral language. Even assuming that this can be done, can we expect that those reading texts that rely on such a sociolegal Esperanto will interpret the terms used in the same way?

Less daunting is to proceed along functionalist lines, which would require closer engagement with and more deliberative application of this method than usually

[15] Jaakko Husa, A New Introduction to Comparative Law 194 (2015).

[16] Catherine Valcke, *Reflections on Comparative Law Methodology—Getting Inside Contract Law*, *in* Practice and Theory in Comparative Law 22, 31 (Maurice Adams & Jacco Bomhoff eds., 2012).

[17] Moshe Cohen-Eliya & Iddo Porat, *American Balancing and German Proportionality: The Historical Origins*, 8 Int'l J. Const. L. 263 (2010); Jacco Bomhoff, *Genealogies of Balancing as Discourse*, 4 Law & Ethics of Hum. Rts. 109 (2010).

[18] Nora V. Demleitner, *Challenge, Opportunity and Risk: An Era of Change in Comparative Law*, 46 Am. J. Comp. L. 647, 654 (1998) further notes that the epistemological load in the analytical or theoretical constructs derived from a particular national setting can extend to an ethnocentric sense of superiority in the description and evaluation of foreign approaches.

[19] David Nelken, *Defining and Using the Concept of Legal Culture*, *in* Comparative Law—A Handbook 109, 124 (Esin Örücü & David Nelken eds., 2007).

practiced by comparative constitutionalists.[20] A core feature of the classic method of functionalism is the formulation of the object of inquiry in system-neutral terms precisely to counter the risk of (hidden) epistemological bias.[21] While this method has received its fair share of criticism, I agree with Catherine Valcke that it does not insist that "*all* the social functions be the same across *all* legal systems"; rather, it is sufficient that the social function used as the point of reference to launch the comparative inquiry is shared across the jurisdictions concerned.[22] To return to the example of the Council of State: the comparatist could frame her inquiry as focused on uncovering the institutional structures in place to assist Heads of State in the exercise of the powers that formally are the preserve of their office.

What is more, the choice of a particular terminology and interjurisdictional linguistic nuances may reveal interesting insights about prevailing values or belief systems in other legal systems. For example, the ability for judges to assess laws against the constitution is typically referred to as "judicial review" in the United States and has been taken often as the preferred shorthand in much of the English literature.[23] Its reference to the identity of the institution that carries out the activity in question continues to speak to the original justification for this type of jurisdiction as articulated by Chief Justice Marshall in *Marbury v Madison*.[24] Conversely, several non-English jurisdictions use wording that emphasizes the yardstick that is applied, viz. the constitution—*Verfassungsgerichtbarkeit* in German or *contrôle de constitutionnalité* in French—as opposed to any of the other recognized standards of review that acts of public authorities can be measured against, such as *Verwaltungsgerichtbarkeit* in German-speaking jurisdictions (which connotes the exercise of administrative jurisdiction) or *contrôle de conventionnalité* in French-speaking jurisdictions (which refers to the use of international conventions as the benchmark of review). In brief, the analysis of paired legal terms across languages can thus provide a worthwhile object of inquiry in its own right for concept formation, or at least constitute another factor to consider in making sense of the internal logic of different constitutional orders.[25]

[20] *See* Mark Tushnet, *The Possibility of Comparative Constitutional Law*, 108 Yale L. J. 1225, 1238–69 (1999) for a discussion of the potential of functionalism.

[21] Konrad Zweigert & Hein Kötz, An Introduction to Comparative Law 34–36 (3rd ed., 1998).

[22] Valcke, *supra* note 16, at 33.

[23] Though it should be noted that it does not always cover the same practice. In the UK, it is generally understood to refer to judicial checks on executive actions (due to the prevailing doctrine of parliamentary sovereignty), while some Canadian scholarship similarly uses the term to refer to scrutiny of administrative acts, with judges reviewing legislation in light of the Charter referred to as "constitutional review" or "constitutional adjudication."

[24] *William Marbury v. James Madison*, 5 U.S. 137 (1803).

[25] This means that comparative studies should systematically include a short statement setting out how leading concepts are understood and which, if any, national legal constructs are used.

A Multilingual Discourse Marked by Fragmentation

Another important aspect of the interplay between language and comparative law has to do with how the former may shape the contours and focus of the latter. The rise of English as the lingua franca is a well-known phenomenon that has affected many areas of our lives. When it comes to legal scholarship, the current discourse is English-centered and conducted mainly through journals, monographs, and edited volumes published by reputable publishing houses in English-speaking jurisdictions. To be sure, having a shared medium of communication holds the promise to vastly expand the academic comparative dialogue in depth and breadth. The pool of prospective participants is enlarged beyond those from English-speaking jurisdictions, as the pervasiveness of legal education in the English language means that there will be scholars from non-Anglophone jurisdictions who can contribute to the field of comparative constitutional law. In doing so, they can infuse the field with insights about a wider range of jurisdictions and topics, thus boosting the scope for concept formation and theory-building.[26]

The difficulty lies in realizing this vast potential. To start with, how many scholars from such jurisdictions who study constitutional topics are truly capable of producing the kind of academic work that meets the requirements set by the leading (English) journals and publishing houses? And even assuming the requisite ability exists, the willingness and time to do so may be lacking. Legal scholars are expected to contribute to the domestic constitutional discourse, critically evaluate new legislative or constitutional initiatives, effect judicial accountability by assessing the legal quality of court decisions, or discuss the constitutional implications of major events in a country's public or political life. Recent scholarship has put forward a stronger conception of the role of the constitutional academy as "knowledge institutions"[27] or "constitutional actors,"[28] playing a part in protecting constitutional democracy. In countries that have a small legal academy[29] or high levels of constitutionally salient activity, the domestic responsibilities for scholars may severely limit their capacity to (also) contribute to the wider comparative constitutional literature.

As such, while it may be said that non-native speakers will eventually have a sustained advantage as they are able to take cognizance of materials from multiple jurisdictions, the fact remains that the (mainstream English-centric) field today is dominated by native speakers, whose interests in particular topics or legal systems

[26] *Cf.* the compelling call to this effect in RAN HIRSCHL, COMPARATIVE MATTERS (2014).

[27] Vicki Jackson, *Legal Scholarship and Knowledge Institutions in Constitutional Democracy* (Summer 2019) AALS News 1.

[28] Liora Lazarus, *Constitutional Scholars as Constitutional Actors*, 48 FED. L. REV 483 (2020).

[29] This may be, but not does not need be, correlated to the population size of the country: other factors include the number of students able to go to law school (which itself is influenced by financial considerations as well as the availability of places, which may be determined by the State) and the existence of barriers to pursuit of a scholarly career upon graduation.

accordingly have a formative influence on the content and direction of the field. In contrast to the general discipline of comparative law, levels of multilinguism also tend to be lower. While it is by now widely accepted that it would be too demanding to insist on complete mastery of a foreign language before considering a researcher to be competent to work on (linguistically) foreign systems,[30] it cannot be denied that linguistic abilities matter.

Perhaps, most pertinently, the existence of a lingua franca should not make us forget the continued existence and development of comparative constitutional law discourses in other languages. These can be interjurisdictional, for instance among German-, French-, or Spanish-speaking scholars,[31] or intrajurisdictional, viz. when it is accepted practice in a country that writings about domestic constitutional topics regularly feature comparisons with foreign approaches and ideas. For the most part, those different national discourses exist and develop alongside, but not in conversation with, the English scholarship read and produced by the mainstream comparative constitutional community—and the latter is the poorer for it.[32]

To give just one example: the English discourse has witnessed the publication of several works devoted to the idea of constitutional dialogues between courts and legislatures and the possible means for such dialogues to happen.[33] These works have been predominantly written by native speakers and focus predominantly on English-speaking (common law) jurisdictions.[34] An important impetus for this body of scholarship was provided by developments in Canada, the United Kingdom, and New Zealand in the 1990s, which saw these jurisdictions devise new procedural responses to better defend constitutional values (particularly fundamental rights protection) without accepting unqualified judicial supremacy to achieve this objective. Judicial decision-making techniques and, to a lesser extent, procedural designs that similarly aim to mediate between court-enforced constitutional supremacy and democracy, can however also be found in non-English jurisdictions—which moreover often possess a longer genealogy. The German and Italian constitutional courts, for instance, can decide that a law is only barely

[30] *See e.g.* Mitch Lasser, *The Question of Understanding*, *in* COMPARATIVE LEGAL STUDIES: TRADITIONS AND TRANSITIONS (Pierre Legrand & R. Munday eds., 2003).

[31] There may be colonial path-dependencies at stake here: Latin American scholars may be more comfortable with Spanish literature and those on the African continent with writings in French, while scholars from Japan or South Korea may be predisposed toward scholarship in German.

[32] This malady also affects general comparative law: *see e.g.* BASIL MARKESINIS, COMPARATIVE LAW IN THE COURTROOM AND CLASSROOM (2003).

[33] *See e.g.* from among a rich literature: Mark Tushnet, *Weak-Form Judicial Review and "Core" Civil Liberties*, 41 HARV. C.R.-C.L. L. REV. 1 (2006); Rosalind Dixon, *The Forms, Functions and Varieties of Weak(ened) Review*, 17 INT'L J. CONST. L. 904 (2019); Aileen Kavanagh, *The Lure and Limits of Dialogue*, 66 U. TORONTO L.J. 83 (2016); Kent Roach, *Dialogic Judicial Review and Its Critics*, 23 SUP. CT. L. REV. 49 (2004); YAP PO JEN, CONSTITUTIONAL DIALOGUE IN COMMON LAW ASIA (2015).

[34] For a notable exception: see Mark Tushnet's discussion of Japan (with Rosalind Dixon) in his chapter *Weak-Form Review and Its Constitutional Relatives: An Asian Perspective*, *in* COMPARATIVE CONSTITUTIONAL LAW IN ASIA 102 (Rosalind Dixon & Tom Ginsburg eds., 2014).

constitutional and, therefore, require the legislature to ensure a more constitutional state of affairs; or find that a law is unconstitutional without declaring its invalidity, just like their Spanish counterpart, to give the legislature space to rectify the situation; meanwhile, the technique of (re)interpreting legislation to make it conform to constitutional requirements and hence save it from annulment is ubiquitous among constitutional courts in non-English-speaking jurisdictions.[35] All these techniques have been the subject of rich commentary in German, Italian, French, and Spanish-language scholarship, to name a few,[36] but have taken up only limited bandwidth in the English-language comparative constitutional discourse. Elsewhere in Europe, many of the Scandinavian countries have special parliamentary committees that are responsible for preenactment review of legislation, which sometimes has been paired with a formal threshold criterion for judicial intervention. In Finland, for instance, courts may refuse to apply laws only if their application "would be in evident conflict with the Constitution,"[37] while Swedish courts, before 2011, could similarly do so only when the friction between the constitution and the law to be applied in a specific case was "obvious."[38]

The failure to consider these and other mechanisms[39] is a missed opportunity. It stymies our collective thinking about the available range of judicial techniques or design options to calibrate the court–legislature relationship, including their respective merits and the conditions under which those approaches thrive (or languish). In the terminology used by Ran Hirschl, this instantiation of what he calls the "concept formation through multiple descriptions" mode of comparative law, thus, remains incomplete and underinclusive.[40] In addition, there is a risk that the English literature implicitly endorses the existence of a common/civil law divide in relation to the debate about weak/strong forms of constitutional adjudication, when the difference may be one of form rather than substance.

Turning to possible ways forward, it seems to me that there is a debate to be had about scholarly responsibilities regarding the use of our respective linguistic abilities to expand access to foreign materials as well as expectations about what should count as a meaningful contribution to the field. To start with, concerted efforts should be devoted to producing scholarship that offers contextual translation,[41]

[35] For a comparative overview with translated excerpts, *see* Maartje De Visser, Constitutional Review in Europe: A Comparative Analysis 291–324 (2015).

[36] The same is true in South Korea or Taiwan, whose constitutional courts have embraced similar decisional techniques, as noted in Wen-Chen Chang, *Book Review: Constitutional Dialogue in Common Law Asia*, 15 Int'l J. Const. L. 264 (2017).

[37] Constitution of Finland, ch. 2, § 106.

[38] Swedish Instrument of Government, ch. 11:14.

[39] In Mongolia, for instance, judicial decisions on the constitutionality of legislation can be rejected by parliament, requiring the constitutional court to re-examine the matter: Constitution of Mongolia, art. 66(3).

[40] Hirschl, *supra* note 26, 238–42.

[41] *Cf.* Paul Bohannan, *Ethnography and Comparison in Legal Anthropology*, *in* Law in Culture and Society (Laura Nader ed., 1997). *Contrast* Max Gluckman, Politics, Law and Ritual in Tribal Society (2017).

whereby both the literal and the actual (invested and culturally charged) meaning of constitutional concepts are translated into another language. Doing so not only enables the scholarly community to better appreciate the specific culturalist 'baggage' that general concepts carry with them; it also offers the prospect of more nuanced theory-building, as it encourages us to question whether certain concepts are truly similar across jurisdictions and whether our classic vocabulary is sufficiently capacious to cover the full plethora of lived constitutional practices. Superb exemplars of such works include Donald P. Kommers and Russell Miller's *The Constitutional Jurisprudence of the Federal Republic of Germany*,[42] Manual José Cepeda Espinosa and David Landau's *Colombian Constitutional Law*,[43] or László Sólyom and Georg Brunner's *Constitutional Judiciary in a New Democracy: The Hungarian Constitutional Court*,[44] which offer translated excerpts of judgments, supported by annotations that explain how leading notions—such as dignity, equality, privacy, federalism, or democracy—are understood in Germany, in Colombia, and also in Hungary before that country's Fidesz-led constitutional transformation. At the same time, there is a need to move beyond court-centricity. There is a pressing need for contextual translational efforts to engage with legislative and executive materials that are a part of the small-c constitution and/or purport to give meaning to formal constitutional provisions, in line with the emerging turn to take political constitutionalism seriously, including in jurisdictions with strong-form review systems.[45]

On a related note, an earlier tradition in general comparative law of publishing leading scholarly treatises in multiple languages deserves to be revived and expanded. This is particularly relevant for countries practicing the civil law tradition, which tend to be non-English-speaking, and which generally have a strong doctrinal and jurisprudential culture. Several civilian scholars have had a formative influence on constitutional theory and practice in their jurisdiction, including the workings of systems of constitutional justice.[46] In this regard, it is worth pointing out that there may be close links between the academy and the constitutional judiciary, evidenced among others in the fact that several constitutional courts count legal scholars among their members or that judges may join (or return to) the academy upon their retirement from the bench.[47] The "pre-judicial"

[42] Donald P. Kommers & Russell A. Miller, The Constitutional Jurisprudence of the Federal Republic of Germany (3rd ed., 2012).

[43] Manuel José Cepeda Espinosa & David Landau, Columbian Constitutional Law—Leading Cases (2017).

[44] László Sólyom & Georg Brunner, Constitutional Judiciary in a New Democracy: The Hungarian Constitutional Court (2000).

[45] *See e.g.* Conor Casey & David Kenny, *The Gatekeepers: Executive Lawyers and the Executive Power in Comparative Constitutional Law*, 20 Int'l J. Const. L. 664 (2022).

[46] Examples from the European continental tradition include Robert Alexy's work on proportionality, Peter Häberle's idea of constitutional theory as cultural science, or Louis Favoreu's efforts to champion the work of the French *Conseil constitutionnel.*

[47] Constitutional court judges tend to serve for a fixed term rather than for life, as in decentralized systems of constitutional adjudication.

or extrajudicial writings produced by these individuals may provide important insights into the principles underlying the case law or the system that is being constructed.[48] For a good understanding of how constitutions are conceived and operate in civil law countries, it is hence important to extend translation efforts to scholarly writings, which should be treated as much as part of the constitutional canon as foundational judgments are. More generally, adding such non-English scholarly voices to the mainstream discourse may have ramifications for the range of conceptual insights on which we can draw or even the choice of what counts as a salient topic to be investigated.

Alongside translations of handbooks and treatises, the compilation of casebooks should be encouraged on account of their valuable role as a resource for comparative research alongside their extant role as a pedagogical tool. This is especially so when such casebooks feature primary materials from a diverse range of foreign jurisdictions alongside commentaries by scholars well versed in (and preferably from) those jurisdictions. Turning from books to shorter works of scholarship, journals could require that articles are preceded by multilingual abstracts, so that those who are not sufficiently proficient to read the entire piece can at least partake of the core arguments advanced, or even accept the publication of articles in multiple languages.[49] Book review sections offer another promising avenue: these should be used to highlight new monographs or treatises in a foreign language, with emphasis placed on how these new works relate to older writings on (comparative) constitutional law in that language as well as to the topics *du jour* in the English discourse. While none of these suggestions will entirely resolve the current linguistic fragmentation within comparative constitutional scholarship, they will help counter unconscious tendencies to treat the English-language discourse as presenting a comprehensive and authoritative account of thinking about constitutional questions from a comparative perspective and enrich that discourse by integrating at least parts of the foreign language literature.

Expectations in Communication with a Foreign Readership

A final aspect that speaks to the interplay between language and comparative law shifts the focus away from the materials under study to the communication

[48] For a contemporary example, changes in the approach of the Italian constitutional court regarding the sequencing of preliminary questions of constitutionality (which are authoritatively resolved by the Italian constitutional court) and the compatibility with EU law (which are authoritatively resolved by the Court of Justice of the European Union) have been attributed in part to influential writings by Augusto Barbera and Marta Cartabia, both of whom were later appointed to the Italian constitutional court.

[49] The *International Journal of Constitutional Law* has for instance begun to publish issues in Spanish, while the *World Comparative Law* journal accepts manuscripts in German, French, or Spanish, albeit on an exceptional basis.

pertaining to these materials between scholars and their audience. This relationship has been implicated in the earlier discussion but warrants consideration on its own as it influences the use and usefulness of comparative works by other members of the scholarly community. It has been noted that there is an implicit quality to much comparative writing, notably as far as methodology is concerned. Among others, this has led to calls for a more deliberate use of principles of case selection,[50] which should be understood as extending to an expectation to specify and account for the eventual choice of the principle chosen. In a similar vein, good comparative writing should address how relevant linguistic issues have been dealt with. While this may seem self-evident, only a minority of scholarship explains how information about foreign legal systems was obtained and how any challenges in accessing or converting materials from one language to another have been dealt with. Greater engagement with these issues can be supported on several grounds. It would enable readers to verify the credibility of the research design and better assess the robustness of the conclusions presented. It would also provide non-native readers with a clearer indication as to whether they can confidently rely on the comparative study in their own work. Here, it may be helpful to refer to a series of guidelines that John Reitz has suggested before deciding to make use of secondary literature about foreign law:

> Does the author possess the necessary linguistic knowledge? . . . Has she made good use of translations of important, relevant legal literature from the foreign country if there are any? Has he reported on actual practices in the country based on his own experiences or on reliable reports by others? Do the author's comments appear to be informed by a deep understanding of the nation's cultural and religious traditions and history?[51]

It is difficult to answer these questions with confidence if the scholarly work in question remains largely, if not entirely, silent.

Another important aspect of the communication between author and audience concerns the manner in which the foreign constitutional order is represented. General comparative scholarship distinguishes between the adoption of an internal point of view, whereby the other system is presented in a manner that resonates with those from that system, and a neutral perspective often associated with the use of functionalism.[52] The former typically finds favor with advocates of contextualism or culturalism, as it is seen to offer a more authentic rendition of the foreign constitutional system ("living like a local"). This is the kind of reconstruction

[50] Hirschl, *supra* note 26.
[51] John C. Reitz, *How to Do Comparative Law*, 46 Am. J. Comp. L. 617, 633 (1998).
[52] *See*, classically, Konrad Zweigert & Hein Kötz, An Introduction to Comparative Law 34–43 (3rd ed., 1998).

sought by those offering constitutional ethnographic studies[53]—involving the application of what in general comparative law is known as the method of "deep-level comparative law."[54] In writing or reading accounts that purport to depict the foreign system "from within," a fully internal perspective is, however, neither possible nor desirable. As (most of the) audience and the author would have grown up in different legal systems, the latter cannot treat the former as she would her domestic readership, with whom she shares a general understanding of the larger cultural, social, economic, political, and ideological whole within which legal rules and institutions are embedded. The comparatist needs to acknowledge and address this cognitive gap to ensure that her work is intelligible to her non-national readership. Doing so will result in a rendering of the system unlike that which would be presented to a local audience, which may extend to the account provided not being as "deep" or "thick"[55] because of the difficulties or suitability of conveying the full suite of extralegal local conditions. In a related vein, John Bell has argued that the reconstruction of the foreign system is unavoidably subjective: it is based on the comparatist's personal selection of information as well as her decisions on how to order and present this information.[56] I agree with Bell that this is not a serious concern as long as local legal professionals do not think that the picture painted of their system is clearly flawed or deceptive. For those consuming ethnographic studies and other works adopting an interior perspective, the key point is to be mindful of this subjectivity. This means that recognizing that what is communicated is not necessarily a (full) representation of national orthodoxy, as those members of the national constitutional academy who decide to write for a foreign audience may do so in pursuit of a particular agenda rather than with the aim of providing a "neutral" account simply intended to expand the knowledge horizons of that foreign audience.

A last aspect concerns the identity of the audience and the implications thereof for communicating findings. The comparative constitutional community is heterogenous, including when it comes to linguistic abilities. This brings us back to the issue of English as the lingua franca: it cannot be assumed that materials written in English can be readily read and understood by all members of that community, especially by those living in the Global South. In our writing, we should accordingly be mindful of thinking of ways to ensure accessibility and epistemic justice. This will, among others, entail reflections about the appropriate choice of medium to convey ideas and the allocation of resources to ensure that contemporary

[53] *Cf.* Kim Lane Scheppele, *Constitutional Ethnography: An Introduction*, 38 Law & Soc. Rev. 389 (2004).

[54] Coined by Mark van Hoecke, *Deep Level Comparative Law*, *in* Epistemology and Methodology of Comparative Law (Mark van Hoecke ed., 2004).

[55] *Cf.* Clifford Geertz, The Interpretation of Cultures 310–23 (1973).

[56] John Bell, *Legal Research and the Distinctiveness of Comparative Law*, *in* Methodologies of Legal Research. What Kind of Method for What Kind of Discipline? 155 (Mark van Hoecke ed., 2011).

theory-building work originally prepared in English is presented in non-English venues too.

Final Remarks

Language can be seen as an intuitive challenge for those who embark on comparative constitutional research: its intricate entanglement with law is often overlooked and not engaged with explicitly. This chapter has argued that this is a missed opportunity at best, and arguably presents a hazard for the collective quality of the scholarly discourse. Indeed, the methodological strengthening of our discipline requires a fuller reckoning with linguistic pathologies. One of the gravest risks for the comparatist here is misunderstanding on account of a failed or incomplete lexical or conceptual translation. This calls for some methodological modesty and sensibility, especially when engaging with materials from a constitutional system in a language that one is not (intimately) familiar with. There are two further challenges to be cognizant of. First, we should recognize that language may not always operate as a bridge that connects and includes scholars as well as ideas from different jurisdictions; it can act as a funnel instead. This is evident in the existence of multiple scholarly discourses that are fragmented along linguistic lines with limited cross-referencing, as recounted earlier. Another aspect worth mentioning here is the court-centric focus that has characterized much of the scholarship. While there are growing calls to cast the net wider,[57] the simple reality is that the easier availability of translated judgments in English as compared to other primary documents—notably those produced by the political branches, who do not often invest in making these accessible to audiences outside the jurisdiction, especially if these documents are confidential and subject to official secrets restrictions—makes it difficult to shift our focus away from the courts. The corollary of the "funnel" challenge is a possible limit to the intellectual growth of the field, which is antithetical to the core aim of comparative law to break out of ethnocentric thinking and associated cultural biases.

The second aspect of the linguistic challenge looks at language as a frame: in short, the medium *is* the message. This refers to the choice of labels to classify legal systems or describe phenomena. As Kim Lane Scheppele has said, "it is crucial to get the metaphors right for highlighting key features of the matter under discussion."[58] For instance, how suitable is the term "dialogue" to describe the interplay

[57] *See e.g.* Maartje De Visser and Jaclyn Neo, *What Would a Pluralist Institutional Approach to Constitutional Interpretation Look Like? Some Methodological Implications*, 20 Int'l J. Const. L 1884 (2022).

[58] Kim Lane Scheppele, *The Migration of Anti-Constitutionalist Ideas: The Post-9/11 Globalization of Public Law and the International State of Emergency*, *in* The Migration of Constitutional Ideas 347, 347 (Sujit Choudhry ed., 2006).

between courts and legislatures, given that it suggests a back-and-forth between these institutions that does not always materialize, while it also appears to overlook the contributions of other actors (including the government, nonpartisan advisory bodies, or even the people) in shaping the meaning given to constitutional provisions? And should Singapore be labeled as belonging to the group of countries practicing authoritarian constitutionalism,[59] or rather as an exemplar of communitarian constitutionalism?[60] Language is implicated in those and other questions, which are set to become more pronounced in the face of a growing push to create new typologies and engage in novel concept formation.

So what can be done? In addition to the suggestions set out earlier in this chapter, there are further ways to harness the inclusive and framing attributes associated with language more fully. To start with, we should actively foster crosslinguistic collaboration in research design and execution to navigate the challenges attendant on legal-conceptual translation. This is not only relevant for those seeking to offer thick descriptions of a small set of foreign jurisdictions, but also matters for those interested in large-n studies to ward off the risk of using monojurisdictional thinking and concepts as universalizable standards when such is not warranted. Further, we could apply the idea of dialogue as an actual mode of scholarship. This would entail deliberately bringing scholars from different jurisdictions and traditions into conversation with one another to share their understanding of, and approach to, a certain constitutional doctrine or institution.[61] Such a dialogical approach should preferably be iterative and feature a deliberate effort to provide participants with regular and repeated opportunities to speak with one another and exchange views on the chosen topic. Technological advances, including familiarity with a growing range of online communication tools, are a clear boon in this regard. Finally, as the field of comparative constitutional law continues to accept the relevance of other disciplines, it would be worthwhile to invest in forging a stronger connection with sociolinguistics or literary theory. The former could possibly help expand the conceptual toolkit for studying how the general public uses constitutional language, tying in with debates about legal consciousness and mobilization, constitutional literacy, and popular constitutionalism. The latter could offer new perspectives on the meaning of the constitution: for instance, by probing the degree to which this text is the product of a culture rather than its authors and how it in turn helps to create culture, or through the identification of unconscious elements embedded in the constitution, from emotions[62] to gendered norms to

[59] Mark Tushnet, *Authoritarian Constitutionalism*, 100 Cornell L. Rev 391 (2015).
[60] Li-Ann Thio, *Constitutionalism in Illiberal Polities*, *in* Oxford Handbook of Comparative Constitutional Law 133 (Michel Rosenfeld & András Sajó eds., 2012).
[61] Good examples are the *Symposium in Honor of the Late Louis Favoreu: France's Exceptionalism in Constitutional Review*, 5 Int'l J. Const. L. 1 (2007); Dialogues on Italian Constitutional Justice—A Comparative Perspective (Vittoria Barsotti et al. eds., 2021).
[62] For instance, András Sajó has argued that constitutions seek to convey and appeal to human emotions rather than rationality: Constitutional Sentiments (2011).

class differences. In sum, there is incredible untapped potential when it comes to the role and significance of language in constitutional comparisons. As such, this chapter should ultimately be read as an invitation to scholars to devote more systematic and explicit attention to the effects of language on our collective ways of thinking, the identification and framing of questions as well as our conception of legal solutions.

8

Reasonable Disagreement: Mark Tushnet, John Rawls, and a Democratic Point to Constitutionalism

Frank I. Michelman

Prelude: Three Scenes

Three memories surge to mind. The earliest is of a major academic conference, held at Yale in 1981, on "Legal Scholarship: Its Nature and Purposes."[1] The event was largely designed (so it struck me at the time) as a showcase for a waxing Critical Legal Studies (CLS) insurgency in our law schools. Mark Tushnet gave a paper on "Legal Scholarship: Its Causes and Cure,"[2] for which I served as designated commentator from the liberal-legal side of the aisle.[3] It was my first-ever serious exchange with Professor Tushnet. I have been learning from him ever since.

Suffice it to say about Mark's paper for that occasion that it found, as a chief cause of embarrassment to the mainstream legal scholarship of its day, a predominant attachment there to something he called "liberal theory." Roughly, that was the idea that people resolve anxieties about abusive or arbitrary treatment from the state, which they have empowered as their protector against the depredations of others in civil society, by supposition of an objectively fair and impersonal rule of law to which the state, like all of us, is subject.[4] But, as noted then by Mark, "the acquiescence of individuals to the liberal rule of law depends upon their continued . . . faith in its objectivity."[5] Twentieth-century Legal Realist investigation had shaken deeply (if not utterly destroyed) the basis for belief in the actuality and even possibility of the requisite objectivity in liberal-legal methodology. The demonstrations of the Realist scholarship therefore could not be "accommodated within the

[1] *See Papers from the Yale Law Journal Symposium on Legal Scholarship: Its Nature and Purposes Held at the Yale Law School on February 13–15, 1981*, 90 Yale L.J. 955 (1981).

[2] *See* Mark Tushnet, *Legal Scholarship: Its Causes and Cure*, 90 Yale L.J. 1205 (1981).

[3] *See* Frank I. Michelman, *Politics as Medicine: On Misdiagnosing Legal Scholarship*, 90 Yale L.J. 1224.

[4] *See* Tushnet, *supra* note 2, at 1206.

[5] *Id.* at 1207. It is not too early to notice a parallel to John Rawls, whose proposed "liberal principle of legitimacy" envisages the exercise of rule in accordance with a short table of higher norms ("constitution"), which "all citizens may reasonably be expected to endorse in the light of principles and ideals acceptable to them as reasonable and rational." John Rawls, Political Liberalism 217 (1993).

Frank I. Michelman, *Reasonable Disagreement: Mark Tushnet, John Rawls, and a Democratic Point to Constitutionalism*
In: *Redefining Comparative Constitutional Law.* Edited by: Vicki C. Jackson and Madhav Khosla, Oxford University Press.
 DOI: 10.1093/9780191996344.003.0008

legal sphere" without undermining liberal theory.[6] Mainstream legal scholarship of the day accordingly proceeded in disregard of those demonstrations, protective of liberal theory at the cost of scholarly credibility; and that was the legal academic malaise Tushnet had set out to diagnose. Of my response on that occasion to this argument from Mark,[7] I need only say that it entered a protest against a Crit vocabulary of that time in which the term "liberal"—as in "liberal legalism," "liberal rule of law," "liberal society"—was decidedly not one of endearment.

A second memory comes from later in that same decade. Its occasion was one of the annual "schmoozes" that Mark Tushnet organized and chaired at Georgetown Law in that period, among law and politics scholars keen on exploring possible new directions for constitutional law and theory. At one of those events, apropos I do not recall what topic or issue under discussion, Mark felt moved to make the declaration: "You know, I am a liberal." I distinctly recall that prefatory "You know"—as if to signal "you might not all be expecting this, but . . . ." I had not been expecting it. It sat me up straight.

The third memory is much younger, from a month or so prior to this writing. It comes from a Zoom-based colloquium of law and politics professors around a recent publication of mine. Mark Tushnet found occasion, in reference to an abstract idea of the "liberal" or "liberal-democratic" as an identifiable strain or tendency in a given society's political culture or conversation, not to define it but rather to say: "I know it when I see it."

Constitutionalism ("As Such")

In what follows, a central bone of contention will be the political-theoretic category "constitutionalism." I will understand by that term a political and social practice, publicly recognized and relied upon by citizens at large, of expected submission by ground-level political actors (including officials, legislative bodies and their members, voters, and any common-law judiciary that may exist) to some prior established constraints—"entrenched" until altered by specially onerous institutional processes tailored to that purpose—on their choices of legislative policies and directives. Note that my definition stipulates neither that the practice must exist as a part of a country's positive law (it might, but it also might be purely customary or conventional), *or* that it be subject to policing by any supposedly transpolitical agency such as a supreme court or constitutional council, *or* that its dictations of constraint on ordinary politics touch on any particular topic (say, religion) in any particular way (say, prescribing freedom in the exercise thereof). You can call this, if you like, constitutionalism thinly institutionalized. It corresponds closely to

[6] *Id.*

[7] *See* Michelman, *supra* note 3.

what Mark Tushnet recently has named as "constitutionalism-as-such"—in contradistinction to a particular form of it (legalist with strong judicial review and rights more thickly listed) that can be seen as "dominant today."[8]

But let us now compromise to this extent on purification of our working idea of constitutionalism: We give that idea a prodemocratic spin by specifying further that the principles of constraint on ordinary politics are such as to mesh with a broadly held (if somewhat vaguely apprehended) commitment to democracy, meaning government by and among citizen equals in a broadly speaking free society. The principles thus will be receptive to political institutional forms, and norms of conduct within them, that are fitting to such a commitment. But then the demand for thinness comes immediately roaring back, by a proviso that these principles appear in a generalized form, abstracted from predetermination of reasonably contestable ground-level policies in the pursuit of lofty democratic commitments—because, in a democracy, those should be left to resolution by the rule of current majorities.

Take an example. Democracy, we may all agree, presupposes freedom of expression. Lots of us tend to think that decides, for a democracy, the question of hate-speech regulation—even as we divide over which way it decides it! Constitutionalism-as-such, while embracing a principle of freedom of expression, leaves the question of hate-speech policy to ordinary political resolution. It does so given the community's assumed recognition and acceptance of the reasonability of arguments both pro and con the consistency of various concrete proposals with democratic freedom of expression.[9] On that condition—which we may regard as quite frequently the case with respect to countless issues of state policy—withdrawal of that topic from the ordinary forms of majoritarian resolution is an undue encroachment on democratic political authority.

Reasonable Disagreement

As Tushnet says, "the idea of reasonableness is doing a lot of work here."[10] It does so throughout his writings on constitutionalism in relation to democracy. The proposition of an expectation, in free societies, of reasonable disagreement among reasonable citizens over the consonance of disputed ground-level policies with

[8] Mark Tushnet, *Review Essay: For Constitutionalism*, 56 VERFASSUNG UND RECHT IN ÜBERSEE [VRÜ] 464, 465 (2023) (Ger.).

[9] MARK TUSHNET & BOJAN BUGARIČ, POWER TO THE PEOPLE: CONSTITUTIONALISM AFTER POPULISM 9 (2021): "On some accounts . . . [laws restricting hate speech] violate ideals of freedom of expression. On other accounts . . . such laws are required to ensure that everyone can participate in civic life on an equal basis. Proponents of each view will of course provide elaborate arguments rooted in stories about individual autonomy, democratic self-governance, and the like . . . [E]ach view is reasonable."

[10] Tushnet, *supra* note 8, at 25.

lofty commitments to civic freedom and equality will prove key to Mark Tushnet's thought about a democratic point to constitutionalism.

It is not, though, that Tushnet proposes, anywhere that I can see, any precise definition for the idea of reasonability. Here is the closest I can find that he comes (in concert with Bojan Bugaric):

> Spell out what you think constitutionalism requires, and ask yourself whether someone with a substantially different political agenda from yours [but subject to our vague pro-democratic commitment to civic freedom and equality] would be unreasonable were she to reject the constraints on policy choices that [your thicker] version imposes.[11]

The unstated assumption is that you very frequently will not so find if you are honest with yourself and respectful of the others. But then for you nevertheless to insist on having the constitutional constraint on policy choice be tipped your way, regardless of a majority's opposite view, would mark you—Tushnet and Bugaric say—as antidemocratic.[12] It is of some interest to our inquiry that Tushnet and Bugaric here expressly notice a kinship between their prodemocratic defense of constitutionalism duly thinned out and the idea of John Rawls that higher-order principles of justice for a liberal society should correspond to those that would be chosen from behind a veil of ignorance.[13]

Constitutionalism *vis-à-vis* Democracy

Constitutionalism-as-such, institutionally and prescriptively thinned out as you may please, remains contentious in the respect of its contested compatibility with democracy in purer or unsullied form. Take our notion of a "constitutional democracy." Presumably, that has in view a political order to which we would (otherwise) attach the descriptor "democratic," but in which constitutionalism also figures as an organizing theme. But how is that possible without welching on the promise of democracy as an order of free self-rule by the people of a country? "How can a people be self-governing," as Tushnet recently has put the question, "if they are unable, without extraordinary effort [entrenchment, remember, is an element of constitutionalism-as-such], to obtain from their government policies that on reflection and after deliberation a majority of them prefer?"[14] You can offer

[11] Tushnet & Bugarič, *supra* note 9, at 35; MARK TUSHNET, WEAK COURTS, STRONG RIGHTS: JUDICIAL REVIEW AND SOCIAL WELFARE RIGHTS IN COMPARATIVE CONSTITUTIONAL LAW 103 (2008) ("The criterion . . . is this: Did the legislator do something that is not at all oriented to the nation's constitutional traditions?").

[12] Tushnet & Bugarič, *supra* note 9, at 35.

[13] *See id.* at 35 n.47.

[14] Tushnet, *supra* note 8, at 7.

in response that a *proper* conception democracy already insinuates constitutionalism,[15] but that only seems to deepen the puzzle, by making of democracy a notion that both presupposes constitutionalism and repels it.

Our business here will be with a certain line of response to the puzzle in that form. The constitutionalism prerequisite to democracy—so goes this line—is itself democratized, by leaving any and all questions of the more precise meanings and concrete applications of abstract entrenched constraints on ordinary majoritarian politics to resolution by "the people themselves" in their conduct of such politics.[16] Notably, that is meant to apply even to constraints regarding the institutional forms *for the conduct of that politics*, given that a wide variety of such forms can be defended as consonant with democracy, depending on conditions at a given time and place and the sort of issue up for decision. But how, you ask, can the extant institutional forms for majority rule be subject to on-the-fly majoritarian modification, without leaving order and stability in shambles? An answer from Tushnet is that publicly settled institutional forms for majoritarian rule can normally and presumptively govern, as required for the orderly day-to-day operation of that rule, while remaining open to occasional deviations, departures, and revisions whose democratic credentials the people themselves can recognize without destabilizing their government.[17] Still that answer leaves hanging the question of why devotees of democracy would allow for constitutionalism *any room at all* in the play of political rule by fairly counted, credibly deliberative majorities.

Tushnet *vis-à-vis* Rawls

In the year 2000, I reflected[18] on Mark Tushnet's suggestion of that time that what ultimately matters for continued constitutional-democratic health in a country such as the United States is not which side Supreme Court majorities come down on in the kinds of legal-doctrinal wrangles composing the daily run of that tribunal's constitutional cases (Mark's examples included cases on criminalization of flag-burning, race-based affirmative action, and incidental burdens to religion from otherwise valid laws); it rather is the spirit and terms in which the core issues behind those legal wrangles are framed and discussed in the country's politics at large. No matter, in Mark's view, that he as lawyer might see this or that adjudicative outcome as reflecting a quite wrong view of our constitutional law in place. As

[15] *Compare id.* at 2–3 (positing a conception of democracy as entailing that "policy on . . . important subjects be subject to the *reliably determined, reasonably stable, and reasonably deliberative* preferences of contemporary majorities") (emphasis supplied).

[16] Larry Kramer, The People Themselves: Popular Constitutionalism and Judicial Review (2004).

[17] *See* Tushnet, *supra* note 8, at 30–33.

[18] *See* Frank I. Michelman, *Populist Natural Law (Reflections on Tushnet's "Thin Constitution")*, 34 Univ. Richmond L. Rev. 461 (2000).

long as people credibly aspiring to the abstract liberal values of the Declaration of Independence, or to American "fundamental guarantees of equality, freedom of expression, and liberty"—our "thin constitution," as Mark then would have it[19]—could fairly take either side of the case, adjudicative outcomes either way are subcritical political events. The American habit of submission in such matters to the constitutional-legal dictates of the Supreme Court might count—Mark thought that it did count—as a setback to democracy here for no good reason, but neither that habit nor a reversal of it should count as a dire threat to the survival of American constitutional faith.[20]

That view of Tushnet's might, I went on then to say, stretch constitutionalism thinner "than some of Tushnet's liberal-minded readers will find they can swallow." I mentioned that I thought that "some" would not include John Rawls. Tushnet asks of us, I wrote, "about what John Rawls does in his most recent explanations of the idea of public reason."[21] (I did not explain but promised to do so in future work.)

Comparing the respective ideas of Tushnet and Rawls on the service (or disservice) to democracy of a practice of constitutionalism, we find an impressive overlap on this question between the two bodies of thought. We will also, though, find in the end at least one seeming sharp discrepancy between them. Rawlsian thought expressly endorses allowance to a non- or counter-popular tribunal—typically but not necessarily envisaged as a supreme or constitutional court—of a decisive, immediate say over the constitutional acceptability, hence the intrasystemic validity, of ground-level lawmaking when challenged as noncompliant with constitutional norms.[22] True, Rawls would limit any such judicial strikedown power to legislative actions that the court finds to lie outside a wide space of reasonable debate over the meanings and applications of abstractly constitutionalized principles and values—thus bringing his view into seeming neighborhood with Tushnet's. But I read Tushnet as a holdout against even that much concession away from democratic-majoritarian control over the contents of the country's laws in force. Constitutionalism *à la* Tushnet does, of course, accept that there must be an outer bound to the space of reasonable debate over constitutional meanings and applications, but it would leave the placement of that bound, with respect to this or that issue under active debate, to decision by ordinary democratic politics. I will ask here, before ending, whether this discrepancy between the stances of Rawls and Tushnet possibly signals some deeper division between the two bodies of thought over the political value or values to be served by constitutionalism in relation to democracy. I will conclude that it probably does not.

[19] *See* Mark Tushnet, Taking the Constitution Away from the Courts 11 (1999).
[20] *See id.* at 153 ("noise around zero").
[21] Michelman, *supra* note 18, at 487.
[22] *See* Frank I. Michelman, Constitutional Essentials: On the Constitutional Theory of Political Liberalism 54, 168–71 (2022).

Rawls in a Nutshell: Constitution and Liberal Legitimacy[23]

In the briefest possible terms, the Rawlsian idea of the point of constitutionalism in and for a democracy runs like this. We want a basis upon which democratic citizens can possibly hope to justify to each other as all free and equal their coercive impositions—political majorities over dissenters—by votes touching fundamental matters over which citizens in modern free societies are bound to find themselves in moral, philosophical, and faith-based disagreement. "[I]n the light of what principles and ideals"—Rawls poses the question—"must we exercise [coercive legislative] power if our doing so is to be justifiable to others as free and equal?"[24]

That is where, for Rawls, the idea of constitutionalism comes in. Citizens in deep disagreement about ground-level policies and laws enacted by democratic majorities over dissent could still agree (Rawls offers it as a hope) on acceptance of a set of relatively abstract directive principles for sorting disputed laws and policies into those that are and are not to be admissible among them, even in the knowledge that future applications would sometimes be repugnant to them.[25] Constitutionalism thus figures centrally in what Rawls posits as "the liberal principle of legitimacy" for democratic-majoritarian government.[26]

Note that it is, expressly by name, a *liberal* principle that Rawls there offers in response to you and me wondering how we can justify to free and equal cocitizens (ourselves included) our expectations of their (and our) normal willing compliance with laws that they (or we) may detest. Now, obviously, not all citizens in any of our countries are liberal. But then it is not literally *every* citizen to whom Rawls thinks such justification need or should be offered (or could possibly be provided). Rather, Rawlsian justification occurs within the fold of those who reciprocate back and forth among them a liberal respect and regard for each other as "free and equal." By Rawls' stipulation, justification is fulfilled by a showing of the compatibility of contested laws with a higher-normative constitution-in-force whose terms "all citizens may reasonably be expected to endorse in the light of principles and ideals acceptable to them as reasonable and rational."[27] Rawls stipulates for reasonability squared. And "reasonable" there does not just signify a general willingness to face the facts and hear the other side. That category, for Rawls, subsumes, as well, the proliberal inclinations conveyed by the "free and equal" formula. A constitution acceptable to all reasonable citizens accordingly will chime with a cluster of liberal-leaning intuitions about human individuality, dignity,

[23] I draw this condensed account of the Rawlsian view of constitutionalism's place in a democracy from passages spread throughout MICHELMAN, *supra* note 22. I will make occasional more specific references to pertinent passages in that book or in works of Rawls, but will not always be able to do so.

[24] RAWLS, *supra* note 5, at 217. Rawls calls that "the problem of political liberalism." *See id.* at xx; Michelman, *supra* note 22, at 20–21.

[25] *See* Michelman, *supra* note 22, at 21–22, 34–36.

[26] RAWLS, *supra* note 5, at 137, 217.

[27] *Id.* at 217.

agency, and, in those respects, equality.[28] But it will do so only vaguely, abstractly, because if the specifications get too thick, they will not pass the test of acceptability to all reasonable citizens.

Rawlsian Proceduralism

As with Tushnet, a lot of work is being done here by a posited fact of reasonable disagreement over applications to concrete policy choices of high-level political values like civic freedom and equality. Rawls takes the position, though, in a direction that Tushnet perhaps does not, or anyway not as far as Rawls does.

That direction is that of *the procedural*.[29] The idea of the procedural, as we use it here, is one of resort to a previously accepted platform of background or framework terms for getting past disagreements over matters on the collective table that all concerned share a wish to have resolved one way or another. In the Rawlsian principle of legitimacy, a country's constitution serves as a table of terms for a procedural response to the special challenge of democratic political justification in the pluralized conditions of a modern free society. That table is our recourse for a deflection of divisive questions of substance (does this law or policy merit the respect or rather the contempt of a right-thinking person?), to a different question (is this law or policy constitutionally kosher?) for which the answer is to be publicly apparent, or at any rate is to be ascertainable by means that could be less open to divisive dispute than are the deflected concrete-policy disputes.

To say that a constitution is to serve, as envisaged by Rawls, as a platform for the procedural justification of majoritarian political coercion among persons reciprocally recognized as free and equal, is not to say that the constraints of a constitution so serving are addressed only to matters we would class as procedural (voting; representation; allocation of powers), or that its guarantees respecting basic rights and liberties extend only to those that a theorist such as Jeremy Waldron might see as intrinsic for a democracy "in good working order."[30] In the conception of Rawls, a constitution acceptable on its face to reasonable and rational, free and equal citizens must include principles of due and high regard for individual conscience, dignity, security, and equality, touching on those concerns in ways not obviously restricted to the conduct of politics.[31] Think freedom of religious exercise. Think

[28] *See* Michelman, *supra* note 22, at 24–25, 92–95.

[29] For the procedural character of Rawls' proposition on the point of constitutionalism for a democracy, *see id.* at 25–28.

[30] Jeremy Waldron, *The Core of the Case Against Judicial Review*, 115 Yale L.J. 1346, 1360 (2006) (stipulating for "a democracy in good working order"). *Compare* Tushnet, *supra* note 8, at 8 (remarking that among the topics that constitutionalism as such might withdraw from unhindered ordinary politics are "core structures of decision-making and fundamental rights essential to the creation and maintenance of mainstream understandings of democracy").

[31] In politics, writes Rawls, unlike in pure gambling, the acceptability and legitimacy of the procedure depend "on the justice of its likely outcome, or on substantive justice," and "any liberal view" must in

freedom of choice of a marital or sexual or other intimate partner, or of which relatives to include as members of your residential family, or of the use of birth control. Think freedom from the degradations and burdens imposed by legally authorized segregation or exclusion by race or sex in public facilities and services. I doubt we should suppose Mark Tushnet's thin constitution to be totally void of all such concerns except insofar as he might tie them to the exercise of fair and deliberate majority rule.

Implications for Judicial Review

The proceduralizing ambition of the Rawlsian principle of legitimacy carries implications for the question of judicial constitutional review. The abstraction of the terms of constraint in a constitution cast for wide acceptability across a modern free society will frequently, in such a society, leave open to fair dispute questions of the compatibility with those terms of contentious concrete policy choices. A constitution cast in such terms thus cannot work *procedurally* as a response to the problem of reasonable political disagreement, without also including agreement on an institutional set up to resolve such applicative disputes in a manner that will count, for the time being, as authoritative for the country's conduct of its politics. Now that set up, evidently thinks Rawls, cannot just be one of referral of these constitution-applicative issues to resolution by the same majoritarian forums and processes in which the issues arise. It must be distinct from those forums, and it must be accorded some measure of decisive authority over them, at least for the immediate and shorter term (meaning until longer-term social, political, and legal processes might bring about a change in the separated tribunal's own resolutions of applied constitutional meanings).[32]

Rawls finds no logical necessity that the distinct institutional set up be a supreme court or any court or courts of law. It could be a distinctly more ambient and popular sort of process as long as that could operate to deliver timely resolutions in a manner transparent to citizens and trusted by them.[33] A supreme court might or might not have a participant role in such a process. If it did, and if the court happened over time to be granted or to gain a leading or superinfluential voice, that might be (as Rawls sometimes seems to suggest) simply a matter of path dependency, the court having become historically entrenched as trusted constitutional arbiter; or it might be because the habitus of legal discourse is found after all—*pace*

that way and to that extent "be substantive." John Rawls, *Political Liberalism: Reply to Habermas*, 92 J. Phil. 132, 170 (1995). *See* Michelman, *supra* note 22, at 27–28.

[32] *See* Michelman, *supra* note 22, at 41–44 (shorter run), 78–82 (longer run).

[33] *See id.* at 44.

CLS—to have some worthwhile virtues for a process of continued development and modulation, over transgenerational time, of the cluster of constitutional meanings on which political stability and legitimacy are believed to depend.[34]

We come then to a final, and crucial, point I need to establish about the Rawlsian-proceduralist conception of judicial review. A constitutional or supreme court's own bottom-line best answer to the constitutional compatibility of some or other questioned concrete policy may differ from the answer implicit in the acts of a democratic legislative body enacting that policy into law. That difference may arise within the space—and that space may be quite wide—of reasonable disagreement, among citizens judging reasonably, over the meanings or applications of abstract constitutional norms.[35] A Rawlsian reviewing court's authority to issue interdicts against a democratic lawmaker's policy choice should accordingly be limited to instances of the court's finding that choice *to lie outside the bounds of that space of reasonable disagreement* over constitutional meanings and applications. It is only in the case of such a judicial finding that the court is authorized to exercise a decisive power of disallowance.

So, at any rate, I have found to be the message from John Rawls.[36] Whether it quite brings Rawls' stance on judicial constitutional review in a democracy into unison with Tushnet's is a question to which I now turn.

The Matter of Weak-form Judicial Review

John Rawls, as I read him, would confine judicial constitutional oversight to ruling on the outer bounds of reasonable disagreement over constitutional meanings and applications. That may bring to mind the conception of "weak-form" judicial review for which Mark Tushnet has stood among our leading expositors.[37] Should our association of Mark with weak-form review stop there, as a negative stance against strong-form review? Or do we take Mark also to be engaged in explaining how judicial review (in the weak form) might work as a positively *preferred* (not just relatively tolerable) feature of institutional design for a country he would regard as democratically well ordered? The more we find Mark's stance to be one of more or less qualified positive support, the stronger will be the correspondence we find between his view and that of Rawls.

[34] *See id.* at 84–87 (offering a Rawlsian conception of the judicial role in a longer-term process of modulation in constitutional meanings and application).

[35] I note here that public recognition of some interest in personal liberty, dignity, or equality as "constitutional" in import does not signify, for either Rawls or Tushnet, that the interest may not, by constitutional prescript, be limited or encumbered by a sufficiently conscientious judgment of override by conflicting constitutional or comparably weighty concerns. On Rawls, *see* Michelman, *supra* note 22, at 53–54, 166–67 & 191.

[36] *See* Michelman, *supra* note 22, at 166–71.

[37] *See, e.g.*, TUSHNET, *supra* note 11.

In Mark's classification, a weak-form court is one that accepts (and comports itself accordingly) that its pronouncements on matters constitutional are in normal course rejectable in the immediate term by other constituted political agencies up to and including whole electorates—the court's voice to that extent becoming one more or less respected voice among others. A court's posture is oppositely "strong-form" insofar as the court counts on the country to treat its adjudicative pronouncements on constitutionality as fixtures thenceforward in the country's established constitutionalist practice, intrasystemically binding as such on other political agents and revisable only by formal constitutional amendment or subsequent reversal by that court.[38]

A "time-continuum" thus is what differentiates weak-form from strong-form review. "Strong-form systems allow the political branches to revise judicial interpretations in the longish run, weak-form ones in the short run."[39] In other words, when the court and the political branches disagree over the compatibility of some policy or statute with constitutional principles and directives, it is not *ever*, in a weak-form practice, the court that has the last and decisive word. That is of course quite in line with Mark's case for a constitutionalism thinned out to make way for reasonable disagreement and democratic self-government. "Weak-form systems of judicial review," he writes, "hold out the promise of reducing the tension between judicial review and democratic self-governance, while acknowledging that constitutionalism requires that there be some limits on self-governance."[40]

Mark's interest in weak-form review may thus seem quite straightforwardly suggestive of pro constitutionalist leanings on his part. (Otherwise, why not get rid of the tension by just tossing aside constitutionalism?) A practice of weak-form (excluding or sharply limiting strong-form) judicial review might arise in a country informally, by unplanned accident or evolution, perhaps in consequence of political struggle. The practice also might arise as a duly deliberated formal choice of institutional design. And a positive choice, then, for an institution of constitutional review, weak-form or strong-form, would seem to signal rejection of what we might call an ultimate populist conception of demotic political power completely non-answerable—I mean as a political-cultural matter, never mind a legal-institutional one—to any so-called constitution (or one that is not "thin" to the point of sheer vapidity).

In order, in Mark Tushnet's case, to nail down such an inference to a proconstitutionalist stance from an interest in weak-form judicial constitutional review, we would have to consider three explanations for that interest on his part that do not insinuate any positive embrace by him of constitutionalism as a

[38] *See id.* at 22–23. By "pronouncements," here, we may understand not just a court's punctual thumbs-up or thumbs-down on this or that law's constitutionality but the court's full *ratio decidendi*—say, the steps in its reasoning that would be taken as binding on lower courts in the system.

[39] *Id.* at 34.

[40] TUSHNET, *supra* note 11, at 23.

preferred element in the politics of a country he would like to live in. First, a comparative constitutional investigator could develop for classificatory purposes an institutional design category of weak-form judicial review, neither asserting nor insinuating any evaluative stance toward what is thus categorized and described. Second, a democracy-minded observer and theorist might judge that weak-form constitutional review is anyway less obnoxious to democracy than strong-form is. They might accordingly prefer it to strong-form in settings where judicial constitutional review in some form is for the time being irretrievably anchored—even if, ideally, they would prefer a total absence of constitution talk from the conduct of their country's politics. Third, a democracy-above-all sort of observer could positively favor weak-form review on the ground that this practice might improve the procedural function of democracy and anyway cannot really impair it. Review by weak-form courts, the thought would run, can call attention to legislative "blind spots" or "burdens of inertia"[41] or to other failures of deliberation up to the mark of a democracy in good working order—the court's interventions thus creating useful junctures for reconsideration while not usurping the authority of democracy itself to decide the conditions of its own endurance as such. All those reasons for interest in weak-form review are in fact visible on the face of Tushnet's work on this topic.

They do not, however, exclude, as an additional (and the maybe also a primary) reason for Mark's pursuit of this topic a wish finally to establish the cohesion of a positive attachment to constitutionalism—a constitutionalism complete, I mean, with protoliberal inflections—with a positive attachment to genuinely popular government. In the title of Mark's most recently circulated address to the topic—"For Constitutionalism"[42]—we find what we might take as a sign of a receptivity (at least) on Mark's part to such an upshot. But it is not entirely clear. "We *could* be for constitutionalism," that paper concludes (meaning constitutionalism-as-such, detached from juridification, authoritative judicial oversight, and a thick enumeration of rights).[43] As advocates for constitutionalism (in case we are) we could say that "constitutionalism is a conversation among equals, nothing more."[44]

That leaves still up in the air whether Mark can be counted as himself a positive subscriber to constitutionalism complete with protoliberal inflections. For further evidence there, we can look to his book-length work (with Bugarič) on the relation of constitutionalism to contemporary populism. In the face of widespread concern and belief that this populism poses, as such, a lethal threat to liberal democracy (and merits resistance on that ground), Tushnet and Bugarič maintain that while that is no doubt true of some manifestations of populist ascendancy we see around the world, it is not true of populism as such or of a populism toward which they

[41] Rosalind Dixon, *The Core Case for Weak-Form Judicial Review*, 38 Cardozo L. Rev. 2193, 2208–10 (2017).
[42] *See* Tushnet, *supra* note 8.
[43] *Id.* at 41 (emphasis supplied).
[44] *Id.* (emphasis supplied).

would be sympathetically disposed. The argument, in short, is that you can be simultaneously sympathetically disposed toward liberal-tinctured thin constitutionalism and toward a practice of government genuinely and wholly by the people acting by majoritarian institutional forms. Over and over, the book's argument for tolerance toward populism is quite specifically directed to a liberal-minded readership.[45] It is not immediately evident what might motivate such an effort by authors not themselves disposed toward broadly speaking liberal government, associating their idea of constitutionalism with that proliberal disposition.[46]

Rapprochement

John Rawls would concede to a supreme court a modicum of shorter-run decisive authority over constitutional applications. To be sure, that authority would be restricted to setting an outer bound to the space of reasonability in resolving those applications, with all choices within that space to be left to ordinary democratic politics. In Mark Tushnet's work we find a distinct aversion to even that much concession away from majoritarian democratic rule—thus, a push toward limiting the court's voice to an interlocutory or commendatory mode. Does that gap of views signal some deeper-lying difference in their respective conceptions of the point of constitutionalism in and for a democracy?

A ground for Rawls' stance is clear enough in his work. He has in view a constitution whose terms are sufficiently abstract to allow it, in conditions of reasonable pluralism, to be found acceptable by all reasonable and rational citizens. But then such terms will themselves, in such conditions, become topics of disagreement at the point of application to disputable concrete policies. In order, then, to serve procedurally as a platform for the justification of coercion of dissenters from majoritarian legislation, the constitution will have to encompass agreement on some institutional setup to resolve for the country, in the immediate or shorter run, those predictable disagreements over applied constitutional meanings and applications. A supreme or constitutional court might reasonably be chosen as that setup. And while a due regard for the claim in a democracy to popular self-rule should confine a reviewing court's authority to decision of whether a law or policy issuing

[45] *See, e.g.*, Tushnet & Bugarič, *supra* note 9, at 1 (pointing out the wide space for reasonable disagreement over applications of freedom of expression among citizens all appealing to values of "individual autonomy, democratic self-governance, and the like"), 5 (asking readers to allow for "varieties" of "democracy and liberal constitutionalism"), 15 (setting up as "important values," possibly to "compete with" freedom of expression, "social stability, personal privacy, [and] civic equality"), 22–23 (supposing as an aim for constitutionalism the protection of "individual liberty" as "a good thing for people to have . . . because it lets people choose the kind of life they want to live, free from domination"), 209–10, 214–15 (bespeaking a tolerant appreciation for country-by-country variations in what will work best as institutional and cultural "guardrails" for "liberal constitutionalism").

[46] *Id.* at 4 ("our friends are under attack").

from democratic politics lies within or beyond the bounds of any reasonable constitutional construction, reservation to a court of *just that much* decisive authority is requisite to the proceduralizing ambition of the Rawlsian constitutional conception.

From Tushnet's apparent aversion to even such a limited concession of decisive judicial authority, one could infer that his attribution of a point to constitutionalism in a democracy rests on some premise other than the Rawlsian one of need for a procedural platform of justification for majoritarian political coercion in a democracy.[47] And what, then, might that be? It might be simply a presupposition on Mark's part that the democracy in view should be in some distinct (if also broad and loose) way or sense a liberal democracy. The presupposition could, but need not, flow from some heavily theorized conception of democracy as always, in essence, a derivation from some broadly speaking liberal or protoliberal intuitions of human individuality, dignity, agency, and (in those respects) equality; or it could more simply be a felt preference, historically or culturally conditioned as it might be, for a democracy compatible with such intuitions: constitutionalism, then, as "the condensate of the citizenry's varying ways of understanding that each individual citizen is part of the common enterprise of self-government under the constitution."[48] Either way, for a Tushnet so disposed, the question of an allowance for decisive judicial authority would come down to one of empirical political sociology for the country at hand, about "the relative size of risks to rights and equality" with and without a judicial or other overseer in place to rope in the people from going over the edge.[49]

Should such be the case with Mark Tushnet, then a rapprochement with Rawls would be in the offing. By Rawlsian lights, political justification rides on procedures of appeal to a constitution, but specifically and only to a constitution (should there be one in force) whose essentials fall in line with principles and ideals reasonably held by reasonable citizens. Such ideals and principles already, for Rawls, incorporate those protoliberal intuitions I mentioned, of human individuality and so on.[50] A public practice of justification by appeal to them mirrors back to us what we already have, in the case that we do have it. We know it when we see it.

[47] But not necessarily. Tushnet recently has suggested how reduction of a reviewing court's voice to one of interlocutory recommendation only, on matters of constitutional compliance, could still be compatible with a Rawlsian justificatory-procedural function for a country's constitution. *See* Mark Tushnet, *Constitution as Recommendation*, 50 PHIL. & SOC. CRITICISM 1023 (2024).

[48] Tushnet, *supra* note 8, at 41.

[49] *Id.* at 39–40. *Compare* TUSHNET, *supra* note 11, at 228 (concluding that a choice for weak-form over strong-form review reflects not only a recognition of the fact of frequent reasonable disagreement over applications of abstract constitutional principles, but a weighing of "the imperfections of both unchecked political processes and unchecked judicial power in arriving at the best specifications of what constitutional provisions mean").

[50] *See* Michelman, *supra* note 22, at 24–25, 92–95.

9

The Challenge to Liberal Constitutionalism

Pratap Bhanu Mehta

Introduction

The dominant paradigm of liberal constitutionalism has a basic set of ingredients: the entrenchment of individual rights to protect the basic freedom of individuals; the affirmation of at least the formal political equality of all citizens; the creation of institutional checks and balances; formally defined limitations on the power of government; and the preservation of institutions and practices that allow citizens to exercise political agency and engage in practices of political justification. This paradigm of liberal constitutionalism has often been challenged from many directions. Mark Tushnet has been prescient in anticipating these challenges and thinking about their analytical foundations. Most recently, Tushnet (with his co-author Bojan Bugarič) has written powerfully about the populist challenges to liberal constitutionalism, urging us, rightly, to distinguish between "Right" populism that is exclusionary and a possible "Left" populism whose aim is to deepen forms of self-government and possibly secure more economic justice.[1] Both populisms have some similarities: both are attacks on the power of entrenched elites; both can have a certain kind of impatience for existing institutions and forms of adjudication, where these serve to contain rather than serve the needs of the people; and both can make appeals to the authority of the people, where the "people" are identified independently of the processes through which they are constituted or their will is expressed.

It seems quite right to distinguish between different forms of populism based on their substantive aims. Some populists aim at deepening democracy whereas others are more authoritarian. But there is one feature of populism that often makes it a threat to liberal democracy. This involves an appeal to the idea of the "people" in a very specific way. Often the invocation of the "people" is rhetorical. But the desire to enact it can be a threat to every element of liberal constitutionalism outlined above. The claim that there is a people that can speak through a singular will, or that popular sovereignty is undivided, can lead to a suspicion of checks and balances. These are seen, not as limitations on power, but as ruses to

[1] Mark Tushnet & Bojan Bugarič, Power to the People: Constitutionalism in the Age of Populism (2021).

Pratap Bhanu Mehta, *The Challenge to Liberal Constitutionalism* In: *Redefining Comparative Constitutional Law.* Edited by: Vicki C. Jackson and Madhav Khosla, Oxford University Press. © Pratap Bhanu Mehta 2025.
DOI: 10.1093/9780191996344.003.0009

divide and thwart the will of the people.[2] It can sometimes put pressure on the protection of individual rights. Individuals seen as dissenting from popular will come to be understood as, in some ways, the enemy of the people. They are not merely asserting their individual rights to free expression; they are standing in the way of popular will. While the energies of populism can reflect the agency of citizens, in that it is created by their active participation, it can also thwart that energy by "predeciding" what the people stand for, before debate has taken place. Often populist leaders claim to personify what the people allegedly stand for, and refuse to engage in practices of political justification.

This chapter examines two different ways in which populisms that arise through the democratic process try to re-enact the myth of the unified people, and in doing so convert political disagreement into a more existential threat to the political order. I will discuss two ways in which this can happen. The first has to do with the way in which democratic proceduralism mobilizes what I call the myth of consent. A legitimate political system relies on the thought that it is based on widespread consent of the people. In part we protect their right to dissent, because it is only the possibility of withholding consent that assures us that when consent is given, it is in fact genuine. But under the pressure of populism, dissent is not seen as a precondition for ascertaining genuine consent, but as a threat to the basic legitimacy of the state.

The idea of the people is invoked in a second, further way—through an appeal to nationalism. The turn to nationalism also serves the same function. It is a way of securing the unity of the people that also cannot explain challenges to its own unity. We often find in many "right-wing" populist movements a tendency to suppress dissent or curtail individual rights, in the name of the people. Sometimes this is motivated by an impulse to authoritarianism. But in this chapter, I want to explore a more disquieting possibility. All liberal democracies are premised on the thought that differences of opinion and points of view are not only to be welcomed and cherished. But they also welcome the thought that forms of political action—open dissent, protest, assembly, if done within the bounds of law—can invigorate public argument and democracy. It is a feature of many "right-wing" populisms, however, that it regards "dissent" from the will of the people not just as disagreement, but as a way of subverting their authority. It in a sense converts disagreement into a *threat*, and places citizens who disagree as potentially subversive of the state. It is in this sense that populism can convert opposition into enemies, rather than treating them merely as citizens who disagree. One manifestation of this is the fact that in many legal jurisdictions protest is increasingly criminalized, or at least regulated heavily. But the disquieting thought is that the source of unease

[2] The very checks and balances that are designed to preserve democracy can be seen in some circumstances as thwarting legitimate majorities. For a recent account of this, *see* Steven Levitsky & Daniel Ziblatt, Tyranny of the Minority (2023).

in democracies about dissent stems from a logic inherent in democratic nationalism itself.

Dissent and the Myth of Consent

In a democracy, dissent is valued—it is the dissent of citizens that deepens the practices of public justification in a democracy. Dissent itself is invigorating for a democracy. Many would go one step further and argue that there is a *right* to dissent; that there is something particularly important about human dignity that such a right captures. And yet, while we emphasize the importance of dissent, actual dissent in any political order always invokes anxiety. There is a familiar anxiety—a self-serving anxiety of holders of power—that dissent will displace them, attenuate their power, or diminish that power. Power always resents and fears dissent. Today's dissenters may, in turn, also fear other dissenters. It is often true of dissenting groups that they fear internal dissent, or that they, in a sense, turn out to be those people who clamp down on dissent when they themselves come into power. So, there is a kind of perpetual anxiety around dissent. It is a self-serving, if understandable, anxiety. Dissent is seen as altering the structures of power. At least those who crush dissent take it seriously. They recognize its subversive potential. This is unlike what is sometimes found in cases defending dissent. These accounts emphasize its communicative or expressive value. But the form of change it brings about does not really challenge the basic institutional structure of society.[3]

There is, however, a different kind of worry about dissent. To dissent is to act against something. George Eliot was right when in *Felix Holt* she observed that "the right to rebellion is the right to seek a higher rule, and not to wander in mere lawlessness."[4] Without speaking in the name of a higher rule, without being grounded in moral judgment, dissent is simply the disposition to subvert, where the means become the ends. In this sense, the Gandhian idea of dissent, which is grounded in *satyagraha*—a rebellion grounded in truth—may capture something truer than the mere word dissent does. Like Eliot's claim, it involves the idea that the claims being advanced by the dissenters are potentially subject to the logic of public justification. They are being done in the name of a common good in a way that can be justified to fellow citizens. Even civil disobedience that is legitimate and not mere rebellion has to appeal to common standards of justice that citizens share.[5]

This is the basis on which established institutions can express skepticism about dissent. Dissenters are seen as not merely those who disagree but as actors crossing

[3] For a discussion of issues pertaining to dissent in a democracy, *see* TIMOTHY ZICK, MANAGED DISSENT: THE LAW OF PUBLIC PROTEST (2023).

[4] GEORGE ELIOT, FELIX HOLT: THE RADICAL 173 (1866).

[5] *See* JOHN RAWLS, A THEORY OF JUSTICE 320 (1971).

the bounds of legitimate political action. The Supreme Court of India's recent decision on the protests at "Shaheen Bagh," which followed a new citizenship law, reveals this skepticism:

> India, as we know it today, traces its foundation back to when the seeds of protest during our freedom struggle were sown deep, to eventually flower into a democracy. What must be kept in mind, however, is that the erstwhile mode and manner of dissent against colonial rule cannot be equated with dissent in a self-ruled democracy.[6]

There are forms of dissent that might be appropriate to colonial rule, or maybe in authoritarian states, but these forms of dissent are not appropriate in self-ruled democracy. In fact, you can extend the point further: Dissent, in the form that was being enacted in Shaheen Bagh, might have been a mode of activity more suitable to a colonial, authoritarian regime than to a democracy.

Why is this claim important? There is something intuitively appealing about the idea that, as citizens enjoy freedom of expression in a democracy, words and deliberation are the currency through which they should articulate their disagreement. If words do indeed work, then perhaps there would be no need for protest. Moreover, in a democracy we can supposedly cashier the rulers for misconduct by voting them out of office during the next election. One can speak as one wants and one can vote as one wants. The bounds of legitimate activity are, in a sense, governed or enabled by these modes of expression. Anything outside these institutional channels is potentially subversive. Moreover, one might ask, can the dissenter claim a certain kind of representative status?

The problem with the dissenter in a democracy, one might say, is that they claim unilateralism. The dissenter sets themselves up as a final judge and arbiter against public institutions, and against settled forms of representation and authorization. The dissenters' seeming unilateralism—their sovereign pronouncement over the sovereign, as it were—seems to be part of the problem. Indeed, political equality demands that we forgo, as Hobbes highlighted, the right to unilateral judgment. If one can decide by oneself what is correct then one is not granting another equal political standing. It seems to be this kind of paradox that the Supreme Court of India may have been hinting at when it suggested that certain forms of protest were not permissible in a democracy. The thought is: In a perfectly functioning democracy, all relevant moral considerations have been taken into the account. In such a case, where the respect due to all persons has been granted, why would one need dissent?

[6] Amit Sahni (Shaheen Bagh, In Re) v. Commissioner of Police (2020) 10 SCC 439, 446.

One might be tempted to say that that is precisely the point. One dissents precisely because our structures of democracy are flawed, because representative processes are not responsive, and because the vulnerable and marginalized are poorly protected. One may even assert that, although the Supreme Court calls on us to abide by our civic obligations, it does not ask whether these civic obligations are binding on people who do not have a fair share in the scheme of cooperation. If the basic scheme of social cooperation does not itself respect the equality of persons, why should the onus of cooperating on civic obligations fall on those protesting? Why should the burden of abiding by these civic obligations fall only on them in the absence of a framework that grants them minimal standing and reciprocity? Why are courts and legislatures so keen to remind us of our duties only when there is a protest? Does not protest serve as an epistemic function of drawing attention to the problems that might otherwise go unnoticed in a democracy?

This defense of dissent has empirical and descriptive support given the reality of our public institutions. But it is not an easy answer for any established institution to accept. It is hard for any settled democratic process to concede its potential illegitimacy in this way; it is hard for a supreme court to concede that there might be areas within a nation where the rule of law does not prevail. For public institutions, to admit the imperfection of one's political order is often viewed as a way to delegitimize it. To grant protest legitimacy is to do just that.

There is a further conceptual challenge. If one protests before all other formal means of addressing the problem have been exhausted—means such as approaching one's legislator, petitioning the judiciary, seeking bureaucratic review, and so forth—one might ask why these settled means to address disagreement have not been used. One is not even trying to resolve disputes through the mechanisms that exist within the system. Yet, alternatively, if one chooses to protest after all such means have been used, and used in vain, then one is effectively engaging in unilateralism. One is not accepting the authority of the means with which one has engaged. The paradox is plain: to prematurely dissent is to reject the mechanisms provided by democracy; to dissent after democracy has pronounced its verdict is to claim a sort of sovereign status. In either instance, the dissenter casts a shadow over the legitimacy of the state.

In standard analyses that underline the importance of pluralism, dissent is understood within the framework of toleration. But in political terms, dissent has a more specific meaning: it implies a withdrawal of consent. Indeed, the dissenter wants to be seen as refusing consent. When one says that a law is discriminatory—as the protestors were asserting in the case of India's citizenship law—it is not the same kind of disagreement that one has over standard government policy or any statute, say one that alters the tax rate. In protesting against a law that punishes people for who they are, one's dissent is performing a kind of refusal of assent to that law. Dissent, in this sense, always carries a taint of disobedience with it, and rightly so.

So, one way of thinking of dissent is that dissent is, literally speaking, the opposite of consent. One might say that dissent shares the same relationship to consent as heresy shares to faith. In principle, genuine faith requires the possibility that one might choose wrongly; that is what guarantees that faith is freely chosen. Similarly, the possibility of dissent is what makes consent genuine. But, in practice, just as a heretic is seen as an affront to faith, the dissenter becomes an affront to claims to consent. Just as the logic of faith cannot tolerate heresy, the logic of consent cannot tolerate dissent. The paradox in the case of democracy is that the more a government claims popular sovereignty as the basis of its own legitimacy, the more dissent is a conceptual threat. When a democracy mobilizes consent as a legitimizing principle, it struggles to accommodate dissent. When protestors enter the streets, when they occupy public spaces, when they hold large meetings, they are puncturing the myth of consent. In our increasingly mediatized environment, with the rise of social media and the like, this refusal of consent that protest represents can be played out spectacularly, and often in decontextualized ways. Ernest Renan once observed that a "nation's existence is . . . an everyday plebiscite."[7] The consent that underwrites legitimacy also has to be performed daily. But if this is true—if the enactment of consent requires a daily performance—then protest by its very nature punctures that performance. As in the case of terrorism, a ruling regime may lose the battle of legitimacy if protest is addressed post facto—once the crowds have gathered, once the television cameras have entered the stage, and once, as it were, the poetry of the protest has been written. What modern states have grasped is that to preserve the myth of their own legitimacy and consent, they have to ensure that protest is not a spectacular performance.

This attempt at preempting protest is also revealing in a further way. If we see cases involving protests, courts may well initially be rather supportive and may go to great lengths to emphasize the right to protest. But the moment that protests become more significant—the moment they begin to *matter*—courts also begin to become more skeptical of such protests. We notice this, for example, in case of the Occupy Wall Street protests in Zuccotti Park.[8] The irony is that the more rules there are that exist to preempt protest, the more the protestor is placed in the position of formally disobeying the law. And that is precisely what the state would like to demonstrate, for such a demonstration would show that the protestor is not motivated by Eliot's higher rule but merely by the refusal to consent. As Jackie Esmonde showed more than two decades ago, the weaponization of bail—the logic of discretion in bail hearings—is a powerful illustration of this.[9] What was noticeable in bail cases involving dissent, Esmonde showed, was not the kinds of considerations

[7] Ernest Renan, *What Is a Nation?*, *in* WHAT IS A NATION? AND OTHER POLITICAL WRITINGS 247, 261 (M.F.N. Giglioli trans. ed., 2018).

[8] Waller v City of New York, 2011 N.Y. Slip Op. 21412.

[9] Jackie Esmonde, *Bail, Global Justice, and the Limits of Dissent*, 41 OSGOODE HALL L.J. 232 (2003).

that one might expect—such as whether the person would interfere with the investigative process—but the underlying construction of the dissenter, whose crime is not to disagree with a particular law but to in fact challenge the legitimacy of the state. This construction of the dissenter is, in a way, like the situation of a person in the informal sector in a country such as India: they exist in a zone of illegality that is created by the discursive practices of the state itself. This line, the pressure to blur the line between the protestor and criminal, the dissenter and criminal, is, of course, buttressed greatly by nationalism—the one ideology that requires an undifferentiated myth of consent and unity.

Nationalism and Preserving the Nation

There is another specific challenge to liberal constitutionalism that remains undertheorized: the challenge of nationalism. In fact, in constitutionalism, as in liberal theory in general, there is a certain embarrassment about using the term "nationalism." The existence of a nation within which a constitution operates is something often taken for granted. The process of nation-building is a process that precedes the constitution; indeed, the "nation" is one of its enabling conditions. Because of liberal constitutionalism's reliance on the concept of the nation, the line between liberal constitutionalism and populism is in practice much thinner than we acknowledge.

We often take it for granted that the political communities within which constitutions operate are bounded. We assume that they have some minimal form of horizontal solidarity. The communities are bounded in the sense that they can set the terms of membership: whom to admit, whom to leave out, and on what terms such decisions can be made. It is also assumed that the successful operation of constitutionalism requires some kind of mutual commitment among citizens to one another. We need a shared commitment to justice, a sense of belonging, a willingness to sacrifice when the nation is under threat. And while a liberal constitution fragments government power to provide for checks and balances, it also appeals to the "people" as repositories of some kind of constituent power. It is for this reason that, from John Stuart Mill onwards, there has been skepticism as to whether liberal constitutionalism can indeed flourish in deeply divided societies where citizens do not have a minimum commitment to each other or do not display the right kind of solidarity.[10]

Sometimes a constitution itself can create this kind of solidarity by laying out the terms of a new social contract where all members of the community feel included. Indeed, one of the hallmarks of liberal constitutionalism has been just this: that

[10] *See* John Stuart Mill, Considerations on Representative Government (1853), ch. 16.

the constitution can itself create new sources of social solidarity. Liberal constitutionalism has relied on a couple of distinctions to make an uneasy accommodation with nationalism. The first is a distinction between civic and ethnic social solidarity. In ethnic solidarity, claims are grounded in the existence of a community that is considered in some senses to be "pre-political"—based on attributes such as religion, language, or ethnicity. The constitution is meant to give expression to the agency, identity, and emotional valence of this pre-political community. In the case of civic conceptions of solidarity, however, there is no pre-political community to which the constitution gives expression; our identity and allegiances are formed through the constitution.

These standard distinctions between civic and ethnic nationalism, however, do less work in sustaining liberal constitutionalism than is commonly assumed. Consider how in many "right-wing" populist challenges to liberal constitutionalism—for example, in the case of Hindu nationalism—there is a braiding of both elements.[11] In some respects, these movements draw their support from two, at first glance, incompatible sources. On the one hand, they appeal to an "ethnic" identity. On the other hand, they position themselves as a political movement that is completing the project of liberalism, rescuing it from its inconsistent applications. Whether or not this braiding of the two strands is ideologically consistent is less of an issue. But the fact that the ethnic dominance can get coded through the language of civic nationalism so easily and so consistently should give us pause. Strikingly, it is neither that difficult for "white supremacists" to formally speak in the language of civic constitutionalism nor for Hindu Nationalists to present themselves as agents of a true liberalism to replace minority-ism. In fact, it is also often the case that it is easier to speak the language of civic nationalism after the relatively unquestioned ethnic dominance of one group.

This easy alignment of civic and ethnic strands should give us pause. Often it turns out to be the case that civic nationalisms are some kind of ethnic nationalisms in disguise. Even if the distinction is genuine, however, one should not automatically assume that a civic nationalism has no deleterious consequences for liberal nationalism. This is the case, I would argue, for three reasons. First, the question of a bounded community always raises the question of membership—and it is in determining membership that the arbitrary power of the state is most clear. Second, as has often been pointed out, even civic nationalism puts out tests of solidarity: In order to have standing you have to express the right kind of solidarity. The fear of "antinationals" is common to both ethnic and civic nationalisms. If one does not conform to current understandings of what shared political values require, one can be as antinational as if one did not belong to the appropriate ethnic group. Indeed, modern populist movements are quite successful at converting political

[11] *See generally* Pratap Bhanu Mehta, *Hindu Nationalism: From Ethnic Identity to Authoritarian Repression*, 10 Stud. Indian Pol. 47 (2022).

disagreements into charges of sedition or antinationalism. This is visible across democracies as diverse as France and India.

Finally, civic nationalisms can be as impatient with institutional plurality as ethnic nationalisms. Although liberal constitutionalism is careful in its analyses of checks and balances in the context of government power, it is not always as clear about issues of representation; that is, about the effective power of different kinds of groups to shape the collective democratic discourse. It has, for the most part, preferred what Adam Pzeworski has called the veil of anonymity.[12] Formal political equality has meant drawing a veil of anonymity over the identities of citizens, whether in terms of class or ethnicity. This is actually quite an attractive ideal. The aim is to free individuals from the tyranny of compulsory identities, and to claim that who one is has no bearing on the opportunities we get to exercise. In practice, though, this anonymity can also be a cloak for the domination of particular groups, where disregarding identities is a cloak for not confronting questions about the distribution of power.

It actually turns out quite often that, on these three dimensions, ethnic and civic conceptions of nationalism can coincide. They can both use exclusionary and arbitrary criteria of membership; they can both convert criticism of dominant political understanding of the political order into a form of dangerous dissent; and they can both prefer a certain formal homogeneity that occludes questions about the distribution of power among groups. Both can be hostile to minority rights and empowerment. Of course, the argument is not that ethnic and civic nationalisms are identical in all respects. However, their "elective affinity" suggests that the project of liberal constitutionalism cannot necessarily be salvaged by recourse to civic nationalism. There is a deep incompatibility between liberal constitutionalism and nationalism. The challenges that "right-wing" populism, which is usually nationalist in orientation, pose to liberal constitutionalism are not unique to it. Exclusionary membership, justifications for executive power when "national" interests are at stake, hostility to political claims about power sharing, and suspicion of identity-based federalisms have all often been central to liberal constitutionalism as well.

How does nationalist populism impinge on constitutionalism? It is true, as Mark Tushnet and Bojan Bugarič have argued, that not all forms of populism are a threat to constitutionalism.[13] The populist critique of elite power can reinvigorate democracy in certain contexts. It can expose the narrow social bases of the corruption of ruling elites who actually exercise power within democracies. Nor is it true that a populist style of politics that is suspicious of existing institutions and of existing checks and balances is necessarily antidemocratic. It often seeks to advance the claim that these institutions and these checks and balances are, in their current

[12] Adam Przeworski, Democracy and the Limits of Self-Government 67 (2010).
[13] Tushnet & Bugarič, *supra* note 1.

form, nothing but ruses to entrench the power of small elites or prevent legitimate redistribution of economic power.

Populism becomes a threat to democracy when it seeks to redefine the very terms of membership in a political community. Almost all constitutions do not just delineate rights and apportion authority between different branches of government; they are also instruments of creating national identities in a variety of ways. At the most basic level, most constitutions operate with a conception of citizenship: who can be a member of a particular community, and to whom this privilege can potentially be extended. Citizenship can take a variety of forms. Principally, there have been three forms of citizenship. The first is a territorial conception of citizenship, where, subject to certain conditions, all those born into a territory are considered citizens. The second is forms of citizenship that depend on membership in a cultural, linguistic, or religious group (*Kulturnation*). The third is a form of citizenship that overlaps with the second, but is in theory distinct. This is a form of citizenship based on descent, tropes of blood and ancestry, and the historical continuation of a community of descent into the present and future (*Volksnation*). In principle, the first form of citizenship is the most compatible with liberal values. It does not regard a particular culture or identity as being a prerequisite for citizenship.[14] However, all constitutions make provisions for defining membership in the political community and the kinds of political allegiances expected of citizens.

But the challenge for liberal constitutionalism is as follows. Liberalism has a well-articulated theory of citizens' rights. It does not, and cannot, have a well-articulated theory of political membership. There are, at an elementary level, broadly two theories of political membership. The first, as in the case of *Kultur* and *Volksnation*, is based on some kind of ascriptive characteristic that gives the community its identity. This involves elevating "cultural attributes" or accidents of "descent" to be a normative ground for membership. The other relies on the much broader rights of a political community to set the terms of its own membership. If a political community is sovereign, it has a right to take decisions on whom to exclude or include from membership. This is, in essence, the Rawlsian framework.[15] This is the basis for almost all exclusions for immigration. Even in cases where an immigrant claims that they have all the citizenship qualities and virtues for being the member of a particular society, that society nevertheless has the right to exclude them.

What is striking is that neither of these arguments are specifically liberal arguments. In general, there is no *liberal* answer to the question of membership. Each of the two answers relies on what one might think of as "accidents." There is either membership in an already existing political community, or some ascriptive

[14] *See generally* Nira Yuval-Davis, *Gender and Nation*, *in* WOMEN, ETHNICITY AND NATIONALISM: THE POLITICS OF TRANSITION 23–35 (Rick Wilford & Robert L. Miller eds., 1998).

[15] *See* JOHN RAWLS, THE LAW OF PEOPLES 9 (1993).

characteristic, or, in the case of those given citizenship for economic reasons, an instrumental characteristic that happens to be useful. They are accidents in that they are partial, and from a normative point of view arbitrary. Indeed, it is hard to imagine a bounded community that, to some extent, does not define itself through the embrace of these arbitrary characteristics. Even for the most liberal of societies, a consistent, principled approach to immigration has proved to be elusive.

Typically, assertions of nationalist populism seek to narrow the terms of membership by restricting immigration, a phenomenon witnessed during both the Trump presidency and the Brexit episode. In some cases, populist nationalisms have gone a step further. Some states have created, or are trying to create, a system of what one might term *constitutional national privilege*—the conscious privileging of members of an ethnically defined community over others. Historically, such arrangements were quite common—for instance, in the aftermath of the breakup of Yugoslavia. Recently India enacted a Citizenship Amendment Act that does two things: it moves India more toward a *Volksnation* conception of the nation, and it also subtly enshrines the view that Muslim refugees would be less eligible for a path toward naturalization than other refugees. At one level, such laws are blatantly discriminatory and violate even the most basic norms of equality. They are also, often, a recipe for conflict, since they breed resentment. Yet in other ways, these laws simply replicate different forms of citizenship that have been legitimized and accepted in many different countries. Hindu nationalists would argue, for example, that there is, in principle, nothing illegitimate about ethnic privilege in citizenship pathways: a number of countries ranging from Israel to Germany allow for such privileges. The problem for liberal constitutionalism is that it is difficult normatively to delegitimize such laws without normatively delegitimizing the principle on which such laws are based.

In the context of nationalism, another feature of populism relates to legitimate opposition. Part of the tension over the will of the "people" can be traced to a republican suspicion of representation and pluralism. If the people are to have a unitary will, and if this will cannot be represented, then the only language available for understanding political difference is a language of betrayal, rather than the language of political differences. This was an argument made as early as the French Revolution. On this view, the Rousseauian claim that the sovereignty of the people can never be divided and that it cannot be represented leads to a conundrum. If the will of the people is unitary, what explains *differences*? Furthermore, if there are these differences, then how is one to ascertain the will of the people? One way out of this puzzle is to see who can effectively perform the will of the able—and, in doing so, represent the other side as *betraying* that will, rather than as merely carrying an alternative interpretation of it. In order for such performance to take place, one has to castigate as an enemy of the people anyone who represents an alternative viewpoint. In that sense, rhetorical invocations of "the people" understood as a unitary entity always run the risk of being antipluralist. Most modern democracies have given up on the Rousseauian idea of popular sovereignty in this sense: they are both pluralist and representative. But if popular sovereignty is no longer the principal source of populist bias against liberal principles, its close cousin is: namely, nationalism.

On such a view, a democracy can have divergent points of view and can be organized through representation. Most modern populisms are not against institutions of representation. What is important is that the people come together in a unitary well by benchmarking their national identity. We are Indian in virtue of "X" or American in virtue of "Y." Sometimes this kind of benchmarking of identity can be quite productive: it is a reminder to citizens of what gives their particular community a distinct identity. Yet one of the features of nationalism is that it is difficult to make room for its own contestation. The opposition is delegitimized or stigmatized, not because it has a different point of view on policy matters, but because its views are represented as *antinational.* It is not an accident that the rhetoric of national populists is often against forces that are seen to challenge their version of the national identity or their benchmarking of nationalism. As a political style, nationalist populism thrives by not so much finding enemies of the *people*, which is a nebulous term in any case, but enemies of the *nation*, which are often measured by certain taboos. These taboos can frequently take expression in the law as well. For example, a political doctrine articulated by a citizen that questions a country's territorial claims might be deemed not just as a disagreement, but an act of *sedition.* Much like Jacobin popular sovereignty, nationalism is an ideology that requires an undifferentiated myth of consent and unity. Nationalism almost inevitably ends up, formally or informally, in tension with or hostile to civil liberties. The *raison d'être*, the guiding principle, of nationalism is, in a sense, the myth of consent and unity. Any suggestion of difference is seen as an assault on that foundational myth.

Conclusion

In studying the challenge to liberal constitutionalism, we need to look at two sources that stem from the logic of democratic mobilization itself. The first is the myth of consent, the need of democracies to mobilize consent. As I argued earlier in the chapter, the question arises: Under what conditions are acts of protest seen, not just as natural disagreements, but instead as questioning the foundational legitimacy of the state? Where populists draw this line determines the degree of pluralism and freedom they are willing to tolerate.

The second form of democratic mobilization seeks to maintain national cohesion by regulating the terms of membership, the historical identity of a political community, or even special privileges for a community in matters of citizenship. A proper study of comparative constitutionalism requires us to focus therefore not just on limitations to government power, entrenchment of rights, and institutionalization of checks and balances, but on the ways in which consent is mobilized, whether in the management of dissent or in the resort to nationalism. In doing so, we may discover the uncomfortable truth that it is not only many "right-wing" populists who give our constitutional order an authoritarian turn, but also liberal constitutionalism's reliance on nationalism—without often naming it. Lawyers have often found great comfort in the *constitutional* element of *constitutional patriotism*.[16] But the real problem, as one wit once put it, is that even constitutional patriotism needs a *patrie*!

[16] For Tushnet's classic contribution on constitutional patriotism, *see* Mark Tushnet, *Forms of Judicial Review as Expressions of Constitutional Patriotism*, 22 L. & PHIL. 353 (2003). On constitutional patriotism, *see generally* JAN-WERNER MULLER, CONSTITUTIONAL PATRIOTISM (2008).

10
The Architecture of Constitutionalism

Peter Cane

Introduction

This chapter is about tripartite, functional separation of powers (SP). In mainstream Western constitutional theory, SP is the main conceptual tool used both to analyze and assess constitutional structures not only of individual constitutional systems but also, comparatively, of two or more systems. The discussion is mainly concerned with SP as a tool for analysis rather than evaluation, although analytical use of SP, of course, is not evaluatively neutral. About SP, Mark has written:

> The three-branch model of government served constitutionalists well for centuries. At some point in the twentieth century, however, its inconsistency with the actual form of modern governments became clear . . . The accumulation of experience suggests . . . that scholars of constitutional law could profitably devote attention to conceptualizing the actual institutions of the modern state in more complex ways, if only by proliferating the identification of its branches.[1]

By tracing the historical development of the SP concept, I aim to show, first, that SP was never a very sharp analytical tool, and, second, that it cannot be much sharpened by adding institutions and functions to the mix. A better strategy, I argue, is to start with the main problem addressed by SP—which I take to be excessive concentration of power, however measured—and analyze the many different solutions and combinations of solutions that have been devised within a framework that brings together two aspects of constitutional structure: allocation and distribution of power on the one hand, and its limitation and control on the other.

Separation of Powers in Early England

In the early 11th century, England was probably the most developed and organized polity in Europe. There, politics were practiced and government was conducted within a dense framework of constitutional rules and principles. At the apex of

[1] Mark Tushnet, Advanced Introduction to Comparative Constitutional Law 128 (2nd ed., 2018). Mark operationalized this suggestion in The New Fourth Branch (2021).

Peter Cane, *The Architecture of Constitutionalism* In: *Redefining Comparative Constitutional Law*. Edited by: Vicki C. Jackson and Madhav Khosla, Oxford University Press. © Peter Cane 2025. DOI: 10.1093/9780191996344.003.0010

government stood the monarch. After William of Normandy seized the English Crown by force, he proceeded to carve up the spoils (especially land) among his leading supporters while leaving untouched much of the established framework of politics and government. Over the course of two or three centuries, post-Conquest monarchs reinvented this system of government, developing sophisticated central and local bureaucracies, a bicameral Parliament and a network of central and local courts, all theoretically and, to a significant extent, practically under monarchical control. In this system, governmental power was highly concentrated. The ultimate, earthly locus of all governmental power was the monarch.

Despite this concentration of power, at least since the early 13th century, the English monarchy had been (in theory, anyway, and often in practice) "limited," not "absolute." In classical terms, "the one" (the monarch) shared power with two other social groups or "estates": "the few" (the land-owning barons and senior clerics, institutionally embodied in the House of Lords) and "the many" (institutionally embodied in the House of Commons), in a mixed polity. The "common people" did not share power directly but through a relatively small group of representatives who were chosen by the rich and the powerful and so were, themselves, typically rich and powerful. This was not "democracy" as we understand it today but, at best, meritocracy and, at worst, plutocratic oligarchy. The monarch had certain unilateral powers to make general laws (in the form of "decrees" or "ordinances") but also shared power to propose and enact general laws (in the form of "statutes") with the two Houses of Parliament acting in unison. By the 13th century, the monarch rarely acted personally as a judge and did not generally interfere with the day-to-day activities of the royal courts. So far as "administration" was concerned, the monarch and the royal bureaucracy focused primarily on foreign affairs and security, both internal and external. In the absence of a standing army, military power was shared between the monarch and the aristocracy, often with the financial support of the Lords and Commons in the form of general taxation. Domestic government—social and economic regulation and enforcement, welfare, and so on—was mainly conducted locally by and under the control of royal appointees. From the middle of the 14th century, the most important local government officials were the Justices of the Peace.

During the dynastic battles of the Wars of the Roses in the 15th century, the monarchy was governmentally weak, consumed with its own survival. The creation of the Tudor dynasty in 1485 ushered in a long century of increasing concentration of political and governmental power in the monarchy. The Tudors made strategic use of Parliament when it suited their state-building agenda, but sidelined it as much as they could. They established a new set of "conciliar" courts (most notably the Court of Star Chamber) over which the monarch exercised considerable control, and one of the main functions of which was supervision of government administration at both central and local levels. After Henry VIII's break from the Roman Church in the 1530s, English monarchs also became the ultimate earthly repositories of religious power, although ecclesiastical courts continued to compete for jurisdiction with royal courts until their abolition in 1641. Regulation of religious practice remained a significant tool of government policy well into the 19th century. This Tudor spree of monarchical power-acquisition culminated, in the early 17th century, in the increasingly strident claims of Divine Right by the Jacobean monarchs, against which Parliamentarians and some judges (notably Sir Edward Coke) reacted in various ways that led, eventually, to regicide, a civil war, and a brief flirtation with republicanism.

It was in this climate that the idea of separation of powers first emerged—as a suggested antidote to excessive concentration of power in the monarchy. Debate focused on the relationship between the monarch and Parliament. The biggest issues in dispute were the extent of royal, unilateral power to levy taxation and to dispense selectively from the operation of general laws and whether the monarch ruled by Divine Right or Right of Parliament. Royal judicial (law enforcement) activity was not a large bone of contention because, on a day-to-day basis, the common-law courts had operated independently of royal interference for centuries and because, in 1641, the controversial conciliar courts established by the Tudors had been abolished. This helps to explain why 17th-century separation-of-powers theory was two-branch (legislative and executive), not three-branch (legislative, executive, and judicial). The upheavals of the 17th century ended with the establishment of the bicameral Parliament as the undisputed monarch-maker and reduced formal royal participation in the legislative process to a power of veto, which has not been exercised since 1708. Henceforth, the prime function of the monarch was to be administration.

Montesquieu and Blackstone

In Montesquieu's (partly descriptive and partly normative) account, the English system of government in the early 18th century was one in which legislative power and executive power were allocated to different institutions; in which legislative power was shared among the three estates of the realm; and in which the formal roles of the monarchy and the aristocracy in the legislative process were less than that of the representatives of the common people. For Montesquieu, the significance of the separation of legislative power from executive power lay in (or, perhaps, depended upon) preservation of the sharing of legislative power among the estates of the realm. Put differently, in his scheme, separation of powers qualifies and strengthens mixed government and balanced constitutionalism, chiefly at the expense of the monarchy.

In early, two-branch theory, courts were typically modeled as machinery for execution of the law; any problem this created was easily addressed by guaranteeing the independence of the judges from monarchical control over the way the law was executed in individual cases. This approach, however, ignored the role of the common-law courts in controlling government and in making (common) law—the courts were the major source of general law until the 19th century. In Montesquieu's account, judicial power was exercised by lay juries that were summoned only as and when needed. There was no "standing judiciary"[2] and the judge was "only the mouth that pronounces the words of the law."[3] Like his predecessors, Montesquieu had no conception of the judges as belonging to one or other of the three estates. Judges were mere servants; and the significant issue was who controlled them, not which estate they belonged to. In this light, it is ironical that Montesquieu, who described the courts as "invisible and null,"[4] should be credited with conceptualizing the exercise of judicial power as a third function of government.

By contrast, Blackstone understood and, indeed, championed the common law and stressed the constitutional importance of judicial independence from external control.[5] It followed that courts be recognized as standing, professionalized institutions distinct from both the legislature and the executive—a "third" branch of government. However, the idea that courts exercised a distinct "judicial function" that should be "separated" from the other two government functions was less obvious. When Blackstone speaks of "judicial power" he apparently refers to the activities of separate judicial institutions, not a type of power clearly distinguishable from legislative and executive power.[6]

The American Founders

It is primarily to the American revolutionaries that we owe the full-blown, three-branch, normative version of separation of powers. The American Founders made at least four important contributions to constitutional practice and theory. First, they departed from the traditional understanding of constitutional balance. The polity was henceforth to be understood as consisting of the singular "People," not plural estates of monarch, nobles, and commons; and the focus of balancing was no longer to be legislative power. Instead, each of the three governmental powers was to be characteristically associated with a distinct institution (or "branch") of government and a balance of powers between those institutions was to be established by giving each a (minor) share of the powers of the others. Rather than separation and balance being seen as distinct principles of constitutional design,

2 M.J.C. Vile, Constitutionalism and the Separation of Powers 113 (2nd ed., 1998).
3 Montesquieu, The Spirit of the Laws 163 (A.M. Cohler, B.C. Miller & H.S. Stone eds., 1989).
4 *Id.* at 158, 160.
5 Vile, *supra* note 2, at 111–15.
6 *See, e.g.*, William Blackstone, Commentaries on the Laws of England, Book I: Rights of Persons 173 (259–60) (Wilfrid Prest & David Lemmings eds., 2016).

balance was now seen as an aspect of separation. In Montesquieu's account, separation preserved and promoted liberty by maintaining balance; for the Founders, preservation and promotion of liberty was the point of separation itself. As a result, ideas of balance between sociopolitical and socioeconomic groups and interests more or less disappeared from constitutional theory.[7] Separation of powers and balance of interests were amalgamated into a single principle under which three distinct branches of government, each exercising a characteristic function, would check-and-balance each other. The reimagining of sovereignty as residing in "the People" left no room in constitutional theory for the idea of civil society as a site of conflict between competing interests. Social conflict was governmentalized.

The second innovation of the American Founders was fundamentally to reconceptualize the "constitution": instead of referring, as in earlier times, to the nature or makeup of the polity,[8] it now referred to a document that codified constitutional law. This brought with it the idea of "constituent power" as a species distinct from legislative, executive, and judicial power. In the US scheme, constituent power resided in the People, and the People, via the Constitution, delegated the other three powers to the three branches of government respectively. Because the constitutional document was a code, it more or less removed from the system the idea of "inherent" governmental power, which is fundamental to English constitutionalism. In the US legal system, the theory is that all governmental power derives from the People through the Constitution. Constitutional codification transforms a predominantly "political" ("organic," "institutional," "material") constitution into a predominantly "legal" constitution. The Constitution and the politics it frames are pulled apart and put in different boxes.

The third contribution of the American Founders lies in their understanding of the place of courts and judicial power in the constitutional scheme of government. The 17th-century English theorists and Montesquieu had associated courts with the rule and execution of law; in their minds, courts had nothing to do with constitutional balance, concern with which focused on the legislature. The American Founders, by contrast, conceptualized courts as one component of a tripolar, institutional balance of power established by the Constitution. The logical conclusion, spelled out in 1803 in *Marbury v Madison*, was that federal courts had power to enforce the Constitution against both the executive and the legislature. The US Supreme Court was the first constitutional court. Its creation articulated and institutionalized one of the roles of courts that earlier theorists had ignored, namely control of the government.

[7] Perhaps the apotheosis of this development may be found in Jon Michaels' theory of "administrative separation of powers," which is analytically a form of power-sharing. *See* Jon D. Michaels, *An Enduring, Evolving Separation of Powers*, 115 Colum. L. Rev. 515 (2015); *On Constitutional Custodians and Regulatory Rivals: An Account of Old and New Separation of Powers* 91 N.Y.U. L. Rev. 227 (2016).

[8] *See e.g.* Montesquieu, *supra* note 3, at 21.

A fourth, fundamental innovation of the US Founders was federalism. US federalism rests on a division of governmental tasks (defined in terms of legislative competences) between the federal and subfederal polities rather than a division of governmental functions. Federalism is sometimes described in terms of "vertical," as opposed to "horizontal," separation of powers. In fact, however, federalism is better understood in terms of balance of power between local and national interests and constituencies than in terms of institutional/functional separation of powers. In general, modern theoretical analysis of governmental layering has been analytically impoverished by the integration of ideas of mixed government into separation-of-powers theory at the time of the American Founding.

The embedding of (three-branch) separation of powers in the design and text of the US Constitution transformed it from analytical and normative theory into binding legal principle. From the US, it found its way into the parliamentary world via the Australian Constitution (1901) and constitutional documents that the British bequeathed to newly independent colonies in the middle of the 20th century. In the later 20th century, the dominance of the US in the export trade in constitutional technology and in the globalizing world of the legal academy entrenched three-branch theory even more deeply into the mindset of constitutional lawyers and theorists worldwide. US academic leadership of the revival of comparative study of public law has also had a significant impact on the globalization of constitutional theory. Over that period, however, the worlds in which Montesquieu and the revolutionaries lived, and which they sought to reflect and mold in their writings, have largely disappeared. Indeed, in many parts of the world, the circumstances of the 18th-century politics of Great Britain and the USA have never existed. The significance of geopolitics and the passage of time has been magnified by the transformation of separation-of-powers theory from essentially ideological to primarily formal.

Separation of Powers in Britain since Montesquieu

In the course of the 18th and 19th centuries, the internal logic and dynamics of the English Revolutionary settlement were fatally undermined by two, related, political developments. One was the gradual transfer of control over the political executive (the "Cabinet") from the monarch to the House of Commons and development of the principle of "ministerial responsibility" to Parliament. As a result, much of the executive power that the 17th-century settlement had allocated to the monarch passed to "the Government"—the monarch's ministers—and the forum of answerability for its exercise from the monarch to Parliament. The other, related, political development was the gradual broadening of the franchise.

Together, these seismic events reversed the separation of executive from legislative power on which Montesquieu and the 17th-century theorists had pinned their hopes of liberty. Progress toward universal suffrage, coupled with a winner-takes-all, first-past-the-post electoral system, led to the formation of a very small number of extra-Parliamentary political groupings ("parties") that organized social interests and constituencies differently than the traditional pattern of monarch, nobles, and commons. Moreover, rather than sharing power, parties exercised power serially and exclusively. The legislative power of the aristocracy was significantly reduced by the Parliament Acts of 1911 and 1949. By the end of the 20th century, the dominance of the hereditary aristocracy in the House of Lords had come to an end; and effective control of its membership had passed from the monarch to the government. In the meantime, pluralization and fragmentation of civil society led to the institutionalization, if not the constitutionalization, of nonelectoral, interest-group politics.

The second half of the 20th century witnessed wave after wave of radical change in the design of the UK Constitution. Under the quasi-federal, mixed government arrangements of the European Union, legislative competences were shared between the UK Parliament and the EU's lawmaking organs. Legislative "sovereignty," too, was shared with the EU: in case of conflict, directly effective EU law would henceforth prevail over UK law, conferring on the courts an unprecedented power of judicial review of parliamentary legislation. Under German influence, EU quasi-federalism also divided power between the center and the localities along legislative/executive lines. Britain's exit from these arrangements in 2020 was foreshadowed by a referendum in 2016. This was the product of highly effective deployment of electoral power to exploit the perceived inability of party-based, first-past-the-post politics to reflect the plurality and diversity of socioeconomic and sociopolitical groupings and interests within civil society.

Much more could be said, but this is enough to make the basic point that (three-branch) separation-of-powers theory is of little use in understanding and analyzing the shifts and swings in the distribution of governmental power in the UK in the 200 years since Montesquieu first proposed the theory and the American Founders turned it to their own purposes.

Separation of Powers in the US since the Founding

What happened to the theory in the US after 1789? The Founders were republicans, intent on promoting the public interest, not "democracy" as such. In *Federalist* 60, Alexander Hamilton expressed the opinion that the dominant (land-owning) interest in civil society should "preponderate in the government" over "the mercantile interest."[9] To this extent, anyway, the Constitution in its original form, in

[9] ALEXANDER HAMILTON, JAMES MADISON & JOHN JAY, THE FEDERALIST PAPERS 298 (Lawrence Goldman ed., 2008).

which neither the President nor the Senate was popularly elected, was designed to incorporate an element of mixed government. The franchise in the US was already very considerably wider than in Britain, and the Founders made no proposal or provision for its further extension. The sovereignty of the people could be expressed safely in the exercise of constituent power, but direct electoral power was potentially more dangerous. However, the electoral cat was already out of the political bag, and extra-Congressional parties developed in the US decades before their extra-parliamentary counterparts in Britain. As suffrage expanded and electoral laws were democratized, interest-aggregating, party politics fundamentally modified the operation of the elaborate system of separated and shared powers that the Founders had constructed. It is hardly an exaggeration to say that in the US today, the capacity to mobilize and demobilize electoral power, a power that Montesquieu ignored and the Founders sought to cabin, dominates the practice of politics and the conduct of government. In 2006, David Levinson and Richard Pildes proposed that the US system of government was one of "separation of parties, not powers."[10] I would go further. Separation theory itself is past its analytical best-by date.

The Founders considered the legislature to be the strongest and "most dangerous" branch, largely because of its policymaking power. For self-defense, the President was given a legislative veto. Over the past two centuries, of course, the balance of power between the President and Congress has dramatically changed and the lion's share of policy-initiation has passed to the presidency. On the other hand, the Founders considered the judiciary to be the weakest and least dangerous branch. The proposed role of the courts in the US constitutional scheme was that of guaranteeing compliance by other governmental institutions with the Constitution and with constitutionally compliant statutes and treaties, without the benefit of either "purse or sword." This function can be contrasted with the "constitutional" role of the courts in the UK system, which includes *making*, as well as enforcing, constitutional law. However, of course, when it fills constitutional gaps, the US Supreme Court itself *effectively makes* constitutional law. In both systems, gap-filling constitutional "common law" yields to gap-filling, "constitutional" statutes;[11] and in both systems, non-legal, political, "conventional" norms play a crucial gap-filling function.

Regarding the executive branch, in *Federalist* 69, Alexander Hamilton went to considerable lengths to reassure critics that the US Presidency would be much weaker than the British monarchy. Unlike the monarch, the President would have no inherent, "prerogative" powers but only such powers as the Constitution itself

[10] *See generally* Daryl J. Levinson & Richard H. Pildes, *Separation of Parties, Not Powers*, 119 HARV. L. REV. 2312 (2006).

[11] These have been dubbed "super statutes": William N. Eskridge Jr. & John A. Ferejohn, *Super Statutes*, 50 DUKE L.J. 1215 (2001).

granted. On the other hand, the Founders were acutely aware of the desirability of "energy" and dispatch in the conduct of government, which implied that the President should have some latitude for unilateral action, unencumbered by the checks and balances built into the system. The extent of the freedom of the President to exercise power unilaterally has, of course, become one of the most contentious and debated issues in US constitutional law and theory. The idea of separation of executive power from legislative power provides no guidance because what is at stake is not the President's power to legislate but the power to take specific action that cannot be described simply and merely as applying legislation. Nor does the concept of checks and balances help, because the issue is not whether executive power should be checked and balanced, but to what extent and in what areas. What is needed, and what the Constitution does not provide, is a theory of positive executive power.

Nor did the Founders theorize "bureaucratic" or "administrative" power. For Montesquieu, bureaucrats and administrators were rather like the judges—because they did not fit neatly into any of the estates, they were invisible. The Founders were similarly blind. In the American colonies, as in England, Justices of the Peace and other local officials were actively engaged in administrative activity. William Novack has traced such activity in the 19th-century states,[12] and Jerry Mashaw has uncovered the extent of administrative activity of the US federal government in the same period.[13] With the growth of federal economic regulation and the invention of the multifunctional regulatory agency in the late 19th and early 20th centuries, entrepreneurs glimpsed potential legal advantage in the apparent mismatch between new governmental arrangements and the Constitution's three-branch model of separation of powers. Progressives countered with distinctions between two types of power and functions—executive and bureaucratic, and political and administrative—which eventually led to the informal recognition of a new, bureaucratic "fourth branch." Because the relationship between the executive and the bureaucracy is quite different in parliamentary systems than it is in the US system,[14] the concept of the fourth, bureaucratic branch finds much less purchase in the former, despite the enormous growth of the bureaucracy associated with increased demand by citizens for government involvement in social and economic life. In recent years, the idea and language of a "fourth branch" has been attached to the plethora of non-judicial bodies—such as ombuds, auditors, inspectorates, and complaint bureaus—created to review the executive in the face of increasing concentration of governmental power in that branch. Such bodies, so it has been

[12] William J. Novack, The People's Welfare: Law and Regulation in Nineteenth-Century America (1996).

[13] Jerry L. Mashaw, Creating the Administrative Constitution: The Lost One Hundred Years of American Administrative Law (2012).

[14] This statement is elaborated in Peter Cane, Controlling Administrative Power: An Historical Comparison, 91–94 (2016).

said, constitute an independent, fourth "integrity" (or "accountability") branch. Institutions in this branch are not courts, and the functions they perform are not judicial. Their job is to "hold government accountable" to various legal and extra-legal values and principles of good governance—a role they share with the legislature, of which some such bodies are conceptualized as delegates or agents.

Taking Stock

Varieties of Powers and Functions

Identifying discrete governmental "powers," "functions," and "institutions" (like identifying discrete social "interests" and "constituencies") is an exercise in interpretive modeling. I want to argue that the preceding narrative has uncovered at least nine "powers" in the sense in which this word is used in the phrase "separation of powers." Two hypotheses underpin this argument: first, that the constitutional theory we have inherited from the "Age of Revolution" reflects 18th-century political circumstances and does not fit constitutional theorizing about twenty-first century politics; and second, that the growth of global constitutional theory hinders analysis of local circumstances.[15]

1. *Constituent power*. This I define as the power to make legal, constitutional norms. Such norms may or may not be embodied in a codified constitutional document and they may or may not have the status of "higher law." The location and distribution of constituent power may vary from one polity to another. In the US, for instance, it resides ultimately in the People; in the UK it resides in Parliament and the courts. The significance of constituent power is reinforced by the suggestion that the average life of codified constitutions is about 19 years.[16] Constituent power is an increasingly important political tool in the hands of so-called populists.
2. *Electoral power*. I define electoral power as the power to control or effectively influence exercise by individuals of the right to vote for ("elect" as opposed to "select" or "appoint") others to represent them in governmental processes. An electoral system is democratic to the extent that suffrage is universal among adults, and elections are "free and fair." "Democracy" is widely considered to be the goal of, and the gold standard for assessing, constitutions and constitutional arrangements. Integral to electoral politics are

[15] Space prevents proper exposition of these hypotheses.

[16] Zachary Elkins, Tom Ginsburg & James Melton, The Endurance of National Constitutions 207 (2009). *But see* David S. Law & Ryan Whalen, *Constitutional Amendment versus Constitutional Replacement: An Empirical Comparison*, *in* Routledge Handbook of Comparative Constitutional Change 74 (Xenophon Contiades & Alkmene Fotiadou eds., 2020).

political parties that organize and mobilize electoral power. Early-modern constitutional theorists and constitution-makers were deeply suspicious of electoral power and gave it, at best, a limited role in constitutional arrangements. Meritocracy and expertise were much preferred to (or, at least, seen as essential brakes on) democracy and the popular will.[17]

3. *Lawmaking power.* Leaving aside the exercise of constituent power, there are two main ways of making law. One is directly to promulgate general rules and the other is to generate general rules as a byproduct of making individual decisions or resolving disputes. Law made in the former way is typically called "statute law" or "legislation." Law of the latter "incidental" or "interstitial" sort is typically referred to as "common law." In England, legislative power originally belonged to the monarch. Parliament originally advised the monarch but, by the 18th century, had assumed plenary legislative power. The significance of legislation as a source of law started to increase in the 19th century; and as demand for law grew, increasing amounts of legislative power were delegated by Parliament to the Executive, where most now resides. The power to make common law also originally resided in the monarch but was eventually lodged in senior courts.
4. *Policymaking power.* I understand "policy" to refer broadly to nonlegal, public norms made by governmental institutions. The power to make policy is a "discretionary" power: it gives the policymaker a choice. Policymaking may be preliminary to lawmaking but it may also be freestanding. The freestanding, "inherent," policymaking power of English monarchs was traditionally called "prerogative power." Prerogative powers were personal to the monarch and could be exercised without the consent of any other person or body ("unilaterally"). They were of greatest importance in the areas of foreign affairs and national security. The nature and extent of unilateral, policymaking power conferred by the US Constitution on the President (for instance) are matters of great complexity and contention because the Constitution does not (explicitly) address these issues. This silence reflects the 18th-century preoccupation with legislatures and legislative power.
5. *Implementing and interpreting power.* This I define as the power of one government official or delegate to implement law or policy made by another. The power to implement typically carries with it a power of interpretation. The location and extent of the power to interpret is one of the most difficult and contested issues in public law because there is no agreed line between interpretation and policymaking. Outside the context of implementing and

[17] Today, the distinction between democracy and meritocracy provides valuable insights into the Chinese constitution. *See, e.g.*, DANIEL BELL, THE CHINA MODEL: POLITICAL MERITOCRACY AND THE LIMITS OF DEMOCRACY (2015).

interpreting codified constitutions, constitutional theory tends to relegate study of implementing and interpreting power to subconstitutional "administrative law." This reflects the fact that it was not until after the "age of revolution," in the 19th century, that a clear distinction was drawn between policymaking and policy implementation.

6. *Coercive power*. This is the power of "the sword," of arms and weapons, of physical force. It is typically wielded by military and police forces. The constitutional and political significance of this power was transformed by the development of professional, standing military forces (especially armies) and (later) police forces with their own institutional structures, and the associated decline in the involvement of citizens, as such, in policing and military activities. The US Founders associated coercive power with the executive branch. However, the relationship between institutions that exercise implementing power on the one hand and coercive power on the other varies greatly from one system to another, to the point where some governmental systems are appropriately called "military regimes" or "police states." Pakistan and Myanmar provide examples of constitutional systems that can be convincingly analyzed and theorized only by taking account of military power.
7. *Scrutiny (or "oversight") power*. This is the power of one governmental official or agency to monitor or review exercises of power by another governmental official or agency. Very early in English history, this power was exercised by Parliament (primarily over the monarch, in the name of the interests of the other estates) and the judges (primarily over royal officials in the name of common and statutory law). The US Founders understood it to be the prime function of federal courts as guardians of the Constitution. In some systems, scrutiny in the name of the Constitution is undertaken by a Constitutional Court, distinct from other courts. Proliferation of nonjudicial, non-Parliamentary "integrity" institutions has been a feature of many systems in the past half-century.
8. *Religious and ecclesiastical power*. Historically, there is an intimate connection between sacred and secular power. In early English history power over hearts and minds, conscience and thoughts, was claimed by religious authorities, while power over bodies and actions was claimed by secular authorities. Henry VIII realized the value of combining secular and religious power. This helps to explain why freedom of thought, religion, and conscience from government interference and regulation was central to much 18th-century revolutionary rhetoric. Today, probably only Iran would count as a theocracy. However, for instance, senior clerics are still entitled to seats in the UK House of Lords; religious courts operate alongside secular courts in Malaysia; and religion and caste are central features of constitutional politics in India. Even in thoroughly secular "liberal democracies,"

separation of "religion" from "politics" remains highly contested territory.[18] "Radicalization" is a contemporary manifestation of the power of religious ideas. There is a widespread view that effective control over bodies and actions presupposes effective control over hearts and minds. This is the territory of "identity politics."

9. *Socio-politico-economic power.* Distribution of power among "estates," "interests," and "constituencies" within "civil society" was central to political and constitutional theory until ideas of institutional and functional distribution started to take hold in the 17th century. By the beginning of the 19th century, civil society had been homogenized into "the People" and ideas of democracy stressed political equality at the expense of material (and other forms of) equality. Political parties became the new "estates"; but, as their name implies, they were placed on the political side of the constitution/politics divide. Inevitably, however, the demand for political equality soon began to breed demands for social and material equality as well. By the 1950s the realization that the People is not an homogeneous entity and that civil society is a site of contestation rather than consensus found its way into pluralistic US political theory and the concept of "interest representation" made famous by Richard Stewart.[19] The idea was that electoral democracy needed to be supplemented by "participatory democracy" that allowed competing social, political and economic interests to participate in various government activities and processes between elections. In the US, for instance, this type of power is manifested in the US administrative rule-making process and in the activities of the "lobbying industry." Many aspects of such modern "mixed government" phenomena lie under the radar of global constitutional theory, of more interest to students of politics and subconstitutional administrative law than to constitutionalists.

There are other areas in which ideas of mixed government are salient but largely absent from mainstream constitutional theory. One is "multilevel" governance. Both federalism and localism are helpfully analyzed in terms of sharing of power among various social and geographical constituencies. In some postcolonial polities, a major focus of constitutional politics is the representation of indigenous groups, as such, in governmental processes. It could even be argued that our understanding of privatization and outsourcing might be enriched by viewing them as forms of power-sharing.

[18] A classic is RAN HIRSCHL, CONSTITUTIONAL THEOCRACY (2010). The author's analysis is affected by his separationist ideology.

[19] Richard B. Stewart, *The Reformation of American Administrative Law*, 88 HARV. L. REV. 1667 (1975).

Functions and Institutions

Identification of more than three "powers" raises the thorny theoretical issue of the relationship between functions and institutions. In the minds of the early English theorists and Montesquieu, there were two main governmental institutions: the monarchy and Parliament. Courts lurked somewhere in the background but were not considered to be autonomous institutions. The main concern of separation of powers was to regulate the relationship between the monarchy and (the Lords and Commons in) Parliament. The US Founders, as we have seen, rejected the whole idea of power-sharing between estates and reconceptualized civil society as the unitary "People." They also reconceived power-sharing in terms of "checks and balances" exerted by each of three "branches" of government on the other two. Each branch was allocated the lion's share of one of three abstract powers and a minor share in the other two powers. This narrowed the theoretical focus to three functions and three institutions. In the US, the theoretical rot set in with the invention of "independent agencies" that did not fit easily into any of the three branches.

Start thinking along such lines and the realization soon dawns that there are all sorts of institutions that perform functions essentially similar to those performed by the three branches, including religious organizations, military and police forces, "tribunals" and other court-like bodies outside the constitutional "judiciary," private sector government contractors and delegates, international organizations, "non-state actors," and so on. All sorts of institutions have various shares in the exercise of various (and more than three) functions and powers. Three-branch separation-of-powers theory is inadequate to the task of explaining individual systems, let alone comparing various systems that differ from one another in significant ways. Consider, for instance, that the Constitution of Taiwan recognizes five different branches and powers,[20] or that the Chinese Constitution divides the judicial branch into two: judges and procurators.[21]

So where can we go from here? I want very briefly to make three recommendations.

Rethinking the Architecture of Government

Mixed Government and Separation of Powers

My first suggestion is that we disentangle the concepts of mixed government and the balanced constitution from that of separation of powers. The balanced

[20] Jiunn-rong Yeh, The Constitution of Taiwan: A Contextual Analysis, 51–90 (2016).
[21] Qianfan Zhang, The Constitution of China: A Contextual Analysis, 183–85 (2012).

constitution rests on the idea that in order to be well governed, the many and various, often competing, interests of its citizens should be represented and have a voice in government. Separation of powers, I would say, addresses the different problem of excessive concentration of public power, not the responsiveness of government to its citizens' concerns. In my opinion, these two ideas are intertwined in an unhelpful way in the constitutional theory we have inherited from the early-modern revolutionary period. Practical problems that can arise from conflation of the two ideas can be seen in the postcolonial constitutional histories of nations in which constitutions embodying separation of powers were superimposed on "patrimonial" societies without regard to how the two patterns of governance would interact. I would also argue that in order to understand "populism" it is necessary to acknowledge the continuing importance of ideas of mixed government in constitutional systems that are not well designed to deal with deep social division and stratification. Again, I would argue that ideas of mixed government provide better ways of understanding supranational arrangements such as the European Union, and transnational arrangements such as those of concern to scholars of "global administrative law," than does the concept of separation of powers.

The post-World War II development of human rights may, perhaps, be understood partly as an attempt to constitutionalize protection of the interests of social groups by means other than representation and power-sharing. One widely observed result of these developments has been "juridification" and "judicialization" of politics. In the absence of representation in public policymaking and lawmaking, citizens seek influence through non-representative channels. The representative, political process, on the one hand, and non-representative, legal processes, on the other, may reflect different, cross-cutting ways of carving up the interests of and divisions within civil society. Direct participation in policymaking and lawmaking processes (whether formal or informal) may be based on yet different patterns of social interest and organization. Aspirations for mixed government were not suppressed by their submersion in separation of powers. Witness the fact that no sooner had the US Constitution come into operation than political parties began to form and play a decisive role in distributing public power.

Concentration and Diffusion of Power

My second suggestion would be to reconceptualize separation of powers in terms of its original aim of preventing undue concentrations of public power. As an analytical tool, I would argue that the image of a spectrum, with high concentration of power and high diffusion of power at either end, is more helpful than separation of powers. In this chapter I have identified many more than three types of public power, and the ways in which these powers are allocated and distributed vary from one polity to another, often very significantly. Take a very obvious example: the distinctions between presidentialism, semipresidentialism, and parliamentarism. In order fully to understand the implications, for the desideratum of avoiding excessive concentration of public power, of the various ways in which powers are distributed between the executive and the legislature, it is necessary also to analyze the ways in which various powers are distributed among other relevant institutions, of which there are many more than the classic three.

Controlling Governmental Power: Sharing and Exclusivity

My third suggestion is that we disentangle the issue of how power is allocated and distributed from the issue of how it is controlled; or, in other words, that we distinguish the concept of separation of powers from that of checks and balances. Instead of understanding checks and balances as an adjunct or qualification of separation of powers, I recommend that we treat it as a mode of controlling power, not of distributing it. Doing that, I would argue, enables us to distinguish in a helpful way between checks and balances as a mechanism of control, and a different mechanism that I have elsewhere called "accountability."[22] The awkwardness of putting the two ideas (allocation and control) together is obvious from the fact that no sooner does theory recommend that powers be separated than it changes its mind and says they should be shared. It would be analytically preferable to think about power distribution in terms of the extent to which power is "shared" or "exclusive." When power is shared between institutions, those institutions must act in concert to exercise the power. By contrast, when power is exclusive, it can be exercised unilaterally. Sharing of power facilitates control of power by "checking and balancing" its exercise. By contrast, controlling the exercise of exclusive power by "holding to account" requires accountability mechanisms that themselves enjoy exclusive power (to hold to account) that can be exercised independently of the institution being held to account. For the control of power, sharing operates prospectively to constrain decisionmaking and action by requiring various institutions to cooperate. By contrast, exclusivity operates retrospectively to hold institutions accountable for decisions made and action taken. The presidential veto in the US system is a paradigm example of constraining—"checking and balancing"—by sharing. Ministerial responsibility to Parliament in the UK system is a paradigm example of retrospective "accountability" for the past.

Elsewhere I have argued that there is a demonstrable association between diffusion of power and prospective control on the one hand, and between concentration of power and retrospective control on the other.[23] This insight provides a helpful perspective from which to view judicial independence. The independence

[22] Cane, Controlling Administrative Power, *supra* note 14.
[23] *Id.*

of the judiciary from control by the executive (for instance) is of most obvious importance in cases where the judiciary is scrutinizing the executive at the behest of a citizen; and one might hypothesize that the more concentrated power the executive enjoys, the more important judicial independence and identification of a distinct "judicial power" would be. This hypothesis is supported by the case of Australia, where the High Court has reacted to concentration of legislative, executive, and bureaucratic powers in the executive by going to great lengths to distinguish judicial power from the other powers and to claim the exclusive right to exercise that power in order to provide retrospective protection for citizens against the government and for the States against the Commonwealth. By contrast, the US Supreme Court has shown less concern about contamination of judicial power by legislative and executive power, thus signaling, I would say, that the Court is understood as having a share in the exercise of each of these other powers.[24]

Conclusion: Law and Theory

Three-branch separation-of-powers theory as expounded in the eighteenth century is not now, and was not then, a sharply honed analytical tool. As theorists, I think we can do much better; and as comparativists, we need to do better. I have made some suggestions about how we might improve our analytical toolkit. Others may have different and better suggestions. Still, there is an elephant in the room: the relationship between law and theory, norm and analysis. In some systems, three-branch separation of powers is embedded in constitutional law. In Australia, for instance, the tripartite arrangement of the Constitution has been interpreted as ruling out the creation of multifunctional agencies. Analytical legal theory must, of course, reflect and accommodate legal facts. The way I would do this is to distinguish between separation of powers as part of the law in some jurisdictions and separation of powers as an analytical tool. Our tools for analyzing distribution and control of governmental power must be able to take account of legal separation of powers while at the same time acknowledging the fact that law requiring separation is only one element of the landscape being mapped. Taking constitutional architecture and design seriously counsels the abandonment of separation of powers as a theoretical tool of analysis.

[24] Peter Cane, *The Common Law, the High Court of Australia, and the United States Supreme Court*, *in* Apex Courts and the Common Law 66, 79–82 (Paul Daly ed., 2019).

11

Global Values in National Constitutions

Richard Albert

Introduction: The Globalization of Constitutionalism?

Mark Tushnet has made many provocative claims in his extraordinary scholarly career. One of the most memorable appeared in an essay published 15 years ago in the *Virginia Journal of International Law*.[1] He argued that the globalization of constitutional law is inevitable.[2] The claim is provocative because the countries of the world seemed then, and seem still today, quite far from agreeing to be bound by anything resembling a world constitution. Creating the legal infrastructure for world constitutionalism was the ambition of instruments such as the Universal Declaration of Human Rights but that project remains incomplete, perhaps unlikely ever to take root in our polarized world. What would the text say, who would enact and enforce it, and how ever could all countries voluntarily subordinate their domestic constitutional law to a supranational agreement? These questions today remain unanswered.

Tushnet of course appreciated the substantial hurdles standing in the way of a world constitution. That is why he neither proposed nor endorsed the creation of a global constitutional document to which all countries would be legally bound. Instead, he foresaw the inevitable globalization of constitutional law taking the form of a convergence in how judges interpret constitutional rights and structures across jurisdictions.[3] The globalization of constitutionalism would therefore occur by interpreting existing national constitutions, not by making a brand new constitution for the world.

Too little time has elapsed to evaluate conclusively whether Tushnet was right. But his provocative claim prompts a question worth asking about the current state of the project of global constitutionalism: Have countries taken steps to globalize constitutionalism, beyond enacting a single world constitution and reinterpreting their national constitutions? The answer is yes. Over the past generation, countries have increasingly designed and redesigned their national constitutions to incorporate global values within them. The aggregate effect has been to inch progressively toward the globalization of constitutional law in piecemeal fashion, one country

[1] Mark Tushnet, *The Inevitable Globalization of Constitutional Law*, 49 VA. J. INT'L L. 985 (2009).
[2] *Id.*
[3] *Id.* at 987.

Richard Albert, *Global Values in National Constitutions* In: *Redefining Comparative Constitutional Law*. Edited by: Vicki C. Jackson and Madhav Khosla, Oxford University Press. © Richard Albert 2025.
DOI: 10.1093/9780191996344.003.0011

at a time, just as Tushnet had foreseen—only this convergence has come from the new generation of constitutional design, not from the judicial interpretation of national constitutions.

In this chapter prepared for a book commemorating the virtually peerless scholarly career of Mark Tushnet, I build on his claim of the inevitable globalization of constitutional law by shining a light on the creative constitutional design strategies countries have deployed to integrate the global values of international law into their national constitutions. I begin by outlining Tushnet's thesis that countries will ultimately build an informal world constitution by converging on their interpretation of national constitutional rights and structures. I then identify and illustrate three models of domestic constitutional design used to advance the project of global constitutionalism, as seen today around the world: (1) applying international law directly to all national legal actors; (2) prohibiting constitutional amendments that violate international law; and (3) requiring judges to interpret the national constitution in conformity with international law.

Recognizing that world constitutionalism is a multigenerational project that will succeed only if reformers seek to innovate along parallel tracks, I conclude with a question that doubles as a suggestion for advocates of global constitutionalism: In addition to pursuing existing strategies toward world constitutionalism, why not also devote energies to building the legal, political, and intellectual infrastructure for an international constitutional court armed with global jurisdiction?

Globalization by Constitutional Interpretation: A View from Tushnet

Tushnet qualified his claim that the globalization of constitutional law is inevitable. He made clear that he is not concerned with "a constitution of the international order or a global constitution."[4] Nor did he suggest that authoritarian states will join democratic ones in embracing what he describes as "rule of law constitutionalism."[5] He instead envisaged the globalization of constitutional law through "convergence among national constitutional systems in their structures and in their protections of fundamental human rights."[6] Convergence, for him, did not necessarily entail uniformity.[7] It entailed nations agreeing "on statements of constitutional principles on high or intermediate levels of abstraction or on quite specific details," though "even convergence on the most abstract level can be important and consequential."[8] Tushnet stressed that he would make "no claims about the

[4] *Id.*
[5] *Id.*
[6] *Id.*
[7] *Id.*
[8] *Id.*

magnitude of those processes' effects, or, putting it another way, about the extent to which those effects will be offset by counterpressures in particular nations,"[9] nor any claims "either about the rate at which the globalization of constitutional law will occur."[10]

Tushnet was primarily interested in globalization processes as they occurred in "nations that compete internationally for investment and human capital, with classes of lawyers able to assert some autonomous pressure on a nation's government."[11] Tushnet identified top-down and bottom-up processes that would lead to convergence, including transnational litigation and supranational decision-making along with the interests of investors in constitutional protections for property rights and also in political stability and predictability in general.[12] Tushnet also suggested that domestic lawyers with crossborder and transnational business dealings "will prefer some degree of convergence of constitutional systems"[13] because "domestic lawyers will face lower costs in transacting with lawyers in nations with familiar constitutional systems than in transacting with lawyers in nations with dramatically different constitutional systems."[14]

Using the United States as his principal case study, Tushnet framed the globalization of constitutional law as a contest among states, though he wondered whether the race would be one to the top or bottom.[15] There would be "nothing inevitable about the direction" in which the constitutional law of states would converge, given the role of ideology in judicial decision-making.[16] Tushnet explained that "there is no reason to think that the 'top' with respect to any specific constitutional guarantee is the most robust protection offered anywhere in the world."[17] Still, as he explained, "because the globalization of domestic constitutional law is inevitable, notions of separation of powers—or of legislative supremacy qualified by the existence of judicial review—will need to accommodate themselves to that globalization."[18]

Globalization by Constitutional Design

Today we know a lot about national constitution-making efforts that build a constitution atop a regime of national rights, namely civil rights, economic

[9] *Id.*
[10] *Id.*
[11] *Id.*
[12] *Id.* at 989–92.
[13] *Id.* at 993.
[14] *Id.* at 994.
[15] *Id.* at 988.
[16] *Id.* at 994.
[17] *Id.* at 1003.
[18] *Id.*

rights, political rights, and social rights. But we know much less about national constitution-making efforts that seek to build a constitution atop a regime of international human rights. Are there national constitutions that integrate global values of international human rights into their architecture? If yes, how do these constitutions advance the project of world constitutionalism? And what can we learn from them?

There are many examples of national constitutions around the world, both current and superseded, that make a strong commitment to international human rights. I have identified three different models of constitutional design intended to embed global values into national constitutions. Each of these three models is built to achieve the same purpose—to respect and protect international human rights and the global values they represent—but they each adopt a different strategy to that end. By *strategy*, I mean the way a national constitution expresses in the text of its domestic higher law its commitment to the global values of international human rights.

There are three major models of globalization by constitutional design. The first is the direct application of international law. It applies international law directly to national actors, without requiring any intermediate step. The second is a prohibition on constitutional amendments that violate international law. It forecloses certain amendments made to the national constitution. And the third is a judicial mandate to interpret the national constitution in conformity with international law. It prescribes the judicial interpretation of the national constitution. These three models of globalization by constitutional design take a different path to the same destination.

Directly Applying International Law

One strategy to advance the project of global constitutionalism is to apply international law directly to all national actors and their actions. Under this strategy, which we can describe as direct application, the national constitution incorporates within its text an explicit rule that gives international law direct application within the national jurisdiction, without requiring an intermediate step between the enactment of international law and its application to the country.

This model for globalizing constitutional law is reflected in the design of the Constitution of Bosnia and Herzegovina. Enacted in 1995, the Constitution is rooted in international law. Consider its preamble: it declares a commitment to international human rights, asserting that "Bosniacs, Croats, and Serbs, as constituent peoples (along with Others), and citizens of Bosnia and Herzegovina" are to be "guided by the Purposes and Principles of the Charter of the United Nations."[19] The preamble also acknowledges its inspiration from the "Universal

[19] BOSNIA & HERZEGOVINA CONST. prmbl.

Declaration of Human Rights, the International Covenants on Civil and Political Rights and on Economic, Social and Cultural Rights, and the Declaration on the Rights of Persons Belonging to National or Ethnic, Religious and Linguistic Minorities, as well as other human rights instruments."[20]

The first article of the Constitution requires the country to remain a Member State of the United Nations.[21] The first rule in the Bill of Rights commits the country to ensuring "the highest level of internationally recognized human rights and fundamental freedoms."[22] These codified constitutional rules are strong expressions of the country's commitment to international law. But they are not the distinctive element of the strategy of direct application.

The Constitution puts into operation its commitment to international law by combining the direct application of international law with the subordination of domestic law. The Constitution declares that the European Convention on Human Rights shall apply directly in Bosnia & Herzegovina.[23] The Constitution makes clear what this rule of direct application means: the European Convention on Human Rights "shall have priority over all other law,"[24] including any domestic constitutional law. This rule requires all governmental actors, including courts and agencies, to "apply and conform to the human rights and fundamental freedoms" enumerated in the European Convention on Human Rights.[25] The Constitution therefore gives precedence to the international law of human rights over the local rules of constitutional law.

The entire Constitution of Bosnia and Herzegovina is built around a commitment to the global values of international human rights. The Constitution entrenches enforcement mechanisms toward this end. For instance, all actors in Bosnia and Herzegovina are required to "cooperate with and provide unrestricted access to . . . any international human rights monitoring [bodies, persons, or organizations],"[26] including those established specifically for Bosnia and Herzegovina, the International Tribunal for the Former Yugoslavia, and "any other organization authorized by the United Nations Security Council with a mandate concerning human rights or humanitarian law."[27] This requirement of unrestricted access is an extraordinary commitment to accountability and transparency in how the country conducts itself with respect to rights and freedoms—and it shows the constitution's commitment to respecting the global values of international human rights.

There are three other architectural features of the Constitution of Bosnia and Herzegovina that illustrate how this model of direct application doubles as a

20 *Id.*
21 *Id.* at art. I(1).
22 *Id.* at art. II(1)
23 *Id.* at art. II(2).
24 *Id.*
25 *Id.* at art. II(6).
26 *Id.* at art. II(8).
27 *Id.*

comprehensive command upon the entire jurisdiction: (1) the selection of judges for the Constitutional Court; (2) the funding of international human rights organizations and obligations; and (3) the specific enumeration of more than a dozen international human rights agreements into the Constitution given direct application.

First, the Constitution specifies that the Constitutional Court is to have nine members.[28] Of those, four are to be selected by the House of Representatives of the Federation and two by the Assembly of the Republic Srpska; the three remaining seats on the Constitutional Court are to be chosen by the President of the European Court of Human Rights among candidates who are not citizens of the country or residents of a neighboring state.[29] The Court's jurisdiction includes matters referred by any court in the country on whether a given law respects the European Convention on Human Rights and is consistent with public international law.[30] This is further evidence of the Constitution's integration of international law into domestic constitutional law.

Second, the Constitution requires governmental institutions to adopt an annual budget that meets the country's international obligations, including its responsibility to finance international bodies charged with protecting and promoting international human rights.[31] There is a safety valve embedded into the Constitution in case an agreement cannot be reached in any given year: the budget of the prior year is adopted automatically on a provisional basis, ensuring that the country can maintain its obligations pending the negotiation of a new annual budget.[32]

Third, the Constitution gives direct application to more than just one international human rights agreement. An annex to the Constitution enumerates 15 international human rights agreements given direct application in the country, including the 1965 International Convention on the Elimination of All Forms of Racial Discrimination; the 1966 International Covenant on Civil and Political Rights; the 1966 Covenant on Economic, Social and Cultural Rights; the 1979 Convention on the Elimination of All Forms of Discrimination against Women; the 1984 Convention against Torture and Other Cruel, Inhuman or Degrading Treatment or Punishment; the 1992 European Charter for Regional or Minority Languages; the 1994 Framework Convention for the Protection of National Minorities; the 1948 Convention on the Prevention and Punishment of the Crime of Genocide; and the 1961 Convention on the Reduction of Statelessness.[33] This is a robust list of international human rights agreements given direct application in

[28] *Id.* at art. VI(1).

[29] *Id.* at art. VI(1)(a)–(b). This rule may be changed by Parliament after the initial appointment of the judges of the Court. *See id.* at art. VI(1)(d).

[30] *Id.* at art. VI(3)(c).

[31] *Id.* at art. VIII(1).

[32] *Id.* at art. VIII(2).

[33] *Id.* at Annex I.

Bosnia and Herzegovina, with a view to hoisting global constitutionalism over domestic constitutionalism.

Prohibiting Constitutional Amendments

A second strategy to globalize constitutional law through domestic constitutional design is to prohibit constitutional amendments. This model of amendment prohibition incorporates the global values of international human rights into national constitutions by limiting the power of constitutional amendment, specifically by prohibiting amendments that violate international law. A good expositor of this constitutional design strategy is the Constitution of Switzerland.

International law infuses every part of the Swiss polity. Both the national and subnational entities are required to respect international law,[34] and so too are the people.[35] The importance of international law is especially visible in relation to how the Swiss Constitution may be reformed.

The Swiss Constitution may be partially or totally revised at any time.[36] A partial revision may be initiated by the people or the Federal Assembly.[37] Yet whether the people or the legislature initiates the partial revision, the proposal "must not violate mandatory provisions of international law."[38] The same is true of total revisions, which may be proposed by either the people, the Federal Council or the Council of States, or the Federal Assembly.[39] Any proposal for a total revision must not violate the mandatory provisions of international law.[40] The reform rules in the Swiss Constitution therefore impose an irrevocable limitation on the power of all actors to revise the Constitution. No change, whether big or small, may violate the global values of international law.[41]

It is not unusual for constitutions to impose substantive limitations on constitutional reform.[42] These unamendable rules establish explicit restrictions on the subject matter of formal amendments. They may be designed to restrict reforms in relation to virtually any principle, value, or rule that constitutional designers wish to elevate in importance above others. For instance, some constitutions preclude reforms that violate secularism,[43] republicanism,[44]

[34] Swiss Const., art. 5(4).
[35] *Id.* at art. 139(3).
[36] *Id.* at art. 192(1). I have described these two changes as constitutional amendments and constitutional dismemberments, respectively. *See* Richard Albert, Constitutional Amendments: Making, Breaking, and Changing Constitutions 191–92 (2019).
[37] Swiss Const., art. 194(1).
[38] *Id.* at art. 194(2).
[39] *Id.* at art. 193(1).
[40] *Id.* at art. 193(4).
[41] *Id.* at arts. 193(4), 194(2).
[42] *See* Richard Albert & Bertil Emrah Oder, *The Forms of Unamendability*, *in* An Unamendable Constitution? Unamendability in Constitutional Democracies (2018).
[43] *See, e.g.*, Portugal Const. art. 288(c).
[44] *See, e.g.*, Italy Const., art. 139.

federalism,[45] or democracy.[46] Others prohibit reforms that suppress or diminish fundamental rights and freedoms,[47] create a single-party state,[48] redraw national borders,[49] or violate the separation of powers.[50] The constitutional design options for unamendability are endless.

In Switzerland, the rules of reform make the country's commitment to international law unamendable. These rules apply also to the creation of a new constitution, which may be enacted in Switzerland using the procedures of total revision. In our conventional understanding of constitutionalism, the constitution-making power is qualitatively different from the constitution-changing power.[51] Yet both powers are treated as similarly limitable and indeed are jointly limited by the Swiss Constitution insofar as both are subject to the restrictions of international law.

We ordinarily understand the power to make a new constitution to be unlimited. We refer to the power to make and legitimate a new constitution as constituent power.[52] According to the conventional theory of constitution-making, this constituent power is typically unbounded, meaning that the constituent power can write anything into or out of the constitution it creates.[53] Yet in Switzerland, the Constitution restricts how it may be totally revised. This purports to operate as a constraint on constituent power when seeking to replace the constitution.[54] Constituent power in Switzerland is therefore limited by the rule that the new constitution may not violate international law. This is an extraordinary rule to find in a constitution, no matter the content of the limitation.

Controlling Judicial Interpretation

We have so far canvassed two strategies constitutional designers have used to incorporate global values in domestic constitutions. The first is to design a framework for the direct application of international law within a country without any need for intervening steps by local actors between the enactment of an

[45] *See, e.g.*, BRAZIL CONST., art. 60(4).
[46] *See, e.g.*, CZECH REPUBLIC CONST., art. 9(2).
[47] *See, e.g.*, NAMIBIA CONST., art. 131.
[48] *See, e.g.*, CAPE VERDE CONST., art. 313(1)(g).
[49] *See, e.g.*, FRANCE CONST., art. 89.
[50] *See, e.g.*, GREECE CONST., art. 110(1).
[51] *See* Mark Tushnet, *Constitution-Making: An Introduction*, 91 TEX. L. REV. 1983, 1985–94, 2006–07 (2013).
[52] *See* MARK TUSHNET, ADVANCED INTRODUCTION TO COMPARATIVE CONSTITUTIONAL LAW § 2.2 (2nd ed., 2018).
[53] *See* Mark Tushnet, *Peasants with Pitchforks, and Toilers with Twitter: Constitutional Revolutions and the Constituent Power*, 13 INT'L J. CONST. L. 639, 645 (2015).
[54] Although there is an ongoing debate whether constituent power can be constrained in this way, my own view aligns squarely with Tushnet's own, which is that "obviously, we cannot proceduralize revolution itself." *Id.* at 649. *See* Richard Albert, *The Structure of Constitutional Amendment Rules*, 49 WAKE FOREST L. REV. 913, 973–84 (2014).

international agreement and its effect in the country. The second is to impose a limitation on how the constitution may be reformed: there can be no reforms that violate international law. The third category is to mandate how judges must interpret the constitution.

The Constitution of South Africa is a good example of this third constitutional design strategy. Under this model, the strategy is to incorporate global values into national constitutions by targeting the judicial branch, specifically by placing onto courts the responsibility for ensuring respect for international human rights. In South Africa, the specific constitutional design is found in Section 39. It codifies a set of instructions for judges on how to interpret the Bill of Rights.[55]

The South African Bill of Rights is described in the Constitution as the "cornerstone of democracy" in the country.[56] It "enshrines the rights of all people in our country and affirms the democratic values of human dignity, equality and freedom."[57] The rights are the ones we might expect in a modern liberal democracy: the right to life,[58] the right to freedom and security of the person,[59] the right to privacy,[60] the right to freedom of religion,[61] the right to freedom of expression,[62] the right to form a political party,[63] the right to human dignity,[64] and many more.

Back to Section 39. It is a model for the third strategy to globalize constitutional law by constitutional design. It specifies how judges are to interpret the Bill of Rights. Here is its full text:

39. Interpretation of Bill of Rights

1. When interpreting the Bill of Rights, a court, tribunal or forum—
   a. must promote the values that underlie an open and democratic society based on human dignity, equality and freedom;
   b. must consider international law; and
   c. may consider foreign law.
2. When interpreting any legislation, and when developing the common law or customary law, every court, tribunal or forum must promote the spirit, purport and objects of the Bill of Rights.

[55] South Africa Const., art. 39.
[56] *Id.* at sec. 7(1).
[57] *Id.*
[58] *Id.* at sec. 11.
[59] *Id.* at sec. 12.
[60] *Id.* at sec. 14.
[61] *Id.* at sec. 15.
[62] *Id.* at sec. 16.
[63] *Id.* at sec. 19(1)(a).
[64] *Id.* at sec. 10.

3. The Bill of Rights does not deny the existence of any other rights or freedoms that are recognised or conferred by common law, customary law or legislation, to the extent that they are consistent with the Bill.

Section 39 codifies an important difference in how the Constitution requires judges to treat international law versus foreign law. Judges "must"[65] consider international law when interpreting the Bill of Rights, while they "may"[66] consider foreign law when interpreting the Bill of Rights. To put it another way, the South African Constitution requires judges to consult international law when interpreting the Bill of Rights, but it simply authorizes them to look to foreign law, if they so choose. This difference is critical to understanding the judicial mandate as a constitutional design strategy to globalize the domestic constitutional law of states.

Section 39 requires South African judges to interpret each of the rights in the Bill of Rights with reference to the global law of international human rights. This is a mandatory rule. Judges are required to look to global values in international human rights law to give meaning to all rights in the Bill of Rights, including the right to equality, the right to be free from torture, the right to adequate housing, and the right to assembly, just to name a few examples. That is a peremptory requirement. In contrast, South African judges may, only if they wish, look to foreign constitutions to inform their understanding of a given right in the Bill of Rights. But referring to foreign law is not required. Judges are merely authorized to do it.

The authors of the South African Constitution made this distinction with one major purpose in mind: to ensure as much as possible that the new South African republic would treat rights consistently with the global values of the international law of human rights. After decades of South African authorities violating the basic fundamental rights of persons, the designers of the country's revolutionary constitution said, "no more." The new Constitution would usher in a newfound respect for rights, but not rights as understood with reference only to local norms. The new Constitution would create a culture of respect for rights as understood by the international community of states. Section 39 is the foundation for this high aspiration. It represents the third of three strategies that modern constitutions have deployed to incorporate global values into domestic constitutional law.

Conclusion—The Path Not (Yet) Taken: An International Constitutional Court

There are many paths for realizing the project of global constitutionalism. One path, described by Mark Tushnet as inevitable, is the convergence of constitutional

[65] *Id.* at sec. 39(1)(b)
[66] *Id.* at sec. 39(1)(c).

interpretation toward a shared, global understanding of constitutional rights and structures. We may well be approaching that world, but many miles remain before it becomes a reality. Another path is to enact a single world constitution. This, too, has a great distance to travel. In this chapter, I have identified another set of strategies that may help reformers achieve the goal of global constitutionalism: to design constitutions to incorporate global values within the domestic legal order.

I have introduced and illustrated three basic constitutional design strategies used to embed the global values of international law into a national constitution. The first strategy is to design a national constitution to apply international law directly to all national legal actors, as seen in the Constitution of Bosnia and Herzegovina. The second strategy is to prohibit constitutional amendments that violate international law, which is reflected in the Constitution of Switzerland. The third strategy is to impose a mandate on judges to interpret the national constitution in conformity with international law, a model adopted by the Constitution of South Africa.

Each of these three strategies seeks the same objective—to respect international law—but each targets a different category of actors. The strategy of direct application is the most sweeping, as it applies to all actors and actions in order to create a truly national commitment to international law. The strategy of amendment prohibition applies to amending actors, though in the Swiss case it raises the question whether it is in fact possible to limit constituent power in the remaking of a national constitution. The third strategy, of a judicial mandate, is the narrowest. Yet although it constrains only one branch of government, it could be especially effective if it is applied by a strong and determined court.

None of these three models is perfect. But all three models are worth considering by any country seeking to make a real commitment to international law within its national constitution. Protecting the global values of international law is an urgent challenge for constitutional states in our present day. Constitutional states must think creatively, and must learn from other states, if they wish to find the best way to honor their shared obligations to the international law of nations.

There is yet another option to consider—a much more controversial one. That option is to create an international constitutional court. It is a controversial option for the same reason that enacting a single world constitution is controversial: we ordinarily associate constitutions with the nation-state, with national borders, and with a domestic high court. Of course, there already are supranational adjudicatory bodies operating around the world, for instance the International Court of Justice, the International Criminal Court, the European Court of Human Rights, the Court of Justice of the European Union, the Inter-American Court of Human Rights, the Caribbean Court of Justice, and the Court of Justice of the Andean Community, to identify only a few. But a constitutional court for the entire world seems much different from current supranational courts.

Nonetheless, the idea of an international constitutional court has secured some support in some corners of the world. Early in the 2010s, the President of Tunisia convened and chaired an *Ad Hoc Committee for the Establishment of an International Constitutional Court*. The Committee issued a report explaining why and how to create the Court.[67] As proposed by the Committee, the Court would have 21 judges elected by the General Assembly of the United Nations.[68] The Assembly would select these 21 judges from a closed list of 42 candidates chosen by a college of judges that would include representatives from the International Court of Justice and the International Criminal Court. Those 42 candidates would themselves have been drawn from a list of roughly 200 nominees, one from each of the member states in the United Nations.

The Court would have two principal functions: giving advice and resolving disputes. The Court would issue advisory opinions at the request of governments, political parties, professional groups, non-governmental organizations, and multinational organizations at the international, regional, or sub-regional level.[69] The Court would also rule on what the report defines as "serious violations of democratic principles and democratic conditions for elections."[70] The Court would hear complaints from political parties, professional groups, non-governmental organizations accredited by the state as part of an electoral process, and multinational organizations at the international, regional, or subregional level.[71] In exercising both of these functions—advice-giving and dispute resolution—the Court would be guided by what the report describes as "the principles and rules relating to democracy and universal and regional civil liberties."[72] These principles and rules are found, according to the Committee, in the Universal Declaration of Human Rights, the International Covenant on Civil and Political Rights, the Treaty on European Union, the European Convention on Human Rights, the Charter of the Organization of American States, the American Convention on Human Rights, the Inter-American Democratic Charter, the Constitutive Act of the African Union, and the Harare Principles.[73]

The overriding goal for the Court would be to advance the values of democracy and constitutionalism, to offer the peoples of the countries of the world an external recourse for domestic violations of democracy, and to reduce the gap between what their constitution promises and what it delivers. As envisioned by the Committee's detailed report, the international constitutional court would ultimately become

[67] Ad Hoc Committee for the Establishment of an International Constitutional Court, Project of the Establishment of an International Constitutional Court (2013).
[68] *Id.* at 18.
[69] *Id.* at 19.
[70] *Id.*
[71] *Id.*
[72] *Id.*
[73] *Id.*

the world's most powerful Court.[74] Like the other ideas proposed for globalizing the domestic constitutional law of states, this idea for a new international constitutional court is far from reality, perhaps farther than any of the others.

There are many paths to a global constitution. It is doubtful that any of them will ever lead to a constitution for the world—either in form or function—as the odds at present are quite low. Yet advocates of a global constitution must brainstorm and pursue strategies to achieve their objective. It may well be that the judges of the national courts of the world will inevitably globalize their domestic constitutional law, as Mark Tushnet predicted.[75] Or it may be more efficacious to adopt constitutional design strategies to globalize constitutional law using one of the three models I have illustrated with reference to the Constitutions of Bosnia and Herzegovina, South Africa, and Switzerland. Or perhaps the optimal plan is to pursue all paths concurrently, working on parallel tracks to make real an aspiration that was conceived long ago but that today remains as far away as ever.

[74] For further details on the Committee's proposal, *see* Richard Albert, *Edward J. Bloustein Jurisprudence Lecture: Does the World Need an International Constitutional Court?*, 3 RUTGERS INT'L L & HUM. RTS. J. 1 (2023).

[75] Tushnet, *supra* note 1.

12

The Constituent Power and Its Limits

*Aharon Barak**

The Theory of the Constituent Power

The Distinction Between Constituent Power and Constituted Power

The theory of constituent power distinguishes between two types of constitutional powers:[1] The first is the primary power, the constituent power.[2] This power is granted by the sovereign, the people.[3] This is the highest constitutional authority. There is no superior authority. This authority of the constituent assembly determines the content of the constitution and the procedures through which it may be amended. The constituent power has the authority to determine which constitutional principles and provisions are unamendable, or "eternal." The constituent power operates so as long as the constitution has not yet entered into force, or has not yet been fully adopted. When the constitution enters into force, the constituent power "vanishes."[4] The constituent power would resume operating in the event that the constitution is abolished, and a new constitution would be adopted by the same primary constituent power that established the abolished constitution,

* After this chapter was written, the Supreme Court of Israel gave a judgment (HC5658/23) which followed my approach—as expressed in an article I wrote in Hebrew—and ruled that the Supreme Court has the authority to review a constitutional amendment that exceeds the constituent authority by undermining Israel's values as a Jewish and democratic state as provided by Israel Declaration of Independence. The Court also ruled that it has the authority to declare such an amendment as unconstitutional and void.

[1] Claude Klein, *Following the Bank Mizrahi Case—The Constituent Power in the View of the Israeli Supreme Court,* 28 Laws 341, 356 (1997); Sharon Wintel, *Eternal Paragraphs in the Constitution: The Strict Normative Standard in Establishing a New Constitutional Order* (2005) (PhD dissertation, The Hebrew University of Jerusalem); Claude Klein, *A Propos Constituent Power: Some General Views, in* National Constitutions in the Era of Integration 31 (A Jyränki ed., 1999); Martin Loughlin & Neil Walker, The Paradox of Constitutionalism: Constituent Power and Constitutional Form (2007); Illan Rua Wall, Human Rights and Constituent Power: Without Model or Warranty (2012); Constituent assemblies (Jon Elster et al. eds., 2018); Lucia Rubinelli, Constituent Power: A History (2020); Yaniv Roznai, *The Boundaries of Constituent Authority*, 52 Conn L. Rev. 1282 (2021).

[2] For further inquiry *see* Yaniv Roznai, Unconstitutional Constitutional Amendments: The Limits of Amendment Powers 121 (2017).

[3] *Id.* at 110 ("Once the constituent power has fulfilled its extraordinary constituting task, it 'becomes dormant' . . . Thus, by establishing a constitution, the constituent power is 'digging its own grave' . . . 'The sovereign himself had retired into the clouds'").

[4] On the basic norm, *see* Hans Kelsen, Pure Theory of law (Max Knight trans., 1967).

Aharon Barak, *The Constituent Power and Its Limits* In: *Redefining Comparative Constitutional Law.*
Edited by: Vicki C. Jackson and Madhav Khosla, Oxford University Press. © Aharon Barak 2025.
DOI: 10.1093/9780191996344.003.0012

or by a new primary constituent power. On some occasions, the constitution itself determines such provisions. However, if such provisions are absent from the constitution, the matter would be determined according to the orders of the body authorized for this under the legal system in place. This body is determined by the basic norm. It might be the current constituent assembly and it might be a new constituent assembly. These bodies would operate based on the existing basic norm; however, there may be a change in the basic norm, and that change will be reflected in the new constituent assembly.

The other constitutional power is a secondary constituent power, the constituted power.[5] The authority of the constituted power is mandated by the primary constituent power. As Tushnet puts it, "after the constituent power creates a constitution, every action taken within that constitutional framework is an exercise of constituted power."[6] The constituted power, as a derived and mandated power, has the authority to amend the constitution, subject to the boundaries dictated by the constituent power. The authorities of the legislative branch and the executive branch are derived authorities that are mandated by the constituent authority. An additional derived authority is that of the constituted power which has the authority to amend the constitution. This authority may be explicitly prescribed under the constitution itself (amending clauses), which also determines who may exercise this authority. In the absence of express provisions regarding the authority to amend the constitution, authority implied by the language of the constitution should be recognized. One should not assume that amending the constitution is not possible in the absence of express provisions pertaining to its amendment. It is hard to accept an "eternal" constitution.

The Constituted Power to Amend the Constitution

The constituted power to amend the constitution is a limited power. Its scope of authority is determined by the constituent power. Thus, the constituted power cannot exceed the scope of the authority granted to it by the constituent power.[7]

One may ask if it is possible to recognize an implied provision for amending the constitution when it is found among an explicit provision that deals with amendment.[8] This is a matter of interpretation. The main question is whether the conditions stipulated in the amendment clause also constitute a negative

[5] On the secondary constituent power, *see* Roznai, *supra* note 2, at 105.

[6] Mark Tushnet, *Constitution-Making: An Introduction*, 91 Tex. L. Rev. 1983, 1989 (2013).

[7] Roznai, *supra* note 2, at 109.

[8] Aharon Barak, *On the Implication in the Written Constitution*, *in* 3 Selected Essays: Constitutional Inquiries 203, 218 (2017).

arrangement which excludes the possibility of additional implied conditions. If the interpretative answer is negative, that is, that the established arrangement does not exclude additional conditions, then it is necessary to examine what those implied conditions for amendment of the constitution are.[9] In certain legal systems courts ruled that the constituted power to amend the constitution does not need to be the base for establishing a new constitution.[10] In my opinion, the normative basis for that conclusion is in the constitutional purposive interpretation of the amendment clause of the constitution. As with every purposive interpretation of the constitution, interpretation of the amendment clause should be done from a broad perspective. The assumption should be that the amendment clause only allows amendments which guard the essence and the identity of the constitution.

As mentioned, the constituted power is limited.[11] Not every constitutional amendment is constitutional. Hence the approach that one should not allow unconstitutional constitutional amendments, using the amendment clause of the constitution. Within this framework developed the conception by which amendments of the basic structure of the constitution are unconstitutional.[12] Interpreting the constitution as a whole leads to the conclusion that provisions of amendments in the constitution presuppose the existence of a complete constitution. The implied meaning of the constitutional text therefore does not recognize constitutional amendments which harm the constitution's basic structure. From this stems the "basic structure of the constitution" doctrine which was adopted by the Supreme Court of India[13] and is accepted in other legal systems.[14] It is important to emphasize that prohibiting amendments in the basic structure of the constitution prevents deep constitutional amendments which change the identity of the constitution and the democratic character of the regime. Therefore, changes in the republican nature of the governing regime, and harm to the separation of powers, rule of law, judicial independence, and human rights, are prevented as well. Every constitution has its elements and foundations which characterize its basic structure.

Is it possible to annul the implied meaning of the basic structure of the constitution by a constitutional amendment, which explicitly declares that every constitutional amendment that was made according to the express language of the amendment clause is constitutional? The Supreme Court of India answered this question in the negative.[15] Just as the constituted power cannot change

[9] *See generally* ROZNAI, *supra* note 2, at 110.
[10] *Id.*
[11] *Id.* at 106 ("Constituted power is the power created by the constitution and is an ordinary, limited power, which functions according to the forms and mode that the nation grants it in positive law.")
[12] *Id.* at 105.
[13] *Id.* at 42.
[14] *Id.* at 47.
[15] Minerva Mills Ltd. v. Union of India, AIR 1980 SC 1798 (India).

the express meaning of the amendment clause, it cannot change the implied meaning of the amendment clause that is inferred from the language of the constitution. This approach does not rule out the possibility of making amendments in the basic structure of the constitution; however, such amendments would not be made by amending the existing constitution through the amendment clause. Rather, such amendments would be possible by establishing a new constitution. A new constitutional authority that is not subordinate to the essence and to the identity of the constituent power could determine new constitutional provisions that are based on a different basic structure. It seems that this would only be possible if the basic norm that stood at the foundation of the constituent power had been replaced.

In a conflict between a constitutional norm which was created by the constituent power and a constitutional norm which was created by the constituted power, the constitutional norm created by the constituent power prevails. Roznai thinks that in the relation between the constituent power and the constituted power the principle of *lex superior derogat inferiori* applies, according to which a superior law prevails over an inferior law.[16] In my opinion, however, the constitutional norms created by the constituent power and the constituted power are at the same normative level.[17] Nonetheless, if the amending constitutional norm does not meet the constitutional conditions (implied or expressed) set out by the constituent power, then the amending constitutional norm cannot be established into a valid constitutional amendment. Thus, the constituent power's constitutional norm prevails over the constituted power's constitutional norm, not because the latter is subordinate to the former, but because the former determines the requirements for the latter to be valid. Therefore, when those requirements are not met, we do not face a valid amendment, and there is no collision between the norms.

From my perspective, it is not befitting to divide between two constitutional levels. It is more appropriate to recognize one constitutional level, as determined by the constituent power, with constitutional amendments within determined by the constituted power. It holds true, as Roznai explains, that the constituted amendment power is a *sui generis* power, and should not be identified with other institutional powers.[18] I agree with Roznai on that matter and it is therefore inappropriate to equate the unconstitutionality of a statute that violates a constitutional norm, with the unconstitutionality of an unconstitutional amendment that does not meet the constitutional requirements. The former (the statute) is at a

[16] *See* Roznai, *supra* note 2, at 137.

[17] Rivka Weil, *What Is the Opinion of the People? On the Relationship between Constitution Adoption Procedures and Amendment Procedures*, 10 L. & Gov't 449, 483 (2007).

[18] Roznai, *supra* note 2, at 110, 113.

subconstitutional normative level, and the latter (the constitutional amendment) is at a constitutional normative level.

The Constituent Power

Presenting the Questions

This article focuses solely on the constituent power. Consequently, I aim to answer two types of main question. The first question asks whether the constituent power is an absolute power, or an unlimited power, or whether there are limitations on the constituent power. In other words, can we recognize norms that were set by the constituent power as unconstitutional? There is a vast body of legal scholarly work focusing on such questions, and this has expanded greatly in recent years.[19] Mark Tushnet explains this phenomenon: "In recent years the idea, originally articulated in the era of the French Revolution, that constitutions ultimately rest on a 'constituent power' has become increasingly prominent in theorizing about constitutional fundamentals."[20]

It seems that a main reason for this relates to the increase in courts reviewing the constitutionality of constitutional amendments.[21] Naturally, this also led to examination of the question to what extent this judicial involvement extends the constitutionality of the establishment of a new constitution. This is the second type of main question that I discuss in this chapter. In essence, this chapter addresses the question whether it is possible to accept the authority of the judicial branch

[19] Klein, *supra* note 1; Yaniv Roznai, *Supranational Law, Globalization and the Constituent Authority—A Study and Comparative Trends*, 22 L. & Gov't 49 (2021); Roznai, *supra* note 5; Roznai, *supra* note 1; Rubinelli, *supra* note 1; Lech Garlicki & Zofia A. Garlicka, *External Review of Constitutional Amendments? International Law as a Norm of Reference*, 44 Isr. L. Rev. 343 (2011); Richard Kay, *Constituent Authority*, 59 Am. J. Comp. L. 715, 722 (2011); Ulrich K. Preuss, *The Implications of "Eternity Clauses": The German Experience*, 44 Isr. L. Rev. 429, 432 (2011); David Landau, *The Importance of Constitution-Making*, 89 Denv. U.L. Rev. 611, 616 (2012); Joel I. Colón-Ríos, Weak Constitutionalism: Democratic Legitimacy and the Question of Constituent Power (2012); Richard Stacey, *Popular Sovereignty and Revolutionary Constitution-Making*, *in* Philosophical Foundations of Constitutional Law 161 (David Dyzenhaus & Malcolm Thorburn eds., 2016); Joel I. Colón-Ríos, *Five Conceptions of Constituent Power*, 130 Law Q. Rev. 306 (2014); Dieter Grimm, *The Achievement of Constitutionalism and Its Prospects in a Changed World*, *in* The Twilight of Constitutionalism? 3–22 (P. Dobner & M. Loughlin eds., 2010); George Duke, *Inherent Constraints on Constituent Power*, 40 Oxford J. Leg. Stud. 795 (2020); Joel I. Colón-Ríos, Constituent Power and the Law (2020); David Landau, *Constitution-Making Gone Wrong*, 64 Ala. L. Rev. 923 (2013); Roznai, *supra* note 2; Roznai, *supra* note 1; Yaniv Roznai, *The Theory and Practice of "Supra-Constitutional" Limits on Constitutional Amendments*, 63 Int'l & Comp. L.Q. 557 (2013); Andrew Arato, The Adventures of the Constituent Power Beyond Revolutions? (2017); Rubinelli, *supra* note 1; Martin Loughlin, The *Concept of Constituent Power*, 13 Eur. J. Pol. Theory 218 (2014); Richard Albert, *Four Unconstitutional Constitutions and Their Democratic Foundations*, 50 Cornell Int'l L.J 169 (2017).

[20] Tushnet, *supra* note 6.

[21] The discussion of that phenomenon has widely benefited from Roznai, *supra* note 2.

to exercise judicial review over the constitutionality of norms created by the constituent power. Is a new constitution subject to judicial review of its constitutionality? This discussion opens with the former question and examines different constitutional solutions, the first of which is the solution relying on natural law.

Solutions Relying on Natural Law

Arguably, natural law, by definition, is external and superior to any positive law, including the constitution or its amendments.[22] Therefore, some hold that the constituent power is limited by virtue of the principles of natural law. According to this approach, the principles of natural law limit and mandate the constituent power. Roznai explains such claims, noting their foundations in the writings of legal scholars from the 18th and 19th centuries.[23]

In my opinion the natural law approach is inappropriate, as my approach to law is positivist in its essence. Accordingly, natural law can be valid only to the extent that it has been absorbed by the legal system. Hence, we should not recognize natural principles above constitutional principles.[24] By this approach natural law cannot be the source of limiting the constituent power, as natural law itself is subject to the constitution.

Solutions Relying on International Law

Some hold that the constituent power is limited by the peremptory provisions of international law. According to this approach, the peremptory provisions of international law are superior to constitutional law and have the power to limit the constituent power.[25]

I reject that approach, as my approach is based on a dualist approach (as practiced in common law systems, such as the United States, Canada, Australia and Israel).[26] According to the dualist approach, international law can be a source of the internal law only if it had been adopted by an internal law source of law such as a statute or the constitution, which adopts international law provisions, or

[22] Garlicki and Garlicka, *supra* note 13, at 355 (stating that "[b]y definition, natural law constitutes an external and superior norm of reference that autonomously exists above all written laws (including constitutions and constitutional amendments")).

[23] Roznai, *The Theory and Practice of "Supra-Constitutional," supra* note 19.

[24] I do not agree with the opinion of Judge Y. Sussman, LB 1/65 Yardur v. Chairman of the Central Election Committee for the Sixth Knesset, P.D. 19(3) 365 (1965) (Isr.). My approach identifies with the interpretive approach of President S. Garnet.

[25] For a description and critique of this approach, *see id.* at 562; Roznai, *The Theory and Practice of "Supra-Constitutional," supra* note 19, at 572.

[26] *See* J.G. Starke, *Monism and Dualism in the Theory of International Law*, 17 BRIT. Y.B. INT'L L. 66 (1936).

the local common law system, which adopts customary international law. These legal sources are subject to the constitution, and thus cannot limit the constituent power. It should be noted that, indeed, monistic approaches too may sometimes subordinate the international law to the constitution.[27]

Solutions Relying on the Interpretation of the Constitution

Can we base upon the constitution itself, which was established by the constituent power, the imposition of limitations of the constituent power? As we have seen, the limitation of constitutional amendments can be based upon the constitution. However, such limitations relate to the constituted power.[28] In my opinion, the imposition of limitations on the constituent power cannot be based on the language of the constitution and its interpretation. Just as the constitution does not create the power which established it, the constitution does not create limits on that power. Such limitations, as far as they exist, should be based upon points of reference that are outside of the constitution itself. I discussed that approach in my ruling in the *United Mizrahi Bank* case:

> It seems to me that that most appropriate view is that the Knesset is endowed with constituent authority. This power derives from the central constitutional fact that Knesset was given the authority to enact a constitution for Israel. The Knesset does not create this authority for itself. It is not granted to the Knesset by a Basic Law or by any other law enacted by the Knesset. In order to frame a constitution, which will be placed above the law in the normative hierarchy, there must be an Archimedean foothold located outside the constitution or the law, which provides the Knesset with the authority to adopt a constitution. The constitution cannot create the authority by which it will be created.[29]

Thus, for example, a provision in the constitution by which human rights or certain institutions cannot be changed ("eternity clauses") might be a base for a claim which limits the constituted power to amend the constitution, but does not limit the constituent power. In German constitutional law, for instance, the constitution determines that one cannot amend the right to human dignity, which enjoys perpetuity.[30] According to my viewpoint, an eternity clause in the constitution does not have the power to establish the argument according to which even after the

[27] *See, e.g.*, Bundesverfassung [BV] [Constitution] Apr. 18, 1999, SR 101, art. 193 (Switz.).
[28] *See supra* note 11.
[29] CivA 6821/93 United Mizrahi Bank Ltd. v. Migdal Cooperative Village, PD 49(4) 221, 355–356 (1995) (Isr.) (hereinafter *United Mizrahi Bank*).
[30] Grundgesetz [GG] [Basic Law], arts 1 & 79(3) (Ger.), translation at https://www.gesetze-im-internet.de/englisch_gg/index.html.

repeal of the constitution, the constituent power is not authorized to establish in a new constitution provisions according to which the right to human dignity is not eternal.[31]

Solutions Relying on Points of Reference that are Outside of the Constitution

Limits by Basic Principles Agreed Upon in Advance Between the Members of the Constituent Power

Assume that a new constituent power repealed the old constitution. The agreement between the members of the constituent power determined that the new constitution would be based upon certain principles. However, with the establishment of the new constitution, these agreed principles were not respected. Does the agreement reached have the power to limit the new constituent assembly?

My answer to this question is no. The agreement in the framework of the new constituent power did not oblige it in its actions. In my opinion, that agreement also cannot oblige the constituted power to amend the constitution in a way that the agreed principles would be fulfilled. An interesting example is the constitution of South Africa. Following elections, a temporary constitution was established in 1994. The temporary constitution established numerous principles which determined the content of the permanent constitution. It was also determined that the Constitutional Court of South Africa, which was established under the temporary constitution, would examine drafts of the permanent constitution, and only after it will confirm that the principles were fulfilled, then the permanent constitution would enter into force. Following this, the Court examined some provisions and determined that they do not comply with the principles set forth under the temporary constitution.[32] It was only after the Court determined that the draft was amended in a way that made it consistent with the fundamental principles that the permanent constitution entered into force, in 1996.[33]

Can we learn from the South African example that agreeing on fundamental principles in advance has the potential to limit the constituent power? In my opinion, this is not the lesson which should be learned from this example. What we can learn from it is that the social powers underlying this consensus on the fundamental principles were strong enough to prevent members of the constituent

[31] See discussion with regard to that question in German constitutional law at Christoph Möllers, *We Are (Afraid of) the People: Constituent Power in German Constitutionalism*, *in* The Paradox of Constitutionalism: Constituent Power and Constitutional Form 87, 96 (Martin Loughlin & Neil Walker eds., 2007). *See also* Roznai, *supra* note 1, at 1399.

[32] Certification of the Constitution of the Republic of South Africa, 1996 (4) SA 744 (CC).

[33] Certification of the Amended Text of the Constitution of the Republic of South Africa, 1996 (2) SA 1 (CC).

power from acting contrary to such consensus. The sticking point that exists outside of the constitution in the South African example is not the limits that were agreed on in the temporary constitution, but rather the social power that stood at the foundation of the permanent constitution.[34]

Limits by Virtue of Constitutionalism Principles

One can argue that the constituent power is limited by several fundamental principles that are at the foundation of the concept of "constitution."[35] According to this approach, the constituent power was intended to establish a constitution, and a constitution is based on number of fundamental principles. It follows therefore that the principles which define the concept of "constitution" are also the limits on the constituent power.[36]

In my opinion, such approach should not be accepted. One needs to separate between the fundamental principles of the constitution and the constituent power. The constitution's fundamental principles, which are at the foundation of the constitution, could limit the constituent power if they had a "supraconstitutional" status. However, these principles, in my opinion, do not have a "supraconstitutional" status.[37] We need to distinguish between constitutional "supraprinciples" and "supraconstitutional" principles. The first are principles which encompass the constitution and are, most of the time, part of it (implicitly or explicitly). Therefore, they cannot limit the constituent power. On the other hand, "supraconstitutional" principles could limit the constituent power had we recognized their "supraconstitutional" status as standing above the constitution. Such an approach would uphold my view that limiting the constituent power needs to base itself on a point of reference found outside of the constitution. Thus, there is no basis for this approach. We do not recognize that there is a constitution above a constitution. We do not recognize "supraconstitutional" values. All we have left with is to base the limits of the constituent power on constitutional "supraprinciples." However, this is impossible as they do not consist of any point of reference that is outside the constitution.

[34] *See* Roznai, *supra* note 1, at 140 ("it is fair to say that constituent power voluntarily accepted upon itself these limitations rather than being obliged by them").

[35] *See* Carlos Bernal, who claims that "there cannot be a constitution without constitutionalism" in Carlos Bernal, *Constitution-Making (Without Constituent) Power: On the Conceptual Limits of the Power to Replace or Revise the Constitution*, *in* CONSTITUTIONAL CHANGE AND TRANSFORMATION IN LATIN AMERICA 21, 34 (Richard Albert et al. eds., 2019).

[36] *See* Roznai, *supra* note 1, at 1404.

[37] Preuss, *supra* note 19. *See* Roznai, *supra* note 1, at 1405; *see also* Shouvik Kumar Guha & Moiz Tundawalla, *Constitution: Amended It Stands?*, 1 NUJS L. REV. 533, 543 (2008); Dietrich Conrad, *Constituent Power, Amendment and Basic Structure of the Constitution: A Critical Reconsideration*, 6–7 DELHI L. REV 1, 12 (1977–78) (emphasizing the need for free debate, freedom from arbitrary arrest, and freely conducted elections in order for there to be a genuine exercise of constituent power(; MURPHY F. WALTER, CONSTITUTIONAL DEMOCRACY: CREATING AND MAINTAINING A JUST POLITICAL ORDER 516 (2007).

Limits by Virtue of the Principle of the Constituent Power

Some argue that the constituent power presupposes the existence of some liberties, such as freedom of speech and freedom of choice, without which the constituent power would lack legitimacy.[38] Roznai explains:

> In order to protect the very idea of constituent power; in order for constituent power to be exercised in the future and to allow and facilitate the people's exercise of constituent power, those rights which form the basis of constituent power must be protected ... Minimum core of rights that are necessary for constituent power to be exercised and re-exercised must be kept ... One cannot use "constituent power" in order to undermine the very notion of "constituent power."[39]

He then notes:

> This limitation is of course one of legitimacy, not of legality.[40]

I agree with this. The very principle of the constituent power makes some limits of the constituent power justified, but that is not enough. They need to have a legitimate basis in order for these justified limitations to affect the scope of the constituent power. In my view, such a legitimacy is based in the sovereignty of the people. Indeed, the principle of sovereignty of the people is the external point of reference on which we can base the limits of the constituent power. Given the importance of this claim, we will now discuss the idea in more depth.

Limitations Anchored in the Principle of Sovereignty of the People

In my opinion, the external point of reference that can limit the scope of the constituent power is the will of the people or the sovereignty of the people. I insisted on this in my ruling in the *United Mizrahi Bank* case, where I stated that "[t]he enactment of a constitution always requires a point of reference from outside the legislative body."[41] With regard to this external reference point, I mentioned: "This point of reference must come from the people, to whom sovereignty belongs. Indeed at the foundation of the Knesset's constituent authority is the concept that the Knesset's constituent authority is derived from the sovereign, from the people."[42]

Later in my ruling I based this approach on three models: Kelsen's basic norm model (the "Grundnorm"); Hart's rule of recognition model; and the best

[38] *See* Roznai, *supra* note 1, at 1405; *see also* Guha & Tundawalla, *supra* note 37; Conrad, *supra* note 37; Walter, *supra* note 37.

[39] *See* Roznai, *supra* note 1, at 1405–06.

[40] *Id.* at 1406.

[41] United Mizrahi Bank, *supra* note 29, at 356. *See also* Kay, *supra* note 19 (which states that the initial constituent authority is external to the constitution it constitutes).

[42] United Mizrahi Bank, *supra* note 29, at 356.

interpretation model for the entirety of social and legal history, formulated by Dworkin.

According to my approach, the constituent power is not authorized to establish a constitution that violates the sovereignty of the people.[43] It is therefore the case that a provision in the constitution by which all of its provisions are eternal, or by which only some of its adult citizens have the right to vote, is unconstitutional.[44] In this context we can suggest, in the spirit of Judge Barak-Erez's ruling in the *Hason*[45] case, that the constituent power is not authorized to "break the tools." In explaining this approach, Judge Barak-Erez writes that it is aimed at "breaking the tools"

> in the sense of irreversible destruction of the constitutional system. For example, if a Basic Law would seek to negate the egalitarian characteristics of the election process, it would cut the ground from under its legislation, since with the damage to equal participation in the elections, it would not be possible to undo what was done. The same goes for a Basic Law that would seek, for example, to add a significant period to the term of office of the Knesset that adopts that amendment, beyond the term of office it was elected for.[46]

The concept of "the people" or "the sovereignty of the people" (or "popular sovereignty") is certainly vague.[47] Disagreements will surround these concepts. However, the ambiguity of these concepts is no different from the ambiguity surrounding other proposals to limit the constituent assembly. Moreover, as will be seen, according to my view, the external reference point in Israel is the fundamental values of the Declaration of Independence. Before us is a written text that indicates the will of the people.

According to my approach, the external reference point on which the constitution is built is the will of the people. This will is being heard from the most supreme authority in the legal system. The identity of this authority is determined according to the basic norm (in Kelsen's theory), or according to the rule of recognition (in Hart's theory), or according to the best interpretation model for the entirety of social and legal history (in Dworkin's theory). The supreme authority in the legal system is the body that authorizes the establishment of the constitution through the constituent power. From this legal structure it follows that the scope of the constituent power cannot exceed the authority bestowed upon it by the supreme authority in the legal system. Indeed, when the people, by means of

43 *See, e.g.*, Kay, *supra* note 19; Landau, *supra* note 19.

44 Yaniv Roznai, *Necrocracy or Democracy? Assessing Objections to Constitutional Unamendability*, *in* AN UNAMENDABLE CONSTITUTION? 30 (Richard Albert & Bertil Emrah Oder eds., 2018).

45 HCJ 5555/18 Hason v. Israel Knesset (July 8, 2021) (Isr.).

46 *Id.*, J. Barak-Erez's ruling, ¶ 16.

47 Dieter Grimm, *Does Europe Need a Constitution?*, 1 EUR. L.J. 282 (1995); Stacey, *supra* note 19; Kay, *supra* note 19.

the supreme authority in the legal system, order the establishment of a constitution, the authority that establishes the constitution, the constituent power, cannot exceed the authority granted to it by the supreme authority. It is therefore the case that when the superior authority in the legal system orders the establishment of a constitution that is based on equality between the people, the constituent assembly is not authorized to establish a constitution that discriminates between people and violates equality. It is important to emphasize that I do not think that the order of the supreme authority in the country is at a higher normative level than the constitution which was established by the constituent power. In addition, I do not think that in the legal system there are two constitutions, of which one is superior to the other. My approach is that in a legal system there is only one constitution, which is the constitution that was established by the constituent assembly. Nonetheless, the scope of authority of the constituent assembly is not unlimited. It was limited by the people, who expressed their will through the supreme authority in the country.

Judicial Review of a Constituent Power that Acts Beyond Its Powers

The common rule in all constitutional democracies is that if a statute enacted by the legislator contradicts the constitution, the constitution has the upper hand.[48] This conclusion is articulated in the well-known rule that a superior norm prevails over an inferior norm (*Lex superior derogat inferiori*).[49] The supremacy of the constitutional norm is expressed, among other things, in that the court is authorized to declare on a contradiction between the constitution and the statute, and to determine what the required constitutional remedy is.[50] Such a constitutional remedy may be declaring the invalidity of the contradicting statute.

As discussed above, in a collision between the provisions of a constitution and an amendment to that constitution, the constitution prevails. This conclusion derives from the subordination of the constituted power to the constituent power.[51] In addition, as discussed, in many legal systems courts are authorized to determine that the constitutional amendment is unconstitutional and to determine what the required constitutional remedy should be. A natural (but not the sole) remedy is a declaration of invalidity of the amendment.

What is the outcome in a case where the constituent power enacts a constitutional provision that it does not have the authority to enact, since that provision contradicts the people's will which is articulated through the instruction of the supreme authority in the country? In my opinion, the rule according to which a

[48] Aharon Barak, Basic Law: Human Dignity and Liberty and Basic Law: Freedom of Occupation 1719 (2023) (Hebrew).
[49] *Id.* at 319.
[50] For further inquiry regarding constitutional remedies, *see id.* at 2355.
[51] *See id.* ch. A.2.

superior norm prevails over an inferior norm does not apply where the constituent power exceeds its scope of authority. The reason for this is that the word of the supreme authority in the state (which is the expression of the sovereignty of the people) is not a constitutional norm that has a higher normative status than the constitutional norm enacted by the constituent power. Moreover, the approach according to which a constitutional amendment that contradicts the word of the supreme legal authority in the state is an unconstitutional constitutional amendment also does not apply. The reason for this is that we are not dealing with an amendment to the constitution, but rather with a constitutional provision that exists in the original constitution. Against this background arises the question whether the court has the authority to rule that the constituent power exceeded its authority, and to determine an adequate remedy.

In my opinion, the limits on the scope of authority of the constituent power have a preeminent legal and social importance. The denial of judicial review would render these limits a dead letter and the sovereignty of the people would be severely damaged. There is therefore no escape from recognizing the court's authority to determine if the constituent power exceeded its authority, and, if the court has determined so, to rule on the appropriate remedy.

The question of judicial review of the constituent power's deviations from the scope of its authority was raised in Israel in the *Hason* case.[52] Numerous judges recognized the court's authority for judicial review of the constitutionality of a Basic Law, which is a supreme constitutional norm in Israel. Judge Vogelman stated in his opinion that he "is inclined to the approach by which [judicial review] derives from the substantive limitations of the constituent power. This is in order that those limitations not become a dead letter."[53] Judge Hendel stated that "there might be importance to judicial review which is based on unwritten fundamental values. As for the extreme situation, where fundamental rights are violated to their very core, I think that the question changes. In such circumstances the door is opened for judicial review, as demanded by justice and by the role it plays."[54] Judge Barak-Erez recognized an authority for judicial review in cases of "breaking tools," in which irreversible destruction of the system is caused.[55] Judge Mazuz stated that "the source of authority for limiting the constituent authority of the Knesset in cases of it violating the core identity characteristics of the State of Israel as Jewish and Democratic" is in the Declaration of Independence. According to him, "the constitutional assembly had been authorized to imbue those principles, of Jewish and Democratic, but was not authorized to diverge from them or cancel them."[56] Deputy Chief Judge Melcer mentioned that the Knesset as a constituent authority

[52] HCJ 5555/18 Hason v. Israel Knesset.
[53] *Id.*, J. Vogelman's ruling, ¶ 4.
[54] *Id.*, J. Hendel's ruling, ¶ 3.
[55] *Id.*, J. Barak-Erez's ruling, ¶ 16
[56] *Id.*, J. Mazuz's ruling, ¶ 9.

is not omnipotent. It has a fiduciary duty to fulfill the objectives for which it was granted authority, and these objectives present the limits of this authority. The Deputy Chief Judge stated that the "Declaration of Independence created the framework for establishing the constitution, thus the constituent authority was intended to fulfill in the constitution the 'history and ideology,' and the concept of 'I believe' in the people, which were articulated in the first and third parts of the Declaration of Independence respectively, and that authority is limited by these principles."[57]

Several judges stated that judicial review of the constitutionality of the Basic Laws should not be recognized. Judge Mintz stated that "we must respect the superior normative status of the constituent norm and not to divide it into segments and review each of these segments."[58] Judge Sohlberg wrote that "whoever wishes to exercise judicial review of the Basic Laws as such, needs to prove the existence of constitutional norms that are higher than higher, above the Basic Laws. However, our law does not recognize a norm which stands above the Basic Laws; not explicitly nor implicitly."[59] Chief Judge Hayut stated that "the conclusion according to which the Knesset as a constituent authority is not 'omnipotent' and has certain narrowed limitations that limit it, does not necessarily teach that it can be used as a basis for judicial review by the court."[60]

In my opinion, in the Israeli context there is a reference point that is external to the constitution on which judicial review of the Knesset's constituent power can be based. This external point of reference operates in the interpretive plane, which leads to narrowing the scope of the constituent authority. This external point is the Declaration of Independence, which ordered the election of the constituent assembly. According to my approach, the DNA of the constituent assembly is the DNA of the Declaration of Independence. The Declaration of Independence determines the vision of the people and their "I believe." It is a "distilled expression of the constituent narrative of Israel."[61] This narrative is based, among other things, on the provisions of the Declaration of Independence by which Israel "will ensure complete equality of social and political rights to all its inhabitants irrespective of religion, race or sex; it will guarantee freedom of religion, conscience, language, education and culture."

57 *Id.*, Deputy C.J. Melcer's ruling, ¶ 5.
58 *Id.*, J. Mintz's ruling ¶ 1.
59 *Id.*, J. Sohlberg's ruling, ¶ 8.
60 *Id.*, C.J. Hayut's ruling, ¶ 8.
61 HCJ 466/07 Galon v. Attorney General, PD 65(2) 1 (2012) (Isr.).

13
Toward Deeper Dialogue: Constitutional and International Law

Cheryl Saunders

Introduction

It is a pleasure to contribute to this volume to celebrate Mark Tushnet's extraordinary contributions to comparative constitutional law. I begin by expressing my appreciation to Mark for the formative role he has played in developing the field of comparative constitutional law. I still remember how impressed I was by the ambition of that early article in the *Yale Law Journal* in 1999,[1] while mentally pushing back against the catch-all of bricolage, which subsequent scholarship has done so much to unpack. I have always found his work thought-provoking and instructive, even when—perhaps particularly when—I did not entirely agree.

I also recall with belated, retrospective affection one memorable project on which we worked together as coeditors, with Thomas Fleiner: the *Routledge Handbook of Constitutional Law*.[2] To try to capture different comparative experiences we asked authors to work on the thematic chapters in pairs. We learned a lot about our fellow scholars from that bold experiment. We also found that, where the pairing presented the opportunity, chapters were constructed around the generalities that international law demands, rather than grappling with the complexity of difference and, so, the challenge of comparison, at the level of constitutional law.

This leads me to my present theme, which I hope is a suitable tribute to Mark.

In this chapter, I put a case for an informed dialogue between those working in the fields of constitutional law and international law respectively, in the interests of both. I have in mind more than an exchange of basic information about the mechanics of the two fields, which are familiar enough and readily accessible to those interested. What I am after, at least in the short term, is deeper, mutual comprehension of what might loosely be described as the worldview of each of them, as a basis for collaborative action on appropriate matters. The ambition of the project should extend as dialogue occurs.

[1] Mark Tushnet, *The Possibilities of Comparative Constitutional Law*, 108 Yale L.J. 1225 (1999).
[2] Routledge Handbook of Constitutional Law (Mark Tushnet, Thomas Fleiner & Cheryl Saunders eds., 2013).

Cheryl Saunders, *Toward Deeper Dialogue: Constitutional and International Law* In: *Redefining Comparative Constitutional Law*. Edited by: Vicki C. Jackson and Madhav Khosla, Oxford University Press. © Cheryl Saunders 2025.
DOI: 10.1093/9780191996344.003.0013

The chapter falls into two substantive sections. In the first section, I build the case for dialogue conceptually. This section begins by describing the foundations of the relationship between constitutional and international law, which are uncontroversial and generally well known. It continues by showing that, nevertheless, the subdisciplines tend to operate in isolation from each other, each pursuing their own vision, producing a silo effect. It argues that, even as constitutional and international law have become increasingly interdependent, this modus operandi has effectively continued, with each subdiscipline unilaterally adapting its principles and practices in response to the changed conditions, to the extent that adaptation has occurred at all. The outcome has reinforced the silo effect, with results that are unsustainable, at least in the real world.

The second, shorter, section of the chapter demonstrates some of the practical consequences that arise. It draws generally on the large and widening field of the making and implementation of new or amended constitutions. It has a particular focus on the relationship between peacemaking and constitution-building, in which the two subdisciplines are apt to collide. Various solutions are possible, but none of them will be reached without the dialogue and mutual understanding for which this chapter calls.

Building the Case

Foundations

The coexistence of domestic and international law is a product of a world order constructed around states. States are defined as having a people, a territory, a government, and the capacity to enter into relations with other states.[3] The definition assumes, without specifying, that there will be bodies of law within states and between states. It also assumes, without specifying, that the responsibility for implementing both bodies of law within a state lies with the state concerned.

Most, although not all, states now are members of the United Nations, the Charter of which recognizes them as formally equal and sovereign, subject to the inroads that the Charter itself makes.[4] Of course, the picture is, and always has been, more complex than this. The concept of a state, which derives from the experiences of polities that centralized authority within relatively well-defined borders, is unfamiliar and undeveloped, sometimes to the point of being functionally fanciful in parts of the world.[5] In addition to the so-called sovereign states that

[3] Montevideo Convention on the Rights and Duties of States art. 1, Dec. 26, 1933, 1761 U.N.T.S. 411.

[4] UN Charter art. 2.

[5] Raza Saaed, *The Ubiquity of State Fragility: Fault Lines in the Categorisation and Conceptualisation of Failed and Fragile States*, 29 Soc. & Legal Stud. 767 (2020).

comprise the polities formally accepted as having international legal personality, there are others not so recognized which effectively operate as states.[6] There also are various categories of polities that exercise a more limited form of independent self-government in association with a sovereign state.[7] In practice, as opposed to form, states are very far from equal, economically and geopolitically. The standard account of the world of states that gives rise to the bodies of law with which this chapter is concerned nevertheless is adequate enough for present purposes.

As this account suggests, international law and domestic law are inherently interdependent to a degree. International law may draw on and feed back into domestic law and practice in a variety of ways, in an iterative process.[8] International institutions necessarily have distinctive characteristics, but draw some inspiration from domestic constitutional design and operation. States rely on international law to achieve outcomes on matters that serve their interests but are beyond their jurisdiction and control. International law relies on state law and institutions to give many of its norms legal and practical effect.

Acting as a form of hinge between the two bodies of law is the constitution of each state. Every state has, or is in the process of creating, a constitution of some kind. Most state-level constitutions have similar properties in the sense of being codified, entrenched, and regarded as fundamental law, enforceable through a judicial process. This traditional concept of the modern constitution provides the authority for the exercise of public power within the state.[9] It draws its legitimacy from the exercise of sovereign authority by the state, in a way that usually is ascribed to a sovereign people.

National constitutions have a face to the outside world as well. Most obviously, they create the institutions and authorize the processes whereby the state exercises its capacity to enter into relations with other states, explicitly or implicitly. In addition, however, every constitution is drafted with an eye to the reactions of some part of the outside world. This inevitably is the case in setting or assuming the boundaries of territory and citizenship,[10] but the point can be substantiated in other ways as well. An imperial power typically had some sway in relation to constitutions drafted in the context of decolonization.[11] Powerful neighbors may

[6] Rowan Nicholson, Statehood and the State-like in International Law (2019)

[7] William Thomas Worster, *Functional Statehood in Contemporary International Law*, 46 Brook. J. Int'l. L 39 (2020).

[8] An Hertogen, *The Persuasiveness of Domestic Law Analogies in International Law*, 29 Eur. J. Int'l L. 1127 (2018).

[9] Dieter Grimm, *The Achievement of Constitutionalism and its Prospects in a Changed World*, *in* The Twilight of Constitutionalism? 3 (Petra Dobner & Martin Loughlin eds., 2010).

[10] Chaihark Hahm & Sung Ho Kim, Making "We the People": Constitutional founding in postwar Japan and South Korea (2015); The Double-Facing Constitution (Jacco Bomhoff, David Dyzenhaus & Thomas Poole eds., 2020).

[11] The nature and extent of this influence differed. In Australia, for example, where the Constitution was drafted before full independence was achieved, it finally was promulgated in an Act of the Imperial Parliament, from which it derived binding force: Commonwealth of Australia Constitution Act 1900 (Imp).

influence the substance or constitution-making process of less powerful states.[12] Some of the earliest constitutions were written to ward off colonization or other forms of external influence by simulating what was assumed to be modernity.[13] International institutions have presided over the creation of new states and their admission to the United Nations since 1945 and continue to do so. The creation of new states now is relatively rare but requires recognition by other states when it occurs.[14] The credentials of the constitution of the new state are not acknowledged as a consideration in these processes but at the very least contribute to the context by reference to which the recognition of statehood occurs.

And occasionally, in a small number of cases which nevertheless offer precedents, international actors appear effectively to have imposed a constitution on another state. The examples typically cited for this purpose are Germany and Japan in the wake of World War II, although even in these cases small but significant steps were taken to support the evolution of a sense of local ownership.[15] A more recent but less encouraging example is Bosnia-Herzegovina, still struggling to achieve normality under a constitution approved in the Dayton Accords.[16] These and other less clear-cut examples, including Iraq, have prompted occasional scholarly speculation about an internationalized *pouvoir constituant*.[17] For the moment, this possibility remains speculation. It has no purchase in either the theory and practice of states or in the formal stance of international institutions.[18]

These aspects of the relations between state constitutions and international law and institutions typically have attracted little attention, until recently, in either constitutional or international law. They have been reinforced, however, by global developments since the fall of the Berlin Wall and contribute to the larger picture that would now provide the setting for interdisciplinary dialogue. The next section sketches the relative indifference of the subdisciplines to each other, as matters stand, as a prelude to examining the implications of more recent developments.

[12] Prabindra Shakya, *Why Nepal's Federalism Debate Matters to India and China*, ConstitutionNet (June 17, 2014), https://constitutionnet.org/news/why-nepals-federalism-debate-matters-india-and-china.

[13] Linda Colley, The Gun, the Ship and the Pen 294 (2021).

[14] Timor-Leste and South Sudan are examples. Bougainville may be another.

[15] Jo Eric Khushal Murkens, From Empire to Union: Conceptions of German Constitutional Law since 1871, at 146–52 (2013); Koseki Shoichi, The Birth of Japan's Postwar Constitution (Ray A. Moore trans., Westview Press, 1998).

[16] European Commission, *Key Findings of the 2022 Report on Bosnia and Herzegovina* (Nov. 22, 2022), https:/ec.europa.eu/commission/presscorner/detail/hr/country_22_6093.

[17] Alexandra Kemmerer, *The* Pouvoir Constituant *in Times of Transition: A Comment on Andrew Arato and Philipp Dann*, in Demokratie in der Weltgesellschaft 507–17 (Hauke Brunkhorst ed., 2009).

[18] *See* United Nations, Guidance Note of the Secretary-General of the United Nations on United Nations Constitutional Assistance 3 (Sept. 2020) (describing constitution making as a "sovereign process"), https://peacemaker.un.org/sites/peacemaker.un.org/files/SG%20Guidance%20Note%20on%20Constitutional%20Assistance_1.pdf.

Silos

The relationship between domestic and international law is formally determined by the choice between monism or dualism, or one of the many variants on them that blur the distinction.[19] The choice lies with the state, and patterns differ significantly across the world. The relationship may be specified in the constitution, or may be simply an assumption that underpins the legal system. On one version of monism, some or all of the international legal norms by which the state is bound may override the constitution itself.[20] Even in this situation, however, the relationship lies in the hands of the state, through power to amend or, if necessary, remake the constitution.[21]

Subject to this schema, the two subdisciplines of constitutional and international law tend to operate in intellectual silos. The explanation lies in deep differences between them, which I ascribed earlier to their respective disciplinary world views. At their core are different perspectives on the nature of law and the sources of their own legitimacy, which influence the assumptions that they make and their attitude to the other.

Constitutional law assumes a source of sovereignty within the state from which the legitimacy of a constitution derives and on which the exercise of all public power draws. In democracies, sovereignty is at least notionally assigned to the people. This underpins the cycle of elections and public accountability on which democracies rely, including for the making and implementation of law within the territory of the state. Constitutions sit at the apex of integrated domestic legal and political systems and most are enforceable through courts, as well as through political processes. The authoritative sources on which domestic law draws directly, subject to the constitution, are internal to the state or under its control and their substance is determined by state institutions, directly or indirectly. In the event of conflict between constitutional and international law, the former prevails within the state, from the perspective of constitutional law, unless moderated by monism or domestic law. The potential for conflict is lessened, although by no means eradicated, by the assumed parameters of the field. Constitutions focus primarily on the control of public power within the state, rather than on the exercise of external sovereignty by state institutions. The law interpreted and applied by domestic courts is primarily domestic rather than international law.

[19] Madelaine Chiam, *Monism and Dualism in International Law*, Oxford Bibliographies (Jun. 27, 2018), https://www.oxfordbibliographies.com/display/document/obo-9780199796953/obo-9780199796953-0168.xml (last accessed Nov. 30, 2023).

[20] Robert Kolb & Momchil Milanov, *Dualism/Monism*, Max Planck Encyclopedia of Comparative Constitutional Law (Aug. 2020), [31], [33], https://oxcon.ouplaw.com/display/10.1093/law-mpeccol/law-mpeccol-e248 (last accessed Nov. 30, 2023).

[21] The qualification avoids the possibility that the relationship between domestic and international law might be treated as unamendable in some constitutional contexts.

By contrast, lacking a sovereign, international law is challenged by enforceability, despite ingenious contemporary attempts to minimize the difficulty. Different international law regimes have tackled this challenge differently, contributing to the fragmentation of the corpus of international law.[22] International law draws its legitimacy from the actual or deemed collective support of states, through treaties or customary international law, elaborated in the writings of jurists. The link between states and international law norms becomes attenuated over time through treaty interpretation and the incremental evolution of international law through the decisions and actions of international institutions. In the event of conflict with domestic, including constitutional law, international law prevails in the international sphere, drawing on the logic of collective authority and a presumption of hierarchical authority. As with constitutional law, however, conflict is sidestepped by the self-imposed parameters of the field: international law does not take account of the internal organization of states in evaluating state compliance.

This account now is out of date, for reasons to be canvassed in the next section. No doubt it also is somewhat superficial and incomplete. It reflects the starting points of each subdiscipline accurately enough, however, to explain the degree of disciplinary separation. As a result, operating within their respective spheres, constitutional law and international law have developed as distinct and complex bodies of theory, law, and practice, each of which has generated a rich scholarly literature. Both have their own, sometimes anguished, internal debates, reflecting their principal preoccupations. In constitutional law, including its comparative counterpart, these include the appropriate role and scope of judicial review, the limits of constitutional amendment and the threats of democratic decay. In international law, they include fragmentation, enforcement, and deadlock in the operation and renovation of key global institutions.

In some respects the concerns of the subdisciplines overlap, in ways given new focus by the pressures of globalization. The tensions between particularism and universalism,[23] in particular, are common to both. So are the related criticisms of the assumptions of both subdisciplines emanating from the so-called Global South, or Third World.[24] The differences between the disciplines ensures that even these debates are taking place in isolation from each other, however, denying these important questions the rounded examination that they deserve.

[22] For an argument that international law diverges between states as well as regimes, *see* ANTHEA ROBERTS, IS INTERNATIONAL LAW INTERNATIONAL? (2017).

[23] Neil Walker has an interesting take on this old question in constitutional law: Neil Walker, *Of Law and Boundaries*, *in* THE OXFORD HANDBOOK OF GLOBAL LEGAL PLURALISM 427 (Paul Schiff Berman ed., 2020).

[24] Contributions in *Third World Approaches to International Law Review* provide an introduction to the field, https://twailr.com/ (last accessed Nov. 30, 2023).

Evolving Practice

The seeds of the current relationship between constitutional and international law were laid with the creation of the United Nations in 1945 and the pivot toward the protection of human rights in the postwar context, following the Universal Declaration of Human Rights in 1948.[25] The implications of these developments for the dynamics of the relationship took new shape, however, after the end of the Cold War in 1989, with rapidly accelerating speed. The collapse of the Soviet Union lifted the constraints on international institutions that were attributable to bipolar geopolitics and removed bipolar competition over systems of government, at least temporarily. These developments coincided with extraordinary innovations in information technology, which took hold over the decade of the 1990s, eventually enabling the almost instantaneous transmission of knowledge and news about constitutional and international developments.[26] The new age of globalization saw a rapid increase in the actual and virtual mobility of people, for an array of professional, personal, and humanitarian purposes, contributing to a greater sense of global connection, the sharing of values, and the spreading of views.

The changes over this time that deserve particular attention for present purposes can be grouped into three categories.

The first concerns the reach and depth of international law, which in turn is connected to the newfound flexibility of international institutions. The United Nations (UN) is a convenient starting point, where geopolitical changes freed the Security Council, the General Assembly and other UN bodies from the constraints that bipolar competition had imposed. A period of growth followed, in the reach and energy of international law, in areas that overlapped with domestic, including constitutional law. This was most obviously the case with human rights law, but international criminal law and international economic law offer other familiar examples. The greater reach of international law was partly attributable to the obvious mechanism of treaty, as new treaties or protocols to existing treaties were made and treaty accessions rapidly accelerated.[27] In addition, however, it stemmed from the much more loosely defined corpus of customary international law and of the sources on which it might draw,[28] and to the incremental growth of international

[25] G.A. Res. 217 (III) A, Universal Declaration of Human Rights (Dec. 10, 1948), https://www.un.org/en/about-us/universal-declaration-of-human-rights.

[26] Science and Media Museum, *A Short History of the Internet* (Dec. 3, 2020), https://www.scienceandmediamuseum.org.uk/objects-and-stories/short-history-internet#:~:text=Consequently%2C%20the%20number%20of%20websites,around%2010%20million%20global%20users.

[27] To illustrate the point by reference to human rights treaties: Australian Human Rights Commission, *Timeline of Major National Human Rights Treaties*, https://humanrights.gov.au/our-work/projects/timeline-major-international-human-rights-treaties.

[28] *See e.g.* the claims concerning the "elevation" of the jurisprudence of international criminal tribunals to norms of customary international law: Roozbeh B. Baker, *Customary International Law in the 21st Century: Old Challenges and New Debates*, 21 Eur. J. Int'l L. 173 (2010).

law through decisions and other actions of international institutions.[29] These latter developments encouraged conceptualization of the subjects of international law as extending well beyond states[30] and broadened the scope of international vis-à-vis domestic law without needing to demonstrate state acquiescence.

A parallel development involved advances in techniques within different international law regimes to enhance compliance with international law, in ways designed to overcome limitations on enforcement. These developments also lessened the reliance of international law on participating states. Examples include the treaty monitoring procedures established in connection with most of the human rights conventions, which interact with state reports or deal with complaints or communications;[31] the elaborate dispute resolution procedures of the World Trade Organization;[32] Investor-State Dispute Settlement procedures (ISDS);[33] and sanctions regimes under the auspices of the Security Council.[34]

A second category of changes in global practice over the past three decades or so concerns constitution-making and the sometimes related activities of peacemaking and peacebuilding. The catalyst, once again, was the events of 1989. The end of that phase of the bipolar world led to an extensive new wave of constitution-making, as new states were created and existing states made new constitutions or substantially revised existing ones. Almost all this constitutional activity was directed toward democratization, broadly around a set of institutions and principles associated with liberal/social constitutional democracy. It is not clear to what extent this phenomenon was orchestrated by the victors of the Cold War, but it seems likely also to have been driven by a desire on the part of leaders and peoples in states around the world to achieve the prosperity and relative individual autonomy offered by established, democratic systems.

Constitutions made at this time for this purpose inevitably looked to democratic constitutions elsewhere. Many, perhaps most, of these constitutional projects also involved active assistance from external advisers, provided through states or institutions within states, international NGOs, intergovernmental organizations, and regional or international bodies.[35] As time has gone on, this activity has increased, becoming systematized and professionalized. One effect has been a greater degree of apparent convergence of the text and institutional design of many of the

[29] The General Comments of Human Rights Treaty Bodies are an example: UN Office of the High Commissioner for Human Rights, *General Comments*, https://www.ohchr.org/en/treaty-bodies/general-comments.

[30] Jan Klabbers, International Law 67–90 (2013).

[31] UN Human Rights Documentation, https://research.un.org/en/docs/humanrights/treaties.

[32] World Trade Organization, *A Unique Contribution*, https://www.wto.org/english/thewto_e/whatis_e/tif_e/disp1_e.htm.

[33] Joachim Pohl, Kekeletso Mashigo & Alexis Nohen, *Dispute Settlement Procedures in International Investment Agreements: A Large Sample Survey*, OECD Working Papers on International Investment 2012/02 (2012), https://www.oecd.org/daf/inv/investment-policy/WP-2012_2.pdf.

[34] UN Security Council, *Sanctions*, https://www.un.org/securitycouncil/sanctions/information.

[35] Comparative Constitution Making (David Landau & Hanna Lerner ed., 2019).

constitutions of the world, although outcomes remain widely variable, depending on context.

External involvement in state constitution-making is potentially sensitive. Physical presence within the state requires at least tacit agreement by the state and an invitation of some kind from someone qualified to give it. External actors also pay at least formal deference to state sovereignty. Initially, external involvement in constitution-making was described in terms of technical or rule of law assistance, although the purpose now is more explicitly acknowledged.[36] The official guidance to UN institutions involved in constitution-building assistance also insists on the need for "national ownership and leadership."[37] Significantly, however, the latest version of the UN guidance defines national ownership as requiring broad inclusion; a requirement determined by international standards rather than by reference to local expectations of what "ownership" might involve. Tellingly also, it requires international actors to whom the guidance note applies to promote "international economic and social norms and standards."[38]

The increasingly ambitious role of international institutions suggests other possible bases for involvement in national constitution-making. The Sustainable Development Goals (SDG), formulated by the General Assembly, offer multiple points of entry, including the commitment to "fostering peaceful, just and inclusive societies."[39] A justification for UN involvement that is explicitly grounded in the Charter, however, is the achievement and maintenance of "international peace and security."[40] The SDGs themselves are in part justified as a "shared blueprint for peace."[41] And conflict is a driver of many constitution-making projects. An unwelcome feature of the unipolar world that evolved from 1989 was the growing prevalence of intrastate conflict. Such conflict may have implications for international stability, quite apart from its consequences for the peoples of the states involved. It attracts international attention on that basis, to a degree and in ways that vary with the nature of the conflict. More often than not, resolution of intrastate conflict requires, or is deemed to require, commitments about the governance of the state for the future, secured through constitutional change. The relevance of the tension between peacemaking and constitution-building for the relations between international and constitutional law is explored as a case study in the following section of the chapter. The point here is to notice conflict resolution as an element in the involvement of international institutions in constitution-making and engagement in the internal constitutional affairs of states, which has become increasingly pronounced in recent decades.

[36] Guidance, *supra* note 18.
[37] *Id.* at 3.
[38] *Id.*
[39] UN, *The 17 Goals*, https://sdgs.un.org/goals.
[40] UN Charter art. 1.
[41] UN, *supra* note 39.

The final set of changes that occurred over these decades with implications for the dynamics of the relationship between constitutional and international law involves institutionalized regional collaboration with domestic constitutional impact. One form of such collaboration is regionalized commitment to human rights protection through a treaty, which may also establish a regional court for the purpose. The European Convention on Human Rights (ECHR) is an example, bringing together 46 member states of the Council of Europe,[42] and vesting jurisdiction to interpret and apply the Convention in the European Court of Human Rights. The ECHR came into force in 1953 and confirmed its "living instrument" approach in 1978.[43] Like many other transnational human rights movements, however, it developed new intensity after 1990.[44] The advisory European Commission for Democracy through Law also was established in 1990, under the auspices of the Council of Europe, and played a significant role in the democratization processes in central and eastern Europe.[45]

Equally significant are movements toward institutionalized regional integration, of which Europe again is an exemplar, although there are developed regional arrangements also in Africa, Latin America, and elsewhere.[46] The European Union had its foundations in the immediate aftermath of World War II but achieved new levels of sophistication over the decade of the 1990s, formally becoming a Union, with European citizens, in 1993.[47] The deepening integration of the European Union blurred the boundaries between domestic and international law. It created a level of government above the state as a polity with federal and confederal characteristics. It flirted for a while with the transformation of the treaties on which it was built into a constitution of a kind.[48] It circumscribed the constitutions of its member states around "shared values" to a considerable extent, the limits of which remain unsettled. It prompted a rich outpouring of scholarship examining these unique arrangements, introducing new theoretical perspectives into both constitutional and international law. It became an important building block for theories of global constitutionalism.

[42] European Convention of Human Rights, 1950, https://www.echr.coe.int/documents/d/echr/convention_ENG.

[43] Tyrer v. The United Kingdom (1979–80) 2 EHRR 1.

[44] Ed Bates, The evolution of the European Convention on Human Rights 20 (2010).

[45] For further details on the Venice Commission, *see* https://www.venice.coe.int/WebForms/pages/?p=01_Presentation#:~:text=The%20European%20Commission%20for%20Democracy,advisory%20body%20on%20constitutional%20matters.

[46] Micha Wiebusch, *The Role of Regional Organizations in the Protection of Constitutionalism*, International IDEA Discussion Paper 17/2016 (2016), https://www.idea.int/sites/default/files/publications/the-role-of-regional-organizations-in-the-protection-of-constitutionalism.pdf.

[47] Treaty on European Union, 1993 (the Maastricht Treaty).

[48] European Parliament, *Draft Treaty Establishing a Constitution for Europe (Not Ratified)*, https://www.europarl.europa.eu/about-parliament/en/in-the-past/the-parliament-and-the-treaties/draft-treaty-establishing-a-constitution-for-europe.

Reactions

Both constitutional and international law and practice reacted to the global changes in the contexts in which they operate in a variety of ways, the most prominent of which are sketched in this section. As a generalization, however, their reactions preserved, to the point of reinforcing, the disciplinary silos. There has been relatively little recognition of growing interdependence in ways that call for mutual understanding, interdisciplinary respect, and collaboration to meet overlapping interests.[49]

Both the expansion of international law into matters internal to states and the increasing extraterritorial engagement of state actors, exercising the external sovereignty of the state, have affected constitutional law and practice. The nature and extent of these effects differ between regions, however, and between states within regions. In parts of the world, including the vast and diverse Asia-Pacific region, they are relatively muted, to the extent that they are noticeable at all.

In one familiar manifestation of impact, international human rights norms increasingly are adopted or adapted, albeit selectively, for the purposes of national and sometimes subnational constitutions. They are a convenient and obvious source on which to draw in designing domestic constitutional instruments, whether or not international advisers also are involved. They may be accompanied by an explicit constitutional authority or duty for domestic courts to draw on international legal sources in interpreting the rights provisions, although without requiring them to be followed.[50] Even without such encouragement, many, although not all, courts with a constitutional jurisdiction may refer to international law for the purposes of constitutional interpretation, applying it where they deem it appropriate to do so.[51] This development has the effect of eroding the distinction between monism and dualism, but without eradicating it altogether, at least from the domestic standpoint.[52]

The impact of global activity in domestic law may raise new and unfamiliar challenges with which constitutional law is not equipped to deal with readily and without controversy. The challenge in *Miller* to the withdrawal of the United Kingdom from the European Union treaties without legislation was one example.[53] The issue raised indirectly in *Allister* is another, about how to explain domestic legislation that accords supremacy to the Northern Ireland Protocol, in

[49] Even where dialogue is beginning to open up, it tends to be confined to particular international law regimes; the impact of international arbitration on national constitutions, for example. This makes sense from the standpoint of international law but is a niche interest for constitutional lawyers.

[50] For example, S. Afr. Const. § 39, 1996.

[51] Vicki Jackson, Constitutional Engagement in a Transnational Era (2013).

[52] David T. Bjorgvinsson, The Intersection of International Law and Domestic Law 15–17 (2015).

[53] R (Miller) v. Secretary of State for Exiting the European Union [2017] UKSC 5.

a constitutional system grounded in a theory of parliamentary sovereignty.[54] An example of a very different kind is drawn from Australia, where in *M68* the High Court was required to decide whether Commonwealth action in relation to "regional processing centres" established in neighboring countries at the instance of Australia, with Australian logistical support and Australian funding, breached Australian constitutional doctrine arising from the constitutional separation of judicial power.[55] In circumstances in which local law authorized the actual detention, a majority of the Court dismissed the claim. Whatever the outcome in these cases, which varied, they point to a need for both theoretical and conceptual development in at least some constitutional contexts, in order to respond adequately to the challenges posed by internationalization.[56]

The implications of internationalization for the operations of constitutional government and the sources on which domestic law might draw is beginning to be reflected in scholarship on constitutional law. It feeds into Martin Loughlin's concern about the implications of "cosmopolitanism" and "ordo-constitutionalism" for constitutional democracy.[57] It is an element in the practices tackled by Vicki Jackson in her work on constitutional "engagement."[58] Early foundations for more systemic projects have been laid in a few collections that bring together the perspectives of constitutional and international scholars.[59] As might be expected, the puzzle of the relationship between constitutional and international human rights has been one of the first issues to attract attention.[60] Typically, this work emanates from the Global North and has not begun to tackle the even more complex relationship of constitutional and international law in the Global South.[61] And even in the Global North, the dimensions of this work that are relevant for present purposes have not made much of an impression on general constitutional scholarly discourse.

The emergence of a field presently referred to as Foreign Relations Law, which also is attracting some comparative attention, is an example of burgeoning interest of another kind in the constitutional implications of international law.[62] It is still in

[54] In the matter of an application by James Hugh Allister and others for Judicial Review [2023] UKSC 3; for a critique, *see* Mark Elliott, *Nothing to See Here? Allister in the Supreme Court*, PUBLIC LAW FOR EVERYONE (July 6, 2023), https://publiclawforeveryone.com/2023/07/06/nothing-to-see-here-allister-in-the-supreme-court/.

[55] Plaintiff M68/2015 v. Minister for Immigration and Border Protection [2016] HCA 1.

[56] For an attempt to provide a theoretical framework in the European context *see* CORMAC S. MACAMHLAIGH, NEW CONSTITUTIONAL HORIZONS: TOWARDS A PLURALIST CONSTITUTIONAL THEORY (2022).

[57] MARTIN LOUGHLIN, AGAINST CONSTITUTIONALISM (2022).

[58] JACKSON, *supra* note 51.

[59] For example, RULING THE WORLD (Jeffrey L. Dunoff & Joel P. Trachtman eds., 2009).

[60] A superb example is Gerald L. Neuman, *Human Rights and Constitutional Rights: Harmony and Dissonance*, 55 STAN. L. REV. 1863 (2003).

[61] The terminology is used in the sense developed in THE GLOBAL SOUTH AND COMPARATIVE CONSTITUTIONAL LAW (Philipp Dann, Michael Riegner & Maxim Bonnemann eds., 2020).

[62] THE OXFORD HANDBOOK OF COMPARATIVE FOREIGN RELATIONS LAW (Curtis A. Bradley ed., 2019); *see also* Bomhoff et al., *supra* note 10, part III.

its infancy, however—at this point, a niche interest among constitutional scholars around the world, and more likely to attract the attention of international lawyers.[63] It remains to be seen whether the insights drawn from comparison will spark more interest in constitutional changes to enhance the accountability of state actors for decisions taken in the exercise of external sovereignty.

At least as marked as the various ways in which constitutional law and practice have begun to actively engage with international law has been a pushback against it. The trend has been most evident in Europe, where interdependence is most marked, within the structures of both the Council of Europe and the European Union. It was evidenced spectacularly by the withdrawal of the United Kingdom from the European Union.[64] Only marginally less spectacular has been the defiance of EU standards by some of its member states, including Hungary and Poland,[65] and Russia's withdrawal from the Council of Europe and the European Court of Human Rights.[66] The potential for pushback is reflected also in the inclusion of a clause in the European treaties to respect the "national identities" of the member states,[67] which in turn contributed to the burgeoning comparative constitutional jurisprudence on constitutional identity and its doctrinal significance.[68] Some, but by no means all, of these developments can be attributed to the rise of authoritarianism and democratic decline. And while these examples are confined to Europe, there are no signs elsewhere in the world that other states are more inclined to surrender substantial authority to an aspect of an international order. If anything, the pandemic years showed states reasserting authority to protect their populations in priority to requests for international collaboration.

The patterns of reactions in international law and relations to the developments of the past 30 years were similarly intradisciplinary. The expansion of the range and depth of international law encouraged still further expansion and prompted debates within the discipline over its justification and legitimacy. One result is that acknowledged subjects of international law have extended beyond states and international institutions and it is clear that the category is not closed. Others for

[63] Campbell McLachlan, *Five Conceptions of the Function of Foreign Relations Law*, *in* Bradley, *supra* note 62, at 87, 88: "outside the United States, the field enjoys no wide currency or commonly accepted scope."

[64] European Commission, *The EU–UK Withdrawal Agreement* (2019–20), https://commission.europa.eu/strategy-and-policy/relations-non-eu-countries/relations-united-kingdom/eu-uk-withdrawal-agreement_en.

[65] *Poland and Hungary in European Commission's Rule of Law Spotlight Again*, EURONEWS (July 13, 2022), https://www.euronews.com/my-europe/2022/07/13/poland-hungary-in-european-commissions-rule-of-law-spotli.

[66] Council of Europe, *Russia Ceases to Be a Party to the European Convention on Human Rights* (Sep. 16, 2022), https://www.coe.int/en/web/portal/-/russia-ceases-to-be-party-to-the-european-convention-on-human-rights.

[67] Treaty on European Union art. 4(2), originating in the Maastricht Treaty, 1992.

[68] Elke Cloots, *National Identity, Constitutional Identity and Sovereignty in the EU*, 45 NETH. J. LEGAL PHIL. 82 (2016). While Cloots challenges the legitimacy of the link, she also substantiates it and further confirms the tendencies that it reflects.

whom subject status is claimed include individuals, in the face of the development of relevant international law regimes including, most obviously, those dealing with human rights and international criminal law.[69] This also chimes with the moral recognition of the peoples of the world as sharing a common humanity irrespective of national borders, even though it is not reflected in the realities of global life.

Theories of global constitutionalism are another, significant, international law response to the developments that have occurred. The core claims for global constitutionalism focus on perceptions of the constitutionalization of the international legal order itself, encompassing both the extent to which it resembles a form of constitutional order, in form, operation, and aspiration, and a desirable trajectory for its future development. Given the inequalities of the international order and the inherent limitations imposed by its nature and composition, these claims are contested.[70] Relevantly for present purposes, however, they are said to have implications for the status of national constitutions as well, which have been perceived as components of a "compound constitutional system," supplemented by international law.[71] This perception draws some support from the extensive involvement of international actors in constitution-building projects in some states. It has also been claimed as a response to the "hollowing out" of traditional democracy within states, necessitating remedial developments at the international level. Such theories have little purchase in reality in the operation of either level of government, however, and no purchase at all in constitutional theory.

Evolving global interdependence exposes a widening range of matters on which active collaboration between states is needed. They include economic and social inequality, climate change, pandemic control, and population movements. Each is challenging; each requires the capabilities that both state and international law can bring to bear. These generalities suggest the value of dialogue. The next section, however, uses the particular context of peace and constitution-making to demonstrate the need for dialogue in more concrete terms.

Illustrating the Case

Many examples might be used to demonstrate the need for enhanced mutual understanding between constitutional and international law. They include international advocacy for the incorporation of international human rights and other norms directly into constitutions, international pressures for adherence to international understandings of transitional justice in the wake of conflict, advocacy

[69] Klabbers, *supra* note 30, ch. 4, 6. Cf. the somewhat more cautious stance in James Crawford, Chance, Order, Change: The Course of International Law 449–50 (2014).

[70] Crawford, *supra* note 69, at 451.

[71] Anne Peters, *The Globalization of State Constitutions*, *in* New Perspectives on the Divide between National and International Law 251, 257 (Janne Nijman & André Nollkaemper eds., 2007).

of neoliberal policies by international economic institutions, and the inclusion of international arbitration clauses in international investment treaties. Whatever the merits of the international law regimes in each of these fields, attention needs to be paid to their suitability in particular domestic contexts, to which they may need to be adapted, if adopted at all. This is the province of domestic law; often, specifically, constitutional and/or comparative constitutional law.

The example on which I focus here is the resolution of intrastate conflicts that require changes to the way the state is governed. The example is significant, at a time when much global conflict is centered within a particular state and arises from causes for which a political settlement is likely to be needed. Common terms of such a settlement include power-sharing, minority rights protection, and greater localized autonomy, to deal with grievances arising from inequality, discrimination, and exclusion. The issues are challenging, and their effective and timely resolution is likely to be critical for those involved.

This familiar enough situation presents problems of implementation and enforcement which the two subdisciplines of constitutional and international law view differently, and to which neither has a complete answer.[72]

From the standpoint of constitutional law, an agreement between parties on terms for ending an intrastate conflict is highly significant in practice but may have no higher legal status than that of an executive agreement, absent provision to the contrary in the constitution itself. Again from this standpoint, the most obvious way to secure compliance with key aspects of the political settlement in the agreement is by including them in an entrenched constitution. This cannot necessarily be guaranteed, however. Constitutional changes that are consistent with the terms of a peace agreement cannot always readily be secured in accordance with expected or required procedures, whether a new constitution is contemplated or amendment of an existing constitution is sought. Success in these circumstances may require considerable commitment to and respect for the underlying peace agreement on the part of constitutional stakeholders whose support may be required for the legitimacy and legality of constitutional change but who may have had limited involvement in peace negotiations.

Even when formal change is made, consistently with the peace agreement, the possibilities of amendment, or unanticipated interpretation, present challenges in relation to its implementation over time. These challenges can be managed to a degree through techniques of constitutional design that have been honed in other contexts, including variable degrees of entrenchment and constitutional guidance

[72] Much of what follows draws on earlier research in Anna Dziedzic & Cheryl Saunders, *Constitutional Implementation for Sustainable Peace*, Melbourne Legal Studies Research Paper Series No. 836 (Jun. 2019), https://papers.ssrn.com/sol3/papers.cfm?abstract_id=3442666; Anna Dziedzic & Cheryl Saunders, *Constitutional Implementation for Sustainable Peace: Update on the Bougainville Case Study*, Melbourne Legal Studies Research Paper Series No. 929 (Dec. 2020), https://papers.ssrn.com/sol3/papers.cfm?abstract_id=3795159.

on interpretive method. Comparative research may identify other solutions as well, which could be adapted to new contexts. Questions so far unanswered, however, include the following. Would it be helpful for the goal of peacebuilding to be incorporated into the concept of a transformative constitution? Should the concept of a "peace constitution" be developed instead, as a distinct category? At what point should such a constitution normalize, so that it no longer is understood through the lens of an aging peace agreement? While these are questions for constitutional law to tackle, an appreciation of their dimensions requires knowledge of peacemaking law and practice from the domain of international law.

From the standpoint of international law, on the other hand, international peace and security is core business, and agreements on which peace can be built are both critical and hard to secure. An agreement to bring an end to an intrastate conflict does not naturally fall under the aegis of international law unless, perhaps, other states become parties, as with the Dayton Accords,[73] or the UN Security Council endorses the agreement in some substantive way, in exercise of its authority under the Charter.[74] In the absence of these conditions, international lawyers have argued for an expansion of the categories of those deemed subject to international law so as to cover all, or some, intrastate peace agreements,[75] or the development of a new field of international law, lex pacificatoria.[76] In the context of these arguments, it sometimes also is claimed that postconflict constitutions may themselves be peace agreements.[77] If any of these possibilities were to eventuate, failure to implement the relevant provisions of the peace agreement through constitutional law could become a matter for international law. At least to this domestic constitutional lawyer, however, that seems an unsatisfactory answer to the undoubted problems of the enforcement of peace agreements through postconflict constitutions. Both constitutional change and its implementation over time need the legitimacy and commitment that only local ownership offers. At the same time, in many cases, local ownership needs to be buttressed by international support to safeguard the security and economic viability of a state struggling with transition to a new constitutional order.

Neither constitutional law nor international law alone can fully bridge the gap between peace agreements and constitutions. While the former offers the most obvious framework within which resolution should be attempted (or so a constitutional lawyer claims), contributions may be needed from international law as well.

[73] Formal parties were the Republic of Bosnia and Herzegovina, the Federal Republic of Yugoslavia, and the Republic of Croatia. A range of other states were signatories or witnesses.

[74] Vijayashri Sripati, Constitution-Making under UN Auspices, ch. 6 (2020).

[75] Scott P. Sheeran, *International Law, Peace Agreements and Self-Determination: The Case of the Sudan*, 60 Int'l & Compar. L. Q. 423 (2011).

[76] Christine Bell, On the law of Peace—Peace Agreements and the Lex Pacificatoria (2008).

[77] Laurie Nathan, *The Real Deal? The Post-Conflict Constitution as a Peace Agreement*, 41 Third World Q. 556 (2020).

Sometimes, moreover, the tables are reversed so that interstate elements of a peace agreement clearly locate it within the field of international law, necessitating insights from comparative constitutional law to maximize its chances of working in practice.

Prospects

There has been a case for dialogue between constitutional and international law since international institutions began reaching into domestic law in the interwar period, at the latest.[78] It took on new urgency in the decades from 1990, marking the current phase of internationalization and globalization triggered by the end of the Cold War. That opportunity was largely missed. Thirty years later the idea is beginning to gather support, in the face of mounting evidence of the mutual interdependence of the two subdisciplines in tackling a host of critical issues. In the context of the case study used in this chapter, for example, experience suggests that the current practice of operating largely in intellectual isolation from each other is not making a sufficient difference on the ground, in terms of either working constitutions or sustainable peace. In the face of evidence of this kind, the borders of the subdisciplines also may be expanding in ways that may demand more effective collaboration. Thus—and none too soon, in my view—the external face of a constitution is becoming a more significant feature of constitutional law and a new focus for study by comparativists. Conversely, international lawyers are looking past domestic constitutions to cities and subnational levels of government in pursuit of effective global responses to the existential threat of climate change.[79]

Both subdisciplines currently share challenges, which also should make dialogue productive and worthwhile. Both are grappling with the phenomenon of the rise of authoritarianism, including the likelihood that at least some of its roots lie in the inequality and anonymity that, in various ways, are products of globalization. Mark has offered further fuel for this debate with his piece "The Globalisation of Constitutional Law as a Weakly Neo-Liberal Project."[80] Both subdisciplines also are facing the need to adapt principle, method, and theory to adequately include the Global South, in a more accurate reflection of the state of the world, in ways that are constructive and not merely deconstructive.[81]

[78] Guy Fiti Sinclair, To Reform the World (2017).

[79] Daniel C. Esty & Dena P. Adler, *Changing International Law for a Changing Climate*, 112 Am. J. Int'l L. Unbound 279 (2018).

[80] Mark Tushnet, *The Globalisation of Constitutional Law as a Weakly Neo-Liberal Project*, 8 Glob. Constitutionalism 29 (2019).

[81] Dann et al., *supra* note 61; Naz Khatoon Modirzadeh, *Let Us All Agree to Die a Little: TWAIL's Unfulfilled Promise*, 65 Harv. Int'l L.J. 1 (2023).

It is to be hoped that the opportunity for dialogue and constructive collaboration is not passing as the contexts in which both subdisciplines operate change. Democratization has faltered, whatever the original catalysts for it over the decades from the 1990s. Constitutional systems everywhere will face major new challenges from climate change which may strike at the very roots of statehood, in terms of territory, people, and government.[82] The war in Ukraine threatens to undermine the raison d'être of the current world order, even if the conflict does not escalate further. And on any view, a multipolar world has returned, bringing with it more vigorous competition over systems of government and greater potential for disagreement in international affairs. It remains only to discover how many poles there turn out to be, and what impact this has on the relationship between constitutional and international law.

[82] Montevideo Convention on the Rights and Duties of States, Dec. 26, 1933, 1761 U.N.T.S. 411.

14
Ancillary Powers of Constitution-Making Bodies

David Landau

An important aspect of Mark Tushnet's recent work has been constituent power, and the way that the theory influences both constitutional amendment and constitution-making.[1] This scholarship raises central concerns that animate Tushnet's other work—in particular, a skepticism of the regulatory power of law, and particularly courts, and a worry that legal discourse may be used to obfuscate the political sphere, where disputes should really be decided.[2] Relatedly, ruminating on constituent power highlights important questions of the limits of law, or, as Tushnet puts it, moments where "law runs out and we must deal with power."[3]

This chapter will use Tushnet's work on constituent power to illuminate ongoing theoretical and practical struggles to restrain or limit constituent assemblies, particularly in Latin America. This chapter explores an aspect that is intertwined with constituent power: ancillary powers of Constituent Assemblies. By ancillary powers, I mean those powers of a Constituent Assembly that go beyond the core action of writing a new constitutional text, such as legislating, organizing elections, and reconstituting other state institutions or replacing their officials.

These ancillary powers of constitution-making are often overlooked, but they can be quite consequential. Indeed, in some recent constitution-making experiences, these collateral powers have been as central as the drafting process itself. Moreover, ancillary powers have become a concern to analysts of constitution-making because they consolidate power in a constitution-making body in ways that have been used for antidemocratic ends. In Venezuela in 1999 and Ecuador in 2008, for example, constituent assemblies wielded their ancillary powers to limit or eliminate institutions in opposition-held hands and to replace the membership of institutions such as high courts, ombudspersons, and local officials, replacing opponents with regime loyalists. The result is a radically changed political context,

[1] *See* Mark Tushnet, *Peasants with Pitchforks, and Toilers with Twitter: Constitutional Revolutions and the Constituent Power*, 13 Int'l J. Const. L. 639 (2013); Mark Tushnet, *Constitution-Making: An Introduction*, 91 Tex. L. Rev. 1983 (2013); Mark Tushnet, *Amendment Theory and Constituent Power*, *in* Comparative Constitutional Theory 552 (Gary Jacobsohn & Miguel Schor eds., 2018).

[2] *See* Mark Tushnet, Taking the Constitution Away from the Courts (1999).

[3] Tushnet, *Peasants with Pitchforks*, *supra* note 1, at 654.

David Landau, *Ancillary Powers of Constitution-Making Bodies* In: *Redefining Comparative Constitutional Law.* Edited by: Vicki C. Jackson and Madhav Khosla, Oxford University Press. © David Landau 2025.
DOI: 10.1093/9780191996344.003.0014

one in which authoritarian actors are able to consolidate nearly all state power and the opposition is quickly swept away.

Given these problems, two prominent analysts of constituent power, Joel Colon-Rios and Andrew Arato, have recently called for conceptualizing the theory in ways that limit constituent assemblies to the work of preparing a new constitutional text, and essentially eliminating ancillary powers.[4] I use Tushnet's conception of constituent power to illuminate two difficulties with these proposals. The first is that it is surprisingly difficult to even draw the line between the core function of a constitution-making body and an ancillary function, a point I illustrate by considering the transitional provisions commonly found in constitutional texts. The second, perhaps deeper, problem is that the wielding of ancillary powers is highly contextual, and they can sometimes have important prodemocratic purposes.

The rest of this chapter is organized as follows. The next section briefly describes the concept of ancillary powers and explores the importance of their abuse as a tool of authoritarian consolidation, drawing on recent examples from Latin America. The chapter then examines scholarly efforts to shape or restrain notions of constituent power to avoid abuse, emphasizing the proposals of Colon-Rios and Arato to limit the ancillary functions of constitution-making bodies. It goes on to use Tushnet's conception of constituent power to suggest both analytic and normative difficulties with attempting to limit constituent power. The chapter concludes by emphasizing Tushnet's view that political, rather than legal, considerations ought to be at the forefront of constitution-making moments, or at the least that his views demand great caution when theorizing in this area.

Ancillary Powers of Constitution-Making Bodies and their Abuses

Ginsburg and Elkins use the concept of an "ancillary power" of a constitutional court to refer to tasks other than the central one of adjudicating constitutional disputes.[5] They find that these other tasks are surprisingly common: 55 percent of constitutional courts around the world have powers to supervise or regulate elections; 39 percent have powers to review treaties; 30 percent have powers to adjudicate charges (such as impeachment) against an executive; and 29 percent have the power to consider sanctions or bans against political parties.[6] These ancillary powers can be very consequential. Consider party bans, which can be used in a militant democracy sense to reduce antidemocratic threats, but can also be used

[4] *See* JOEL COLON-RIOS, CONSTITUENT POWER AND THE LAW (2020); ANDREW ARATO, THE ADVENTURES OF THE CONSTITUENT POWER: BEYOND REVOLUTIONS? (2017).

[5] *See* Tom Ginsburg and Zachary Elkins, *Ancillary Powers of Constitutional Courts*, 87 TEX. L. REV. 1431 (2009).

[6] *Id.* at 1443 tbl.1.

to suppress minority groups or to attack the democratic opposition on behalf of authoritarians.[7] In Cambodia in 2017, for example, the Supreme Court used its party-banning power to disband the only major opposition party, the National Rescue Party, leaving the authoritarian Cambodian People's Party with every single parliamentary seat.[8]

One could make a useful analogy with constitution-making bodies. Their core task, of course, is to write a new constitution. But in fact, recent work has shown that they carry out other tasks at least fairly frequently. First, constitution-making bodies sometimes issue legislation, either directly (such as by issuing a decree) or by selecting a body that has (often temporary) legislative powers. Second, constitution-making bodies sometimes take on tasks that involve reorganizing state institutions. They might, for example, remove officials from power, schedule new elections, or reduce or enhance the power of other bodies, such as legislatures or courts.

As with the ancillary powers of courts, the ancillary powers of constitution-making bodies can be extremely consequential and can sometimes even overshadow the core task of writing a new text. Moreover, they can be linked with the abuse of constitution-making to erode rather than fortify democracy, undermining what Dixon and I have called the "minimum core" of the democratic order.[9] Constitution-making moments can be dangerous moments for democracy.

Across several recent experiences, the basic story has been similar. A single party or coalition with authoritarian goals convokes a constitution-making process and manages to achieve the votes to dominate the constitution-making body. Of course, the text of the constitution is itself a key instrument. Constitution-making processes, at least in theory, put in play the entire institutional order at once. So would-be authoritarians may find it an especially efficient tool to seize power. They can increase the power of the regime while weakening checks on its exercise.[10]

But a narrow focus on constitutional text misses much of what can make constitution-making moments such efficient tools of authoritarianism. In one sense, constitution-making is usually part of a longer process of democratic decline, where regimes also deploy other tools both before and after the constitutional replacement. In another sense, a constitution-making process might play a role as a critical juncture, putting the political system of a country on a new track. This critical juncture is not only about the text, but also about the way in which a constitution-making moment can change the political context.

[7] *See* Samuel Issacharoff, *Fragile Democracies*, 120 Harv. L. Rev. 1405 (2007).

[8] *See* Prak Chan Thul and Amy Sawitta Lefevre, *Cambodia's Main Opposition Party Dissolved by Supreme Court*, Reuters, Nov. 26, 2017, https://www.reuters.com/article/us-cambodia-politics/cambodias-main-opposition-party-dissolved-by-supreme-court-idUSKBN1DG1BO.

[9] *See* Rosalind Dixon and David Landau, *Competitive Democracy and the Democratic Minimum Core*, *in* Assessing Constitutional Performance 268 (Tom Ginsburg & Aziz Huq eds., 2016).

[10] *See* David Landau, *Abusive Constitutionalism*, 47 U.C. Davis L. Rev. 189 (2013).

The wielding of constituent power theory in some recent constitution-making processes in Latin America serves as an illustration. There, the idea that the "people" retain ultimate authority to replace their constitution has often been understood to mean that the constitution-making body, once elected, cannot be restrained and can make any changes to the constitutional order that it wishes. More dramatically, it has sometimes been held to mean that once convoked, the constitution-making body stands above all other state institutions, and can reconstitute, reorganize, or even directly stand in for those bodies whenever it wishes.

The 1991 constitution-making process in Colombia provided an influential precedent for authoritarians elsewhere in the region, even though the 1991 constitution strengthened Colombian democracy and helped to provide an exit from a deep political and social crisis. In allowing the referendum and election calling the Assembly, which was not expressly contemplated as a mode of change in the 1886 constitutional text, the Supreme Court emphasized the theory of constituent power—that the people maintained the inherent power to replace their constitution. That power led the Court (by a narrow margin) to approve the selection of a Constituent Assembly, while throwing out aspects of the presidential decree calling it that narrowed the competence of that body.[11] The president had attempted (on the basis of a multiparty pact) to restrict the Assembly to treating only certain constitutional topics; the Court held that as a reflection of the original constituent power of the people, the Assembly had to have the power to change any pieces of the constitutional order that it wished.[12]

Once convoked, the Assembly did not limit itself to replacing the constitution. It made a controversial decision to revoke the mandate of the Congress and to call immediate new elections for that body.[13] It also retained a kind of legislative power after its drafting work had been completed. The transitional provisions of the new constitution gave the president considerable power to adopt key laws by decree during a set period of time; the Assembly also chose from its own membership a special body (the "small constituent assembly") charged with approving or vetoing those presidential decrees.[14] The Assembly's ancillary activities were controversial at the time (especially the revocation of the congressional mandate), but they had fairly broad support because the Congress was so unpopular, and they had a prodemocratic rather than an antidemocratic impact. The 1991 constitution ultimately helped to rejuvenate an exhausted constitutional order on behalf of a broad multiparty coalition.

[11] *See* Decision No. 138, Oct. 9, 1990 (S. Ct. Col.).
[12] *Id.*
[13] *See* Camilo Calderon, Revocatoria del Congreso en 1991, Credencial Historia No. 162, July 21, 2017, https://www.banrepcultural.org/biblioteca-virtual/credencial-historia/numero-162/revocatoria-del-congreso-en-1991.
[14] *See* Const. Col., trans. arts 5–6 (1991).

The example of the Colombian constituent process proved attractive elsewhere in the Andes in the following years, where it was used to justify constituent assemblies, called outside the existing constitutional order, and which spent much of their time on "ancillary activities." Consider the 1999 Venezuelan process and the 2008 Ecuadorian process. In both cases, populist outsiders (Hugo Chavez and Rafael Correa) won election on a platform that argued existing institutions were illegitimate. Once elected they faced substantial opposition, in Congress and elsewhere, from traditional political actors and parties. They asserted a unilateral right to proceed with a constituent process anyway, after approval of the idea of constitutional replacement by popular referendum.[15] Both assemblies were dominated by supporters of the president, and both wrote constitutions that were both innovative and which tended to centralize power in the new presidents. Both also spent a considerable amount of time on ancillary activities outside of the drafting process itself.

The Venezuelan Constituent Assembly asserted its sweeping powers early and aggressively, waving the banner of original constituent power. In one of its early sessions, the Assembly summoned President Chavez to appear before the Assembly. Chavez humbly placed his presidential mandate before the Assembly, stating that he could only continue in power if the Assembly agreed. The Assembly then voted on whether Chavez should continue in office, and agreed overwhelmingly that he should do so.[16] Given that Chavez supporters had won more than 90 percent of the seats in the Assembly, there was of course never any realistic danger that Chavez would be deposed from power. Rather, the purpose of this dramatic scene—the country's president putting himself underneath the Assembly and later being re-sworn in in front of it—was to make a point: The Assembly was supreme, and it had full power over *all* Venezuelan institutions. The President of the Assembly was explicit on this point: he called the ratification "an act of sovereignty of the National Constituent Assembly" and stated that "the implication from the legal point of view is that all the powers are under the jurisdiction of the Constituent Assembly."[17]

These powers were then used to target the many Venezuelan institutions that were still bastions of the opposition. The Assembly issued decrees reducing the Congress to a rump and closing down the Supreme Court, as well as replacing key local officials and union leaders.[18] It also arrogated to a National Legislative Commission (which it selected) all legislative power for more than a year, much longer than the time it had actually spent on drafting the new constitution.[19] The

[15] *See* Landau, *supra* note 10, at 203–07.

[16] *See La Asamblea Constituyente ratifica a Chávez en su cargo*, El Mundo, Aug. 10, 1999, https://www.elmundo.es/elmundo/1999/agosto/10/internacional/chavez.html.

[17] *Id.*

[18] *See* David Landau, *Constitution Making Gone Wrong*, 64 Ala. L. Rev. 923, 946–48 (2013).

[19] *See* Joshua Braver, *Hannah Arendt in Venezuela: The Supreme Court Battles Hugo Chavez Over the Creation of the Venezuelan Constitution*, 14 Int'l J. Const. L. 555, 568 (2016).

Commission passed a number of key laws. Many of these moves were eventually upheld by the Supreme Court, which accepted that they were an incident of original constituent power.[20] The Assembly became what Braver has aptly called a "despotic and all-powerful actor."[21]

The story in Ecuador is fairly similar. After an initial fight about whether the Assembly wielded "original constituent power," the Assembly again dissolved the Congress and exercised direct legislative powers for a transitional period.[22] It also replaced key officials held by the opposition, such as the Attorney General and Comptroller.[23]

In the contexts in which constitution-making in Venezuela and Ecuador occurred, the wielding of ancillary powers had an antidemocratic impact, unlike in Colombia. In both cases, they allowed demagogic presidents to sweep away muscular but declining opposition movements that retained majority power in legislative bodies, as well as considerable power in the courts, other checking institutions, and at the local level. They also allowed these bodies to take rapid steps to reconstitute the legal order. The stage was set for a centralization of power that led to something like a competitive authoritarian regime in both contexts. In both cases, the ancillary powers of the Assembly appear to be at least as important to the outcome as the drafting function.

The *reductio ad absurdum* of such a sweeping conception of constituent power occurred in Venezuela from 2017 to 2020, when Chavez's successor Nicolas Maduro called a constituent assembly. Maduro's purpose was not to replace or even to amend a constitution with which he was ideologically aligned. Instead, it was to repress the opposition, which had won an overwhelming congressional majority at the end of 2015, as the country slid into a severe economic crisis. Maduro argued (and a packed Supreme Court agreed) that he could call such an assembly on his own, without even needing to hold a referendum.[24] The opposition boycotted the assembly elections and Maduro's allies won every seat, but vote totals were so low that the regime apparently used fraud to boost them.[25] The new assembly

[20] The full engagement of the Court with the constitution-making process is more nuanced: it made some tentative and ultimately unsuccessful efforts to rein in the Assembly. For recounting and analysis of these decisions, see Braver, *supra* note 19, at 569–78; Landau, *supra* note 18, at 943–49.

[21] *See* Braver, *supra* note 19, at 568.

[22] *See* Catherine M. Conaghan, *Ecuador: Correa's Plebiscitary Presidency*, 19 J. DEMOCRACY 46, 57 (2008).

[23] *See id.*

[24] For debate about the legality of this maneuver, see José Ignacio Hernández G., *Symposium on "Venezuela's 2017 (Authoritarian) National Constituent Assembly"—Pursuing Constitutional Authoritarianism*, INT'L J. CONST. L. BLOG, Sept. 1, 2017, http://www.iconnectblog.com/2017/08/symposium-on-venezuelas-2017-authoritarian-national-constituent-assemblyjose-ignacio-hernandez-g.

[25] *See What Has Venezuela's Constituent Assembly Achieved?* BBC NEWS, Aug. 30, 2017, http://www.bbc.com/news/world-latin-america-41094889.

immediately issued a series of decrees, including one asserting that it now held all legislative power, and thus effectively replaced the legislature.

One of the assembly's first decrees removed the national General Prosecutor (who had turned against Maduro).[26] It scheduled snap new elections for a number of posts, including the president (allowing Maduro to win a new term under very unfair electoral conditions), and required all new local officials to be sworn in by the assembly itself. This effectively disqualified opposition mayors who refused to recognize the assembly's legitimacy.[27] Further, the assembly issued a series of important laws, such as a law "Against Hate, For Peaceful Coexistence and Tolerance," which placed vague, draconian restrictions on speech.[28] It created a "Truth and Reconciliation Commission," which was an instrument of the regime's goal to attack opposition figures rather than a genuine attempt to achieve either truth or peace.[29]

What the assembly never did in its three years of life was to write a new constitution or even change a single article of the 1999 Venezuelan constitution. All of its work was carried out using ancillary powers. Its real purpose was to subordinate and bypass the opposition-held legislature, thus acting as a kind of superlegislature or omnicompetent political body, placed above the constituted institutions created by the existing constitutional order itself. As authentic representative of the "people," in other words, the assembly could do whatever it wanted. Predictably, once the Maduro regime regained control over the Congress in new (and dubious) elections held in 2020, the assembly was dissolved.[30] The assembly was no longer a necessary instrument.

Thus, constitution-making bodies can do many things beyond redrafting constitutional texts. These ancillary tasks—such as reconstituting or closing other institutions, scheduling elections, and legislating—may have an affinity with certain theories of constituent power, particularly the very strong variant that has been important in recent years in Latin America. Moreover, these ancillary powers seem important in at least some constitution-making episodes. At least in some cases, they might be used to strengthen a new democratic constitutional order, as suggested by Colombia. But ancillary powers also seem to be a potent tool for abuse by authoritarian actors, as the Venezuelan and Ecuadorian examples show.

[26] *See* Gaceta Oficial 6.322 Extraordinario, Aug. 5, 2017.

[27] *See* Gaceta Oficial 41.259, Oct. 20, 2017 (officials must be sworn in front of Assembly); Gaceta Oficial 41.265, Oct. 26, 2017 (mayoral elections); Gaceta Oficial 6.361 Extraordinario, Jan. 23, 2018 (presidential elections).

[28] *See* Ley constitucional contra el odio, por la conviviencia pacifica y la tolerencia, Gaceta Oficial 41.274, Nov. 8, 2017.

[29] *See* Ley Constitucional de la Comisión para la Verdad, la Justicia, la Paz y la Tranquilidad Pública, Gaceta Oficial 6.323 Extraordinario, Aug. 8, 2017.

[30] *See Nicolás Maduro anuncia la disolución de la Asamblea Constituyente*, El Mundo, Aug. 18, 2020, https://www.elmundo.es/internacional/2020/08/18/5f3bfbfcfc6c8361348b460e.html.

Shaping Constituent Power

The abuse of constitution-making processes, often carried out under the guise of constituent power, has led to theorizing on whether the theory of constituent power can be controlled, restricted, or shaped in some way.[31] Perhaps the most dramatic proposal is that of Sergio Verdugo, who argues in a recent piece that constituent power is so problematic that it should simply be junked.[32] However, Verdugo does not identify an alternative theory to conceptualize constitution-making processes, and such an alternative is not readily available. The basic idea that "the people" ultimately have the power to remake their constitutional order is deeply baked into notions of democratic sovereignty. That is, although the roots of constituent power theory are complex and include staunch critics of liberal democracy such as Schmitt, the theory itself seems intertwined with modern liberal democracy.[33]

Friendlier critics of constituent power have sought to fix or shape the theory, reducing its ambiguities which are ripe for abuse, rather than replacing it entirely. One line of thought seeks to give greater definition to the term "people." Constituent power commonly has a majoritarian valence—it is often triggered by a simple majority vote in a referendum, and constitution-making bodies frequently make decisions by a simple majority vote within the institution. The majoritarian nature of constitution-making seems dangerous, even paradoxical. Ordinary politics is ringed with constraints that temper simple majoritarianism, constraints that can oddly be swept aside during constitution-making.[34] Moreover, theory would seem to predict that constitution-making should be more consensual, not less consensual, than ordinary politics, since it is setting the basic ground rules of the polity.[35] Vicki Jackson argues that democratic consent should be seen as a necessary, but not sufficient, condition for an authentic exercise of constituent power, since democracy is only one of the values that a good constitution should embody.[36] Recent social science also tends to support the idea that constitution-making bodies controlled by a single, dominant political force are associated with worse democratic outcomes than those that require negotiations among multiple political forces.[37]

[31] *See* David Landau & Rosalind Dixon, *Constraining Constitutional Change*, 50 Wake Forest L. Rev. 859 (2015).

[32] *See* Sergio Verdugo, *Is It Time to Abandon the Theory of Constituent Power?* 21 Int'l J. Const. L. 14 (2023).

[33] *See* Rosalind Dixon & David Landau, Abusive Constitutional Borrowing: Legal Globalization and the Subversion of Liberal Democracy 117–18 (2021).

[34] *See* Landau, *supra* note 18, at 932.

[35] *See* Donald L. Horowitz, Constitutional Processes and Democratic Commitment 4–5 (2021) (calling for constitution-making via consensus whenever possible).

[36] *See* Vicki C. Jackson, *Constituent Power or Degrees of Legitimacy*, 12 Vienna J. Int'l L. 319, 338 (2018).

[37] *See* Gabriel L. Negretto and Mariano Sanchez-Talanquer, *Constitutional Origins and Liberal Democracy: A Global Analysis, 1900–2015*, 115 Am. Pol. Sci. Rev. 522 (2021).

Thus, some scholars have suggested that the "people" in constituent power should be conceptualized to require a more consensual, and more durable, showing of support. As Jackson notes, the people is better seen as a multivocal rather than univocal concept, given divisions and disagreements between groups and individuals.[38] For example, one might regulate the meaning of the term "people" that is central to constituent power by requiring a sufficient showing of (super)majority popular will to trigger an assembly in the first place. A related idea is to regulate the process through which the new constitution is written, for example, by requiring certain kinds of voting rules for electing an assembly or for voting within it, or a certain level of deliberation in writing the new constitutional text.[39] Scheppele has argued that constituent power without these characteristics of durability and consensus is effectively fraudulent and should be deemed an inauthentic exercise.[40]

This kind of fix is intuitively appealing, but it is also problematic. The "people" is inevitably an abstraction, one which is hard to operationalize in any particular way. The Hungarian constitutional process criticized by Scheppele, for example, was written by a two-thirds supermajority of the Hungarian Parliament, not a simple majority. The trouble was that, given the electoral rules, which were written for ordinary politics and privileged governability by giving the largest party a substantial bonus in number of seats, Fidesz found itself in a position to write the new text unilaterally.[41] Chile, more recently, has had two of the most highly regulated constitution-making processes in memory. In a first process, which resulted in a failed referendum in 2022, the Constitutional Convention was required to have a two-thirds vote to adopt constitutional text, on the assumption that in that way the major political movements would have influence. But the right fared terribly in the elections while the left cleaned up, and the right-wing (and even center) parties ended up being frozen out of the decision-making coalition.[42] The 2023 elections for the subsequent Constitutional Council were a kind of mirror image: rules were designed to require a supermajority for the Council to overrule a draft prepared by a consensus of political experts, but this time the right cleaned up, with right-wing parties essentially winning enough seats to ignore the constraint and write a draft unilaterally.[43] The concept of the "people," as expressed through referenda and elections, is difficult to pin down.

[38] *See* Jackson, *supra* note 36, at 322.

[39] *See* Kim Lane Scheppele, *Unconstitutional Constituent Power*, *in* Modern Constitutions 154 (Rogers M Smith & Richard R Beeman eds., 2020).

[40] *See id.*

[41] *See* Miklós Bánkuti, Kim Lane Scheppele & Gábor Halmai, *Hungary's Illiberal Turn: Disabling the Constitution*, 23 J. Democracy 138, 138 (2012).

[42] *See* Sergio Verdugo, *The Paradox of Constitution-Making in Democratic Settings. A Tradeoff between Party Renewal and Political Representation?*, Int'l J. Const. L. Blog, Sept. 24, 2022, http://www.iconnectblog.com/the-paradox-of-constitution-making-in-democratic-settings-a-tradeoff-between-party-renewal-and-political-representation.

[43] *See* Vanessa Buschschlüter, *Chile Constitution: Far-Right Party Biggest in New Assembly*, BBC News, May 8, 2023, https://www.bbc.com/news/world-latin-america-65524068.

A second approach to shape or fix constituent power is to limit the scope of a constitution-making body's powers, for example, by conceptualizing it as only having authority to write a new constitution, rather than to carry out any other tasks. In other words, constitution-making bodies, properly understood, do not have the ancillary powers that they have often assumed.

A few of the most prominent and thoughtful scholars working on constituent power have argued for this last route. Andrew Arato, for example, has argued for recovering a tradition of "double differentiation," where constituent assemblies cannot interfere in the work of ordinary political institutions such as legislatures, just as ordinary legislatures cannot interfere in the constitutional drafting work of constituent assemblies.[44] Each would proceed within its own sphere, and thus constitution-making bodies would need to focus exclusively on their core task of writing a new constitution. They would not have ancillary powers.

Joel Colon-Rios has made a similar proposal from a theoretical perspective that works more explicitly with the theory of constituent power.[45] Colon-Rios argues that there is a distinction between "sovereignty" and "constituent power."[46] Constituent assemblies are themselves delegated constituent power by the sovereign people. This means that their power is not absolute, but rather is bounded by the explicit and implicit terms of the grant. Colon-Rios argues that constituent assemblies are selected for a particular task and cannot arrogate legislative or other non-drafting powers to themselves.[47] They are bound by the terms of the delegation to carry out the task for which they were selected: writing a new constitution.

These arguments are interesting refinements of constituent power theory, but they are also motivated by pragmatic concerns—particularly regarding the Latin American cases with which both Colon-Rios and Arato are familiar. The idea is that restraining a constitutional assembly's ability to carry out ancillary tasks will limit the authoritarian abuses of constituent power outlined above. As already noted, much of the damage to the democratic system in Venezuela and Ecuador stemmed from the assemblies' carrying out other tasks, such as legislating and reorganizing or shutting down other state institutions.

Restricting Ancillary Powers

Can and should constituent power theory be shaped or restrained in these ways? Mark Tushnet's work on constituent power suggests some of the problems with

[44] *See* ARATO, *supra* note 4, at 96.

[45] *See* COLON-RIOS, *supra* note 4; Joel Colon-Rios, *Constitution Making and Constituent Power*, *in* COMPARATIVE CONSTITUTIONAL LAW IN LATIN AMERICA 227 (Rosalind Dixon & Tom Ginsburg eds., 2017).

[46] *See* Colon-Rios, *supra* note 4, at 226.

[47] *See id.*

the proposals outlined here. Tushnet argues against a "sociological" definition of constituent power that requires that acts by the people take any particular form in order to be valid.[48] He argues instead that constituent power is a purely conceptual placeholder denoting any potentially revolutionary change in a legal order. Tushnet suggests that constitution-making moments are moments where law effectively runs out—and, here as elsewhere, the real drivers of events are politics rather than law.[49] This is true even with respect to revolutionary changes made from within the constitutional order (say, by ordinary amendment mechanisms), and eternity clauses and doctrines such as the unconstitutional constitutional amendment doctrine are best understood as suggestions rather than commands to future exercises of constituent power.[50] The identification of a change as involving the constituent power can thus often only be made in retrospect, when one observes the degree of change made to a constitutional order, and whether or not it was successful. Tushnet's arguments suggest that it may be difficult or impossible to define constituent power, either by giving shape to the term "people" or by limiting the scope of its exercise.

Tushnet's critiques have obvious applicability to the attempts to give greater shape to the term "people" that is at the core of the constituent power theory. In this section, I argue that they also suggest problems with the efforts of Arato and Colon-Rios to restrict or eliminate the exercise of "ancillary powers" by constitution-making bodies. I suggest two, overlapping issues: (1) it is difficult to draw the line between "constitution-making" functions and "ancillary" functions, a problem best illustrated by the (oft overlooked) importance of transitional provisions; and (2) in some cases, it may not even be desirable to limit ancillary powers, because these may play a prodemocratic rather than an antidemocratic function in some cases. I take these two points in turn.

Ancillary Powers and Transitional Provisions

The line between writing the constitutional text and engaging in ancillary tasks such as legislating or reorganizing institutions is surprisingly difficult to draw. In extreme cases, of course, the problem is clear: take the 2017 Venezuelan Constitutional Assembly, which never undertook any serious steps to replace or even amend the 1999 constitution, but which instead spent all its time issuing decrees that enacted legislation and reorganized other institutions.

But in many other (and more typical) cases, the line is slippery. Transitional provisions do not offer the only manifestation of this difficulty, but they do offer

[48] *See* Tushnet, *Peasants with Pitchforks*, *supra* note 1.
[49] *See id.* at 654.
[50] *See* Tushnet, *Amendment Theory and Constituent Power*, *supra* note 1.

perhaps its clearest manifestation. Constitutions often (although not inevitably) contain a separate section on transitional norms, often at the end of the text. These transitional provisions are widely varied in form and content, and almost completely overlooked by the scholarly and policy literatures. Yet they are immensely important and are often recognized as such by participants.

I do not aim to paint a full portrait of transitional norms here (I have done so in another recent paper[51]), but they have a few stock characteristics. One is that they are usually intended to be temporary in nature, rather than permanent in the sense of the constitutional text. They serve as a bridge during a transition period, during which the constitution is starting to be implemented. They can be used to *delay* full implementation of the constitution, for example, by allowing existing officeholders or legal frameworks to remain in place for a period of time. In this sense, they may provide stability or serve as a political compromise with the old regime. Transitional provisions can also be used, however, to *accelerate* the implementation process, often by providing temporary rules for the composition of key institutions, or by granting special powers to key officials. Finally, transitional provisions can offer a *roadmap* for at least the initial stages of the implementation process, for example, by providing duties on the branches of government to pass laws or construct policies within a set timeframe.

In a formal sense, transitional provisions are simply part of the constitutional drafting process. They usually take effect, for example, at the date when the constitution itself goes into effect. But they also tend to set rules for reorganizing or abolishing existing institutions. And sometimes, they give the constitution-making body itself power to pass certain laws and to exercise other powers. In this sense, they fulfill many of the ancillary functions outlined above.

In the 1991 Colombian constitution, for example, the transitional articles ordered the existing Congress to cease all of its functions, while calling rapid elections for a new Congress using the altered electoral rules.[52] The transitional provisions also endowed then-president Cesar Gaviria with extraordinary powers to issue decrees having force of law in key areas needed to implement the constitution, while also giving a Special Commission selected by the Assembly (and partly composed of Assembly members) power to propose and prepare decrees, as well as to veto the decrees issued by the president.[53] In other words, in Colombia the ancillary powers of the Convention were largely exercised via the transitional provisions.

In the 1999 Venezuelan constitution, the situation was different. The transitional provisions, again, gave the Constituent Assembly certain powers, including the power to pass the new law governing the regime of the capital district (Caracas) and the power to appoint the National Ombudsperson.[54] However, most of the

[51] David Landau, *Transitional Norms in Constitutions*, 50 YALE J. INT'L L. (forthcoming 2025).
[52] *See* CONST. COL., trans. arts. 1–3 (1991).
[53] *See id.* trans. arts. 5–11.
[54] *See* CONST. VEN., trans. arts. 1, 9 (1999).

Convention's ancillary functions were carried out by separate decrees issued by the Assembly. Some of these were issued while the constitution was being written: these decrees sharply limited congressional power and reorganized the judiciary, for example.[55] But the most consequential decrees were issued after the constitutional text had been approved via referendum. This second set of decrees dissolved the Congress and state legislative assemblies, while replacing many mayors and union officials, as well as justices of the Supreme Court.[56] The Assembly also issued a decree replacing the Congress with a national legislative commission selected by the Constituent Assembly.[57]

A comparison of the two experiences suggests the interchangeability of transitional provisions and other mechanisms (such as decrees) to carry out ancillary functions. Most of the decrees issued by the 1999 Venezuelan Assembly, at least those issued after the referendum, could have been done by using transitional provisions instead. This was, indeed, the mechanism used in Colombia.

Still, a few subtler suggestions for drawing a line may exist. One possible criterion might be temporal: the constitution-making body is free to include provisions that reorganize state institutions (or even grant special implementation powers) once it has completed its work, via transitional provisions or other means. Indeed, these tasks seem like a central part of constitution-making. But the Assembly cannot interfere with the other branches of government while it is undertaking its work, for example, by issuing "decrees" that are separate from its core task of writing a constitution. This temporal criterion is a coherent line, but one might wonder whether it would make much difference to the abuses outlined in Venezuela and Ecuador. In Venezuela, as just noted, the most significant decrees were actually issued after the new constitution had been approved by referendum.

Another criterion might be more functional in nature: the constitution-making body can delegate ancillary functions to others, but it may not assume legislative powers for itself. In this sense, the problem in Colombia and Venezuela might be that the assemblies created and elected bodies, partially composed of their own members, that exercised legislative power after the constitution-making process had concluded. These were essentially full congressional powers in the case of Venezuela, and proposal and veto powers in the case of Colombia. Again, a "no self-dealing" principle has some intuitive appeal, here as elsewhere. But it is another

[55] *See* Gaceta Constituyente (Diario de Debates), Agosto–Septiembre 1999, No. 7, Aug. 12, 1999; Gaceta Constituyente (Diario de Debates), Agosto–Septiembre 1999, No. 8, Aug. 17, 1999; Gaceta Constituyente (Diario de Debates), Agosto–Septiembre 1999, No. 11, Aug. 25, 1999; Gaceta Constituyente (Diario de Debates), Agosto–Septiembre 1999, No. 14, Aug. 30, 1999. *See also* Landau, *supra* note 18, at 946–47.

[56] *See* Gaceta Constituyente (Diario de Debates), Noviember 1999–Enero 2000, No. 51, Dec. 22, 1999; Gaceta Constituyente (Diario de Debates), Noviember 1999–Enero 2000, No. 62, Jan 30, 2000. *See also* Braver, *supra* note 19, at 568; Landau, *supra* note 18, at 948.

[57] *See* Gaceta Constituyente (Diario de Debates), Noviember 1999–Enero 2000, No. 51, Dec. 22, 1999, at 3–4.

example of a criterion that may have little practical effect. Would the results in Venezuela have been different, for instance, if President Chavez had been invested with power to choose the temporary Special Legislative Commission, instead of the Assembly? And at a deeper level, as explored in the next section, there are interesting questions about whether stopping a constitution-making body from dealing directly in the implementation process is always a good idea.

The Positive Side of Ancillary Powers

There is no question that ancillary powers can be used antidemocratically. In Ecuador and Venezuela, these powers aided incumbents with authoritarian ambitions by allowing them to sweep away opponents and install allies across the political landscape. But—and this is a point made again and again in Tushnet's work—the impact of these kinds of powers is highly dependent on the political context.

Take, again, Colombia in 1991. The existing political order had been constructed decades before, in a pact called the National Front that ended a period of extensive civil strife, followed by a dictatorship. The two parties agreed to share most major political posts in the country, including rotating the presidency, while divvying up the Congress, Supreme Court, and Cabinet.[58] Even after the National Front formally ended, its vestiges endured and led to an increasing sense that the system was incapable of responding to social needs: the so-called blocked society.[59] Against a backdrop of drug-fueled violence, political assassination, and repression in the 1980s, and following on the heels of a series of failed attempts to change the 1886 constitution, the social demand for a new constitution became overwhelming. A student movement eventually fueled the events that led to the convoking of the 1991 Constituent Assembly, with the involvement of new president Cesar Gaviria. The assembly itself was a pluralistic body, composed of a mix of older political actors (such as the two traditional parties) and new movements such as the demobilized M-19 guerilla group, which won the second-largest block of seats.[60] Most decisions were made by consensus or ample majority, and close votes were unusual.[61]

Against this backdrop, the assembly's "ancillary" decisions come into greater focus. The assembly decided to vest extensive implementation powers in the

[58] *See* Robert H. Dix, The Politics of Colombia (1987).

[59] *See* Mario Latorre Rueda, *Colombia, una sociedad bloqueda? Articulo 120: Espiritu Nacional y participacion Adecuada y Equitativa*, *in* Hechos y Critica Politica 121 (Mario Latorre Rueda ed., 1986).

[60] *See* John Dugas, *La Constitucion Politica de 1991: un pacto politico viable?*, *in* La Constitucion de 1991: un pacto politico viable? 15, 38 (John Dugas ed., 1993).

[61] *See* Gabriel L. Negretto, Making Constitutions: Presidents, Parties, and Institutional Choice in Latin America 187–88 (2013).

president, with a special body selected by the assembly itself serving as a potential veto on the president's decisions. Together, these two bodies were given power to pass decrees—laws governing the 1991 Constitution's new institutional order, including the Constitutional Court—very quickly. It is fascinating that the assembly made these implementation decisions at the same time as it undertook a well-documented effort to limit presidential decree powers on other issues, because of a widespread sense that executive power had been abused. Yet these special powers proved successful: they allowed the new order to be constructed quickly and comprehensively, in a way that was sympathetic to the constitutional regime. The initial implementation process would almost certainly have proven less successful if it had been left in the hands of the Congress.

The more controversial decision—indeed, perhaps the most controversial decision the assembly made—was to prohibit the Congress from undertaking new legislation and to cut the existing congressional term short while calling new elections. There was a clear element of self-interest in this decision: the upstart parties in the assembly, such as the M-19, were driving forces behind it and sought in part to create new political space for their movements.[62] But the decision also responded to the social reality that the Congress was widely viewed as having little legitimacy, including by many adherents of the traditional parties. And adherents reasonably calculated that implementation of the new constitutional order would have been far more difficult with the existing Congress in place, rather than a new body that was elected using very different rules. As the then-presidential secretary stated, the attitude of many political forces was that "if one wanted a deep reform, it was fundamental to revoke the congressional mandate and call new elections under the new constitutional order."[63]

The Venezuelan Constituent Assembly in 1999 utilized a more aggressive vision of its powers. It curtailed congressional power earlier, and eventually shut down and replaced officials from a wider range of institutions, including the Supreme Court. And it put a body it selected directly in charge of implementation for a long period of time, rather than merely being vested with a veto power over presidential implementation decisions as in Colombia.

But the most important difference between the two constitution-making episodes was in political context, rather than in the design or wielding of legal rules. The Colombian Assembly followed a pluralistic logic, with most of the major

[62] The negotiated outcome with the Liberal Party was that members of the Constituent Assembly would be ineligible for election to the new Congress, a decision that proved fateful for the M-19. *See* Lawrence Boudon, *Colombia's M-19 Democratic Alliance: A Case Study in New-Party Self-Destruction*, 28 Lat. Am. Persp. 73, 79 (2001).

[63] *See* Calderon, *supra* note 13. Analyses in hindsight have suggested that the revocation ultimately did not fulfil its goals, and that for various reasons, the new electoral rules failed to produce an improved Congress. Juan Sebastián Lombo, *Revocatoria del Congreso: el cambio político que nunca fue*, El Espectador, June 11, 2021, https://www.elespectador.com/politica/revocatoria-del-congreso-el-cambio-politico-que-nunca-fue/.

parties and movements (new and old) agreeing that the old order had to be swept away. The Venezuelan Assembly worked at the behest of a single, newly dominant movement headed by a charismatic populist with authoritarian tendencies.[64] The Venezuelan Assembly worked relentlessly to remove or weaken enemies of the new administration, and by the end of its tenure it had succeeded in transforming the political context. The goal in both cases was to sweep away aspects of a discredited old order.[65] But the Venezuelan Assembly did so more thoroughly than in Colombia and did so in the service of a dominant political movement with authoritarian ambitions, rather than a pluralistic set of actors who sought institutional changes for overlapping reasons.

Conclusion

This chapter introduces the concept of an ancillary power of a constitution-making body, which it defines as powers other than the drafting of a constitutional text. These powers, which include tasks such as legislating and reorganizing or reconstituting state institutions, are rarely emphasized in the literature, but can be important. Indeed, in some recent constitution-making episodes, their abuse has played a central role in undermining the democratic order.

This chapter also uses Tushnet's ideas about constituent power as inspiration to explore two difficulties with recent scholarly attempts to restrict ancillary powers: an analytic difficulty in distinguishing ancillary authority from the ordinary exercise of drafting a new constitutional text, and a normative difficulty with restricting functions that may sometimes play a valuable and prodemocratic role.

Ultimately, Tushnet's arguments pose a challenge for all of us seeking to theorize about constituent power. His descriptive view is that constitution-making moments are often moments where "law runs out" and reliance on legal restraint is thus futile; the accompanying normative view may be that, here as elsewhere, reliance on legal form can mask contestation that is better cast in openly political terms. At the least, those views ought to serve as a warning, albeit hopefully not as an invitation to stop trying to improve theories of constitution-making.

[64] *See* Ana María Bejarano and Renata Segura, Ni una asamblea más sin nosotros. *Exclusion, Inclusion and the Politics of Constitution-Making in the Andes*, 2 CONSTELLATIONS 217, 225 (2004).

[65] *See* Jorge González-Jácome, *From Abusive Constitutionalism to a Multilayered Understanding of Constitutionalism: Lessons from Latin America*, 15 INT'L J. CONST. L. 447, 465–66 (2017).

15
Legal Reasoning Matters

Dieter Grimm

Judicial Review Contested

Constitutional courts and constitutional adjudication are preferred subjects of research in comparative constitutional law. But there seems to be a lack of interest in legal reasoning and the method of constitutional interpretation in various legal systems. This attitude is favored by the assumption of legal realists, widely found in North America, that judges, when they decide cases, are not guided by the law, but by extralegal criteria or motives. Views such as this are not alien to Mark Tushnet. For him, judges, no less than politicians, "have an incentive to maximize the sphere of their power and responsibilities."[1] If this is true, "taking the Constitution away from the courts"[2] is indeed democratically more plausible than taking it away from the politicians who have a popular mandate and are accountable to the electorate.

Others go even further than Tushnet and think not only that judges are as biased as politicians in understanding the constitution, but also that they do not care much about the law in general. In his book on the jurisprudence of eight constitutional courts, David Robertson attributes this attitude to political scientists who deal with judicial review.[3] But it is by no means limited to political scientists. It will be found with legal scholars as well. Jeremy Waldron, for instance, views judicial opinions as "artificial and distorted," hiding rather than revealing what motivated the judges when they decide a case.[4] For Larry Kramer, descriptions of adjudicating where justices are "studiously pondering weighty questions of principle before crafting careful explanations that reflect deeply on the theoretical dilemmas they have faced" are "romanticized accounts."[5]

That courts are better prepared to determine the meaning of a constitutional provision than the political branches of government is questioned. Mark Tushnet discusses it under the heading "The Question of Capacity" and concludes that the "contrast between courts and legislatures is so overstated as to be worthless for

[1] Mark Tushnet, Taking the Constitution Away from the Courts 26 (1999).
[2] *Id.* at 154.
[3] David Robertson, The Judge as Political Theorist: Contemporary Constitutional Review 13 (2010).
[4] Jeremy Waldron, *The Core of the Case Against Judicial Review*, 115 Yale L.J. 1346, 1383 (2006).
[5] Larry D. Kramer, The People Themselves: Popular Constitutionalism and Judicial Review 240 (2004).

Dieter Grimm, *Legal Reasoning Matters* In: *Redefining Comparative Constitutional Law.* Edited by: Vicki C. Jackson and Madhav Khosla, Oxford University Press. © Dieter Grimm 2025. DOI: 10.1093/9780191996344.003.0015

someone trying to argue against a populist constitutional law that focuses on democracy and legislative responsibility" (as he himself advocates).[6] The problem is therefore just "one of choice between self-interested institutions."[7] For Waldron, a comparison between judicial and parliamentary deliberation ends in favor of parliament, where the "real issues," not interpretation and doctrine, are at stake.[8] Others reproach the US Supreme Court for having given up deliberating at all; instead, the judges vote immediately after oral argument.[9]

Behind this skepticism about courts, there seems to be a fundamental distrust in the capacity of legal reasoning to objectively determine the meaning of a constitutional provision. It is especially Jeremy Waldron who insists that in matters of fundamental rights a consensus about their meaning is philosophically, not only empirically, impossible.[10] Courts have no superior insight. If they nevertheless retain the last word in matters constitutional, nothing less than democracy is at stake, because they withdraw important political questions from the democratic process and thereby deprive the people of their right to decide about the direction of politics in free elections. Under such circumstances, what matters is not *how* a constitutional provision is interpreted, but *who* interprets it. Waldron's view culminates in the assertion that "legislation just *is* the adjudication of those controversies."[11]

While some conclude that no criteria for a correct interpretation exist, others assume that constitutional interpretations are "correct" only within the boundaries of an institution (the so-called departmentalism), not crossborder.[12] There is even a line of research which denies that constitutional courts are established in the interest of constitutional law. Different explanations are given that are supposed to be more realistic.[13] Ran Hirschl rejects them all and argues that judicial review is a hegemonic project of politicians who want to stabilize and maintain their power by providing for a seemingly neutral court that will be inclined to decide political controversies in their favor; that is to say, just the opposite of the common understanding according to which constitutional courts exist to enforce the requirements of the constitution against whoever is in power.[14]

To be sure, judges who are biased or do not care about the constitution, courts that do not deliberate, politicians who establish constitutional courts not for the

[6] TUSHNET, *supra* note 1, at 69.
[7] *Id.* at 27.
[8] Waldron, *supra* note 4, at 1385, 1391.
[9] KRAMER, *supra* note 5, at 240.
[10] JEREMY WALDRON, LAW AND DISAGREEMENT 1, 211 (1999).
[11] *Id.* at 309. See also the advocate of a nonlegal, political constitutionalism, RICHARD BELLAMY, POLITICAL CONSTITUTIONALISM: A REPUBLICAN DEFENCE OF THE CONSTITUTIONALITY OF DEMOCRACY 5 (2007): "The democratic process *is* the constitution."
[12] The origins can already be found with Thomas Jefferson: see KRAMER, *supra* note 5, at 106.
[13] See Tom Ginsburg & Mila Versteeg, *Why Do Countries Adopt Judicial Review?* 30 J.L. Econ. & Org. 587, 588 (2013).
[14] See Ran Hirschl, *The New Constitutionalism and the Judicialization of Pure Politics*, 75 FORDHAM L. REV. 721 (2006).

sake of the constitution but in the interest of preserving their power, do of course exist. The question is only whether these attitudes are inherent in judicial review or at least the rule for constitutional adjudication or whether, what legal realists call romanticism or professional ideology of judges, is possible, not only in ideal situations but also in the real world, namely to have legal reasoning not as an ex post justification of otherwise found results but as a true ground for the decision, so that constitutional courts are established to make the constitution matter and can indeed fulfill this function and that judges exist who try to decide cases to the best of their legal knowledge and skills; in short: whether the realist description is the pathological case, whereas the other way is the rule.

In Europe, American-type legal realism does not play an important role in the debate on constitutional adjudication. Here, the dominant view is that, in spite of the vagueness of many constitutional provisions, the interpretation of constitutional law and the application to cases is a procedure that can be classified as legal and in fact guides judicial behavior in the majority of jurisdictions. Admittedly, constitutional courts have considerable political influence, but nevertheless are conceived as legal institutions. In this respect, legal science in Europe differs to a certain extent from political science, which (with rare exceptions, such as David Robertson) tends to describe constitutional courts as political actors and judicial review as a political activity, without however making itself familiar with legal reasoning or the content of constitutional judgments.

The different perceptions of constitutional courts and constitutional adjudication can be explained in part by the different research interests of the two disciplines. Political science is interested in the impact of the constitution on politics and the relationship between the court and the other branches of government. Legal science, to the contrary, is primarily, although not exclusively, interested in the competencies of constitutional courts and the legally correct interpretation and application of the constitution. The object is, however, the same for both disciplines, and therefore it is not sufficient simply to state that one and the same institution is seen as political by one and as legal by the other discipline. On the one hand, constitutional adjudication has beyond doubt a political impact, but on the other hand, it has this impact by dealing with the constitution as law.

Judicial Review—Legal or Political?

Judicial Review as Function of the Constitution

If this is true, the question is no longer whether constitutional courts are legal or political institutions and whether constitutional adjudication is a political or a legal activity, but in what sense and to what extent it is legal and in what sense and to what extent it is political. This suggests a more differentiated approach that distinguishes between the object, the effect, and the process of constitutional adjudication.[15] Viewed like this, it is obvious that judicial review typically deals with political issues. Constitutional law is the part of the law that regulates political behavior, and constitutional courts are established to enforce constitutional law vis-à-vis government. Hence, the object of judicial review is inevitably political. The same is true for its effect. Constitutional courts can annul or request political acts against the will of the democratically elected representatives of the people. This is not a usurpation; it is their task.

Legal realism is content to take the fact that the object and the effect of judicial review are political as sufficient to characterize it as being altogether political. It neglects the third question that concerns the process of ascertaining the meaning of the constitution and applying it to cases and controversies. However, the character of judicial review, legal or political, cannot be determined without taking constitutional law into account, which judicial review is all about. Constitutions can exist and matter without constitutional adjudication. But constitutional adjudication makes no sense without a constitution, more specifically a constitution that has the quality of law, whereas a purely political constitution lacks the binding force that the law conveys on a normative text.[16] This is why a merely political constitution does not fulfill the expectations that were and still are combined with modern constitutionalism.

In the constitution, the people determine the conditions under which their representatives may exercise public power. The constitution not only organizes the government and distributes the power among the various organs, but also regulates the exercise of political power by the organs. It is the constitution's very purpose to withdraw certain subjects from the democratic process and from electoral change and to impose constraints on elected majorities. Constitutions are about limited government. They achieve this by virtue of being law. However, constitutional law can fulfill this function only if it is superior in rank to all other law or legal acts. The superiority of the constitution grounds in its attribution to the people themselves, whereas the rest of the law emanates from the organs of the people who have to act in accordance with the constitution.

Rejecting constitutional adjudication because it constrains the democratic process ignores that it does so in enforcing constitutional law, which, because of its popular origin, is higher law. But the nature and function of constitutions are either not discussed or reduced to a nonlegal role and hence not regarded as binding. In Ran Hirschl's argument, the content of the constitution does not appear at all.

[15] See Dieter Grimm, *What Exactly Is Political about Constitutional Adjudication?*, *in* Judicial Power: How Constitutional Courts Affect Political Transformation 307 (Christine Landfried ed., 2019).

[16] See Bellamy, *supra* note 11.

When he finds that judicial review concerns politics or even megapolitics[17] and is illegitimate because of its object, he does not even ask whether the subject matter of a judgment has been regulated by a constitutional provision, but creates the impression that the constitutional court acts on its own impetus. He tacitly assumes that the character of the constitution as law is irrelevant for its judicial agents, so that the existence or the absence of a constitutional basis for the judgment does not make a difference.

As a consequence of Jeremy Waldron's view that the meaning of fundamental rights is necessarily subject to "reasonable disagreement," any assertion about the meaning of the Bill of Rights for a certain case and controversy is simply a subjective opinion of the individual interpreter. For Mark Tushnet, the constitution enjoys high authority and deserves high respect, but cannot claim binding force or at least cannot claim primacy over all other law or legal acts; even less can Supreme Court rulings claim supremacy. The other branches of government may disregard the rulings of the Supreme Court.[18] This is especially asserted for fundamental rights. He emphasizes the importance of human rights, but finds it sufficient if they are guaranteed on the level of ordinary rather than higher law.[19] However, as such they are not binding for the legislature. For him, the constitution has a different function: It "sets the terms of the discourse."[20]

Larry Kramer's target is judicial supremacy.[21] The constitution is a product of the people. Therefore, authentic statements about the meaning of constitutional provisions can be expected only from their author, the people. The Supreme Court does not express what the constitution means, but what the judges mean. The two are not identical. The court's rulings should be considered by their addressees but not have binding effect on them. For Kramer, this is the American tradition, while the assertion of the contrary is just "bluster and puff."[22] *Marbury v. Madison* was an aberration that had never found general consent, and only very recently had the attitude gained ground that the constitution was a document for legal professionals and not for the people to interpret. Kramer wants to restore the American tradition. The Supreme Court "is ultimately supposed to yield to our judgments about what the Constitution means and not the reverse."[23]

Only Waldron considers that the people themselves as bearer of the constituent power may have decided in favor of constitutional adjudication. He accepts such a decision as an expression of popular will, but understands it as a renouncement of democracy.[24] For him, judicial review and democracy are irreconcilable. Mark

[17] See Ran Hirschl, *The Judicialization of Mega-Politics and the Rise of Political Courts*, 11 Ann. Rev. Pol. Sci. 93, 94 (2008).
[18] Tushnet, *supra* note 1, at 6.
[19] *Id.* at 165.
[20] *Id.* at 185.
[21] Kramer, *supra* note 5, at 233.
[22] *Id.* at 221.
[23] *Id.* at 248.
[24] Waldron, *supra* note 4, at 1359.

Tushnet and Larry Kramer are not compelled to deal with this problem because they talk only about the American system, where the constitution does not explicitly provide for judicial review. Rather, it was the Supreme Court that found judicial review implied in the supremacy of constitutional law. Supremacy of constitutional law meant for Chief Justice Marshall supremacy also of the Court's rulings on the meaning of the constitution. Although often criticized because of this opinion, the Supreme Court has never reversed it.[25]

However, in the US, the people, who, according to Tushnet, Kramer, and others, are the authentic interpreters of constitutional law, cannot express themselves in the legal process, but only in general elections. In elections they decide on persons or political parties who run for public office, indirectly evaluating their political views or platforms, performances, or intentions. This may imply the candidates' or parties' understanding of constitutional provisions with regard to certain issues. However, elections are highly aggregated expressions of confidence for a candidate or a party. As such, they are inapt to promote particular constitutional understandings. Just as little can the result of an election be interpreted as the popular decision of a particular constitutional issue. But even if this were possible, it still remains an open question how the people could oblige the representatives to follow the opinion of the voters.

Since none of the authors, in spite of their assertion that the constitution should be given back to the people, brings the people back in, the result is that the constitution may be a venerable but not a binding document. If the authors mentioned want to bring the people back in when constitutional issues are at stake, but do not give them any power to intervene as decision-makers, the power taken away from the judiciary accrues with the representatives of the people. They are not subjected to external bonds. The constitution binds them only insofar as it means what they think it means. Under these conditions, the assertion that "the people themselves" decide constitutional conflicts makes sense only if the representatives are identified with the people and the will of the elected representatives not only is attributed to the people, but *is* the will of the people.

The Founding Fathers were, however, far from such an identification. They had experienced not only the consequences of the English concept of parliamentary sovereignty but also the practice of the American state parliaments in the short interval between independence and the foundation of the United States. The Founders' answer was the rejection of the English model and the differentiation between people and representatives. The people should be sovereign—not Parliament, as in England—while parliaments could act only on behalf of the people. Their relationship was one between master and servant. The position of an organ of the people is incompatible with sovereignty of the organ. This is the

[25] Plyler v. Doe, 457 U.S. 202 (1982).

central theme of the whole constitutional debate.[26] This was the great innovation of the American Revolution that then led to the modern constitution.

The constitution emerged because the people, although sovereign, is not capable of governing. It rather determines who shall govern for a certain period of time. This difference entails the problem of all political representation: that the representatives may alienate themselves from their masters and no longer pursue the interests of the people, but their own interests. The means to solve this problem was the constitution, the next ingenious invention of the American Revolution. In the constitution, the people determine the terms under which the representatives are authorized to rule. But these terms can fulfill their purpose only if they are binding on the representatives, which means nothing else than law. In the American Revolution, the notion of constitution changes its meaning. Previously descriptive, it became prescriptive.[27] It does not describe reality, but addresses expectations to reality. It claims obedience.

It was just the historical achievement of the American Revolution of the 18th century to invent the constitution as law.[28] All the ingredients of what was to become the modern constitution were already there, but they were philosophy, not law. Fundamental rights existed in England, but they were not attributed to the people and not entrenched above Parliament, which in England enjoyed sovereignty.[29] The novelty of the American Constitution and the Bill of Rights was that they were attributed to the people as the source of all public power and therefore superior to any government act. The aim was a government of laws and not of men. Denying the constitution the quality of law means to turn the wheel back to the prerevolutionary age and to destroy the most important achievement of the American Revolution.

However, although binding law, the constitution does not enforce itself. It takes effect through law-conforming behavior. This is true for all law, but for constitutional law to a heightened degree. If ordinary law is violated by its addressees, the law enforcement agencies of the state will react, if necessary, with physical force. The addressees of constitutional law are the highest state authorities. If they violate the constitution, there is no superior power to enforce it. This specific weakness of constitutional law provoked a further groundbreaking invention of the Americans,

[26] See Edmund S. Morgan, Inventing the People: The Rise of Popular Sovereignty in England and America (1988); Gordon Wood, The Creation of the American Republic 1776–1787 344 (1998).

[27] See Dieter Grimm, *The Concept of Constitution in Historical Perspective*, *in* Constitutionalism: Past, Present, and Future 89 (2016).

[28] See Wood, *supra* note 26; Grimm, *supra* note 27, at 3, 41; Gerald Stourzh, *Constitution: Changing Meanings of the Term from the Early Seventeenth to the Late Eighteenth Century*, *in* Conceptual Change and the Constitution 35, 47 (Terence Ball & J.G.A. Pocock eds., 1988).

[29] See Gerald Stourzh, *The Declaration of Rights, Popular Sovereignty and the Supremacy of the Constitution: Divergencies Between the American and the French Revolutions*, *in* 577 La Révolution Américaine et l'Europe. Colloque international du Centre National de la Recherche scientifique [PINCITE] (1979).

namely judicial review, although this did not find its way into the text of the constitution but was inferred from it by the Supreme Court. It gave bite to the constitution, as can be seen if one compares the relevance of constitutional law in political systems with and without judicial review.

Capability of Constitutional Law to Instruct Judicial Behavior

It is therefore necessary to proceed to the third question: whether the process of adjudicating, namely applying constitutional provisions to cases and controversies, is also political or can be qualified as legal. For Alexander Hamilton, the judiciary was "the least dangerous branch" of government. It has "neither force nor will, but merely judgment."[30] Chief Justice Marshall called it "the very essence of judicial duty" to decide conflicts between constitutional law and ordinary law.[31] Marshall realized that this duty could not be fulfilled without expounding and interpreting the constitution. Yet, he left no doubt that this was a legal operation. The advocates of populist constitutionalism or majoritarian democracy deny that. For them, the judiciary is a dangerous branch, at least if constitutional law is concerned. Who is right?

Evidently, constitutional adjudication is not political in the sense that legislative acts, presidential measures, international negotiations, and the like are political. Rather, the arena changes when a political issue is brought before the court. The actors change, the criteria change, and the procedure changes. The actors are legal professionals, while politicians are reduced to the role of appellant and respondent. The judges owe their position to a political decision, but, once in office, they are independent from politics in fulfilling their function and the outcome of elections does not affect their work. The criteria for deciding are legal norms, not political expediency, desirability, repercussions on elections, and so on, and the process is one of ascertaining the meaning of the relevant constitutional provision with regard to the case at hand. It is perceived as a matter of cognition, not of will.

It may, of course, be that all this is irrelevant, if legal norms are unable to instruct judicial behavior, or if judges do not feel themselves bound by legal norms. The doubts regarding the first alternative stem from the nature of legal norms. They are designed to cover an unforeseeable number of future cases and are, therefore, formulated in a more or less abstract and general way, whereas the cases to which they apply are always individual and concrete. The gap between the norm and the case has to be bridged by interpretation. This is true for all law, but for constitutional law in a heightened degree, since constitutions contain the foundational norms of the political and social order and thus resemble principles more than rules. As a

[30] THE FEDERALIST NO. 78 (Alexander Hamilton).
[31] Marbury v. Madison, 5 U.S. 137, 178 (1803).

consequence, constitutional provisions are usually not immediately applicable to a case. This is particularly true for fundamental rights and maxims such as democracy, rule of law, and so on.

Consequently, the case at hand cannot be solved without additional input, regardless of who interprets the constitution: the government, administrative agencies, lawyers, or judges. The highest interest is, however, that in judges, because they claim the last word if the meaning of the constitution is contested. All depends on how this input is generated. If one assumes that where the determinacy of the text ends, political reasoning starts, so that the additional input is necessarily political, one must conclude that the process of adjudicating is also politics and should therefore not be in the hands of judges, but should rather be performed by elected and accountable politicians. However, before drawing this conclusion, one should concede that precisely this is the question which requires further exploration. Is there a specifically legal way of interpreting legal norms?

Functionally complex societies, which predominate today, are characterized by the fact that each of the various subsystems of society follows a logic or code of its own. These systems operate according to this code, measure success and failure by it, and are susceptible to expectations from other systems if they can be translated into their own code. The specific contribution of each system to society as a whole depends on the ability to operate according to its logic and not to be submitted to the logic of other systems. This does not mean that the various systems are completely independent from each other. They are rather interdependent, meaning that no system can exist without the performance of other systems, yet without being allowed to instrumentalize those systems for their own purposes. Guaranteeing this is one of the functions of fundamental rights.[32]

This means that the legal system must be allowed to operate according to legal criteria. It is true that the vast majority of legal norms that are administered in the legal system are produced in the political system. But once enacted the law is disconnected from politics and operates henceforth according to the legal logic. The political logic counts for the making of law, not for its application. It is the function of judicial independence to guarantee just this. The guarantee works mainly vis-à-vis the political system, which in most countries is also responsible for the appointment of judges. But here again, once appointed, judges are usually irremovable and not subject to renewal—and certainly not to instructions from the other branches of government. Vis-à-vis non-political actors, it is mainly the criminalization of corruption that protects the independence of the judiciary.

[32] A function of fundamental rights that is recognized by the German Constitutional Court, but not in the US. For a theoretical foundation, *see* NIKLAS LUHMANN, GRUNDRECHTE ALS INSTITUTION. EIN BEITRAG ZUR POLITISCHEN SOZIOLOGIE [FUNDAMENTAL RIGHTS AS INSTITUTION: A CONTRIBUTION TO POLITICAL SOCIOLOGY] (1965).

Operating legally in this protected sphere is not mission impossible. Judges have means to reach solutions in a legal way, even if the text of the constitution or a statute is no longer conclusive, but leaves doubts as to its meaning. Legal arguments are available in dealing with textual indeterminacy. What counts as a legal argument may be contested and is at times severely contested. But there is no doubt that nonlegal arguments are not acceptable. The question which argument falls within the realm of law and which not can only be determined within the legal system. It may be determined differently in time and space and it is not immunized against influences from outside. But these influences have to pass a legal filter and have to be translated into legally valid arguments. Not every argument passes the filter and not any result can be justified legally.

Thus, doctrine, method, and precedents narrow the space that the text leaves open. In Germany and countries that are influenced by German jurisprudence, doctrine has adopted the specific form of "Dogmatik." It is a product of the continuous work with the law in which legal scholars and legal practitioners participate, an equivalent of which seems to be lacking in the United States.[33] It furnishes proven and widely accepted understandings of norms for recurring problems. Dogmatik thus relieves the judge of the requirement to be always starting from scratch and contributes to the consistency of case law. The legal quality of the solution reached is provided by using specific legal methods of interpretation. Precedents that are binding in common law systems lack this quality in civil law systems, but they nevertheless inform their doctrine.

However, doctrine and method, although products of legal reasoning, do not share the authority of the law. They work through conviction instead of authority. They are neither uncontested nor unchangeable. Normally each time has its predominant doctrine and method. They narrow the space of uncertainty, structure the path toward the solution of the cases, and often carry over the initial differences among the judges. This does not exclude that at the end of the deliberation in the court, two or more solutions to a case compete—but this does not excuse the individual judges from the requirement to find what for them, and according to their best knowledge, is the "right" solution. Legal education in Europe centers on the question what the correct interpretation and application of the law is, knowing that there may be more than one correct solution.

Yet, however refined doctrine and method may be, it remains an inconclusive test. Undeniably, the process of finding the legally "correct" solution is influenced by factors that are not legal in the strict sense. However, they enter the process of legal argumentation only through the medium of legal norms, and can be shaped by them. Therefore, they should not too willingly be reduced to subjective

[33] See Alexander Somek, *Two Worlds of Legal Scholarship and the Philosophy of Law*, *in* Common Law–Civil Law: The Great Divide? 141 (Nicoletta Bersier, Christoph Bezemek & Frederick Schauer eds., 2022). The American "restatements" are no such equivalent.

preferences or interests. Often they are general concepts or background assumptions of a just order or the function of the judiciary. But to admit this is not to express approval of rational choice theories that imagine judges as having the sole purpose to maximize their own or their institution's power without paying attention to the law, using it only in order to disguise their findings as being determined by the law.

Willingness of Judges to Follow Constitutional Law

Likewise, it cannot be taken for granted that judges do not see themselves as bound by the law. It would of course be naïve to deny that there are judges who disregard the law in favor of their own preferences or the self-interest of the institution, or render decisions in such a way that conflicts with the powerholders are avoided. In political systems that have been captured by populist parties, this may even be the rule. But it would be rash to assume that it is true for judges in general. Rather, it should be regarded as what it is: a perversion of judicial review. In systems where the rule of law is taken seriously, judges will feel bound by the law, in spite of its gaps, ambiguities, and contradictions. Legal reasoning under conditions of indeterminacy is their business, not only when they apply ordinary law, but also in constitutional law cases.

Legal education is an indicator. It is centered on legal reasoning. If one takes the German case, legal studies are focused on the correct interpretation of norms. Legal education used to be and still mainly is judge-centered. The final exam is a state exam with professors and judges acting as examiners. After graduation from law school, a practical training of two years follows, which the graduates spend with various legal agencies, most of them courts, where they learn how to handle cases and to write opinions. The training ends with a second state exam, with which the trainee acquires the necessary qualification to become a judge and which also opens the doors to all other legal professions. This exam is again judge-centered and usually conducted by judges. The degree trainees obtain is decisive for their professional perspective. The judiciary usually recruits only candidates who graduated at above average levels.

On the bench, judges continue to work along the lines they have been taught in law school and during the practical training. They follow this pattern when handling cases and deliberating. If Larry Kramer complains that the Supreme Court no longer deliberates, this is true of the United States but not of constitutional or highest courts in general. A recent, invaluable book by Gertrude Lübbe-Wolff, herself a former justice of the German Constitutional Court, discusses the ways in which constitutional courts or apex courts deliberate and arrive at a solution.[34]

[34] Gertrude Lübbe-Wolff, Beratungskulturen. Wie Verfassungsgerichte arbeiten und wovon es abhängt, ob sie integrieren oder polarisieren [Deliberating Cultures.

Roughly 80 countries appear in the book, a number that has no parallel in any comparative research I know. Deliberation is the rule. Most courts deliberate before they decide. Many deliberate extensively.

In Germany, the deliberation is prepared by a lengthy memo by the judge rapporteur. The memo presents the case and the decisions of the lower courts, and gives a summary of the briefs and the statements the Court may have invited; it contains an account of academic writing on the subject matter, and often also of foreign jurisprudence that dealt with the same problem. The memo ends with a reasoned proposal for the decision, but does not add a draft opinion. Doctrine structures the memo and the deliberation. It is a step-by-step operation. Urged to follow a certain order in solving a legal problem, like the prongs of the proportionality test, judges find it easier to overcome initial differences. In the German Court it is normal for judges to change their mind on the result or the reasoning because of the arguments exchanged in the deliberation. Secrecy of deliberation seems to be a precondition for this to happen.

The draft opinion is written only after deliberation and voting. It is discussed and, if deemed necessary, modified or altered in a second deliberation. Informal agreements by groups of justices prior to the deliberation are considered inappropriate. The opinion is the product of the deliberation. The central part of the opinion is the concretization of the relevant constitutional provisions in view of the case at hand. It has the case in mind, but is not limited to the case. The concretization may serve as a starting point for later cases. The concretized norm is applied to the case. It is not rare that social science evidence about the segment of social reality that is the object of legal regulation is introduced in order to make sure that the decision of the court will be suitable to reach the purpose of the constitutional provision in the given state of reality.

Gertrude Lübbe-Wolff describes the position of the German Court in the following words:

> In spite of a number of highly contested debates that occur from time to time, the Federal Constitutional Court has been able to mobilize a high degree of confidence and acceptance for its jurisprudence, for itself, and—more important—indirectly also for the constitution that it interprets. This is mainly due to the way in which it succeeds to integrate constructively the various views in its deliberation, to discern the justified core of the contrasting views, to find well-balanced solutions, not to disintegrate into internal factions and to not to systematically favor specific political tendencies.[35]

How Constitutional Courts Work and On What It Depends, Whether They Integrate or Polarize] (2022).

[35] *Id.* at 15 (my translation).

The book also shows how a different style of deliberation or the omission of a deliberation and a different way of dealing with controversies among the judges may produce the opposite effect.

This is an institutional aspect of constitutional adjudication—a relatively small one, but one which is neglected in the research on the institutional arrangements of judicial review. The other neglected aspect is not institutional but substantive. It is the opinions in which constitutional courts tell why they reached a certain result and how it follows from the constitution that they expound. Of course, the making and the representation of a decision may fall apart. The opinion is not an account of the process of deliberation within the court. It is the justification of the result on which all or the majority of judges finally agreed. Of course, one cannot exclude that opinions conceal the true motives that lead the court in deciding a case. But again, this is the pathological, not the regular case. Normally the opinion reveals the views that, in the eyes of the judges, justified the result.

Therefore, opinions are a source of information about judicial decision-making. One can see which alternatives were considered. If there are dissenting opinions one can also see which major controversies divided the court. Inconsistencies or gaps in an opinion often indicate hidden controversies. The opinion allows a conclusion as to which arguments counted as legal. Although judges usually do not talk about their method of interpretation, it is normally possible to ascertain whether they followed a certain method, which one it was, and whether they applied it consistently. One can see whether empirical expertise was employed in order to find an interpretation that has a chance to be effective and whether the judges were aware of the consequences of their decision in the real world.

As an example of a scholar from a common law country and in addition a political scientist who supports this view, one can mention once more David Robertson. After having compared the jurisprudence of eight constitutional courts or apex courts he comes to the conclusion that "legal and constitutional values inevitably take a high priority for such people (e.g. judges), even as political actors." Robertson continues: "Seeking private motivations, tends to direct attention away from something I regard as crucial—the study of the role of judicial argument, methodology, and logic." He adds: "My method is to take judicial argument seriously as one of the major, if not the sole determinant of the decisions courts make. I prefer my approach because it simply seems beyond credibility that so many thousands of professionally socialized and able men and women should be lying or deluding themselves in their arguments."[36]

The latter is a plausibility argument, and as such less convincing than empirical findings. But legal realists do not have superior insight into the decision-making of judges, either. The individual considerations and the collective deliberations are a

[36] ROBERTSON, *supra* note 3, at 20.

black box for them as well as for observers like Robertson. The realists have but a theory, rational choice, that was developed for decision-making in other systems, and which is by no means uncontested and not necessarily transferable to the legal system. What one has, however, are the opinions in which reasons for the decision are given. They may at times be not good or not coherent reasons, but they are what judges or the majority agreed upon, and it is unlikely that this is all done with the intention to hide the true motives. The question whether courts operate legally or politically cannot be sufficiently answered if those courts' opinions are ignored.

Judicial Review and Democracy: Neither Contradiction nor Condition

These considerations show that judicial review can be handled in a legal manner. But that does not mean that judicial review is necessary, although there are authors who, from a philosophical point of view, assert that only political systems with judicial review can claim legitimacy.[37] The argument is drawn from the paramount importance of human rights for the legitimacy of a political system. Without a possibility for individuals to have their rights enforced against government, rights are regarded as an empty promise. In the view of these authors, recognition of human rights entails judicial review. From a constitutional point of view, however, one would admit that the people as constituent power may reject judicial review. Even if one accepts that the constituent power of the people is limited by certain fundamental principles of international law, an obligation to adopt judicial review would not be among them.

However, just as the people in their capacity as constituent power may reject judicial review, they may decide to adopt it. This is the case in Germany where constitutional adjudication was seen as a safeguard of rather than a threat to democracy after the experience of a failed democracy in 1933. The Basic Law declares fundamental rights binding for all state powers including the legislature and stipulates that the decisions of the Constitutional Court on the constitutionality of laws have themselves the force of law. The same is true for many countries that turned toward liberal democratic constitutionalism in the second half of the 20th century. For them, too, judicial review meant strengthening, not weakening democracy. Waldron's argument that a decision for judicial review is a rejection of democracy loses much of its strength if judicial review can be exercised in a legal way.

Whether advocates of popular or populist constitutionalism such as Mark Tushnet and Larry Kramer would defend their rejection of judicial review or

[37] ALON HAREL, WHY LAW MATTERS (2014); JACOB WEINRIB, DIMENSIONS OF DIGNITY (2016); Mattias Kumm, *The Turn to Justification: On the Structure and Domain of Human Rights Practice*, *in* HUMAN RIGHTS: MORAL OR POLITICAL? 238 (Adam Etinson ed., 2018).

judicial supremacy even if the people had explicitly decided in favor of it in the constitution is an open question. They confine their argument to the United States where such an explicit decision is lacking. Behind their rejection of judicial review is a strictly majoritarian understanding of democracy. The constitution is reduced to organizational and procedural provisions, but cannot impose substantive requirements on politics. Fundamental rights may not claim binding force for the legislature. If they exist, they are only binding for administrative agencies of the state, not for the political branches of government. The whole burden of legitimizing public authority is then carried by the election, which, in order to fulfill this function, has to be free.

However, free elections, able to hold the representatives accountable to the people, have a number of preconditions, without which they would not fulfill their function. It is not enough that voters have a choice among various candidates and political parties and are free from pressure or fear when they exercise their right to vote. It is also necessary that parties can be formed and candidates nominated freely and that they can compete without the competition being influenced by the state, which in practice means by the ruling party that disposes of the legislative and financial means of the state. Of particular importance in this respect is the transparency and control of campaign financing. Furthermore, it seems necessary that the voters can freely inform themselves about parties and candidates, their past performance and their promises for the future. This presupposes a free public discourse, maintained by free media.

It is apparent that the majority principle cannot guarantee this freedom. To the contrary, it endangers the preconditions of free elections because it gives the elected majority an unrestricted mandate, with the possible consequence of abolishment of democracy by a democratic vote. This is not just a hypothetical case: It is what happened in Germany in 1933. And if this is the worst case, there are other abuses too. An uninhibited majority can use the legislative power or the financial means of the state to enhance their own chances to win the next election and to minimize the chances of the minority. In short, it can use its power to perpetuate its rule. The preconditions of a free election can only be guaranteed by fundamental rights which bind the legislature. Democracy depends on them. Would it not then at least be necessary to allow judicial review insofar as it protects the integrity of the democratic process?[38]

But this might not be sufficient. Freedom in the public sphere also presupposes a certain degree of freedom in the private sphere. Citizens who have to fear pressure, discrimination, obstacles placed in their path by powerholders are not free in their participation in the public sphere. It would be rash to call this risk merely hypothetical. It happens all the time in various countries in spite of their claim to

[38] See JOHN HART ELY, DEMOCRACY AND DISTRUST (1980).

be democratic. Moreover, fundamental rights do not only exist for democracy's sake. They protect individual dignity and autonomy in the first place and democracy insofar as collective self-government seems to be the political system that is best compatible with individual self-development. A free society rests on both pillars. Individual rights and democracy complement each other. Without their counterpart, both have a self-destructive tendency.[39]

On the other hand, democratic legitimacy of a political system does not depend on judicial review. The binding force of the legal constitution is independent from the power of the judiciary to enforce it. There are examples of countries where constitutional law and fundamental rights are in principle respected without constitutional courts enforcing them. This is largely a matter of the legal culture of states. However, countries with a legal culture of law-abidance are small in number. In particular, many of the recent constitutional democracies seem to lack this cultural background. There is more historical evidence for the irrelevance of constitutional law in countries without judicial review than there is the opposite. Even if constitutional courts cannot guarantee that the constitution is respected, they enhance the chances of this if they are able to operate independently and stay within the scope of their function.

The question of whether to adopt or reject judicial review is therefore not a principled but a pragmatic one.[40] On the one hand, it cannot be denied that judicial review implies a democratic risk, whose source is the indeterminacy of many constitutional law provisions, which makes a genuine judicial input necessary—and the more so the older the constitution is, or the more difficult it is to adapt it to new challenges by way of amendment. On the other hand, there is the risk of an irrelevant constitution. This risk affects the substantive parts of the constitution more than the organizational ones. The existence of risks on both sides makes weighing inevitable. The outcome is not predetermined. What seems reasonable under the conditions of one country may not be advisable under the conditions of another. Every country that understands itself as a liberal democracy must make this choice for itself.

[39] See Dieter Grimm, *Rule of Law and Democracy*, *in* RULE OF LAW VS MAJORITARIAN DEMOCRACY 43 (Giuliano Amato, Benedetta Barbisan & Cesare Pinelli eds., 2021).

[40] See Dieter Grimm, *Constitutional Adjudication and Democracy*, *in* 2 JUDICIAL REVIEW IN INTERNATIONAL PERSPECTIVE, LIBER AMICORUM IN HONOUR OF LORD SLYNN OF HADLEY 103 (Mats Andenas ed., 2000).

16

The Political Paradox of African Constitutionalism Revisited: Kenya's *BBI* Case

Catherine O'Regan[*]

Mark Tushnet's contribution to the development of the contemporary discipline of comparative constitutional law has been extraordinary. His insightful and acerbic writing has traversed the field, and, as importantly, he has been a mentor to many young scholars in the field. It is an honor and pleasure, therefore, to provide a chapter in this volume to mark that contribution.

The discipline of comparative constitutional law has grown substantially in the past two decades, both in terms of the quantity of scholarship that has been produced and in relation to the jurisdictions that are considered in the scholarship, but Africa remains somewhat underexamined. Yet the past 30 years have seen an extraordinary process of constitutional renewal in Africa. In southern and east Africa, for example, 8 of the 24 countries have adopted a new constitution since 2000[1] and a further 11 countries did so in the previous decade.[2]

In the early 1990s, in a seminal article, Kenyan scholar Okoth-Ogendo memorably described constitutions in Africa as reflecting a political paradox; that is, Africa had "constitutions without constitutionalism."[3] Okoth-Ogendo observed that in Africa there was widespread acceptance that African states need constitutions, for "without a constitution, a state can have no legitimate or sovereign existence,"[4] and that most African constitutions commence with an assertion of sovereignty. Yet despite the commitment to having a constitution, Okoth-Ogendo argued that many African political elites did not accept "the classical notion that the purposes of constitutions are to limit and control state power."[5] He thus

* The author would like to thank Professor Christina Murray for her helpful comments on an earlier draft.

[1] Burundi (2005), Comoros (2001), Democratic Republic of Congo (2005), Kenya (2010), Rwanda (2003), Swaziland or Eswatini (2005), Zambia (2016), aZimbabwe (2013).

[2] Djibouti (1992), Ethiopia (1995), Eritrea (1997), Lesotho (1993), Madagascar (1998), Malawi (1994), Mozambique (1990), Namibia (1990), Seychelles (1993), South Africa (1996), Uganda (1995).

[3] H.W.O. Okoth-Ogendo, *Constitutions without Constitutionalism: Reflections on an African Political Paradox*, *in* State and Constitutionalism in Africa 65 (Issa G. Shivji ed., 1991).

[4] *Id.* at 68.

[5] *Id.*

Catherine O'Regan, *The Political Paradox of African Constitutionalism Revisited: Kenya's* BBI *Case* In: *Redefining Comparative Constitutional Law*. Edited by: Vicki C. Jackson and Madhav Khosla, Oxford University Press. © Catherine O'Regan 2025. DOI: 10.1093/9780191996344.003.0016

summarized the political paradox as "the state elites' search for the formal means by which to preserve the integrity of the 'constituted polity' without being embroiled in a maze of constitutional law whose function, in classical theory, is to control and supervise constitutionality."[6] Okoth-Ogendo identified various techniques commonly adopted by African political elites to achieve their goal of constitutions that did not impose constraints, including coups d'état; simply ignoring provisions of the constitution; and, perhaps most interestingly, the conversion of constitutions into instruments of political warfare.[7] This last technique, he argued, was often achieved through processes of constitutional amendment, with the result that political decisions or strategies were often translated into processes of constitutional amendment,[8] and in the process "the Constitution lost of its claims to being the basic law."[9]

This chapter engages with the question whether Okoth-Ogendo's paradox can be said to have survived the new wave of constitution-making in Africa through the lens of a seminal case that recently made its way through the Kenyan courts: the *BBI* case,[10] challenging the introduction of the Kenyan Constitutional Amendment Bill of 2020 as unconstitutional in terms of the Kenya Constitution 2010. The *BBI* case raises questions about the limits of the constitutional amendment power under that Constitution and about whether Okoth-Ogendo's political paradox still obtains in Kenya.

Clearly, the questions posed by Okoth-Ogendo concern the relationship between the constitutional framework and the courts' interpretation of it, on the one hand, and politics and social relations, on the other. This relationship has been a key theme in Mark Tushnet's writing throughout his career. In several of his writings in the 1970s and 1980s, Tushnet explored the question to what extent law is autonomous of politics and social relations. In his astringent review of Lawrence Friedman's *A History of American Law*,[11] Tushnet disparaged Friedman's claim that the legal system "works like a blind, insensate machine. It does the bidding of those whose hands are on the controls. The laws . . . reflect the goals and policies of those who call the tune."[12] Not so, argued Tushnet: Friedman is ignoring "the possibility that some changes in the law may be explicable solely in terms of the autonomous internal dynamics of the legal process and the possibility that the legal order may become an active influence, to some degree, on the social and economic

[6] *Id.* at 69.
[7] *Id.* at 71–72.
[8] *Id.* at 73.
[9] *Id.*
[10] For the Supreme Court decision, *see* Attorney-General and Others v. Ndii and Others, 2022 KESC 8 (KLR) (Kenya), http://kenyalaw.org/caselaw/cases/view/231325/. Decisions in the other courts are cited later in this chapter.
[11] . Mark Tushnet, *Perspectives on the Development of American Law: A Critical Review of Friedman's* A History of American Law 1977 Wis. L. Rev. 81 (1977).
[12] *Id.* at 82.

order." Moreover, he argued, Friedman ignored the ideological functions of the legal order, which he defined "as a means of persuading both oppressor and oppressed that their conditions of existence are just."

The empirical question whether law operates in any sense autonomously of politics and social relations, and, if so, how and in what circumstances, is closely related to the questions that animated Okoth-Ogendo's account of African constitutions. Okoth-Ogendo's account suggests that the difficulty in Africa was that constitutional law rarely if ever operated autonomously of politics. He argues that African political elites not only acted to ensure that constitutions did not constrain power, but also operated as an instrument for the appropriation of power.[13]

In assessing whether Okoth-Ogendo's paradox persists, and to what extent, doctrinal and critical accounts of emerging African constitutional jurisprudence are of central importance. Of course, whether constitutions function in a framework of constitutionalism is not to be determined only by how courts engage with constitutional questions. For the ways in which legislatures, executives, regional governments, security services such as police and the army, political parties, and, in many parts of Africa especially, traditional leadership behave are all important indicators of the hold of constitutions. Yet for lawyers, in particular, the work of courts is necessarily an important part of the analysis. And doctrinal engagement with the work of courts, it seems to me, is one of the ways in which academic lawyers can and should engage in the project of constitutionalism.

This argument will not come as a surprise to Mark Tushnet. In one of his most recent pieces of writing, "Writing while quarantined: a personal interpretation of Contemporary Comparative Constitutional Law," he compares the reception of critical scholarship of US constitutionalism in the 1970s and 1980s to the current reception of critical scholarship in comparative constitutional law. He argues that in the 1970s and 1980s US progressives were hostile to critical scholarship on US constitutional law because

> [t]hey were fighting to maintain [...] the gains made by the Warren Court. Those offering critical perspectives, assertedly from the Left, were like a Fifth Column: Not only might the critics weaken the resolve of the Warren Court's defenders, but those defenders had to divert some energy from the fight against the Burger Court to explain why the critics were wrong.[14]

He asserts that the same phenomenon is abroad today, as the third wave of constitutionalism appears to be faltering and lapsing into forms of democratic decay and

[13] Okoth-Ogendo, *supra* note 3, at 73.

[14] Mark Tushnet, *Writing While Quarantined: A personal interpretation of contemporary constitutional law*, 15 Vienna J. on Int'l Const. L. 53 (2021).

authoritarianism. He argues that critical perspectives are coming under pressure as they did in the US in the 1970s and 1980s, and for much the same reason.

This chapter is informed—as was much of the debate about the BBI case—by the anxiety about the future of constitutionalism in the democracies of southern and east Africa. It does not deny the value of critical scholarship rooted in social science but asserts the central value of doctrinal scholarship rooted in law too.

The *BBI* case is a case of high constitutional significance. In it, the courts were approached to constrain the conduct of the political branches of government, and particularly to restrain them from amending the constitution. As Sam Issacharoff has noted, it is such cases that put courts at particular risk: "In repeated engagements with entrenched political power, a confrontational judiciary is at grave risk of emerging the loser."[15] And, as he also notes, "the flight from principle in the face of consolidating political power appears to be a path fraught with peril. If judges do not have claim on a broader principle for confronting the political branches, then why should they not stand down in the face of the political will of the majority?"[16] Constitutional cases should thus be cogently decided for profound reasons of democratic and legal principle but also perhaps for reasons of institutional endurance.[17] We can never know the extent to which unarticulated reasons motivate a court's decision, but we can assess whether the articulated ones are plausible and legally cogent.

Accordingly, an important task for comparative constitutional law should be to subject constitutional jurisprudence to evaluative scrutiny. This chapter will thus situate the *BBI* case within its historical context. It will then identify two of the key issues in the case that are relevant to the persistence of Okoth-Ogendo's paradox, and outline the reasoning in the decisions of, in particular, the High Court and the Supreme Court. In conclusion, I shall consider the extent to which it can be said that the case is an exemplar of a new direction in constitutional adjudication, and of resistance by courts to the preservation of the political paradox identified by Okoth-Ogendo.

As noted above, a major premise of this chapter will be that comparative constitutional lawyers should recognize that thoughtful doctrinal analysis of constitutional jurisprudence in domestic settings is important, perhaps particularly in societies where levels of political distrust are high. As comparative constitutional lawyers, we need to recognize that the project of deepening doctrinal critique and engagement with court decisions may be of enduring value.

[15] Samuel Issacharoff, Fragile Democracies: Contested Power in the Era of Constitutional Courts 264 (2015).

[16] *Id.* at 265.

[17] *See* Theunis Roux, The Politics of Principle: The First South African Constitutional Court, 1995–2005 (2013).

The Historical Background to the *BBI* Case

The BBI case cannot be understood without an appreciation of Kenya's political and constitutional history. Kenya gained independence from Britain in 1963, and its 1963 Constitution was adopted following negotiations between the British government and Kenyan leaders.[18] The 1963 Constitution established a parliamentary democracy with a bill of rights, justiciable by the courts. But this constitutional framework did not last long. It was subject to repeated amendment first under the leadership of Jomo Kenyatta and then under that of Daniel arap Moi. Indeed, there were 38 amendments to Kenya's 1963 Constitution before it was replaced by the 2010 Constitution.[19] The first of these constitutional amendments was introduced by Jomo Kenyatta's government in 1964, the year after independence. It established Kenya as a republic and introduced a system of presidential government in place of the parliamentary system established in the 1963 Constitution.[20] The second amendment, introduced in the same year, disestablished the autonomous regional governments, which had been protected by a special majority under the 1963 Constitution, and created a unitary government.[21] Kenyatta was followed as president by Daniel arap Moi, who introduced a system of *de jure* one-party rule in the 19th constitutional amendment adopted in 1982.[22] Moi's authoritarian and corrupt politics led to prolonged civil society resistance, and persistent demands for constitutional change.[23] In the early 1990s, Moi conceded and some constitutional changes were introduced. Notably, the provision of the Constitution that had prohibited opposition parties was repealed, and presidential term limits were introduced. However, Moi won the next two rounds of presidential elections and remained as president till 2002.

Pressure for fundamental constitutional change continued to build and in 1997 the Constitution of Kenya Review Act (the Review Act) was passed. After intense political contestation, a Constitution of Kenya Review Commission was

[18] See for a fuller account Yash Ghai, *Constitutions and Constitutionalism*, *in* OXFORD HANDBOOK OF KENYAN POLITICS 207 (Nic Cheeseman, Karuti Kanyinga & Gabrielle Lynch eds., 2020).

[19] LUIS FRANCESCHI & P.L.O. LUMUMBA, THE CONSTITUTION OF KENYA: A COMMENTARY 707 (2nd ed., 2019).

[20] *See* The Constitution of Kenya (Amendment) Act, No. 28 (1964) and the discussion of the first 18 amendments to the 1963 Constitution, which were enacted between 1964 and 1979, in FRANCESCHI & LUMUMBA, *supra* note 19, at 32–43.

[21] The Constitution of Kenya (Amendment) (No. 2) Act, No. 38 (1964). *See* discussion in FRANCESCHI & LUMUMBA, *supra* note 19, at 705.

[22] The 19th amendment to the 1963 Constitution, introduced by the Constitution of Kenya (Amendment) Act (1982). Again, *see* FRANCESCHI & LUMUMBA, *supra* note 19, at 42.

[23] *See* David W. Throup, *Daniel arap Moi and One-Party Rule (1978–1991)*, *in* Cheeseman, Kanyinga & Lynch, *supra* note 18, at 56–68, 64–66; and Bruce J. Berman, Jill Cottrell & Yash Ghai, *Patrons, Clients and Constitutions: Ethnic Politics and Political Reform in Kenya*, 43 CANADIAN J. AFR. STUD. 462, 463 (2009).

established, under the chairpersonship of Yash Ghai.[24] The Commission implemented an energetic program of public education and consultation. More than 37,000 submissions were received from the public and hearings were held in each of Kenya's then 210 constituencies.[25] The Commission produced a draft Constitution in 2002. It was at this time that Moi stood down from politics, elections were held, and a new government was established led by Mwai Kibaki, leading a new political party. It was the first change of government Kenya had seen since Moi had come to power in 1978, and it was a time of tremendous hope.[26] The draft constitution prepared by the Review Commission was referred, as the legislation required, to a national constitutional conference (comprising all the members of Parliament, political party representatives, and representatives from civil society), which debated and adopted a text.[27]

At this time, there was another important development. A constitutional challenge was brought to the provisions of the Review Act on the basis that it did not provide for the constitutional text to be submitted to the people of Kenya in a referendum.[28] A majority of the court upheld the argument that the amendment power provided for in s 47 of the 1963 Constitution did not empower Parliament to adopt a new constitution without a referendum and found the Review Act to be unconstitutional. Ringera J, one of the majority, reasoned, "Indeed if the process of constitutional review is to be truly people driven, 'Wanjiku' (the mythical common person) must give her seal of approval, her very imprimatur to the proposed Constitution."[29] The following year, Parliament amended the Constitutional Review Act to provide for a referendum following parliamentary ratification of the new text.

Once the national constitutional conference had finalized the text, it was sent to Parliament. At that moment, however, the newly appointed government led by Kibaki intervened and substantial modifications were introduced to the text undermining many of the core elements of the draft.[30] The draft Constitution was then put to the country in a referendum, in accordance with the amended Review Act, in November 2005, but it was rejected by 58 percent of those who voted.[31]

[24] See the full discussion of this process in Jill Cottrell & Yash Ghai, *Constitution Making and Democratization in Kenya (2000–2005)*, 14 *Democratisation* 1, 5 (2007). See also Franceschi & Lumumba, *supra* note 19, at 43–48.

[25] Cottrell & Ghai, *supra* note 24, at 9–10.

[26] *See* Berman, Cottrell & Ghai, *supra* note 23, at 463–64.

[27] *See* Cottrell & Ghai, *supra* note 24, at 12.

[28] *See* Njoya and Others v. Attorney General 2004 eKLR, Civil Application 82 of 2004, decided on March 25, 2004, http://kenyalaw.org/caselaw/cases/view/16582.

[29] *Id.* at 16.

[30] *See* Cottrell & Ghai, *supra* note 24, at 16; and Christina Murray, *Political Elites and the People: Kenya's Decade-Long Constitution-Making Process, in* Gabriel L. Negretto, Redrafting Constitutions in Democratic Regimes: Theoretical and Comparative Perspectives 190, 195 (2020).

[31] *See* James D. Long, *Civil Conflict, Power-Sharing, Truth and Reconciliation, 2004–2013, in* Cheeseman, Kanyinga & Lynch, *supra* note 18, at 82–95, 84–85.

The referendum campaign was described by a Kenyan academic as having been marred by "outright lies, misuse of state power and nativist appeals to tribal hysteria,"[32] with President Kibaki campaigning for a Yes vote and Raila Odinga for a No vote. Yash Ghai, who had played a leading role in the draft constitutional text that had been produced by the Review Commission, concluded later that "[i]n one sense, the referendum was a triumph for the democratic will. It was clear that many people were disgusted at the way the government had hijacked the process. But it is also clear that the exercise turned into a popular vote of confidence in the government as a whole."[33]

The ensuing 2007 elections were bitterly contested by Kibaki, now leading a newly formed Party of National Unity, and by Raila Odinga, leading the Orange Democratic Movement, supported among others by William Ruto. When the election commission announced that Kibaki had won the elections at the end of December, violent protests "with frightening ethnic dimensions"[34] broke out across the country, lasting for several months. By the time they had subsided, an estimated 1,200 people had been killed and 700,000 displaced.[35]

A panel of eminent African leaders, led by UN Secretary General Kofi Annan, intervened to negotiate a settlement between the two major parties. The negotiated settlement led to the establishment of the Kenyan National Dialogue and Reconciliation (KNDR) team, which was given several tasks, including halting the violence and restoring order, addressing the humanitarian consequences of the violence, resolving the political crisis, and initiating institutional reforms. One of the first things the KNDR did was to propose the establishment of a commission of inquiry into the causes of the postelection violence, which reported in October 2008. The Commission concluded that the violence had not been "opportunistic" but had been at least in some places directed by political elites, and had been exacerbated by an "apparent collapse" of state institutions and security forces.[36] Following the Commission's report, the Prosecutor of the International Criminal Court initiated an investigation, which led to charges against four people, including political leaders Uhuru Kenyatta and William Ruto. The charges concerned crimes against humanity, including murder, deportation or forcible transfer of population, and persecution.[37] By 2016, the charges against Kenyatta had been withdrawn and the charges against Ruto dismissed.

[32] *See* Makau Mutua, Kenya's Quest for Democracy: Taming Leviathan (2008), cited in Murray, *Political Elites*, *supra* note 30.

[33] *See* Cottrell & Ghai, *supra* note 24, at 16.

[34] *See* Collins Odote, *The 2013 Elections and the Peace Narrative (2013–2015)*, *in* Cheeseman, Kanyinga & Lynch, *supra* note 18, at 108.

[35] Long, *Civil Conflict*, *supra* note 31, at 87.

[36] *Id.* at 89.

[37] See arts. 7(1)(a), 7(1)(g), & 7(1)(h) of the Statute of Rome. *See also* Njoki Wamai, *International Relations and the International Criminal Court*, *in* Cheeseman, Kanyinga & Lynch, *supra* note 18, at 562, 564.

Other elements of the negotiated settlement included a resolution to the political crisis. In February 2009, Kibaki and Odinga signed a National Accord to establish a government of national unity in which Kibaki served as president and Odinga served in a new prime ministerial position. The Cabinet was composed of members of both the Party of National Unity and the Orange Democratic Movement.[38] Finally, the negotiated settlement required the Government of National Unity to take steps toward constitutional reform. The settlement included an agreement to tackle poverty, regional inequality within the country, and youth unemployment.

It was agreed that constitutional reform was to be undertaken in a staged process. A committee of experts (the Committee) was established in December 2008. Its mandate was to identify the core contentious issues and seek to make proposals that would garner broad consensus.[39] The process drew on the 2005 draft constitution prepared by the Constitution of Kenya Review Commission, as well as the amendments introduced by Parliament to that draft. The staged process also provided for a period of public consultation, but made clear that decisions on the contested issues would be taken by a multiparty Parliamentary Select Committee (the PSC), following which the draft text would be returned to the Committee for review and revision. The Committee would then send the draft Constitution to Parliament for adoption, after which it would be put to a referendum of all voters. In this way the process required popular input, but also sought to ensure that there was elite support of the draft.[40]

Once the Committee had drawn up its proposals there was provision for public consultation, following which the proposals were revised and then forwarded to the PSC.[41] One of the key proposals of the Committee was the establishment of a parliamentary system of government but this proposal was rejected by the PSC, which insisted on the retention of a presidential system.[42] The Committee then revised the draft in light of the PSC proposals, adopting some, including the decision concerning presidential government, but also revising and rejecting others.[43] The draft was then sent to Parliament, which could amend the draft only by a special majority of 65 percent. Although many amendments were proposed, none received the requisite support, and Parliament thus adopted the draft unchanged.

The draft was then put to a referendum in August 2010. Both Kibaki and Odinga supported the adoption of the Constitution, but Ruto campaigned for a no vote, as

[38] *See* Long, *Civil Conflict*, *supra* note 31, at 88–89.

[39] *See* the informative account of the constitution-making process by one of the Committee of Experts, Professor Christina Murray, in Christina Murray, *Making and Remaking Kenya's Constitution*, *in* CONSTITUTION MAKERS ON CONSTITUTION MAKING: NEW CASES 37, 50–54 (Tom Ginsburg & Sumit Bisarya eds., 2022).

[40] *See* Murray, *Political Elites*, *supra* note 30, at 200–01.

[41] *Id.* at 199–204.

[42] *See* Murray, *Making and Remaking Kenya's Constitution*, *supra* note 39, at 57–58.

[43] Murray, *Political Elites*, *supra* note 30, at 203.

did, for example, the churches.[44] In the end, 67 percent of those voting supported the adoption of the Constitution.[45]

The Kenyan Constitution 2010 came into force in late August 2010. The 2010 Constitution introduced an upper house (a new Senate) and a system of devolved government which saw the establishment of 47 county governments, with elected governors, county assemblies, and county executives. It also provides for an extensive bill of rights, and for a range of independent accountability institutions. Finally, it regulates constitutional amendments carefully, as is more fully described below.

Perhaps not surprisingly, the adoption of the new Constitution did not put an end to the intense political rivalry which had characterized Kenyan politics since the end of one-party rule in 1992. As Collins Odote perceptively remarked, the 2007 postelection violence "shattered the perception" that Kenya was an island of peace in a conflict-riven region. The violence that followed the 2007 election thus cast a long shadow over the 2013 elections, which again saw a bitter contest between two realigned groups of politicians—alignments which were built at least in part on an ethnic calculus. Kenyatta and Ruto (who had previously been an ally of Raila Odinga in opposition to Kenyatta) joined forces, under the banner of the Jubilee Alliance, to contest the presidency against Odinga and Musyoka (who had served as vice president in the Government of National Unity). All four of these politicians had been active in the 2007 elections and had served in the Government of National Unity after 2008. A new independent body, the Independent Election and Boundaries Commission, had been established under the new Constitution to manage the elections. Unfortunately, newly introduced electoral technology malfunctioned and Kenyatta and Ruto's narrow electoral win in the elections was contested, but this time in the Supreme Court rather than on the streets.[46] The Supreme Court upheld the results.

The 2017 presidential elections were again contested by the incumbent, Kenyatta, leading the Jubilee Alliance with Ruto, and by Odinga, now leading the National Super Alliance with Musyoka and others. Again, the establishment of the main coalitions in advance of the elections was guided by ethnic calculations.[47] As in 2013, there were difficulties with the electoral technology, and when the Independent Election and Boundaries Commission announced that Kenyatta had won the election with 54 percent of the vote Odinga and his allies again challenged the decision in the Supreme Court.[48] The Constitution sets a tight time frame for electoral petitions, requiring the Supreme Court to deliver a decision within

[44] *Id.*
[45] *See* Murray, *Political Elites*, *supra* note 30.
[46] *See* Odote, *The 2013 Elections*, *supra* note 34, at 97.
[47] *See* Marie-Emmanuelle Pommerolle, *The 2017 Elections and Electoral (In)justice (2015–2017)*, *in* Cheeseman, Kanyinga & Lynch, *supra* note 18, at 109.
[48] *Id.*

21 days. The Supreme Court somewhat unexpectedly, following its decision on the challenge to the 2013 elections, upheld the challenge and set aside the electoral result, ordering that the election be rerun within 60 days.[49]

Shortly before the election was rerun the National Super Alliance withdrew and the consequence was that the Jubilee Alliance and Kenyatta won. The National Super Alliance vigorously contested the legitimacy of the announced election outcome, and on January 30, 2018, in an unofficial inauguration ceremony held in a public park in central Nairobi, Odinga was sworn in as the "People's President," as his supporters called him.[50] Just six weeks later, Kenyatta and Odinga, at a public meeting subsequently dubbed "the Handshake," announced an (unpublished) accord purportedly to end the political tension in Kenya.

Following the accord's announcement, President Kenyatta appointed the Building Bridges to Unity Taskforce (the BBI Taskforce) to make proposals to "build lasting unity" in Kenya.[51] Following an interim report by the Taskforce in November 2019, President Kenyatta appointed a Steering Committee to implement the BBI Taskforce's proposals. Following the Steering Committee report, the Constitution of Kenya Amendment Bill 2020 (the 2020 Constitution Amendment Bill), containing a wide range of amendments to the Constitution, was produced and the BBI Steering Committee then set about collecting signatures for the constitutional amendments to be introduced by a popular initiative. Key amendments in the Bill included the introduction of the office of prime minister and two deputy prime ministers, to be appointed by the president, with the prime minister to serve as leader of government business in Parliament;[52] the recognition of the office of "Leader of Official Opposition," who would become the third most senior officer in Parliament after the Speaker and the prime minister;[53] and the establishment of a new office of Judicial Ombudsman, to be nominated by the president and approved by Parliament, who would serve as a member of the Judicial Service Commission[54] and receive and investigate complaints against judges, including disciplining judges. The Bill also proposed an increase in the number of constituencies in Parliament from 290 to 360.[55] It was this Amendment Bill, and the process whereby it was to be introduced, that led directly to the *BBI* case.

[49] *See* Odinga and Musyoka v. IEBC and Others 2017 KESC 42 (KLR) (Kenya), Election Petition 1/2017, http://kenyalaw.org/caselaw/cases/view/140716/.

[50] *See* Pommerolle, *The 2017 Elections, supra* note 47, at 110.

[51] *See* Terms of Reference to the BBI Taskforce set out in David Ndii and Others v. Attorney General and Others 2020 KEHC 738 (KLR) (Kenya), Petition E282 of 2020, consolidated with Petitions E397, E400, E401,E402, E416, and E421 of 2020, and Petition 2 of 2021, High Court, ¶ 3, http://kenyalaw.org/caselaw/cases/view/205553/.

[52] *See* The Constitution of Kenya (Amendment) Bill, cl. 24 (2020).

[53] *See* The Constitution of Kenya (Amendment) Bill, cl. 15 (2020).

[54] *See* The Constitution of Kenya (Amendment) Bill, cls. 36–38 (2020).

[55] *See* The Constitution of Kenya (Amendment) Bill, cl. 11 (2020).

The Political Paradox Revisited

Before turning to the *BBI* case, several aspects of this history require comment, as they may illuminate some aspects of the political paradox of "constitutions without constitutionalism" identified by Okoth-Ogendo. First, the persistent use of constitutional amendment by Kenyan leaders between 1963 and 2010 to seek to avoid the limits placed on their authority by the Constitution, but without abrogating the Constitution itself, demonstrates how those leaders sought to preserve the quintessential paradox identified by Okoth-Ogendo. As mentioned above, there were 38 amendments to Kenya's 1963 Constitution before it was replaced by the 2010 Constitution.[56] The Constitution of Kenya (Amendment) Bill 2020 (which contained the amendments relating to the BBI) was both similar and different to the constitutional amendments that preceded it. It was an amendment introduced by the political elite, in a manner that was perceived to serve their interests, but it was different in that it was clearly an attempt at an elite pact,[57] unlike the amendments introduced by Moi and Kenyatta in the first three decades after independence.

The second insight to be drawn from this history, however, is that alongside the incessant resort to constitutional amendment by those in power over these decades, there has also been a vocal campaign for constitutional reform waged by civil society actors. These civic actors have continued to assert the possibility of constitutionalism in Kenya, despite the ongoing resistance to it by political leaders. As outlined above, civic protest led to a constitutional reform process from the late 1990s which was derailed by Kibaki's government and resulted in the popular rejection of the proposed new constitution in 2005. But the demand for constitutional reform did not abate and in the aftermath of the 2007 postelection violence constitutional reform was put back on the agenda, and led to the adoption of the 2010 Constitution.

Third, the repeated resort to constitutional amendment by political leaders resulted in widespread skepticism in Kenya about constitutional amendments championed by political leaders, and that skepticism was one of the drivers of the demands for constitutional reform in a "people-driven" process. That skepticism probably led to the specific provisions of the 2010 Constitution concerning constitutional amendment. As noted above, the 2010 Constitution regulates constitutional amendments carefully. There are two processes for introducing

[56] Franceschi & Lumumba, *supra* note 19, at 707.

[57] *See* Yaniv Roznai & Duncan M. Okubasu, *Stability of Constitutional Structures and Identity amongst "Political Settlement": Lessons from Kenya and Israel*, 1 Compar. Const. Stud. 101, 102 (2023).

constitutional amendments: The first is through a parliamentary initiative, which requires two-thirds support in both houses of parliament, and the second is by popular initiative, which requires the support of at least a million voters and either the support of a simple majority of both houses of parliament or, failing that, popular support in a referendum.[58] Any amendment (whether introduced as a parliamentary or popular initiative) that relates to the supremacy of the Constitution, the territory of Kenya, the sovereignty of the people, the national values and principles of governance, the Bill of Rights, the president's term of office, the independence of the judiciary and other independent accountability institutions, the functions of Parliament, and the objects, principles, and structure of devolved government, may not take effect without approval in a referendum.[59]

In such referendums, amendments to what might be described as the core principles of that Constitution must be approved by a majority of voters and with reasonable levels of support across the country (20 percent of registered voters in half the 47 counties must support the amendment).

Finally, there is the changing role that courts have played in Kenya over the past 60 years. In the early years courts were generally deferential to government, but after the 1990s and the rise of popular demands for constitutional reform, courts became more robust in their consideration of challenges to constitutional amendment. Noteworthy in this regard is the 2004 High Court decision holding that the failure of the Review Act to provide for a referendum before a new constitutional text to be adopted was unconstitutional.[60] Just as noteworthy is the fact that Parliament immediately amended the Review Act following the High Court decision to provide for a referendum where the constitutional text could be referred to the people.

These four aspects of the history demonstrate that while political leaders may have continued to sustain the political paradox, growing popular resistance to it by civil society actors was a key driver of constitutional reform in 2010. Accordingly, the 2010 Constitution removed the power to amend core constitutional provisions from Parliament acting alone. Instead it provided that amendments to core provisions of the constitution require a referendum. The 2010 Constitution, therefore, sought to end one of the techniques that had enabled Kenyan political leaders to preserve the political paradox. The question, then, is how successful the 2010 Constitution has been in achieving that goal.

[58] *See* CONSTITUTION art. 256 (2010) (Kenya).
[59] *See* CONSTITUTION arts. 255, 257 (2010) (Kenya).
[60] *See Njoya*, *supra* note 28.

The *BBI* Case

In the High Court

Following the publication of the 2020 Constitutional Amendment, eight separate constitutional petitions were filed in the High Court to challenge its constitutionality. The High Court consolidated the petitions and a panel of five judges heard the case over three days in March 2021. Two issues were most salient to a consideration of the survival of the political paradox under the new constitutional framework: does the Basic Structure doctrine of interpretation apply in Kenya? And what is the remit of a popular initiative to amend the Constitution and, in particular, may it be initiated by the president?

The first question was whether the Basic Structure doctrine, originally developed by the Indian Supreme Court in the *Kesavananda* case,[61] applies in Kenya. In *Kesavananda*, the Indian Supreme Court held that the Indian Parliament may not amend the basic features of the Indian Constitution even if it follows the procedures set out in Article 368 of the Indian Constitution. Article 368 provides that a two-thirds majority of those present and voting in both houses of parliament is all that is required to amend the Indian Constitution, save where federal structures or relationships are affected or the powers of the judiciary or president are to be amended, in which case the amendment will require, in addition, ratification by the legislatures of half of the states. The Basic Structure doctrine established in *Kesavananda* is now a deeply rooted principle of Indian constitutional law, and has also been followed in other jurisdictions. The question before the Kenyan High Court (and in due course the Kenyan Court of Appeal and Supreme Court) was whether it was a principle of the Kenyan Constitution as well.

The Kenyan High Court held unanimously that the Basic Structure doctrine does apply in Kenya. It reached this conclusion after reviewing the history of the making of the Kenyan Constitution 2010, and especially by noting the centrality of public participation to the making of that Constitution, in contradistinction to the many processes of constitutional amendment initiated (effectively) by presidents in the years between 1963 and 2010. The Court also cited the decision in *Njoya and others v Attorney General*, discussed above, which found that the adoption of a new constitution had to be ratified by referendum.

Having recounted this history, the High Court concluded that "the stable canon of principles of interpretation of the Constitution which have emerged . . . yield the conclusion that Kenyans intended to protect the Basic Structure of the Constitution . . . from destruction through gradual amendments."[62] The High Court identified

[61] Kesavananda Bharati v. State of Kerala (1973) 4 SCC 225 (SCI).

[62] *See* David Ndii and Others v. Attorney General 2020 KEHC 738 (KLR) (Kenya), ¶ 469, http://kenyalaw.org/caselaw/cases/view/212141/.

four processes that were required for constitution-making: civic education; public participation; constituent assembly debate, involving consultations and public discourse; and a referendum.[63] The Court acknowledged that there was no clause in the Constitution which explicitly rendered any Article unamendable but held that the scheme of the Constitution in the light of its history meant that the power to amend the Constitution was substantively limited. The Court held that the "essence of the constitutional order" may only be changed by the exercise of primary constituent power, which would require civic education, public participation, the establishment of a constituent assembly for consultation and deliberation, and a referendum.[64] There was no discussion in the judgment of how Articles 255 to 257 of the Constitution might intersect with the Basic Structure doctrine asserted in the judgment (although those Articles were considered when the Court addressed the question who may launch a popular initiative). And the Court did not provide a clear definition of what constitutes the Basic Structure of the Kenyan Constitution. The Court held that the Basic Structure consists of "the foundational structure of the Constitution as provided in the Preamble, the eighteen chapters; and the six schedules of the Constitution"[65] but went on to say that "it is *not* every clause in each of the eighteen chapters and six schedules which is inoculated."[66] It is "the core edifice, foundational structure and values of the Constitution" that are protected.[67]

With regard to the second question, that is, who may initiate a popular initiative, the High Court noted that this provision had been carried forward to the 2010 Constitution from the original 2005 draft Constitution which had failed.[68] It held that the popular initiative was intended to be a route to be pursued by registered voters and civil society institutions, not by government institutions and officers,[69] and that it was clear that in 2020 it was President Kenyatta who had initiated the Constitutional Amendment Bill using a process which was reserved for "the ordinary citizenry . . . [and] cannot be undertaken by the President or State Organs under any guise."[70]

It is clear from the High Court judgment that the Court considered the history of constitutional amendment and reform in Kenya to be of paramount importance in interpreting the Constitution and in determining its approach to the question whether the Basic Structure doctrine applied in Kenya. The Court was obviously concerned about the history of what it called "hyper-amendment" of the Constitution, even citing Okoth-Ogendo's seminal article in this regard.[71] The

63 *Id.*
64 *Id.* at ¶ 472.
65 *Id.* at ¶ 474 (f).
66 *Id.* at ¶ 474 (g).
67 *Id.*
68 *Id.* at ¶ 478.
69 *Id.* at ¶ 481.
70 *Id.* at ¶ 497.
71 *Id.* at ¶ 407.

Court also relied on the precedent in the *Njoya* case which concerned the interpretation of the 1963 Constitution. On the other hand, the Court paid relatively little attention to the text of the 2010 Constitution, and little or none to the amendment clauses of that Constitution. What is clear, however, from the reasoning of the Court is that its view was that the Constitution did not permit the president to seek amendment of the Constitution in a manner that would undermine its core principles.

A Brief Note on the Court of Appeal Decision

On appeal, the majority of a seven-member bench of the Court of Appeal reached the same conclusion as the High Court.[72] All seven judges wrote separately. On the question whether the Basic Structure doctrine was applicable in Kenya, six of the seven judges held that it was,[73] and five judges held that the Basic Structure doctrine limited the amendment powers set out in Articles 255 to 257 of the Constitution.[74] As in the High Court judgment, the judgments emphasized Kenya's political and constitutional history in reaching their conclusions. The Court held unanimously that the president may not initiate constitutional amendments through the use of the popular initiative route which was a form of popular participation preserved for individuals. There was one dissent, from Sachele JA, who held that the Basic Structure doctrine had no place in the Kenyan Constitution. She noted that the referendum requirement in the 2010 Constitution for amendments that affect core aspects of the Constitution had its historical roots in the work of the Constitution of Kenya Review Commission.[75] She also noted that in the ten years since the 2010 Constitution had come into force there had been 21 attempts to amend the Constitution (10 introduced in Parliament and 2 by way of popular initiative) and that all had failed.[76] She also noted that the Constitution of Kenya Review Commission had emphasized the importance of achieving a balance between flexibility and rigidity.[77] Justice Sichale however joined the rest of the judges of the Court in concluding that it was not open to the president to rely on the popular initiative provisions of the Constitution to introduce a constitutional amendment.[78] "This was not a Wanjiku-driven process," she remarked.[79]

[72] *See* IEBC v. David Ndii and Others 2021 KECA 363 (KLR) (Kenya), Court of Appeal decision, http://kenyalaw.org/caselaw/cases/view/217967.

[73] Musinga J.A., Nambuye J.A., Okwengu JA, Kiage J.A., Gatembu J.A., and Tuiyott J.A.. Sichale J.A. dissented.

[74] Musinga J.A., Nambuye J.A., Kiage J.A., Gatembu J.A., and Tuiyott J.A.. Okwengu J.A. and Sichale J.A. dissented.

[75] *See* IEBC v. David Ndii and Others, *supra* note 72, judgment of Sichale J., at ¶ 40.

[76] *Id.* at ¶ 42.

[77] *Id.* at ¶¶ 43–47.

[78] *Id.* at ¶ 75.

[79] *Id.*

In the Supreme Court

On appeal to the Supreme Court, in which seven judges also heard the matter, a different result was reached:[80] Six of the seven judges held that the Basic Structure doctrine does not apply in Kenya.[81] However, six of the seven judges agreed with the Court of Appeal and the High Court that the president could not rely on the popular initiative process in the Constitution to initiate a constitutional amendment,[82] and five of the seven judges held that the president had imitated the 2020 Constitutional Amendment.[83]

In her judgment, Chief Justice Koome noted, as Sichale JA had done in the Court of Appeal, that the Constitution of Kenya Review Commission had held that it was important for a new constitutional text to achieve balance between rigidity and amendability.[84] In her view, the tiered process of constitutional amendment provided in Articles 255–257 of the 2010 Constitution balanced flexibility and rigidity, as well as recognizing the need "to ring-fence that core or fundamental commitments of the Constitution."[85] She pointed out that neither the High Court nor the Court of Appeal had carefully considered the amendment procedures provided in Articles 255–257, nor had they, save for Sichale J, considered what conclusions should be drawn from the unsuccessful attempts to amend the Constitution between 2010 and when the case was heard. She concluded that

> in a case where the amendment process is multi-staged; involves multiple institutions; is time-consuming; engenders inclusivity and participation by the people in deliberations over the merits of the proposed amendments; and has down-stream veto by the people in the form of a referendum, there is no need for judicially-created implied limitations to amendments power through importation of the basic structure doctrine.[86]

With regard to whether the president could initiate the process of constitutional amendment through reliance on the popular initiative procedure, Chief Justice Koome adopted a purposive analysis of Article 257. She noted that the proposal for a popular initiative process for amending the Constitution had arisen at the National Constitutional Conference in 2005, where the Final Report of

[80] *See* Attorney-General and Others v. David Ndii and Others 2022 KESC 8 (KLR) (Kenya), Supreme Court, http://kenyalaw.org/caselaw/cases/view/231325/.

[81] Koome C.J., Mwilu D.C.J., Wanjala S.C.J., Ndungu S.C.J., Lenaola S.C.J. and Ouko S.C.J.. Ibrahim S.C.J. dissented.

[82] Koome C.J., Mwilu D.C.J., Ibrahim S.C.J., Wanjala S.C.J., Lenaola S.C.J. and Ouko S.C.J.. Ndungu S.C.J. dissented.

[83] Koome C.J., Mwilu D.C.J., Ibrahim S.C.J., Wanjala S.C.J. and Ouko S.C.J., Ndungu S.C.J. and Lenaola S.C.J. dissented.

[84] *See* judgment of Koome C.J., Attorney-General and Others v. David Ndii, *supra* note 80, at ¶ 190.

[85] *Id.* at ¶194.

[86] *Id.*, at ¶ 205.

the relevant technical committee had stated that the popular initiative was an "innovation where the citizens can on their own motion initiate amendment to the Constitution."[87] She held therefore that "amending the Constitution through a popular initiative was intended to be a citizen-driven and citizen-centred process"[88] and is "therefore a preserve of the citizens, 'the Wanjiku' in Kenyan popular lexicon."[89]

Conclusion

There was thus a sharp disagreement in the *BBI* case, between the judgments of the High Court and the majority in the Court of Appeal, on the one hand, and the majority in the Supreme Court, on the other, over the question whether the Basic Structure doctrine was an implied principle of the Kenyan Constitution. The Supreme Court decided, by a substantial majority, it was not. In reaching its conclusion, the Supreme Court paid close attention to the amendment provisions in the 2010 Constitution, something that neither the High Court nor the Court of Appeal had done. Despite the difference in the approach to constitutional interpretation, the outcome in all the courts was that the Constitution of Kenya (Amendment) Bill 2020 was found to be unconstitutional. Yet it is also not clear that the difference between the High Court and Court of Appeal approach which did conclude that the Kenyan Constitution contains a Basic Structure doctrine, and the Supreme Court approach which held that it did not, will make a significant difference in practice. It is clear that amendment of the 2010 Constitution is far harder than amendment of the 1963 constitution was: 22 amendments (if one includes the ill-fated 2020 amendment) have now failed since 2010. Any substantive amendment of the Constitution which affects core principles as set out in section 255 of the Constitution will, in addition to parliamentary support, require the support of voters in a referendum.

What is plain from all the judgments written in this case in the three courts is that the Kenyan courts were not willing to be partners in enabling the process of constitutional amendment proposed by President Kenyatta in the Constitution of Kenya Amendment Bill 2020. To that extent, they resisted the preservation of the political paradox observed by Okoth-Ogendo. Again and again the judgments state that the pattern of constitutional "hyper-amendment" is not to be repeated under the 2010 Constitution. These judgments illustrate that the courts were adamant that they would act autonomously of political power, and especially in the case of

[87] *Id.* at ¶ 237.
[88] *Id.* at ¶ 238.
[89] *Id.* at ¶ 241.

the Supreme Court majority decision with fidelity to the text of the Constitution. Okoth-Ogendo might well have applauded.

And yet, it may be fitting to end with a note of caution, as perhaps Okoth-Ogendo would have as well. The historical account of this case demonstrates that the political elites in this case, notably President Kenyatta, intended to use the mechanism of constitutional amendment for political purposes. That he should have done so is not surprising as constitutional amendment has long been one of the core tools of political elites in Africa, as Okoth-Ogende noted. But the Supreme Court decision in *BBI* has made plain that amending Kenya's 2010 Constitution in any substantive manner will now likely be beyond the direct control of politicians. What is not clear is how the Kenyan political elite will respond to this line drawn by the courts. The political paradox arises, as Okoth-Ogendo also observed, because "contemporary elites in Africa are preoccupied with the perfection of ways, means, and techniques of their own survival" which "are most unhealthy for the growth of constitutionalism."[90] Until it becomes clear how Kenyan political leaders respond to the consequences of the *BBI* decision, it will be too soon to say that the Kenyan Constitution of 2010 has ended the political paradox of African constitutionalism.

[90] *See* Ogendo, *supra* note 3, at 80.

17

Rights as the Domain of Weak-Form Review

Jeremy Waldron

Weak-form Review

In a system of weak-form judicial review, courts scrutinize legislation for its conformity to the provisions of a Bill of Rights, but they do not have final power to strike down or limit the application of legislation that is incompatible with the Bill of Rights. In Canada, lawmakers at the national or provincial level may legislate "notwithstanding" the relevant provisions of Charter of Rights and Freedoms, either in the first instance or in response to an adverse court ruling. So judicial power is weaker in Canada than in a system of strong judicial review such as that of the United States. In New Zealand the system of review is weaker than it is in Canada. The Bill of Rights Act (NZBORA) provides bluntly in section 4 that

> [n]o court shall, in relation to any enactment (whether passed or made before or after the commencement of this Bill of Rights) hold any provision of the enactment to be impliedly repealed or revoked, or to be in any way invalid or ineffective; or decline to apply any provision of the enactment—by reason only that the provision is inconsistent with any provision of this Bill of Rights.

New Zealand courts are not left entirely toothless. They have an obligation to search for and apply an interpretation of any legislation they are considering which avoids conflict with the rights provisions of the NZBORA if that is possible. That is true also in the version of weak judicial review that one finds in the United Kingdom. In addition, the United Kingdom's Human Rights Act (HRA) provides that, if a court is satisfied that some legislation is incompatible with a HRA right and if the right and the legislation cannot be reconciled interpretively, then the court may make a formal declaration of its incompatibility. Such a declaration opens the path to possible fast-track amendment (at the discretion of a Minister of the Crown). But the British system of review is still weak. Absent ministerial amendment, a declaration of incompatibility "does not affect the validity, continuing operation or enforcement of the provision in respect of which it is given" (UK HRA, s. 4(6)).

Is weak judicial review a form of *constitutional* review? Does weak-form review establish a distinct version of *constitutionalism*? It is tempting to say *no*. So long as compatibility with the relevant Bill of Rights is not in itself made a condition of legislative validity, the Bill of Rights is not really operating as part of the *constitution*

Jeremy Waldron, *Rights as the Domain of Weak-Form Review* In: *Redefining Comparative Constitutional Law.* Edited by: Vicki C. Jackson and Madhav Khosla, Oxford University Press. © Jeremy Waldron 2025.
DOI: 10.1093/9780191996344.003.0017

of the country concerned. "Half Measures on British Freedoms," proclaimed *The New York Times* when the HRA was enacted.[1]

But there is room for a more accommodating perspective. Certainly the provision made for weak-form review is part of the complex apparatus for lawmaking in the United Kingdom, New Zealand, and Canada. No account of that apparatus would be satisfactory if it omitted mention of such provision. Weak-form review is a constitutional alternative to strong judicial review. It does some (but not all) of the work that strong judicial review does in the United States, only it does it differently and in a way that is more subservient to representative institutions. Weak-form review occupies the same space as strong judicial review. So why wouldn't we also say that weak-form review is *a* version of constitutionalism, albeit a *different* version of constitutionalism? That is the position of Stephen Gardbaum, who talks about this "new Commonwealth model" as a "third model of constitutionalism that stands between the two polar models of constitutional and legislative supremacy."[2]

Whatever one's views on the merits of weak-form versus strong-form review, there is one other feature of weak-form review that might undermine its constitutionalist credentials. Weak-form review (in the United Kingdom, New Zealand, and Canada) does not apply to legislation touching *all* issues of constitutional concern. It has but a limited domain. The application of weak-form review, in the countries that have it, is confined to issues of rights. It is not extended to constitutional issues in general; certainly not to issues such as federal structure or separation of powers.

Whether or not we think this feature of weak-form review should detract from its constitutional status, it is certainly worth considering in its own right. What is the reason for this limited domain? And how are other constitutional issues dealt with in systems that have weak-form judicial review for issues about rights? In at least one of the countries with weak-form review—Canada—issues about the allocation of power between national and provincial legislatures seem to be dealt with using *strong*-form review when they come to court. Now it is usually thought that rights matter more than structural issues. So why, we might ask, are *rights*—of all things—given this weaker protection?

Mark Tushnet has long been one of our most thoughtful commentators on the contrast between weak-form and strong-form judicial review.[3] But he does not address the questions I have raised. He has no hesitation in describing weak-form review as a form of *constitutional* review and mostly he does not seem to notice its

[1] Editorial, *Half Measures on British Freedoms*, N.Y. TIMES, Nov. 17, 1977, at A22.

[2] Stephen Gardbaum, *The New Commonwealth Model of Constitutionalism*, 49 AM. J. COMPAR. L. 707, 709 (2001).

[3] See the following by MARK TUSHNET: WEAK COURTS, STRONG RIGHTS: JUDICIAL REVIEW AND SOCIAL WELFARE RIGHTS IN COMPARATIVE CONSTITUTIONAL LAW (2008); *Alternative Forms of Judicial Review*, 107 MICH. L. REV. 2781 (2003); *New Forms of Judicial Review and the Persistence of Rights- and Democracy-Based Worries*, 38 WAKE FOREST L. REV. 813 (2003); *Weak-Form Judicial Review: Its Implications for Legislatures*, 2 NEW ZEALAND J. PUB. & INT'L L. 7 (2004).

limited domain. I say "mostly," for there are a couple of passages where he comes close to recognizing the issue: "Weak-form systems," he says in a piece published in the *New Zealand Journal of Public International Law*, "have focused on human rights protections."[4] However, instead of questioning the whys and wherefores of this specific focus, he proceeds instead to raise questions about *human* rights, noticing the importance of the International Covenant on Civil and Political Rights in inspiring the HRA, the NZBORA, and the Canadian Charter. That *is* important, as we shall see shortly.[5] But it does not answer our question.

Tushnet also says that "weak-form systems hold out the promise of protecting liberal rights in a form that reduces the risk of wrongful interference with democratic self-governance."[6] But again, he does not explore the exclusivity of this focus. He mostly just assumes that countries that have weak-form review are evolving an alternative conception of constitutionalism, albeit one that he worries may prove unstable (perhaps liable to escalate into strong-form judicial review, or collapse back into simple acceptance of parliamentary supremacy).

Constitutional Status?

For American commentators, it may be hard to see the point of the questions I am raising.[7] Americans are accustomed to seeing their Bill of Rights as part of the Constitution, perhaps the most important part; so rights-based judicial review is bound to seem constitutional in character. But strong judicial review emerged in the United States—in *Marbury v. Madison* 5 U.S. (1 Cranch) 137 (1803)—in response to a constitutional issue that had nothing to do with rights. It was about the role played by the Constitution in ordaining and limiting the jurisdiction of the US Supreme Court. The decision in *Marbury* rested on the Constitution's explicit establishment of its own structuring terms as higher law, rendering void (in Chief Justice Marshall's analysis) any statutory provision—even a provision of a momentous statute like the 1789 Judiciary Act—purporting to confer additional jurisdiction on the Court.

If rights were not necessarily part of the constitution, then the "higher law" logic of *Marbury v. Madison* might not apply to legislation that was incompatible with rights. But there is now no room to question their constitutional status in the US. Once the Bill of Rights was added to the Constitution in 1791, specifically through the path of constitutional amendment—its terms taking their place alongside later

[4] Tushnet, *Weak-Form Judicial Review*, *supra* note 3, at 7.

[5] *See infra* text accompanying note 28.

[6] Tushnet, *New Forms of Judicial Review*, *supra* note 3, at 814.

[7] Tushnet acknowledges in *Weak-Form Judicial Review*, *supra* note 3, at 7 that his own "perspective is of course that of a scholar of United States constitutional law, and [his] initial comments are framed with reference to the United States experience."

structural amendments as well—it made sense to extend the argument in *Marbury v. Madison* to rights as well, and to treat them too as higher law enforceable by the courts.[8] Now, we know that the trajectory of the establishment of judicial review of legislation in Canada, New Zealand, and the United Kingdom was quite different (and centuries later) from its trajectory in the United States. But, as I said earlier, weak-form review seems to operate in the Commonwealth countries I have mentioned in the space in which strong-form review operates in the United States. Doesn't that mean, therefore, that, like strong-form review, it *is* constitutional in character? Aren't my questions just semantic quibbles?

I do not think so. It is not just a matter of whether we *call* weak-form review a form of constitutional review. It is partly a matter of the basis of the provision that has been made for it in the systems concerned. I will talk about that in a moment. Also, in the self-understanding of American jurisprudence, the protection of individual rights is not just treated as something imperative and effective; it is comprised in the very document that establishes the whole basis of government. The legitimacy of Congress, for example, as a legislature is bound up *both* with its serving the functions and observing the limits set out in Article One of the Constitution *and* in its observing the rights constraints laid down in the Bill of Rights and subsequent amendments. Together, those elements are what Congress's legitimacy depends on. A bill abridging free speech or taking private property without just compensation would be no more an authentic Act of Congress than a bill purporting to become law without a vote in the Senate or without being presented to the President for his signature. That—if you like—is the heavy significance of constitutional status.

Now, Professor Tushnet says that, in the countries that have them, weak-form limits on courts' powers over legislation are also *laid down in the constitutions concerned*.[9] Is this right? In the United Kingdom, the prohibition on strong-form review and the grant of the power of weak-form review, including the power to make Declarations of Incompatibility together with the legal consequences of such declarations, are all set out in a statute, namely, the Human Rights Act of 1998. In the New Zealand case, such matters are set out in the text of the New Zealand Bill of Rights Act of 1990 sections 2–7, again a piece of legislation enacted in the ordinary way. Indeed, the NZ statute was passed on a majoritarian basis along "bitterly divided party lines."[10] At a glance, this statutory provision seems quite different from conferring powers of judicial review in a constitution.

[8] But it did take a while before American courts began striking down legislation on these grounds. (I am grateful to Mark Graber for this point.)

[9] Tushnet, *Alternative Forms of Judicial Review*, *supra* note 3, at 2786.

[10] Gardbaum, *supra* note 2, at 727. In Britain, the HRA was passed with crossparty support. But it was not unanimous. It was also marked by a high intellectual level of debate: Lord Campbell was heard to protest in the House of Lords about "'these escoteric [*sic*] lectures on law at this time of night,' having 'never heard anything like this after dinner' in the eighteen years he had been in the Lords." (*See* K.D. Ewing, *The Human Rights Act and Parliamentary Democracy*, 62 Mod. L. Rev. 79, 79 (1999).)

However, appearances can be deceptive, because the two countries I have mentioned lack codified constitutions. In each case the country's constitution consists of many scattered texts, most of them statutory (such as the Act of Union, the Parliament Acts, and the Act of Settlement in the United Kingdom). As Tushnet acknowledges, "[p]articular systems may have a number of texts that, taken together, are the nation's constitution."[11] So the relevant provisions may be constitutional in quality even though they are not found in something called *the* constitution. Whether that is enough, though, to confer the "heavy" significance I mentioned on the previous page is another question.

As "mere" statutory provisions each in a Westminster system, the HRA and the NZBORA are of course vulnerable to simple legislative amendment or repeal. But not all statutes are equal. The political obstacles to such an exercise would be formidable and some commentators speculate that the judiciary might oppose it. Conventions (in the British sense) might be developing informally to protect these special statutes from repeal. This, I think, is a possible source of some of the instability that Tushnet talks about: If the HRA gradually acquires higher-law status, then weak-form review might morph into strong-form review in the United Kingdom.

Actually, it is a little more complicated than that. Concerning the status of the HRA and the NZBORA, *two* things establish them as *weak* in relation to judicial review.

First, they are both pieces of legislation enacted in the ordinary way. No attempt was made to entrench them or secure for them any basis of extraordinary enactment that would consecrate them as "higher law." Indeed, that category barely exists in a Westminster-style system of parliamentary sovereignty. Neither of the relevant statutes can be said to be "entrenched." Each of them looks vulnerable to explicit amendment and repeal by ordinary majoritarian legislation;[12] indeed, each of them looks vulnerable also to *implicit* repeal by ordinary majoritarian legislation enacted subsequently if it is on its terms contrary to the provisions of the NZBORA or the HRA, as the case may be. That is what we are imagining might change.

But, *second*, quite apart from the basis of their enactment and their vulnerability to various forms of repeal, both pieces of legislation contain provisions that go out of their way explicitly to forbid strong judicial review. (I quoted the relevant provisions near the beginning of this paper.) That second point is important. Without it,

[11] Tushnet, *Weak-Form Judicial Review*, *supra* note 3, at 11.

[12] People say these bills of rights can be overturned by a simple majority. That is not quite true: both parliaments have elaborate procedures for enactment, amendment, and repeal, which require multiple majoritarian decisions (First Reading, Second Reading, Committee Stage, Third Reading), not the crude and singular majority procedure that courts use when they make their decisions. Also, the British Parliament is bicameral, so that majority decisions are required also in the House of Lords (though ultimately, under the Parliament Act, the Commons can prevail in the event of conflict between the two Houses).

it is possible to imagine Bill of Rights legislation morphing into entrenched higher law through the development of constitutional conventions, the emergence of judicial customs, shared understandings in the political class, and so on. Maybe this is improbable anyway. But as long as the relevant legislation explicitly disclaims strong-form review, it is much less likely to happen.

Canada's version of weak-form review is shaped quite differently from that of the United Kingdom or New Zealand: It consists in provision that is made for "Parliament or the legislature of a province [to] expressly declare in an Act of Parliament or of the legislature, as the case may be, that the Act or a provision thereof *shall operate notwithstanding*" the rights in the Canadian Charter of Right and Freedoms. Still, that provision is made in section 33 *of the Charter*. Now, although the Charter too is part of a statute, the statute in question is much more explicitly *constitutional* in character—much more likely to be regarded as higher law—than the relevant rights statutes in the British or New Zealand cases. The Charter is part of the 1982 Constitution Act, which is the closest Canada comes to having a codified and entrenched constitution. Even so, my general point remains: The notwithstanding clause is not an aspect of Canada's *overall* constitutional scheme. It is embedded specifically in that part of the scheme that applies to rights. It seems to have no application to the provisions of the Canadian Constitution that determine legislative competence, for example the provisions that distinguish the powers of the national legislature from those of provincial legislatures.

When Structural Issues Arise

What happens in these systems with other constitutional issues (like federalism or separation of powers)? Three possibilities present themselves:

(i) there might be strong judicial review over legislative violations of structural provisions; or
(ii) there might be no power of judicial review at all over such violations; or
(iii) there might be weak judicial review over such violations.

In none of these jurisdictions have I seen any evidence of (iii), that is, of the arrangements for weak-form review expanding out from the realm of rights to govern other constitutional matters. Nor am I aware of any doctrine corresponding to (ii), disqualifying the courts decisively from reviewing legislative violations of constitutional rules in any way at all. Still, the situation varies as between these three countries.

In New Zealand the question barely arises. From a constitutionalist perspective, New Zealand seems to have the worst of all worlds. Its structural constitution has been radically simplified over the years. It once had a provincial structure but now it is a unitary state, so there are no issues of federal legislative competence. It once had a bicameral legislature, but it was made unicameral in the early 1950s. And any constitutional restraints imposed historically by Great Britain no longer apply. So it is hard to imagine courts finding anything to strike down in this area.[13] That is not because the judiciary is disqualified from doing so (as it is in s. 4 of the NZBORA), but because there are so few nonrights-based constitutional constraints on the legislature available for judicial enforcement. I guess maybe the rules in New Zealand's 1986 Constitution Act constraining the dismissal of judges or governing the initiation of money bills might under certain circumstances require courts to rule on the constitutionality of legislation. Or maybe New Zealanders' appreciation of the 1840 Treaty of Waitangi will evolve toward the imposition of constitutional constraints in the legislature's dealings with *tangata whenua*. In either of these eventualities, though, there is no indication that enforcement of such constraints will be subject to (anything like) the NZBORA limitation on judicial authority. At best (or worst) a background doctrine of parliamentary sovereignty would kick in to preclude strong judicial review.

In the UK, the recent decision of the Supreme Court in *R (Miller) v Secretary of State for Exiting the European Union* [2017] UKSC 5 seems to be an instance of (i), though it is not strictly speaking review of legislation, but rather of an executive position regarding legislation.[14] It is certainly strong judicial review concerning the powers of Parliament. Also, there are robust structural constraints in the Act of Union and associated statutes dating from the beginning of the 18th century when England and Scotland were united. If Parliament purported to legislate in violation of one of these constraints—if, for example, it were to attempt to disestablish the Presbyterian church in Scotland and replace it with the Church of England[15]—it is not clear what would happen. Some jurists say dogmatically that Parliament's will would prevail in virtue of its sovereignty. Others imagine that a judicial challenge to vindicate the guarantees laid down in the Protestant Religion and Presbyterian Church Act might well succeed. The UK was never wholly a unitary state; Scottish law has had a measure of independence from English law, and laws were sometimes passed specifically for Northern Ireland. Britain became much less of a unitary state after 1999 with the devolution of governmental powers to assemblies in

[13] There is one case—R. v. Lander [1919] NZLR 305—in which the Court of Appeal refused to apply legislation concerning extradition because it did not comply with powers laid down in the New Zealand Constitution Act 1852. I owe this citation to GEOFFREY PALMER AND ANDREW BUTLER, TOWARDS DEMOCRATIC RENEWAL: IDEAS FOR CONSTITUTIONAL CHANGE IN NEW ZEALAND n.127 (2018).

[14] Note that the term "weak-form review" does not apply to judicial review of executive or administrative action. In the countries under discussion, all such judicial review is strong-form in character.

[15] *See* the Protestant Religion and Presbyterian Church Act, 1707, which contains language binding the newly established joint Parliament of Great Britain to uphold the position of the Presbyterian Church in Scotland "for all time comeing," https://www.legislation.gov.uk/aosp/1707/6.

Cardiff, Edinburgh, and Belfast. In 2014, the UK Supreme Court gave its decision in *Agricultural Sector (Wales) Bill—Reference by the Attorney General for England and Wales* [2014] UKSC 4. The case concerned legislation by the Welsh Assembly regulating the wages of agricultural workers and the question was whether the enactment went beyond the competence of the Cardiff assembly, encroaching unconstitutionally on the domain of the Westminster Parliament. In the event, the court held that it did not; but it was clear that, had there been a contrary finding, the Welsh legislation would have been held invalid. There was no equivalent of section 4(6) of the HRA to rescue it.

The disparity that interests me is clearest in the case of Canada. There it is widely recognized that constitutional review has two separate domains: the division of powers between the federal and provincial governments, and the rights guaranteed in the Charter.[16] The latter is definitely weak-form review by virtue of the "notwithstanding" clause; but that clause has no application to the former. And Canada *does* allow strong-form review on questions of legislative competence. It has long been established that the Canadian courts and indeed the Judicial Committee of the Privy Council (when that functioned as Canada's highest court) could review and strike down provincial legislation if it impinged substantially on matters entrusted by the Constitution to the federal legislature. And the relevant legislatures would have no comeback. Charles Haines points out that an act of Ontario to prevent the profanation of the Sabbath was held void because an infraction of the act was made an offense against the criminal law, which was held to have been reserved for the exclusive authority of the Dominion Parliament.[17] Also, a provision of British Columbia's Cattle Protection Act, requiring that a Dominion railway company be liable for injuries to cattle unless its railroads were properly fenced, was invalidated by the Privy Council.[18] (Take that, Ronald Coase!) Actually, this might apply to national legislation too. In *Regina v Bittle*, 21 Ont. Rep. 605 (1892), sections of the Canada Temperance Act of 1878 were held invalid for encroaching on the domain of provincial legislation.[19] Haines noted that some Canadians have said there is a vast difference between declaring bills ultra vires and declaring them unconstitutional, but Haines responded, persuasively, that "the difference, if there is any, is not readily discoverable."[20] Now, these are all old cases, predating by many decades

[16] *See* Center for Constitutional Studies, *Judicial Review* (July 4, 2019), https://www.constitutionalstudies.ca/2019/07/judicial-review/.

[17] Charles Haines, *Judicial Review of Legislation in Canada*, 28 Harv. L. Rev. 565 (1915).

[18] Madden v. Nelson & Fort Sheppard Railway [1899] AC 626.

[19] *See* Haines, *supra* note 17, at 572.

[20] *Id.*, 582–83.

the enactment of the notwithstanding clause. But jurisdictional litigation of this sort continues in Canada, and there is no indication that it involves anything other than strong-form review. An illustration is a recent case dealing with constitutional authority over interprovincial pipelines.[21,22]

Advantages of Weak-form Review

Is it possible to make sense of any of this? Well, make sense of what, exactly? If strong-form review works, as it does in Canada, for constitutional issues involving jurisdictional boundaries, then why not do away with the notwithstanding clause in Charter matters and have strong review for rights as well? Analogously, in the United Kingdom and perhaps also in New Zealand, if there is no in-principle objection to strong-form review on constitutional matters that do not involve rights, then why not have it for rights issues? Why give lesser protection to rights when stronger protection is available in the constitutional repertoire of the country in question? Or we can put the question the other way round. If weak-form review is such a good idea, why not have it on all constitutional matters? Why restrict it to rights?

Like Mark Tushnet, I am convinced that weak-form judicial review *is* a good idea. I think it fulfills a valuable function in a democratic system. I am known as a critic of strong-form review,[23] but something like the British system, with its Declarations of Incompatibility, seems admirable, because

> [i]t combines ultimate parliamentary responsibility with a "canary in the coalmine" function for the judiciary, exercising whatever expertise they may have in matters of rights to alert the polity formally and publicly to the dangers posed by certain pieces of legislation.[24]

[21] *See* discussion in Eric Adams, *Canada's Constitution, and the Contradiction that Works*, THE GLOBE AND MAIL May 3, 2018. *See also* Rogers Communications Inc v. Châteauguay (City), [2016] 1 SCR 467. *See also* B.L. STRAYER, JUDICIAL REVIEW OF LEGISLATION IN CANADA (1968).

[22] Something similar applies in Australia, so far as encroachments of state legislation on federal prerogatives is concerned and vice versa. On those matters, there is strong-form review in Australia. *See* Adrienne Stone, *Judicial Review Without Rights: Some Problems for the Democratic Legitimacy of Structural Judicial Review*, 28 OXFORD J. LEGAL STUD. 1 (2008). Now, Australia has no bill of rights at the national level, weak-form or otherwise, so the disparity I am considering does not (yet) arise. But there is a weak-form bill of rights in the Australian state of Victoria; there the 2006 Charter of Human Rights and Responsibilities is weak-form in the way that New Zealand's Bill of Rights Act is. If Victoria's provision is viewed as a laboratory for a national bill of rights, then Australia is kind of heading toward the Canadian situation—with a clear juxtaposition of strong-form and weak-form provision.

[23] *See* Jeremy Waldron, *The Core of the Case against Judicial Review*, 115 YALE L.J. 1346 (2006).

[24] Jeremy Waldron, *Judicial Review of Legislation*, THE ROUTLEDGE COMPANION TO PHILOSOPHY OF LAW 435 (Andrei Marmor ed., 2014).

Or, as Tushnet puts it, "weak-form systems hold out the promise of protecting liberal rights in a form that reduces the risk of wrongful interference with democratic self-governance."[25] It reduces the risk of judges being seen as enemies of representative democracy.

Merits aside, it arguably was not open to either Britain or New Zealand to eschew all forms of special protection for rights in their laws. Here I think Tushnet is right to point to the influence of regional and global human rights institutions.[26] Britain is subject anyway to the decisions of the European Court of Human Rights and treaty-bound to respect them. The HRA is in effect a domestication of the European Convention. And all three countries are parties to the International Covenant on Civil and Political Rights, Article 2(2) of which requires them "to take the necessary steps, in accordance with its constitutional processes and with the provisions of the present Covenant, to adopt such laws or other measures as may be necessary to give effect to the rights recognized in the present Covenant."

Article 2(3) of the ICCPR requires parties to the treaty to ensure that any person whose rights and freedoms have been breached has an effective remedy. Legal scholars sometimes argue that the lack of express remedies in the NZBORA means that New Zealand does not meet this requirement.[27] So there is and has been pressure of various forms to do *something* about rights and give them a high-profile presence in the public law of the countries concerned. Also, these countries are known to take rights seriously. They are free and open societies. Their states are good citizens in the international human rights arena (or at least New Zealand and Canada are).[28] But that returns us to an earlier question: Why, then, on issues about *rights* of all things, do they hesitate or draw back? (Or: Why weak judicial review specifically on *legislation* affecting rights, for they have no problem with strong judicial review of executive actions that violate their respective rights statutes?) Why not use strong judicial review to protect rights from parliamentary attack?

Why Frame Things This Way?

Our questions about weak-form review are tangled. It is partly a matter of background and foreground, of path-dependency. From an American perspective, with a strong background of constitutional commitment, we ask: Why deny rights the benefit of strong judicial review? Why make an exception for them? Same question

[25] Tushnet, *New Forms of Judicial Review*, *supra* note 3, at 814.

[26] *See supra* text accompanying footnote 5.

[27] *See, e.g.*, Anthony Mason, *Human Rights: Interpretation, Declarations of Inconsistency and the Limits of Judicial Power*, 9 NEW ZEALAND J. PUB. INT'L L. 1 (2011). *See also* UN HUM. RTS. COMM., *Concluding Observations of the Human Rights Committee: New Zealand* (Apr. 28, 2016), paragraph 10: "The State party should . . . (c) consider entrenching the Bill of Rights Act 1990 and strengthening the role of the judiciary . . . in assessing the consistency of enacted laws with the Act and the Covenant."

[28] The UK's position is less respectable because of its continual conflicts with the ECtHR and the existence of strong political currents that favor cutting loose from the ECHR.

for Canada: There has been no problem over the decades with judges striking down laws that go beyond the stipulated boundaries of national and provincial legislatures, so why introduce a "notwithstanding" clause for rights when it was not felt necessary for structural constitutional review?[29] On the other hand, if, like lawmakers in the United Kingdom or New Zealand, we assume a background—a starting point, a sort of default position—of parliamentary sovereignty and very limited power for judges, then a certain amount of timidity is to expected in latter-day experiments with judicial review. But again, why is it harder to overcome that timidity on rights than on other issues?[30]

Certainly, if we were looking for an originalist answer to our questions—Why did those who set up these arrangements frame them in this way? What was their intent?—we would make reference to the not altogether consistent hesitation and unease that attended enactment of a Bill of Rights in New Zealand and, to a lesser extent (because they were already familiar with the idea through the workings of the ECtHR), in the United Kingdom.

The NZBORA was the child of Sir Geoffrey Palmer, law professor and politician (Prime Minister from 1989 to 1990). The version he sponsored as Minister of Justice in 1985 did aspire to higher-law status with supermajoritarian entrenchment and it would have permitted strong judicial review. But Palmer's Labour Party colleagues and many ordinary New Zealanders combined their general lack of enthusiasm for the whole project with grave misgivings about the politicization of the judiciary that it would involve. Palmer's proposal was mangled in Committee and what emerged was the weak-form version of judicial review that we have been discussing. In that rather unedifying episode, I am not aware of there having been any discussion of the specific issue addressed in this chapter. In New Zealand, as we have seen, there is not much of a tradition of strong judicial review anyway to contrast with the weak-form review that emerged finally in the NZBORA in 1990. The legislative debates, such as they were, just concentrated on rights-adjudication and didn't really address the question I have posed. Also, there has been no real discussion of this in subsequent academic analysis of the NZBORA.

However, it is worth noting that Sir Geoffrey continues to worry away at the Bill of Rights project, and in his and Andrew Butler's latest (2016) proposal for

[29] *See* Stone, *supra* note 22, for a most helpful exploration of the distinction between rights-based and structural constitutional review and whether the arguments brought against the former can be applied to the latter. (I am grateful to Rosalind Dixon for this reference.)

[30] I talk here about backgrounds and default positions. These are not just technical matters. Both backgrounds furnish important considerations of political morality for those who cleave to them. That is pretty clear in the case of American-style constitutionalism with its strong connection to liberty. On the other side, a background commitment to parliamentary sovereignty is bound up with democratic ideals; it is not just a Diceyan technicality. *See* Gardbaum, *supra* note 2, at 760, for the proposition that "parliamentary sovereignty [has] provided a long and largely successful tradition of constitutionalist democracy." The parliamentarist background is also connected with a strong political uneasiness about committing controversial issues of public policy to judges, though it has to be said that defenders of parliamentary sovereignty have had few problems on this ground with judicial review of executive action.

constitutional reform he has actually unified rights and other constitutional issues so far as the stronger form of WFR he now proposes is concerned.[31] So, section 68 of the proposed constitution for which he is lobbying provides as follows:

a. All courts have jurisdiction to determine the question of the inconsistency of any law or conduct with this Constitution . . .
b. When deciding a constitutional matter within its jurisdiction, a court or tribunal . . . [m]ust declare that any law or conduct that is inconsistent with the Constitution is invalid to the extent of its inconsistency.

There is no discrimination here between violating rights and violating other constitutional rules.

But it is still weak-form review. The declaration envisaged here as a remedy is conditional on its confirmation by the Supreme Court and it would be subject to the power of Parliament to legislate subsequently to affirm the Act in question, "notwithstanding the decision of the Supreme Court." That would convert NZ's present arrangements into something more like the Canadian "notwithstanding" version of weak-form review, though with five crucial differences:

(i) the "notwithstanding legislation" would be reactive rather than preemptive of the Court's finding;
(ii) the proposed New Zealand "notwithstanding" clause would present itself as a license to legislate notwithstanding the Court's decision rather than, as in Canada, notwithstanding the relevant Charter right itself;[32]
(iii) the "notwithstanding" legislation would have to be passed by a 75 percent supermajority in the House of Representatives;
(iv) the "notwithstanding" legislation would have to be reviewed by Parliament and renewed every five years;[33] and
(v) most importantly for our inquiry, this whole procedure would apply to all aspects of constitutional review, not just provisions about rights.

Palmer and Butler do not focus specifically on (v) in their comments; what they say about these proposed arrangements for judicial review is almost all about

[31] Geoffrey Palmer & Andrew Butler, A Constitution for Aotearoa New Zealand (2016).

[32] *See* Waldron, *supra* note 23, at 1357 n.34 on the Canadian situation: "[T]he real problem is that section 33 requires the legislature to misrepresent its position on rights. To legislate notwithstanding the Charter is a way of saying that you do not think Charter rights have the importance that the Charter says they have. But the characteristic stand-off between courts and legislatures does not involve one group of people (judges) who think Charter rights are important and another group of people (legislators) who do not. What it usually involves is groups of people (legislative majorities and minorities, and judicial majorities and minorities) all of whom think Charter rights are important, though they disagree about how the relevant rights are to be understood."

[33] This is an additional suggestion, put forward in Palmer and Butler, Towards Democratic Renewal, 137–38.

rights. But the terms of the provision encompass all constitutional matters, and even though New Zealand is a unitary state the Palmer/Butler proposal would have a greater number of nonrights-based restrictions on legislation than there are at present.

The United Kingdom's HRA was the latest of the three versions of weak-form review that we have been considering and, as Janet Hiebert observes, that gave British lawmakers a chance to reflect on the other two.[34] They thought they needed to sail between the Scylla of a "notwithstanding" clause that would be very rarely used and the Charybdis of New Zealand's overdeferential arrangement. There seems to have been no awareness in the British discussion of the questions we have identified about the disparity in treatment between rights issues and nonrights issues of constitutional structure.

In all of these debates—with the arguable exception of Sir Geoffrey Palmer's 2016 proposal—I do not think it ever occurred to anyone to raise as an issue the possibility that weak-form review might apply to nonrights questions of constitutional propriety. The players were all fixated on how (or whether) to set up a Bill of Rights and on the role the judiciary would play in upholding *that*.

Interpretation

This does not stop us from asking interpretive questions about how the disparity might be understood and justified. We do not have to treat it as a careless anomaly or an unrationalized product of path-dependency. An originalist asks about what the framers of these arrangements for weak-form review had in mind; that leads to a dead end in this case. But we might also ask, more abstractly: What sense *can* be made of these arrangements (whether such rationale has ever occurred to anyone or not)? In other words, we might take a Dworkinian approach:[35] Let's see if it is possible to justify the disparity between the form of review prescribed for rights and the form of review prescribed or allowed for other constitutional issues. What happens if *we* try to present it in a good light—make it the best it can be—for the purposes of comparative analysis?

Some Possible Resolutions

I want to emphasize that it is a *disparity* we are investigating. We are not trying to justify weak-form review or to say—as I believe—that it is actually better than

[34] JANET HIEBERT, PARLIAMENTARY BILLS OF RIGHTS: THE EXPERIENCES OF NEW ZEALAND AND THE UNITED KINGDOM 248 (2005).

[35] *See* RONALD DWORKIN, LAW'S EMPIRE ch. 2 (1986).

strong-form judicial review. I have said something along those lines. But now what we want to make sense of is the use of weak-form review for rights only and not for other constitutional issues. When legislators and judges disagree about rights, what reason is there to make provision for the legislature's view to prevail when we do not allow it to prevail when there is disagreement on constitutional issues not involving rights?

In an oral presentation based on this chapter, I toyed with the idea that some of Mark Tushnet's critical scholarship on rights from the 1980s (long before he became interested in weak-form review) might be relevant to these questions. In a paper published in 1984, Tushnet noticed a few things about the way American courts dealt with rights in constitutional cases.[36] They spoke and acted as though rights were matters of principle, something like "trumps" (if we can still use that word) over considerations of public policy. But constitutional rights provisions were (are) vague and drafted in such loose terminology that even if they were not indeterminate in their abstract meaning, they certainly became so once the courts were done with them. "[T]he language of rights is so open and indeterminate that opposing parties can use the same language to express their positions."[37] Competing rights could be invoked so readily and courts had to resort so often to balancing tests to resolve such competition that rights really never had the power that liberal theorists claimed they had. Courts would stretch or shrink them to order, to accommodate competing pressures of all sorts—all the time under a pretense that the right represented an abiding principle that never changed. Frankly, courts were simply engaged in amateurish and inconsistent policymaking. And Tushnet saw this as unsatisfactory, perhaps fraudulent.

Might these ideas be of some assistance in answering our questions? Tushnet's 1980s critique of rights is certainly important. And so is his 2000 book *Taking the Constitution Away from the Courts*. It provides a fine basis for an argument against strong judicial review and, if we combine it with the canary-in-the-coalmine function of weak-form review (referred to earlier), it might add up to a good defense of the HRA, if not the NZBORA. Courts may be serviceable in their solemnity in drawing attention to possible rights abuses, but we would be in a sorry state (exemplified by the current US situation) if it were left up to courts to "resolve" the policy issues that disputes about rights inevitably generate.

But so far that does not address the disparity. To do that, we would have to show that Tushnet's indeterminacy critique is *likely to be more true of rights discourse than of structural constitutional discourse*. Is it? Australian scholar Adrienne Stone considers the possibility that "the vague and abstract language that characterizes constitutional rights is absent or much less common in the structural sphere."[38]

[36] Mark Tushnet, *An Essay on Rights*, 62 TEX. L. REV. 1363 (1984).
[37] *Id.* at 1371.
[38] Stone, *Judicial Review without Rights*, *supra* note 22, at 8.

That may be true of some structural provisions, such as the minimum age for the US President, but is it true on other structural matters? These seem capable of generating indeterminacies and antinomies as numerous and as intractable as those generated by rights provisions.

What about the comparative importance of rights and structural issues? Several times in this paper I have asked, "Why confine weak-form review to rights—to *rights* of all things, when we know that rights matter so much?" We cannot approach an answer to this question without noting that the moral importance of rights—and they are important—does not preclude the possibility of good-faith disagreement about what they require. So if the answer turns out to have anything to do with greater or lesser controversy in various constitutional domains, we should not assume that such controversy is diminished with regard to rights by everyone's awareness of their moral importance. It would be convenient (though it would aggravate our problem) if it were the case that, the more morally important the rule, the less disagreement there is likely to be—and a lot of liberal political philosophy kind of assumes that—but that is unfortunately not the case.[39] Since many issues of rights *are* controversial—as well as morally important and deeply felt—then perhaps the final decision about them should be left in the hands of representative institutions which respect the diversity of people's views.[40]

Can one approach the same point also from the other direction? I have heard it said that structural constitutional rules matter less, and so we should not be so upset when a decision one way or another is imposed by unelected judges. These matters need to be settled; indeed, everyone ought to be able to see that it is more important that they be settled than that they be settled rightly. Strong-form review achieves this decisively through a judicial verdict: We do not need the sort of dialogue back and forth that some versions of weak-form review involve.[41] There are two questions here: (1) Is settlement particularly important for structural issues? (2) Is it true that which option we settle on matters less in the case of structure than in the case of rights?[42]

On (1), Adrienne Stone states the position about settlement very clearly, though I am not sure she is convinced. She wonders whether strong judicial review

> is necessary to provide for the settlement of federal disputes because federal disputes—more than other kinds of constitutional disagreements—are especially in need of settlement by a third party. When a parliament and a citizen

[39] I argue this extensively in JEREMY WALDRON, LAW AND DISAGREEMENT (1999).
[40] *See id.* 105–18, for the connection between legislative majoritarianism and respect.
[41] This possibility was put to me by Frank Michelman in discussion.
[42] Is this why structural litigation is rarer? (Is it?) At the meeting, it was suggested that most structural issues are so settled they do not get litigated—for example, equal representation of states in the Senate (credit Sanford Levinson). But federalism is an exception: US v. Morrison 529 U.S. 598 (2000), for example. There is a good discussion of the moral issues that might be at stake in Stone, *supra* note 22.

> disagree about the meaning of a right it is clear, in the absence of judicial review, whose view prevails. In a federal conflict—where for example two democratically elected parliaments take conflicting views of the extent of their legislative powers—it is by no means obvious, without some form of adjudication, whose view should prevail.[43]

Stone says the most this shows is that we need *some* provision for final settlement to avoid see-sawing between rival legislative solutions. But it does not have to be a court. Where rival theories of the appropriate balance between nation and prince or state are circulating in the community, maybe some representative mechanism for settling the matter would be more respectful.

This is especially the case where the rival views of constitutional structure are deep and heartfelt. So, on point (2), not everyone agrees that matters of constitutional structure are like rules of the road—technicalities requiring simple settlement for the sake of coordination with no real merits pertaining to either option. People take federalism very seriously, and they engage in heartfelt controversy about an appropriate balance between various levels of government. The same is true of separation of powers, and for that matter the establishment of the Presbyterian church in Scotland. In oral discussion of this chapter, participants emphasized that so-called structural issues often have significance for individual rights and freedom; certainly that is true of the theory of separation of powers.[44] Some rights, such as the right to vote, are both crucial for constituting political structures and of the utmost importance to individuals. We should not be misled by the idea of a simple contrast between rights-oriented and structural issues. Too often the latter category becomes just a grab-bag for any considerations that are not explicitly phrased as rights.[45]

I did see one other intriguing suggestion in the Canadian literature along the lines of the point about structure, coordination, and settlement. On a website addressing judicial review in Canada, the following point is made:

> When a court strikes down legislation on division of powers grounds, it does not mean that the content of law itself violates the constitution. Rather, it means that the institution which enacted the law (a provincial legislature or Parliament)

[43] Stone, *Judicial Review without Rights*, *supra* note 22, at 27. She also cites A.V. DICEY, INTRODUCTION TO THE STUDY OF THE LAW OF THE CONSTITUTION xcv–xcvi (8th ed., 1915): "under every federal system there must almost of necessity exist some body of persons who can decide whether the terms of the federal compact have been observed."

[44] *See* MONTESQUIEU, THE SPIRIT OF THE LAWS (Anne Cohler, Basia Miller & Harold Stone eds., 1989) Book XI, Chapter 6 for connection between liberty and the separation of powers.

[45] And this is not to mention the John Hart Ely point that rights can be construed as strategies to secure the importance of procedural or representational considerations in case the latter are affected by structural defects in a given political system. *See* Gardbaum, *supra* note 2, at 753, for some discussion of Ely in this connection.

> violated the Constitution. Consequently, if there is a strong public interest in enacting this legislation, the appropriate institution can enact this act. Conversely, when a court strikes down legislation on Charter grounds, it means that the content of the law violates the Constitution, and no legislature could properly enact this law.[46]

That is an interesting contrast. It suggests, once again, that it matters less who has the final decision on structural matters. Were rights to be attended with strong-form review, there would be no comeback for those who disagreed with a decision of the court (short of the near impossible business of trying to enact a constitutional amendment). That may be a reason for weakening the judicial position, to give some recourse to those who disagree with the court. Where structural matters are attended with strong-form review, however, a judicial decision is not really the last word. If the attempt to pass a bill with a particular content is struck down because it was put forward at the federal rather than the state or provincial level (or vice versa), proponents of the measure are not without recourse. They can try again, though this time at the level the courts have deemed appropriate, with more or less exactly the same legislative content. They have that option, even though they are afflicted with strong judicial review.

This is an argument of the right sort, I think. But it may be a little too abstract. In its abstraction, it ignores the differential political costs that may attend legislative endeavors at different levels. And perhaps it is too blithe in its assumption that "exactly the same content" can be reproduced in the federal context (where state legislation has been blocked) or in the state context (where federal legislation has been blocked). Still—along with the limited force of the settlement argument—it is the best I can come up with.

[46] Center for Constitutional Studies, *Judicial Review*, *supra* note 16.

18

Common Law and the Liberation of Self-Interest from Regulation

David C. Donald

Introduction: Free Markets Like Common Law

In the year in which I first had the pleasure of meeting Mark Tushnet, he argued that a revitalized federalism was necessary to allow liberal individualism to support an institution requiring civically minded citizens.[1] He proposed a civic government in which "[b]oth proponents of and objectors to specific projects are . . . strongly committed to the community as a whole and are likely to work things out."[2] Nevertheless, he also observed that "[o]ur intellectual universe has been impoverished by the success of the Framers' enterprise, so that we scarcely understand the ways in which federalism served republican goals."[3]

Indeed, 20 years later the Framers' success had reached such a zenith, and understanding such a nadir, that not only commitment to the community but also protective institutions other than litigation fell into disfavor. Civil law Europe[4] and Asian financial centers[5] worked hard to follow the US push for deregulation and common law. The world's premier economic development organization instructed developing countries to join as well:

> Common law countries regulate the least . . . Heavier regulation is generally associated with more inefficiency in public institutions—longer delays and higher

[1] Mark V. Tushnet, *Federalism and the Traditions of American Political Theory*, 19 GA. L. REV. 981 (1985).

[2] *Id.* at 995. Tushnet later notes: "I cannot deny that a mushy romantic utopianism infects the last few paragraphs. They may underestimate permanent human drives toward domination and individualism in their easy assumption that things can be worked out." *Id.* at 997.

[3] *Id.* at 992.

[4] Attempting to keep up with the leader, European countries and the European Union tried to make their law more like that of the US, deregulating capital markets, encouraging litigation, and paying executives in stock-options, among other adjustments. *See* David C. Donald, *Endowment, Fundamentals and Fashion in the Market for Corporate Law*, *in* FESTSCHRIFT FÜR THEODORE BAUMS ZUM SIEBZIGSTEN GEBURTSTAG 305 (Helmut Siekmann ed., 2017).

[5] An example of Hong Kong's cloying relationship with British law is the adoption of an unnecessary stewardship code. *See* David C. Donald, *Stewardship in the Hong Kong International Financial Centre*, *in* GLOBAL SHAREHOLDER STEWARDSHIP 284 (Dionysia Katelouzou & Dan W. Puchniak eds., 2022).

David C. Donald, *Common Law and the Liberation of Self-Interest from Regulation* In: *Redefining Comparative Constitutional Law.* Edited by: Vicki C. Jackson and Madhav Khosla, Oxford University Press. © David C. Donald 2025.
DOI: 10.1093/9780191996344.003.0018

> cost—and more unemployed people, corruption, less productivity and investment, but not with better quality of private or public goods.[6]

Codified rules tend historically to arise from principles that already exist in the common, or customary, law,[7] and regulation often makes those rules binding *ex ante* or easier to enforce *ex post* against socially undesirable behavior.[8] In 2004, the World Bank instructed developing countries that regulation was *per se inefficient* because rules delay profit-seeking, dampening the market forces that bring employment, investment, and productivity.

At century's end, planned economies everywhere were of course being reorganized to liberate market forces, reshaping politics in particular on the Eurasian landmass from Paris to Shanghai.[9] This new faith that human interaction propelled by self-interest contains a self-adjusting balance finer than anything planning could devise instructed humanity to strip away the clumsy, cerebral artifacts, such as regulation, that it had devised.[10] By peeling away law's distortion of the natural market ecosystem, individuals were given the "freedom to choose."[11] As Von Hayek explained, because any lawmaker's or planner's view of a complex situation is inherently imperfect, policymakers must understand "how to dispense with the need of conscious control and how to provide inducements which will make the individuals do the desirable things without anyone having to tell them what to do."[12] Hayek sees economics since Adam Smith as finding this in markets: "the essential utility of the price system consists in inducing the individual, while seeking his own interest, to do what is in the general interest."[13]

Synergic movements of myriad self-interested individuals "discover" one, common, good.[14] Once this natural force had been revealed to humanity, regulation by its very nature was understood to pollute the ecosystem of selfish wants. In

[6] WORLD BANK, DOING BUSINESS IN 2004: UNDERSTANDING REGULATION xiv (2004).

[7] Watson sees this happening in Rome: *see* ALAN WATSON, EVOLUTION OF WESTERN PRIVATE LAW 32–35 (2001). Glenn has explained on the basis of extensive study that common, or customary, law is found in all jurisdictions. H. PATRICK GLENN, ON COMMON LAWS 45–49 (2009).

[8] This is Louis Loss' explanation of how the US securities laws arose from principles of tort and contract. *See* LOUIS LOSS & JOEL SELIGMAN, FUNDAMENTALS OF SECURITIES REGULATION 910 (5th ed. 2004).

[9] No country pursued this course more drastically or successfully than the Peoples' Republic of China. *See* e.g. DALI L. YANG, REMAKING THE CHINESE LEVIATHAN 25 (2004).

[10] MILTON FRIEDMAN, CAPITALISM & FREEDOM: A LEADING ECONOMIST'S VIEW OF THE PROPER ROLE OF COMPETITIVE CAPITALISM 13 (2002).

[11] "Economic freedom is an essential requisite for political freedom. By enabling people to cooperate with one another without coercion or central direction, it reduces the area over which political power is exercised . . . the free market provides an offset to whatever concentration of political power may arise." MILTON FRIEDMAN, FREE TO CHOOSE: A PERSONAL STATEMENT 2–3 (1979).

[12] Friedrich A. Hayek, *The Use of Knowledge in Society*, AM. ECON. REV. 519, 527 (1945).

[13] *Id.* at 529.

[14] "Price discovery" is generally accepted to be the action of markets. It is general usage that markets do not "invent" or "create" a price, they "discover" it. That price is deemed transcendent, waiting for self-interested buyers and sellers to discover it. *See* Robert Schwartz et al., *The Dynamic Process of Price Discovery in an Equity Market*, 36 MANAGERIAL. FIN. 554 (2010).

this framework of belief, the minimalist nature of common law was championed because it leaves a field of behavior open until *after* actionable damage occurs and is thus uniquely compatible with the self-policing forces of markets. Alexander Hamilton's argument in *Federalist 1* that citizens should "[establish] good government from reflection and choice" rather than "[depending] for their political constitutions on accident and force"[15] had been superseded by the discovery that history's most powerful force—self-interest—was beneficent.

Common law and market forces share several characteristics. First, each supplies its product only in response to demand, because each is driven by the self-interest of a person seeking a ruling or remunerative transaction. Where lawyers are compensated by contingent fees, the similarity is complete, because obtaining the ruling *is* a remunerative transaction. Second, neither common law nor market forces clutter the landscape with unwanted products, so that no rule or product comes into existence without a buyer. Third, both common law and market action occur within a substantively agnostic, procedural framework which aspires to neutrality. While a few "market failures" are acknowledged,[16] these are exceptions that prove the rule. Last, common law and markets operate with such openness because they both assume the presence of an unseen ordering force that ultimately defines justice in the one case and fair price in the other. Common law remains tacitly understood "by the best minds"[17] until the case in controversy is decided, and an efficient asset price abides within the laws of economics until concrete offer and acceptance "discover" it. The *raison d'être* of both common law and market action is thus to let the best assertion prevail before the higher law by allowing self-interested interaction within a neutral framework to summon forth justice or price.

This chapter will explore how the academy and governments alike have embraced a beneficent, *natural* force from the late 20th century and advocated the peeling away of *unnatural* legal and governmental layers of law and regulation. Liberating the natural forces of self-interest valorized common law as a lighter, plaintiff-driven substitute for *ex ante* regulation. Comparative legal studies championed common law, in part merging its newfound esteem with earlier, nationalistic arguments praising law forged by a freedom-loving, Anglo-Saxon culture.[18] A very significant difference between an economic efficiency argument and one couched in Anglo-Saxon nationalism is that when common law is seen aligned with a universal, natural force, no cultural heterogeneity argument can be raised against its adoption.

[15] THE FEDERALIST NO. 1 (Alexander Hamilton).

[16] *See, e.g.*, George A. Akerlof, *The Market for "Lemons": Quality Uncertainty and the Market Mechanism*, 84 Q. J. ECON. 488 (1970).

[17] *See* the discussion in the third section.

[18] These earlier themes are found in Maitland writing before World War I. *See* FREDRIC MAITLAND & FRANCIS MONTAGUE, A SKETCH OF ENGLISH LEGAL HISTORY 37 (2005 [1915]).

The chapter is organized in five sections. Following this introduction, the chapter will examine the discovery of free market forces as a universal good and question the validity of such discovery. It will go on to examine more recent positions taken in comparative scholarship on common law and civil law. It will then review some of the most salient social impacts of liberating self-interest from law, after which it concludes.

Unleashing the Self to Discover the Common Good

As the 20th century approached its end, history too was "ending," as it had for Europe in the mid-19th century.[19] The world seemed ready to converge on certain truths that had now become self-evident: that markets are the best arbiters of value and quality; that free and uninhibited exercise of self-interest creates optimal social results; and that government regulation of such free behavior imposes costs in most cases that exceed its benefit.

Although both the philosophy and the psychology popular at the time supported the idea that competition among individual preferences discovers the general good better than a dutiful search for it,[20] the arguments of economists were clearly the most influential.[21] As mentioned in the introduction, Hayek expresses the message well: we can "dispense with the need for conscious control" because "the essential utility of the price system consists in inducing the individual, while seeking his own interest, to do what is in the general interest."[22] Paul Samuelson and Eugene Fama, together with the great popularizer Milton Friedman, carried this notion into the social sciences, public policy, and public perception.[23] Ayn

[19] The self-aggrandizement of culture certainly did not originate in the United States. As Georg WF Hegel explained to his students, "[w]orld history travels from east to west; for Europe is the absolute end of history, just as Asia is the beginning." GWF Hegel, Lectures on the Philosophy of History 197 (HB Nisbet trans., 1975). This is the thread that Francis Fukuyama picked up when declaring that US "liberal democracy" was history's absolute end. Francis Fukuyama, The End of History and the Last Man 338 (2nd ed. 2006).

[20] Popular culture's turn from society to the individual is explained in some depth by examining the biographies and career paths of the socially committed man, Adolf Berle, and individualist, Michael Jensen, in Nicholas Lemann, Transaction Man: The Rise of the Deal and the Decline of the American Dream (2019); also *see* John Kay & Paul Collier, Greed Is Dead: Politics after Individualism (2020).

[21] This rise of economics as the defining discipline of society has been the topic of extensive academic commentary. Some leading monographs are: Noam Chomsky, Profit Over People: Neoliberalism and Global Order (1999); Joseph Stiglitz, Globalization and Its Discontents (2002); Michael Sandel, What Money Can't Buy: The Moral Limits of Markets (2012); Thomas Piketty, Capital in the Twenty-First Century (2013); John Kay, Other People's Money: Masters of the Universe or Servants of the People? (2015); and Binyamin Appelbaum, The Economist's Hour: False Prophets, Free Markets, and the Fracture of Society (2019).

[22] Hayek, *supra* note 12, at 527, 529.

[23] *See* Andrew Lo, Adaptive Markets: Financial Evolution at the Speed of Thought (2016) and Appelbaum, *supra* note 21, for a historical overview of this process.

Rand emerged as a leading philosophical novelist in a world championing self-interest,[24] and her protégé Alan Greenspan (Federal Reserve Chair 1987–2006) was perhaps the world's most important banker at century's end.[25] Oreskes and Conway have shown that the triumph of market force over reasoned government in the public mind was aided by a generously funded, long-term propaganda campaign.[26]

Efficient market forces were understood as capable of reduction to mathematical principles following the model of physics,[27] but how did economists discover this hitherto hidden force of prosperity? The most robust, statistically supported analyses of market efficiency were found in a rarefied view of regulated securities markets. Eugene Fama, following earlier work by Samuelson, found that an "efficient" market is a market which "adjusts rapidly to new information"[28] as "the market realizes"[29] the information is "associated" with changes in return.[30] This information is "evaluated precisely"[31] because, as Gilson and Kraakman explain, "modern finance assume[s] that investors are fully rational (or that the market acts as if they are)."[32]

If financial actors are fully rational and market prices always efficient, politicians and policymakers can dodge risky decisions potentially endangering their careers by letting "market forces" decide, as Greta Krippner shows was done beginning in the 1970s.[33] John Kay reports that key advisors in the Clinton White House saw the "bond market" as something like an oracle to which government should look for approval.[34] Arguments such as those of Myron Scholes—that because traders

[24] *See* JENNIFER BURNS, GODDESS OF THE MARKET: AYN RAND AND THE AMERICAN RIGHT 269–70 (2009).

[25] As Greenspan put the matter: "It hardly makes any difference who will be the next president. The world is governed by market forces." Cited in QUINN SLOBODIAN, GLOBALISTS: THE END OF EMPIRE AND THE BIRTH OF NEOLIBERALISM 1 (2018).

[26] NAOMI ORESKES & ERIK M. CONWAY, THE BIG MYTH: HOW AMERICAN BUSINESS TAUGHT US TO LOATHE GOVERNMENT AND LOVE THE FREE MARKET (2023).

[27] "Samuelson found his inspiration in modern mathematical physics. In fact, the mathematical physicist Edwin Bidwell Wilson mentored Samuelson at Harvard, which Samuelson described in a fascinating 1998 article on the intellectual origins of his thesis." LO, *supra* note 23, at 210.

[28] Eugene Fama et al., *The Adjustment of Stock Prices to New Information*, 10 INT'L ECON. REV. 1 (1969).

[29] This anthropomorphizing of "the market" into a being that "realizes" things is phrasing still reflected more than 60 years later in our financial media. This shorthand anthropomorphizing usage lumps together as having a single will, heterogenous persons trading securities for different reasons, on different time horizons and with different compensation profiles, differing amounts of funds available, and using differing levels and quality of technology.

[30] Fama, *supra* note 28, at 20.

[31] Eugene Fama, *Efficient Capital Markets: A Review of Theory and Empirical Work*, 25 J. FIN. 383 (1970) 383, 396, 415.

[32] Ronald Gilson & Ranier Kraakman, *The Mechanisms of Market Efficiency Twenty Years Later: The Hindsight Bias*, 28 J. CORP. L. 715, 723 (2003).

[33] "Policymakers deliberately allowed fluctuation in the federal funds rate in order to work behind the 'camouflage of market forces.'" GRETA R. KRIPPNER, CAPITALIZING ON CRISIS 135 (2011).

[34] James Carville, Clinton policy adviser, WALL ST. J. (Feb. 25, 1993), cited in JOHN KAY, OTHER PEOPLE'S MONEY: MASTERS OF THE UNIVERSE OR SERVANTS OF THE PEOPLE? 247 (2015).

risked the most they would self-regulate better than government could[35]—led Alan Greenspan to advocate successfully that Congress outlaw the regulation of derivative instruments, in 2000.[36]

Once market forces became the heartbeat of US society, doubts arose as to whether investors really do rationally decide the underlying value of companies issuing securities. Evidence has indicated that they do not. Information driving price is mainly data about the trader's own portfolio and liquidity needs in connection with the trading activity of others.[37] Trading expresses a subjective preference. In all likelihood, objective "market efficiency" was not discovered, but rather invented. This corresponds to what George Soros has long argued by characterizing market prices as "reflexive."[38] Applying Keynes' beauty contest analogy,[39] Soros explains that the intelligent trader "looks for the flaws" in existing narratives about price and works on "convincing people" to accept one narrative or another:

> The fact that a thesis is flawed does not mean that we should not invest in it as long as other people believe it in and there is a large group of people left to be convinced. The point was made by John Maynard Keynes when he compared the stock market to a beauty contest ... Where I have something significant to add is in pointing out that it pays to look for the flaws; if we find them we are ahead of the game because we can limit our losses when the market also discovers what we already know.[40]

Market price, in this sense, is less a beneficial confluence of reason than the sum result of posing and bluffing: guessing "what average opinion expects the average opinion to be," to use Keynes' phrase. Real market efficiency would require, as Andrew Lo explains, an "infinite chain of reasoning ... as though a buyer and seller were trapped in a hall of mirrors: the seller knows that the buyer knows that the

[35] Myron S. Scholes, *Global Financial Markets, Derivative Securities, and Systemic Risks*, 12 J. Risk & Uncertainty 271, 280, 283–85 (1996).

[36] *See* The Commodity Futures Modernization Act of 2000, H. R. 5660, 106th Cong. (Dec. 14, 2000).

[37] In their analysis of the May 6, 2010 "flash crash" the government task force examined in detail the trading activity of 15,000 accounts, finding that nearly all buy and sell orders were triggered by information on market price, movement in market prices seen against historical models, percentage of trades measured against all trades, relationships between prices in primary and derivative markets, and internal risk management needs dictating the holding of long and short positions for hedging purposes. *See* U.S. Commodity Futures Trading Comm'n & U.S. Sec. & Exch. Comm'n, Findings Regarding the Market Events of May 6, 2010: Report of the Staffs of the CFTC and SEC to the Joint Advisory Committee on Emerging Regulatory Issues (Sept. 30, 2010).

[38] George Soros, The New Paradigm for Financial Markets: The Credit Crisis of 2008 and What It Means 8 (2008) ("In order to establish and protect the status of economics as a science, economists have gone to great lengths to eliminate reflexivity from their subject matter.").

[39] See John M. Keynes, The General Theory of Employment, Interest and Money 156 (1936) ("It is not a case of choosing those which, to the best of one's judgment, are really the prettiest, nor even those which average opinion genuinely thinks the prettiest. We have reached the third degree where we devote our intelligences to anticipating what average opinion expects the average opinion to be.").

[40] George Soros, Alchemy of Finance 25 (2003).

seller knows that the buyer knows . . . that the asking price is too high."[41] Yet psychology shows "most humans can only see four levels deep into the hall of mirrors of intention,"[42] making fully rational pricing impossible. Indeed, when market fundamentalists remove the reflective thinking of government policymakers from their model of an operational society, they later try to pack all that thinking back into the self-interested decision of the rational agent, as Tversky and Kahneman explain:

> A particularly unrealistic implication of the rational agent model is that agents make their choices in a comprehensively inclusive context, which incorporates all the relevant details of the present situation as well as expectations about all future opportunities and risks. Much evidence supports the contrasting claim that people's views of decisions and outcomes are normally characterized by narrow framing and by the related notion of mental accounting.[43]

Lo argues that we may consider markets to "have a few bugs," but the data shows they are entirely constituted of behavioral quirks: "We aren't rational actors with a few quirks in our behavior—instead, our brains are collections of quirks. We're not a system with bugs; we're a system of bugs."[44] Market stability arises when most traders have the same quirks, or habits and expectations, and markets crash because of "maladaptive" behavior.[45] Robert Shiller has offered numerous historical examples of transitions from adaption (bubbles) to maladaption (crashes).[46] This "accident and force" view of human behavior is something that the US constitutional Framers might well have seconded, and why they sought to check such "bugs" through reflection, choice, and checks and balances.[47]

Market efficiency is an article of faith, not a tenet of science. But it is a faith that changed our world. The belief that markets spin raw selfishness into social good has the corollary that public duty exercised in government impedes rather than promotes the social good. Ronald Reagan captured this sentiment perfectly in his "nine most terrifying words: I'm from the Government, and I'm here to help."[48] It followed that laws and regulations restricting self-affirming profit extraction were weakened and taxes to support government action were cut. In Europe, governments sold off large industrial and commercial holdings, sometimes in areas of

[41] Lo, *supra* note 23, at 109–10.
[42] *Id.*, at 112.
[43] Daniel Kahneman, *A Perspective on Judgment and Choice: Mapping Bounded Rationality*, 58 Am. Psych. 697, 706 (2003).
[44] Lo, *supra* note 23, at 186–87.
[45] *Id.*, at 189.
[46] Robert J. Shiller, Irrational Exuberance 185 (2nd ed., 2005).
[47] The Federalist No. 51 (James Madison).
[48] Ronald Reagan, *News Conference—I'm here to help*, Reagan Foundation (Aug. 12, 1986), https://www.reaganfoundation.org/ronald-reagan/reagan-quotes-speeches/news-conference-1/.

essential services and often at bargain prices, to private buyers.[49] So strong was this historical current that President Reagan not only could deregulate at home but also was able to convince Russian premier Mikhail Gorbachev to "tear down" the Berlin Wall and end the experiment of a planned economy.[50] As Piketty remarks, the eventual "collapse of the communist countermodel was undoubtedly a powerful reason for the renewal of faith—in some cases unlimited faith—in the self-regulated market and private ownership of the means of production."[51]

Uncivil Comparative Law Scholarship

With the conviction that enabling (rather than constraining) self-interest was the route to the common good, and the collapse of the socialist countermodel, US politicians could assure Americans and the rest of the world that the unrestricted churning of free markets was "on the right side of history."[52] Catching this wave perfectly, a team of economists referred to as LLSV[53] "discovered" comparative law and explained why history reached its pinnacle in late 20th-century United States: it was the inexorable culmination of an Anglo-Saxon genius that began in the late 12th century with the creation of common law.[54] Just as Virgil discovered history in the path from Aeneas to Caesar Augustus, so too could LLSV discover a noble line from Henry II to the Washington Consensus. Common Law embodied the virtues found on the right side of history. It enabled rational actors to *demand* law and judges to *supply* it, but only on the basis of skillful argument.[55]

This is why LLSV could boast discovery in their empirical investigation of a key to economic development.[56] The logic of this "legal origin" theory was simple and

[49] "In effect, privatization reverses a centuries-long process whereby the state took on things that individuals could not or would not do." TONY JUDT, ILL FARES THE LAND 116–17 (2010). Also *see* TONY JUDT, POSTWAR: A HISTORY OF EUROPE SINCE 1945 (2005).

[50] Andrew Glass, *Reagan challenges Gorbachev to 'tear down' Berlin Wall, June 12, 1987*, POLITICO (June 11, 2017).

[51] THOMAS PIKETTY, CAPITAL AND IDEOLOGY 835–36 (2020).

[52] MICHAEL SANDEL, THE TYRANNY OF MERIT: WHAT'S BECOME OF THE COMMON GOOD? 53 (2020). Sandel observes that repeated use of the term "the right side of history" by US presidents from Clinton to Obama "reflected their confidence, following the fall of the Berlin Wall and the breakup of the Soviet Union, that history was moving ineluctably toward the spread of liberal democracy and free markets."

[53] This team is usually referred to as LLSV, which stands for Rafael La Porta, Florencio Lopez-de-Silanes, Andrei Shleifer, and Robert W. Vishny.

[54] Rafael La Porta, Florencio Lopez-de-Silanes, Andrei Shleifer & Robert W. Vishny, *Legal Determinants of External Finance*, 52 J. FIN. 1131, 1149 (1997). Rafael La Porta, Florencio Lopez-de-Silanes, Andrei Shleifer & Robert W. Vishny, *Legal Investor Protection and Corporate Governance*, 58 J. FIN. ECON. 3, 9 (2000); Rafael La Porta, Florencio Lopez-de-Silanes & Andrei Shleifer, *What Works in Securities Law*, 61 J. FIN. 1, 15–16 (2006); Rafael La Porta, Florencio Lopez-de-Silanes & Andrei Shleifer, *The Economic Consequences of Legal Origins*, 46 J. ECON. LIT. 285, 286 (2008).

[55] *See* e.g. Paul H. Rubin, *Why Is the Common Law Efficient*, 6 J. LEGAL STUD. 51, 53 (1977).

[56] From a terminological perspective, the "common law" argument was somewhat problematic because LLSV generally gave higher ratings to US law although there is very little *US* common law. In the area of securities regulation, federal courts do interpret federal statutes, but that type of statutory interpretation is not generally understood as common law. "Common law" arises in the US primarily in the

convincing: markets bring prosperous development; common law protects investors best, causing the strong markets to develop (e.g. New York and London); therefore, common law causes prosperous development.[57] This explains why the World Bank, in its report quoted at the opening of this chapter, could issue a blanket recommendation of common law. Because judges would create no more law than had been requested, the remaining set of possible actions would stay government-free, a world open and ready for molding by creative innovation. Further, common law can be found to be agnostic on questions of allocative or distributive justice,[58] and its focus on protection of private property rights against encroachment of the state[59] places it squarely on the side of free markets and property-owning individuals.

It mattered little that the "legal origin" theory was false. Mark Roe explained that LLSV neglected to factor two world wars and a Cold War into their calculation of European market development.[60] John Coffee explained to LLSV that, "[i]ronically, it is the most statutory (and thus civil law-like) aspects of corporate governance in common law countries whose value the LLS&V research seems to affirm."[61] Indeed, far from being flexible and court-centered, US securities regulation is expressed in thousands of pages of rules.[62] Curtis Milhaupt and Katharina Pistor found LLSV supported the origin argument about hundreds of years of common law with only "recent economic performance—mostly using data from the 1990s," rather than looking at a more comprehensive period.[63]

These refutations and the financial crises in 2001 (the "dot.com bubble") and 2008 (the "global financial crisis"), caused largely by US institutions governed by

US states, so that we may speak of New York or Delaware common law. Thus, the term "common law" was used imprecisely.

[57] *See* La Porta et al., *Legal Determinants*, *supra* note 54, at 1149. The connection between financial development and economic development also became very problematic. *See* e.g., ADAM TOOZE, CRASHED: HOW A DECADE OF FINANCIAL CRISES CHANGED THE WORLD (2018).

[58] Richard A. Epstein, *The Social Consequences of Common Law Rules*, 95 HARV L. REV. 1717, 1718 (1982).

[59] The protection of private property is seen as a major virtue of common law when championed by LLSV, and although writing in the 21st century, they support their argument with reference to common law's protection of minor nobles against the crown about 800 years earlier, at the time of the Magna Carta, in 1215. *See* Frank B. Cross, *Identifying the Virtues of the Common Law*, 15 SUP. CT. ECON. REV. 21, 24–35 (2007).

[60] Mark J. Roe, *Legal Origins, Politics, and Modern Stock Markets*, 120 HARV. L. REV. 460, 501–02 (2006).

[61] John C. Coffee, Jr., *Law and the Market: The Impact of Enforcement*, 156 U. PA. L. REV. 229, 249 (2007).

[62] A very compact version of just the Securities Act of 1933 (regulating primary market sales of securities) and the Securities Exchange Act of 1934 (regulating secondary market sales of securities) before the enactment of the 850 page Dodd Frank Wall Street Reform Act of 2010 consisted of more than 300 pages. The rules written for the '33 and '34 Acts (again prior to adding more than 1,000 pages for the Dodd–Frank Act rules) consisted of about 2,000 pages of densely packed regulations.

[63] CURTIS MILHAUPT & KATHARINA PISTOR, LAW & CAPITALISM: WHAT CORPORATE CRISES REVEAL ABOUT LEGAL SYSTEMS AND ECONOMIC DEVELOPMENT AROUND THE WORLD 23 (2008).

US law, did not significantly dampen the steam of the common law engine. Its momentum continued to be considerable—in part due to the "network strength" of the US currency, law, and language in the world, as I have argued elsewhere,[64] and also because the belief persists that freewheeling capital markets are at the core of American democracy.[65]

When market force is society's best tool for development and plaintiff-driven common law is understood as society's best form of lawmaking, the "red tape" of regulation will be cut. *Post hoc* judicial solutions are preferred to *ex ante* licensing or supervision because they let freedom reign until someone (with access to a lawyer) complains. Legislatures and regulators should not attempt to address broad-based social problems with generally accessible solutions, for this could inhibit a better answer that could arise through profit-seeking. Law should react to concrete problems raised in court by persons with concrete interests and the means to advocate them.

Both market action and common law make reference to a transcendent perfection that materializes in competition. In the 17th century, Sir Matthew Hale defined common law as "a river that is altered by many tributaries yet remains the same," or like the fabled ship Argos—changed over the years of the Argonauts' adventure, yet remaining self-same.[66] Two hundred years later, Holmes concurs: "The substance of the law at any given time pretty nearly corresponds, so far as it goes, with what is then understood to be convenient."[67] In our own era, Sir John Baker's analysis of English common law echoes this: "The law today is not what particular courts or parliaments in the past have said it is, but . . . may be perceived as being what the courts ought to do, in the opinion of the best legal minds of the day, even if those are not the minds currently controlling the decisions of the highest appellate court."[68] Similar to Baker's idea that the "best minds" are ready to state what the law is, Melvin Eisenberg tells us that "[t]he common law does not consist of doctrinal propositions found in binding official texts. Rather, it consists of the rules that would be generated at the present moment by application of the institutional principles that govern adjudication."[69] The "institutional principles of adjudication" are for Eisenberg similar to procedural frameworks also referenced by Hale, Holmes, and Baker.[70]

[64] David C. Donald, *Legal System Network Effects and Global Legal Development*, 10 Notre Dame J. Int'l & Comp. L. 267 (2020).

[65] As President Joseph Biden found it necessary to assure his audience during his 2023 State of the Union Address when proposing significant government action in the economy: "Look, I'm a capitalist. I'm a capitalist." President Joseph Biden, *State of the Union Address* (Feb. 7, 2023), https://www.whitehouse.gov/state-of-the-union-2023/.

[66] Sir Matthew Hale, The History of the Common Law 40–43 (1971).

[67] Oliver W. Holmes, The Common Law 21 (2009).

[68] John H. Baker, The Law's Two Bodies: Some Evidential Problems in English Legal History 5 (2001).

[69] Melvin A. Eisenberg, The Nature of the Common Law 3 (1988).

[70] *Id.* at 44.

The virtue of the common law is that it will be just as it should be when needed by the *best minds*, and will not trouble their clients until then. The difficulty is defining how those best minds will specify the correct law. As Tushnet explains, Holmes ducked this issue entirely after joining the Supreme Court by sticking very close to written texts.[71] H. Patrick Glenn sees a similar evasive tactic in the genesis of English common law. It was "a series of procedural routes (usually referred to as remedies) to get before a jury and state one's case,"[72] devised in essence to control a conquered territory while escaping responsibility for the details of justice. Leaving ultimate decisions to the jury served to "co-opt the population to [the Norman kings'] work, so if actual decisions were left to the local folks . . . the judges could just get the right questions asked . . . and be off to another town."[73] This is structurally identical to how Krippner sees governments using financial markets—rather than decision-making—to evade responsibility for difficult apportionments of entitlements between constituencies.[74]

Civil law is very different in that it aims to grasp and define positive law (*Recht* or *droit*).[75] Although the mature common law of Rome evolved into civil law as expressed in Justinian's Code and Digest,[76] and both the United Kingdom and United States seem to be following a similar path as they pile up more statutory declarations of substantive rights, this evolutionary aspect is not highlighted in turn-of-the-century texts praising common law.[77] Civil law is not seen as a phase in relation to common law, but as a smothering blanket of rules issued by government, not dissimilar from how a planned economy is understood to treat economic innovation.

Modern civil codes such as those written in France or Germany attempt to synthesize legal principles present in society and condense them in comprehensive frameworks that can be grasped and even applied by average citizens without legal training.[78] This process is memorialized in the document's title, *Bürgerliches Gesetzbuch* ("Citizens' Law Book"). Grewal highlights the network development differences between social networks springing organically from individual market decisions and those consciously designed by sovereign government:

[71] Mark V. Tushnet, *The Logic of Experience: Oliver Wendell Holmes on the Supreme Judicial Court*, 63 Va. L. Rev. 975, 1011 (1977).

[72] H. Patrick Glenn, Legal Traditions of the World 243 (4th ed. 2010).

[73] *Id.* at 239.

[74] As Kripper explains, "rather than decisions about allocation moving into the strong light of public debate and discussion where a new social consensus could be forged, these decisions drifted ever further into the shadowy realms of the market." Greta R. Krippner, Capitalizing on Crisis 20 (2011).

[75] Glenn, *supra* note 72, at 160–64; Randall Lesaffer, European Legal History: A Cultural and Political Perspective 270–73 (2009).

[76] Peter Stein, Roman Law in European History 18–21, 32–35 (1999).

[77] Glenn, *supra* note 72, at 240.

[78] On the German Civil Code, *see* Konrad Zweigert & Hein Kötz, Einführung in die Rechtsvergleichung [Introduction to Comparative Law] 142–147 (3rd ed., 1996).

> Instead of wandering blindly into circumstances that emerge, unforeseen, as the result of many different individuals' actions . . . we can become part of a unified political body in order to consider the kind of world we would like to live in . . . The difference between these two ways that we make our social world—over time through the accumulation of interdependent, individual decisions, or all at once in an act of political construction—reveals the deep way in which we can use politics to overcome the vagaries of history.[79]

Grewal's description of deliberate network construction not only echoes that of Tushnet cited at the outset of this chapter, but also resembles both the creation of civil law (statutory law) and the image of "reason and choice" evoked by Hamilton in *Federalist 1*. Nevertheless, at the turn of the century this was considered weak in the protection of individual property rights, even leading to lower ratings of bonds issued by civil law countries under their domestic law.[80] As long as the public clings to a belief that a greater force born of self-interest leads to better and higher results than do reason and choice, an "act of political construction" will not be feasible. Rather, political deconstruction—whatever that means[81]—will be on the agenda.

Peeling Away an Inheritance of Thoughtful Protections

During the early stages of dismantling "New Deal" and "Great Society" government, in late 1987, Professor Mark Tushnet mentioned to students (including the author of this chapter) taking his course "Federal Courts and the Federal System" that in litigation of a takeover battle, one powerful oil company had recently sought to protect itself from another such company through use of constitutional civil rights provisions,[82] and thus students should be alert to counterintuitive uses of the law. Perhaps Professor Tushnet was at some level concerned about alternative uses for the brilliant strategies he had recently recounted in his monograph *The NAACP's Legal Strategy against Segregated Education, 1925–1950*,[83] which

[79] David S. Grewal, Network Power: The Social Dynamics of Globalization 294 (2008).

[80] Bertrand du Marais et al., *Rating the Law: How Financial Rating Agencies are Assessing the Legal Risks of Financial Transactions*, *in* Law and Economics of Risk in Finance 15–34 (Peter Nobel & Marina Gets eds., 2007).

[81] Mark V. Tushnet, *Trust the Science but Do Your Research: A Comment on the Unfortunate Revival of the Progressive Case for the Administrative State*, 98 Ind. L.J. 335, 336 (2023) (referring to the Trump Administration promise to deconstruct the administrative state).

[82] Pennzoil Co. v. Texaco Inc., 481 U.S. 1, 6 n.6 (1987): "Texaco also argued that application of the Texas bond and lien provisions would violate the Due Process and Equal Protection Clauses of the Fourteenth Amendment to the Federal Constitution."

[83] Mark V. Tushnet, The NAACP's Legal Strategy Against Segregated Education, 1925–1950 (1987).

explains how a team of dedicated lawyers conducted a nationwide litigation campaign to reach *Brown*[84] and end legal segregation despite paralysis on the issue in Congress.

At century's close, there indeed was continued use of litigation to protect or advance civil and human rights—what most would call the positive side of individual liberty—but there were also those counterintuitive and unsettling uses of similar strategies by powerful interests.[85] Much of this litigation sought to empower strong actors and "peel away" regulatory safeguards that had been erected to assist the vulnerable during the first three quarters of the 20th century. In the areas of financial regulation and commercial and labor law, well-funded groups used litigation and lobbying to free up space for the financial industry and other powerful actors to pursue their interests. Groups seeking open space for the vigorous and affluent include the Mackinac Center, the Cato Institute, the National Right to Work Foundation,[86] the Securities Industry Association,[87] the International Swap and Derivatives Association,[88] and the Business Roundtable.[89] Powerful actors used strategic litigation to "make new legal rights from old cloth"[90] while fighting for a freer world in which private actors would be at liberty to pursue profit unencumbered by "red tape" imposed by "out-of-touch regulators."[91]

With unions retreating, tax rates falling, and financial markets surging, society changed. Data from the Federal Reserve Bank of St. Louis shows the ratio of wages to investment income growing steadily in tandem from 1950 until 1994, and then diverging sharply, with wages flattening out and investment income heading upwards (save for brief periods of market corrections).[92] From the mid-1990s, executive compensation tied to stock and options led to the top 1 percent of the

[84] Brown v. Board of Education of Topeka, 347 U.S. 483 (1954).

[85] One of the most far-reaching was probably the litigation culminating in Citizens United v. Federal Election Commission, 558 U.S. 310 (2010), which gave corporations the freedom to spend without limit on political campaigns.

[86] The last three organization supported, e.g., *Friedrichs v. California Teachers Association*, 136 S. Ct. 1083 (2016), seeking to outlaw unions for public sector employees.

[87] For example, *Shearson/Americal Express Inc. v. McMahon*, 482 U.S. 220 (1987), allowing the securities industry to force arbitration of any customer disputes with broker-dealers.

[88] Int'l Swaps & Derivatives Ass'n et al. v. U.S. Commodity Futures Trading Comm'n, 887 F.Supp.2d 259 (2012) (preventing the CFTC from imposing position limits on trading without extensive investigation).

[89] The Bus. Roundtable v. Sec. & Exch. Comm'n, 905 F.2d 406 (1990) (vacating an SEC rule to ensure equal voting rights among shareholders of listed companies).

[90] "[W]hat distinguishes the common law from the civil law is the latitude it gives private lawyers in fashioning the law. They don't just advise on existing law, they constantly make new legal rights from old cloth." Katharina Pistor, The Code of Capital 169 (2018).

[91] "It is barely too much to say that the new, deregulated world of national and international finance was made for the investment banks." Tooze, *supra* note 57, at 51.

[92] *Corporate profits versus labor income*, The FRED Blog (Aug. 8, 2018), https://fredblog.stlouisfed.org/2018/08/corporate-profits-versus-labor-income/.

population taking home about 21 percent of income while the bottom 50 percent took home only about 12 percent in 2018.[93] In 2023, the distribution of wealth between the very wealthy and ordinary people is approaching the levels present when *Lochner*[94] was decided.[95] The changes have not just been economic, and have included mass belief that the US government is an evil cult; an attempted *coup d'état*; and complete denial of election results. Expression of individual preferences is at an all-time high, but the results are not what Hayek or Samuelson expected.

Conclusion: Speak Market

Late in the 20th century, scholars and governments unearthed a secret that apparently had been hidden for millennia: reason, civic duty, and government were only second-best tools for ordering society. Policy analysis rests on the "proposition that, given agreement on social goals, reason can be used to realise those goals,"[96] but agreement on a common goal had been lost and the good-faith search for those goals was abandoned. Indeed, the search was deemed unnecessary because Left and Right alike agreed that giving free rein to self-interest in an orderly market would bring out the common good.[97]

In this vein, common law was found superior because it allows each person to seek and earn their own justice. It also became the more effective tool because consensus in lawmaking proved harder and harder to reach. While government by elected officials fell into paralysis, the Supreme Court has increasingly carried the burden of the nation's most pressing problems.

This turn to government-by-litigation was not without its successes, as progress in individual human rights shows. However, the polity has been fractured and an inheritance of protections designed for ordinary people is being stripped away. Examining this as one period in the long-term history of humanity, Yuval Harari sees us reverting to the mean: All of human history until the "late modern era" took place under enormous economic inequality, so the current trend can be understood as swinging away from an aberration.[98]

[93] Thomas Piketty, Capital and Ideology 523 (2020).

[94] Lochner v. New York, 198 U.S. 45 (1905).

[95] *See*, e.g., Oxfam, Survival of the Richest How we must tax the super-rich now to fight inequality 15–19 (2023), https://oxfamilibrary.openrepository.com/bitstream/handle/10546/621477/bp-survival-of-the-richest-160123-en.pdf.

[96] Mark V. Tushnet, *Post-Realist Legal Scholarship*, 15 J. Soc'y Pub. Tchrs. L. n.s. 20, 23 (1980).

[97] Sandel, *supra* note 21, at 13.

[98] Yuval Noah Harari, 21 Lessons for the 21st Century 82–83 (2019). Indeed, pursuant to a "data religion" already seen in valorizing stock market prices over government planners, the lives of ordinary humans could be dissolved into something akin to an animal existence under the analytic scrutiny of algorithms and their owners. Yuval Noah Harari, Homo Deus: A Brief History of Tomorrow (2015), ch. 11.

If the administrative infrastructure and the moral superstructure of civic duty are stripped away, and humanity stands again where it did before the efforts of the Enlightenment or the Progressive (Victorian) era began, perhaps we should invoke the close of Roberto Unger's *Knowledge and Politics*, duly updated for the 21st century American belief system, and pray: "But our days pass, and still we do not know you fully. Why then do you remain silent? Speak [market]."[99]

[99] Roberto Mangabeira Unger, Knowledge and Politics 295 (1975).

19

Dialogic Judicial Review and First World Autocracies

Po Jen Yap

Dialogic judicial review is a judicial practice whereby the pursuit of legislative objectives can be constructively modified, but not foreclosed, by judicial input into the lawmaking process.[1] Also termed "weak-form judicial review"[2] by Mark Tushnet, this responsive model of judicial review is most commonly found in constitutional systems which adopt creative structural mechanisms that expressly preserve the legislature's right to *disagree* with the judicial interpretation of rights via the ordinary course of politics,[3] such that the use of a constitutional amendment to overrule the courts is unnecessary. But the existence of these structural mechanisms is not a prerequisite for a dialogic approach to constitutional discourse to occur. Even in the absence of these structural devices, so far as any court enforces constitutional rights in a way that leaves sufficient decisional space to the legislature or allows the legislature to respond in disagreement using the ordinary political process—without resorting to a constitutional amendment—an interbranch constitutional dialogue on rights can occur.[4]

Over the course of Tushnet's long, luminous career, he has made three important observations on this dialogic model of judicial review. First, he argues that weak-form review is potentially unstable as, over time, it may escalate into strong-form judicial review, or, conversely, degenerate back into parliamentary supremacy.[5] Second, while Tushnet generally prefers weak-form review over strong-form, he believes that "only strong-form review offers some reasonable prospect of dealing with the problems posed by classical sedition laws and restrictions on

[1] Leighton McDonald, *New Directions in the Australian Bill of Rights Debate*, Pub. L. 22 (2004).

[2] Mark Tushnet, *New Forms of Judicial Review and the Persistence of Rights and Democracy-Based Worries*, 38 Wake Forest L. Rev. 813, 814 (2003).

[3] Peter Hogg & Allison Bushell, *The Charter Dialogue Between the Courts and Legislatures (Or Perhaps the Charter of Rights Isn't Such a Bad Thing After All)*, 35 Osgoode Hall L.J. 75 (1997); Kent Roach, The Supreme Court on Trial: Judicial Activism or Democratic Dialogue (1st ed., 2001); Alison Young, Democratic Dialogue and the Constitution [PINCITE] (2017); Geoffrey Sigalet, Grégoire Webber & Rosalind Dixon, Constitutional Dialogue: Rights, Democracy, Institutions (2019); Rosalind Dixon, Responsive Judicial Review (2023).

[4] Po Jen Yap, Constitutional Dialogue in Common Law Asia (2015).

[5] Tushnet, *supra* note 2, at 814–15.

Po Jen Yap, *Dialogic Judicial Review and First World Autocracies* In: *Redefining Comparative Constitutional Law.* Edited by: Vicki C. Jackson and Madhav Khosla, Oxford University Press. © Po Jen Yap 2025.
DOI: 10.1093/9780191996344.003.0019

the franchise."[6] Third, according to Tushnet, the argument for weak-form review is less compelling in dominant party democracies than in countries with stronger norms of electoral competition.[7]

Singapore is a dominant party democracy, which Tushnet is intimately familiar with. Not only is Tushnet well versed in its laws, he is a discerning consumer of its cuisine; but the latter is a story for another time. Tushnet has argued that Singapore embodies a model of "authoritarian constitutionalism"[8]—a hybrid political system between liberal democracies and illiberal regimes. According to Tushnet, an authoritarian constitutional system is controlled by a dominant party which makes all the relevant public policy decisions in that system,[9] operates elections not tainted by fraud but where the electoral rules are *transparently* manipulated to facilitate the incumbent's victory,[10] protects human rights "at an intermediate level,"[11] and creates *independent* courts that perform weak-form review.[12] As Tushnet admits, such authoritarian constitutional systems are incredibly rare.[13] In fact, Singapore is the only extant example that Tushnet is able to name.

One may then ask: Why are authoritarian constitutional systems—as defined by Tushnet—so rare? What makes Singapore so exceptional? In my view, this particular hybrid system is uncommon because it is what I term a First World autocracy—an autocratic system that is concurrently an advanced economy. And First World Autocracies are rare birds indeed. The International Monetary Fund has classified 40 countries and territories as advanced economies, and these jurisdictions include the United States, Germany, the United Kingdom, Japan, Canada, Australia, Taiwan, and similar.[14] But only *three* jurisdictions in this league of high society are *not* competitive democracies: Singapore and the two Special Administrative Regions governed by China—Hong Kong and Macau.

For a developed economy to grow and flourish, commodities and capital must flow seamlessly. The regulatory framework must be efficient and transparent, its infrastructure modern and highly networked, its courts independent and capable of adjudicating *commercial* disputes—even against state actors—freely and fairly. We see this in both Singapore and Hong Kong. Singapore topped the Heritage

[6] Mark Tushnet, *The Relation Between Political Constitutionalism and Weak-Form Judicial Review*, 14 German L.J. 2249, 2262 (2013).

[7] Mark Tushnet & Rosalind Dixon, *Weak-Form Review and its Constitutional Relatives: An Asian Perspective, in* Comparative Constitutional Law in Asia 102, 104 (Tom Ginsburg & Rosalind Dixon eds., 2014).

[8] Mark Tushnet, *Authoritarian Constitutionalism*, 100 Cornell L. Rev. 391 (2015).

[9] *Id.* at 449.

[10] *Id.* at 414.

[11] *Id.* at 396.

[12] *Id.* at 450.

[13] *Id.* at 454.

[14] IMF, *Countering the Cost-of-Living Crisis*, World Economic Outlook Report 103 tbl.A (Oct. 2022), https://www.imf.org/en/Publications/WEO/Issues/2022/10/11/world-economic-outlook-october-2022.

Foundation's Index of Economic Freedoms in 2023.[15] Hong Kong topped it for 25 years but was dropped from the rankings in 2021, the city now lumped together with the rest of China. But by other matrices, both cities still fare very well. In the Swiss-based International Institute for Management Development (IMD) World Competitiveness Ranking of 2023, Singapore comes fourth and Hong Kong is seventh.[16] In the 2023 Schroders Global Cities Index—an annual scorecard of a city's economic, environmental, transport, and innovation factors—Singapore is eighth and Hong Kong ninth.[17] In the 2023 Global Financial Centres Index, both cities are also neck and neck, with Singapore in third place and Hong Kong fourth.[18]

But even as both jurisdictions scale the economic ladder, their governments equally prize political dominance within their own systems. Singapore has been ruled by the People's Action Party since the country's independence in 1965, and Hong Kong has been governed by the Communist Party of China since the establishment of the Special Administrative Region in 1997. And neither has any intention of relinquishing control. For a dominant party to remain in power indefinitely, it has to regularly modify the electoral rules to preserve its incumbency—or even extend its lead—and rely on an optimal mix of co-optation, repression, censorship, and propaganda to buttress its hegemony.[19] We see that too in Singapore and Hong Kong.

Keeping an economy open and humming, while its political system is closed to competition, requires immense statecraft and finesse. Succeeding at both is hard. And this explains why there are so few First World autocracies around.

In this chapter I shall seek to explore the constitutional role that the courts play in these First World autocracies. Specifically, I argue that dialogic or weak-form review is the only viable and effective path for courts operating in such autocracies. The judicial use of strong-form review to address problems posed by sedition laws and restrictions on the franchise—as Tushnet suggests[20]—would be counterproductive, as this would only be to the detriment of the courts. At the same time, I argue that dialogic review is not judicial abdication. I will also show how weak-form review has enhanced rights protection in Singapore and Hong Kong, and has imposed soft but meaningful controls on state power in these autocracies. Precisely because these autocracies want to remain First World economies, the perceived independence of the courts must be preserved for their governments to retain talent

[15] The Heritage Found., 2023 Index of Economic Freedom, https://www.heritage.org/index/.

[16] IMD/World Competitiveness Ctr., IMD World Competitiveness Ranking 2023, https://www.imd.org/centers/wcc/world-competitiveness-center/rankings/world-competitiveness-ranking/2023/.

[17] Schroders, Schroders Global Cities Index (2023), https://www.schroders.com/en/global/individual/media-centre/san-francisco-takes-top-spot-in-schroders-global-cities-index/.

[18] Z/Yen, The Global Financial Centres Index (2023), https://www.longfinance.net/programmes/financial-centre-futures/global-financial-centres-index/gfci-33-explore-the-data/gfci-33-rank/.

[19] *See* Adam Przeworksi, *Authoritarianism, Authority, and Representation*, 60 Asian Surv. 347 (2020).

[20] Tushnet, *supra* note 6, at 2262.

and continued investment in the economy. Governments in First World autocracies are sensitive to global businesses' perception of the regime's commitment to the rule of law as that directly impacts the entity's economic future. This is unlike military dictatorships and banana republics, where the rent-seeking behavior of autocrats is driven primarily by the self-interest of its cabal.[21] Therefore, in First World autocracies, so long as the courts respect the regime's plenary agenda-setting powers, the government will in turn acquiesce to the judiciary's calibrated show of force to preserve rights.

Singapore

Since gaining independence in 1965 Singapore has been governed by the same political party, the People's Action Party (PAP). The PAP has consistently controlled more than 85 percent of the elected seats while garnering 60–70 percent of the popular vote. With its relentless supermajority in Parliament, the PAP government can pass legislation and even constitutional amendments with ease, such that it makes all relevant public policy decisions in the country.

Singapore's electoral system is unique insofar as it provides for both single-member constituencies (SMCs) and multimember group constituencies in parliamentary general elections. Such multimember group constituencies are known as Group Representative Constituencies (GRCs), and each GRC is formed by merging three to six single wards into one mega-constituency.[22] The GRC system was first introduced, following a constitutional amendment in 1988, with the stated purpose of ensuring racial diversity in Parliament—at least one team member must be from a racial minority community.[23] But the GRC system also benefits the PAP, as the latter has relied on this system to ensure the election of new candidates of ministerial caliber; these promising freshmen are fielded in GRC teams alongside party stalwarts with mass electoral appeal.[24] And to further cement its political advantage, the ruling PAP regime strategically skews the political competition in its favor by redrawing preexisting electoral boundaries before *every* general election.[25]

The PAP government's hegemony is also attributable to the extraordinary control it exercises over public expression in Singapore. Foremost is its control over

[21] How Dictatorships Work: Power, Personalization, and Collapse (Barbara Geddes, Joseph Wright & Erica Frantz eds., 2018).

[22] Constitution of the Republic of Singapore, art. 39A.

[23] *Id.* art. 39A(2).

[24] For early discussions of the electoral advantages which the GRC system conferred upon the PAP, see Kevin Tan, *Constitutional Implications of the 1991 Singapore General Elections*, 13 Singapore L. Rev. 26, 46–51 (1992); Li-Ann Thio, *The Post-Colonial Constitutional Evolution of the Singapore Legislature: A Case Study*, Singapore J. Legal Stud., 1993, at 80, 106–07.

[25] Po Jen Yap, Courts and Democracies in Asia 26 (2017).

print media located or operating within Singapore. The Newspaper and Printing Presses Act[26] requires a person to first obtain a license before he or she can print, publish, or circulate a newspaper in Singapore, and this license can be refused or withdrawn by the Minister of Communications and Information at his or her discretion.[27] Furthermore, any newspaper that publishes in Singapore must create two classes of share: ordinary shares and management shares. Each management shareholder has 200 times the voting rights of an ordinary shareholder[28] over any resolution relating to the appointment/dismissal of a director or any staff member of the newspaper company, and the former share type can only be owned by Singapore citizens or corporations that have been approved by the said minister.[29] In recent years the Singapore government has further expanded its regulatory control over expressive conduct to cyberspace. In 2019, Parliament passed the Protection from Online Falsehoods and Manipulation Act (POFMA). POFMA empowers ministers to issue executive directions against "false statements of fact" communicated online. These directions may require these statement-makers to either correct their statements, by amending them to add the government's chosen response to it,[30] or remove those statements entirely.[31] The Public Order Act[32] also requires an organizer of a public assembly, even if it is a demonstration by *one* person,[33] first to obtain a permit from the Commissioner of Police;[34] further, licenses for outdoor political protests are not granted in practice. Outdoor demonstrations organized by Singapore citizens in Speaker's Corner—a small park—are exempted from these licensing requirements.

Singapore's Constitution formally grants courts the power of judicial review. Article 4 of the Constitution expressly states that "any law enacted by the Legislature . . . which is inconsistent with [the] Constitution shall, to the extent of the inconsistency, be void." However, in view of the PAP's overwhelming control over Parliament, and its unfettered ability to introduce even constitutional amendments, Singapore's courts have shied away from the constitutional invalidation of legislation. Notably, when the government lost a constitutional decision before the Court of Appeal in 1988 for the first and last time, the government swiftly overturned that decision via a series of constitutional and statutory amendments within a month of the judgment. In that seminal decision, in *Chng Suan Tze v Minister of Home Affairs* (1988), the Court of Appeal quashed the preventive detention orders issued under the Internal Security Act (ISA) against alleged Marxist conspirators

26 Newspaper and Printing Presses Act 1974.
27 *Id.* §§ 21, 22.
28 *Id.* § 10(11).
29 *Id.* § 10(1)(c).
30 Protection from Online Falsehoods and Manipulation Act, § 11.
31 *Id.* § 12.
32 Public Order Act, ch. 257A.
33 *Id.* § 2(1).
34 *Id.* §§ 7(1), 7(2) & 16(1)(a).

on a technicality,[35] but also concluded *obiter* that the ministerial discretion to detain personnel under the ISA would be subject to an "objective" review by the courts. This decision proved to be sufficiently disquieting to the government, and subsequent statutory and constitutional amendments restricted judicial review in ISA cases to only narrow procedural grounds.[36]

Since the government's swift rebuke of the Singapore Court of Appeal's perceived judicial overreach in *Chng Suan Tze*, the nation's highest court has abstained from invalidating any legislation that comes its way. The mandatory death sentence for drug trafficking was upheld on the basis that the Constitution does not expressly prohibit inhumane punishment and "it would not be appropriate for [judges] to legislate new rights into the Singapore Constitution under the guise of interpreting existing constitutional provisions."[37] Judicial caning is also constitutional, as the constitutional right to life and liberty had no application to "punishment to be imposed on a convicted person after trial."[38]

On issues pertaining to electoral competition—for which Tushnet advocates strong-form review—the Singapore courts are equally subdued. In *Vellama d/o Marie Muthu v Attorney-General* (2013),[39] Singapore's Court of Appeal determined that the prime minister had a constitutional duty under Article 49 of the Constitution to call for a by-election within a "reasonable time"[40] when a casual vacancy in a SMC arose. Unfortunately, the Court subsequently qualified this ruling in *Wong Souk Yee v Attorney-General* (2019)[41] by holding that the constitutional duty to call for a by-election imposed by Article 49 *only* applied to SMCs and not GRCs, and this is so even if the vacancy would render the GRC without any racial minority. One should also note that in Singapore, only 15 percent of the elected seats are constituted as SMCs; the other 85% are constituted as GRCs. The decision in *Wong Souk Yee* essentially makes by-elections redundant in Singapore.

While Singapore's court of final resort has upheld the constitutionality of every legislation in the country and has validated all the electoral changes introduced by the PAP to entrench its hegemony, the judiciary under the leadership of the incumbent Chief Justice Sundaresh Menon is not a rubber-stamp. It merely asserts its control and advances human rights dialogically in the realm of *statutory* interpretation. This strategy has been defended by Chief Justice Menon in the following terms:

[35] Po Jen Yap, Constitutional Dialogue in Common Law Asia 73–77 (2015).
[36] Constitution of the Republic of Singapore, art. 149; Internal Security Act, § 8B.
[37] Yong Vui Kong v. Public Prosecutor [2010] 3 SLR 489, 59.
[38] *Id.* at 64.
[39] Vellama d/o Marie Muthu v. Attorney-General [2013] 4 SLR 1.
[40] Vellama v. Attorney General [2012] 4 SLR 698, [84].
[41] Wong Souk Yee v. Attorney-General [2019] 1 SLR 1223.

What underlies this approach is the belief that a court which is respected by the other branches of government can effectively shape the debate and ensure the legality of government actions by setting out its concerns openly and potentially obviating a binary clash between the Judiciary and the Executive.[42]

Dialogue on Ouster Clause

Ouster clauses are disconcerting because they strip courts of jurisdiction, thereby removing independent judicial oversights over executive action, as we have seen in the aftermath of *Chng Suan Tze*. In recent years, however, the Singapore courts have begun to resist these statutory encroachments on judicial power.

Tan Seet Eng v Attorney-General (2015)[43] involved a challenge to a preventive detention order issued under the Criminal Law (Temporary Provisions) Act (CLTPA),[44] which allowed the government to detain without trial persons "associated with activities of a criminal nature."[45] The Minister of Home Affairs' decisions on such detentions are also deemed final.[46] On the facts, the detainee was alleged to have financed football match-fixing activities in Europe, Africa, and the Middle East from Singapore.

Notwithstanding the ouster clause, the Court ruled that it had the power to objectively review the grounds of the detention to determine whether the Home Affairs Minister had acted within the scope of his statutory powers,[47] and on the facts quashed this detention order. In doing so, the Court noted that the constitutional and statutory amendments to overrule its earlier attempt to assert "objective" review in *Chng Suan Tze* applied only to detentions under the Internal Security Act, and not to other forms of preventive detention.[48]

When reviewing the disputed detention, the Court of Appeal (CA) also added two glosses to the legislation. First, even though the CLTPA merely requires the detainee's association with activities to be of "a criminal nature"[49] for detention to be justified, the CA ruled that such "activities must be of a *sufficiently serious* nature that it leads the Minister to be satisfied that it is *necessary* to act."[50] Second, the threat posed by this sufficiently serious criminal activity must exist *in Singapore*.[51] Although the applicant was operating "*from* Singapore,"[52] and his actions were

[42] Sundaresh Menon, *The Rule of Law: The Path to Exceptionalism*, 28 Singapore Acad. L.J. 413, 421 (2016).
[43] Tan Seet Eng v. Attorney-General [2016] 1 SLR 779.
[44] Criminal Law (Temporary Provisions) Act, *hereinafter* CLTPA, ch. 67 (Singapore).
[45] *Id.* § 30(1).
[46] *Id.* § 30(2).
[47] Tan Seet Eng at 62.
[48] *Id.* at 98.
[49] CLTPA, § 30(1).
[50] Tan Seet Eng at 135.
[51] *Id.* at 147–48. See also Menon, *supra* note 42, at 422–23.
[52] *Id.* at 146.

"reprehensible and should not be condoned,"[53] the Court opined that there was "nothing to suggest whether (or how) these activities could be thought to have a bearing on the public safety, peace and good order *within* Singapore,"[54] and his detention was therefore *ultra vires*.[55]

In compliance with the judicial order, the applicant was freed, but six days after this judgment was handed down, he was re-detained under a new CLTPA detention order, which this time set out the grounds relied on by the government to establish the existence of the relevant threat *in Singapore*.[56] Nevertheless, the government also released three other detainees on its own accord after reviewing this decision. And in 2018, the government tabled amendments to the CLTPA to statutorily list nine distinct crimes that justified preventive detention: unlicenced moneylending; drug trafficking; involvement in a secret society; human trafficking; and robbery with firearms, among others.[57]

The CA next confronted an ostensible ouster clause in *Nagaenthran v Public Prosecutor* (2019).[58] Singapore imposes a mandatory death sentence on persons who traffick certain prescribed drugs. However, a discretion is granted to the courts to impose a life sentence in lieu if the Public Prosecutor certifies to the court that the accused has substantively assisted the Central Narcotics Bureau in disrupting drug trafficking activities.[59] Notably, the Misuse of Drugs Act further inserts this particular provision, found in Section 33B(4):

> The determination of whether or not any person has substantively assisted the Central Narcotics Bureau in disrupting drug trafficking activities shall be at the sole discretion of the Public Prosecutor and no action or proceeding shall lie against the Public Prosecutor in relation to any such determination unless it is proved to the court that the determination was done in bad faith or with malice.[60]

Even though the law states that this determination of the accused's assistance shall be at the sole discretion of the Public Prosecution (PP), the Court deftly decided that this clause "does not purport to exclude the jurisdiction of the courts to supervise the legality of the PP's determination"[61] on the "usual grounds of judicial review, such as illegality, irrationality and procedural impropriety."[62] In the Court's view, all Section 33(B)4 did was to grant the PP immunity from lawsuits,[63] and the

[53] *Id.*
[54] *Id.*, emphasis in original.
[55] *Id.* at 148.
[56] Sundaresh Menon, *supra* note 42, at 422–23.
[57] CLTPA, Fourth Schedule.
[58] Nagaenthran v. Public Prosecutor [2019] 2 SLR 216.
[59] Misuse of Drugs Act, § 33B.
[60] *Id.* § 33B(4).
[61] Nagaenthran at 51.
[62] *Id.*
[63] *Id.*

relevance of the first clause in the disputed provision was to merely vest "the *merits* . . . of the determination"[64] solely with the PP, leaving room for the courts to review its *legality*.[65] Given that this is the "true nature and interpretation"[66] of Section 33B(4), the Court held that it was moot for the Court to decide whether the law could oust the Court's power of judicial review altogether, but the CA did suggest *obiter* that such a statutory course of action "would be constitutionally suspect for being in violation of Art. 93 of the Singapore Constitution [which vests judicial power in the Supreme Court] as well as the principle of the separation of powers."[67]

Dialogue on Drug Offenses

Singapore imposes a mandatory death sentence on persons convicted of trafficking certain controlled drugs above a prescribed amount.[68] The courts have regularly upheld this draconian statutory feature.[69]

But even as these drug laws are upheld as constitutional, there has been a recent quiet judicial revolution where the CA has added new layers of due process into this penal regime. Notably, all these enhancements were achieved dialogically as the Court engaged in statutory interpretation.

In *Saravanan Chandaram v Public Prosecutor* (2020),[70] the CA overruled a 24-year-old precedent[71] that had previously defined a cannabis mixture to include both (1) a mixture of cannabis and another plant of noncannabis origin *and* (2) a mixture of different parts of the cannabis plant. In *Saravanan*, the CA ruled that a cannabis mixture would only include the first mixture, and not the second. This ruling is significant because it basically wiped out a category of cannabis mixture that would trigger the death penalty in Singapore. But notably, the CA did so under the rules of statutory interpretation. First, the CA relied on a textual reading of "mixture"—there was no "mixture" to speak of if the plant matter consisted solely of cannabis.[72] Second, according to the CA, when the impugned law was passed in 1993, the "specific purpose"[73] behind the legislation as evidenced in the parliamentary materials was to impose the death penalty on persons who traffick a mixture of cannabis with other vegetable matters such as tobacco. And Parliament's original intent further buttressed the CA's textual reading of the term "mixture."

[64] *Id.* at 67.
[65] *Id.* at 74.
[66] *Id.* at 51.
[67] *Id.* at 74.
[68] Misuse of Drugs Act, Second Schedule.
[69] Yong Vui Kong v. Public Prosecutor [2010] 3 SLR 489.
[70] Saravanan Chandaram v. Public Prosecutor [2020] SGCA 43.
[71] Public Prosecutor v. Manogaran s/o R Ramu [1996] 3 SLR(R) 390.
[72] Saravanan Chandaram v. Public Prosecutor [2020] SGCA 43, at 92, 104.
[73] *Id.* at 100.

Singapore's drug laws also presume persons to have known the nature of a controlled drug when they are found in possession of them.[74] When the accused persons are found in possession, the burden of proof is on them to prove the absence of the relevant knowledge. Furthermore, the Singapore courts had previously taken the view that the relevant *mens rea* codified in this statutory presumption was not just actual knowledge, but also willful blindness.[75] In other words, when the accused persons were found in possession of drugs, it would not suffice for the accused just to prove they had no actual knowledge of the nature of the drugs; they had to also prove they were *not willfully blind* to the drug's nature. But in *Gobi v Public Prosecutor* (2020),[76] the CA overruled its prior line of case-law and decided that willful blindness would no longer be a feature of this statutory presumption, and the accused would no longer need to rebut this *mens rea* element.[77] This issue is often a question of life and death as persons found in possession of controlled drugs above a prescribed amount are presumed to be in possession for the purpose of drug trafficking,[78] and trafficking triggers the death penalty. After *Gobi*, if the prosecution is arguing that the accused persons are willfully blind to the drug's nature, the burden is now on the prosecution to prove beyond reasonable doubt that the accused have a clear, grounded, and targeted suspicion about the nature of the disputed item and had deliberately refused to pursue reasonable means of verification.[79]

Vis-à-vis statutory interpretation, the legislature can always reclaim the field with the passage of other legislation if it disagrees with the Court's reading of the preexisting one. These judicial innovations may impose additional enactment costs on the legislature if it disagrees with the judicial decisions in question; but after deliberation and careful consideration, "the better-informed government decision-makers will only be willing to act when their true interest in the policy is sufficiently strong."[80] And this give-and-take facilitates a constitutional dialogue on rights interpretation where the courts collaborate in a common enterprise with the political branches to promote public welfare.[81]

[74] Misuse of Drugs Act, § 18(2).

[75] Tan Kiam Peng v. Public Prosecutor [2008] 1 SLR 1; Masoud Rahimi bin Mehrzad v. Public Prosecutor and another appeal [2017] 1 SLR 257.

[76] Gobi v. Public Prosecutor [2020] SGCA 102.

[77] *Id.* at 98(a).

[78] Misuse of Drugs Act, § 17.

[79] Gobi at 98(c).

[80] Matthew Stephenson, *The Price of Public Action: Constitutional Doctrine and the Judicial Manipulation of Legislative Enactment Costs*, 118 YALE L.J. 2, 11 (2008).

[81] Yap, *supra* note 4, at 106.

Hong Kong

The Hong Kong Special Administrative Region (HKSAR) was established in 1997 after Britain returned its former colony to the People's Republic of China. The head of the HKSAR government—the Chief Executive (CE)—is currently elected by an Election Committee composed of only 1500 members.[82] The Election Committee is overwhelmingly stacked with pro-Beijing delegates, thereby ensuring that only a pro-Beijing candidate can be selected as Chief Executive.[83]

The Hong Kong Legislative Council is a unicameral body. Following an overhaul of the electoral system in 2021, it is now composed of 90 members elected by three electoral methods: 20 seats in the Legislative Council are constituted via universal suffrage in Geographical Constituencies (GC) elections;[84] 30 seats[85] are constituted via Functional Constituencies (FC), a system in which the right to vote depends upon a person's membership or registration in a recognized social, economic, industrial, commercial, political advisory, or professional body represented in the legislature,[86] and furthermore, for the most part it is only the recognized corporate bodies operating in these professions—and not individuals working in these professions—that can vote; and 40 seats are reserved for members chosen by the Election Committee of the Chief Executive.[87] All Legislative Council candidates must be pre-vetted by a Candidate Eligibility Review Committee Law—staffed by senior government officials—to ensure that prospective lawmakers would abide by the Hong Kong Basic Law, the city's mini-Constitution. All these measures were introduced by Beijing in 2021 to ensure that only "patriots" can govern Hong Kong.

In June 2020, Beijing annexed a new national security legislation (NSL) to Hong Kong's Basic Law.[88] Frustrated with the months of civil unrest that rocked the city in 2019, and with the local government's inability to pass national security law "on its own,"[89] Beijing decided to take matters into its own hands and custom-make a bespoke one for Hong Kong. The NSL criminalizes four main offences: secession, subversion of state power, terrorism, and foreign collusion; however, these offences are all vague and poorly defined.[90] The enforcement and prosecution decisions

[82] Hong Kong Basic Law, Annex 1.

[83] SIMON YOUNG & RICHARD CULLEN, ELECTING HONG KONG'S CHIEF EXECUTIVE 79, 91 (2010).

[84] Hong Kong Basic Law, Annex 2.

[85] *Id.*

[86] For a critique of the FC system, see Simon Young & Anthony Law, *Privileged to Vote: Inequalities and Anomalies of the FC System*, *in* FUNCTIONAL CONSTITUENCIES: A UNIQUE FEATURE OF THE HONG KONG LEGISLATIVE COUNCIL 59 (Christine Loh ed., 2007).

[87] Hong Kong Basic Law, Annex 2.

[88] The Law of the People's Republic of China on Safeguarding National Security in the Hong Kong Special Administrative Region (*hereinafter* NSL).

[89] Hong Kong Basic Law, art. 23.

[90] *See* THE NATIONAL SECURITY LAW OF HONG KONG RESTORATION AND TRANSFORMATION (Hualing Fu & Michael Hor eds., 2022).

made under the NSL are entrusted to local officials[91] and Hong Kong courts are also empowered to adjudicate the vast majority of cases brought under this law.[92] But it is noteworthy that it is the Chief Executive of Hong Kong who decides on the list of judges who will hear these national security cases, though these national security judges are to be appointed from the pool of *pre-existing* Hong Kong judges,[93] and the specific rostering of individual judges for any case is the sole responsibility of the chief judge of the relevant court concerned.[94] In rare serious cases where foreign governments are involved or the Hong Kong government is unable to enforce the law effectively, the Chinese procuratorate and courts are legally empowered to take over from local counterparts.[95] The law opens up the chilling possibility that for these exceptional cases, the offenders, if in Hong Kong, can be extradited to the Mainland to face trial. Finally, the power of interpreting this national security law lies with China's Standing Committee of the National People's Congress,[96] which expressly allows Mainland officials to overrule the Hong Kong judiciary's interpretation of this criminal law.

As of January 1, 2023, no one had been extradited to Mainland China to face trial under the NSL, but 90 people had been charged under this law, 47 of whom are pro-democracy activists who, prior to the 2021 election revamp, had organized an informal election primary to field candidates who can win seats in the Legislative Council and subsequently block the passage of the government's budget, thereby forcing the CE's resignation.[97]

The regressive political developments in Hong Kong are deeply troubling, but this does not mean that its judges are constitutionally neutered like their Mainland counterparts. Present circumstances notwithstanding, the Hong Kong judiciary enjoys significant autonomy from the local government. Under the Basic Law, the Hong Kong judiciary is empowered to exercise its judicial powers independently, free from any interference.[98] Judges are appointed by the Chief Executive, on the recommendation of the Judicial Officers Recommendation Commission (JORC). But in practice, all candidates put forward by the JORC are appointed and it is the Chief Justice who chairs the nine-member JORC that shapes the composition of the bench, especially the crucial Court of Final Appeal (HKCFA).[99]

[91] NSL, arts. 16, 18.
[92] *Id.* art. 40.
[93] *Id.* art. 44.
[94] Chief Just. of Ct. of Final Appeal, Statement on Behalf of the Judiciary (July 2, 2020), https://www.info.gov.hk/gia/general/202007/02/P2020070200414.htm.
[95] NSL, art. 55.
[96] *Id.* art. 65.
[97] Austin Ramzy & Tiffany May, *Hong Kong Charges 47 Democracy Supporters With Violating Security Law*, New York Times (Feb. 28, 2021), https://www.nytimes.com/2021/02/28/world/asia/hong-kong-security-law-arrests.html.
[98] Hong Kong Basic Law, art. 85.
[99] Albert H.Y. Chen & Po Jen Yap, The Constitutional System of the Hong Kong SAR: A Contextual Analysis 117 (2023).

Beijing is empowered under the Basic Law to overrule any constitutional decision of the HKCFA by a Legislative Interpretation.[100] But this is not to say that the courts are politically irrelevant in Hong Kong's constitutional landscape. The Hong Kong judiciary has built up a history of invalidating legislation since the Bill of Rights Ordinance was enacted in the territory in 1991.[101] Like all political practices, judicial practices are path-dependent,[102] such that Hong Kong judges can appeal to history and *stare decisis* for continuing the practice of enforcing human rights against the Hong Kong government. Furthermore, Beijing cannot and will not reverse every decision by the HKCFA as it does not want to appear to be rescinding from its commitment to allow the HKSAR to "exercise a high degree of autonomy and enjoy . . . independent judicial power,"[103] as this would adversely impact Hong Kong's long-term viability as an international financial center and China's own long-term goal of reunifying Taiwan.

While the "patriots-only" legislature will be united in defending the Chinese Central Government's core interests in Hong Kong, these lawmakers do not owe their political allegiance to the Chief Executive of the HKSAR (who is not drawn from any political party) or a singular political party in Hong Kong. Notably, the largest political party in Hong Kong—the Democratic Alliance for the Betterment and Progress of Hong Kong—only took 19 out of 90 seats in the Legislative Council at the most recent 2021 election held after the electoral overhaul. Trade-based FC legislators remain electorally accountable only to their narrow sectoral constituents. What the 2021 electoral overhaul did was to entrench Beijing's domination in the Legislative Council, but the electoral revamp did not resolve intraparty division. Trade unionists and tycoons still coexist uneasily in the Legislative Council, as do nationalists and conglomerates who want Hong Kong to remain attractive to international investors. They may all be Beijing loyalists but their conflicting socioeconomic visions and contrasting policy prescriptions are not easily bridged.

Where Beijing's core interests are not at stake, where there are intra-party divisions on policy, the HKCFA retains significant discretion to shape the law. This is because both the Chinese and Hong Kong governments want to keep the city as a top international financial center that is attractive to business investors and overseas talent. And to do that, the rule of law in Hong Kong must be perceived to be upheld, and the government cannot neuter its judiciary or overrule it at every turn. Therefore, while the HKCFA can do little to countermand Beijing's hegemony over the political system, the Court can "dialogue" strategically with the government

[100] Hong Kong Basic Law, art. 158.

[101] Yash Ghai, *Sentinels of Liberty or Sheep in Woolf's Clothing? Judicial Politics and the Hong Kong Bill of Rights*, 60 Mod. L. Rev. 459 (1997).

[102] Alec Stone Sweet, *Path Dependence, Precedent, and Judicial Power*, *in* On Law, Politics, and Judicialization 112 (Martin Shapiro & Alec Stone Sweet eds., 2002).

[103] Hong Kong Basic Law, art. 2.

on policy prescriptions and rights protections that are less objectionable to the regime.[104]

Trimming and Political Rights

"Trimming" has been defended by Cass Sunstein as a heuristic for judges to attend carefully to competing positions and attempt to steer between the poles when reaching a particular legal result.[105] Judges "trim" either by striking a middle path or preserving what is most essential to competing reasonable positions, so that political conflict is reduced and people who hold competing positions do not feel humiliated or excluded by the outcome.[106] And we may observe how the HKCFA has dialogically trimmed the excesses of the local government's restrictions on political rights, while upholding the core pillars of the legislation.

In *Kwok Wing Hang v Chief Executive in Council* (2020),[107] the HKCFA upheld the Chief Executive in Council (CEIC)'s power to invoke the Emergency Regulations Ordinance (ERO) to make regulations on any occasion of public danger, and also upheld the constitutionality of the Prohibition on Face Covering Regulation (PFCR)—the subsidiary legislation enacted pursuant to the ERO.

The context of this litigation may be explained briefly. For most of 2019, Hong Kong was rocked by civil unrest. The protests originally arose in opposition to the government's attempt to pass an extradition law that would allow for Hong Kong residents to be extradited to other regions and countries, including Mainland China, to face trial for alleged offenses committed there. Even though the bill was eventually withdrawn, the unrest continued as protestors pressed on with other demands, including amnesty for arrested protestors and an independent inquiry into alleged police brutality. Notably, many protestors wore masks during the protests to prevent identification and to shield themselves from the effects of tear gas and pepper spray used regularly by the police. In response to escalating street violence, the CEIC invoked the ERO to enact the PFCR, which bans facial covering in all public assemblies.

Notably, the HKCFA upheld the ban on facial covering at all assemblies, including lawful and peaceful ones. For the Court, it was proportionate to dampen the emboldening effect of a facial covering at all assemblies, especially since the "desire for anonymity, does not lie at the heart of the right to peaceful assembly."[108]

But more innocuous and subtle is what the HKCFA did with the ERO. Notably, Section 2(2)(g) of the ERO stipulates that regulations made by the CEIC may

104 See Chen & Yap, *supra* note 99, Chapter 6.
105 Cass Sunstein, *Trimming*, 122 Harv. L. Rev. 1049, 1051 (2009).
106 *Id.* at 1053.
107 Kwok Wing Hang v. Chief Executive in Council [2020] HKCFA 42.
108 *Id.* at 134.

provide for "amending any enactment, suspending the operation of any enactment." Section 2(4) of the ERO further provides that "A regulation . . . shall have effect notwithstanding anything inconsistent therewith contained in any enactment." The upshot of these two provisions would be that the ERO—on its face—would have allowed the CEIC to pass regulations that can override all rights in the Bill of Rights Ordinance (BORO).

The HKCFA nevertheless neutralized the draconian effects of the ERO by ruling that any regulations enacted pursuant to the ERO must not restrict any "fundamental rights protected under the ICCPR and the BORO as guaranteed under article 39 of the Basic Law unless the regulations satisfy the prescribed by law requirement and proportionality analysis."[109] In short, rights-infringing emergency legislation has to be constitutionally justified, like all other local laws in Hong Kong. Notably, the lower court only held that the ERO cannot override Section 5 of BORO,[110] which only pertained to nonderogable rights in public emergencies, such as the right against torture. But under the HKCFA's formulation, the entire BORO regime remains applicable when the ERO is invoked.

Dialogue on Criminal Due Process

Apropos of criminal laws, the HKCFA has also actively engaged in dialogic review. Instead of deeming an impugned governmental practice unconstitutional *per se*, such that legislation is invalidated, the HKCFA regularly uses the common law and the rules of statutory interpretation to reach right-friendly outcomes.

One such method is the judicial use of common law presumptions. In *Kulemesin v HKSAR* (2013), the HKCFA ruled that that where offence-creating penal provisions were silent or ambiguous as to the *mens rea*, "the more serious the offence in terms of penalty and social obloquy, the less likely it is that the presumption of *mens rea* will be held to have been supplanted."[111] Where a serious offence carrying severe penalties was involved, the CFA held that the following alternative regime on *mens rea* could apply:

> [T]he prosecution need not set out to prove *mens rea*, but if there is evidence capable of raising a reasonable doubt that the defendant may have acted or omitted to act in the honest and reasonable belief that the circumstances *or likely consequences* of his conduct were such that, if true, liability would not attach, he must be acquitted unless the prosecution proves beyond reasonable doubt the absence

[109] Kwok Wing Hang, *supra* note 107, at 69.
[110] Leung Kwok Hung v. Secretary for Justice [2020] HKCA 192 at [293].
[111] Kulemesin v. HKSAR, (2013) 16 HKCFAR 195, 59.

of such exculpatory belief or that there were no reasonable grounds for such belief.[112]

One must note what the HKCFA was doing here. In essence, the Court was construing ambiguous penal statute in ways that advanced substantive values of due process. But at the same time, these new principles are mere common law clear-statement rules that allow the legislature to override the Court's presumptions by ordinary legislation. In other words, the Legislative Council can simply respond in disagreement and statutorily remove the due diligence defense in express terms if it so chooses. But until the legislature does so, the HKCFA has imposed a new default rule that enhances criminal due process for the accused charged with serious crimes.[113]

Even with Hong Kong's draconian NSL, the HKCFA has not simply capitulated to everything the government seeks. In its first substantive NSL ruling in *HKSAR v Lai Chee Ying* (2021),[114] the HKCFA had to interpret the statutory requirements for bail under the NSL. Article 42(2) of the NSL reads: "No bail shall be granted to a criminal suspect or defendant unless the judge has sufficient grounds for believing that the criminal suspect or defendant will not continue to commit acts endangering national security."[115] While the HKCFA accepted that the requirements for bail under the NSL are "more stringent"[116] than the position under the ordinary criminal law, where a presumption in favor of bail exists, the Court also ruled *against* the government when the former concluded that bail conditions should *not* be presumptively excluded from consideration when judges decide whether to grant bail under the NSL.[117] Therefore, lower court judges, in deciding whether to grant bail to the accused charged under the NSL, have to assess whether the preventive effect of appropriate bail conditions would suffice, instead of inflexibly imposing a custodial order pending trial. And the HKCFA defended this ruling using the ordinary rules of *statutory* interpretation:

NSL [Article] 4 and NSL [Article] 5 expressly stipulate that . . . rights, freedoms and values are to be protected and adhered to in applying the NSL. They provide the context in which NSL [Article] 42(2) must be construed and applied. As far

[112] *Id.* at 83(b).

[113] In HKSAR v. Choi Wai Lun (2018) 21 HKCFAR 167, 70, the HKCFA determined that a penal provision that criminalized indecent assault on a minor did not impose absolute liability but merely absolved the prosecution from proving "mens rea as to the girl's age, but the accused has a good defence if he can prove on a balance of probabilities that he honestly and reasonably believed that the girl was 16 or over."

[114] HKSAR v. Lai Chee Ying, [2021] HKCFA 3.

[115] NSL, art. 42(2).

[116] HKSAR v. Lai Chee Ying at 53(b).

[117] *Id.* at 57.

as possible, NSL 42(2) is to be given a meaning and effect compatible with those rights, freedoms and values.[118]

Express Findings of Unconstitutionality

In the past two decades, the HKCFA's express findings of unconstitutionality have been reserved for decisions that did *not* encroach on Beijing's core concerns or impede the HKSAR government's ability to maintain law and order.[119] Specifically, the Court's most progressive and consequential decisions in the past 20 years have pertained to LGBT rights.

In *W v Registrar of Marriages* (2013),[120] the HKCFA determined that it was unconstitutional to prohibit postoperative transsexuals from marrying in the capacity of their acquired gender. Next, in *QT v Director of Immigration* (2018),[121] the HKCFA upended the Immigration Department's discriminatory practice of limiting spousal dependant visas to expatriates who were in heterosexual marriages and extended equal access to these visas to persons in same-sex civil partnerships. Finally, in *Leung Chun Kwong v. Secretary for Civil Service* (2019),[122] the HKCFA ruled that it was unconstitutional for the Civil Service to deny spousal benefits to same-sex couples married overseas, and for the Inland Revenue to prohibit these couples from electing for joint-tax assessment, when both benefits were conferred on married heterosexual couples. While the HKCFA accepted that the government was entitled to protect the traditional family constituted by heterosexual marriage, the HKCFA was "unable to accept the proposition that heterosexual marriage would be undermined by the extension of [these] benefits to same-sex married couples . . . Heterosexual marriage is not promoted by the differential treatment in question."[123] Finally, in 2023—after the passage of the NSL and the electoral overhaul—the HKCFA unanimously ruled that it was unconstitutional for the Commissioner of Registration to require female-to-male transgender persons to undergo full sex reassignment surgery before they could alter their gender markers on Hong Kong Identity Cards.[124]

These express findings of unconstitutionality all pertained to judicial orders that the HKSAR executive government would grudgingly enforce, even if it may not agree with the Court on the merits. Beijing is simply indifferent to gay rights in Hong Kong. Furthermore, these are issues where there are ideological cleavages

[118] *Id.* at 42.
[119] Po Jen Yap, *Twenty Years of the Basic Law: Continuity and Changes in the Geoffrey Ma Court*, 49 Hong Kong L.J. 209 (2019).
[120] W v. Registrar of Marriages (2013) 16 HKCFAR 112.
[121] QT v. Director of Immigration (2018) 21 HKCFAR 324.
[122] Leung Chun Kwong v. Secretary for Civil Service (2019) 22 HKCFAR 127.
[123] *Id.* at 72.
[124] Q v. Commissioner of Registration [2023] HKCFA 4.

within the pro-Beijing coalition in Hong Kong such that the local government does not have the political capital to cobble a constitutional amendment to overrule the courts. Notably, many business-friendly lawmakers in the pro-Beijing coalition support marriage equality.[125] On issues where the pro-Beijing coalition is divided, any potential backlash against the courts would be unlikely, and the HKCFA can therefore in such instances assert its authority more decisively and give a more generous expression of the Basic Law.

Conclusion

Mark Tushnet has advocated for strong-form judicial review to address problems posed by sedition laws and restrictions on the franchise,[126] and he deems weak-form review less compelling in dominant party democracies than in countries with stronger norms of electoral competition.[127] In the same vein, Stephen Gardbaum has also developed a comparative political process theory of judicial review which argues for robust judicial intervention when authoritarian governments entrench their powers by fortifying their political systems against competition or accountability.[128]

But as we have discussed above, the Singapore government has used the constitutional amendment to overrule its highest court when the latter has attempted to assert review over the country's national security laws. With supermajoritarian control of the seats in Parliament, the hegemonic regime easily revised the Constitution to limit judicial review to procedural irregularities in the detention orders. Beijing has foisted a National Security Law on Hong Kong and created a "candidate eligibility review committee" to vet potential Chief Executive and legislative candidates. China has stayed its hand so far on Hong Kong judges. But if the local judges were to overreach and strike down these laws, a sweeping overhaul of judicial appointments would soon follow.

Judges operating in dominant party regimes must weigh the consequences of antagonizing their semipermanent governments, which can clip their wings in retaliation. Such policy considerations are the "anti-modalities"[129] of constitutional adjudication—constitutional taboos more honored in the breach. These are extralegal considerations that judges must heed in politically sensitive disputes if they want to remain independent and effective for other cases.

[125] Regina Ip, *Why Using Chinese Tradition to Oppose Same-Sex Marriage in Hong Kong Is Misguided*, South China Morning Post (Dec. 1, 2018), https://www.scmp.com/comment/insight-opinion/hong-kong/article/2175645/why-using-chinese-tradition-oppose-same-sex.

[126] Tushnet, *supra* note 6, at 2262.

[127] Tushnet & Dixon, *supra* note 7, at 104.

[128] Stephen Gardbaum, *Comparative Political Process Theory*, 18 Int'l J. Const. L. 1429 (2020).

[129] David E. Pozen & Adam M. Samaha, *Anti-Modalities*, 119 Mich. L. Rev. 729 (2021).

But equally, in First World economies such as Singapore and Hong Kong, the regimes prize the economic value of an independent judiciary, which allows these tiny jurisdictions to attract global investments and remain the world's leading financial centers. And therefore the government will also acquiesce to any calibrated judicial show of force to assuage international investors' concerns regarding whether the rule of law remains a cornerstone of the city's governance. The pathologies of First World autocracies are such that only dialogic judicial review can facilitate a constructive and sustainable model of rights protection in this unique subset of hybrid regimes.

20

We the Fourth Branch? The People as an Institution Protecting Democracy

Yaniv Roznai[*]

Introduction

Democracy around the world is in crisis.[1] In attempts to establish how constitutional democracy can survive, scholars have focused on courts and on constitutional design.[2] What type of governmental institutions are required in order to protect democracy? Is the traditional separation of powers between the three branches of government sufficient, in an era of populism and democratic erosion, to protect democracy? In a series of studies, Mark Tushnet provided the first general theory of a new "fourth branch" of government: a group of institutions, such as electoral committees, anticorruption agencies, and ombuds audit agencies, whose role is to protect constitutional democracy.[3]

These institutions can serve as protectors of democracy due to their distinct independence and forms of expertise, even though—as Tushnet shows—they do not always succeed in protecting constitutional democracy, as they can be abused or involved in partisan and intraparty struggles. In this short chapter I take on Tushnet's concept of fourth branch institutions protecting democracy and apply it to the people. To demonstrate how the people can protect democracy, I describe the civil protest that took place in Israel in 2023 against the government's proposed judicial overhaul plan. In their study, Ginsburg and Huq argued that "[c]onstitutions cannot save democracy: Only democrats can."[4] The Israel case shows that determined and organized citizens can, if acting effectively, save democracy even when it is under severe threat from a populist government.

* I wish to thank Adi Tal for her terrific research assistance, and the editors for their kind invitation, for their useful comments and for organizing this book honoring one of our giants in the field. I am truly honored to be part of it.

[1] Constitutional Democracy in Crisis (Mark A. Graber, Sanford Levinson & Mark Tushnet eds., 2018).

[2] *See, e.g.*, Tom Ginsburg & Aziz Z. Huq, How to Save a Constitutional Democracy (2018).

[3] Mark Tushnet, The New Fourth Branch: Institutions for Protecting Constitutional Democracy 5 (2021).

[4] Ginsburg & Huq, *supra* note 2, at 240.

Yaniv Roznai, *We the Fourth Branch? The People as an Institution Protecting Democracy* In: *Redefining Comparative Constitutional Law*. Edited by: Vicki C. Jackson and Madhav Khosla, Oxford University Press. © Yaniv Roznai 2025.
DOI: 10.1093/9780191996344.003.0020

In the next section, the concept of fourth branch institutions is reviewed. The chapter then describes the civil protest movement against the judicial overhaul. It goes on to raise the idea of the people as an institution protecting democracy.

Fourth Branch: Institutions Protecting Democracy

In democratic regimes, the function of protecting democracy can be distributed between different institutions.[5] Tushnet shows how the South African Constitution, for example, identifies different institutions, such as the public protector, the state auditor, and the election commission as "institutions supporting constitutional democracy."[6] According to his definition, institutions protecting democracy are "institutions whose *specific* charge is to protect one or another dimension of democratic functioning, such as electoral fairness or the use of public funds for public purposes."[7] Electoral commissions, for example, aim to ensure that the electoral process is free and fair, and its results accurate. In his pioneering work, Tushnet explored the design features as well as the actual functions of such institutions protecting democracy, as well as the risks associated with their actions.[8]

In a somewhat similar vein, Tarunabh Khaitan recently claimed that fourth branch institutions can be best understood as guarantor institutions: "a tailor-made constitutional institution, vested with material as well as expressive capacities, whose function is to provide a credible and enduring guarantee to a specific non-self-enforcing constitutional norm (or any aspect thereof)."[9] Khaitan's framework encompasses electoral commissions, human rights commissions, central banks, probity bodies (such as anticorruption bodies), attorneys general, auditors general, and what Vicki Jackson terms "knowledge institutions" such as statistics bureaus and census boards, information commissioners, and the like.[10]

I do not here aim to glorify the ability of fourth branch institutions to protect democracy or to critically question this ability. Obviously, as Tushnet shows, there are success stories and failure stories, of fourth branch institutions.[11] What I wish

[5] Mark Tushnet, *Institutions Protecting Democracy: A Preliminary Inquiry*, 12 Law & Ethics Hum. Rts. 181, 182 (2018).

[6] *Id.* at 183, referring to S. Afr. Const. 1996, ch. 9.

[7] *Id.*

[8] *Id. See also* Mark Tushnet, *Institutions for Protecting Constitutional Democracy: An Analytic Framework, with Special Reference to Electoral Management Bodies*, 16 Asian J. Compar. L. S10 (2021); Mark Tushnet, *Institutions Protecting Constitutional Democracy: Some Conceptual and Methodological Preliminaries*, 70 Univ. Toronto L.J. 95 (2020); Rosalind Dixon & Mark Tushnet, *Democratic Constitutions, Poverty and Economic Inequality: Redress through the Fourth Branch Institutions?*, 51 Fed. L. Rev. 285 (2023).

[9] Tarunabh Khaitan, *Guarantor Institutions*, 16 Asian J. Compar. L. S40, S42 (2021).

[10] *Id. See* Vicki Jackson, *Knowledge Institutions in Constitutional Democracies: Preliminary Reflections*, 7 Can. J. Compar. & Contemp. L. 156 (2021).

[11] Tushnet, *supra* note 5, at 167–75.

to do is to raise the option of conceptualizing also "the people," when acting as an ad hoc massive and organized civil protest movement, with the aim to deal with a major offense of liberal democracy in order to block it as another, unique, type of fourth branch institution.

For Tushnet, institutions protecting democracy are all "public institutions with some degree of responsibility, usually indirect, to the electorate."[12] This is not true, almost by definition, of civil society organizations, although one could include them within the scope of the study by focusing on the legal arrangements—freedom of the press and freedom of association—that are used to preserve their ability to protect constitutional democracy."[13] Their study, Tushnet claimed, "would require examination of the ways in which and the degree to which actors within them are socialized to take preserving constitutional democracy as one of their goals."[14] In the next section I provide a relatively detailed account of events occurring in Israel in 2023 in order to show how the civil society movement managed to create sufficient power to slow down, and perhaps even to block, a significant and dangerous attempt to undermine the democratic order. The connection to institutions protecting democracy seems natural because the main goal of the civil protest movement was preserving Israel's democracy.

The People as an Institution Protecting Democracy: The 2023 Protest Movement and the Judicial Overhaul in Israel as a Case Study

Between 2018 and 2022, usually the period of a single government, Israel experienced a political crisis with five elections taking place. None of the prominent political figures involved managed to assemble a sufficiently robust coalition government capable of effectively governing the nation. This prolonged political instability (caused also by Benjamin Netanyahu's criminal indictment) concluded with Netanyahu, the leader of the Likud party, forming a new coalition in December 2022 which signified a dramatic shift to the right on the Israeli political spectrum, particularly in its religious composition.

Soon after the formation of the government, on January 4, 2023, Minister of Justice Yariv Levin announced in a special press conference "a judicial reform." In this speech, Levin outlined four pivotal topics of the reform: (1) "the Override Clause," which would grant the Knesset the authority to override Basic Laws and Supreme Court rulings; (2) restructuring the judicial selection committee in a manner that would provide the coalition the authority to appoint judges to the

12 TUSHNET, *supra* note 3, at 5.
13 *Id.*
14 *Id.*

Supreme Court and to other, lower, courts; (3) limiting judicial review, by removing courts' authority to hear petitions or appeals that challenge governmental decisions on ground claim of being "unreasonable," by limiting constitutional review only to the Supreme Court sitting *en banc* and striking down unconstitutional laws by a supermajority of 12 out of 15 judges, and removing courts' authority to review basic laws, shielding them from judicial review; (4) authorizing ministers to choose their own legal counsel, instead of appointment by independent committees and providing that legal advice of governmental lawyers will not be binding.[15] The coalition agreement between all parties stated that they will support the judicial reform. The implications of the so-called reform[16] were to weaken the judicial and the attorney general, precisely the two independent bodies that can block governmental power, thereby strengthening the already extremely strong executive and providing the coalition absolute powers of legislation, turning the government into an unlimited one. Even many of those who believe that reform of the judicial system is required[17] thought that this revolutionary reform went too far.

Criticized for its potential impact on the democratic character of the state, on separation of powers and checks and balances, the announcement led to protests on January 7 in Tel Aviv, attended by 20,000 people. The momentum carried into the following week. A few days later, on January 12, in an unusual speech delivered at the annual conference of the Israeli Association of Public Law, Supreme Court President Esther Hayut strongly criticized the proposed reform, describing it as an "unrestrained attack on the legal system" and accusing it of undermining judicial

[15] For a thorough analysis of the so-called judicial reform, *see* the group of articles all published in a special symposium of the 56 Israel Law Review 289–540 (2023): Iddo Porat, *Political Polarisation and the Constitutional Crisis in Israel*; Yaniv Roznai & Amichai Cohen, *Populist Constitutionalism and the Judicial Overhaul in Israel*; Tamar Hostovsky Brandes, *The Constitutional Overhaul and the West Bank: Is Israel's Constitutional Moment Occupied?*; Yaniv Roznai, Rosalind Dixon, & David E. Landau, *Judicial Reform or Abusive Constitutionalism in Israel*; Guy Lurie, *The Attempt to Capture the Courts in Israel*; Tom Ginsburg, *The Long Hand of Anti-Corruption: Israeli Judicial Reform in Comparative Perspective*; Mordechai Kremnitzer, *Releasing the Government from Acting Reasonably; or, the Government Says Goodbye to Reasonableness*; Manal Totry-Jubran, *Constitutionalising Israel's Constitutional System*; Gábor Halmai, *Is There a 'Constitutional Moment' in Israel and Hungary?*; David Kretzmer, *The "Constitutional Reform" and the Occupation*; Joshua Segev, *Reforming the Israeli High Court of Justice: Proposed Versus Desirable*; Daniel Friedmann, *Politics in Legal Disguise*; Ofra Bloch & Barak Medina, *The Two Revolutions of Israel's National Identity*; Yoav Dotan, *Israel's Constitutional Moment.*

[16] Since its proposal, I refused to call the reform a "reform" but rather a judicial overhaul or a revolutionary change, because its implications on the legal system were revolutionary; it was by no means a reform that keeps the constitutional framework intact. For a conceptualization of revolutionary constitutional change, *see* Gary J. Jacobsohn & Yaniv Roznai, Constitutional Revolution (2020). In a recent judgment the European Court of Human Rights also referred to "the so-called 'reform of the judiciary'" and not judicial reforms, as these were violations of rule of law. I thank Laurent Pech for highlighting this: Wałęsa v. Poland, App. No. 50849/21 (Nov. 23, 2023), https://hudoc.echr.coe.int/eng?i=001-229366.

[17] For such an argument *see, e.g.*, Yonatan Green, *The Peculiar Case of the Israeli Legal System*, 24 Federalist Soc'y Rev. (Sep. 1, 2023), https://fedsoc.org/fedsoc-review/the-peculiar-case-of-the-israeli-legal-system.

independence.[18] Attorney General Gali Baharav-Miara also expressed concerns in a comprehensive legal opinion, highlighting substantial problems related to the so-called reform: "Every one of the proposed arrangements raises substantial problems that go to the root of the principle of the separation of powers, judicial independence and the professionalism of the judicial branch, protection of individual rights, the rule of law, and the preservation of proper governance."[19] The "Brothers and Sisters in Arms" ("Achim Laneshek") organization, composed of reserve members from several Israeli Defense Force (IDF) units working together to stop the judicial overhaul and protect Israel's democracy due to concern that it might impact the IDF (for example by weakening the judicial or legal oversight of military actions), was founded around the same time. As the legislation was accelerated, thousands of former IDF soldiers, including reserves, pilots, special combatants, and individuals from various other units, joined in the space of weeks.[20]

On January 21, the protests expanded to major cities such as Haifa, Jerusalem, and again Tel Aviv, now with more than 130,000 participants. As the so-called reform gained rapid momentum on a weekly basis, the corresponding protest grew in parallel. A pivotal shift occurred on January 28 when the protesters relocated to Kaplan Junction, a central point at the entrance to Tel Aviv. During this period the Israeli Law Professors' Forum for Democracy was founded, comprising around 150 permanent faculty members from law faculties in Israeli academic institutions.[21] Concerned about the legal reform, they volunteered to give lectures, write position papers, record videos, and talk at rallies about how the reform will affect Israel's democracy.[22] Also in the legal field, in a response to the judicial overhaul, a group of private lawyers from the leading law firms in Israel—known as the "The Black Robes"—organized a massive billboard campaign against the "override clause" and various protests near the Tel Aviv Court. In addition to this group, the then chair of the Israeli Bar Association, Avi Himi, protested very vocally against the judicial overhaul, claiming that it would destroy Israel's democracy.

On February 8, MK Simcha Rothman, chair of the Knesset's Constitution, Law and Justice Committee announced his plans to vote swiftly on approval of the bill concerning the judicial selection committee for its first reading in the Knesset on February 13. In response, Brothers in Arms organized a three-day march to

[18] *See* Yaniv Roznai & Shani Shnitzer, *Navigating the Ship in Stormy Waters: President Esther Hayut and the Israeli Constitutional Crises 2018–2023* Int'l J. Const. L. (forthcoming).

[19] Jeremy Sharon, *Attorney General: Judicial Overhaul Plan "Would Give Government Unrestrained Power,"* Times of Israel (Feb. 2, 2023), https://www.timesofisrael.com/attorney-general-judicial-overhaul-plan-would-give-government-unrestrained-power.

[20] For further information, *see* Brothers and Sisters for Israel, https://www.brothersandsistersforisrael.org/.

[21] *See* Israeli Law Professors' Forum for Democracy, https://www.lawprofsforum.org/en.

[22] For an elaboration on the work of legal scholars against the judicial overhaul, *see* Ittai Bar-Siman-Tov, Tamar Hostovsky Brandes, Eliav Lieblich, Yaniv Roznai & Adam Shinar, *Scholactivism in the Service of Counter-Populism: The Case of the Constitutional Overhaul in Israel* Int'l J. Const. L. (forthcoming).

Jerusalem, involving influential figures such as former directors of the Mossad and retired generals, in an aim to create public pressure that might prevent such voting. The march ended in a mass demonstration in Jerusalem—held on the same day as a national general strike—outside the Knesset building during the voting. More than 100,000 people gathered in the demonstration. While the demonstration unfolded outside the Knesset, inside the Knesset's Constitution, Law and Justice Committee passed the amendment to "Basic-Law: The Judiciary" concerning changing the composition of the judicial selection committee. The changes were approved with nine votes in favor and seven against, and the bill was placed for vote at the plenary.

These events marked the rise of another important and unexpected movement—the Start Up protest. High-tech companies account for 25 percent of Israeli taxes and more than 50 percent of Israeli exports. The Start Up protest group claimed that the judicial overhaul would affect the economy, would put the right to property at risk, and would therefore affect investors. Protests began on January 24, in the form of a one-hour strike led by tech company executives. Within a month, it evolved from an initiative of individuals into an organized movement, with thousands of tech employees actively participating. On the day of the national strike, 300 Israeli high-tech companies allowed their employees to join the strike. By the end of February, more than 150,000 people were demonstrating in Tel Aviv, with thousands more participating across the country. During that period, a central headquarters was established to unite the majority of organizations protesting against the judicial overhaul.

The criticism went beyond the so-called reform's content to also take in the pace of the process. Fundamentally transforming the legal system should involve a deep and extended procedure, involving in-depth deliberations and learning, with broad public support. However, the Knesset Constitution, Law and Justice Committee debated the bill rapidly, excluded inputs from the Committee's legal counsel and ignored opinions of experts throughout the process. As a result, the opposition then chose to abstain from the Committee's debates.

On March 1, the Knesset's Constitution, Law and Justice Committee was scheduled to discuss and vote on the bill, which included an override clause and constrained the High Court's judicial review power. This led to a "national disruption day" with many large demonstrations and protests across the country throughout the day. Ultimately, after heated debates, the Committee approved the bill with the support of nine members as the opposition chose to boycott the vote. One week later, on March 9, the central headquarters declared a "day of resistance," involving actions such as blocking highways, protesting at Ben Gurion International Airport, and organizing a major demonstration in Tel Aviv. The protesters stated that the total number of participants across the nation was approximately 400,000.

On March 14, the bill easily cleared its first plenum vote of the Knesset by a margin of 61–52. In a special speech a day later, on March 15, President Isaac Herzog announced a compromise proposal for a judicial reform ("the people's directive").[23] Although President Herzog has no formal constitutional role in the process, he believed it necessary for him to intervene to stop the ongoing crisis. Faced with a divided nation and escalating tensions, the president engaged with individuals, scholars, and civil society organizations from diverse backgrounds to in order to bridge the gap between the opposing sides and navigate an end to Israel's crisis. However, President Herzog's proposal was rejected by the coalition only a few minutes after its announcement.[24]

On March 25, Minister of Defense Yoav Gallant publicly announced his opposition to the so-called reform, urging his coalition members to halt the proposed legislation, which he said could threaten Israel's security, and calling for negotiations between the ruling coalition and the opposition. In response, on March 26, Prime Minister Netanyahu announced Gallant's removal from office. This was a significant moment in the ongoing protests. Thousands of demonstrators filled the streets of Tel Aviv, Haifa, and Jerusalem, blocking main roads and igniting multiple fires on Tel Aviv highways. The protesters demanded Gallant's reinstatement and an end to the passage of the legislation. On March 27 the chairman of Israel's General Federation of Labour ("Histadrut"), Arnon Bar David, declared a general strike until Gallant was reinstated as Minister of Defense and demanded a halt to the legislative process. The chairman of the Israel's Airports Authority announced a strike and the Israel Medical Association followed suit. On March 27, President Herzog called for the legislation to be halted. In response to this growing public pressure, the legislation was put on hold, in order to try and reach a compromise. In addition, Gallant's dismissal did not come into effect, and he retained his position as Minister of Defense. The unprecedented public pressure succeeded in its aim. For the time being, at least.

On March 28, representatives from both the coalition and the opposition were appointed for negotiations at the president's residence. They were accompanied by legal experts.[25] The objective was to engage in in-depth discussions on key reform topics, seeking broader agreements. However, between March and May the negotiations started to falter, with the two sides unable to find common ground. The lack of trust between the parties was extremely acute and influenced the process. The fact that the bill concerning the judicial selection committee was still on the Knesset's agenda and was ready for a second and third vote at the plenary at any time only aggravated the situation, as the opposition feared it was negotiating with

[23] An English version of the proposal is available at https://www.mitve-haam.org/_files/ugd/f35a26_8eb0f820ae1b4d32bd178cc2b7cf4352.pdf. For a comparison between the government's proposal and the President's proposal, *see The People's Framework: Understanding President Herzog's Judicial Compromise Proposal*, Israel Policy Forum, https://israelpolicyforum.org/wp-content/uploads/2023/03/The-Peoples-Framework.pdf.

[24] For full disclosure, this author was one of the professional consultants of the President's team working on the proposal.

[25] For full disclosure, this author was one of the experts appointed by one of the opposition parties to participate in the negotiations.

a gun to its head. Throughout this period the protesters continued to demonstrate every Saturday night.

Two important elections took place in June. The first was the Israeli Bar Association election, which saw a record turnout: 50.8 percent of about 77,000 eligible voters. There were two main candidates: Efi Neve, who supported the coalition's so-called reform, and Amit Becher, an antijudicial reform candidate. Becher received 73 percent of the vote, against just 20 percent for Neve, and was chosen as the chairman of the Bar Association. This vote was a clear statement by the legal profession that it objects to the judicial overhaul. In response, a few days later the coalition promoted a bill that would eliminate the Bar's licensing authority, its power to sanction lawyers for misconduct, and its representations in the judicial selection committee.[26]

The second important election came when the Knesset voted for its representatives for the judicial selection committee: two out of nine members, with the custom that one member of Knesset is from the coalition and the other from the opposition. The Knesset indeed selected an opposition representative, Karine Elharrar, but failed to select a representative from the coalition, in a clear attempt to postpone the entire process. In response, the opposition announced that they would pause negotiations until such a representative had been selected. The coalition took advantage of this announcement and decided to continue and promote the so-called reform unilaterally—only this time, instead of attempting to enact the entire package in a quick "blitz," it would do so incrementally. In the language of the protest movement, this shift was "from the Hungarian Blitz to the Polish Salami." The coalition decided that the first salami slice would be to abolish the "reasonableness" standard, which it believed it would be the least contentious element in the so-called reform.[27]

Accordingly, on June 26, the Knesset's Constitution, Law and Justice Committee met to discuss the bill removing from the courts the authority to apply the "reasonableness" standard when reviewing decisions or actions of the Cabinet, the prime minister, or ministers. Accordingly, the protesters stepped up their demonstrations. On July 3, demonstrations unfolded place across the country, with people blocking high roads and the entrance to the airport. Commissioner of Police Yaakov "Kobi" Shabtai notified Tel Aviv police chief Amichai Eshed that he would be removed from his job and moved to a different position. Eshed announced his resignation, saying the removal was due to "political considerations" and that he had been asked by Minister of National Security Itamar Ben-Gvir to order police officers to handle those protesting against the judicial reform more forcefully but

[26] Michael Bachner, *Knesset Passes Preliminary Reading of Bill to Sap Bar Association of Key Powers*, Times of Israel (July 5, 2023), https://www.timesofisrael.com/knesset-passes-preliminary-reading-of-bill-to-sap-bar-association-of-key-powers/.

[27] Kremnitzer, *supra* note 15.

had refused. Following this resignation, thousands of protesters across the country spontaneously took to the streets.[28]

On July 19, more than 1,000 Air Force reservists, including 500 pilots, announced that they would stop their volunteer service. Similar announcements were made by the intelligence reserve and combat reserve. On July 22, 100 leaders from the secret service organizations in Israel, including the Mossad and the Israel Security Agency ("Shabak"), including former Chiefs of Staff and retired generals, sent a letter to Prime Minister Netanyahu calling for the suspension of the reform. They were concerned that the removal of the reasonable standard would affect the independence of important gatekeepers, would weaken judicial supervision on governmental decisions, and would leave them vulnerable to prosecution in the International Criminal Court.

Less than a month after the bill was brought for deliberation in the committee, on July 24, the Knesset voted on the part that removes the reasonableness standard from the judicial toolkit when it comes to decisions of the Cabinet and the ministers (in contrast with the unelected bureaucracy). On that day, thousands of protesters arrived in Jerusalem from Tel Aviv after a four-day march. Meanwhile, the opposition boycotted the third vote and the bill passed by a vote of 64–0, while thousands of protesters gathered in front of the Knesset. Former Supreme Court President Aharon Barak issued an exceptional statement stating that the reasonableness law will "damage the fundamental values of Israel as a Jewish and democratic state." In his view, "it threatens to undermine the rule of law, proper administration, the purity of morals in government, and the basic rights of every person in Israel."[29] The Israeli Business Forum, representing Israel's largest private sector companies, declared an impending strike, urging an immediate halt to the legislation.[30]

Various petitions were submitted to the High Court of Justice challenging the constitutionality of this law. But in this chapter I am interested not in the court's authority to review this constitutional amendment but in the public protest. It was an unprecedented collective action by the civil society and the public at large, unique both in its size—hundreds of thousands of protests every week—and in its endurance—the demonstrations persisted every week for 39 weeks in a row. They were halted only due to the horrifying October 7 massacre and the war that broke out in Gaza in response.

[28] Carrie Keller-Lynn & TOI Staff, *Thousands Take to the Streets, Block Roads after Tel Aviv Police Chief Steps Down*, Times of Israel (July 5, 2023), https://www.timesofisrael.com/thousands-take-to-the-streets-block-roads-after-tel-aviv-police-chief-steps-down/.

[29] Michael Starr, *Aharon Barak: Reasonableness Bill Will Damage Israel's Values*, The Jerusalem Post (July 23, 2023), https://www.jpost.com/israel-news/article-752083/.

[30] TOI Staff, *Business Forum, Tech Companies to Strike Ahead of Final Votes on Reasonableness Law*, Times of Israel (July 24, 2023), https://www.timesofisrael.com/business-forum-tech-companies-to-strike-ahead-of-final-votes-on-reasonableness-law/.

The People as a Fourth Branch?

Separation of powers is a basic idea within constitutional theory.[31] The principle of separation of powers, as described by Montesquieu in his *The Spirit of the Laws*, famously centered on three governmental branches: legislative power; executive power; and judicial power. This separation of powers was needed in order to prevent abuse of power, because "*c'est une expérience éternelle que tout homme qui a du pouvoir est porté à en abuser.*"[32] In order to prevent this abuse of power it would be necessary, according to Montesquieu, to organize the government in such a way that power would check power. In other words, this separation of governmental powers results in a power block.[33]

In a famous article entitled "The New Separation of Powers," Bruce Ackerman argues against exporting the American separation of powers system of an independently elected presidency to check and balance a popularly elected congress, but rather calls in favor of a "constrained parliamentarianism" model, in which a prime minister and his or her cabinet are authorized to remain in power as long as they can retain the support of a democratically elected chamber of deputies. Other independent institutions, including a constitutional court, must perform a checking function.[34]

These theories and models focus on *horizontal separation of powers* between different political actors and governmental branches. And likewise, other institutions supporting constitutional democracy presented earlier in the chapter, such as election commissions or ombudsmen, are horizontal institutions. I have elsewhere briefly argued that there is another type of separation of powers: a *vertical* one, between *the people and the government*. This separation of powers is the oldest but at the same time the newest one, recently flourishing in constitutional design.[35]

In traditional constitutional theory a distinction is made between *constituent power* and *constituted power*, formulated by Sieyès in his famous pamphlet "What Is the Third Estate?" on the eve of the French Revolution.[36] Constituent power is the power to create a constitution. Constituted power is a power created by the constitution. A constitution cannot constitute itself and it presupposes a

[31] For a comparative reconstruction *see* CHRISTOPH MOELLERS, THE THREE BRANCHES: A COMPARATIVE MODEL OF SEPARATION OF POWERS (2013).

[32] CHARLES LOUIS DE SECONDAT, BARÓN DE MONTESQUIEU, I DE L'ESPIRIT DES LOIS 162 (Gonzague Truce ed., 1961).

[33] *See, e.g.*, James T. Brand, *Montesquieu and the Separation of Powers*, 12 OR. L. REV. 175 (1933).

[34] Bruce Ackerman, *The New Separation of Powers*, 113 HARV. L. REV. 634 (2000). *Cf.* Clindy Skach, *The 'Newest' Separation of Powers*, 4 INT'L J. CONST. L. 93 (2007) (arguing that the constitutional model being imported by new democracies around the world is neither the constrained parliamentary model nor American Presidentialism model but rather semipresidentialism, most often associated with the French Fifth Republic).

[35] Yaniv Roznai, *The Newest-Oldest Separation of Powers*, 14 EUR. CONST. L. REV. 430 (2018).

[36] Emmanuel-Joseph Sieyès, *What Is the Third Estate?*, *in* POLITICAL WRITINGS 136 (Michael Sonenscher ed., 2003).

constitution-making power. This power cannot itself be constituted. Tushnet has written extensively on how the theory of constitution-making power should be conceptualized and comprehended.[37] This separation between constituent and constituted powers is the very first separation of powers, which is prior to the separation of constituted powers.[38] One method for the people to act as another blocking power or a "gatekeeper" is through various formal or informal direct participation mechanisms that provide citizens the tools and option to approve or reject constitution-making or constitutional reform proposals.[39] It can provide a check on the other governmental branches. As Andreas Auer stated, "the governing bodies, particularly government and parliament, have to accept the fact that the people . . . may make binding decisions they disapprove and dislike."[40] Indeed, when constitutional reforms reach the people for their consideration, they often vote with the government, but sometimes they vote against the government's proposals.[41]

Consider the following examples in which major constitutional reforms were rejected by the people: In 2005 Kenyans rejected a proposal for a new constitution that would have entrenched presidential powers, even though many government officials, including President Mwai Kibaki, had campaigned for its adoption.[42] In 2013 a slim majority of Irish voters rejected a proposal to abolish the Senate and reconstitute the legislature as a unicameral parliament.[43] In Italy in December 2016, voters overwhelmingly decided against a major constitutional reform that would have modified the Senate's structure, the constitutional status of the regions, and the confidence relationship between the government and parliament.[44] That same year, in Colombia, a majority of voters rejected a peace plan carefully negotiated by the political elites to end decades of civil war.[45] This trend seemed to represent "a rebuke to the governing elite."[46] This manifests the revival of the vertical separation

[37] *See, e.g.*, Mark Tushnet, *Constitution-Making: An Introduction*, 91 Tex. L. Rev. 1982 (1984); Mark Tushnet, *Peasants with Pitchforks, and Toilers with Twitter: Constitutional Revolutions and the Constituent Power*, 13 Int'l J. Const. L. 639 (2015); Mark Tushnet, *Amendment Theory and Constituent Power*, *in* Comparative Constitutional Theory 317 (Gary Jacobsohn and Miguel Schor eds., 2018).

[38] Andrew Arato, The Adventures of the Constituent Power 76 (2017).

[39] Zachary Elkins, Tom Ginsburg & Justin Blount, *The Citizen as Founder: Public Participation in Constitutional Approval*, 81 Temple L. Rev. 361, 367 (2008).

[40] Andreas Auer, *Editorial—The People Have Spoken: Abide? A Critical View of the EU's Dramatic Referendum (In)experience*, 12 Eur. Const. L. Rev. 397, 402 (2016).

[41] *See* Matt Qvortrup, *Western Europe*, *in* Referendums Around the World 19 (Matt Qvortrup ed., 2018).

[42] Catherine O'Regan, *The Political Paradox of African Constitutionalism Revisited: Kenya's BBI Case* (this volume).

[43] John Fitzgibbon, *Ireland's Decision to Retain the Seanad Is Not the End of the Country's Political Reform Process*, LSE Eur. Pol. & Pol'y (EUROPP) Blog (Oct. 9, 2013).

[44] Gianfranco Pasquino & Marco Valbruzzi, *Italy Says No: The 2016 Constitutional Referendum and Its Consequences*, 22 J. Mod. Italian Stud. 145 (2017).

[45] Aila M. Matanock & Miguel García-Sánchez, *The Colombian Paradox: Peace Processes, Elite Divisions & Popular Plebiscites*, 146 Daedalus 152 (2017).

[46] *Id.*

of powers between constituent and constituted powers, placing the people themselves as a check on the power of governments. As Qvortrup writes, referendums have tended to have the effect of "a democratic safeguard" against overzealous politicians and hasty legislation.[47]

A second method for the people to act as a check on governmental power, as another blocking mechanism, is through the "right to resist and protest" movement, as we have seen in Israel. While the future of the so-called judicial reform is still unclear, what seems to be clear is that the massive public protests and civil resistance managed to block, or at least delay, vast parts of the government's judicial overhaul plan. On its facts, this is remarkable. The most rightwing homogeneous coalition Israel has ever had possessed a clear majority—64 out of 120 members of the Knesset—and in theory could have easily enacted the judicial overhaul. If not for the protest movement, the judicial overhaul would have been enacted swiftly, especially considering the extremely weak mechanisms of checks and balances in the Israeli system: no bicameralism; no president with veto power; no regional element in the elections; a unitary system and not a federal one in which a vertical separation of powers exists; neither part of a supranational institution such as the EU nor subordinated to a supranational tribunal such as the European Court of Human Rights, as are members to the European Convention on Human Rights.[48] Furthermore, there is a relatively small and weak legislature, controlled by the relatively strong and large executive. And other fourth branch institutions are weak: the state comptroller is a relatively weak institution without real teeth, there is no human rights ombudsman, and the central elections committee is politically dominated. The only strong institutions are the Supreme Court and the Attorney General, which is precisely why the judicial reform targeted these two institutions. With the Knesset being controlled by the executive, there are hardly any political checks on governmental power. And in this case, the people acted as a fourth branch—an institution, aside from the judiciary, that managed to function as a speed bump and a stop sign vis-à-vis a populist constitutional project, and protected democracy.

True, the protest movement did not succeed in completely stopping the judicial overhaul; after all, part of the reform was enacted. However, consider events in late March 2023, when the coalition negotiated the reform with the opposition, as equals, under the auspices of the President: This exceptional political event was enabled only thanks to the protest movement. The opposition itself had no real power without the public protest. At the time of the writing of this chapter, almost a year has passed since the new government announced its judicial overhaul but failed, eventually, in promoting it in its entirety. The civil protest, which made the national flag its symbol (implying that this protest protects the identity of the

[47] *See* Matt Qvortrup, *Two Hundred Years of Referendums*, *in* Qvortrup, *supra* note 41, at 263.
[48] *See* Roznai & Cohen, *supra* note 15, at 18.

state), had huge success. It managed to convince a large percentage of the public of why the so-called reform was objectionable, as opinion polls consistently showed. And, as aforementioned, it also had the support of trade unions, business leaders, leading academics, and—more critically—thousands of military reservists, including fighter pilots, who threatened to refuse to volunteer for military service.

It is important to note that the civil protest movement included many different groups with diverse aims; some groups aimed to promote various democratic values such as gender equality, ending the military occupation, or changing the religious status quo in Israel. However, the main and general claim of the protest movement, and the reason why the protest managed to remain all-inclusive and broad, was to protect democracy. In that respect, it was portraying itself as a conservative movement: it was not necessarily, at least in the early stages of the protest, about *promoting* Israel's democracy but about *protecting* it against what was perceived as a significant threat to the democratic order.

The right to resist is nowadays recognized in many constitutional documents.[49] For example, Article 20(4) of the German Basic Law anchors the "Right of resistance" and provides that "All Germans shall have the right to resist any person seeking to abolish this constitutional order if no other remedy is available."[50] This provision, Tushnet correctly notes, complements the eternity clauses (Article 79(3)).[51] The fundamental constitutional values of the state are protected by formal unamendability. If the constitution-amender violates this unamendability, the court can block the constitutional reform by striking it down as unconstitutional. But apart from the judiciary, also the people themselves—if no other remedy is available—have the right to resist the abolishment of the constitutional order, and so protect the democratic order. Interestingly, this amendment did not appear in the original Basic Law of 1949 but was inserted as an amendment in 1968 as a counterweight to constitutional amendments granting the government extensive emergency powers.[52]

Tom Daly has elaborated on how the citizen can function as "democracy-defending," not only through rights of resistance but also through constitutionalizing civic education and citizens' assemblies.[53] As for civic education, Daly writes:

> If the right of resistance is a measure of last resort . . . an alternative approach is the preventive measure of ensuring adequate civic education, which . . . can arm the citizens with enough knowledge to appreciate the fundamental values of the

[49] *See, e.g.*, Tom Ginsburg, Daniel Lansberg-Rodriguez & Mila Versteeg, *When to Overthrow Your Government: The Right to Resist in the World's Constitutions*, 60 U.C.L.A. L. Rev. 1184 (2013).

[50] Art. 20(4), Basic Law for the Federal Republic of Germany.

[51] Tushnet, *Constitution-Making: An Introduction*, *supra* note 37, at 2005.

[52] Georg Gesk, *Right to Resistance and Terrorism—the Example of Germany*, 13 German. L.J. 1075, 1078 (2012).

[53] Tom Gerals Daly, *Designing The Democracy-Defending Citizen*, 6 Const. Stud. 189 (2020).

> democratic state, discern the falsity in the siren song of the authoritarian populist, and identify unconstitutional . . . threats against the system.[54]

In order for citizens to act as democracy-defenders they must have some kind of constitutional education, some constitutional literacy.

Constitutional literacy is of great importance to sustaining constitutional democracy.[55] Also in that respect, the Israeli case provides a very interesting illustration. In order to counter the populist judicial overhaul and the often abusive borrowing rhetoric behind it, legal scholars played a vital role in providing reliable information on the judicial system, on case law and on comparative law, through accessible means, such as videos, op-eds, short papers, and speeches in rallies and in homes, to provide the greater public with much more constitutional knowledge regarding what they are protesting about and why.[56] Liora Lazarus correctly notes that

> [t]he fight to stem the tide of authoritarianism depends on establishing a defense of the rule of law which has real purchase on the public imagination. This narrative must be capable of persuading the broader public of the essential value of constitutionalism. If we fail to establish this counter-narrative, liberal democracy as a whole is threatened.[57]

The Israeli protest against the judicial overhaul succeeded in providing such a narrative.

The main claim I wish to make in this chapter, therefore, is that the people themselves, when acting collectively, are another type of *branch*, which is vertically separated from governmental-instituted organs and which may be regarded as an institution protecting democracy that can block or slow attempts by populist governments to undermine the democratic order. Constitutional regimes organize all society's fundamental political institutions.[58] "The people" may be regarded as another type of institution.[59] Of course, "the people" is very different in many aspects

[54] *Id.* 202. On civic education and constitutional design, *see also* Mark Tushnet, *Constitutional Design as if Civic Education Mattered*, 41 Soc. Phil. 210 (2010).

[55] Maartje De Visser & Brian Christopher Jones, *Unpacking Constitutional Literacy* 13 Glob. Constitutionalism 1 (2023); Vicki C. Jackson, *Law Schools and Civic Education*, AALSNews (Fall 2019), https://www.aals.org/about/publications/newsletters/aals-news-fall-2019/law-schools-and-civic-education/.

[56] Bar-Siman-Tov, Brandes, Lieblich, Roznai & Shinar, *supra* note 22.

[57] Liora Lazarus, *Brexit in the Supreme Court: When Populists Attack the Rule of Law, Everyone Loses*, The Conversation (Sept. 27, 2019), https://theconversation.com/brexit-in-the-supreme-court-when-populists-attack-the-rule-of-law-everyone-loses-124302?fbclid=IwAR2GsL_g3HozjmRNv7elL-efq9Tft8K7dL_RE4-merzceWcXA7vjb8ob28s.

[58] Mark Tushnet, *Foreword: The New Constitutional Order and the Chastening of Constitutional Aspiration*, 113 Harv. L. Rev. 29, 36 (1999).

[59] There is an old tradition of considering the people of Rome as an institution—*populus Romanus*. *See* Tim Cornell, *Populues, in* Oxford Classical Dictionary (2016), https://oxfordre.com/classics/display/10.1093/acrefore/9780199381135.001.0001/acrefore-9780199381135-e-5248. When the people are regulated by the constitution—for example, for a referendum—they should be regarded as a

from what Tushnet regards as institutions protecting democracy or from what Khaitan describes as guarantor institutions. In contrast with fourth branch institutions, the people neither have special expertise nor are accountable to any actors.[60] They are, however, independent, at least when it comes to independence from the ruling party or coalition. Yet, being dependent upon fundraising, the people are not independent from economic influence by other financial actors. So, there is a great risk of manipulation. However, those who care about democracy must stand up for its protection. Protecting democratic values cannot be left only to the courts; it must also be done in the streets.[61] In that respect this idea also corresponds with Tushnet's general approach, urging the people themselves to take responsibility for protecting their liberties and the constitution and not rely solely on the judiciary.[62]

Conclusion

In a *Guardian* article about the Israeli protests against the judicial overhaul, Jonathan Freedland wrote: "everyone who cares about democracy, including those who are distant from Israel, should desperately want those protesters to succeed. We need them to win."[63] We need them to win because this will be an optimistic sign that people can object against populist governments and counter populist constitutional projects. And if in Israel, with this unprecedented protest movement, the people do not win, then it would be hard to see how other, smaller and less determined protests will prevail.

Without overly romanticizing it, I think that the Israeli case study shows that a collaborative and coordinated effort by large segments of the society allows the people themselves to act an institution protecting democracy. On November 18, 2023 the John McCain Prize was awarded to "the People of Israel." The Prize was accepted by a representative of the abovementioned Achim Laneshek, the non-governmental organization of reserve men and women from units in the Israeli Defense Forces which was founded to protest against the judicial overhaul but, since the October 7 terrorist attack, has focused its activities on providing aid and relief to many communities all over Israel. "Members of Achim Laneshek,"

constitutional organ. *See* Yaniv Roznai, *We the Limited People? On the People as a Constitutional Organ in Constitutional Amendments*, 110 Sup. Ct. L. Rev. 103 (2023).

60 Khaitan, *supra* note 9, at S44.

61 Julian Scholtes, *The Complacency of Legality: Constitutionalist Vulnerabilities to Populist Constituent Power*, 20 German L.J. 351 (2019).

62 Mark Tushnet, Taking the Constitution Away from the Courts (2000).

63 Jonathan Freedland, *Israelis' Defiance of Netanyahu Holds a Lesson for Anyone Who Cares about Democracy*, The Guardian (July 28, 2023), https://www.theguardian.com/commentisfree/2023/jul/28/israelis-benjamin-netanyahu-democracy-protests-donald-trump?CMP=Share_AndroidApp_Other.

the press release states, "have gone from demonstrating for democracy in the streets to demonstrating their commitment to democracy by mobilizing to assist the country's fight against terrorism." Eyal Nave, the representative from Achim Laneshek, said: "Democracy is fragile. It requires constant vigilance and attention. We are a team of action so when the people of Israel needed us the most, we answered the call."[64] This was an institution protecting democracy.

Tushnet writes that "[a] nation with enough institutions supporting constitutional democracy might be able to protect against specific threats as they arise."[65] In Israel there was a specific threat but not enough institutions supporting democracy, and this is when the people came to play a significant role. The unprecedented and unexpected protest movement was especially important in light of the relatively weak political mechanisms of checks and balances in the Israeli system. It is true that there is a strong and independent Supreme Court in Israel. But the court can do only so much. Alexander Hamilton famously wrote that "[t]he judiciary . . . has no influence over either the sword or the purse."[66] Interestingly, in the Israel case, the two most influential bodies in the protest movement were Achim Laneshek and the Start Up protest, two bodies that represent, in many ways, the sword and the purse.[67] Indeed, the Israeli case demonstrates how "people acting in and through civil society's institutions might effectively influence and constrain the government."[68]

Which brings me to a word of caution for comparative constitutional law. Because of the dominance of these two bodies in public life in Israel—the high-tech industry being so dominant for the economy, and the military reserves playing such an important role in society—their involvement in the protest movement was significant in ways that could make Israel a unique case. It might be difficult to draw analogies for countries without compulsory enlistment and whose economies do not depend so much on a particular industry.

To conclude, if Frank Vibert labeled administrative institutions protecting democracy as "the rise of the unelected,"[69] in this chapter I wish to emphasize "the rise of the people" as the old-new power that can protect democracy. Tushnet is accurate in his instinct that institutions protecting democracy "is an interesting and useful one for studying constitutional structures comparatively."[70] I believe that the role of the people themselves in protecting democracy is an important

[64] The HFX John McCain Prize for Leadership in Public Service Presented to The People of Israel, Nov. 18, 2023, https://halifaxtheforum.org/press/the-hfx-john-mccain-prize-for-leadership-in-public-service-presented-to-the-people-of-israel/

[65] Tushnet, *supra* note 3, at 22.

[66] Federalist No. 78.

[67] I thank Ronit Levine-Schnur, the founder and chair of the Israeli Law Professors Forum for Democracy, for providing this important observation.

[68] Mark Tushnet, *The Constitution of Civil Society*, 75 Chi.-Kent L. Rev. 379, 412 (2000).

[69] Frank Vibrent, The Rise of the Unelected: Democracy and The New Separation of Powers (2007).

[70] Tushnet, *supra* note 3, at 201.

and interesting inquiry, both theoretically and comparatively, and I hope that the Israeli case can provide a useful starting point for future inquiries.

I cannot conclude this chapter without thanking Mark Tushnet, who has been a great source of inspiration for me and for many others in the field. We all owe Professor Tushnet a great deal, and for this we say: Thank you.

21

Constitutional Design and Political Parties

Sujit Choudhry[*]

Introduction

In *Why the Constitution Matters*, Mark Tushnet asserts that "the Constitution matters because political parties matter."[1] But what exactly does Mark mean? As he observes, one of the striking features of the American constitution is that "no matter how hard you look, you're not going to find anything about political parties in the Constitution, much less anything about internal party structures."[2] The reason is the Framers' strong aversion to "factions" of self-interested politicians who would fight over the spoils of power as opposed to pursuing the broader public interest. Nevertheless, Mark argues that "there's some connection between the Constitution and political parties even though they aren't mentioned"—specifically, "federalism, the presidency, and the First Amendment."[3] Federalism provided the institutional platform for the rise of national political parties, which were historically coalitions of state and metropolitan political parties—although the incentive to organize national parties increased with growing federal power. The president can uniquely project a unifying ideology for a party. Finally, the First Amendment protects internal party organization from government regulation and has profoundly affected the law of political finance.

To be sure, as Franita Tolson argues, the effect and perhaps the purpose of the 12th Amendment was to spur the creation of political parties, by requiring the president and vice-president to be presented together.[4] Nevertheless, as a general matter, Mark's observation holds. I want to use it as a springboard for comparative investigation. The *absence* of political parties from the American constitution stands in stark contrast to their *prevalence* in constitutions across the world. The terms "political party" or "political parties" appear in 155 of 193 constitutions currently in force.[5] Other constitutional provisions that refer to fractions of legislatures or to leaders of the opposition also entrench aspects of political party systems.

* I thank Adem Abebe, Joel Bakan, Sumit Bisarya, Sam Issacharoff, Vicki Jackson, Madhav Khosla, Rick Pildes, and Kimana Zulueta-Fuelscher for helpful comments.

1 Mark Tushnet, Why the Constitution Matters 13 (2010).

2 *Id.* at 14.

3 *Id.* at 32.

4 Franita Tolson, *The "Independent" State Legislature Theory*, 10 Tex. A&M L. Rev. 549.

5 This data is from the Constitute Project, www.constituteproject.org (last accessed Nov. 25, 2023).

Sujit Choudhry, *Constitutional Design and Political Parties* In: *Redefining Comparative Constitutional Law.* Edited by: Vicki C. Jackson and Madhav Khosla, Oxford University Press. © Sujit Choudhry 2025.
DOI: 10.1093/9780191996344.003.0021

Nevertheless, political parties have attracted minimal attention in the literature on constitutional design.[6] Moreover, in the clutch of recent books on democratic decline and populism, Sam Issacharoff stands alone in devoting sustained attention to the role of political parties, notwithstanding that the breakdown of party systems has enabled takeovers of political parties by populist outsiders, as Levitsky and Ziblatt argue.[7] To paraphrase Nancy Rosenblum, political parties are the orphans of comparative constitutional law.[8]

In this chapter, I taxonomize constitutional provisions that reference political parties thematically according to their function. A focus on constitutional texts has obvious limitations. The wording of constitutional texts says nothing about their interpretation. Constitutional texts may be parchment barriers that are ignored. These provisions must be implemented through detailed regulatory schemes often overseen by specialist institutions such as "fourth branch" electoral management bodies.[9]

Nonetheless, a study of constitutional texts can pay dividends. Constitutions have both *regulative* and *constitutive* functions.[10] Constitutions are *regulative* by conferring legal status, rights, and powers on individuals and collectivities, creating institutions and setting out rules regarding their composition and decisionmaking procedures, organizing power vertically and horizontally, and setting limits on institutional power. But these particulars also *constitute* a vision of "constitutional morality" that provides an overarching account for these specific choices in constitutional design, as Madhav Khosla has explained in the context of India.[11]

This way of thinking about constitutions raises two questions which I explore in this chapter. How do constitutions rely on political parties to discharge their regulative function? Can we abstract away from the details of constitutional design to develop a constitutive account of the role of political parties in constitutional democracies?

[6] Exceptions include: Daryl J. Levinson & Richard H. Pildes, *Separation of Parties, Not Powers*, 119 HARV. L. REV. 2312 (2005–06); Sujit Choudhry, *"He Had a Mandate": The South African Constitutional Court and the African National Congress in a Dominant Party Democracy*, 2 CONST. CT. REV. 1 (2009); Richard Pildes, *Political Parties and Constitutionalism*, *in* COMPARATIVE CONSTITUTIONAL LAW 254–64 (Tom Ginsburg & Rosalind Dixon eds., 2011); Tarunabh Khaitan, *Political Parties in Constitutional Theory*, 73 CURRENT LEGAL PROBS. 89 (2020); Tom Daly & Brian Christopher Jones, *Parties versus Democracy: Addressing Today's Political Party Threats to Democratic Rule*, 18 INT'L J. CONST. L. 509 (2020); Stephen Gardbaum, *Comparative Political Process Theory*, 18 INT'L J. CONST. L. 1429 (2020).

[7] STEVEN LEVITSKY & DANIEL ZIBLATT, HOW DEMOCRACIES DIE (2018); SAM ISSACHAROFF, DEMOCRACY UNMOORED: POPULISM AND THE CORRUPTION OF POPULAR SOVEREIGNTY (2023).

[8] NANCY ROSENBLUM, ON THE SIDE OF THE ANGELS: AN APPRECIATION OF PARTIES AND PARTISANSHIP 1 (2008).

[9] *Constitutional Democracy and Electoral Commissions: A Reflection from Asia* (Symposium Issue), 16 Supp. S1 ASIAN J. COMPAR. L. S1 (2021).

[10] Sujit Choudhry, *Group Rights*, *in* OXFORD HANDBOOK OF COMPARATIVE CONSTITUTIONAL LAW 1099–23 (Michel Rosenfeld & Andras Sajó eds., 2012).

[11] MADHAV KHOSLA, INDIA'S FOUNDING MOMENT: THE CONSTITUTION OF A MOST SURPRISING DEMOCRACY (2020).

Political Parties and Constitutional Design: A Taxonomy

As Ingrid van Biezen has explained, in the 20th century the movement to adopt constitutional provisions in relation to political parties can be traced to the new postauthoritarian constitutions of Italy (1947) and Germany (1949).[12] Both Germany and Italy had been one-party states, whose governing parties had come to power by competing in electoral politics, capturing the state from within, and ending electoral competition. Their new constitutions entrenched commitments to multiparty democracy that were designed to prevent democratic backsliding from occurring again.

Constitutional provisions that refer to political parties have broadened in scope and fall into six categories: (a) basic function; (b) the right to form political parties; (c) militant democracy; (d) access to public resources; (e) legislative design; and (f) the separation of party and state. In this section, I provide an overview of constitutional provisions in each category.

Basic Function

Constitutions describe the basic role of political parties in a constitutional system. There are two major models, which use different languages to describe that role: the German model and the French one.

Article 21(1) of the German *Grundgesetz* provides: "Political parties shall participate in the formation of the political will of the people." Other constitutions that link political parties to the "political will" include the postauthoritarian constitutions of Spain (Art. 6) and South Korea (Art. 8(2)). By contrast, Article 4 of the French Constitution provides: "Political parties and groups shall contribute to the exercise of suffrage." This formulation has been adopted widely across Francophone Africa (e.g. Benin, Art. 5).

There may be little difference between describing the role of political parties in terms of "political will" or of the "exercise of suffrage." Both convey the fundamental idea that political parties are constituent institutions of constitutional democracy, by serving as mechanisms through which the political opinions of individual citizens are ascertained, consolidated, and formed, and then expressed in political institutions through the collective political process of elections. These provisions update and extend an older set of constitutional provisions that define the basic institutions of the state as the executive, the legislature, and the judiciary, and which set out their core functions. Both the German and French models elevate political parties to the constitutional plane, and firmly establish their status as

[12] Ingrid van Biezen, *Models of Party Democracy: Patterns of Party Regulation in Post-War European Constitutions*, 4 Eur. Pol. Sci. Rev. 327 (2012).

necessary institutions of constitutional democracy, as opposed to contingent features of political practice.

But these provisions also presuppose that political parties are *unlike* the executive, legislature, and judiciary. As Jan-Werner Müller has explained, political parties are intermediary institutions, because they occupy a space *between* the people and the state and are distinct from both.[13] They are created by citizens, to reflect their interests, and to mobilize them politically to change policies and laws. In this respect, they are like institutions of civil society, such as unions and organized religion, that allow individuals to formulate joint positions and act collectively and *challenge* state power. But the distinctive purpose of a political party is to elect public officials who *wield* state power within public institutions under public law. Political parties are therefore like public institutions. These provisions also convey that political parties are instruments for the people, *on whose behalf* they coordinate public control of elected institutions and state functions. They also presuppose that political parties are institutions that exist for democratic purposes and are constrained by that purpose.

Finally, these provisions impliedly entrench multiparty democracy, and hence, political competition, because they refer to political *parties* in the plural. These provisions are particularly important in transitional contexts, where the previous regime was undemocratic and multiparty democracy is a radical break from the past. The principal enforcement mechanism may be the public, not the courts. These provisions can serve as focal points for political mobilization by citizens to defend the very idea of multiparty democracy against a governing political party trying to establish its dominance by clearly stating a basic feature of the constitutional order.

The Right to Form Political Parties

Bills of rights create the permissive legal environment for the creation of political parties in the manner of the American constitution. The liberal freedoms of expression, association, and assembly together require the negative toleration of political parties by the state. Political parties are products of the joint activity of individuals to associate, assemble, and engage in political expression collectively.

A constitutional alternative is to expressly entrench the right to form political parties, to put the existence of this right beyond doubt. Once again, this may be particularly useful in a transitional context, where multiparty democracy must be established or renewed after a period of civil war and/or autocracy. Many constitutions do so, in one of two ways.

[13] Jan-Werner Müller, *Democracy's Critical Infrastructure: Rethinking Intermediary Powers*, 47 Phil. & Soc. Criticism 269 (2021).

Constitutions may expressly guarantee the right to form and belong to political parties, by including such a right as an illustrative example of the scope of a generic right to freedoms of assembly and association. For example, Article 21 of the Barbados Constitution provides that "no person shall be hindered in the enjoyment of his freedom of assembly and association, that is to say, his right to assemble freely and associate with other persons and in particular to form or belong to political parties or to form or belong to trade unions or other associations for the protection of his interests."

Such formulations do not spell out precisely what activities individuals can engage in once they have formed political parties. Disagreements would have to be settled by constitutional interpretation. There is considerable value in communicating to citizens in a transitional context what political parties can do. The second approach addresses this concern, by entrenching a separate right to form political parties and specifying their protected activities. The leading example is South Africa, where Article 19(1) guarantees the right "to form a political party" and also entrenches the rights "to participate in the activities of" a political party—a guarantee of internal party democracy (discussed further below)—to "recruit members for" a political party, and "to campaign for a political party or cause."

Militant Democracy

Karl Loewenstein first developed the concept of "militant democracy" based on his diagnosis of the Nazis' rise to power in Weimar.[14] The Nazis formed a political party, contested elections in which they fielded candidates, took up their seats in the Reichstag, participated in the legislative process, and formed the government through a constitutional mechanism at the invitation of the president, before seizing power unconstitutionally.

Militant democracy is a set of constitutional techniques to constrain the potential threat posed by political parties to constitutional democracy from within. The leading example is Article 21(2) of Germany's *Grundgesetz*, which provides: "Parties that, by reason of their aims or the behaviour of their adherents, seek to undermine or abolish the free democratic basic order or to endanger the existence of the Federal Republic of Germany shall be unconstitutional. The Federal Constitutional Court shall rule on the question of unconstitutionality."

Article 21(2) provides that a party may be unconstitutional either because of its *ideology* or its *activities*. It applies not just to parties but also to their *adherents*, preventing party leaders from disavowing the anticonstitutional conduct of party members. It protects "the free democratic basic order," which has been interpreted

[14] Karl Loewenstein, *Militant Democracy and Fundamental Rights*, 31 Am. Pol. Sci. Rev. 417 (1937).

to include the inviolability of human dignity (Art. 1), and democracy, federalism, the separation of powers, and constitutional supremacy (Art. 20). Finally, it vests in the Federal Constitutional Court the legal power to determine whether parties are unconstitutional.

Other subsections of Article 21 add more details. Article 21(1) mandates that parties' "internal organization . . . conform to democratic principles." Finally, Articles 21(3) and (4) establish two consequences for an unconstitutional party—loss of state financing or dissolution.

Article 21 has inspired militant democracy provisions globally. Many provisions concern the ideology and activities of political parties. Article 6 of the Constitution of Croatia provides, for example, that "[p]olitical parties which by their programs or violent activities aim to demolish the free democratic order endanger the existence of the Republic of Croatia are unconstitutional."

But many militant democracy provisions go further than Article 21(2) and specifically prohibit political parties that aim to use violence and/or use it. An example is the Georgian constitution, where Article 23(3) provides: "The establishment and activity of a political party that aims to overthrow or forcibly change the constitutional order of Georgia . . . shall be inadmissible." Some countries prohibit parties from having paramilitary wings. For example, Article 91(2)(c) of the Kenyan constitution provides: "A political party shall not . . . establish or maintain a paramilitary force, militia or similar organisation." Constitutions may contain broadly worded bans on any paramilitary organizations which encompass those operated by political parties. For example, Article 42 of the Constitution of Paraguay provides: "Secret associations and those of a paramilitary character are prohibited."

These provisions are motivated by historical experiences where political actors turned to violence and/or had armed military wings. The contexts vary. A constitution may be part of a post-civil war settlement, in which opposition forces agree to lay down arms and compete by creating political parties and contesting elections (e.g., Mozambique). Another scenario is a transition from military rule, to prevent the risk that old regime elements establish a paramilitary organization drawn from former military personnel, especially where the regime operated extralegally (e.g., Paraguay). These provisions also reinforce the state's monopoly on force and support constitutional provisions regarding civil–military relations, including civilian control and oversight of the military.[15]

Constitutions now employ militant democracy provisions for two sets of purposes beyond the protection of constitutional democracy from antidemocratic parties and violent overthrow. First, militant democracy provisions often ban parties which organize or promote hatred, based on race, region, religion, tribe, ethnicity, and/or language. These provisions are found in diverse societies in

[15] SECURITY SECTOR REFORM IN CONSTITUTIONAL TRANSITIONS (Zoltan Barany, Sumit Bisarya, Sujit Choudhry & Richard Stacey, eds., 2019).

which these differences have served as the basis of political mobilization. These provisions fall into two subcategories. Some constitutions prohibit political parties formed based on race, region, religion, tribe, ethnicity, and/or language. For example, Algeria's constitution (Art. 57) provides that political parties "may not be founded on a religious, linguistic, ethnic, gender, corporatist or regional basis." Others prohibit parties that promote hatred and/or division as opposed to those organized on that basis, such as Albania's constitution, where Article 9 prohibits parties "that incite and support racial, religious, regional or ethnic hatred." Article 91(2)(a) of Kenya's constitution combines both strategies: "[a] political party shall not . . . be founded on a religious, linguistic, racial, ethnic, gender or regional basis or seek to engage in advocacy of hatred on any such basis." The targeted political parties may seek to advance the interests of a specific group, a majority or a minority. They are not necessarily antidemocratic, but may be. A majority party may seek to make the state an ethnocracy or theocracy, whereas a minority may seek power-sharing, autonomy, and/or secession.

Second, militant democracy provisions ban political parties whose programs would undermine national unity, national sovereignty, and/or territorial integrity. This responds specifically to secessionist mobilization by minorities, which may be irredentist and advocate accession to an ethnic kin state. A well-known example is Article 68 of Turkey's constitution:

> The statutes and programs, as well as the activities of political parties shall not be contrary to the independence of the State, its indivisible integrity with its territory and nation, human rights, the principles of equality and rule of law, sovereignty of the nation, the principles of the democratic and secular republic; they shall not aim to promote or establish class or group dictatorship or dictatorship of any kind, nor shall they incite citizens to crime.

The Constitutional Court of Turkey has interpreted Article 68 to ban Kurdish political parties advocating for federalism and/or secession.[16]

In addition, militant democracy provisions are now not just *negative* (what a political party cannot stand for or do) but *positive* (what a political party must stand for and achieve). Of note are "national character" provisions in many African constitutions, requiring political parties to operate across the state as a whole and not represent a region or ethnic group. Such provisions do not relate to parties' goals or conduct but rely on the premise that membership determines both. These provisions trace their origins to the "federal character" requirements in Article 223(1)(b) of the Nigerian constitution for the leadership of political parties: "The constitution and rules of a political party shall [. . .] ensure that the members of the

[16] Ödül Celep, *The Political Causes of Party Closures in Turkey*, 67 Parliamentary Affs. 371 (2014).

executive committee or other governing body of the political party reflect the federal character of Nigeria."

The change of terminology, from *federal* in the Nigerian constitution to *national* in other constitutions, reflects the application of this idea in nonfederal states, where political cleavages may be territorial or nonterritorial.[17] Moreover, whereas the Nigerian provision applies to party leadership, the national character requirement applies to parties themselves. The goal is to limit political competition to national parties that appeal across ethnic lines and aim to govern through a multi-intraparty or interparty ethnic coalition. This idea migrated first from Nigeria to other countries in Anglophone Africa (e.g. Constitution of Ghana, Art. 55(4)), and then spread to Lusophone Africa (e.g. Constitution of Angola, Art. 17(2)(a)) and Francophone Africa (Constitution of Burundi, Art. 78) in post-civil war contexts.

Now I turn to *internal party democracy*, which furthers a number of goals: A democratically governed party is less likely to become dominated by a single person or clique, and therefore poses less of a threat of autocracy if it wins power; internal party democracy habituates party members in the practice of debate and compromise, preparing them to participate in democratic politics; and internal party democracy helps ensure that party elites remain responsive and accountable to their political supporters.

Provisions on internal party democracy are far less common than those governing a party's goals and activities, likely reflecting a view that party autonomy should not be encroached upon by the state because of the risk of incumbent entrenchment by a governing party. Moreover, most provisions are generic, like Germany's Article 21(1). For example, Article 269(4)(a) of Nepal's constitution provides: "The constitution and rules of the political party should be democratic." A handful of constitutions take a different approach and authorize legislatures to enact laws to establish internal party democracy, such as Article 228 of Nigeria's constitution.

An important constitutional question is which institutions have the power to initiate legal proceedings to determine that political party is unconstitutional and have the power to make that decision. In Germany, the Constitutional Court rules on constitutionality, but the power to initiate such proceedings is vested by legislation in the State Prosecutor, who is politically independent of the political executive. The German approach is widespread in Central and Eastern Europe (e.g. Art. 87(1)(j) of the Constitution of the Czech Republic).

Turkey provides a counterexample. Article 69 provides: "The dissolution of political parties shall be decided finally by the Constitutional Court after the filing of a suit by the office of the Chief Public Prosecutor of the Court of Cassation." The office of Chief Public Prosecutor was for nearly two decades under the control of

[17] TERRITORY AND POWER IN CONSTITUTIONAL TRANSITIONS (George Anderson & Sujit Choudhry, eds., 2019).

Kemalist elites. As Islamist parties—the Refah Party and its successor the Justice and Development Party (AKP)—contested elections and increased their vote share, the Chief Public Prosecutor commenced proceedings in the Constitutional Court which dissolved the Refah Party but not the AKP, which eventually took power.[18]

Access to Public Resources

Historically, the common law and civil law have accorded different legal status to political parties. The common law has viewed political parties as *unincorporated private associations*, free to regulate their internal governance through contracts and by-laws.[19] By contrast, the civil law has seen political parties as *public utilities* because of their important public functions that should be regulated to ensure they serve the public interest.[20] The logic of the public utility view of the role of political parties in constitutional democracies is that constitutions should grant political parties rights to access *public resources* in order for them to deliver their public functions.

Public funding for political parties is the clearest implication of the public utility model. Many constitutions require governments to provide public funding to political parties, while leaving the details to legislative regulation. Brazil's constitution (Ch V, Article 17(3)) provides: "Political parties have the right to resources from party funds and to free radio and television time, as provided by law." By contrast, some constitutions entrench a right to public funding and include a specific formula, such as those of Mexico (Art. 41), Colombia (Art. 109), and Costa Rica (Art. 96). Public financing can dampen political competition, to the advantage of the governing political party and/or a cartel of established political parties and at the expense of emerging political parties with a low seat count. The fairness of these formulas in practice depends on a highly contextualized assessment of their impact in specific political contexts.

In jurisdictions with state-run broadcasters, constitutions may guarantee fair access to airtime on public radio and television, which are a central mechanism for reaching the public at scale and are even more important in countries with high levels of illiteracy. Where state media are dominant, these provisions ensure that governing parties do not monopolize it (e.g. Colombia. Art. 109). These obligations are usually limited to election periods. In other countries, the duty of public

[18] Asli Bâli, *Courts and Constitutional Transition: Lessons from the Turkish Case*, 11 Int'l J. Const. L. 666 (2013).

[19] Anika Gauja, *State Regulation and the Internal Organisation of Political Parties: The Impact of Party Law in Australia, Canada, New Zealand and the United Kingdom*, 46 Commonwealth & Compar. Pol. 244 (2008).

[20] Ingrid van Biezen, *Political Parties as Public Utilities*, 10 Party Pol. 701 (2004).

media to be balanced has been interpreted to allow opposition parties to gain access to media on other occasions too, such as in Ghana, where Article 163 provides that "[a]ll state-owned media shall afford fair opportunities and facilities for the presentation of divergent views and dissenting opinions."

Legislative Design

Constitutions also refer to political parties as part of the rules governing *government formation* in parliamentary or semipresidential systems. Under most constitutions, the president (in semipresidential systems) or the head of state (in parliamentary systems) is simply conferred a power to appoint a prime minister that would command the support of a parliamentary majority, without reference to the party composition of that majority.

But some provisions refer to the appointment of a prime minister from the majority *party*, or the coalition of *parties* that commands a majority, or from the party with the highest number of seats. A parliamentary example is Article 27(2) of the Greek constitution, which provides: "The leader of the party having the absolute majority of seats in Parliament shall be appointed Prime Minister. If no party has the absolute majority, the President of the Republic shall give the leader of the party with a relative majority an exploratory mandate in order to ascertain the possibility of forming a Government enjoying the confidence of the Parliament." A semi-presidential example is Ukraine (Art. 114). In some countries, constitutions use the term "parliamentary faction" (e.g. Ukraine) or "parliamentary group" (e.g. Greece), but in substance, the terms encompass political parties.

Constitutions also institutionalize *opposition* powers, which I define as an institutionalized power possessed by a formally designated party group *or* by a fraction of legislators *or* by a formally recognized opposition leader that encompasses but goes beyond rights of individual legislators to speak and vote against government bills. Regimes of opposition powers have at least two components.[21]

First, opposition powers create an opposition team through provisions that encourage the aggregation of, or coordination among, opposition legislators, to act collectively. The principal way to do so is to create the leader of the opposition as a public office with powers (e.g. committee memberships), which shifts the intraopposition distribution of power away from individual members by providing incentives for opposition legislators to join and not defect from the opposition party. Conversely, if the leader holds office only with the support of the opposition caucus, and there is a formal process for appointment and dismissal, the constitution can regularize that accountability relationship and create transaction

[21] Sujit Choudhry, *Opposition Powers in Parliamentary Democracies* (draft on file with author); David Fontana, *Government in Opposition*, 119 Yale L.J. 384 (2009).

costs to dismissal and a default of incumbency. Creating the office of leader can enhance the legislative coherence and effectiveness of opposition parties, thereby promoting political competition. Barbados (Art. 74(2)) provides a good example.

Second, opposition powers confer opposition rights to scrutinize the conduct of the executive through *oversight powers*, the powers to (a) convene the legislature and constitute a quorum (e.g. Austria, Arts 28(2) and 31) and, once the legislature has been convened; (b) pose oral and verbal questions (e.g. France, Art. 48) and trigger interpellations (focused plenary debates) (e.g. Finland, Art. 43); (c) oversee the executive in standing committees or special commissions of inquiry (e.g. Germany, Art. 44(1)); and (d) propose motions of non-confidence or censure (e.g. Nepal, Art. 100(4)). These oversight powers also simultaneously serve as agenda-setting powers by enabling the opposition to present a countervision for government when exercising them.

Finally, the largest and most detailed set of provisions regarding the role of political parties in legislative design concerns a change in political party membership by members of the legislature, when a legislator "crosses the floor" (defects) to join another political party or a legislator is expelled from their party. The legislator is no longer a member of the party under whose banner they ran in the last election. The response depends on the electoral system and its underlying theory of representation.

Under closed-list proportional representation, voters cast ballots for parties, not candidates. If the legislator leaves their party, floor-crossing is not possible because the seat does not belong to the member, and the seat reverts to the party. In constituency-based systems, voters cast ballots for candidates. If the candidate ran under a party, floor-crossing presents a constitutional choice. If elections are primarily votes for candidates, then the legislator has a direct electoral mandate from their constituents and should be able to join another party or sit as an independent and face their constituents in the next election. But if elections are primarily votes for parties, a legislator no longer has an electoral mandate and should resign.

In the Commonwealth, floor-crossing has historically been an important mechanism for the backbench to check the power of party leaders. However, floor-crossing has been criticized, on the basis that electoral mandates now flow more from party affiliations than individual candidates. In addition, in Africa and Asia floor-crossing has fallen prey to corruption, especially by governments that use inducements (e.g., ministerial positions, patronage) to woo opposition legislators.

Many Commonwealth constitutional systems have resolved this debate in favor of the party representation theory of electoral mandates by banning floor-crossing. The leading example is the Indian "anti-defection" clause in Schedule 10, Article 2(1)(a)), which provides that a legislator loses their seat "if he has voluntarily given up his membership of such political party." The Indian anti-defection clause also enforces party discipline, because it provides that a member loses their seat if "if he votes or abstains from voting in such House contrary to any direction issued by the political party to which he belongs or by any person or authority authorised by it in this behalf" (Art. 2(1)(b)).

Separation of Party and State

Incumbent entrenchment by governing parties is a risk in any constitutional democracy. One mechanism of incumbent entrenchment is declaring a party-state. In some postcommunist constitutions there are provisions that prohibit the state from having a party identity, a direct response to history. For example, Article 20(4) of the Constitution of the Czech Republic provides that "political parties and political movements, as well as other associations, are separate from the state."

A more serious risk is partisan capture by appointing party loyalists to institutions that should operate independently of the governing party. Article 130 of the Weimar Constitution spoke directly to this issue, by providing that "[o]fficials are servants of the whole community and not of a party." Constitutions continue the tradition of separating party and state by prohibiting members of two institutions from being members of political parties—the courts and the security services. A governing party which captured these institutions would control the legal system and the use of force, and could use them to persecute its opponents.

Frequently, justices of the constitutional court cannot be current members of a political party. Article 137(1) of the Slovakian constitution, for example, provides: "[i]f an appointed judge of the Constitutional Court is a member of a political party or a political movement, he must surrender his membership prior to taking his oath." A more difficult issue concerns *past* leadership positions in a political party. In Albania leadership within the past ten years is disqualifying, for *all* judges, not just Constitutional Court judges (Art. 136(4)). Disqualification based on past office holding may exclude qualified individuals, especially in a transitional context where they have been politically active.

There are often specific rules against political party membership for security sector agencies. For example, Article 92 of Burundi's constitution provides: "Members of the defense and security corps as well as active magistrates are not authorized to join political parties." These rules are often part of a broader process of democratization from authoritarian or military regimes, where an important goal is "extracting the security services from politics" and subjecting them to civilian oversight and authority.[22] Another tool to achieve this goal is a constitutional provision stating that the security services are nonpartisan and cannot favor the interests of a political party. For example, Article 239(3)(a) of the Kenyan

[22] Sumit Bisarya & Sujit Choudhry, *Security Sector Reform in Constitutional Transitions*, 23 INTERNATIONAL IDEA POLICY PAPER 20 (2020).

constitution provides: "In performing their functions and exercising their powers, the national security organs and every member of the national security organs shall not . . . act in a partisan manner."

Lessons from Constitutional Design: Positive Functions and Negative Risks

What preliminary lessons can we draw from constitutional design about the status and role of political parties in a constitutional democracy?

In *Party Government*, Eric Schattschneider wrote: "The rise of political parties is indubitably one of the principal distinguishing marks of modern government . . . modern democracy is unthinkable save in terms of the parties."[23] The centrality of political parties to constitutional democracy remains hard to dispute. Democracy minimally consists of free, fair, and regular elections, under the rule of law, among political parties, in which a government stands for reelection against an opposition that seeks to replace it. The idea of government and opposition is short-form for governing and opposition *parties* (or coalitions of parties).[24]

Political parties serve at least ten functions. These include:

a. *Integration and mobilization of citizens*: Since the influence of a single citizen on electoral outcomes is minimal, political parties are a coordinating device that solve a collective action problem, by mobilizing citizens under the banner of a political party to cast their ballots in the same manner and shape electoral results.
b. *Interest aggregation*: Political parties aggregate the interests of party members and interest groups, through brokering, compromise, and negotiation, into a set of policy goals that secure broad support within the party and among its supporters.
c. *Formulating public policy*: Political parties translate these policy goals into specific proposals for public policy found in a party platform that sets out the party's agenda for government.
d. *Simplifying political participation*: Platforms cohere around an ideological orientation and/or questions of identity, which lowers the costs of political choice by enabling citizens to "find some party that reflects their values most closely," without reviewing and considering each separate policy in a platform.[25]

[23] Eric Schattschneider, Party Government (1942).
[24] Elliot Bulmer, *Opposition and Legislative Minorities: Constitutional Roles, Rights and Recognition*, International IDEA Constitution-Building Primer 22 (Stockholm: International IDEA, 2021).
[25] Khaitan, *supra* note 6, at 99.

e. *Structuring the popular vote and enabling political competition*: Political parties and their platforms structure election campaigns into debates about competing governing agendas; in constituency-based systems, they convert elections from a collection of local contests into national campaigns between parties vying for power.
f. *Representation*: Political parties facilitate electoral choice and accountability, by linking individual candidates to political parties.
g. *Accountability*: Citizens can hold governing parties accountable electorally for accomplishing or failing to deliver on their platforms, which also furthers the goal of political competition.
h. *Recruiting leaders for public office*: Political parties identify, recruit, and train future political leaders, and provide them with opportunities and resources to secure public office.
i. *Government selection*: In parliamentary and semipresidential systems, political parties also enable the selection of the government and tests of parliamentary confidence.
j. *Enabling the enactment of legislation*: Political parties enable the work of the legislature, by coordinating individual legislators to act collectively as party members, to set the legislative agenda, propose legislation, offer their collective views, and vote on it.

These are all *positive* functions of political parties that further constitutional democracy. Many of the categories of constitutional provisions surveyed above recognize these functions and/or are means to operationalize them.

Provisions on the basic function of political parties serve the constitutive function of codifying their roles in integrating and mobilizing citizens, interest aggregation, formulating public policy, simplifying political participation, structuring the popular vote and enabling political competition, representation, and accountability. These functions are all implied by the capacious phrases "formation of the political will" and "contribute to the exercise of suffrage." Linking these functions to these provisions can assist political mobilization in response to threats to political parties—for example, from a would-be autocrat seeking to dismantle a party system on the pretext that it stands in the way of the expression of the popular will, when in reality that system is an institutional mechanism to form and express that will.

The right to form political parties, whether as an illustrative example of the rights to freedom of assembly and association or as a standalone right, furthers the same functions in a regulative sense. Those functions can shape the interpretation of the scope of the right, the test for determining if it is infringed, and the proportionality analysis of measures which infringe that right. They can help courts to define when governing parties act for an unconstitutional motive to suppress opposition parties and to condemn incumbent entrenchment, in the manner of the German and Czech constitutional courts.[26] They can also shape the assessment of necessity and proportionality *stricto sensu*, by providing legal scaffolding for courts to organize their assessment of the costs and purported benefits of a challenged measure.

Constitutional provisions regarding legislative design further the goals of structuring the popular vote and enabling political competition; accountability; recruiting leaders for public office; government selection; and enabling the enactment of legislation. The rules for government formation encourage legislators to select a leader who can be appointed prime minister, and to form parties large enough to contend for power. Creating the office of leader of the opposition with the power to dispense patronage encourages aggregation among the opposition. Opposition oversight mechanisms promote accountability and enable the opposition to present its own agenda for governing. Antidefection clauses can promote political competition, by creating a mechanism for party discipline that prevents the fragmentation of political parties.[27]

Constitutional rights to access public resources have both constitutive and regulative functions that support parties in delivering on all these goals. Van Biezen has argued that in Western Europe, the shift from relying on private contributions to public funding has been the principal reason for the "transformation of parties from the traditionally voluntary private associations which perform public roles and occupy government positions, towards parties as public utilities"; conversely, this "ideational transformation concerning the place of political parties in modern democracy" generates constitutional claims to public funding.[28] These provisions challenge the traditional divide between the common law and civil law traditions over the legal status of political parties, which has less significance than it once did. In common law democracies, political parties are now highly regulated by constitutions and political party laws, which impliedly reflects their role as public utilities. Conversely, in the civil law world, constitutions tend to protect political parties from the abuse of public power to safeguard political pluralism. It is preferable to think about regulating political parties in *any* legal tradition in relation to their role as competitors in a political marketplace for partisan control.[29]

Constitutional design also reveals an acute concern with the *negative* risks posed by political parties. As Rosenblum has explained, constitutional democracies have long wrestled with "anti-partyism," the fear that political parties could subvert constitutional democracy and undermine democratic representation and accountability, in three ways: by (a) undermining the unity of a political community exercising popular sovereignty by providing institutional platforms for the

[26] Samuel Issacharoff & Richard Pildes, *Politics as Markets: Partisan Lockups of the Democratic Process*, 50 Stan. L. Rev. 643 (1998).

[27] Madhav Khosla & Milan Vaishnav, 22 *Democracy and defections*, Int'l J. Const. L. 400 (2024), https://doi.org/10.1093/icon/moae037.

[28] Biezen, *supra* note 20, at 702.

[29] Issacharoff & Pildes, *supra* note 26.

accentuation of political disagreements; (b) undermining the role of individual legislators to act in the best interest of their constituents, by requiring them to vote with the party line; and (c) giving rise to a professional political class which places its own personal interests in holding onto power ahead of those of its constituents and creates networks of clientelism and patronage.[30]

The provisions on militant democracy and the separation of party and state reflect a different set of concerns regarding the negative effects of political parties. Unlike Rosenblum's antipartyism objections, these misgivings do not object to the existence of parties *per se*. Rather, they proceed from the premise that political parties play an indispensable role in constitutional democracy, but pose certain kinds of risks which constitutional design can and should mitigate.

Militant democracy provisions serve the constitutive function of conveying the nature of the existential risk that might pose a threat to the constitutional order, and the regulative function of checking that risk.[31] Historically, that threat was understood to come from antidemocratic parties who capture the state from within through peaceful, democratic means, with the collapse of Weimar as the paradigmatic case. The rules on internal party democracy view the threat in the same way, but presuppose that party governance can be a prophylactic. In specific national contexts, the *source* of the existential threat varies. In some countries, the threat is to democracy, but the source of danger is violence from paramilitary organizations allied with a party. In others, the nature of the existential threat is to the *character* of democracy. In what I have termed "divided societies," bans on political parties organized on the basis of ascriptive differences, and "national character" requirements for political parties, are mechanisms to encourage cross-ethnic alliances as the units of electoral competition.[32] The existential threat may be to territorial integrity—leading to bans on secessionist parties.

Finally, the provisions on the separation of party and state check the risk that the parties can capture the state by prohibiting party membership for the courts and security services. But this is not the only way to respond to this fear. As Mark has recently explained, fourth branch institutions (e.g. electoral commissions, anticorruption authorities) which "combine independence to ensure that the institution isn't captured by one party with accountability to ensure that the institution doesn't become a force independent of political parties" are one kind of constitutional design response to partisan capture.[33] This might reflect the reality that, at least in dominant party democracies, partisan capture can be held at bay, but not forever.

[30] Rosenblum, *supra* note 8.

[31] My concept of "existential threat" overlaps with Sam Issacharoff's concept of "fragility," in his *Fragile Democracies*, 120 Harv. L. Rev. 1407 (2007).

[32] Sujit Choudhry, Constitutional Design in Divided Societies: Integration or Accommodation? (2008).

[33] Mark Tushnet, The New Fourth Branch: Institutions for Protecting Constitutional Democracy 20 (2021).

Conclusion

Constitutional provisions on political parties do not exist in isolation from the rest of the constitutional text. For example, as Benjamin Schupmann has argued, militant democracy party bans are closely linked to "eternity clauses" that safeguard the basic structure of constitutional democracy from constitutional amendment by authoritarian populists.[34] Taxonomizing constitutional provisions on political parties based on their function enables these connections to be drawn and explored systematically.

[34] Benjamin Schupmann, Democracy Despite Itself: Liberal Constitutionalism and Militant Democracy (2024).

22

Civic Virtue, Civic Obligation, Knowledge Institutions, and Proconstitutional Actors

*Vicki C. Jackson**

In many important works, Mark Tushnet has critiqued strong forms of judicial review. Whether in writing about the US Constitution or about weak-form judicial review, he has argued against the finality of judicial review and in favor of statutory resolutions. But Tushnet is not only skeptical about judicial review; he is skeptical about the value of entrenchment even of those institutions through which democratic decisions are made, given the tendency of institutional arrangements to favor particular substantive outcomes.

This skepticism is, I think, rooted less in an admiration of legislatures and more in a deep sense of epistemic modesty and a democratic commitment to self-government. In his 2011 paper urging progressives to focus on political (rather than legal) constitutionalism, Tushnet makes two arguments that appear throughout his work: legal constitutionalism will debilitate democratic politics and cedes too ink control over policy to unelected judges; and, moreover, "the rough-and-ready judgments of proportionality made in political constitutionalism . . . are typically at least as good as" those made by courts.[1] In some contrast to Jeremy Waldron's work,[2] Tushnet has more of a warts-and-all approach to the value of political constitutionalism, including legislative log rolling, or compromises for reasons of administrative efficiency.

In another paper about judicial review of "direct legislation" (that is, laws enacted by referendum), Tushnet denied that special standards of judicial review should be applied to direct legislation because of its presumed lack of deliberation (as compared to laws enacted by legislatures). He wrote: "To put it as a provocation, what's so great about deliberation? Or at least, what's so great about deliberation that it should be allowed to displace decisions made directly by the people? When contrasted with backroom dealing, *deliberation* is an open process in which participants invoke public reasons. But direct legislation displays that modest

* With thanks to Madhav Khosla for helpful comments; to Mark Tushnet, Judith Resnik, Rosalind Dixon, Guy Charles, Nick Stephanopoulos, Niel Siegel, Bob Taylor, and Martha Minow for helpful conversations along the way; and to Brandon Broukhim for valuable research assistance.

[1] Mark Tushnet, *Progressive Constitutionalism: What Is "It"?*, 72 Ohio St L J 1073, 1077–79 (2011).

[2] *See, e.g.*, Jeremy Waldron, The Dignity of Legislation (1999).

Vicki C. Jackson, *Civic Virtue, Civic Obligation, Knowledge Institutions, and Proconstitutional Actors* In: *Redefining Comparative Constitutional Law.* Edited by: Vicki C. Jackson and Madhav Khosla, Oxford University Press.
 DOI: 10.1093/9780191996344.003.0022

form of deliberation."[3] In other work he concedes some role for public deliberation, defending weak-form review on the ground that courts might play a procedural role in focusing public, or legislative, deliberation on particular fundamental issues.[4]

On Tushnet's vision, then, in a well-designed polity, all else being equal, politics should play a larger role than it does in US-style constitutionalism and that of some other countries. And this means a larger role for legislative bodies or some equivalent. Whatever the virtues or vices of "direct legislation" through referenda, Tushnet's work, if taken seriously, emphasizes the importance of legislatures, legislators, and the engaged public that elects them and votes on proposed referenda.

Now, if we are going to look to legislatures and democratic publics to play a larger role in developing and sustaining constitutional systems, questions about legislators' role and of what citizenship entails become more important. How should these be approached? For some scholars the answers are decidedly institutional, focusing on the design of electoral systems, the structure of parliaments, the regulation of campaign finances and contributions, and the like. In part under the influence of Tushnet's classic work *The Possibilities of Comparative Constitutional Law*,[5] much of the literature in comparative constitutional law that concerns legislatures at all employs functionalist approaches associated with issues of institutional design. Yet, in his recent book on *New Fourth Branch Institutions*, Tushnet concludes that institutional approaches to the protection of constitutional democracy are difficult to design and that it is hard to anticipate how they will work in practice. In one of the final paragraphs of the book, he writes: "if institutions cannot serve systematically to protect constitutional democracy, and if, as we should, we want to preserve it, we have to strengthen the institutions that generate civic virtue."[6] In other words, he concludes, the success of constitutional democracies may depend more on the orientation (of officials and people) toward civic virtue, that is, toward the public character of office holders and citizens, than it does on the institutions of governance themselves. Highly decentralized governance is one approach Tushnet raises as a possibility, but, as he notes, other institutions, including the family, civil society, and (at least in the past) some forms of commerce, may also promote civic virtue.

So, if one is a constitutional law scholar, what would it mean to take seriously the idea that to promote good constitutionalism and good democracy one needs to promote civic virtue?[7] Some questions, then, and a question about the questions,

[3] Mark Tushnet, *Fear of Voting: Differential Standards of Judicial Review of Direct Legislation*, 1996 ANN. SURV. AM. L. 373, 382 (1996).

[4] *See generally* Mark Tushnet, *Policy Distortion and Democratic Debilitation: Comparative Illumination of the Countermajoritarian Difficulty*, 94 MICH. L. REV. 245 (1995).

[5] Mark Tushnet, *The Possibilities of Comparative Constitutional Law*, 108 YALE L.J. 1225 (1999).

[6] MARK TUSHNET, THE NEW FOURTH BRANCH: INSTITUTIONS FOR PROTECTING CONSTITUTIONAL DEMOCRACY 179 (2021).

[7] Virtues differ from duties—the former reflect internal normative commitments, the latter a sense of fulfilling obligations owed to others. I will return to this distinction at the end. For now I treat civic

which is: Do constitutional law scholars have anything to contribute on the subject?

1. **What is civic virtue?** Defining civic virtue today is challenging.[8] But the idea would embrace at a minimum some orientation (i) to care for the good of the community of which one is a part. In a democratic republic, civic virtue might also embrace (ii) a presumption of honesty in public dealings, since self-government (or government legitimized through popular participation) depends on the accuracy of public evaluation of public servants. In a secular society (in which religious considerations of faith in godly powers or in an afterlife are not central to public policy), civic virtue might also embrace (iii) a set of dispositions toward action based on accurate information and knowledge, rather than on beliefs about the empirical world held based on religious faith or its equivalent.

Other aspects of civic virtue deserve mention: Seeking justice is often thought of as a civic virtue, as is the courage to stand for—and explain in terms others could appreciate—what you believe in. But the performance of these virtues might at times come into conflict with other civic virtues such as tolerance, which, in a heterogenous community, might be just as central in order for a polity to function. Perhaps a norm of reciprocity of reasoning might be an aspect of civic virtue, one implied by the idea of honesty in public dealings—that a reason offered to justify a course of action that favors party A will be respected on similar facts favoring party B.

At a minimum, an orientation that each person has an obligation to the whole community, and to try to promote the good of that community—or, perhaps more modestly, to enable that community to function at some minimal level of adequacy—would be entailed in any idea of civic virtue. Perhaps the best that can be offered is a circular, question-begging statement that defining the requisite level or nature of civic virtue entails a sufficient distribution of the attitudes and behaviors necessary to sustain decent constitutional democracies.

virtue and civic duty as overlapping concepts that contribute to an understanding of the role morality of different public capacities—legislator, elected executive, judges, appointed officials, citizens.

[8] For different emphases, *see, e.g.*, Miriam Galston, *Taking Aristotle Seriously: Republican-Oriented Legal Theory and the Moral Foundations of Deliberative Democracy*, 82 Calif. L. Rev. 329 (1994) (emphasizing willingness to talk, listen, and be open-minded; noting feminist approaches that emphasize compassion); William Galston, *Expressive Liberty, Moral Pluralism, Political Pluralism: Three Sources of Liberal Theory*, 40 Wm. & Mary L. Rev. 869, 878 (1999) (emphasizing self-restraint); Christopher A. Callaway, *Civic Duties, Civic Virtues, and the Barriers to Effective Citizenship*, 43 Hum. Rts. Mag. 23 (2018) (discussing "cardinal virtues of . . . justice, wisdom, courage, and temperance," civic virtues of being "tolerant, self-disciplined, dedicated to the common good, and supportive of . . . government," and finally virtues of "democratic citizens" who are "engaged, well-informed, and open to ideas and perspectives different from their own"); *cf.* American Academy of Arts and Sciences Commission on the Practice of Democratic Citizenship, Reinventing American Democracy for the 21st Century American Democracy, Our Common Purpose 21 (2020) (discussing "virtuous cycle of culture, institutions, and civil society").

2. **Whose civic virtue?** Constitutionalists have devoted much thought to defining what is good judging and judicial reasoning in constitutional interpretation. But a civic virtue-oriented approach to constitutionalism would need also to be more concerned about the attitudes and expectations of public officeholders beyond judicial officers—that is, of those who hold elective or appointive public office in democratic governments. Much ink has been given to defining the role-morality of judges, of what it means to be a judge—about norms of impartiality, openmindedness, and fairness, as well as about specific aspects of being a constitutional judge based on reasoning about the nature and purpose of constitutions.[9] Constitutionalists need to reflect more on the distinct role moralities of officeholding (elective and appointive) and citizenship in constitutional democracies; these moralities would likely differ from the models of judging to accommodate real (and valuable) differences in role.[10]

What would it mean to give comparable attention to the role-morality of other public officials, those holding constitutional lawmaking and decisional offices, such as members of national parliaments and chief executives? Or to the role-morality of political party leaders, or academics?[11] Or of ordinary citizens?[12]

A starting question about representatives might be, *first*, whether an aspiration for impartiality, central to the role conception of judging, has a place, or as central a place, in the role-morality of representing. A *second* question is whether, in contrast to the aspirations for judges to make principled, reasoned, and consistent decisions about the law, for elected representatives decisionmaking based on bargaining, or logrolling, is an appropriate part of their role-morality.[13] A *third* set of

[9] *See generally, e.g.*, RONALD DWORKIN, JUSTICE IN ROBES (2006); AHARON BARAK, THE JUDGE IN A DEMOCRACY (2006); Aharon Barak, *Foreword: A Judge on Judging: The Role of a Supreme Court in a Democracy*, 116 HARV. L. REV. 19 (2002).

[10] *See generally* Vicki C. Jackson, *Pro-Constitutional Representation: Comparing the Role Obligations of Judges and Elected Representatives in Constitutional Democracy*, 57 WM & MARY L. REV. 1717 (2016) [hereinafter Jackson, *Pro-Constitutional Representation*]; William P. Marshall, *The Limits on Congress's Power to Do Nothing: A Preliminary Inquiry*, 93 IND. L.J. 159 (2018); Neil S. Siegel, *After the Trump Era: A Constitutional Role Morality for Presidents and Members of Congress*, 107 GEO. L.J. 109 (2018); Robin West, *Toward the Study of the Legislated Constitution*, 72 OHIO ST. L.J. 1343 (2011).

[11] On the role-morality—or potential civic virtues—of legal scholars, see Liora Lazarus, *Constitutional Scholars as Constitutional Actors*, 48 FED. L. REV. 483 (2020) (arguing the need for independence of judgment by scholars); *see also* Kate O'Regan, 2023 Sir David Williams Lecture on "The Craft of Constitutional Adjudication" (May 4, 2023), https://www.cpl.law.cam.ac.uk/sir-david-williams-lectures/professor-kate-oregan-craft-constitutional-adjudication (arguing the importance of scholars taking doctrine and reasoning of courts seriously).

[12] On constitutional duties of citizens, *see* Mila Versteeg & Erensu Altan, *Constitutional Duties*, AM. J. COMP. L. (forthcoming); *see also* Fernando Berdion Del Valle & Kathryn Sikkink, *(Re)discovering Duties: Individual Responsibilities in the Age of Rights*, 26 MINN. J. INT'L L. 189 (2017); Michael Walzer, *Civility and Civic Virtue in Contemporary America*, 41 SOC. RSCH. 593 (1974) (discussing potential civic responsibilities of American citizens).

[13] For discussion, *see* Eric Beerbohm, *The Problem of Clean Hands*, in NOMOS LIX: COMPROMISE 3, 16–17 (Jack Knight ed., 2018) (arguing that "lawmakers generally have a weightier moral reason to countenance compromise than ordinary citizens," that "compromise can, given certain background conditions, make a piece of legislation more democratic," and that the demands of "deliberative" theories of negotiation—e.g. condemning all threats or misrepresentations—may make "the practice of

questions concerns the role-morality of executive heads of government (who are tasked with carrying out laws and usually have some independent powers to act) and administrative officials (meaning those who are tasked to carry out laws once enacted).

A *fourth* question is: how does the role-morality of administrative policy makers with regulatory authority under statutes differ from that of elected lawmaking representatives or more purely administrative officials? A recent US Supreme Court decision rejected a challenge to administrative rulemaking that was, in part, based on a claim that the agency process manifested a lack of openmindedness in considering public comments; a statutory requirement for opportunity for public comment generally exists for rulemaking, though, the Court held, it can follow rather than precede issuance of a rule.[14] The Court "declin[ed] to evaluate the final rules under the open-mindedness test [because] the text of the APA provides the 'maximum procedural requirements' that an agency must follow in order to promulgate a rule"; the Court would focus on "objective" requirements (notice, opportunity for comment, a statement of basis and purpose, and 30-day notice of effectiveness); while implying there was no requirement of openmindedness, the Court failed to discuss another statutory requirement for "consideration" of "relevant matter."[15] While it might be understandable to say that a court cannot judicially enforce an openmindedness requirement, it is quite another matter to suggest that a statute authorizing regulatory policymaking does not require openmindedness in considering statutorily mandated public comment. Why wouldn't the legislature contemplate such openmindedness—or, to put it slightly differently, why wouldn't a legislative requirement of "consideration" be understood to require genuineness of consideration? The US Court's attitude may be contrasted with the principles of public life set forth in the UK Cabinet Manual (2011), which are "selflessness, integrity, objectivity, accountability, openness, honesty and leadership."[16]

Other questions about civic virtue arise in other settings: Should political party leaders be understood to have duties beyond those of serving the interests of their parties in electoral and policy contests; should they filter out dangerous

negotiation impossible"). *Cf.* Romer v. Evans, 517 U.S. 620, 639–40 (Scalia J dissenting) (arguing that legislatures need not be consistent in the way courts are).

[14] Little Sisters of the Poor Saints Peter & Paul Home v. Pennsylvania, 140 S. Ct. 2367 (2020).

[15] *Id.* at 2385–86; *see* 5 U.S.C. §553(c) ("After consideration of the relevant matter presented, the agency shall incorporate in the rules adopted a concise general statement of their basis and purpose"). The Court's "Syllabus," which is *not* deemed part of the official decision, announced that "The 'openmindedness' test has no basis in the APA." *Id.* at 2371. (The Syllabus is prepared by the Reporter of decisions, who "works closely with the justices" in so doing. *See* Mark Walsh, *SCOTUS Notebook: The Mechanics and Art of Court Decisions*, ABA Journal (June 28, 2012), https://www.abajournal.com/news/article/scotus_notebook_the_mechanics_and_the_art_of_court_decisions) (summarizing Tony Mauro interview with retiring Reporter of Decisions in 2010).

[16] UK Cabinet Office, The Cabinet Manual: A Guide to Laws, Conventions, and Rules on the Operation of Government 26 (2011).

candidates?[17] Is an aspiration to develop public civic virtue incompatible with important commitments to freedom of thought and speech? This question is of particular importance in the context of considering education for civic virtue.[18]

3. **What expectations about public office role-morality, or civic virtue, exist? Do expectations matter?** Assuming there is a core of civic virtue that entails an orientation to the public wellbeing—and recognizing Mark Tushnet's point that the success of institutions depends at least in part on the civic character or virtues of those who work them—we might ask questions about the state of public expectations about the virtues or conduct of representatives.

First, what are public expectations about civically virtuous behavior? Are dishonest acts viewed as normal or shameful? Is refusal to negotiate with members of the other party viewed as good and normal (e.g. because the other party is viewed as mortal enemy), or out of line with expectations (e.g. if the other party is viewed as loyal opposition)?

Second, if there are public expectations about civically virtuous behavior, do they matter in influencing holders of public office? Why might cultural expectations matter? They may matter in at least two ways: first, by influencing a person's self-understanding and thereby functioning as an internal constraint or guardrail; and second, by creating external, social, or reputational incentives to which people respond. (I have elaborated on the importance of social expectations and their possible positive effects on legislators' conduct in other work.)[19] As other scholars suggest,

> instructing Congress that it has a constitutional duty to act in certain circumstances might serve to change political culture. The position that congressional action is optional sends the message that there is no need for members to work together because there are no common responsibilities. The notion that Congress has a duty to act, on the other hand, tells the members that they have common goals and common obligations.[20]

[17] *See* STEVEN LEVIITSKY AND DANIEL ZIBLATT, HOW DEMOCRACIES DIE (2018).

[18] On different conceptions of civic virtue and its relationship to liberal commitments to freedom of thought and tolerance for different views, compare, *e.g.*, William A. Galston, *Pluralism and Civic Virtue*, 33 SOC. THEORY & PRACTICE 625 (2007) (emphasizing pluralism, distinguishing civic from other virtues, and noting a "meta-virtue—namely, the ability to shift from one mode of conduct to another as one crosses the lines between different spheres of one's life") with, *e.g.*, JEAN JACQUES ROUSSEAU, EMILE; OR, CONCERNING EDUCATION 155–57 (Eleanor Worthington, trans., 1889) (contemplating education toward a set of correct beliefs) and AMY GUTMANN, DEMOCRATIC EDUCATION 39 (1987) (emphasizing importance of public education for civic purposes).

[19] *See* Vicki C. Jackson, *Legislatures and Effective Government: Raising Expectations for Representatives*, *in* CONSTITUTIONALISM AND A RIGHT TO EFFECTIVE GOVERNMENT 181 (Vicki C. Jackson & Yasmin Dawood eds., 2022).

[20] Marshall, *supra* note 10, at 171; *see id.* at 167 (suggesting that failures to act on appropriations or nominations that threaten the government's ability to function should be viewed as constitutionally unacceptable).

Yet it may be easier to identify public-spirited judges, virtuous in their role, than to identify public-spirited legislators, because being a good legislator may often occur in private discussions, and is less visible.[21] Many of legislators' dealings will occur in private negotiations, as compared to the work of appellate judges, whose most important work product is published. It is possible that the exercise of civic virtues by members of multimember bodies may be best determined not by examining discrete legislative acts but by examining the legislator's actions over the course of a life in public service, and thus require the skills of political historians and biographers as well as (possibly) legal scholars.[22]

4. Another important question is: **if expectations about civically virtuous conduct matter, how are such expectations likely to be produced?** In *The New Fourth Branch*, Mark Tushnet concludes his inquiry by exploring which institutions can work to develop civic virtue. (A larger message of this recent book might be that relying on institutional solutions will always have limits, especially to the extent that the institutions are produced, structured, or populated by existing political powerholders.) Nonetheless, I agree with Professor Tushnet that institutions can be identified that might be thought to have a particularly powerful role to play.

Tushnet discusses several institutions: "religion, the market, the family and civil society." He argues that religion cannot be relied upon, because of great variations in attitudes toward government among religions. The "doux commerce" theory and related theories based on agrarian or smalltown life, he argues, are obsolete in light of contemporary global markets. But he further argues that one could imagine ways in which markets and family interactions and radically decentralized governance institutions might help foster civic virtue. In so arguing, he emphasizes the role of face-to-face interactions in developing civic virtue—and that of institutions that encourage such face-to-face interactions.[23] Below I discuss several possible components of a renewed effort to promote civic virtue.

Radically decentralized forms of governance and civic education: Tushnet holds out hope for seriously decentralized forms of governance as an approach to protecting democracy. As noted, he argues that such localized governance will "restore the face-to-face" interactions that, according to "doux commerce" theories, tended to generate civic virtue. "Radical decentralization," he writes, "means that people will be working regularly with their co-citizens on projects whose effects on them will be immediately visible . . . They will have to negotiate, bargain, compromise and persuade," which "will encourage them to see things as others see them, not merely as they personally do."[24] Two examples in the sphere of governance are

[21] Jackson, *Raising Expectations*, *supra* note 19, at 191 n.48.

[22] *See, e.g.*, Robert Caro, The Years of Lyndon Johnson: Master of the Senate (2002); Don Orberdorfer, Senator Mansfield: The Extraordinary Life of a Great American Statesman and Diplomat (2003).

[23] Tushnet, New Fourth Branch, *supra* note 6, at 175–79 (for quotations in this paragraph).

[24] *Id.*

offered: panchayat village governance in India and remedies of "engagement" developed by the South African Constitutional Court, each of which occurs in settings small enough to facilitate face-to-face discussion or negotiation among those most directly affected by the issues at hand. And, Tushnet argues, to strengthen democracy we have to strengthen those institutions that contribute to civic virtue.[25]

The virtues he believes will arise in these smaller, more decentralized settings bear some resemblance to the virtues that William James, one of the first generation of philosophical "pragmatists" in the United States, believed democracy required of its citizens: a "tincture of self doubt" and degree of tolerance for different ideas, the development of mutual respect among its citizens, the welcoming of contestation, "overcoming the blindness" of some to the conditions of others, and condemning hatreds and efforts to use or promote violence against others.[26] For James, education was a path to inculcating such virtues; while he focused on university-level education, current scholarship suggests that the institutions of primary, secondary, and tertiary education are all vehicles to promote the emergence of these virtues.[27] In order for this to happen in the United States, however, there may need to be a willingness on both sides of a presently highly polarized debate to identify a minimal list of qualities sought to be developed by education—including tolerance and (where possible) respect for opposing parties, and a willingness to try to persuade others based on evidence. Such a willingness can be very hard to muster when people believe their opponents are evil or deeply morally misguided.

Thick views of civic education across the country may need to await a less polarized time for their development.[28] But perhaps some very elemental ideas, on which agreement could be obtained, would include (i) the importance of evidence-based thinking, combined with some degree of epistemic self-doubt or openness to revision; (ii) tolerance for disagreement; (iii) willingness to compromise; (iv) understanding that the role of government is to advance the public good (however variously it is understood); and (v) the importance of knowledge about how to participate in and influence governments. Such knowledge may be a predicate for the kind of effects of a radically decentralized governance that Prof Tushnet envisions.[29]

Knowledge institutions and civic virtue: In addition to the institutions Tushnet identifies, other possibilities that might contribute to developing civic virtues

[25] *Id.* at 179.

[26] On William James, *see* Joshua I. Miller, A Democratic Temperament: The Legacy of William James 85, 57–59 (2021).

[27] *See also, e.g.*, Danielle S. Allen, Education and Equality (2016); Ronald J. Daniels, What Universities Owe Democracy 86–130 (2021); Mark C. Alexander, *Law-Related Education: Hope for Today's Students*, 20 Ohio N.U. L. Rev. 57 (1993).

[28] On polarization, *see, e.g.*, Pew Rsch. Ctr., As Partisan Hostility Grows, Signs of Frustration with the Two-Party System (2022). A useful example of a relatively thick effort to bridge polarization may be found in the Educating for American Democracy Project, https://www.educatingforamericandemocracy.org (last visited Aug. 6, 2023).

[29] For example, if a local community group wants to stop construction of a building in a particular site, they need to know who has power to stop it, by what means, and under what kind of pressures or argumentation. Likewise, if a group wants to turn a vacant lot into a park, they need to know how to find

include: common experiences (e.g. military or other common service); employment settings that emphasize a public-spirited ethos (including the civil service); and informational and cultural institutions that may be regarded as either part of the world of commerce or as part of civil society (e.g. universities, free press, other NGOs, for-profit news media or entertainment providers, other businesses[30]). Moreover, the words and actions of political leaders may have significant impacts on civic virtue.[31] Each of these requires serious thinking by constitutionalists, although the tools of other disciplines (including sociology, psychology, economics, and history) will be necessary for full evaluation.

The fostering of civic virtue is likely to involve multiple efforts in multiple venues, and among the places that may be looked to for contributing to certain

out who owns it, who has power to make or influence decisions about its use, and what kinds of pressures or arguments are likely to be persuasive.

[30] Although most definitions of civil society exclude the for-profit center—*Commission on Social Determinants of Health: Civil Society Report*, World Health Org. [WHO] (Oct. 2007), https://www.who.int/publications/m/item/commission-on-social-determinants-of-health-civil-society-report ("Civil society refers to the space for collective action around shared interests, purposes and values, generally distinct from government and commercial for-profit actors")—it is a mistake to overlook the impacts of for-profit-motivated cultural products and practices. *Compare* the TV series *The West Wing* (NBC, 1999–2006) (depicting people in the White House as mostly well motivated) or the movie *All the President's Men* (1976) (treating bad conduct as unusual and dishonorable) with the movie *Dave* (1993) (featuring an evil chief of staff). Or consider the positions taken by the business community on the constitutionality of affirmative action and the (negative and positive) impact of their practices. *See, e.g.*, Brief for Major American Business Enterprises as *Amici Curiae* Supporting Respondents at 1, Students for Fair Admissions v. President & Fellows of Harvard College, 143 S. Ct. 2141 (2023) (No. 20-1199) (urging that admitting racially and ethnically diverse student bodies was of high importance to business); Andrew Ross Sorkin et al., *Why Corporate America Is Worried about Affirmative Action*, N.Y. Times (June 30, 2023), https://www.nytimes.com/2023/06/30/business/dealbook/corporate-diversity-affirmative-action.html.

[31] A number of well-regarded judges, for example, have noted the inspirational effect on their own professional lives of Robert F. Kennedy's speeches. For Margaret H. Marshall, former Chief Justice of the Supreme Judicial Court of Massachusetts (noted for her decision finding a right to same-sex marriage under the state constitution in Goodridge v. Dept of Pub. Health, 798 N.E.2d 941 (Mass. 2003)), it was Kennedy's 1966 speech in Capetown, South Africa, during Apartheid, where he proclaimed: "Each time a man stands up for an ideal, or acts to improve the lot of others, or strikes out against injustice, he sends forth a tiny ripple of hope, and crossing each other from a million different centers of energy and daring, those ripples build a current which can sweep down the mightiest walls of oppression and resistance." Marshall, a young university student active in the antiapartheid movement at the time, accompanied Kennedy and his speech influenced her strongly. *See Margaret H. Marshall, '76: "Do What You Can Today"*, Yale L. Sch. Today (Nov. 23, 2022), https://law.yale.edu/yls-today/news/margaret-h-marshall-76-do-what-you-can-today (quoting RFK speech). Judge Patricia Wald, whose contributions were recognized by the American Medal of Freedom award, likewise noted the influence on her life of Robert Kennedy's vision of a politics of social justice. *See* Linda Greenhouse, *The Kind of Judge We Need*, N.Y. Times (Jan. 17, 2019) (quoting Wald's 2008 statement on why she was supporting Barack Obama for president rather than Hillary Clinton). One might compare also the work of Senators McCain and Feingold in enacting campaign finance reform, for which they were honored with the 1999 John F. Kennedy Profiles in Courage Award—*see U.S. Senators John McCain and Russell Feingold Share 10th John F. Kennedy Profile in Courage Award*, https://www.jfklibrary.org/events-and-awards/profile-in-courage-award/award-recipients/john-mccain-1999—with Senator McConnell's public statement in 2010 that defeating the sitting President was his "top priority." *See* Frank James, *Sen. Mitch McConnell Insists: One and Done for Obama*, Nat'l Pub. Radio (NPR) (Nov. 4. 2010, 12:02 PM), https://www.npr.org/sections/itsallpolitics/2010/11/04/131069048/sen-mcconnell-insists-one-term-for-obama.

kinds of civic virtues—or understandings of civic duties—are "knowledge institutions."[32] A characteristic of those institutions, I argue, is a commitment to the development or dissemination of knowledge, which knowledge is to be determined by the independent application of a set of disciplinary standards, developed within the particular institution—which may be an academic discipline, or may be the responsible press (to the extent it survives)—all of which have some commitment to developing or disseminating knowledge about or improved understandings of the world.[33] To the extent that the core of civic virtue is an orientation to be concerned for others, the independent judgment required in the production of knowledge may be thought conducive to the exercise of at least some forms of civic virtue. Indeed, in his book, Mark Tushnet acknowledges the role of "professional norms" based on expertise and a professional commitment to "impartiality" in the application of those norms, although he argues that such professional norms may only weakly constrain the operation of partisan forces on public decisionmaking.[34]

Knowledge institutions include (1) universities and other institutions of higher education and research; (2) the free and responsible press—which I define to include those committed to reporting aimed at disclosing and identifying rather than concealing true facts;[35] and (3) some government offices, charged with producing or acting upon specialized knowledge and typically staffed by career civil servants and professionals in different disciplines. Professional associations are another kind of institution that might be a "knowledge institution," as in the role of associations of lawyers or judges who help develop the disciplinary norms of how law as a profession behaves in proceedings to determine truth in contested legal matters,[36] or in the role of various scientific or academic disciplinary associations.[37]

[32] Vicki C. Jackson, *Knowledge Institutions in Constitutional Democracies: Preliminary Reflections*, 7 Can. J. Comp. & Contemp. L. 156 (2021).

[33] *See id.* at 211–18.

[34] *See* Tushnet, New Fourth Branch, *supra* note 6, at 60–61 (noting role of professional standards and norms).

[35] *See* Vicki C. Jackson, *Knowledge Institutions in Constitutional Democracy: Reflections on "The Press,"* 14 J. Med. L. 275 (2022).

[36] The American Bar Association describes itself as "founded in 1878 on a commitment to set the legal and ethical foundation for the American nation." *About Us*, Am. Bar Ass'c, https://www.americanbar.org/about_the_aba/ (last visited Aug. 6, 2023). Its Model Rules of Professional Conduct (MRPC) require "candor" toward tribunals. *See* Model Rules of Prof. Conduct r. 3.3 (Am. Bar Ass'n 1983) ("A lawyer shall not knowingly: (1) make a false statement of fact or law to a tribunal or fail to correct a false statement of material fact or law previously made to the tribunal by the lawyer; (2) fail to disclose to the tribunal legal authority in the controlling jurisdiction known to the lawyer to be directly adverse to the position of the client and not disclosed by opposing counsel; or (3) offer evidence that the lawyer knows to be false"). The MRPC also impose special responsibilities on prosecutors, *see id.* r. 3.8 (requiring that prosecutors "refrain from prosecuting a charge that the prosecutor knows is not supported by probable cause"; "make timely disclosure to the defense of all evidence or information known to the prosecutor that tends to negate the guilt of the accused or mitigates the offense"; and, upon learning of new material evidence casting doubt on a prior conviction, to disclose the evidence and, where that evidence is "clear and convincing," to take steps to remedy the conviction).

[37] *See e.g.*, American Historical Society, *About the AHA*, Am. Hist. Soc'y, https://www.historians.org/about-aha-and-membership (last visited Aug. 6, 2023) (describing itself as "[p]romoting new

What is the connection between knowledge institutions and civic virtue? A commitment to act for the common good cannot be sustained without attention to what constitutes the common good. The public good, at least in secular terms, requires knowledge about human conditions and plausible evidence-based theories of how those conditions can be improved upon. The public good, in a democracy, also requires knowledge of the acts in office of elected representatives. The public benefits from having habits of mind that are promoted by the ideas of verification, epistemic openness, and critical evaluation of different arguments about matters that are promoted by universities, a free press, and professionals in various fields. Moreover, a commitment of knowledge institutions is to getting at what is accurate and what is not; this entails a degree of honesty about what the facts of a matter are, another feature of civic virtue.[38] There will be much room for reasonable disagreement. But attitudes toward knowledge and truth about the world matter greatly to the exercise of civic virtues in a constitutional democracy.

Proconstitutional attitudes and civic virtue: Governments in free democratic systems must not adopt attitudes of hostility to the free press and higher education institutions; rather, the obligation of governments and legislatures is to protect freedom of the press and the academic freedom of institutions of higher learning. Nor should the heads of government or members of parliament be allowed to intimidate or retaliate against professional civil servants for performing their duties in good faith. Such attitudes or actions are antithetical to the fostering and exercise of civic virtue. Constitutional democracies require "democratic competency" and "trust/honesty" forms of legitimation;[39] constitutional democracy requires some balance between partisan political action on behalf of majorities and impartial action that protects all. In the US the Pendleton Act (1883) and its successors, requiring civil service hiring that is based on merit and forbidding politically

approaches to history education and scholarship and setting professional standards for the discipline"); American Psychological Association, *About APA*, AM. PSYCH. ASS'N, https://www.apa.org/about (last visited Aug. 6, 2023) ("Our mission is to promote the advancement, communication, and application of psychological science and knowledge to benefit society and improve lives"); American Statistical Association, ETHICAL GUIDELINES FOR STAT. PRAC. (AM. STAT. ASS'N 2022), https://www.amstat.org/docs/default-source/amstat-documents/ethicalguidelines.pdf?Status=Master&sfvrsn=bdeeafdd_6/ (last visited Aug. 6, 2023) (defining professional integrity to include "[using] methodology and data that are valid, relevant, and appropriate, without favoritism or prejudice, and in a manner intended to produce valid, interpretable, and reproducible results" and "[opposing] efforts to predetermine or influence the results of statistical practices and resists pressure to selectively interpret data").

[38] *See The Roadmap*, EDUCATING FOR AMERICAN DEMOCRACY, https://www.educatingforamericandemocracy.org/the-roadmap/5designchallenges/ (last visited Aug. 6, 2023) ("civic honesty" and "reflective patriotism" as part of what civics education should aim for).

[39] *See* ROBERT C. POST, DEMOCRACY, EXPERTISE, AND ACADEMIC FREEDOM: A FIRST AMENDMENT JURISPRUDENCE FOR THE MODERN STATE (2012); Bruce Ackerman, *The New Separation of Powers*, 113 HARV. L. REV. 633, 688–97 (2000).

motivated job discipline,[40] should be regarded as fulfilling a constitutional requirement of representative government—that the laws enacted by representatives be administered impartially and based on sound knowledge applied to the statutory objectives.

Central to the idea of civic virtue are the ideas that public officials should act in the public interest and that some solidarity among citizens supports public-interested governance. Governance benefiting only a portion of the public to the exclusion of others is antithetical to democratic norms of equality among those in the polity, and may also be a form of corruption.

Does fostering civic virtue or solidarity require a reinvigorated idea of constitutional (or civic) duties? A virtue is a disposition; a duty is an obligation. They are closely related, but duties are in theory enforceable—by courts, or administrative actors, or constituents. One cannot force someone to be virtuous, but persons can be forced to perform or fulfill duties, or encouraged to do so by the establishment and reinforcement of virtuous norms. Do elected and executive branch officials have duties—do they have "proconstitutional" obligations in the way they conduct their public offices? There are strong reasons to say that they do, and that the scope of those obligations cannot be limited to only what courts regard as justiciable.[41]

US constitutional law is often thought of as reluctant to find *justiciable* constitutional duties, and certainly it is, in comparison to the many other more modern constitutional systems whose texts articulate positive duties of government that the courts are expected to and have adjudicated. As I indicated above in discussing *Little Sisters*, there is a distinction between whether a duty exists and whether that duty is justiciable. "Political constitutionalism" may be centrally concerned with the obligations of political actors to carry out constitutional duties; these are the terms in which Tarun Khaitan, among others, has discussed the "Directive Principles" of the Indian Constitution;[42] and my understanding of Jeremy Waldron's work on

[40] *See* Pendleton Civil Service Reform Act, 22 Stat. 403 (1883) (original civil service statute). Today, the federal civil service is divided into three categories: the competitive service; the exempted service; and the Senior Executive Service (which includes both career and, in certain cases, political appointees). *See* Jon O. Shimabukuro & Jennifer A. Staman, Cong. Rsch. Serv., R45635, Categories of Federal Civil Service Employees: A Snapshot 1, 6 (2019). On recent threats to the civil service's nonpartisan character, *see* Creating Schedule F in the Exempted Service, Exec. Order 13,957, 85 Fed. Reg. 67631 (2020), *revoked by* Exec. Order 14,003, 86 Fed. Reg. 7231 (2021) (Trump-era executive order creating new category within the exempted service for "positions of a confidential, policy-determining, policy-making, or policy-advocating character that are *not* normally subject to change as a result of a Presidential transition") (emphasis added); Jonathan Swan, *A Radical Plan for Trump's Second Term*, Axios (July 22, 2023) (noting that if Schedule F were reimposed, a future president "could fire tens of thousands of career government officials with no recourse for appeals. He could replace them with people he believes are more loyal to him and to his [ideological] agenda. Even if [the President] did not deploy Schedule F to this extent, the very fact that such power exists could create a significant chilling effect on government employees").

[41] *See* Jackson, *Pro-Constitutional Representation*, *supra* note 10, at 1744.

[42] Tarunabh Khaitan, *Constitutional Directives and the Duty to Govern Well*, *in* Constitutionalism and a Right to Effective Government? 193, 201, 204 (Vicki C. Jackson & Yasmin Dawood eds., 2022).

the dignity of legislation is that elected representatives would feel an obligation to properly account for claims of individual rights in considering contentious issues of social policy.[43]

The conventional understanding of the US Constitution—as a "negative" constitution, which provides primarily for what government cannot do rather than for what government must do—is incomplete, for it was also plainly a purpose of the 1789 Constitution to bring into being a working government. The US Constitution's structural articles include a number of "shall" commands (for example, in Article I that a census "shall be made" every ten years, or in Article II that the President "shall take care that the laws be faithfully executed");[44] the Constitution requires the Congress to "assemble" at least once a year.[45] The Fourteenth Amendment's safeguarding of "the equal protection of the laws," as both a textual and a historical matter, connotes a set of positive obligations on governments, as Robin West, among others, has argued.[46]

By providing for the popular election of representatives and requiring that the United States guarantee a republican form of government, moreover, the Constitution plainly grounds its own claim to legitimacy in a commitment to self-governance through regular elections of representatives, whose task it is, presumably, to represent the public. That the US Court treats claims against excessively partisan gerrymandering as nonjusticiable should not obscure agreement (of what appears to be a majority of the Justices at the time) with the position that excessively partisan districting is inconsistent with presuppositions about the role of representation.[47] But the Court's sometimes-vision of itself as possessing "supersupremacy"[48] in the interpretation of the Constitution leads it—and the public—too often to conflate what is constitutionally justiciable with the scope

[43] WALDRON, *supra* note 2.

[44] This "take care" clause, it has recently been argued, is more about imposing duties on the President than granting powers. *See* Andrew Kent et al., *Faithful Execution and Article II*, 132 HARV. L. REV. 2111 (2019). For other accounts of "positive" aspects of the U.S. constitution, see, e.g., SOTIRIOS BARBER, WELFARE AND THE CONSTITUTION 1–3 (2003) (discussing the Preamble's "general welfare" clause); Steven J. Heyman, *The First Duty of Government: Protection, Liberty, and the Fourteenth Amendment*, 41 DUKE L.J. 507, 524–42, 557–63 (1991) (due process clause-based right to protection); Susan Bandes, *The Negative Constitution: A Critique*, 88 MICH. L. REV. 2271, 2308–34 (1990) (arguing for a conception of positive rights); Owen M. Fiss, *Why the State?*, 100 HARV. L. REV. 781, 785–94 (1987) (obligations to protect freedoms of speaking); Shalev Roisman, *Presidential Factfinding*, 72 VAND L. REV. 825, 827–34, 837–45, 852 (arguing "that the President has a constitutional duty to act . . . honestly and based on reasonable inquiry").

[45] U.S. Const. art I, §4 ("shall assemble").

[46] *See* Robin West, *Toward an Abolitionist Interpretation of the Fourteenth Amendment*, 94 W. VA. L. REV. 111, 130 (1991).

[47] *See* Rucho v. Common Cause, 139 S.Ct. 2484, 2506–07 (2019) ("Excessive partisanship in districting leads to results that reasonably seem unjust. But the fact that such gerrymandering is 'incompatible with democratic principles' . . . does not mean that the solution lies with the federal judiciary"). Other parts of the opinion sound less in limits on judicial competence and more as if the Court is saying that the Constitution includes no duty to avoid excessive partisanship in districting.

[48] On supersupremacy, *see* Vicki C. Jackson, *Introduction: Congressional Control of Jurisdiction and the Future of the Federal Courts*, 86 GEO. L.J. 2445 (1998).

of what is constitutionally required—that is, if a question is nonjusticiable, this is (mistakenly) taken to imply that the challenged conduct is constitutionally permissible.

As Mark Tushnet has repeatedly urged, judicial decisions rejecting constitutional challenges may add to the harm caused by the challenged action by implying not only that the courts cannot remedy the harm but that the harm is not a violation of any legal duty or norm, that the conduct is constitutionally legitimate.[49] This risk exists, but could perhaps be mitigated if the courts were more aware of the existence and importance of nonjusticiable obligations of political officials; if the courts refrained from suggesting that no duties exist other than those enforceable by courts; and if courts were willing to express at least advisory opinions to this effect. Thus in discussing *Little Sisters* I suggested that it is one thing to say that courts are not well situated to enforce a norm of openmindedness; it is a very different matter to say that the framework statute for assuring the lawfulness of administrative action does not contemplate such a duty. Government officials may owe duties to the polity, under the Constitution, that are not correlated with (judicially) enforceable individual rights.

Elected representatives should be understood to have a range of constitutional duties, even if they are nonjusticiable.[50] A government "shutdown" for failure to enact a budget should be regarded as a default in the constitutional obligations of the legislature to enable government to act. Persistent failures to nominate and confirm persons for important government positions required to enable existing statutory schemes to work might similarly be regarded as a default of a constitutional duty, albeit nonjusticiable. Failure to take statutory action to preserve the capacity of an independent press to report on government activities[51] is itself a

[49] *See* Mark Tushnet, *Social Welfare Rights and Judicial Review,* 82 TEX. L. REV. 1895, 1914–18 (2004).

[50] On the duties implicit in being an elected representative, see generally HANNA FENICHEL PIFTKIN, THE CONCEPT OF REPRESENTATION (1967). Being a good representative is challenging and the role morality of a representative differs from that of a judge or a private citizens. *See* Jackson, *Pro-Constitutional Representation, supra* note 10; Beerbohm, *supra* note 13; *see also* Michael Walzer, *Political Action: The Problem of Dirty Hands,* 2 PHIL. & PUB. AFF. 160 (1973). For some, representation consists primarily in discerning what constituents want (or if they have no view, what is in their interest), and acting accordingly. For others, representation requires *considering* what constituents want, but then deciding independently on the best course. For this latter view, emblemized by Edmund Burke's famous opposition to mandatory instruction in his *Speech to the Electors of Bristol* (1774), the representative's knowledge and experience in government are critical. *See* RICHARD BOURKE, EMPIRE AND REVOLUTION 385–86, 410 (2015) (explaining how Burke distinguished deliberation, a representative's duty, from "will"); DAVID BROMWICH, THE INTELLECTUAL LIFE OF EDMUND BURKE 225 (2014) (discussing Burke's "idea of the duties of a representative" and "of a knowledge and wisdom specially connected to politics" whereby "a lawmaker by the performance of his duties may come to know things not available to those who elect him"). But even on the former view, knowledge and experience will be helpful in working out compromises with other legislators or in resolving issues on which constituents have no discernible view.

[51] *See* MARTHA MINOW, SAVING THE NEWS: WHY THE CONSTITUTION CALLS FOR GOVERNMENT ACTION TO PRESERVE FREEDOM OF SPEECH 58–61 (2021) ("[T]he First Amendment may itself require the government to take action to strengthen the information and news functions presupposed by democratic governance"); Martha Minow, *Does the First Amendment Forbid, Permit, or Require Government Support of News Industries?, in* CONSTITUTIONALISM AND A RIGHT TO EFFECTIVE GOVERNMENT? 86

failure of proconstitutional representation, as are failures to protect other knowledge institutions (including in the civil service).

The language of constitutional duty might prove helpful, at the margins, in mustering public demands to meet these politically enforceable obligations. And the recognition of constitutional duties in this broader way may, in some small way, contribute to the fostering of civic virtue, by the message that public officials—to be admired for doing their job—need to act in public-spirited ways. Constitutional law professors and judges are engaged in discourses of constitutional rights and duties; it is my hope that these discourses of duties can expand to embrace more of the nonjusticiable but constitutionally vital duties of other branches of government.[52] In all of these ways, then, I join Tushnet's call for attention to the institutions that can contribute to the development of civic virtue.

(Vicki C. Jackson & Yasmin Dawood eds., 2022) ("effort[s] to improve the ecosystem of news . . . may even be required by the First Amendment"); Martha Minow, *The Changing Ecosystem of News and Challenges for Freedom of the Press*, 64 Loy. L. Rev. 499, 539–40, 543–54 (2018) (describing initiatives to protect the press for the government, including Congress).

[52] Different implications may arise for citizens. Although citizens have duties defined in law—duties of military service, for example, or to serve on juries, or (in some polities) to vote, *see supra* note 12—a thin conception of such duties is probably best suited to a polity dedicated to sustaining large spaces for individual autonomy and freedom. For citizens in such polities the distinction between *virtue* and *duty* may be even more important than for elected officials.

23

Popular Constitutionalism during Populist Times

Bojan Bugarič

Introduction

In this short contribution, I would like to argue that Professor Mark Tushnet's scholarship has always been animated by his deep commitment to democratic ideals. Tushnet's writings on different constitutional law topics reveal his consistent commitment to democracy as a foundational value of his constitutional thinking. As a constitutional law scholar, he is particularly interested in the concept of popular constitutionalism.[1] The key feature of popular constitutionalism is that the people ultimately control the interpretation of constitutional law. In his own articulation of popular constitutionalism, Professor Tushnet seeks to retrieve and reinvent this prominent tradition of American constitutionalism. Building upon the work of Larry Kramer's seminal historical account of popular constitutionalism, *The People Themselves: Popular Constitutionalism and Judicial Review*,[2] Professor Tushnet argues that one key feature of this model is that it is a dialogic process: "In popular constitutionalism, everyone—the mobilized people, their political representatives, and the courts—offers up constitutional interpretations all at once."[3] Furthermore, what is distinctive about this model "is that the courts have no normative priority in the conversation."[4] The picture that emerges from the sketches of popular constitutionalism clearly reveals that Professor Tushnet's conceptualization of popular constitutionalism is not the case against judicial review as such, or, even worse, against the courts and their independence.[5] The core

[1] Mark Tushnet, Taking Back the Constitution (2020), particularly Chapter 15, *Popular Constitutionalism versus Judicial Supremacy*. In his earlier magnum opus, Taking the Constitution Away from the Courts (1999), Tushnet uses the term "populist constitutionalism." As I will argue in this chapter, Tushnet uses "popular" and "populist" interchangeably. See also his article *Popular Constitutionalism as Political Law*, 81 Chi.-Kent L. Rev. 991 (2006).

[2] Larry D. Kramer, The People Themselves: Popular Constitutionalism and Judicial Review (2004). For other important work in this tradition, see Richard D. Parker, "Here, the People Rule": A Constitutional Populist Manifesto (1994). For a brief and succinct conceptual account, see R. Gargarella, *Popular Constitutionalism, in* Encyclopedia of the Philosophy of Law and Social Philosophy (M. Sellers & S. Kirste eds., 2020).

[3] Tushnet, *Popular Constitutionalism as Political Law*, *supra* note 1, at 999.

[4] *Id.*

[5] See for example Tushnet's argument defending a weak form of judicial review, Weak Courts, Strong Rights: Judicial Review and Social Welfare Rights in Comparative Constitutional

Bojan Bugarič, *Popular Constitutionalism during Populist Times* In: *Redefining Comparative Constitutional Law*. Edited by: Vicki C. Jackson and Madhav Khosla, Oxford University Press. © Bojan Bugarič 2025.
DOI: 10.1093/9780191996344.003.0023

claim of his work is that judges are no better than citizens in making informed decisions about their political choices. Therefore, it follows almost logically that it would be wrong to give the power over those decisions to nine unelected judges instead to citizens themselves.

His strong belief in the people's judgment is nicely illustrated with this passage from his short contribution to *Dissent* in 2005:

> One T-shirt sold after the 2004 election listed what the Democratic Party has accomplished: Equal Pay. Equal Rights. 40 Hour Work Week. Social Security. Medicare. Clean Water. Clean Air. Safe Food. Freedom of Speech. Voting Rights. All but the last two were achieved primarily through legislation, and some—the social welfare achievements of the modern state—had little connection to the Supreme Court, except when it obstructed them.[6]

Professor Tushnet's argument here is not only that popular constitutionalism's most important "feature may be that the people's interpretations are often different from—even inconsistent with—the views prevailing among elite lawyers,"[7] but also that people are capable, through democracy, of making perfectly sound and good political decisions. As a result, it makes more sense to let people and not judges make the most important political decisions in a democracy. Moreover, as Tushnet argues, from a normative political perspective, popular constitutionalism is appealing because it "expresses democracy's core commitment to popular self-government, while judicial supremacy expresses a commitment to government by elites."[8]

Popular Constitutionalism in the Age of Populism[9]

Around the world, governments characterized by observers as populist have taken power. Many of their actions have been incompatible with tenets of modern liberalism. This has generated commentary suggesting that populism is itself incompatible with constitutionalism. As a result, some constitutional scholars have voiced

LAW (2007). Similarly, for Tushnet judicial independence represents one of the key elements of constitutionalism. See MARK TUSHNET & BOJAN BUGARIČ, POWER TO THE PEOPLE: CONSTITUTIONALISM IN THE AGE OF POPULISM 24 (2021).

[6] Mark Tushnet, *Democracy vs Judicial Review: Is It Time to Amend the Constitution?*, 52 DISSENT 59, 60 (2005).
[7] TUSHNET, TAKING BACK THE CONSTITUTION, *supra* note 1, at 245.
[8] *Id.* at 246.
[9] Parts of this chapter are drawn from Bojan Bugarič, *Could Populism Be Good for Constitutional Democracy*, 15 ANN. REV. L. & SOC. SCI. 41 (2019); TUSHNET & BUGARIČ, *supra* note 5.

concern as to whether Professor Tushnet's advocacy of popular constitutionalism during populist times can be defended on an empirical level.[10]

There is a tendency in current constitutional thinking to reduce populism to a single set of universal elements. These theories juxtapose populism with constitutionalism and argue that populism is by definition antithetical to constitutionalism.[11] Populism, according to this view, "undermines the very substance of constitutional (liberal) democracy. By attacking the core elements of constitutional democracy, such as independent courts, free media, civil rights and fair electoral rules, populism by necessity degenerates into one or another form of anti-liberal and authoritarian order."[12]

In this chapter, I argue that such an approach is not only historically inaccurate but also normatively flawed. There are historical examples of different forms of populism, such as the New Deal in the United States, which did not degenerate into authoritarianism and which actually helped American democracy survive the Great Depression of the 1930s. Looking at the current populist map, we can also find examples of such democratic populists, who seek to protect and defend democracy by making it more responsive, equitable, and inclusive. Hence, it is wrong to argue that there is something intrinsic to populism which makes it incompatible with constitutionalism.

We must therefore distinguish between varieties of populism. There is not a single form of populism, but rather a variety of different forms, each with profoundly different political consequences. Populism always coexists with one or other of a variety of different host ideologies, which significantly determine how populism affects democracy.[13] As more recent empirical studies of the effects of populism over constitutional democracy show, the picture is mixed: Populism has both negative and positive consequences for democracy.[14] While it is clear that certain instances of authoritarian populism lead to democratic backsliding and breakdown, it is also true that democratic populism can foster democratization.

[10] Rosalind Dixon, *Power to the People: Democratic Populism or Egalitarian Liberalism?*, Balkinization symposium on Mark Tushnet and Bojan Bugarič, *Power to the People: Constitutionalism in the Age of Populism*, https://balkin.blogspot.com/2022/03/power-to-people-democratic-populism-or.html.

[11] Cristóbal Rovira Kaltwasser, *Populism vs. Constitutionalism: Comparative Perspectives on Contemporary Western Europe, Latin America, and the United States*, Policy Brief, The Foundation for Law, Justice, and Society (2013); Jan Werner Müller, What Is Populism? (2016); William Galston, Anti-Pluralism: The Populist Threat to Liberal Democracy (2018); Yascha Mounk, The People vs. Democracy: Why Our Freedom is in Danger and How to Save It (2018); Stefan Rummens, *Populism as a Threat to Liberal Democracy*, *in* Oxford Handbook of Populism 554 (Cristóbal Rovira Kaltwasser, Paul Taggart, Paulina Ochoa Espejo & Pierre Ostiguy eds., 2017).

[12] Takis S Pappas, *Populists in Power*, 30 J. Democracy 70 (2019).

[13] Benjamin Moffitt, Populism (2020).

[14] Kirk A. Hawkins & Cristóbal Rovira Kaltwasser, *What the (Ideational) Study of Populism Can Teach Us, and What It Can't*, 23 Swiss Pol. Sci. Rev. 526 (2017).

As a result, "despite the fact that there are good reasons for worrying about the rise of populism, scholars are probably putting too much emphasis on the downsides and thus not considering potential positive effects of populist forces."[15] The limits of the dominant approach, which defines populism in a singular "generic" form, lie precisely in neglecting to analyze the impact of host ideologies on legal and political consequences of various populist forces. Once we couple populist discourse with (host) ideology, we see a much more complicated pattern of interrelationship between populism and constitutional democracy: populism comes in different versions, with quite different impacts on constitutionalism and the rule of law. Examples of democratic, liberal, socially inclusive forms of populism quite clearly show that authoritarianism and antipluralism are not necessarily the key elements of populism. Of course, sometimes conservative and progressive populists slide into authoritarianism. When they do they are best described, as Douglas Johnson puts it, as authoritarians masquerading as populists.[16]

Professor Tushnet offers the most trenchant critique of such a "generic" approach to populism:

> Most academic writing has focused on the right-wing versions. That writing generates critiques of what the authors describe as generic populism, critiques that the authors then apply to left-wing populism. It seems to me, though, that the critiques are mostly concerned with the "right-wing-ness" of the object of study, but present themselves in politically neutral terms—presumably because direct political criticism would seem unscholarly.[17]

Instead of talking about populism in general, Professor Tushnet argues, scholars should direct their attention to the questions posed by specific actions taken by individual populist governments. Most general accounts of populism treat it as a style of politics or form of political discourse devoid of any particular ideology. Coupling populism with different host ideologies, however, shows that populist parties and leaders have very different conceptions of the people, goals, and relations to liberal democracy.

[15] *Id.* at 531.

[16] Douglas A. Johnson, *In Defence of Democratic Populism*, *in* HUMAN RIGHTS IN A TIME OF POPULISM: CHALLENGES AND RESPONSES (Gerald L Neumann ed., 2020).

[17] Mark Tushnet, *Comparing Right-Wing and Left-Wing Populism*, *in* CONSTITUTIONAL DEMOCRACY IN CRISIS? 639 (Mark A. Graber, Sanford Levinson & Mark Tushnet eds., 2018).

Is Populism (Always) Antithetical to Constitutionalism?

Populism as Anti-Liberalism: Is There a Single Formula to Define Populism?

Handbooks, research guides, and companions to populism abound. Authors use the term to refer to a large number of political movements, and no agreed-upon definition has yet emerged. The most commonly used definition of populism under this approach comes from Cas Mudde. According to Mudde, populism is

> a thin-centered ideology that considers society to be ultimately separated into two homogeneous and antagonistic groups, "the pure people" versus "the corrupt elite," and which argues that politics should be an expression of the volonté générale (general will) of the people.[18]

Similarly, Jan-Werner Müller, probably the most widely cited author on this matter, defines populism as "a way of perceiving the political world that sets a morally pure and fully united—but . . . ultimately fictional—people against elites who are deemed corrupt or in some way morally inferior."[19]

As Moffitt correctly notes, both Mudde and Müller highlight two core features of populism: "a) the divide between the people and the elite and b) the homogeneity, unification and moral purity of the people."[20] One of the most important narratives that has developed around populism in the academic literature is that it is a threat to liberal democracy. Mudde and Müller are strong proponents of this view. For both of them, populism's core features imply that populism is at odds with liberal democracy. For Müller, populism is "a profoundly illiberal and, in the end, directly undemocratic understanding of representative democracy."[21] While Mudde allows the possibility that populism can potentially be democratic, he agrees with Müller that it is illiberal. Hence, on both readings, populism's essential trait is a rejection of pluralism: "Populism holds that nothing should constrain 'the will of the (pure) people' and fundamentally rejects the notions of pluralism and, there-fore, minority rights as well as the 'institutional guarantees' that should protect them."[22]

My view is that, to use a tired metaphor, populisms may share a family resemblance, but the family is an extended one whose dispersal around the world has

[18] Cas Mudde, *The Populist Zeitgeist*, 39 Gov't & Opposition 54, 543 (2004).
[19] Müller, *supra* note 11, at 19–20.
[20] Moffitt, *supra* note 13, at 14.
[21] Jan Werner Müller, *The People Must be Extracted from Within the People: Reflections on Populism*, 21 Constellations 484 (2014).
[22] Cas Mudde & Cristóbal Rovira Kaltwasser, Populism: A Very Short Introduction 81 (2017).

produced members who could have little to say to each other at a family reunion. Treating populism as inherently antiliberal and antipluralist is somewhat in tension with another element of the ideational approach to populism. As mentioned earlier, Mudde defines populism as a "thin-centered ideology," suggesting populism has the 'ability to cohabit with other, more comprehensive ideologies.'[23] The implication of the thin-centered nature of populism is that "it does not stand alone as an ideology but it is rather always combined with other ideologies."[24]

Such adaptability of populism is best captured by Paul Taggart's claim that populism is chameleon-like, ever adapting to the colors of its environment.[25] As a thin-centered ideology, populism shares characteristics of other thin-centered ideologies such as nationalism, feminism, and green politics rather than being a thick ideology like liberalism, socialism, or fascism. Hence, there exist several rather different varieties of populism: agrarian, socio-economic, xenophobic, reactionary, authoritarian, and progressive.[26] In order fully to understand the logic of the different populisms, we have to approach them as socially and historically contingent categories. Anna Grzymala Busse argues that instead of analyzing populism per se, we should recognize that it takes a variety of guises.[27]

As mentioned, earlier, some examples of populism quite clearly show that authoritarianism and antipluralism are not necessarily the key elements of populism. Curiously enough, despite the variety of forms that populism can assume, there is a tendency in current academic literature, both in political science and law, to reduce populism to a set of generic elements such as antipluralism, the people's homogeneity and exclusivity, nationalism, a strong single leader, impatience with institutions, direct rule, and vilification of minorities. These theories usually juxtapose populism with constitutionalism and argue that populism as such is antithetical to constitutionalism. Populism, according to this literature, "fundamentally opposes the essence of constitutionalism,"[28] and is "the mirror-image opposite, and a major foe, of contemporary liberal democracy."[29]

Jan-Werner Müller's formulation is probably the most widely cited. He argues that populism is not only antielitist but also antipluralist: populists claim that "they, and they alone, represent the people."[30] In their worldview, there are

[23] Ben Stanley, *The Thin Ideology of Populism*, 13 J. Pol. Ideologies 95, 100 (2008).

[24] Moffitt, *supra* note 13, at 13.

[25] Paul Taggart, Populism 4 (2000).

[26] Margaret Canovan, Populism (1981); Noam Gidron & Bart Bonikowski, *Varieties of Populism: Literature Review and Research Agenda*, Working Paper Series No 13-0004, Weatherhead Center for International Affairs, Harvard University (2013); Cas Mudde & Cristóbal Rovira Kaltwasser, *Populism*, *in* Oxford Handbook of Political Ideologies 493 (Michael Freeden, Lyman Tower Sargent and Marc Stears eds., 2013).

[27] Anna Grzymala-Busse, *Global Populisms and Their Impact*, 76 Slavic Rev. S3 (2017).

[28] Cas Mudde, *Are Populists Friends or Foes of Constitutionalism?*, The Foundation for Law, Justice, and Society 4 (2013), www.ora.ox.ac.uk/objects/uuid:fc657de0-ab0c-4911-8d2b-646101599b65.

[29] Pappas, *supra* note 12, at 70.

[30] Müller, *supra* note 11, at 20.

no opponents, only traitors. The opposition leaders are delegitimized through being cast as not caring about ordinary citizens, but only about the interests of various "liberal" elites. Hence, on Müller's reading, populism's essential trait is a rejection of pluralism. The second element of the 'inner logic of populism' is the non-institutionalized notion of the people: "For them, 'the people themselves' is a fictional entity outside existing democratic procedures, a homogeneous and morally unified body whose alleged will can be played off against actual election results in democracies."[31]

What populists actually assert is "that there is a singular and morally privileged understanding or will that has not been manifest through the formal structures of democratic choice."[32] This leads us to the third element of populism: a populist leader. The role of the populist leader is to do what the people want. The formal structures of liberal democracy have to be put aside if they are preventing the populist leader from fulfilling his role. Populist leaders distrust all the traditional institutions of liberal democracy that stand between them and the wishes of the people. As a result, many of the populist parties openly flout the rule of law and explicitly reject the values of liberal democracy. A corollary of this element is the strong personalization of power, reflected in the fact that strong leaders such as Orbán and Kaczynski have managed to concentrate almost unlimited political power in their own hands.

Müller's definition of populism has many followers in the constitutional law literature. Conceptualized in this way, with the core antipluralist "inner logic," Schmittian understanding of the people,[33] and the strong role of the powerful leader, populism clearly comes into conflict with liberalism's commitment to pluralism, openness, and protection of individual rights. Moreover, after Müller moves from the analysis of populist inner logic to an examination of what populists actually do when in power, populism becomes almost indistinguishable from authoritarianism and dictatorship. The hallmarks of populism in power are colonization of the state, mass clientelism and mass corruption, and the systematic repression of civil society.[34] It is no surprise then that Müller views populism essentially as "a permanent shadow of modern representative democracy, and a constant peril."[35]

In light of the particular type of populism that has evolved in East Central Europe, which is the central focus of his study, most of Müller's claims seem reasonably accurate. The authoritarian populists in Hungary and Poland

31 *Id.* at 27.
32 Aziz Z Huq, *The People Against the Constitution*, 116 MICH. L. REV. 1123 (2018).
33 CARL SCHMITT, THE CRISIS OF PARLIAMENTARY DEMOCRACY (1985).
34 MÜLLER, *supra* note 11, at 44–48.
35 *Id.* at 11.

have successfully institutionalized, through legal reforms, a new version of a semiauthoritarian regime, which sits halfway between "diminished democracy"[36] and "competitive authoritarianism."[37]

However, while Müller's definition relatively accurately captures the "inner logic" of one particular type of populism, authoritarian populism, it leaves out many other possible types of populism which do not necessarily share the same characteristics. Though Müller puts anti-pluralism at the center of his analysis, his presentation, in contrast, could be understood to refer to nearly all forms of political activity by "ordinary" people unified for political purposes only in a project aimed at displacing existing ruling elites with political leaders more attuned to the interests of the people—interests that could in principle vary depending on which groups of ordinary people are most immediately affected by specific policies. The corruption and moral inferiority that Müller sees in populism's description of ruling elites could, again in principle, be a way of characterizing their failure to take the interests of (a possibly pluralist) "ordinary" population adequately into account.

A "selection bias" of generic approaches, criticized by Professor Tushnet, has been given more detailed scrutiny more recently. Thomas Frank critiques Müller for wrongly using the word populist to describe only racist and authoritarian demagogues.[38] Marco D'Eramo and Daniel Steinmetz-Jenkins criticize Müller's definition of populism for excluding a figure like Bernie Sanders from the ranks of the populists.[39] Frank lists several historical figures associated with progressive and democratic populism in the United States: Andrew Jackson, the Populist Party, and FDR. Frank also reminds us of an alternative definition of populism, offered by historian Lawrence Goodwyn. In the opening statement of his book *The Populist Moment*, Goodwyn argues: "This book is about the flowering of the largest democratic mass movement in American history. It is also necessarily a book about democracy itself."[40]

For Goodwyn, populism represented "a vision of democratic participation that was actually more advanced than what we settle for today. Far from being a threat to democracy, Populism was democracy's zenith."[41]

[36] David Collier & Steven Levitsky, *Democracy with Adjectives: Conceptual Innovation in Comparative Research*, 49 World Pol. 430 (1997).

[37] Steven Levitsky & Lucian A. Way, Competitive Authoritarianism: Hybrid Regimes After the Cold War (2010).

[38] Thomas Frank, The People, No: A Brief History of Anti-Populism 35 (2020).

[39] Marco D'Eramo, *They, The People*, 103 New Left Rev. 129 (2017); Daniel Steinmetz-Jenkins, *The Logic of Populism*, 64 Dissent 186 (2017).

[40] Lawrence Goodwyn, The Populist Moment: A Short History of the Agrarian Revolt in America vii (1978).

[41] Thomas Frank, *Forget Trump—populism is the cure, not disease*, The Guardian (23 May 2018).

Populism: From a Single Formula to "Varieties of Populism"

The limits of these theories, which define populism in a singular "generic" form, lie precisely in their neglecting to analyze the impact of host ideologies on legal and political consequences of various populist forces. As Camilla Vergara argues, these theories have contributed to a "totalitarian turn" in the conception of populism toward an identitarian, xenophobic, and oligarchic form of politics clothed in populist rhetoric.[42] We must therefore distinguish between many different forms of populism, each with profoundly different political and constitutional consequences. When we examine the relationship between populism and constitutional democracy, populism should not be considered in isolation from its host ideology.

Margaret Canovan was one of the first scholars of populism who argued that populism comes both in democratic and authoritarian forms. She claimed that populism is "born out of crisis as a cure for the failures of traditional forms of representation."[43] She argued that democracy has two faces, "redemptive" and "pragmatic," and that populism thrives on the tension between the two, representing the invocation of the redemptive face of democracy, as a "corrective to the excesses of pragmatism."[44] For Canovan, populism is a democratizing phenomenon aimed at perfecting democratic representativeness, renewing the political system from within. Similarly, for Hannah Arendt, "these episodes of collective self-assertion are invariably fleeting and in stand in tension with the need for a more stable constitution of collective freedom, embodied in the rule of law, and representative institutions,"[45] and thus represent "a constitutive feature of the modern democratic project."[46] To label them "populist," in a pejorative sense, is to misunderstand this inherent instability of the democratic project. As James Miller argues, the populist "outbursts are essential to the continued vitality, and viability, of modern democracy—even as (and precisely because) they challenge the status quo, destructive though that challenge may be."[47] As Vergara correctly argues, "this normative dimension of populism, as a 'corrective' was gradually lost within the theoretical discussion especially after the 'discursive turn' in the interpretation of the concept in the late 2000s."[48]

In their recent article, Jane Mansbridge and Stephen Macedo argue that there is a "common conceptual core" of populism, which fits all cases of populism, both

[42] Camila Vergara, *Populism as Plebeian Politics: Inequality, Domination, and Popular Empowerment*, 28 J. Pol. Phil. 222 (2020).

[43] Margaret Canovan, *Trust the People! Populism and the Two Faces of Democracy*, 47 Pol. Stud. 8 (1999).

[44] Vergara, *supra* note 42, at 229.

[45] James Miller, Can Democracy Work? A Short History of a Radical Idea from Ancient Athens to Our World 11 (2018).

[46] *Id.* at 11.

[47] *Id.*

[48] Vergara, *supra* note 42, at 230.

left and right, those in the United States, Europe and elsewhere. Their minimal common core defines populism as "the people" in a moral battle against "the elites." As such, this minimum core definition does not preclude either progressive or conservative or authoritarian forms of populism. Furthermore, they argue, the core can be good for democracy, because the core elements "benefit democracy by taking democratic politics back to its normative roots in the wants and needs of ordinary citizens and challenging, on egalitarian and justice grounds, elite political, economic, and cultural domination."[49] They warn that the moral antagonism inherent in populism's core elements has the potential to undermine "the democratic commitment to treating all members of the polity, including members of the elite, with respect [and] the capacity of democracy for negotiation and compromise."[50] However, unlike other authors who attribute to populists the Schmittian concept of politics, they emphasize that the core elements are not inherently in tension with constitutionalism. It is only the associated characteristics that are often dangerous. They come in two different groupings, being strongly suggested but not entailed characteristics, and then frequent correlates. In the first group we find elements such as a homogeneous people, an exclusive people, greater direct popular rule, and nationalism. The second group comprises elements such as a strong leader embodying the people, vilification of minority groups, and impatience with deliberation. Again, the core elements are not antidemocratic and inherently in conflict with liberalism. It is only when the core elements are accompanied by some of the elements from two other groups that populism is created. They conclude that populism is "sometimes healthy for democracy in opposition but rarely healthy in power."[51] I believe that Mansbridge and Macedo's two-pronged definition of populism, with its core and accompanying elements, better fits the complexity and multiplicity of forms that populism can assume. It allows us to see the multifaceted nature of populism, which sometimes comes in democratic form and sometimes in authoritarian or illiberal form.

In another important recent study of populism, Pippa Norris and Ronald Inglehart argue that populism comes in authoritarian and libertarian versions.[52] Their definition of authoritarian populism partially differs from other approaches (Mudde, Müller, Mansbridge, Macedo). What primarily distinguishes authoritarian from libertarian populism is the embrace of authoritarian values such as security, conformity, and obedience, which lead to "prioritising collective security for the group at the expense of liberal autonomy of the individual."[53] For my

[49] Jane Mansbridge & Stephen Macedo, *Populism and Democratic Theory*, 15 Ann. Rev. L. & Soc. Sci. 60 (2019).

[50] *Id.* at 60.

[51] *Id.* at 73.

[52] Pippa Norris & Ronald Inglehart, Cultural Backlash: Trump, Brexit and the Rise of Authoritarian Populism (2019).

[53] *Id.* at 7.

argument, it is important that Norris and Inglehart, like Mansbridge and Macedo, allow the possibility of "varieties of populism" and identify key elements for both types of populism. For the second type, the libertarian populist parties, they argue, it is typical that they "use populist discourse railing against corruption, mainstream parties, and multinational corporations, but this is blended with the endorsement of socially liberal attitudes, progressive social policies and participatory styles of political engagement."[54] They also argue that these parties are less common as a type but their support has also grown in recent years in several European states. Among libertarian populists, Norris and Inglehart include Spain's Podemos Party and the Indignados Movement, Greece's Syriza, the Left Party in Germany, the Socialist Party in the Netherlands, Italy's Five Star Movement, Bernie Sanders in the US, and so on. These examples of democratic, liberal, socially inclusive forms of populism demonstrate, in a more or less perfect form, that authoritarianism and antipluralism are not necessarily the key elements of populism. Despite the current hegemony of authoritarian populism, a far different sort of populism is possible: democratic and antiestablishment populism, which combines elements of liberal and democratic convictions.

Following this line of argument, sociologist Bart Bonikowski argues both that populist claims need not lead to authoritarian governance and that authoritarianism can rely on a variety of other legitimating discourses besides populism. Furthermore, Bonikowski points out that "populism has also been employed by mainstream politicians who operate within the constraints of democratic institutions. And even when populist movements have radical origins, the resulting political outcomes can be benign with respect to democratic stability."[55]

In this vein, Bonikowski mentions the People's Party in the United States and the Brexit campaign in the United Kingdom. Nevertheless, the list of examples of democratic populism is not meant to suggest that this form of populism is an exclusive domain of the political left. As the radical right usually combines populism with nativism and authoritarianism, it is simply empirically less likely to find this kind of populism (democratic) among the radical right-wing parties. As Bonikowski and Gidron show, populism has also been employed by mainstream politicians who operate within the constraints of democratic institutions (McGovern, Nixon, George H.W. Bush, Dukakis, and Clinton).[56] Moreover, radical left populism is, like its radical right counterpart, not immune to antiliberal and authoritarian tendencies.

[54] *Id.* at 11.

[55] Bart Bonikowski, *Ethno-Nationalist Populism and the Mobilization of Collective Resentment*, 68 Brit. J. Socio. 181, 190 (2017).

[56] Bart Bonikowski and Noam Gidron, *The Populist Style in American Politics: Presidential Campaign Rhetoric, 1952–1996*, 94 Soc. Forces 1593 (2016).

If the combination of populism and constitutionalism "sounds odd especially to a European ear,"[57] populist constitutionalism has a strong resonance among many prominent American constitutional scholars.[58] As Joseph Fishkin and William Forbath have recently argued, many populist movements in the United States contributed to the creation of the "antioligarchy" concept of constitutionalism, which sought to empower and protect the democratic nature of the American constitution.[59] In the same way, Bruce Ackerman has argued that the key founding moments of American constitutionalism are best defined as the episodes of democratic populist constitutionalism.[60] Mirroring the minimalist core definition of populism by Mansbridge and Macedo, David Fontana puts forward an argument for "unbundling" the antiestablishment and democratic part of populism from the authoritarian and xenophobic version.[61] And last but not least, in his most recent book on American judiciary, Mark Tushnet presents his case for popular constitutionalism, which in many aspects comes close to populist democratic constitutionalism.[62]

Conclusion

As the analysis of different forms of populism and populist constitutionalism has shown, popular constitutionalism remains an important corrective to liberal constitutionalism. The current populist upsurge, dominated by authoritarian over democratic flavors of populism, doesn't diminish the relevance of popular constitutionalism. Its relevance is poignantly captured by the following conclusion of Professor Tushnet's short essay on this topic:

> Contemporary discussions of populism tend to use the term as a pejorative. Though populisms come in different forms, they are generally reactions to real failures by political elites. Their programs include constitutional changes that often respond to the causes of those failures. Perhaps, whatever their flaws and however much they have contributed to policy failures, existing constitutions

[57] Lucia Corso, *What does Populism Have to Do with Constitutional Law? Discussing Populist Constitutionalism and Its Assumptions*, 3 Rivista Di Filosofia Dei Diritto 444 (2004).

[58] Bruce Ackerman, We the People: Foundations (1991); Kramer, *supra* note 2; Parker, *supra* note 2; Tushnet, Taking the Constitution Away from the Court, *supra* note 1.

[59] Joseph Fishkin & William E. Forbath, The Anti-Oligarchy Constitution: Reconstructing the Economic Foundations of American Democracy (2022).

[60] Ackerman, *supra* note 58.

[61] David Fontana, *Unbundling Populism*, 65 U.C.L.A. L. Rev. 1486 (2018).

[62] Mark Tushnet, Taking Back the Constitution: Activist Judges and the Next Age of American Law (2020).

cannot be improved without running excessive risks of different kinds of failures—authoritarianism, in particular. But, in the light of the failures that generated the resurgence of populism we ought to be open to considering institutional innovations and constitutional changes on their merits. Some might be valuable, others too risky. That the innovations are promoted by populists is not in itself a reason to dismiss them.[63]

[63] Mark Tushnet, *Comparing Right-Wing and Left-Wing Populism*, *in* Constitutional Democracy in Crisis? 650 (Mark A Graber, Sanford Levinson & Mark Tushnet eds., 2018).

24

Pluralizing Constitutionalism

Cora Chan

Introduction

Writings on constitutionalism in the comparative constitutional law field have, until recently, as Professor Mark Tushnet notes, "centred on liberal constitutionalism, to the point where many studies seem to assume that the field is dichotomized between generally liberal constitutionalist nations and authoritarian nations."[1] One of Professor Tushnet's many legacies will be his exposition of strains of constitutionalism other than liberal constitutionalism. He has, for example, crafted sophisticated accounts of authoritarian constitutionalism and illiberal constitutionalism and offered thought-provoking ideas on Ernst Fraenkel's concept of the dual state. His attempts at "pluralizing" constitutionalism[2] have significantly "expand[ed] the conceptual space for comparative constitutionalism."[3] Not only have they brought analytical clarity and allowed us to theorize the many regimes that do not fit into the dichotomized framework of authoritarianism versus liberal constitutionalism; they also have important normative implications for constitutional design and strategy. This chapter draws on Professor Tushnet's contributions on nonliberal constitutionalism and the dual state to examine four issues pertaining to the nature, structure, and significance of the dual state, as well as to the stability of mixed constitutions.

Is Every State a Dual State?

The first issue is whether "every state is a dual state,"[4] an unresolved question in the theory of the dual state that is pointedly raised in Professor Tushnet's work. Dual state theory was developed by Fraenkel to explain the legal system of the Third Reich, and has since been applied to theorize other authoritarian legal systems. The dual state is a bifurcated legal order, with one domain that acts arbitrarily, "unchecked by any legal guarantees" (Fraenkel calls this the "prerogative state"), and

[1] Mark Tushnet, *Varieties of Constitutionalism*, 14 Int'l J. Const. L. 1, 2 (2016).
[2] Mark Tushnet, *Authoritarian Constitutionalism*, 100 Cornell L. Rev. 391, 395 (2015).
[3] Mark Tushnet, *The Possibility of Illiberal Constitutionalism*? 69 Fla. L. Rev. 1367, 1367–68 (2017).
[4] Mark Tushnet, *The Dual State in the United States: The Case of Lynching and Legal Lynchings*, 16 L. & Ethics Hum. Rts. 41, 50 (2022).

Cora Chan, *Pluralizing Constitutionalism* In: *Redefining Comparative Constitutional Law*. Edited by: Vicki C. Jackson and Madhav Khosla, Oxford University Press. © Cora Chan 2025. DOI: 10.1093/9780191996344.003.0024

another that is by and large governed by legal rules or norms and is hence characterized by some degree of regularity and predictability (Fraenkel calls this the "normative state").[5] Two features of the dual state should be noted. First, it exhibits "structural asymmetry."[6] The normative state is subordinate to the prerogative state because the state to which a given matter is assigned is determined by the political authorities in the latter.[7] The presumption is that the normative state has jurisdiction over said matter, but the prerogative state has "jurisdiction over jurisdiction," that is, Kompetenz-Kompetenz. Legal rules govern but only to the extent that the political authorities allow. Second, because the political authorities enjoy the absolute power to determine the boundaries of the dual state's two domains, no sphere of life is "immune from the inroads of the Prerogative State."[8] Everything is potentially political.[9] The prerogative state can and may step in at any time,[10] rendering a nontrivial part of people's lives incapable of regulation by legal rules and norms.[11]

It is generally considered that the type of regime within which a dual state operates is not a full liberal democracy but nearer to the authoritarian end of the spectrum[12] because the structural dominance of the prerogative state renders the dual state significantly deficient on a key criterion for liberal democracy, namely, the rule of law.[13] However, this position may be opposed on the ground that every legal order is a dual state because there are always pockets of absolute discretion by rulers and pockets of law-based governance. Even in regimes deemed liberal democracies, rulers may suspend the rule of law when it comes to states of emergency and national security.[14] Professor Tushnet remarks, for example, that

[5] Ernst Fraenkel, The Dual State: A Contribution To The Theory Of Dictatorship xiii (E.A. Shils trans., 2010). Two points about my terminology are in order. First, I refer to the normative domain of the dual state as being "governed by legal rules." By such usage, I do not mean to imply that the normative domain must satisfy the requirements of the rule of law—not even in the thin sense. All I mean is that the normative domain of the dual state is characterized by a degree of regularity and predictability in contrast to the prerogative domain. Second, my understanding of "legal order" in this chapter is a loose one that includes any system that gives out prescriptions for people's conduct. I therefore consider the dual state as a legal order even though it has a prerogative domain. This paragraph (including this footnote) draws on Cora Chan, *From Legal Pluralism to Dual State: Evolution of the Relationship between the Chinese and Hong Kong Legal Orders* 16 L. & Ethics Hum. Rts. 99, 102, 105–06 (2022).

[6] Jens Meierhenrich, The Remnants of The Rechtsstaat: An Ethnography of Nazi Law 89 (2018).

[7] Fraenkel, *supra* note 5, at 57.

[8] *Id.* at 44.

[9] *Id.* at 57–58.

[10] Meierhenrich, *supra* note 6, at 238.

[11] Chan, *supra* note 5, at 109.

[12] See Chan, *supra* note 5, at 107–09; Meierhenrich, *supra* note 6, at 233–45.

[13] Tom Ginsburg and Aziz Z. Huq identify democratic elections, liberal rights, and the rule of law as the criteria of liberal constitutional democracy. See their How To Save A Constitutional Democracy 10–15 (2018).

[14] Chan, *supra* note 5, at 108. See also David Dyzenhaus, The Long Arc of Legality: Hobbes, Kelsen, Hart 324–25 (2022).

> [l]arge swaths of national security law . . . look a lot like the domain of arbitrariness that is said to characterize the prerogative side of the dual state. And, of course, the fact that [a] court require[s] only that the Home Secretary subjectively believe that . . . detainees ha[ve] hostile associations license[s] the Home Secretary to act arbitrarily in specific cases . . . [Over the years] [s]ome [legal] black holes have disappeared, but many remain.[15]

Accordingly, the objection goes, the dual state is but a generic legal structure that underlies even liberal democratic regimes.

I attempt here to address this objection by drawing on an insight from Professor Tushnet's work on nonliberal constitutionalism, namely, that what ultimately distinguishes various regime types and strains of constitutionalism may not be legal but rather sociological.[16] Comparing the constitutionalism in Hungary and Venezuela with that in Singapore, for example, he speculates that the leadership of the two former countries is "not committed to the idea of constitutionalism as a constraint on power," whereas that of the latter is. If that is indeed the case, then a "normative commitment to constraints on public power . . . might be a truly distinguishing characteristic of authoritarian constitutionalism."[17] If "authoritarian rulers have a direct normative commitment to some degree of constitutionalism," "authoritarian constitutionalism would then be part of the pluralized universe of constitutionalism."[18] Also, Professor Tushnet is inclined to think that self-restraint ("due to socialisation rather than institutions") that "substantially reduces the risk of arbitrary action should count as constitutionalist"[19] and, further, that conventions may contribute to an understanding of illiberal constitutionalism.[20]

My reflection on these insights suggests that what ultimately distinguishes regime types and strains of constitutionalism is not formal legal provisions or institutions, but rather the attitude of the legal and political authorities toward compliance with various constraints, an attitude that determines the effectiveness of those constraints. For example, although the UK Parliament can, in theory, discard all legal constraints upon it, the current UK regime can be deemed constitutionalist because, inter alia, its political and legal authorities have a shared normative commitment to fulfilling the substantial body of fundamental norms embodied in statutes, case law, and rights obligations under international law, even in areas in which rulers apparently enjoy wide discretion. This normative commitment translates into effective constraints on public power. The further a polity departs from

[15] Tushnet, *supra* note 4, at 44.

[16] An alternative way of framing this is that what ultimately makes a rule legal might be its sociological aspects.

[17] Tushnet, *supra* note 2, at 438.

[18] *Id.* at 448.

[19] *Id.* at 416 n.135.

[20] Tushnet, *supra* note 1, at 4.

that commitment, the less effective the constraints on its power are, and the less it can be deemed constitutionalist. Applying this argument to the present discussion, what distinguishes a dual state from a liberal constitutionalist regime is the lack of a normative commitment on the part of the political authorities in the former to constraints on public power. Hence, not every state is a dual state. Whether a dual state structure exists depends on the attitude of the authorities.

The above analysis has two implications for understanding of the dual state. The first is that because the political authorities in a dual state lack a normative commitment to constraints on their power, their incentives for maintaining the normative sphere of the dual state are necessarily purely instrumental. In Professor Tushnet's view, such instrumental incentives may provide too thin an assurance for investors because there is no guarantee that political convenience will not at some point call for them to be assigned to the prerogative rather than the normative state.[21]

The second implication is that in discerning whether a regime is a dual state (or a particular type of regime, for that matter), one needs to examine evidence (or the lack thereof) of the leadership's normative commitment to constraints on its power, evidence that is not limited to formal legal arrangements. The answer to such questions as whether there exists self-restraint based on a normative commitment and whether such restraint leads to effective constraints on power may become clear only over an extended period of time.

Both implications can be illustrated by the case of Hong Kong. Since China resumed sovereignty in 1997, putting an end to British colonial rule, it has governed Hong Kong using the "one country, two systems" model, according to which the city has a high degree of autonomy, including the power of final adjudication, and practices separate economic and legal systems. The model is elaborated in the Hong Kong Basic Law, the city's posthandover constitutional document. This law, on the one hand, contains many hallmarks of liberal constitutionalism. It stipulates an extensive list of fundamental rights enforceable by an independent judiciary, institutes checks and balances, and even promises eventual universal suffrage. Yet, on the other hand, it also contains elements of authoritarianism. For example, it vests the final power of interpreting the Basic Law with Beijing's National People's Congress Standing Committee (NPCSC), a political organ controlled by the Chinese Communist Party. On the face of it, then, there appear to be no limits to when the NPCSC may issue an interpretation. Further, if the NPCSC erodes the guarantees of the Basic Law in the name of an interpretation, there seem to be no avenues of redress. Judging from formal provisions alone, Hong Kong's posthandover legal order appears to have been a dual state from the outset: the guarantees of the Basic Law apply only to the extent that Beijing allows them to.

[21] Tushnet, *supra* note 2, at 440.

However, the dual state did not emerge until 2020. Prior to that year, the foundational principles of the Basic Law—stated to be unamendable therein—functioned as effective limits on Beijing's power;[22] until then, Beijing indeed exercised its power with restraint. To be sure, there were signs of decline in that restraint even before 2020,[23] but Beijing nevertheless abided by the core principles of the Basic Law. However, things took a dramatic turn in 2020, when Beijing enacted a draconian national security law (NSL) for Hong Kong outside the Basic Law framework in response to the large-scale pro-democracy protests in Hong Kong in 2019. The new law, whose final power of interpretation is vested with Beijing, introduces several vaguely worded offenses, including collusion with foreign forces and secession and subversion, which do not require an element of violence, all of which have a maximum sentence of life imprisonment. It designates special personnel within Hong Kong's prosecution, police, and judiciary to handle national security cases—personnel whose appointment can be influenced by Beijing directly or indirectly. Most alarmingly, the NSL stipulates that Beijing can mandate that cases be tried in mainland China in certain circumstances. It thus defies the Basic Law's provisions separating the criminal justice systems of mainland China and Hong Kong—separation that was presumed to constitute the core of the "one country, two systems" concept declared unamendable within the Basic Law.[24] The NSL's introduction therefore suggests that there are no limits to what Beijing can do should it choose to step in, and hence that a nontrivial part of people's lives is no longer regulated by the Basic Law.[25] For present purposes, the main takeaway is that although the formal provisions of the Basic Law appear to give Beijing unbounded political discretion, in practice such discretion was limited by that law's core principles until 2020, when Beijing's normative commitment to constraints broke down.

Nevertheless, the "remnants" of legality from Hong Kong's previous, more liberal era[26]—including a strong rule-of-law tradition and independent courts—have enabled the city to retain a sizable rule-governed sphere even as its legal order has

[22] Chan, *supra* note 5, at 118–23.

[23] *See, e.g.*, Decision of the NPCSC on Issues Relating to the Selection of the Chief Executive of the HKSAR by Universal Suffrage and on the Method for Forming the Legislative Council of the HKSAR in the Year 2016 (adopted at the 10th Session of the Standing Committee of the 12th National People's Congress on Aug. 31, 2014); Interpretation of Article 104 of the BL by the NPCSC (adopted at the 24th Session of the Standing Committee of the 12th National People's Congress on Nov.7, 2016); Decision of the NPCSC on Approving the Co-Operation Arrangement Between the Mainland and the HKSAR on the Establishment of the Port at the West Kowloon Station of the Guangzhou-Shenzhen-Hong Kong Express Rail Link for Implementing Co-Location Arrangement (adopted at the 31st Session of the Standing Committee of the 12th National People's Congress on Dec. 27, 2017).

[24] Cora Chan, *Can Hong Kong Remain a Liberal Enclave within China? Analysis of the Hong Kong National Security Law*, Pub. L. 271, 281–82 (2021).

[25] Chan, *supra* note 5, at 120–21.

[26] See Meierhenrich, *supra* note 6, esp. at 11. This and the following two sentences draw on Cora Chan, *Scholarship in Times of Constitutional Transformation: A View from Hong Kong*, 24 Hum. Rts. L. Rev. 1, 4, 13 (2023).

turned authoritarian. Hong Kong's legal order has thus emerged as a dual state rather than a full-blown, nonbifurcated authoritarian legal order. In cases of no concern to Beijing—which constitute the normative state, and encompass the majority of cases—existing constitutional guarantees still apply. It is only in highly politically sensitive cases which the prerogative state is unable to control via the normative state that the prerogative state is likely to step in. The Hong Kong government has thus sought to assure investors that they are safe. Nevertheless, the first implication highlighted above reminds us that there is no guarantee that "actions [that] are *currently* allocated to" the normative state will not later be reassigned to the prerogative state.[27] Consider the recent controversy over Google's search results for "Hong Kong's national anthem." In 2022, several sporting events broadcast a song that rose to prominence during the 2019 protests ("Glory to Hong Kong"), apparently mistaking it for the city's national anthem (which is actually China's national anthem, "March of the Volunteers"). The organizers claimed that the error was a result of their staff Googling "Hong Kong national anthem," a search that returned "Glory to Hong Kong." The Hong Kong government requested that Google amend its search results, which Google refused to do.[28] Fierce criticism from the Hong Kong government and pro-China politicians and media ensued, with some even suggesting that Google might have fallen foul of Hong Kong's security laws and that legal action might be taken against it.[29] If these laws were read in accordance

[27] Tushnet, *supra* note 2, at 440 (emphasis in original).

[28] Tom Grundy, *Security Chief: Google Refused to Change Search Results for Hong Kong Anthem, "Hurt the Feelings" of Citizens*, Hong Kong Free Press (Dec. 13, 2022, 11:03AM), https://hongkongfp.com/2022/12/13/security-chief-google-refused-to-change-search-results-for-hong-kong-anthem-hurt-the-feelings-of-citizens/.

[29] Press Release, The Government of Hong Kong Special Administrative Region, *LCQ6: Curbing Circulation of Information that Violates Hong Kong National Security Law* (Nov. 30, 2022, 4:15 PM), https://www.info.gov.hk/gia/general/202211/30/P2022113000508.htm; Press Release, The Government of Hong Kong Special Administrative Region, *Transcript of Remarks by S for S after Fight Crime Committee Meeting (with Video)* (Dec. 12, 2022, 9:43 PM), https://www.info.gov.hk/gia/general/202212/12/P2022121200781.htm; 七欖風波 當局倡互聯網搜尋將國歌置頂 *(Controversy from Rugby Seven: Authorities Urge Internet to Pin National Anthem as Top Searches)*, Oriental Daily (Dec. 1, 2022), https://orientaldaily.on.cc/content/%E8%A6%81%E8%81%9E%E6%B8%AF%E8%81%9E/odn-20221201-1201_00176_204/%E4%B8%83%E6%AC%96%E9%A2%A8%E6%B3%A2--%E7%95%B6%E5%B1%80%E5%80%A1%E4%BA%92%E8%81%AF%E7%B6%B2%E6%90%9C%E5%B0%8B%E5%B0%87%E5%9C%8B%E6%AD%8C%E7%BD%AE%E9%A0%82; Edward H. Leung, *Google*拒刪「港獨」歌 政府要採取法律行動 *(Google Refuses to Delete "Hong Kong Independence" Song, the Government Will Take Legal Action)*, Wenweipo (Dec. 13, 2022, 4:39 AM), https://www.wenweipo.com/a/202212/13/AP6397916de4b0e80f8119ce38.html; 外交部回應播錯國歌：互聯網企業有義務向大眾傳遞正確信息 *(Response from Ministry of Foreign Affairs Regarding the Broadcast of Wrong National Anthem: There is Obligation on Internet Enterprises to Deliver Correct Information to the Public)*, Hong Kong Economic Times (Dec. 14, 2022, 4:12 PM), https://invest.hket.com/article/3421349/%E5%A4%96%E4%BA%A4%E9%83%A8%E5%9B%9E%E6%87%89%E6%92%AD%E9%8C%AF%E5%9C%8B%E6%AD%8C%EF%BC%9A%E4%BA%92%E8%81%AF%E7%B6%B2%E4%BC%81%E6%A5%AD%E6%9C%89%E7%BE%A9%E5%8B%99%E5%90%91%E5%A4%A7%E7%9C%BE%E5%82%B3%E9%81%9E%E6%AD%A3%E7%A2%BA%E4%BF%A1%E6%81%AF; Gong Xueming, 播「獨歌」種仇煽暴 法律界促追究到底 *(Broadcasting "Independence songs" to Incite Hatred and Violence Legal Profession Urges In-depth Investigation)*, Takungpao (Dec. 25, 2022, 4:23 AM), https://www.wenweipo.com/epaper/view/newsDetail/1606710521355177984.html.

with Hong Kong's usual common law principles, then it was highly unlikely that Google's conduct would be taken to have broken them. However, given the strong stance of the Hong Kong government (and apparently the Chinese government as well) on the matter, it was not inconceivable (at the time) that Beijing would interfere via an interpretation of the NSL or by some other means to secure the legal result it desired. At the time of writing, the Hong Kong Court of Appeal has granted the Hong Kong government's application for an injunction against certain criminal acts involving the song "Glory to Hong Kong,"[30] so the Chinese government is unlikely to have to intervene, but the saga shows how malleable the line between the normative and prerogative spheres is in a dual state.

Arbitrariness of the Prerogative Sphere

The second issue that I would like to probe into here is what is meant by "arbitrariness" in the dual state. According to Fraenkel, arbitrariness exists at two levels in the dual state. First, the prerogative state acts arbitrarily in deciding whether a given case should be handled by the normative or prerogative state. Second, the way in which matters are handled in the prerogative state is also arbitrary.

Professor Tushnet argues that "the concept of a dual state requires that we have available an analytically useful concept of (legal) arbitrariness and that we don't have such a concept independent of accounts of liberalism as a normative enterprise ... It's not clear to me that the concepts of 'arbitrariness' and whatever counts as its opposite are analytically useful independent of some normative version of liberalism."[31] I would like to defend the usefulness of the arbitrariness concept in the dual state theory by defining it as *normlessness* or, crudely, violation of the thin rule of law, that is, governance by general, clear, prospective, and publicized rules.[32] As long as there are some constraints, however thin, on the authorities' power, governance is nonarbitrary. This thin understanding is in line with Fraenkel's theory, which stresses the unpredictability that comes with arbitrariness.[33] Professor Tushnet appears to reject the thin understanding of arbitrariness on the ground that it would lead to the "troubling" conclusion that nonarbitrary exercises of power are compatible with great substantive inequalities.[34] For example, as long

[30] Secretary for Justice v. Persons Conducting Themselves in Any of the Acts Prohibited Under Paragraph 1(a), (b), (c), or (d) or the Indorsement of Claim, [2024] H.K.C.A. 442.

[31] Tushnet, *supra* note 4, at 50.

[32] See Chan, *supra* note 5, at 102. For different conceptions of the rule of law, *see e.g.* Jeremy Waldron, *The Concept and the Rule of Law*, 43 GA. L. REV. 1 (2008).

[33] This does not mean that the rules in the normative state are always determinate but that on the whole the normative state offers much more predictability and regularity than the prerogative state: Chan, *supra* note 5, at 108–09. See Tushnet, *supra* note 4, at 47–51 for how the application of legal rules in general hinges on sociological considerations.

[34] Tushnet, *supra* note 4, at 6–7.

as the racist principles underpinning the lynching of African-Americans are clearly delineated in previously and publicly pronounced rules, and those rules are followed, the lynching regime cannot be considered arbitrary. My reply to this concern is threefold. First, the definition of arbitrariness suggested here is only for the purpose of elucidating the nature of the dual state. I am not claiming that arbitrariness should be understood in this way for all purposes. Second, I am not arguing that what was most problematic about the Nazi legal order, which the dual state theory was developed to explain, was arbitrariness as defined here. Discrimination against a particular race and religion was of course part of what made the Nazi regime problematic (to say the least), but it is not a defining feature of the concept of the dual state. Third, and relatedly, the dual state is but one of many possible manifestations of injustice. Professor David Dyzenhaus, for example, theorized two other manifestations: the "Apartheid State," exemplified by apartheid South Africa, in which one group is relegated by the legal system to second-class citizen status but is still governed by it,[35] and the "Parallel State," exemplified by the Israeli and Palestinian legal orders, in which one group is governed by an entirely different legal system than the other.[36] Both are to be distinguished from the dual state, in which certain matters are governed by a lawless domain (i.e., the prerogative domain). Once we appreciate these points, it no longer seems problematic that the concept of arbitrariness in the dual state is unable to capture instances of substantive inequality.

In fact, that there are instances of inequality not captured by the dual state framework is made clear in Professor Tushnet's own writing. He highlights the fact that even after the dual state involving the practice of lynching was formally displaced in the US after the 1920s, "many of the substantive and procedural norms of lynching [were incorporated] into the regular criminal justice system—to create 'legal lynchings,'" such that the laws "actually applied in legal lynchings differed from those applied in cases involving (most) white defendants."[37] Even the application of apparently equal law required the "making of social judgments about facts,"[38] judgments that at times reflected social bias against the disfavored group.[39] Hence, in reality, although the regime was no longer formally a dual state, "legalized lynchings were a manifestation of a dual legal system, operating *within* a formally unified one."[40] Indeed, legalization may have "stabilized rather than weakened" inequality by removing part of what makes lynching problematic,[41] namely, that it is formally unregulated by law. It is thus clear that the formal dual state is but one of

[35] DYZENHAUS, *supra* note 14, at 329.
[36] *Id.* at 330–33.
[37] Tushnet, *supra* note 4, at 56.
[38] *Id.* at 54.
[39] *Id.* at 49–50, 56–57.
[40] *Id.* at 56 (emphasis in original).
[41] *Id.* at 58–59.

many possible manifestations of inequality and that one need not be troubled by the concept's failure to encompass grave substantive inequalities.

Complexities in the Dual State

The third issue that I would like to explore is the possible complexities in the structure of the dual state, an issue inspired by Professor Tushnet's detailed exposition of the variants of constitutionalism and penetrating analysis of the practice of lynching in the US from circa 1870s to 1920s. He argues, for example, that lynching was not completely unregulated by norms: it was "law-like—or 'law lite'—rather than a domain of arbitrariness."[42] He also argues that it is possible for constitutionalism to be illiberal: illiberal because the polity contains inequality among groups of citizens, rendering certain groups second-class citizens, but constitutionalist because all citizens are subject to a thin rule of law and "thin constitutionalism," defined as the existence of "some space for civil society," "some protection of [free] expression," and governance "that is in some sense consultative."[43] Inequality among citizens can take at least two forms. In the first, the disfavored group enjoys only the thin rule of law and thin constitutionalism, whereas the favored group enjoys the full panoply of liberal rights.[44] In the second, both groups enjoy the full panoply of liberal rights at a level of specification "compatible with the liberal premise that all people are equal in all respects relevant to governance," but those enjoyed by the disfavored group are specified at a lower level than those enjoyed by the favored group.[45] These analyses inspired me to explore the possible intricacies *within* a dual state. I make two observations.

First, it is possible for the normative state to be subdivided into two domains, such that a dual state is trifurcated rather than bifurcated,[46] with (1) one domain that enjoys liberal constitutionalist guarantees; (2) another that enjoys some degree of regularity and predictability, and thus cannot be characterized as arbitrary; and (3) a third that is arbitrary.[47] Domains 1 and 2 both belong to the normative state, whereas domain 3 belongs to the prerogative state. Rulers have absolute power to decide which of the three domains a given matter is to be regulated by. Second, although every intervention by the prerogative state is an assault on the normative state in that it constitutes a deviation from prevailing rules, sometimes

[42] *Id.* at 51, 54.
[43] Tushnet, *supra* note 3, at 1370.
[44] *Id.* at 1373–74.
[45] *Id.* at 1378–79.
[46] Building on my earlier point that what ultimately distinguishes regime types is the attitude of the legal and political authorities toward compliance with various constraints, the structure of a dual state is ultimately determined by such attitude as well.
[47] See also Julius Yam, *Constitutional Courts in Hybrid Regimes* (DPhil thesis at University of Oxford (on file with author)) (2022).

in doing so the prerogative state seeks to introduce new rules, some of which manage to offer predictability over time.[48] In other words, a prerogative intervention may first shrink the "ratio"[49] of the normative state and then expand it. The prerogative state can thus both threaten and inject life into the normative state.

These two points can be illustrated by the Hong Kong legal order, which, as explained above, emerged as a dual state in 2020. After more than three years of the NSL's implementation, three rather than two domains have surfaced in Hong Kong's criminal justice system. The three domains are outlined below. Beijing, by virtue of possessing the final power to interpret both the NSL and the Basic Law, has the absolute power to determine which of the three domains a given matter is to be governed by.

(1) The first domain contains nonpolitically sensitive cases, to which the full panoply of substantive and procedural guarantees in Hong Kong's liberal common law legal tradition applies.[50] These are run-of-the-mill criminal cases in which Beijing takes no interest and which the courts are free to adjudicate according to their usual principles.

(2) The second domain contains politically sensitive cases to which thinner substantive and procedural guarantees apply, but those guarantees are nonetheless clearly pronounced in advance and offer some predictability. As a result of more than three years of litigation, many of the vague provisions in the NSL have been concretized into principles that can serve as a guide to the courts and litigants. For example, we now know that the courts will not read down the NSL's apparent reversal of the presumption of bail using common law techniques.[51] There are still uncertainties concerning the scope of some NSL provisions, but the basic new rules of the game have been established. Hence, harking back to my second observation above, what started out as an act of the prerogative state—the imposition of the NSL in violation of existing constitutional rules—has gradually acquired a normative character, leading to an expansion of the normative state and a corresponding shrinking of the prerogative state (relative to when the NSL was first introduced).[52]

(3) The third domain contains politically sensitive cases to which not even these thinner guarantees apply, and in which Beijing acts at will. These are cases in which Beijing intrudes into the operation of the normative state,

[48] Chan, *supra* note 5, at 25.

[49] Meierhenrich, *supra* note 6, at 246.

[50] Julius Yam argues that "the existence and size of the liberal normative state is what usually distinguishes the legal order of a hybrid regime from that of a pure authoritarian regime." Yam, *supra* note 47.

[51] HKSAR v. Lai Chee Ying (No. 3), [2021] H.K.C.F.A. 3, [2021] 1 H.K.C. 670 (C.F.A.); Johannes Chan, *Judicial Responses to the National Security Law: HKSAR v Lai Chee Ying*, 51(1) Hong Kong L. J. 1 (2021).

[52] Chan, *supra* note 5, at 25.

> such as by issuing an interpretation of the NSL to change preexisting rules governing national security cases or by transferring a case to the Party-controlled mainland courts. An example is Beijing's intervention on the question of whether defendants in national security cases can hire foreign counsel to defend them, an issue that the NSL does not explicitly address. In a rare instance of a ruling against the government on a security matter, the Hong Kong courts held that top Beijing political target Jimmy Lai could, as have defendants in other complex cases in Hong Kong, hire counsel from London to defend him in his national security trial.[53] This ruling was contrary to the wishes of Beijing, which sees the involvement of foreign barristers as a threat to national security. As a result, the NPCSC issued an interpretation of the NSL (for the first time) to vest the Beijing-controlled Chief Executive and National Security Committee with the power to determine whether foreign counsel is allowed in individual cases,[54] a question that had hitherto been exclusively under the purview of the Hong Kong courts. Following the issuance of the interpretation, the Hong Kong government enacted legislation to elaborate when and how foreign counsel can be admitted in national security cases.[55] Harking back to my second observation above, an act that started out as an act of the prerogative state—that is, an interpretation of the NSL to change the rules governing the deployment of foreign counsel—has gradually acquired a normative character via further stipulations, leading to an expansion of the normative state and a corresponding shrinkage of the prerogative state.[56]

The foregoing analysis shows that Hong Kong is not, as may be postulated, a polity in which a matter either enjoys the full panoply of liberal constitutionalist rights or is subject to the arbitrariness of the prerogative state, and nor is the effect of a prerogative intervention on the normative state one-way in reducing the ratio of the latter.

Both domains of the normative state help to stabilize the dual state, albeit in different ways. The first domain highlighted above gives the dual state the semblance of the liberal (or "thick") rule of law, thereby lending a cloak of legitimacy to the authoritarian regime, while the second concretizes the prerogative state's directives, thereby rendering the authoritarian regime more efficacious. It is perhaps to

[53] Re an application by Mr Timothy Wynn Owen KC, [2022] H.K.C.F.I. 3233; [2022] H.K.C.A. 1689, [2022] 5 H.K.L.R.D. 726 (C.A.); [2022] H.K.C.A. 1751; [2022] H.K.C.A. 1898; [2022] H.K.C.F.A. 23.

[54] Interpretation by the Standing Committee of the National People's Congress of Article 14 and Article 47 of the PRC Law on Safeguarding National Security in the Hong Kong Special Administrative Region (Dec. 30, 2022).

[55] Legal Practitioners (Amendment) Ordinance (2023) Cap.159 (H.K.).

[56] Chan, *supra* note 5, at 25.

the first domain that the Hong Kong government attempts to direct attention when it seeks to assure investors that it is business as usual in Hong Kong.

The Stability of Mixed Constitutions

The fourth and final issue that I wish to discuss is the stability of mixed constitutions, which I define here as constitutions that contain both liberal and non-liberal fundamental elements.[57] Professor Tushnet's discerning analysis of the imperatives that may lead to illiberal constitutionalism or authoritarian constitutionalism becoming full-blown authoritarian or liberal constitutionalism raises—and suggests answers to—the questions of whether mixed constitutions are inherently less stable than pure constitutions such as fully authoritarian constitutions and fully liberal constitutions and whether the imperatives for instability in mixed and pure constitutions differ and, if so, how. Instability plagues any polity that contains opposing forces, even if they are not reflected institutionally. Is the instability of mixed constitutions any different from that of pure constitutions? Professor Tushnet's analysis suggests that it may indeed be different. The sources of instability in the types of nonliberal constitutionalism that he tracks include: the inherent difficulty of sustaining a "dual normative commitment"[58] to authoritarianism and constitutionalism;[59] the potential for the institutions that reflect that dual commitment to generate destabilizing forces;[60] the difficulties of maintaining unequal treatment for two groups of citizens;[61] and the difficulties of laying down clear norms on the distinction between those groups.[62] Some of these sources of instability arise from institutional expressions of the opposing forces of authoritarianism and liberal constitutionalism, expressions that are less likely or less prominent in pure systems. An interesting exercise that would build on Professor Tushnet's seminal work would be to systematically compare the sources of instability in pure and mixed constitutions, as well as those in different types of mixed constitutions, and to distill the conditions for these constitutions to settle into an equilibrium.

Hong Kong provides a good illustration of both the instability of mixed constitutions and of what might be needed to sustain them. As outlined above, Hong Kong's key constitutional document, that is, the Basic Law, contains important elements of both liberal constitutionalism and authoritarianism. The liberal

[57] For various understandings of mixed constitutions, see Yaniv Roznai, *What Are We Talking About When We Talk About "Mixed Constitutions"? Towards a Typology of Constitutional Mixture*, 16(2) L. & Ethics Hum. Rts. 193 (2022); Adam Shinar, *Deconstructing Mixed Constitutions*, 16(1) L. & Ethics Hum. Rts. 167 (2022).

[58] Gila Stopler, *Semi-Liberal Constitutionalism*, 8(1) Glob. Constitutionalism 94, 101 (2019).

[59] Tushnet, *supra* note 2, at 455.

[60] *Id.* at 446–47.

[61] Tushnet, *supra* note 3, at 1374–76.

[62] *Id.* at 1376.

elements—including fundamental rights enforceable by an independent judiciary and the guarantee of eventual universal suffrage—have, at least until recent years, given rise to a rich body of constitutional litigation, a vibrant civil society and community of activist lawyers, and liberal aspirations culminating in social movements, all of which have pushed the constitutional order toward full-blown liberal constitutional democracy. These developments have in turn prompted Beijing to tighten control, pushing Hong Kong toward authoritarianism. In its first two decades under Chinese rule, Hong Kong oscillated between these two opposing forces.[63] Beijing's reaction in 2020 to the 2019 pro-democracy protests marked a significant turn toward authoritarianism. Nevertheless, as explained above, a duality persists in Hong Kong's legal order, meaning that dissonance within that order will also persist. Such dissonance—manifested in, inter alia, tensions between the institutions of the normative and prerogative states—renders the dual state fragile. Given the structural asymmetry in the dual state—which likely reflects an asymmetry in political power—the dual state is more susceptible to evolving into full-blown, nonbifurcated authoritarianism than into full legality.[64] Yet, the remnants of liberal constitutionalist institutions and traditions make it possible to contest state action even in politically sensitive matters.[65] The Hong Kong courts' ruling in 2022 that Jimmy Lai could hire foreign counsel is but one example.[66] Although the ruling was subsequently overturned by an NSL interpretation by Beijing, it shows the possibility of legal contestation and hence of pushing back or slowing down the authoritarian transition. The case of Hong Kong, then, suggests not just the fragility of constitutions with a dual commitment to liberal constitutionalism and authoritarianism, but also what might be needed to sustain such constitutions: rigorous contestation by institutions of the two ideological forces—contestation that settles the mixed constitutional order into an equilibrium.[67] Such contestation enabled Hong Kong to maintain its relatively liberal character in the first two decades of Chinese rule, and will presumably be needed to maintain the city's normative sphere in the post-2020 constitutional era.

[63] Cora Chan, *Thirty Years from Tiananmen: China, Hong Kong, and the Ongoing Experiment to Preserve Liberal Values in an Authoritarian State*, 17(2) INT'L J. CONST. L. 439 (2019).

[64] Chan, *supra* note 5, at 36.

[65] See MEIERHENRICH, *supra* note 6, at 235.

[66] See Re an application by Mr Timothy Wynn Owen KC, [2022] H.K.C.F.I. 3233; [2022] H.K.C.A. 1689, [2022] 5 H.K.L.R.D. 726 (C.A.); [2022] H.K.C.A. 1751; [2022] H.K.C.A. 1898; [2022] H.K.C.F.A. 23.

[67] *See* Cora Chan, *How Hong Kong's Courts Interpret Beijing's Interpretation of the Basic Law May Yet Surprise*, SOUTH CHINA MORNING POST (Nov. 9, 2016, 4:00 PM), http://www.scmp.com/comment/insight-opinion/article/2044385/how-hong-kongs-courts-interpret-beijings-interpretation (last accessed Nov. 25, 2023); CORA CHAN & ALBERT HY CHEN, *Yash Ghai and the Constitutional Project of "One Country, Two Systems" in Hong Kong*, in FURTHERING CONSTITUTIONS, BIRTHING PEACE: LIBER AMICORUM YASH PAL GHAI 303, 312–13 (Humphrey Sipalla & J. Osogo Ambani eds., 2021).

Conclusion

Professor Tushnet's scholarship challenges us to discard crude, narrow, or monolithic approaches to the study of constitutionalism and to imagine new conceptual possibilities. This chapter constitutes a humble attempt to expound on the nature of the dual state and the stability of mixed constitutions in that spirit. The professor's scholarship on the varieties of constitutionalism enables us, among other things, to rationalize systems that do not fit neatly into the bipartite lens of authoritarianism versus liberal constitutionalism and to recognize that nonliberal constitutionalism may be the best option in certain circumstances. In using Singapore to expound on what authoritarian constitutionalism looks like, Professor Tushnet writes: "from a normative point of view the central question . . . is whether a Singapore without authoritarian constitutionalism would be a liberal democracy or a fully authoritarian state. If the latter, authoritarian constitutionalism may be normatively attractive *for Singapore*."[68] Indeed, the desirability of a constitutional system should be evaluated on the ground in light of real-world constraints. If attempts to fully liberalize a system are likely to attract a political backlash that pushes the system toward full authoritarianism, then a system that falls short of liberal constitutionalism—whether in the form of a dual state or not—may be the best option for now, all things considered, and the constitutional design and strategy should follow suit, that is, be in line with a system that falls short of liberal constitutionalism.

[68] Tushnet, *supra* note 2, at 460 (emphasis in original).

25

Competitive Populism

*Madhav Khosla**

On Populism

The preoccupation of comparative constitutional lawyers over the past decade or so has been the rise of authoritarian populism. One routinely acknowledged feature of the new authoritarianism is that it involves democratic erasure rather than outright rupture. Instead of the "dramatic *executive coups* of the past," Nancy Bermeo observes, we face "*executive aggrandizement*."[1] Although populism, by itself—as Mark Tushnet and Bojan Bugarič have carefully shown in *Power to the People*—can come in many possible forms, it does have an authoritarian variant.[2] When that variant manifests, we speak of those in power as "elected authoritarians,"[3] and we speak of the phenomenon at work as "the corruption of popular sovereignty."[4]

In this chapter I should like to reflect on one possible pathway that might follow our present political moment: *competitive populism*.[5] It should be said that this is not necessarily the most plausible or likely pathway. Perhaps many of today's populist regimes will take the path of Venezuela, and become full-fledged authoritarian polities. Military regimes have often been less robust than regimes structured around a single party or leader, with the former being more vulnerable to endogenous factors than the latter.[6] Moreover, present-day authoritarian populists gradually but meaningfully chip away at the rules and practices that enable free and fair elections. Perhaps in time the situation in Hungary, where electoral concerns accumulate with each passing election, will resemble that of countries such

* For valuable comments and criticism, I am grateful to Cora Chan, Sujit Choudhry, Rosalind Dixon, Vicki C. Jackson, David Landau, Pratap Bhanu Mehta, Mark Tushnet, and Milan Vaishnav.

[1] Nancy Bermeo, *On Democratic Backsliding*, 27 J. Democracy 5, 6 (2016).

[2] Mark Tushnet & Bojan Bugarič, Power to the People: Constitutionalism in the Age of Populism 36–53 (2022).

[3] Wojciech Sadurski, *Constitutional Democracy in the Time of Elected Authoritarians*, 18 Int'l J. Const. L. 324 (2020).

[4] Samuel Issacharoff, Democracy Unmoored: Populism and the Corruption of Popular Sovereignty (2023).

[5] The term "competitive populism" has a very specific meaning in the context of India and some other developing nations. It is used to refer to what are seen as almost indiscriminate welfare-related promises where political parties try to do outdo one another in public claim-making. Clearly, that is not how I use the term in this chapter.

[6] *See* Barbara Geddes, *What Do We Know about Democratization after Twenty Years*, 2 Ann. Rev. Pol. Sci. 115 (1999).

Madhav Khosla, *Competitive Populism* In: *Redefining Comparative Constitutional Law*. Edited by: Vicki C. Jackson and Madhav Khosla, Oxford University Press. © Madhav Khosla 2025. DOI: 10.1093/9780191996344.003.0025

as Singapore ever more.[7] Even though we may recognize this reality, the possibility of competitive populism is worth exploring. Or so I should like to suggest.

Some years ago, Steven Levitsky and Lucan A. Way held up for consideration *competitive authoritarianism* as a distinct regime type. In such regimes elections are genuine, but opposition figures are harassed and hassled, and critics are silenced and controlled. Even though the playing field is not level, elections in such regimes are not shams, and democratic institutions, practices, and opportunities are prevalent enough to make such regimes competitive. Those in power can be thrown out of power, even though achieving such an outcome is no easy task. For Levitsky and Way, four institutional domains offered the space for democratic behavior, engagement, and contestation, however imperfectly: elections; the legislature; the judiciary; and the media. In each of these arenas, the authoritarian government exerts pressure and tries to exercise control. Yet, in each domain, there is sufficient space for some kind of opposition voice to express itself. The competition in such regimes is "real but unfair."[8]

There is much in the Levitsky–Way thesis that will seem familiar to us. But there are some core differences between the regimes that they studied and those that contemporary comparative constitutional lawyers have considered. In regimes that have in recent times transitioned to having an authoritarian character, in some form and to some degree, one has witnessed the reconstitution of traditional institutions. Whether one considers apex judicial institutions, media regulatory authorities, fourth branch bodies such as electoral commissions, or others, one finds that authoritarian populists have altered their powers, changed their composition, amended their role, and weaponized their functioning. In contrast to simply closing down institutions or suspending their powers, today's authoritarian populists "work within the inherited institutional structure and subvert it for their purposes."[9] And this subversion, as a number of scholars have shown, can take many forms.[10]

The question of institutional subversion is a significant one. For present purposes, however, I should like to draw attention to a related but different

[7] *See* Kim Lane Scheppele, *How Viktor Orbán Wins*, 33 J. DEMOCRACY 45 (2022). Elections have, of course, long been a feature of authoritarian regimes. *See generally* Jennifer Gandhi & Ellen Lust-Okar, *Elections under Authoritarianism*, 12 ANN. REV. POL. SCI. 403 (2009); Jennifer Gandhi, *Elections and Political Regimes*, 50 GOV'T & OPPOSITION 446 (2015).

[8] STEVEN LEVITSKY & LUCAN A. WAY, COMPETITIVE AUTHORITARIANISM: HYBRID REGIMES AFTER THE COLD WAR 3 (2010). For an early statement, *see* Steven Levitsky & Lucan A. Way, *Elections Without Democracy: The Rise of Competitive Authoritarianism*, 13 J. DEMOCRACY 52 (2002). For a recent reflection in light of populist challenges, *see* Steven Levitsky & Lucan Way, *The New Competitive Authoritarianism*, 31 J. DEMOCRACY 51 (2020).

[9] WOJCIECH SADURSKI, A PANDEMIC OF POPULISTS 49 (2022).

[10] For a helpful taxonomy of varieties of institutional subversion, *see id.* at 48–82. *See also* Kim Lane Scheppele, *Autocratic Legalism*, 85 U. CHI. L. REV. 545 (2018); ROSALIND DIXON AND DAVID LANDAU, ABUSIVE CONSTITUTIONAL BORROWING: LEGAL GLOBALIZATION AND THE SUBVERSION OF LIBERAL DEMOCRACY (2021); Alvin Y.N. Cheung, *Legal Gaslighting*, 72 U. TORONTO L.J. 50 (2022).

question: namely the question of not how deinstitutionalization occurs, but what it presages. Let us assume that an authoritarian populist regime does in fact perform poorly at an election, and thereby manages to lose power. The results of the Brazilian and Polish elections in 2022 and 2023, respectively, suggest that this is not entirely fanciful. What kind of overall constitutional order should we except such a regime to put into place? The traditional political institutions, such as those acknowledged in the account of competitive authoritarianism, have been discredited in major ways. This discrediting is, of course, partly a consequence of the deinstitutionalization that authoritarian populists have unleashed while in power. But the brutal reality is that the functioning of such institutions—legislatures and courts, for example—has been a source of concern, disappointment, and controversy well before the rise of authoritarian populism. To draw on Tocqueville's reading of the collapse of an *ancien régime*, it is precisely the already weakened character of such institutions that may well have facilitated their swift breakdown during authoritarian populism.[11]

In the face of this reality, it will be hard to trust former institutional structures and processes in the same way that we once did; and it will be hard to revive them using the same vision that created them. If the new governing party that follows the present phase of populism has an institutionalist agenda, that agenda might be challenging to satisfy. And if this new governing party is populist, but in a nonauthoritarian way, it will be anti-institutionalist and will have limited interest in building and sustaining institutions. Insofar as this is true, the phase that might follow authoritarian populism could well be a phase of *democracy without institutions*. We will be left in a certain kind of institutional vacuum: the prior institutions, associated with liberal constitutional democracy, will not lend themselves to being rebooted. To be sure, all regimes require institutions for a host of purposes, not least of which are coordination problems. And, over time, there is bound to be some kind of institutional re-imagination and reinvention. *Power to the People* itself leaves us with some tantalizing possibilities in this regard through its reflections on the use of the referendums.[12] Yet, for the immediate future, what I mean to suggest is that it is not clear that institutions will quite serve the standard checking, limiting, and deliberative functions with which they were once associated; and it is not clear that they will occupy the independent domain of legitimation that they once enjoyed.

If this is true, then the real contribution of *Power to the People* may not only be that it helps us disaggregate populism and constitutionalism. More fundamentally, in showing us how populism can take more than one form and can manifest in ways that are conservative as well as progressive, *Power to the People* may in fact

[11] *See* Alexis de Tocqueville, The Ancien Régime and the French Revolution (Jon Elster ed., Arthur Goldhammer trans., 2011 [1856]).

[12] Tushnet & Bugarič, Power to the People, *supra* note 2, at 249–59.

provide a window into the different flanks that could structure political contestation in the future. As Tushnet and Bugarič carefully show, the idea of constitutionalism can exist in several different permutations across different democratic orders. It must have a baseline—popular authorization, legal entrenchment, judicial independence, and organized political parties—but beyond that, a plurality of arrangements can be legitimate. For Tushnet and Bugarič, the goal here is to urge care in criticizing arrangements as "anti-constitutional" simply because they depart from our political preferences.[13] In showing us this plurality, they may well be showing us the possibilities and limits of our political horizons.

On Institutions

Why might we suppose that our political future could involve a contest between different varieties of populism? The basic reason for the possibility of competitive populism is the deinstitutionalization to which I have referred. The perversion of conventional institutions has taken place both before and during the phase of authoritarian populism. Consider the case of the Supreme Court of India, an apex judicial institution that has been respected, even mythologized, among domestic and comparative scholars for some years. Although the Supreme Court has been a prominent actor within India's democratic schema for decades, a certain dissatisfaction with its functioning has been present well before the current populist phase. As one commentator noted several years ago, "[t]he Supreme Court […] has given enough players enough victories to leave them feeling as if they have a stake in keeping the game of political give-and-take going."[14] In some of the areas where the Court has invited most acclaim, such as public interest litigation and social rights adjudication, there has been an emerging sense that its record is less attractive than early enthusiasts assumed.[15] In the years immediately preceding the 2014 general elections in India, which ushered in the government led by the Bharatiya Janata Party (BJP), the Court's dramatic interventions in the domain of accountability and corruption underemphasized a variety of legal niceties.[16] All of this is simply to suggest that the Court's maneuvering as an institutional actor locating and seeking its political space within a democratic system has long been appreciated. Its approach over the past decade or so has largely been dual in nature: a refusal to hear and adjudicate some of the most controversial legal questions, at

[13] *Id.* at 29.

[14] Pratap Bhanu Mehta, *The Rise of Judicial Sovereignty*, 18 J. Democracy 70, 76 (2007).

[15] *See* Madhav Khosla, *Making Social Rights Conditional: Lessons from India*, 4 Int'l J. Const. L. 739 (2010); Anuj Bhuwania, Courting the People: Public Interest Litigation in Post-Emergency India (2016).

[16] *See* Pratap Bhanu Mehta, *The Indian Supreme Court and the Art of Democratic Positioning, in* Unstable Constitutionalism: Law and Politics in South Asia 233, 252–58 (Mark Tushnet & Madhav Khosla eds., 2015).

least in a timely manner; and a clear willingness to approve controversial state actions and to endorse extraordinary state power.[17] Whatever one makes of this approach, it is not entirely out of sync with the Court's prior stance of delivering verdicts attuned to the political climate that persists.

Consider, in a very different way, the case of the Indian Parliament. In recent years, there have been legitimate concerns over abusive practices involving legislative procedures. These include the subversion of parliamentary procedures and norms, as well as the politicization of functionaries such as the Speaker of the House.[18] While such concerns are real and true, there is a longer history of the deinstitutionalization of India's representative chamber. One important element here is the antidefection provisions in the Constitution, inserted nearly four decades ago. In sum, these provisions prohibit legislators from voting against the party whip on all matters, thereby disabling their independence. They reduce the act of voting to a mere performative exercise. Within this schema, the legislature cannot perform its role of holding the executive responsible because the party whip incapacitates its members. Simply put, power has, as a result, moved from the legislature to the political party.[19] A serious assessment of India's antidefection law requires further study, but the point worth making is that the decline and crisis of core public institutions has long preceded the present populist wave.[20]

Such deinstitutionalization is not merely limited to particular institutions. It has a more ideological character. Recall that one basic feature of authoritarian populism is not the absence of legality but the absence of limitations on the exercise of power. As scholars observed in the events following Hungary's 2010 election—to offer but one well-known example—such populism involves the breakdown of checks and balances that typically structure the workings of power in constitutional democracies. The 2012 Hungarian Constitution, commentators observed at the time, gives "the Fidesz government the power to do whatever it wants without constraint, and then entrenches the Fidesz government, its policy preferences [...] and its personnel into a distant constitutional future."[21] The new constitutional schema was

[17] *See generally* Madhav Khosla & Milan Vaishnav, *The Three Faces of the Indian State*, 32 J. Democracy 111, 116–17 (2021).

[18] On the former, *see, e.g.*, Tarunabh Khaitan, *Killing a Constitution with a Thousand Cuts: Executive Aggrandizement and Party–State Fusion in India*, 14 L. & Ethics Hum. Rts. 49, 65–67 (2020). On the latter, *see, e.g.*, Subhash Desai v. Governor of Maharashtra, 2023 SCC Online SC 607.

[19] *See generally* Aradhya Sethia, *Where's the Party? Towards a Constitutional Biography of Political Parties*, 3 Indian L. Rev. 1, 30 (2019); Udit Bhatia, *What's the Party Like? The Status of the Political Party in Anti-Defection Jurisdictions*, 40 L. & Phil. 305 (2021); Madhav Khosla & Milan Vaishnav, *Democracy and Defections*, 22 Int'l J. Const. L. (forthcoming 2024).

[20] For a general reflection on this in the Indian context, *see* Rethinking Public Institutions in India (Devesh Kapur, Pratap Bhanu Mehta & Milan Vaishnav eds., 2017).

[21] Miklós Bánkuti, Gábor Halmai & Kim Lane Scheppele, *From Separation of Powers to a Government without Checks: Hungary's Old and New Constitutions*, *in* Constitution for a Disunited Nation: On Hungary's 2011 Fundamental Law 237, 240 (Gábor Attila Tóth ed., 2012). In general, scholars routinely speak of populism as an attempt to "free political power from legal restraints." Susanne Baer, *The Rule of—and Not by Any—Law: On Constitutionalism*, 71 Current L. Probs. 335, 349 (2018).

one with "no real checks and balances."[22] If conventional constitutional democracy has been associated with the regulation and control of state power, authoritarian populism—indeed, all forms of authoritarianism—has exposed us to a version of *constitutionalism as state power.*[23]

This vision has exposed not only a certain dissatisfaction with prior institutions, but a certain dissatisfaction with the institutional ideology that is centered on checks and limitations. As should be clear, my aim here is in pursuing the thought that even if we assume that a new political configuration enters office upon defeating authoritarian populism, it will find itself in a challenging position with respect to reconstructing institutions. The authoritarian populist narrative—however true or false—has sketched a new institutional vision in both general and specific terms, where limited constitutionalism has been theorized to be a form of bureaucratization at best and elite preservation at worst. In other words, the gradual erosion of conventional institutions has brought with it the gradual erosion of the institutional vision that grounded them. Consider, for example, the 2016 "demonetization" decision of the Government of India declaring that 86 percent of existing currency notes shall no longer be legal tender.[24] There were some intricate legal questions involved here, such as the meaning of "any series of bank notes" under the relevant statute.[25] In particular, the law required that the demonetization of currency could only take place upon the recommendation of the Central Board of Directors of the Reserve Bank of India.[26] For our purposes, what matters is the understanding of the role of the Central Board of Directors in the original demonetization decision and the Supreme Court verdict which upheld the action (years later).[27] As Justice Nagarathna's minority opinion underlined, the Central Board did not play its required role in the impugned instance, not least because the proposal for demonetization was not initiated by the Board. That is to say, "the recommendation did not originate from the Bank [. . .] but was 'obtained' from the Bank in the form of an opinion for demonetization submitted by the Central Government."[28]

[22] Tushnet & Bugarič, Power to the People, *supra* note 2, at 84.

[23] In Tushnet's case study of Singapore, for instance, what gives the regime an authoritarian cast is the regulation of private life, the national security apparatus, the restrictions on free speech, and so forth. Mark Tushnet, *Authoritarian Constitutionalism*, 100 Cornell L. Rev. 391 (2015). In the case of China, to mention the world's largest authoritarian state, studies often note that legal rules do not constrain the party-state. *See* Benjamin L. Liebman, *Legal Reform: China's Law-Stability Paradox*, 143 Daedalus 96, 98 (2014); Taisu Zhang & Tom Ginsburg, *China's Turn toward Law*, 59 Va. J. Int'l L. 306, 316 (2019).

[24] *See* S.O. 3407(E), Ministry of Finance, Government of India (8 November 2016). *See also* The Specified Bank Notes (Cessation of Liabilities) Act 2017.

[25] *See* § 26(2), Reserve Bank of India Act 1934.

[26] This is with respect to demonetarization grounded in § 26. There may be other paths to demonetization outside this statutory provision.

[27] Vivek Narayan Sharma v. Union of India (2023) 3 SCC 1.

[28] *Id.* at 174.

What one witnessed in this instance was not merely a strong executive, but a declaration on the legitimacy and space of public institutions like central banks. The core feature of the episode was not the taking away of legal tender of currency notes, but the complete subordination of the Board—and the conversion of some element of statutory independence into a relationship between the Government of India and the Reserve Bank as one of "interaction/consultation."[29] The key elements in the decision—the emphases on speed and confidentiality and on the singularity of executive judgment—were all attacks on an ideology centered on institutional checks and balances and technocratic expertise. There may be many good reasons to have reservations about this ideology, but what is important to recognize is that the episode did not involve merely institutional subjugation in one specific instance. It consisted in a new institutional vision that called into question the validity and wisdom of the prior order.

This overall approach to institutions is linked to the idea that it is the state, as a general entity, that must be the starting point of any analysis. For the state to perform its constitutive role, it needs to perform a set of functions that cannot be formalized within the existing framework of institutions. The question of membership is an easy example. Consider the 2019 amendment to India's overarching citizenship statute.[30] The change provides for two different tracks to obtain citizenship. If one is a Buddhist, Christian, Hindu, Jain, Parsee, or Sikh from the neighboring nations of Afghanistan, Bangladesh, and Pakistan, and has arrived in India prior to 2015, one is entitled to a fast-track procedure. All others—noticeably *Muslims*—are required to take the standard, lengthier, and more cumbersome path. The stated reason for the law is humanitarian: the law provides a means by which minority groups persecuted across the border can find a home in India. But it does not take much to pierce the stated rationale. If this is indeed the rationale, then why are certain persecuted minorities—Muslim groups such as the Ahmadis in Pakistan—excluded from the law? Moreover, the law makes no mention of religious persecution whatsoever. It simply focuses on one's religious identity; it does not address whether the person or group in question has been persecuted.[31]

Notice how this change interacts in insidious ways with a different endeavor—the creation of an all-India registry for citizens.[32] The purpose of this initiative is to

[29] *Id.* at 106. On the powers and nature of the Reserve Bank of India, *see* Errol D'Souza, *Reserve Bank of India: The Way Forward, in* RETHINKING PUBLIC INSTITUTIONS IN INDIA, *supra* note 20, at 139–79.

[30] The CITIZENSHIP (AMENDMENT) ACT, 2019. For a careful study of this change and of the broader history and legal structure of citizenship in India, *see* Niraja Gopal Jayal, *Reinventing the Republic: Faith and Citizenship in India*, 10 STUD. INDIAN POL. 14 (2022).

[31] The discriminatory character of the law appears quite plainly to violate the equal protection guarantee in Article 14 of India's Constitution, though the Supreme Court is yet to confront this matter. On this guarantee, *see generally* Madhav Khosla, *The Equal Protection Guarantee in India*, in THE OXFORD HANDBOOK OF COMPARATIVE HUMAN RIGHTS (Neha Jain & Mila Versteeg eds., forthcoming 2025) (draft on file with author).

[32] *See* MINISTRY OF HOME AFFAIRS, GOVERNMENT OF INDIA, NOTIFICATION S.O. 2753(3) (NPR) (2019); Assam Public Works v. Union of India (2019) 9 SCC 70.

conduct an all-India enumeration of current residents in order to determine who is an illegal migrant and who is a legal resident. But how is this determination to be conducted? The reality of limited Indian state capacity means that millions lack birth certificates and other identification.[33] In cases where disputes have already begun to arise, courts have rejected the claims of persons who possess several documents and have resided in India for decades.[34] The emphasis has been on the fact that the burden of proving citizenship lies on the person who is claiming that they are a citizen. But how one can one discharge this burden in a country where proper documentation is far from the norm? It is easy to see how exclusions from the registry and the new citizenship law can come together in dramatic ways: A Hindu whose documentation is found wanting and who is thereby excluded from the registry can easily receive citizenship (via the provisions in the Citizenship Amendment Act) whereas a Muslim in the same position has no such option.[35]

The consequences of the national registry project will turn on its bureaucratic reality. They will turn on how the state chooses to create the list of citizens. This basic fact underscores the role of administrative discretion in a populist regime. As a general matter, it is through the exercise of administrative discretion that power is structured and deployed in the modern state. Crudely put, the work is done through administration by administrators. The legal authority of the administrative state has been a source of some controversy in democratic states, especially with its tremendous growth over the past century or so. But, though contests persist over the regulation of the administrative state, there is considerable acknowledgment of its importance. Tellingly, both Pierre Rosanvallon and Adrian Vermeule, to provide prominent examples, recognize the inescapability of administrative discretion.[36] In democracies some kind of equilibrium has emerged, with legislatures and courts granting some degree of autonomy to, and maintaining some degree of accountability over, administrative agencies.

In the case of authoritarian populist states, however, we do not have the same set of checking and balancing institutions; in such a scenario, administrative discretion acquires a completely new meaning. This is government by administration, plain and simple. Here Lord Hewart's picture of despotism by administration is front and center.[37] The system is governed entirely by its own inner rationality.[38]

[33] On state capacity in India, *see generally* Devesh Kapur, *Why Does the Indian State Both Fail and Succeed?*, 34 J. Econ. Persp. 31(2020).

[34] *See, e.g.*, Nur Begum v. Union of India, W.P.(C) 1900/2019, 18 February 2020 (Gauhati High Court).

[35] One is reminded of how citizenship claims—and the erasure of individuals—occurs during the birth of nations. A fine example is the creation of the Slovenian state in 1991. *See* Jelka Zorn, *Ethnic Citizenship in the Slovenian State*, 9 Citizenship Stud. 135 (2005).

[36] *See* Pierre Rosanvallon, Democratic Legitimacy: Impartiality, Reflexivity, Proximity (Arthur Goldhammer trans., 2011); Adrian Vermeule, Law's Abnegation: From Law's Empire to the Administrative State (2016).

[37] *See* Lord Hewart of Bury, The New Despotism (1929).

[38] The link between that rationality and deep forms of politicization is an important one. *See generally* Carol Harlow & Richard Rawlings, *Populism and Administrative Law*, LSE Law, Society and

As D.J. Galligan once noted, what is interesting about administrative discretion is not the potential for actions by "the idiosyncratic official," but that it "allows and even encourages the formation of an internal normative system, without guidance from the outside world as to what the norms should be."[39] The practice of administrative discretion offers an image of a somewhat different kind of "dual state" than the one that Ernst Fraenkel had in mind.[40] In contrast to Fraenkel's structural duality between different domains of law, administrative actions may not merely be about a functional differentiation between the political and the functionalist. Rather, the system can create a duality where the practice of law results in different outcomes for different people.[41] Seen in this way, authoritarian states offer an interesting twist to legal certainty. There is remarkable selective enforcement but there is the certainty that the state can always act.[42]

For all populists alike, whatever else they might compete on, there is an understanding that state-building is impossible without administrative discretion. Consider the debates surrounding India's *Aadhaar* project—the creation of the world's largest biometric database. The project's initial logic was the verification of identity. All states must be able to *identify* their citizens—to know whether Person X is actually Person X. This is a minimum condition for state action. It is hard to deny that states should have the authority to undertake such a verification exercise. The tricky issue lies in determining what follows from this. What lies beyond constructing the project as a mere identity-verifier? Should one's *Aadhaar* details be required to open a bank account? Should they be required to acquire a telephone number? Should such details be connected with one's medical history? The question is what information and services are linked to *Aadhaar*. The issue, that is to say, is one of architectural design. The appropriateness of connecting different kinds of data is not a straightforward matter, but it greatly determines the impact of the *Aadhaar* project.

For myriad reasons, the question of architectural design and linking protocols has been de-emphasized in the *Aadhaar* debate. The focus has been on the collection of data and on the access to the linked data. The Supreme Court decision

ECONOMY WORKING PAPERS 12/2023 7–8 (2023), https://papers.ssrn.com/sol3/papers.cfm?abstract_id=4414379 (last accessed Nov. 19, 2023).

[39] D.J. Galligan, *Authoritarianism in Government and Administration: The Promise of Administrative Justice*, 54 COMMON LEGAL PROBS. 79, 90 (2001).

[40] *See* ERNST FRAENKEL, THE DUAL STATE: A CONTRIBUTION TO THE THEORY OF DICTATORSHIP (2017 [1941]).

[41] For an attempt to think of administrative law within the framework of a dual state, as traditionally understood, *see* Bas Schotel, *Administrative Law as a Dual State. Authoritarian Elements of Administrative Law*, 13 HAGUE J. RULE L. 195 (2021).

[42] This is not the world of The Queen v. Bolton (1841) 1 QB 66, 76 ("It is much more important to hold the rule of law straight than, from a feeling of the supposed hardship of any particular decision, to interpose relief at the expense of introducing a precedent full of inconvenience and uncertainty in the decision of future cases").

that upheld the project also seemed to miss the point.[43] The verdict concentrated on privacy-related worries, and it expressed concern over data theft rather than over how public and private services are connected with the database. Crucially, under the legal framework that exists, the choice of linking, along with a great many other powers, lies with administrators. Indeed, the entire working of the project—from the collection to the authentication to the sharing, and so on, of the *Aadhaar* data—is delegated.[44] While India has traditional excessive delegation (nondelegation) doctrines, the Court's decision shows how the categories and inquiries that such doctrines involve have long failed to keep pace with the complexity involving delegation. But, from the perspective of state-building, how can anybody but administrators be in charge? If the identification of a citizen is the minimum condition for all public policy, then the duplication of identity is a constant worry. As per this account, the need for a confirmable identity is constant and ever-changing. To deny the state the power to shape, alter, and establish protocols in an adaptable fashion is to take neither the task of identification nor the responsibilities of the state seriously.

A deinstitutionalized form of discretionary governance is also visible in a different domain: criminalization. As Nicola Lacey has carefully observed, the relationship between populism and criminalization is somewhat complex—both may well have been caused by the same factors, rather than the former having led to the latter.[45] This is not the occasion for a full-fledged reflection on the historical roots of the growing penal state, but there are some features of India's changing criminal apparatus that bear mentioning. To begin with, there has been a clear expansion of the antiterrorism framework.[46] But, more substantially, there have been new and revised offenses—pertaining, in particular, to "the interest of India" and money-laundering—and new powers granted to central authorities (the National Investigation Agency and the Enforcement Directorate) to investigate and prosecute these offenses.[47]

The distinct feature of the new offenses is the generalized rather than exceptional focus on order. Here, in a play on the Hobbesian narrative, the state needs to demonstrate the dangers of chaos in order to justify itself. The turn to a generalized condition intersects with questions of membership and administration. It intersects with the former insofar as there is a fusing of internal and external dangers. The state's coercive apparatus is no longer one where the police operate locally under certain guidelines as in the case of domestic crimes, and where national

[43] K.S. Puttaswamy v. Union of India (2019) 1 SCC 1.

[44] *See* § 23, Aadhaar (Targeted Delivery of Financial and Other Subsidies, Benefits and Services) Act 2016.

[45] Nicola Lacey, *Populism and the Rule of Law*, 15 ANN. REV. L. SOC. SCI. 79, 90–92 (2019).

[46] *See* Unlawful Activities (Prevention) Amendment Act, 2019 (which authorizes the state to declare *individuals* terrorists). *See also* NIA v. Zahoor Ahmad Shah Watali (2009) 5 SCC 1.

[47] *See* National Investigation Agency (Amendment) Act 2019; Finance Act 2019.

authorities like the military respond to external threats with fewer restraints. Instead, the national authority assumes a far greater role in violence and threats writ large—because the state cannot assume the orderliness of society and the loyalty of its members.

The coming together of internal and external security involves the coming together of the state's law and order functions and its prerogative power. As would have been familiar to Hobbes, the circumstance of being threatened cannot but engender a certain unilateralism—it requires discretion. (As Hobbes saw, this is most powerfully illustrated in cases of preemption.) Given the perceived—or, one might say, constructed—threat, the overall structure of society becomes a space where, to draw on Hamilton, "no constitutional shackles can wisely be imposed."[48] Because the social order is constantly under threat, and because all actors are potential enemies, the state requires the administrative power to ascertain—and preempt and prevent—the validity and urgency of specific threats by specific actors. Given this, it is not altogether a surprise that India's money-laundering law is spectacularly open-ended. Indeed, it has gone so far as to do away with a *mens rea* requirement.[49] The point here is not that there is a suspension of limitations on power or that there is greater control over fact-finding. It is rather that factual artifacts are themselves constructed.

To return to our initial supposition: the reason why the future may well involve a competition between different populisms is because the deinstitutionalized governance structure that authoritarian populism has ushered in will be hard to formalize even once more progressive forms of populism succeed. (It is also the case—and this is a key question raised by Tushnet and Bugarič's work—that nonauthoritarian populism might arrive first, and this may well result in the same kind of hangover, as it were.) Many of our cherished institutional forms have been severely weakened and challenged even in contexts where serious democratic backsliding has not been witnessed. Consider the case of delegated legislation and rulemaking. As Jeff King has emphasized, it is hard to conceive of the modern state in the absence of such secondary legislation.[50] There are, of course, important questions to be asked about safeguards over the long term, and about mechanisms for scrutiny and oversight. But it is one matter to ask these questions, quite another to believe that administrative discretion can be displaced. The substitution of authoritarian populism by a different populism may well use this governance structure in very different ways—indeed, that is what will make such a variant of populism a progressive one.

[48] THE FEDERALIST NO. 20 ("Tyranny has perhaps oftener grown out of the assumptions of power called for, on pressing exigencies, by a defective constitution, than out of the full exercise of the largest constitutional authorities.")

[49] *See* § 3, Prevention of Money-Laundering Act, 2002.

[50] Jeff King, *The Province of Delegated Legislation*, *in* THE FOUNDATIONS AND FUTURE OF PUBLIC LAW 145 (Elizabeth Fisher et al., eds., 2020).

If this brief account of extant and prior institutions holds weight, then it may well be the case that even if authoritarian populism is outvoted by an opposition force that is committed to institutions, this opposition force, although now in power, will be hamstrung by the reality in which it finds itself. This reality, almost a variant of conventional studies on state incapacity, will mean that the institutionally oriented party will have no option but to become a new populist version of itself. To put the point provocatively, it may well have to embrace a certain anti-institutionalism. In a scenario where the institutional wreckage is unsalvageable, competitive populism may be the only possible regime type on immediate offer. The implication here is that what will be crucial after authoritarian populism is not the nature of institutional design but the character of political contestation.[51] The institutional account will be limited because political life will have to confront, in more powerful ways than before, the construction and the working of social power. In an era of competitive populism, what will count is administration rather than rules and texts. The regimes that exist will enjoy considerable constitutive and prerogative power, and a certain discontentment over forms and institutions will persist. If the idea of competitive authoritarianism was centered on "elections without democracy,"[52] the idea of competitive populism is centered on elections without institutions. Insofar as this is true, our world will resemble the classic Levinson–Pildes supposition even more radically than they had supposed.[53] That is to say, the distribution and practice of political power will not only shape the outcomes of popular politics, but could also shape regime types—it could determine whether the regime acquires a more democratic or authoritarian bent.

On Instrumentalism

As I take it, *Power to the People* sought to remind us that the theoretical case for formal institutional channels that govern the people is always going to be a somewhat tricky endeavor. One can at all times try to offer an argument for an institution in Elyian terms—to suggest that the institution tries to make democracy possible rather than to limit it.[54] The challenge is that, if one is focused on giving voice to the people, then one is ultimately interested in some form of authorization. It is hard to dispense with the mechanisms that give primacy to this reality. Even formal defenses of institutional checks and limitations are burdened with having to provide some account of how they give *power to the people*. Tushnet and Bugarič

[51] It is worth taking note of a cycle that follows the converse logic: Perhaps the competition between populisms will result in the victor reconstructing institutions to preserve and entrench their ideology.
[52] Levitsky & Way, *Elections Without Democracy*, *supra* note 8.
[53] *See* Daryl J. Levinson & Richard H. Pildes, *Separation of Parties, Not Powers*, 119 Harv. L. Rev. 2311 (2006).
[54] *See* John Hart Ely, Democracy and Distrust: A Theory of Judicial Review (1980).

appreciate that one cannot, crudely put, have democracy without empowering the people. It is why they take such pains to explore how majority preferences can be ascertained.[55]

Thus far, I have suggested that our future political options may lie between different populisms—between progressive, inclusive variants and authoritarian, repressive ones—and our political reality may remain unmediated by institutions in an era where older institutions have lost their role and newer ones are yet to find stability. As we consider this possibility, let us ruminate over a theme that animates Tushnet and Bugarič's project: we should substantively evaluate what comes out of populism on its own terms, given that what can seem anti-institutional may well be prodemocratic. At one point in *Power to the People*, Tushnet and Bugarič delicately suggest that we should not equate populism with instrumentalism. In most cases, regardless of the leader or decisionmaker involved, legal rules can be marshaled in service of political positions, and populists usually work within rules rather than outside them. Merely because populists deploy rules to serve their ends does not make them instrumentalists, unless the term is diluted of significance and all actors count as instrumentalists because, after all, they all have the same orientation toward rules. As Tushnet and Bugarič observe, "those who describe populists as instrumentalists need to do more than identify a rule that in their view blocks some populist policy; they need to show that no reasonable arguments are available to support that policy."[56] For Tushnet and Bugarič, an overemphasis on formalism is a mistake, in part because formalism does not truly constrain action in ways that we imagine or hope that it might.

This point is well taken, but it invites the following question. Is it possible that one form of populism is closer to rule of law characteristics than other forms? Is there a version of populism that has a greater claim to empowering the people and meeting certain standards of legality? For the sake of argument, let us assume that both variants of populism agree that apex courts should not play a major role in a democratic polity. But perhaps they disagree on what might count as a rule of law polity that is democratically governed. One might say that present critiques of existing institutions are, in certain cases, legitimate, as Tushnet and Bugarič do. But does it follow from such a conclusion that both accounts of populism are equally noninstrumental? It is possible to suggest, in sketching out the difference between variants of populism, that one form of populism might have deeper rule of law characteristics because its substantive characteristics are rooted in a more egalitarian conception of the people. And, insofar as this is true, might it be possible to assert that although populism comes in many forms, not all forms are equally noninstrumental?

[55] *See* Tushnet & Bugarič, Power to the People, *supra* note 2, at 249–70.
[56] *Id.* at 76.

Within the conventional framework of constitutional democracy, when we think in terms of formal institutions, we think of authority being grounded in indirect ways. We pay attention to formal checks and balances, limitations and procedures, and the like. It is possible to conceive of many different variants of populism—situated across the political spectrum—working within rules and institutions, and using these rules and institutions to serve their ends. It is possible—I think that Tushnet and Bugarič come relatively close to this position, and possibly occupy it—to regard legal practice as being constituted by certain kinds of power relations and social orderings, and as furthering the preferences of those who enjoy authority. Under such an account, deference to form and so on is—as in the traditional realist sense—used to achieve the outcome that one wants.[57]

But the one question that does arise is that if this is noninstrumental—and as noninstrumental as any other approach because it does not disregard rules but works within them—then are all forms of noninstrumental legality the same? Crudely put, are they all *equally noninstrumental*? It may be worth exploring the thought that perhaps a certain progressive populism might be possible that empowers everyone, and gives each person an equal voice. This form of empowerment and equality has a thicker sense of noninstrumentalism to it. This conception is democratic, but it is not undisciplined like other variants of populism: it is disciplined by a substantive conception of the rule of law. This conception is noninstrumental in a deeper sense than other conceptions of populism.

Under such an account, the authoritarian variant of populism struggles to have rule of law characteristics because it is partial to certain groups. It does not contain any egalitarian conception and it does not implicate any vision of the common good.[58] Both variants of populism, the progressive one and the regressive one, share a certain approach to the conventional institutions that exist—both utilize them to serve their ends. But their responses to this approach is different. In the former conception, what replaces such utilization is a certain egalitarianism; in the latter conception, what replaces such utilization is another kind of partisanship. Could we argue that if a populist variant is not only authorized by the people like all populism but is based on a conception of mutual respect—that it is genuinely inclusive and toward the common good—this makes it noninstrumental in ways that other variants of populism are not?

The effort at distinguishing between the varieties of populism—at not conflating populism with "authoritarian populism"—is an important one. Tushnet and Bugarič help us notice how populism can also come in inclusive and progressive forms, how it can be a way to challenge elite structures and entrenched forms of power in ways that further rather than upset our democratic sensibilities. The

[57] *See generally* KARL LLEWELLYN, THE COMMON LAW TRADITION: DECIDING APPEALS (1961).

[58] The idea of partiality is an important feature of account of populism. *See* JAN-WERNER MÜLLER, WHAT IS POPULISM? (2016).

supposition that I have been venturing suggests that perhaps we might have an account of populism that may not be *formal* but can still be noninstrumental in a more profound sense than other conceptions which are noninstrumental only in the trivial sense that they work within rules and institutions rather than disregard them. Within such an account, what gives the populist variant a more serious relationship to noninstrumentalism is that it is expressive of equality; it incorporates each person's voice. It is this characteristic that separates it from pure political formalism.

In thinking about competition between populisms, one is—it should be noted—not trying to get the right balance between both populisms. In certain cases, political contestation involves competition between morally symmetrical ideals—one might want a balance, say, between progress and stability or between revolution and order. Unlike circumstances of this sort, the recent wave of authoritarian populism has opened up our politics such that our choices are now wider. The competition is now no longer between morally symmetrical principles, but between, among other things, equal voice and ethnic privilege. A progressive variant of populism may not govern within the framework of institutions that have previously inspired our constitutional politics, but it can still take a form that is noninstrumental in deeper ways than other variants of populism.

The possibility of such an outcome invites two concluding thoughts, which may have particular significance for lawyers. The first relates to our prior discussion on administrative discretion in populist regimes. If we ask how a progressive populist regime exercises administrative discretion differently—and if we connect that question with our present reflections on non-instrumental legality—perhaps the way in which a nonauthoritarian populist regime can achieve a more egalitarian cast is through its exercise of administrative law. It is the site of administrative law making and application that will hold the promise for a progressive populism to be, inelegantly put, even more noninstrumental than other populisms. If such a supposition has force, then the task for lawyers will be to determine what the character of such lawmaking and application might be.

The second thought sits in a somewhat awkward position to our first one. The tempting question raised by Tushnet and Bugarič's study of referendums and the like is not only whether there are better ways of identifying majority preferences than those we presently employ, but also whether particular institutional *forms*, perhaps of the kind that we have not yet sufficiently considered, might be more likely to engender progressive populism. If this is true, then the possibility of a progressive populism, which that has a thicker noninstrumentalist cast, raises the question of whether certain institutional forms may be more conducive to generating that particular kind of noninstrumentalism. Perhaps, in considering constitutional design possibilities, we must attend not only to whether the mechanisms we choose to use—referenda, citizen assemblies, and so on and so forth—reflect majority preferences, but also whether they are likely to engender outcomes that are more egalitarian and consistent with rule of law features than other design options. But, of course, a political endeavor that seeks to answer this may, in turn, mean that we return to the question of institutional architecture. It may, in other words, mean that we return to the place where we began—which is often the nature of politics, and, indeed, constitutional politics.

26

Mapping Power: Constitutionalism and Its Colonial Legacy

Erin F. Delaney[*]

Introduction

An explosion of new work exploring the relationships between and among constitutionalism and imperialism, colonialism, decolonialism, and neocolonialism, among other frames, has led to a concomitant desire to *do something* with this knowledge. In the past few years, the demand that the field engage directly with these legacies has grown louder. In *Global Constitutionalism*, a recent editorial was explicit in its charge to constitutional scholars to "decolonise constitutional law" through "a commitment to analyzing the colonial legacy in constitutional formation, the contemporary rights regime, and international public law, from both theoretical and historical perspectives."[1] Others have called on comparative constitutional law scholars to shift from "the modern, positivist tendency to measure and to rank" to "a focus on relationships of power between legal systems or legal traditions."[2]

These calls reflect the understanding that decolonization is not a "once-off political event, marked by the physical withdrawal of the colonial administration,"[3] but an ongoing process. But what process? Is "decolonization" merely the identification and acknowledgment of the existence and role of imperial power? Is it the creation of space for indigenous autonomy in an otherwise liberal democratic

* In addition to offering my thanks to the editors of this book and the participants at the conference from which it emerged, I would like to acknowledge Rosalind Dixon, Berihun Gebeye, Harshan Kumarasingham, and, in particular, Christina D. Ponsa-Kraus, for their generosity of mind and spirit in commenting on this chapter. Amra Saric, Chris Scheren, and Dylan Steele provided excellent research assistance, and I am, as always, indebted to Northwestern's indefatigable librarians, Tom Gaylord and Sarah Reis.

[1] Jonathan Havercroft, Jacob Eisler, Jo Shaw, Antje Wiener & Val Napoleon, Editorial, *Decolonising Global Constitutionalism*, 9 Global Constitutionalism 1, 6 (2020). *See also* Karen J. Alter, *From Colonial to Multilateral International Law: A Global Capitalism and Law Investigation*, 19 Int'l J. Const. L. 798, 799–800 (2021) (asking how colonialism contributed to the development of global capitalism and arguing for the integration of colonial law into the broad historical trajectory of international law).

[2] Lena Salaymeh & Ralf Michaels, *Decolonial Comparative Law: A Conceptual Beginning*, 86 RabelsZ 166, 187 (2022).

[3] Justin Ngambu Wanki & Carol C. Ngang, *Unsettling Colonial Paradigms: Right to Development Governance as Framework Model for African Constitutionalism*, 18 Afr. Stud. Quart. 67, 67 (2019).

Erin F. Delaney, *Mapping Power: Constitutionalism and Its Colonial Legacy* In: *Redefining Comparative Constitutional Law.* Edited by: Vicki C. Jackson and Madhav Khosla, Oxford University Press. © Erin F. Delaney 2025.
DOI: 10.1093/9780191996344.003.0026

constitutional order?[4] Or does it require the destruction of that very order itself? Is it a process, as Linda Tuhiwai Smith would say, "aimed at *undoing* the multi-faceted impacts of the colonial project and re-establishing strong contemporary indigenous nations and institutions based on traditional values, philosophies and knowledge"?[5]

There are normative prescriptions embedded in these questions. And, certainly, some approaches to decolonizing comparative constitutional law might function to deny agency to current democratic leaders or to discount public preferences in postcolonial contexts, resulting in claims of Western-led performative decolonization or neo-colonialism through "decolonization."[6] In other contexts, abusive borrowing of postcolonial discourse is linked to internal domestic power grabs and authoritarianism.[7]

At minimum, the call to action asks us, as scholars, to do more than look to law. It asks us to map the power structures that produce and maintain the law—law which in turn entrenches those power structures and invests them with legitimacy. A more nuanced empirical and positive understanding is needed to ground the normative debates about how to undertake any project of decolonization. And this brings me to the work of Mark Tushnet, along two important dimensions.

The first is Mark's early involvement with the Critical Legal Studies movement. Mark shared its intellectual commitments to an understanding of law as power and social structure and to a methodology of rich description, which would uncover "unexpressed assumptions" and expose "the consciousness that animates" constitutional law.[8] Here decolonization as deconstruction embodies an agenda: to fully capture the colonial paradigms still at work in postcolonial societies (i.e.,

[4] It is possible, of course, that the very act of creating this space can work to undermine the hegemonic aspects of western governance culture. *See, e.g.*, Sergio Miranda Hayes, *Decolonization in the Constitutional System: Indigenous Rights and Legal Pluralism, A Comparative Study Between Bolivia, Colombia, and Ecuador* (The New School, Working Paper, 2017).

[5] Linda Tuhiwai Smith, Decolonizing Methodologies: Research and Indigenous Peoples 19 (1999) (emphasis added).

[6] *Cf.* Olúfẹ́mi Táíwò, Against Decolonisation: Taking African Agency Seriously (2022) (critiquing decolonialization as a project that denigrates contemporary African agency and exists without clearly defined goals).

[7] In India, certain legal efforts lauded as "anticolonial" rejection of the British legacy are in turn Hindu nationalist efforts to limit the rights of minorities. *See, e.g.*, Amrit Dhillon, *Modi Employs New Tool in India's War against the English Language: Hindi Medical Degrees*, The Guardian (Oct. 22, 2022), https://www.theguardian.com/world/2022/oct/22/modi-employs-new-tool-in-indias-war-against-the-english-language-hindi-medical-degrees (describing Modi's imposition of Hindi on a language-diverse nation); Zia Haq, *Our History Has Mark of Colonial Conspiracy:* PM, Hindustan Times (Nov. 25, 2022), https://www.hindustantimes.com/india-news/our-history-has-mark-of-colonial-conspiracy-pm-101669398772785.html (describing initiatives that seek to rewrite a "decolonized" history, where in actuality such initiatives imply writing complicated Indian history with a heavily one-sided, Hindu-nationalist gloss).

[8] Mark Tushnet, *Critical Legal Studies and Constitutional Law: An Essay in Deconstruction*, 36 Stan. L. Rev. 623, 634–35 (1984).

structural patterns, political regimes, socioeconomic and cultural practices, and, of course, law).[9]

The second is Mark's capacious definition of *constitutionalism*, and his willingness to "unsettle the view that liberal constitutionalism simply *is* constitutionalism, and that all other varieties are defective."[10] Mapping power structures will require looking closely at central aspects of liberal constitutionalism, particularly its purported commitment to self-determination and consent, and asking whether such preconditions are possible in postcolonial settings. Mark embraced, in a 2016 ICON editorial, "adjectival constitutionalism,"[11] or the "study of constitutionalisms identified by some modifier,"[12] and encouraged scholars to engage in the examination of varieties of constitutionalism.[13] In the sections that follow, I take him up on his invitation.

This chapter introduces the concept of *coercive constitutionalism*. All moves toward "decolonizing constitutionalism" recognize the stubborn persistence of the constitutive colonial power asymmetries in postcolonial contexts. Coercive constitutionalism directly engages the paradox at the heart of the postcolonial project—the coexistence of colonial coercion *and* autochthonous agency—and imagines ways in which we might resolve or transcend it. And it is here that we can look to Mark's legacy for guidance. In short, we need his broad and ecumenical scholarly lens—one that encompasses many disciplines and comparative insights—to do this work.

The Continuum of Coercion

In the wake of the American-led invasions of Iraq and Afghanistan following 9/11, there was a resurgence of interest in comparative empire and nation-building.[14] One early scholarly foray into this renewed effort to grapple with the relationship between imperialism and constitution-making was Noah Feldman's contribution to adjectival constitutionalism: *imposed* constitutionalism.[15] In his words, an imposed constitution is one "drafted and adopted in the shadow of the gun," and he referenced constitutions in postwar Japan and Germany as exemplifying the concept.[16] Drawing from his own experiences in Iraq, Feldman sought to identify what was troubling about imposed constitutionalism. He concluded

[9] *See* Wanki & Ngang, *supra* note 3, at 67. In Karen Alter's Foreword, she touches on the problems with engaging with "colonial law" as a distinct category: *see* Alter, *supra* note 1.

[10] Mark Tushnet, Editorial, *Varieties of Constitutionalism*, 14 Int'l J. Const. L. 1 (2016).

[11] Mark cites Diana Kapiszewski for the term. *Id.*

[12] *Id.*

[13] *See, e.g.*, Mark Tushnet, *Authoritarian Constitutionalism*, 100 Cornell L. Rev. 391 (2015).

[14] Phiroze Vasunia, *The Comparative Study of Empires*, 101 J. Roman Stud. 222, 235 (2011).

[15] Noah Feldman, *Imposed Constitutionalism*, 37 Conn. L. Rev. 857, 889 (2005).

[16] *Id.* at 858.

that the inherent tension with—or absence of—self-determination as part of the constitutionalization process challenged the "very phenomenon of democratic constitutionalism itself."[17]

Feldman thus suggested self-determination as the touchstone of democratic constitutionalism, which presumably requires, at minimum, a constitution to which a people *consented*, and more robustly, a constitution that a people themselves drafted and ratified, reflecting autochthonous values and priorities. This particular idealization of democratic constitutionalism has limited purchase, especially in light of historically anemic conceptions of "a people"—before recent years, which "democratic" constitutions could possibly meet the lofty ideal? One might also ask whether this minimum criterion is even necessary for democratic constitutionalism. In describing a paradigmatic imposed constitution, Dieter Grimm has argued that "No German constitution was longer in force than the Basic Law. None achieved a higher significance for the political process and for the societal order. None enjoyed a higher appreciation by the public."[18]

The concept of an imposed constitution "seems simple and clear: A written constitution . . . imposed on a people without their full agreement."[19] But that simplicity quickly unravels. Fred Schauer questioned the usefulness of the term, wondering how often true *imposition* occurred.[20] In his analysis, Schauer glides quickly by colonialism, arguing that "much of the phenomenon of imposition in general, at least prior to the twentieth century, was attributable to colonialism, but colonial constitutional imposition was rare."[21] And he does not discuss the wave of constitutions produced by intentionally decolonizing empires in the mid-twentieth century, which Benedikt Goderis and Mila Versteeg refer to as the "most paradigmatic examples of imposed constitutions."[22] But Schauer's critique goes beyond the empirical claim, suggesting that there exist non-indigenous, non-borrowed, yet non-imposed constitutions which merit attention.[23] More recently, David Law has argued that the very idea of imposed constitutions creates a false and unsustainable dichotomy between "imposed and unimposed," useful only for constructing political narratives to delegitimize—or romanticize—the constitution.[24]

[17] *Id.* at 889.

[18] Dieter Grimm, *The Role of Fundamental Rights after Sixty-Five Years of Constitutional Jurisprudence in Germany*, 13 INT'L J. CONST. L. 9, 14 (2015). My thanks to Berihun Gebeye for this insight.

[19] Yasuo Hasebe, *Imposed Constitutions*, MAX PLANCK ENCYCLOPEDIA OF COMPAR. CONST. L. (2016).

[20] Frederick Schauer, *On the Migration of Constitutional Ideas*, 37 CONN. L. REV. 907, 913 (2005).

[21] *Id.* at 909.

[22] Benedikt Goderis & Mila Versteeg, *The Diffusion of Constitutional Rights*, 39 INT'L REV. L. & ECON. 1, 4 (2014).

[23] Schauer, *supra* note 20, at 913.

[24] David S. Law, *Imposed Constitutions and Romantic Constitutions, in* THE LAW AND LEGITIMACY OF IMPOSED CONSTITUTIONS 34, 55 (Richard Albert, Xenophon Contiades & Alkmene Fotiadou eds., 2018). In Japan, the characterization of the Kenpō as an imposed constitution is used to "undermine the legitimacy of the document in its present form and thus to pave the way for amendment," whereas "to defend the Kenpō as an expression of deeply held values and aspirations is to blunt the case for

Schauer recognizes the problem of hinging analysis on a dichotomy of "imposed" versus "autochthonous" constitutions.[25] In his view, it is all a matter of influence. With a focus on influence, Schauer proposes a turn toward *transnational* constitutionalism: "understanding the patterns of migration of legal and constitutional ideas in the twenty-first century requires that we recognize that mechanisms of political influence, economic incentives, regional cooperation and much else will say far more about who influenced whom."[26] And certainly, identifying and explicating these mechanisms is critical to a broader understanding of constitutional creation.[27]

Pace Schauer, the study of transnational influence can shed important light on the external influences on constitutional development in former colonies as well. For example, in her work on the Cuban Constitutional Convention, 1900–1901,[28] Christina Ponsa-Kraus demonstrates both how geopolitical concerns informed the United States' efforts to influence the Cuban Constitution and how control of Cuba through constitutionalism itself was beside the point. The United States' decision to demand, through the "Platt Amendment," that Cuba include a set of provisions in its constitution limiting its own power to conduct foreign relations and enter into treaties "rendered meaningless all but the most cynical definition of independence."[29] Yet, the demand was *unnecessary* to maintain hegemonic control over Cuba (as Cubans themselves recognized). The effort to impose the Amendment is better understood as an American attempt to force the "codification of the Monroe Doctrine in a constitution" and thus to further the Doctrine's recognition within international law.[30] And, to judge from the statements of the Cuban delegates to the Convention, their resistance to the Platt criteria was "*not* because they thought successful resistance would somehow eliminate the problem of U.S. hegemony . . . but because the express settlement of these relations in the Cuban constitution would undermine its authority as the founding text of the emergent Cuban nation-state."[31]

The work of Kristen Stilt and Donal Coffey on "independence" constitutions in Malaya and Burma is similarly illuminating. Stilt looks at the decision to include an establishment clause in the 1957 Malayan Constitution, showcasing the

amendment." David S. Law, *The Myth of the Imposed Constitution*, *in* The Social and Political Foundations of Constitutions (Denis Galligan & Mila Versteeg eds., 2013) 239, 252.

[25] Schauer uses the term "indigenous," but because that term is also used as a referent to specific indigenous populations within broader (settler) nation states, I am using autochthonous.

[26] Schauer, *supra* note 20, at 916.

[27] For a recent effort to take this call seriously, *see* Elisabeth Perham, *Modes of External Constitutional Advising* (PhD dissertation, University of New South Wales) (on file with author). In her dissertation, Perham explores the role of constitutional advisors in this vein, creating a thoughtful typology and assessment of advisor impact.

[28] Christina D. Ponsa-Kraus, *A Guarantee Clause for the Americas: The United States in Cuba, 1898–1902* (unpublished manuscript) (on file with author).

[29] *Id.*

[30] *Id.*

[31] *Id.*

international and domestic dimensions of the debate.[32] Secular India and Islamic Pakistan, former parts of the British Empire, were both critical reference points that took on political weight beyond their constitutional models. Internal domestic pressures driven by concerns over the ethnic Malay minority also shaped the constitutional discourse. Coffey explores the creation of the 1947 Constitution of the Union of Burma, noting that the specific British influence on the Constitution was "somewhat limited."[33] But he highlights the links between Delhi and Rangoon that influenced the drafting and concludes that the biggest foreign influence on the text was the Irish Constitution of 1937.[34]

Schauer is clearly right at a general level: geopolitical power politics will inform constitutional construction in ways shy of direct compulsion. But, in the context of constitutionalism in the shadow of empire, constitution-making occurs within a broader imperialist dynamic that structures the available options and sets the boundaries of "acceptable" borrowing.[35] The concept of transnational constitutionalism obscures the pervasive influence and agenda-setting powers of the imperial and colonial authorities, which supplement and substitute overt with covert coercion. In Linda Colley's recent study of the development of written constitutions, she identified certain communities—such as those of Pomare II in Tahiti and King Kamehameha III in Hawaii—that turned to constitutionalism in order to protect themselves and their peoples against conquest, by structuring their realms into polities that would be recognizably "civilized" to imperial powers.[36] These constitutions were not imposed, and yet they undeniably arose from something more tangibly coercive than transnational political or economic influence.

Influence shades into coercion when persuasion is accompanied by threat, whether implicit or explicit. At one end of this coercion continuum may exist (constitutional) imposition at gunpoint,[37] and at the other end, just shy of "influence," lies incentive by economic or political loss or benefit. But determining whether an incentive is coercive is a function of the situation of the people(s) on whom

[32] Kristen Stilt, *Contextualizing Constitutional Islam: The Malayan Experience*, 13 Int'l J. Const. L. 407 (2015).

[33] Donal Coffey, *The Drafting of the Constitution of the Union of Burma in 1947* (unpublished manuscript) (on file with author).

[34] *Id.*

[35] *Cf.* Goderis & Versteeg, *supra* note 22, at 17 (indicating connections between the constitutional frameworks of colonizers and the one adopted by the successor state: "[D]ecision of countries to adopt constitutional rights is correlated with past adoption by their former colonizer, countries with the same legal origin, the same religion, the same former colonizer, and the same dominant aid donor").

[36] Linda Colley, The Gun, the Ship, and the Pen: Warfare, Constitutions, and The Making of the Modern World 293, 299 (2021). *See also* Erin Delaney, *Of Constitutions and Constitutionalism*, Balkinization (Oct. 27, 2021), https://balkin.blogspot.com/2021/10/of-constitutions-and-constituti onalism.html (reviewing Colley's book).

[37] *Cf.* Feldman, *supra* note 15, at 880 ("[C]oercion is a sort of continuum in the international context").

it operates.[38] Critically, any analysis of coercion must take into consideration the scope of the domestic population's capacity to resist.

Neither imposed nor transnational constitutionalism provides sufficient purchase for us truly to grapple with the mutually constitutive relationship between coercion and agency in the colonial and postcolonial contexts. A power-mapping exercise must explore both coercion and agency before turning to any of the various normative claims about "what next."

Assessing Agency

Evaluating agency requires disaggregating a complex array of persons and groups, as well as assessing their capacity for informed consent within coercive structures. It demands close analysis of ongoing political power relations, both in the shadow of, and operating parallel to, the colonial (or hegemonic) power; a clear understanding of the cultural and political context to identify those who did not (or were not invited to) participate; and an assessment of the degree or quality of freedom for those in fact deliberating or participating.

Consent itself is complicated. Apparent consent may not reflect autonomous consent. Or consent may be given as a political strategy, but without normative approval; constitutionalization may be a way of organizing resistance, as noted above. The US Indian Reorganization Act of 1934, which gave authorization to tribes to adopt constitutions (approved by the Secretary of the Interior), required a constitutional ratification procedure for those tribes voting to constitutionalize under its terms.[39] Some tribes chose not to constitutionalize. Others voted for constitutionalization, attempted to exercise agency in crafting certain unique constitutional provisions, and then ratified the result. And others "consented" even as they rejected the claim that constitutionalization represented an act of autochthonous agency. As one Comanche elder recalled: "Well, we are going to pass this constitution to get white people off our back. Who needs it? We will not use it anyway."[40]

Assessing the role of autochthonous agency in colonial and postcolonial constitution-making enables us to understand the nature, scope, and effectiveness of coercion in the process. To describe a colonial or postcolonial constitution as "imposed" is to "beg[] the question of upon whom."[41] In his critique of "imposition"

[38] *Cf.* Nat'l Fed'n of Indep. Bus. v. Sebelius, 567 U.S. 519, 577–78 (2012) (rejecting the threat of withdrawal of federal funding for a state program as unconstitutional "when 'pressure [to accept the conditions of the funding] turns into compulsion'").

[39] 25 U.S.C. §5123(a)(1).

[40] Philleo Nash et al., *The IRA Record and John Collier*, *in* Indian Self-Rule: First-Hand Accounts of Indian–White Relations from Roosevelt to Reagan, 108 (Kenneth R. Philp ed., 1986).

[41] *Id.*

as a metric for evaluating constitutions, David Law questions "both the coherence and relevance of the distinction between imposition by domestic political actors and imposition by foreign governments."[42] Even in "classic" examples of imposed constitutions, such as the Kenpō of post-World War II Japan, fruitful analysis of the role of elites, leadership, and the general public in the adoption of the constitution reveals a complex multilateral dynamic that belies the claim of imposition.[43] And evaluations of the mid-20th-century wave of decolonization constitutions have similarly benefited from attention to internal, on-the-ground politics. For example, in Africa, decolonization constitutions were seen by some as a means to facilitate the transferal of power by former imperial powers to domestic elites, without input (or pushback) from local constituencies.[44]

Mechanisms of coercion include agenda-setting (or agenda-limiting) "directed at ensuring the acquiescence of local elites, with fundamental questions of constitutional choice safely remaining in foreign hands."[45] The story of the inclusion of bills of rights in new constitutions by British colonial decisionmakers provides an example.[46] Concerns about the peaceful transfer of power *within* decolonizing entities led the British to prioritize bills of rights, notwithstanding historic British constitutional "hostility" to the concept.[47] Both the British and domestic elites "did not trust that the new political authorities in many soon-to-be decolonized African countries would protect the interests of their principal constituencies—white settlers, domestic urban intelligentsia, and foreign investors," leading to the adoption of "an entrenched constitutional catalogue of rights," as well as courts to enforce them.[48]

[42] Law, *The Myth of the Imposed Constitution*, *supra* note 24, at 241.

[43] *Id.* at 242, 244–46 (suggesting general public welcomed the changes introduced and highlighting the ways in which translation and linguistic nuance was used to control meaning).

[44] Ruth Gordon, *Growing Constitutions*, 1 U. Pa. J. Const. L. 528, 543–44 (1999); John Mukum Mbaku, *Entrenching Constitutionalism in African Countries: Lessons from America's Founding Fathers*, 55 Tex. Int'l L.J. 89, 108 (2019).

[45] Sujit Choudhry, *Old Imperial Dilemmas and the New Nation-Building: Constitutive Constitutional Politics in Multinational Polities*, 37 Conn. L. Rev. 933, 933 (2005).

[46] In his discussion of British imperialism, Harshan Kumarasingham rightly notes that there was "no uniform mechanism either to ready a territory for independence or to establish constitutional measures and institutions to facilitate the process." Harshan Kumarasingham, *Constitution and Empire*, *in* The Cambridge Constitutional History of the United Kingdom (Peter Cane & Harshan Kumarasingham eds., 2021) 496, 528. Indeed, different colonialisms can operate under the umbrella of the same imperialism. *See generally* Sebastian Conrad, German Colonialism (Sorcha O'Hagan trans., 2014). For example, "classic colonialism" might be seen as a capitalist loop of resource extraction (raw materials and labor) and market creation for finished products produced at the metropole, while "settler colonialism" is understood to be driven by an "intention to acquire and occupy land on which to settle permanently." Evelyn Nakano Glenn, *Settler Colonialism as Structure: A Framework for Comparative Studies of U.S. Race and Gender Formation*, 1 Sociology of Race & Ethnicity 52, 67 (2015).

[47] *See generally* Charles O. H. Parkinson, Bills of Rights and Decolonization (2007).

[48] Ran Hirschl, *The Political Origins of Judicial Empowerment through Constitutionalization: Lessons from Four Constitutional Revolutions*, 25 Law & Soc. Inquiry 91, 137–38 (2000).

Although the rough cut of "elites versus others" can be useful (and has different implications for Japan than for African decolonization constitutions),[49] an assessment of agency also requires close and critical attention to the quality and nature of the participation of the broader domestic public. As Semahagn G. Abebe has written, "the system of transplantation of Western legal and political ideals was made by way of disregarding the well-entrenched, informal traditional values that guided the lives of ordinary Africans for centuries."[50] These "relations of assimilation" can lead to a type of *unfreedom*, in the words of James Tully.[51]

Tully suggests that even if people "are permitted and often encouraged to participate in democratic practices of deliberation," they are "constrained to deliberate in a particular way, in a particular type of institution and over a particular range of issues so their agreements and disagreements serve to reinforce rather than challenge the status-quo. Although they are governed through their freedom to some extent, they nevertheless deliberate within the rules rather than over the rules, as the principle of democracy requires."[52] On the one hand, Sudipta Kaviraj has written, colonialism may have "failed in its political objective of gaining permanent compliance," as "the alphabet it presented to the colonial society was broken apart, parcellized, turned around to spell dissent." On the other hand, he concludes, "in a different sense of course that was precisely the mark of its success. Even those who ended colonial rule and inherited their country used this alphabet, now neither wholly alien nor wholly familiar, as the means to their liberation and to construct their own social order."[53]

Ponsa-Kraus likens this kind of coercion to a type of imperial or colonial gaslighting. She suggests that the imperial mindset can be analogized to that of a "gaslighter's 'characteristic desire . . . to destroy the possibility of disagreement,'" by "'destroying the source of possible disagreement—the independent, separate, deliberative perspective from which such disagreement might arise.'"[54] Taken to its logical conclusion, decolonial thinking requires delinking: "not accept[ing] the options that are available to you,"[55] refusing to accept the agenda-setting power, or introducing (or excavating) preexisting alphabets.

[49] John Mukum Mbaku, *Citizenship Laws and Political and Economic Participation in Africa*, 43 N.C. J. Int'l L. 110, 134–41 (2018) (assessing failures in local participation in Côte d'Ivoire).

[50] Semahagn G. Abebe, *The Relevance of African Culture in Building Modern Institutions and the Quest for Legal Pluralism*, 57 St. Louis U. L.J. 429, 433–34 (2013).

[51] James Tully, *The Unfreedom of the Moderns in Comparison to Their Ideals of Constitutional Democracy*, 65 Modern L. Rev. 204, 221 (2002).

[52] *Id.* at 223.

[53] Sudipta Kaviraj, The Imaginary Institution of India 81–82 (2010).

[54] Christina D. Ponsa-Kraus, *Empire by Gaslight: The Legal History of Puerto Rico's Future* (unpublished manuscript) (on file with author) (quoting Kate Abramson, *Turning Up the Lights on Gaslighting*, 28 Philosophical Perspectives 1, 14 (2014)).

[55] Walter D. Mignolo, *Geopolitics of Sensing and Knowing: On (De)Coloniality, Border Thinking and Epistemic Disobedience*, 14 Postcolonial Stud. 273, 276 (2011).

And yet, these statements also introduce a major challenge for scholars seeking to understand and elucidate colonized or postcolonial constitutional constructs and cultures. What to make of the paradoxical phrasing—"[f]reedom to some extent," and "neither wholly alien nor wholly familiar"—as societies undertake new constitutionalization practices and move farther away from overtly coercive constructs? Since the wave of original decolonization constitutions, "constitution making has transformed from mimicking the constitutions of colonial rulers to either autochthonous constitution-making or hybrid processes that fit the local context."[56] Do the current politicians and activists in Puerto Rico understand themselves to be gaslit? And who has the standing (cultural, moral, epistemological) to articulate that contention?

How much do shared powers of agenda-setting, or the *ex post* rationalization of having been "persuaded," create or undermine a sense of agency? In some histories of British decolonization, domestic constitutional drafters put a premium on instantiating a form of parliamentary supremacy; this constitutional "option" was clearly dictated by the context of colonial rule, but the constitutional demand was insisted upon by domestic elites, not promoted by London.[57] For example, in Harshan Kumarasingham's masterful exegesis of the development of "Eastminster," he explains how postcolonial constitutions in India, Pakistan, Ceylon, Malaya, and Nepal were developed "not just [as] a matter of the British intention in 'charter, statute or instruction' but [also by] how those on the ground 'regarded the instruments they received and how they worked them.'"[58] Effective power-mapping must take into consideration the possibility of a compromised consent—but one that might still operate *as agency*.

The Struggle for Synthesis

It is incontrovertible that the legacies of colonialism are still felt today. Theories of path dependency and historical institutionalism confirm what is evident on the ground. As E. Tendayi Achiume recently argued, "colonial-era racial and related inequality in land and property ownership remains central to the socioeconomic marginality of many, and this persisting inequality and marginality are partially

[56] Rangita de Silva de Alwis et al., *Women and the Making of the Tunisian Constitution*, 35 BERKELEY J. INT'L L. 90, 103 (2017). *Cf.* David S. Law & Mila Versteeg, *The Evolution and Ideology of Global Constitutionalism*, 99 S. CAL. L. REV. 1163, 1231 (2011) (suggesting that former colonies—on "their own path"—are now leading the development of the Anglo-American model of rights constitutionalism).

[57] *See* Donal Coffey, *Constituent Power and Parliamentary Sovereignty in Commonwealth Constitutional Legal Systems* (unpublished manuscript) (on file with author); *see also* Dietmar Rothermund, *Constitution Making and Decolonization*, 212 DIOGENES 9, 10–11 (2006).

[58] Harshan Kumarasingham, *Eastminster—Decolonisation and State-Building in British Asia*, *in* CONSTITUTION-MAKING IN ASIA 1, 11 (Harshan Kumarasingham ed., 2016). Even within this construct, Kamarasingham recognizes that "the meaning of Eastminster differs from Kathmandu to Kuala Lumpur," and calls for further study and research. *Id.* at 27.

sustained by neocolonial logics embedded in the constitutions of postcolonial African nation-states."[59] And Liaquat Ali Khan has explained that decolonization in

> the Muslim world did not remove Western codes and constitutions from legal systems, which had penetrated deeply into the legal fabric of daily life . . . The liberated Muslim nations found it daunting, if not impossible, to dismantle the imported legal infrastructure of codes and courts and replace it with classical fiqh developed in the early centuries of Islamic empires.[60]

But Mark Tushnet and Dimitry Kochenov are prescient when they highlight the importance of looking at "the ways in which post-colonial political leaders have adopted or rejected the institutions colonial rulers had imposed upon their nations."[61] Current actors, many democratically elected, often contribute to the perpetuation of colonial legacies through the construction of the postcolonial state.

Coercive constitutionalism encompasses the spectrum of power dynamics at play in postcolonial constitutions. Coercive constitutions incorporate elements of autonomy and choice exercised by domestic constitutional delegates, and/or perceptions of autonomy and choice,[62] along the coercion continuum. For example, colonial deference to self-interested domestic elites may itself create an aura of self-determination,[63] and/or a strong domestic perception of control and autonomy, and/or the possibility of actual autochthonous agency. The admixture will be different in each context.[64]

This power-mapping is relevant to ongoing processes of decolonization. A coercive constitution may be a postcolonial constitution, but in recognizing the interplay of agency and coercion, it must be disaggregated and evaluated, taking the possibility of domestic agency seriously. It cannot be entirely discarded as imposed and yet must also earn its prefix "post." The critical turn can show the fundamental

[59] E. Tendayi Achiume, *Migration as Decolonization*, 71 Stan. L. Rev. 1509, 1546 (2019).

[60] Liaquat Ali Khan, *Jurodynamics of Islamic Law*, 61 Rutgers L. Rev. 231, 284 (2009).

[61] Mark Tushnet & Dimitry Kochenov, *Introduction (the Politics of Constitutional Law), in* Research Handbook on the Politics of Constitutional Law 1, 3 (Mark Tushnet & Dimitry Kochenov eds., 2023).

[62] It may be that people do not understand a constitution to be coerced because it is "theirs" and they chose it, but they might be deluded about the true freedom of their choice. *Cf.* Foluke Ifejola Adebisi, *Decolonising Education in Africa: Implementing the Right to Education by Re-Appropriating Culture and Indigeneity*, 67 N. Ir. Leg. Q 433, 437 (2016) (describing the metaphor used by Valentin Mudimbe of "an African researcher 'who rides up and down a lift believing that he or she is in control of its movement, all the while unaware that Western technicians in fact possess the knowledge of its operation and thus ultimately determine the limits of its freedom'").

[63] *Cf.* Madhavi Sunder, *Enlightened Constitutionalism*, 37 Conn. L. Rev. 891, 900 (2005).

[64] *See* S.A. de Smith, The New Commonwealth and its Constitutions 54 (1964) (noting that, at the time of writing, it was not "possible, on the basis of the information at present available, to make confident generalisations about the respective roles of the British Government and the local governments in the authorship of the more sophisticated constitutional instruments").

internal contradictions, instabilities, and even incoherence of coercive constitutionalism, but the post-postcolonial project has reconstructive aims. It may be true that "deconstructing the postcolonial speaks of what can be,"[65] but it is the reconstruction project that will determine what is.

How should scholars proceed? There are different normative goals of decolonization—and it is important to recognize that a power-mapping approach may have different uses depending on the circumstances. For example, the assumptions of coercive constitutionalism might matter little for a project of *undoing*, such as one resonating with Linda Tuhiwai Smith's argument cited at the opening of this chapter. The attentive disambiguation of the postcolonial constructs followed by the excavation of precolonial indigenous structures of governance requires a view of current populations as denied genuine agency. In this paradigm, scholars should engage in the "project of undoing and unlearning the coloniality of power, knowledge and being and of creating a new sense of humanity and forms of interrelationality."[66] In some ways, these calls dovetail with rejectionist attitudes toward liberal constitutionalism itself, suggesting that "liberal constitutionalism's association with either colonialism, or colonialism's successor paradigm of 'classical modernist' post-colonial nation-state building, makes it inappropriate wholesale for the post-colonial world."[67]

For others, a recognition of coercive constitutionalism might serve, not as a method of unraveling the constitutional tapestry, but as a way of identifying its various threads and by whom it was woven. In countries in which active engagement by postcolonial leaders has attempted a type of constitutional repatriation, Berihun Gebeye sees a syncretism at work: "the process and result of adoption, rejection, invention, and transformation of diverse and seemingly opposite legal rules, principles and practices into a constitutional state with imperial or colonial legacies."[68] Coercive constitutionalism would highlight the coercion and agency in these processes. As a normative project, however, recognizing what has been created, how, and from what starting point is only the first step. The next step requires articulating a normative vision of constitutionalism itself, against which the mapped results can be measured.

One version of that next step might be found in Latin American *transformative* constitutionalism, which addresses not only a revised *what* of constitutionalism—a postliberal constitutional order—but also a more expansive *who*.[69] To use the terms

[65] Adebisi, *supra* note 62, at 438.

[66] Nelson Maldonado Torres, *Fanon and Decolonial Thought*, *in* Encyclopedia of Educ. Phil. and Theory 799. *Cf.* Jan Erk, *Traditional Kingdoms and Modern Constitutions*, *in* Comparative Constitutional Law in Africa 329 (Tom Ginsburg, Rosalind Dixon & Adem Kassie Abebe eds., 2021).

[67] Asanga Welikala, *Theorising Constitutionalism in Buddhist-Dominant Asian Polities*, *in* Buddhism and Comparative Constitutional Law (Tom Ginsburg & Ben Schoenthal eds., 2022).

[68] Berihun Gebeye, A Theory of African Constitutionalism 2 (2021).

[69] On transformative constitutionalism more generally, *see* Michaela Hailbronner, *Transformative Constitutionalism: Not Only in the Global South*, 65 Am. J, Comp. L. 537 (2016); Eric Kibet & Charles

of coercive constitutionalism, it asks: How can agency be enhanced and coercion limited? As Jorge Farinacci-Fernós has written in the context of the 2009 Bolivian Constitution, "the crucial participation of the country's indigenous majority during the drafting process has carried enormous weight" in the Constitutional Assembly as a force for decolonization.[70] Of course, within transformative constitutionalism, it is not possible to erase all vestiges of written constitutionalism's origins. Even in the Bolivian context, the constitution "does include the classical legal features, many of which trace back to the core elements of modern constitutionalism. And yet, its introduction of plurinationality and other pluralist aims has also made it, in the words of the Tribunal Constitucional Plurinacional in Bolivia, a 'constitutionalism that has no precedent.'"[71] In Bolivia, an express goal of emancipatory decolonization served as a backdrop to constitutional reimagination.[72] In other contexts, scholars recommend a more clearly articulated hybridization.[73]

The study of coercive constitutionalism fuels the normative turn: What will resolve and transcend the postcolonial paradox of coexistent coercion and agency? It takes seriously the transnational actors and networks that influence constitution-building in the present. It assesses the threat of neocolonialism. And it offers a close look at the fine-grained aspects of constitutional development, such as agenda-setting powers, timetables, and financial resources, thereby enabling us to identify and evaluate the nature of agency and coercion.

Conclusion

Ultimately, explicating coercive constitutionalism—however it is operationalized and for whatever normative goal—will require confronting challenges. "Western liberal democracy" does not produce one set of constitutional structures. Some may be more coercive than others. The examination of distinct imperialist constitutional visions will illuminate the nature of coercion and the scope

Fombad, *Transformative Constitutionalism and the Adjudication of Constitutional Rights in Africa.* 17 Afr. Hum. Rts. L. J. 340 (2017). My thanks to Neil Modi for discussion on this topic; his doctoral dissertation is tentatively entitled "Mapping Transformative Constitutionalism: A Comparative & Institutional Study."

70 Jorge Farinacci-Fernós, *When Social History Becomes a Constitution: The Bolivian Post-Liberal Experiment and the Central Role of History and Intent in Constitutional Adjudication*, 47 Sw. L. Rev. 137, 150 (2017).

71 *Id.* at 144.

72 *Cf.* Zoran Oklopcic, *Comparing as (Re-)Imagining: Southern Perspective and the World of Constitutions, in* The Global South and Comparative Constitutional Law (Philipp Dan, Michael Riegner & Maxim Bönnemann eds., 2020).

73 Abebe, *supra* note 50, at 435 (arguing that reconciling African traditionalism and Western-style democracy is the best way forward for Africa).

for self-determination in any individual context.[74] Thus, scholars might explore both comparative imperialism and comparative colonialism,[75] acknowledging the possibility of multiple expectations of what constitutionalism is and what it can accomplish, both as a construct and as an aspect of imperialist claims to "universalizing discourses and practices."[76] The deeper, more foundational challenge, however, lies in reckoning with the reality that "the structures of the field of power under colonialism" are "inextricable from certain discursive structures," which in turn are embedded in colonial historiography.[77] "To construct accounts of that construction,"[78] historians and scholars must be attentive to the epistemological weaknesses or blindspots in present-day historiography and broader scholarship, recognizing the threats of epistemic injustice and calls for the decolonization of knowledge itself.[79]

As another recent call to decolonize comparative constitutional law highlighted, the project demands "community, embeddedness, collaboration and community-building,"[80] and I would add the more prosaic needs of interdisciplinarity, funding, and time. And here, once again, I return to Mark. Mark's pioneering work has contributed to a welcome shift in the field from comparative constitutional law to comparative constitutional studies. His wide-ranging scholarship reflects that broader and more ambitious aim. He has written that scholars trained first as lawyers tend to think first about law, and scholars trained first as political scientists tend to think first about power and then law. But Mark thinks about sociology, culture, politics, economics, power, and law. He runs the table. And as an omnivorous reader and enthusiastic supporter of emerging scholars all over the world, he is the consummate collaborator. In short, it is in Mark's ethos that we can find both the path to deconstruction and the tools for reconstruction.

[74] *See* Rothermund, *supra* note 57 (suggesting the "Cartesian mind of the French politicians and administrators" drove their approach to decolonization).

[75] I use the term "imperialism" rather than "empire" intentionally. Imperialism embraces a set of "universalizing discourses and practices" (Vasunia, *supra* note 14, at 229) that functions to enforce some element of metropole-based homogeneity without falling into definitional derailment about whether something (like the United States) is or is not "an Empire." *See id.*; *see also* John M. MacKenzie, *European Imperialism: Comparative Approaches*, 22 Eur. Hist. Q. 415, 416–17 (1992). There is also interesting work distinguishing colonialism and empire: *see* Michael Adas, *Imperialism and Colonialism in Comparative Perspective*, 20 Int'l Hist. Rev. 253 (1998).

[76] Vasunia, *supra* note 14, at 229.

[77] Kaviraj, *supra* note 53, at 41.

[78] *Id.* at 43.

[79] *See, e.g.*, Andrea J. Pitts, *Decolonial Praxis and Epistemic Injustice*, *in* Routledge Handbook on Epistemic Injustice (Ian Kidd, José Medina & Gaile Pohlhaus, Jr. eds., 2017) (asking how to produce a decolonial corpus of scholarship without perpetuating the trends of academic neocolonial expansion).

[80] Tom Gerald Daly & Dinesha Samararatne, *Decolonising Comparative Constitutional Law (and Democratisation Studies)?*, *in* Democratic Consolidation and Constitutional Endurance in Africa and Asia 1, 6 (Tom Gerald Daly & Dinesha Samararatne eds., 2024).

27

The Possibilities of Constitutional Tourism

Jamal Greene

Mark Tushnet is a prolific traveler. Although I have not attempted a precise count, on reflection it is conceivable that an outright majority of significant conferences I have attended in my professional life have also been attended by Mark. On information and belief, the same is true of others, both within the field of comparative constitutional law and in domestic US constitutional law as well. As perhaps the most accomplished public law comparativist the United States has ever known, it is not surprising that Mark has spent a lot of time on the road. Without being overly presumptuous, I want to reflect a bit on what he might have learned in his travels.

I am driven to ask this question based on the challenge Günter Frankenberg put to current and would-be comparative scholars more than 35 years ago. In a single, devastating paragraph, Frankenberg made sure that anyone intrepid enough to enter the field would have an answer to what, exactly, they were doing there:

> Comparative law is somewhat like traveling. The traveler and the comparatist are invited to break away from daily routines, to meet the unexpected and, perhaps, to get to know the unknown. Traveling promises opportunities for learning both about one's own country and culture and about other countries and cultures. Going places and gazing at a strange world do not, however, automatically open up new horizons. More often than not, even exotic trips turn out to be vain attempts to escape from everyday life and to re-invent the traveler's world-view. Tourism as conspicuous consumption occasionally unearths some raw material upon which learning can take place, and "collecting countries" or "making Europe in a week" at best teaches the tourist how little she knows about herself or others. . . . As long as we understand foreign places as like or unlike home, we cannot begin to fully appreciate them, or ourselves. We travel as if blindfolded: visiting only landmarks of our past, that restore confidences and banish fear.[1]

[1] Günther Frankenberg, *Critical Comparisons: Re-thinking Comparative Law*, 26 Harv. J. Int'l L. 411, 411–12 (1985).

Jamal Greene, *The Possibilities of Constitutional Tourism* In: *Redefining Comparative Constitutional Law*. Edited by: Vicki C. Jackson and Madhav Khosla, Oxford University Press.
DOI: 10.1093/9780191996344.003.0027

This paragraph is dispiriting. It seems to suggest that successful comparativists not only cannot be dabblers or dilettantes—we knew that, I guess—but that they cannot really even be "of" a place, grounded in a foundational set of traditions or perspectives on the law, for in being so situated they inevitably transform their subject to fit the mold they have taken with them. To be a tourist is to do what your priors, formed elsewhere, urge you to do, to see, and to experience.

I see at least three ways in which Mark has made himself less vulnerable to these criticisms than others. First is the sheer volume of travel, and here I mean travel in its literal sense. Frankenberg notes the interesting way in which so much of the comparativist's research agenda is generated under contingent and idiosyncratic circumstances. Indeed, he recommends reading forewords and prefaces of comparative books to get a sense of this bias, revealed in "the comparatist's legal education and exposure to specific legal cultures, honeymoons and travels, invitations to conferences, and so on."[2] Mark's travel has been so voluminous that it somewhat mitigates this limitation.

Put to one side for the moment what one may substantively learn from literal travel. Assuming travel contributes to comparative study in some way, Mark's selection of destinations is sufficiently indiscriminate as to allow him to compare A to B and B to C and D to B, E, and G, rather than simply bringing all conversations back to A. I am struck here by Mark's observation, in his pandemic-inspired reflection on the state of comparative constitutional law, that we should not trust foreign scholars we meet at conferences to be especially faithful rapporteurs of their own traditions because they, like we, are the sorts of people who go to conferences.[3] Travel enough in a certain mode and you come to distrust travel, per se, as forcing an encounter with differences in perspective. The restaurant that appeals to you in one place is much the same as the one that appeals to you in another; you have, after all, brought the same person's platinum credit card to both places. The lessons of travel cannot become organic until travel itself becomes mundane. Mark has long understood that.

Mark's second safeguard against comparative public law as being too driven by "conspicuous consumption" emerges out of his orientation as a critical theorist. Frankenberg's criticism aims most directly at normative theorists whose comparative engagement aims to produce an ideal set of judicial and political institutions. Part of the reason the criticism itself feels dated is because of Tushnet's own work, in both domestic and comparative constitutional law. Mark is an eternal skeptic. The form this takes is not to take the shortcomings of the United States to identify other systems as better or in need of the same interventions he thinks necessary in

[2] *Id.* at 443.

[3] Mark Tushnet, *Writing while Quarantined: A Personal Interpretation of Contemporary Comparative Constitutional Law*, 15 VIENNA J. INT'L CONST. L. 53 (2021).

his home jurisdiction. It is, rather, to assume that, in a chaotic society beset with deep disagreement, all robust institutional defenses are too optimistic about the autonomous constraining power of institutions. This is less a particular normative perspective than a commitment, born of years of practice, not to adopt any such perspective, or at a minimum not to become too deeply attached to it. Indeed, Mark's audacious recognition of "bricolage" as a distinctive constitutional design strategy performs his skepticism of too-neat normativity.[4]

This intellectual disposition seems to me well designed to resist the dangers of constitutional tourism. Frankenberg recognized this. "Legal realism and, to a lesser degree, sociological jurisprudence have . . . challenged the idea of a politically neutral normative structure determined by legal reasoning and forming a coherent system," he writes. "The realist message and, of course, its radicalization by critical legal scholars go to a large extent unnoticed in the discourse on comparative law." Although it is fair to say that these perspectives do not dominate the field, it is no longer the case that they go unnoticed.

A third way in which Mark is able to defy Frankenberg's critique is through a related but distinctive feature of Mark's scholarship. Mark is not just an eternal skeptic; his observations are always, inimitably, tentative. All of Mark's ideas are hypotheses. They are always subject to testing, to qualification and revision. For some, this orientation is born of intellectual timidity. Not so with Mark, who does not lack self-confidence. Mark's hesitations, rather, are constitutive. As others (including Mark) have noted, his style of writing can have a halting, meandering style, as one would expect in conversation over a glass of pinot noir after the conference presentations have at last concluded. This style is, if I may, as disciplined as it appears not to be. For Mark, the person who says "I will proceed to tell you why weak-form review (or proportionality or fourth branches or what-have-you) are preferred, and why their critics are mistaken" is the one who lacks discipline. The more inductive "Here are some things—well, a lot of things—I've noticed, some of which seem usually bad and others of which are sometimes good and sometimes not, depending" seems just the right tone for the successful comparativist and the successful tourist alike.

It is in this spirit that one comes to recognize that Mark's canonical *The Possibilities of Comparative Constitutional Law* is not quite what the uninitiated might have expected it to be. The title of the piece could lead someone to believe it to be optimistic or aspirational, but only if that someone does not know Mark. The choice of the more banal "possibilities" over the warmer "potential" is deliberate. "Possibilities" is meant in its most literal sense. The article does not celebrate

[4] Mark Tushnet, *The Possibilities of Comparative Constitutional Law*, 108 Yale L.J. 1225, 1229 (1999).

functionalism or expressivism or bricolage, nor does it denigrate them, nor does it attempt anything like a complete catalog of what each entails, nor does it suggest that there are not other modes of constitutional comparison that might be interesting. Here, as always, Mark's comparative work is an entry point, and often a provocation, rather than a conclusion. He is never so nostalgic as most of us are as tourists. His work lacks the sentimentality that the word "potential" takes as its baggage. And now that he is retired, his journey, as ever, is unfinished.

28

Constituent Power in Constitutional Theory, with a Note on Language and Method

Mark Tushnet

I thank everyone who contributed a chapter to this volume; I have read and appreciated all of them. In this chapter, I address a small number of the many ideas raised in the other contributions; dealing with the others would extend this contribution beyond the bounds of practicality (and readers' patience).

Several chapters in this volume discuss the concept of constituent power and its proper role—if it has one—in thinking about constitutions and their social and legal foundations. I started thinking about that concept well after I had done substantial work in comparative constitutional law, and my ideas continue to develop. This volume provides me with an opportunity to develop them a bit more fully, though I admit that I do not have a fully formed concept, and its defenses, at hand. After presenting my current thinking about constituent power, I conclude this contribution with some reflections on work in comparative constitutional law.

As Sergio Verdugo observes in his critique of arguments giving the concept of constituent power an important place in constitutional theory, the concept "has not achieved the status of a mainstream academic idea in the United States."[1] The concept is ubiquitous in constitutional theory elsewhere—perhaps too ubiquitous when it is deployed in circumstances where other concepts are available to describe and justify the normativity of constitutions (overall) or some of their provisions.[2]

[1] Sergio Verdugo, *Is It Time to Abandon the Theory of Constituent Power?*, 21 INT'L J. CONST. L. 14, 14 (2023). In this connection I think it worth noting that the concept was barely mentioned in the first edition of VICKI C. JACKSON & MARK TUSHNET, COMPARATIVE CONSTITUTIONAL LAW (1999). One reason for its neglect in US constitutional theorizing, I have suggested, is that the manner in which the US Constitution was adopted and its content—which Verdugo calls "reflexive," *supra* at 56—obscured the concept's importance or, alternatively and oddly equivalently, made that importance so obvious that it required no discussion. *See* Mark Tushnet, Foundations of Public Law: *A View from the United States*, *in* QUESTIONING THE FOUNDATIONS OF PUBLIC LAW 209 (Michael A. Wilkinson & Michael W. Dowdle eds., 2018).

[2] Verdugo, *supra* note 1, provides an effective critique of the indiscriminate employment of the concept, though I believe he is mistaken in thinking that excessive use discredits the idea itself.

Mark Tushnet, *Constituent Power in Constitutional Theory, with a Note on Language and Method* In: *Redefining Comparative Constitutional Law.* Edited by: Vicki C. Jackson and Madhav Khosla, Oxford University Press. © Mark Tushnet 2025.
DOI: 10.1093/9780191996344.003.0028

My thinking about constituent power develops from paying attention to two scenarios.[3] The first involves the revolutionary displacement of an existing constitution in a manner inconsistent with that constitution's rules for amendment or replacement.[4] This scenario has at least arguably occurred with some frequency, which means that the concept of constituent power has some real-world purchase. The second scenario is more theoretical than practical, but thinking about it helps flesh out the concept's contours. In this scenario many people—but short of the number required by existing amendment rules—believe that a specific change in the constitution is urgently needed but find the change blocked by the amendment rules, which themselves cannot be changed urgently. Consider, for example, the highly restrictive amendment rules of the US Constitution, which require quite substantial supermajorities for constitutional amendment. Those majorities can in principle be achieved through repeated electoral victories but, in this scenario, that path is unsatisfactory because the change is urgently needed (or at least that is what many people believe).

In both scenarios irregular forms of constitutional change can (or will) be employed.[5] The concept of constituent power explains why or how the ensuing changes have at least the same normative weight as constitutional changes pursuant to the existing constitution's rules for amendment or replacement. I think it worth emphasizing, first, that the concept need not be deployed to explain the normativity of *every* constitutional change—only those that occur irregularly—and second, that not every irregular constitutional change has the appropriate degree of normativity. Indeed, one might say that the concept of constituent power is designed to identify those, and only those, irregular changes that have that degree of normativity.

With this background I turn to my account of constituent power.[6] The starting point is the proposition that people are entitled to govern themselves—to be, as it is sometimes put, the authors of the laws under which they are governed. One

[3] These scenarios parallel, though are not identical to, the two scenarios Verdugo describes, the first "where the conditions for democratic procedures to operate reasonably well are non-existent" and the second "in which th[ose] conditions operate reasonably well." Verdugo, *supra* note 1, at 21.

[4] This is the scenario that provoked Abbe Sieyès's initial development of the concept, and arguably the scenario that generated discussion of the concept by Carl Schmitt and Hans Kelsen with respect to the Weimar Constitution.

[5] Verdugo, *supra* note 1, at 44, observes that "constituent power theory says little about the design choices of constitution-makers" (in, I believe, these scenarios). He is correct but, in my view, that is not a critique of constituent power theory, which is not designed to deal with such choices. For one description of irregular processes in the second scenario, *see* Mark Tushnet & Bojan Bugarič, Power to the People: Constitutionalism in the Age of Populism 243 (2021). *See also* text accompanying notes 20–22.

[6] Verdugo, *supra* note 1, provides a set of criticisms of what he calls the "conventional" account of the constituent power. For present purposes I am willing to stipulate that my account is not the conventional one (though I believe that it has some points of contact with it), and I will sometimes point out how my account renders irrelevant some of Verdugo's criticisms of the conventional account.

implication of that proposition is that real embodied people can, after serious political contestation that can sometimes involve violence, choose whatever constitutional design they want.[7] Although older versions of the concept—what Verdugo calls the conventional account—treat the constituent power as subject to no limits whatever, today I think it best to stipulate that the constituent power is subject to the requirement that their choices must comply with international human rights norms construed to be rather thin or with a wide margin of appreciation.[8]

How do we know when a choice (of ordinary policy or of a constitutional provision or of a constitution as a whole) is that of the people who are entitled to govern themselves? In most cases, the existing constitution's procedures for enacting laws or amending or replacing constitutions—procedural regularity—provides the basis for our conclusion that the people have made the choice.[9] Procedural regularity is absent in our two scenarios, though. Nor can we come up with some list of procedures that underwrite self-governance even though they depart from the existing constitution's procedural mechanisms. The forms that procedural irregularity can take are for all practical purposes innumerable. In addition, as Verdugo suggests, every procedure can be "gamed" to produce an outcome that powerful politicians favor even though in the circumstances at hand the procedure's outcome does not represent the choice of a self-governing people (though under other circumstances it would).[10]

I think it helpful to divide our inquiry into two parts. The first, which I believe to be both central to many discussions of constituent power and in the end unhelpful, asks how we can identify "the people" who are said to be the authors of the irregular constitutional change.[11] The second, which I believe to be dispositive, asks

[7] This modifies substantially the position I took in Mark Tushnet, *Peasants with Pitchforks, and Toilers with Twitter: Constitutional Revolutions and the Constituent Power*, 13 Int'l J. Const. L. 639 (2015), where I connected the concept to an analytically confused combination of real-world and purely conceptual considerations.

[8] *See also* Cheryl Saunders's contribution to this volume. As Verdugo suggests, this constraint, and similarly others that have been suggested, is not all that important because the constraining norms are defined in such general terms that it would be difficult to find an actual exercise of constituent power, as I understand it, that violated those norms. Verdugo, *supra* note 1, at 49–53, especially at 52 ("the requirements often involve open-textured ideas that are easy to formally implement by leaders seeking democratic erosion"). Aharon Barak, in this volume, argues that international human rights norms cannot constrain the constituent power because some nations choose to be dualist and, as such, are not bound by international law until they incorporate it into domestic law pursuant to that law's own procedures. I believe, tentatively, that this is a mistake because the stipulated constraint operates *before* the nation takes a position on whether it will be a monist or dualist polity with respect to international law.

[9] The argument that procedural regularity guarantees self-governance is not a simple one. For a recent detailed exposition, *see* Frank Michelman, Constitutional Essentials: On the Constitutional Theory of Political Liberalism (2022).

[10] The usual example is a referendum organized according to ad hoc rules. The result might represent the people's considered choice but it might not.

[11] This question does not arise in connection with constitutionally regular changes because the procedures identify that people.

how we can identify irregular constitutional changes that result from the exercise of the constituent power.

Verdugo points out that there is "no such thing as a unified people acting with a single voice."[12] He suggests that the theory of constituent power has difficulty dealing with "the fact that society is divided."[13] That is undoubtedly true of some versions of the theory, and in particular of versions offered by some politicians in the course of their efforts to bring about irregular constitutional change.[14] Sometimes constituent power theory is framed as a struggle between a unified "us" and a "them" that is placed outside the true people. Ethnonationalist versions of constituent power theory are especially subject to this criticism. Sometimes explicitly, sometimes implicitly, charismatic leaders and their academic supporters invoke Carl Schmitt's account of constituent power in which constitutional change is endorsed by the people's acclamation, which Verdugo might characterize as sometimes shouting down dissenting voices.[15]

Though political actors using the theory might have a *tendency* toward that kind of discourse, this sort of exclusionary account of the people is not inherent in theory itself.[16] There is nothing in the theory of constituent power that denies the possibility that a nation's people might be pluralistic. As I have suggested in my earlier work, the United States offers an important concrete example of a nation of that sort. Consider two among many pieces of evidence. First, Walt Whitman: "Do I contradict myself? Very well then I contradict myself. (I am large, I contain multitudes.)"[17] Second, the national motto on the nation's currency: "E Pluribus Unum" (emphasizing the "pluribus" as much as the "unum").[18]

How can we understand a concept that has both an exclusionary and an inclusionary version? As a first stab I suggest this: A nation's people are those who commit themselves to the fulfillment of the nation's project. Some nations might "have" an ethnonationalist project, as Victor Orbán and Narendra Modi suggest for today's Hungary and India. Others might "have" a creedal project.[19] As the scare quotes indicate, though, political actors will offer different versions of

[12] Verdugo, *supra* note 1, at 20. *See also id.* at 30 ("denying the unity of the people is a robust line of attack").

[13] *Id.* at 44.

[14] Pratap Bhanu Mehta's discussion of nationalism and "bounded communities" in this collection provides valuable insights into these versions.

[15] *Cf. id.* at 38 (describing situations in which "segments of the society which lack sufficient political influence but which should nonetheless be considered as part of the political community" are excluded from "the people").

[16] I discuss the implications of this tendency below.

[17] Walt Whitman, Leaves of Grass (1855) ("Song of Myself," no. 51).

[18] I believe that another example is presented in Pierre Trudeau's successful re-presentation of Canadian national identity as multicultural or plurinational rather than binational. For a brief discussion, *see* Mark Tushnet, *Autochthony and Influence: The Charter's Place in Transnational Constitutional Discourse, in* Constitutional Crossroads: Reflections on Charter Rights, Reconciliation, and Change (Kate Puddister & Emmett Macfarlane eds., 2022).

[19] For the United States, *see* Mark Tushnet, *What Then Is the American?*, 38 Arizona L. Rev. 873 (1996).

what the national project is: for the United States today, perhaps Christian nationalism; for Hungary and India nationally distinctive versions of liberal constitutionalism. Who the people are will then be determined by the outcome of political contestation.

We cannot know who the nation's people "are," then, when political contests over defining the nation's project are ongoing. Recall that we are dealing with cases in which these contests take the form of seeking irregular constitutional change. Though the question deserves more empirical attention than I can give it here, I suspect that these cases arise when challengers seek to displace an understanding of the nation's project that they believe to be embedded in the procedures for regular constitutional change.[20]

My interim conclusion is that the concept of constituent power can do little real work in periods when some political actors *seek* irregular constitutional change.[21] Here an earlier point about political rhetoric recurs. During these periods some politicians will *claim* that the nation is undergoing an exercise of the constituent power (and others will deny that claim): an irregular constituent assembly is the forum in which the nation's people are revising the constitution; an irregular referendum is the vehicle the people are using to adopt a constitutional amendment. As before, I defer consideration of the question "What are we to make of these conceptually inappropriate uses of the concept of constituent power?"

With prospective use of the concept ruled out as inappropriate, what of a retrospective use? My suggestion is simple: Proponents of irregular constitutional changes will put such changes forward and find out whether they are in fact taken up, or, as I will sometimes put it, whether they stick.

They might hold an irregular referendum, get what they regard as enough votes, and urge people to start behaving (politically) in conformity with the result. For example, the referendum might purport to reallocate seats in one house of the nation's legislature to ensure that some group (indigenous people, for example) has guaranteed seats. Someone—not necessarily the government—conducts an election for those seats. What happens when the winners show up at the legislature? Maybe the officials in charge of seating legislators will say, Fine, nice to have you here. Maybe they will say that there has been no real election and deny seats to the victors. Litigation might ensue. If denied seats, the victors might go to court saying that the constitution had in fact been amended. Maybe the courts will reject the claim—but maybe not. Maybe the courts will say that the irregular amendment and the irregular elections actually did express the will of the nation's people. Parallel outcomes might occur were those who believe the elections were sham

[20] I think this is pretty clearly true in the first scenario, of revolutionary displacement of an existing constitution. The second scenario can be described as arising from a status quo bias where the existing procedures block changes that challengers believe to be urgently required.

[21] Verdugo describes efforts to deploy the concept in such periods as its prospective use.

and unconstitutional to go to court with the aim of keeping the victors out of the legislature.

We can work out a slew of scenarios in which irregular constitutional changes either stick or do not stick. When they do we can say that the constituent power had in fact been exercised. And that is all there is to the concept.[22]

Of course, there are details. Here are a few, in no particular order.

1. For a constitutional change to stick, opposition to it must damp down within some reasonable period. That can happen in a number of ways. Opponents might become reconciled to the change and start working within the reconfigured constitutional system. They might drop out of domestic politics either by emigrating or by becoming internal exiles. Opposition might decline for bad reasons, though, in particular when opponents are subjected to repression. When an irregular change "sticks" as a result of such repression we should be hard-pressed to say in retrospect that the change resulted from an exercise of constituent power. Determining whether such repression has occurred widely enough might be quite difficult empirically and normatively, particular when we recognize the possibility of internal exile.

2. How long do we have to wait to find out whether a change sticks? Sometimes we will know pretty quickly. People might simply ignore the purported change, or the revolutionary government might find itself unable to carry out ordinary governmental activities such as sending out the trucks to collect the trash. Or people might welcome the change and the new government might basically pick up where the old one left off. Sometimes, though, there will be a period of uncertainty.[23] It is not clear to me, though, that anything turns on our being able to use the concept of constituent power immediately after an irregular constitutional change has occurred.[24]

3. Referring to imposed constitutions, Verdugo asserts that the fact that "these constitutions enjoy a degree of social acceptance does not mean that the constituent

[22] *Cf.* Erin Delaney's discussion in this volume of imposed constitutions and in particular her quotation from Dieter Grimm, which can be read to assert that the retrospective endorsement of the German Basic Law gives it its legal validity. *See also* Peter Cane's contribution to this volume, which can be read to offer retrospective validity as a substitute for the analytics of a theory of separation of powers in giving the modern administrative state its legal foundation.

[23] A historical example might come from the Russian Revolution of 1917, which was not consolidated until the new government defeated antirevolutionary forces supported by foreign powers. A more contemporary and contestable one might be the Maduro government in Venezuela. It rather clearly falsely claimed to have resulted from exercises of the constituent power for a period from roughly 2016 through roughly 2022. *Cf.* Verdugo, *supra* note 1, at 54 (referring to "the three-year nightmare of the Maduro-friendly constituent assembly (2017–20)"). Starting in the early 2020s, though, the opposition began to regularize its participation in the nation's government, and it is at least possible to describe the Venezuelan government in 2023–24 as the outcome of irregular constitutional changes that have now stuck.

[24] The uncertainty does, as Verdugo suggests, make it difficult or impossible to say in the moment whether an irregular constitutional change represents a choice by the people mobilized or a minority's tyrannical exercise of power. *Cf.* Verdugo, *supra* note 1, at 46.

power theory has a space to justify them from a descriptive point of view."[25] I am not entirely sure whether this objection is limited to cases of imposed constitutions or whether Verdugo means to suggest that the concept of constituent power is not connected at all to questions of social acceptance. I note, though, the connection between my account of the constituent power and H.L.A. Hart's influential discussion of the concept of law. Hart offers what he calls a descriptive sociology according to which the regular behavior of people recognized as public officials *is* the law. Public officials clearly play an important role in my account of "sticking." Without fully committing to a Hartian account of law in general, about which I am woefully underqualified to comment, I do suggest that treating the concept of constituent power as connected to a descriptive sociology clarifies its content.

4. My account of the constituent power, like others we have examined briefly, is subject to important rhetorical distortions. Verdugo argues that political actors will deploy retrospective accounts like mine to create "romantic narrative[s]" that "invisibilize" groups and create a false story of national unity that lacks sufficient "resembl[ance to] the facts" of irregular (and regular) constitutional development.[26] This means that the account will have a tendency to treat "the people" as a retrospectively created fiction.[27] This criticism echoes one discussed earlier, that the concept of constituent power leads people to ignore the pluralism that actually characterizes real polities. And my response here echoes my response there: the concept of constituent power does not in itself require that we ignore pluralism. Again to use a US example: history professor Woody Holton's history of the US Constitution's creation has the title "Unruly Americans and the Origins of the Constitution."[28] They were unruly—pluralistic, divided—*and also* Americans.

5. Though in my account the concept of constituent power is properly used only retrospectively, politicians may well use it in the moment: "We're going to convene a constituent assembly that will exercise the constituent power to create a new constitution." Courts have been asked to determine the legality of the actions taken pursuant to such claims.[29] My inclination is to say that they should stay out of these cases—or, more formally, should treat the actions the politicians take as exercises of their right of free political expression.[30] The politicians will convene the assembly, their opponents will make prudential judgments about whether to

[25] Verdugo, *supra* note 1, at 67.

[26] Verdugo, *supra* note 1, at 58, 67–68, 48.

[27] *Id.* at 48.

[28] Woody Holton, Unruly Americans and the Origins of the Constitution (2007).

[29] Most notably, I think, in Venezuela and Colombia, but also in Spain in connection with an irregular referendum sought to be held regarding whether the people of Catalonia wished to secede from Spain.

[30] The trickiest issue here, I suspect, is whether politicians actually holding power—such as Hugo Chávez in Venezuela—can use public resources to support the project of irregular amendment. The Irish jurisprudence on this question seems to me the best developed (in opposition to using public resources) but also somewhat questionable.

participate or abstain, the assembly will "promulgate" a new constitution, and then we'll see what happens.

I have reconstructed the idea of constituent power to avoid some prominent criticisms, most notably that it cannot deal with the fact of pluralism and political division in processes of irregular constitutional change. A quite different type of criticism runs through the foregoing, though. Verdugo writes that one version of a retrospective account can be "used in undesirable ways."[31] And that is true of many other versions or components of other versions: many, perhaps all, can be misused by political actors seeking immediate political advantage.[32]

The problem Verdugo identifies is not uncommon in legal doctrine and political theory. We have a doctrine or theoretical concept that, as stated, can sometimes lead us to desirable outcomes. In practice, though, in the hands of willful or ignorant users the doctrine or concept will generate undesirable outcomes. A good example is provided by Carl Schmitt's idea that we can identify when the constituent power has been exercised by seeing whether a leader's claims about it having been exercised is accepted by "acclamation," which I take to be manifested by incontrovertible support by substantial supermajorities. Often leaders will make such a claim without actually having that degree of support (though perhaps with the support of an ordinary majority). And, having made the claim, they leverage the concept of acclamation and constituent power to generate an account of the legality of their actions. Yet, there is another side to the story: sometimes the leader will indeed have the requisite degree of support—or, in Schmitt's terms, the leader's policies will be accepted by acclamation.[33]

What can we do? We have a standard approach in the domain of legal doctrine. We have a doctrine that, when applied directly (in a first-order way), sometimes does well and sometimes does badly. We then make a second-order determination: net out the good and bad (not always a simple calculus, of course) and keep the doctrine if the net is good, discard it if the net is bad.

Can we do the same with political theory concepts? Verdugo does not actually perform the suggested calculus, though the tenor of his article is that the concept of constituent power should be abandoned. There is, though, a key institutional difference between second-order analysis in legal doctrine and in political theory. We have legal institutions that can purge the system of doctrines that on net do badly: higher courts can reverse lower courts that use the doctrine (whether for ill—more often if the net is bad—than for good, but even when the doctrine happens to produce good results). I doubt that there is such an institution in the domain of political theory. Perhaps the community of scholars could come to a

[31] Verdugo, *supra* note 1, at 58.

[32] For some examples, *see id.* at 20 ("can trigger opportunistic behaviors by politicians seeking to circumvent procedures that do not favor them").

[33] David Landau's contribution to this volume identifies cases in which an issue collateral to that of the concept of constituent power promoted good outcomes and cases in which it promoted bad ones.

general agreement that the concept of constituent power should be abandoned but there will inevitably be dissidents—and there is nothing the community can do about them. Even more, there is nothing the community can do about opportunistic political leaders who, perhaps drawing upon what the academic dissidents write, use (which is to say, misuse) the concept.

Further, what would it mean to abandon the concept? Here we must keep in mind the two scenarios in which it appears to provide the basis for treating as lawful constitutional changes brought about by irregular means. We could of course deny that such changes are lawful. I believe that there are simply too many cases in which irregular changes have settled in for that course to be attractive, especially cases fitting the first—revolutionary displacement—scenario.[34] Alternatively, we could come up with some term other than "constituent power" to explain why irregular constitutional changes are lawful. Indeed, "irregular but law-creating changes" might be a decent replacement.

That approach might work for academics. I doubt that it would work in political rhetoric. Some political leaders will adapt and replace "constituent power" with "irregular but lawful change" in their rhetoric. Others (probably the better politicians) will say, "The academics call it 'irregular but lawful change'; I call it 'constituent power,' and it's yours to exercise."

I do not want to end this part of my discussion by hinting that we are stuck with the concept of constituent power. The term itself identifies something that I believe must be part of the conceptual toolbox of constitutional theorists, whatever name they give it: that sometimes irregular constitutional changes are lawful.

Maartje De Visser's contribution to this volume explores the importance of facility in more than one language for the field of comparative law generally. My discussion of the concept of constituent power is an argument in the domain of constitutional theory that is provoked and illuminated by discussions about constitutional law and theory outside the United States.[35] How important is facility in several languages for work such as the foregoing?

From a purely personal point of view it had better be the case that "multilingualism" is not all that important because, as I have said in somewhat embarrassed tones in conversation, the only language I have is English.[36] As De Visser observes, many jurisdictions, including ones to which I have devoted a fair amount of

[34] Indeed, I must confess a lurking sense that were we to trace any constitution back far enough we would find irregularity somewhere. *Cf.* BRUCE ACKERMAN, 1 WE THE PEOPLE: FOUNDATIONS (1991) (arguing that the US Constitution's most important provisions have irregular foundations; I note that in my view Ackerman's case is stronger with respect to some provisions than with respect to others).

[35] I note that my work in comparative constitutional law is a mash-up of constitutional theory and functional analysis, as De Visser observes. I believe that much of what I say about issues of language facility applies to functional analyses as well.

[36] I can struggle through reading French and have written one article that involved research in French-language sources but all my other work relies entirely on resources available in English. (The article is Mark Tushnet, *Amendment Theory and Constituent Power*, *in* COMPARATIVE CONSTITUTIONAL THEORY 317 (Gary Jacobsohn & Miguel Schor eds., 2018).)

attention (Canada, the United Kingdom, Ireland, India), are Anglophone; English is today the academic lingua franca;[37] many constitutional courts publish versions of their decisions translated into English;[38] and today Google Translate is a tool each of us can use to get usable though imperfect translations into English.[39] Still, much remains out of reach to me.

De Visser begins with the importance of multilingualism for general comparative law. That discipline historically has focused on comparative legal *doctrine*, in which variations in specific verbal formulations might matter a great deal. It might be, though, that once we move toward constitutional theory or functionalism those specifics become less important.[40]

The reason is that we are interested in the conceptual and practical problems associated with the theoretical concepts and functional arrangements we are studying, and those problems have some but only some connection to the linguistic formulations used to describe concepts and arrangements.[41] A sufficiently rich primary and secondary literature in English dealing with those concepts and arrangements is likely to get one pretty far.[42] Consider for example a political

[37] For a discussion of English as a general lingua Franca, *see* the wonderful Philippe Van Parijs, Linguistic Justice for Europe and the World (2011).

[38] There is an article to be written (perhaps it already has been written and I am unaware of it) about the criteria different courts use to choose which of their opinions they will translate into English. Comparing the databases of the translations of decisions by the Supreme Court of Israel made by the Court itself and those made by the Israeli Supreme Court Project at Cardozo Law School (now suspended, I believe) might be a place to begin.

[39] Google Translate has problems dealing with idiomatic or colloquial expressions, but in my experience, places one in hailing distance of decent translations of technical (legal) language, which one can clean up on one's own. For recent overviews of Google Translate's accuracy, *see* "Research versus Practice: How Accurate Is Google Translate?," https://phrase.com/blog/posts/is-google-translate-accurate/#how-to-use-google-translate-best-practices(last updated Nov. 8, 2023); Nadiia Mykhalevych, "How Accurate Is Google Translate," Preply blog, Oct. 23, 2023, https://preply.com/en/blog/how-accurate-is-google-translate/.

[40] After writing an article on problems associated with developing a doctrine predicated in what I called a "general right to liberty" and then elaborating its analysis in an article that used examples from German constitutional law, I discovered that the German formulation of that concept is "general freedom of action"—and that German constitutional law addressed the problems I associated with a general right to liberty. *See* Christian Bumke & Andreas Voßkuhle, German Constitutional Law: Introduction, Cases, and Principles 101 (2019). The precise verbal formulation, that is, was relatively unimportant; the underlying concepts were. (The first article is Mark Tushnet, *The Doctrinal Structure of a General Right to Liberty, in* Three Essays on Proportionality Doctrine, https://papers.ssrn.com/sol3/papers.cfm?abstract_id=2818860. The second is Mark Tushnet, "Verhältnismäßigkeit und das Problem regulatorischer Subventionen (Proportionality and the Problem of Regulatory Subsidies)," in Rechtsdiskurs, Rechtsprinzipien, Rechtsbegriff: Elemente einer diskursiven Theorie fundamentaler Rechte–Symposium zum 75. Geburtstag von Robert Alexy (Carsten Bäcker ed., 2022) (written in English and translated by the editorial team).

[41] One qualification: Sometimes scholars think that if one starts with a specific linguistic formulation some other formulations necessarily follow or are ruled out. As a general proposition that seems to me plainly mistaken, though defending that claim is beyond the scope of this chapter.

[42] My personal experience is that such a literature can be effectively supplemented by what Jamal Green calls constitutional tourism, which involves informal "interviews" with "informants" who help me identify some specifics associated with the concepts and arrangements as they arise in their jurisdictions. (As with all quasi-anthropological exercises one has to be sensitive to the interests and potential biases of one's informants.)

theorist interested in *ideas* initially offered by Rousseau or Kant, whose only language is English. Such a theorist has a rich English-language literature on those ideas. Undoubtedly there are works in French and German (and Farsi!) that might help the theorist think about the ideas of interest but the theorist has to consider whether the effort to learn those languages is worth whatever marginal payoff there will be to her thinking.[43]

One way to put the point is this: Monolingualism is undoubtedly a problem for a scholar interested in *explicating* legal doctrines and concepts used in a legal system that employs a language that the scholar cannot read. It is a smaller problem, though, for the scholar interested in *exploring* the concepts and their associated problems. Not, I emphasize, "no problem at all," but the proof is in the pudding: How interesting are the arguments and conclusions offered by the monolingual scholar?

[43] I recall that I once read a parenthetical description in English of the argument in an article in German by a German legal scholar (I believe the scholar was Claus-Wilhelm Canaris), that sounded as if the German scholar was making an interesting and subtle argument about the state-action/horizontal effect doctrine. It was not worth my time, though, to track the article down and get it translated. (Today I might actually try to use Google Translate on the article.)

Index

For the benefit of digital users, indexed terms that span two pages (e.g., 52–53) may, on occasion, appear on only one of those pages.

The manufacturer's authorised representative in the EU for product safety is Oxford University Press España S.A. of El Parque Empresarial San Fernando de Henares, Avenida de Castilla, 2 - 28830 Madrid (www.oup.es/en or product.safety@oup.com). OUP España S.A. also acts as importer into Spain of products made by the manufacturer.
Printed and bound by CPI Group (UK) Ltd, Croydon, CR0 4YY
14/09/2026
02216284-0009